The Life and

Thought of

Josiah Royce

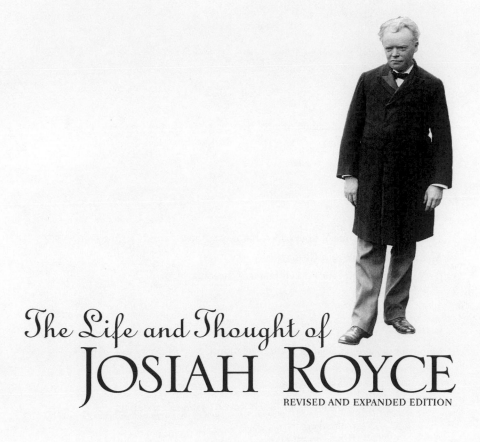

The Life and Thought of

JOSIAH ROYCE

REVISED AND EXPANDED EDITION

JOHN CLENDENNING

VANDERBILT UNIVERSITY PRESS
NASHVILLE AND LONDON

Revised and expanded edition 1999

99 00 01 02 03   5 4 3 2 1

This publication is made from paper that meets the minimum requirements of
ANSI/NISO Z39.48-1992 (R 1997)—
Permanence of Paper for Printed Library Materials. ∞

Library of Congress Cataloging-in-Publication Data

    Clendenning, John, 1934–
      The life and thought of Josiah Royce / John Clendenning . —
    Rev. and expanded ed.
      p. cm. — (The Vanderbilt library of American philosophy)
    Includes bibliographical references and index.
    ISBN 0-8265-1312-3 (alk. paper)
    ISBN 0-8265-1322-0 (pbk. : alk. paper)
    1. Royce, Josiah, 1855-1916. 2. Philosophers--United
    States--Biography. I. Title. II. Series.
    B945.R64 C54 1998
    191--dc21
    [b]
                                  98-25325
                                     CIP

Published by Vanderbilt University Press
Printed in the United States of America

For Rosey
. . . forever

Contents

Illustrations *(following page 254)*

1. Josiah Royce, 1914
2. Josiah Royce, circa 1860
3. Josiah Royce, 1875
4. Josiah Royce, circa 1885
5. Josiah Royce, circa 1890
6. Royce's mother, Sarah Eleanor Bayliss Royce
7. Royce's sister, Mary Royce Ingraham
8. Royce's sister, Harriette Royce Barney
9. Royce's sister, Ruth Royce
10. Royce's sister-in-law, Anna Head
11. Royce's niece, Eleanor Ingraham
12. Josiah and Katharine, circa 1914
13. Royce's wife and sons
14. Royce's first son, Christopher
15. Royce's second son, Edward
16. Royce's third son, Stephen
17. Royce's daughter-in-law, Marion Woodworth Royce
18. Royce's grandson, Randolph
19. Josiah Royce, Meadeville, Pennsylvania, 1902
20. With Margaret Gilman, 1902
21. William James and Josiah Royce, 1903

Preface

When the first edition of this book was published in 1985, neither I nor anyone else anticipated that a revision would be needed in the foreseeable future. Indeed one noted scholar paid the book a high compliment by calling it "definitive." However, the discovery of a large collection of new unpublished materials, as well as other recent developments, has prompted me to undertake this enlarged and very substantially revised edition. This discovery, in context with the evolution of the Papers of Josiah Royce, is itself a story worth telling.

In the years following his death in 1916, Royce's family and friends sorted through his professional papers searching for writings that would assure his lasting philosophical significance. In 1930, this important effort resulted in the establishment of the Papers of Josiah Royce in the Harvard University Archives, a rich core of rare, mostly unpublished, texts—ranging from his earliest to his final work—that served the needs of scholars for several decades. For me, this collection was an indispensable resource in my studies of Royce's life and thought. However, the original body of papers was incomplete. Being an archive dedicated rather narrowly to the preservation of Royce's writings, it contained no incoming correspondence and almost nothing that pertains to his personal character or family history. All of this sensitive personal material remained with Royce's widow, Katharine, until 1944 when her health failed and she was forced into a nursing home.

Soon afterward, these papers were acquired by her youngest son, Stephen, who moved them to his home in Michigan and eventually stored them in his office building. Efforts to recover this material while Stephen was alive were unsuccessful. Understandably protective of family privacy, he became a shield that repelled biographical inquiry. Even after his death in 1954, despite the sincere efforts of the philosopher's grandson, access to whatever might have survived seemed impossible. So by the time I wrote my book, it was generally assumed among Royce scholars that these remaining papers would never be available—or indeed, that they no longer existed.

Then, in 1988, through a wholly unexpected revelation, the new owner of Stephen Royce's office building in Crystal Falls, Michigan, while preparing to sell the property, opened some boxes and found the missing papers. Inquiries were made, and eventually, thanks to Harley P. Holden, the curator of the Harvard University Archives, this important addendum has been absorbed into the Papers of Josiah Royce. With Frank M. Oppenheim, I undertook an overview of this new material in 1989 and coauthored an article, "New Documents on Josiah Royce," which we published in *Transactions of the Charles S. Peirce Society*. In 1996, I revisited the collection for a detailed examination.

Being fair to the first wave of scholarship, I cheerfully acknowledge that the new material does not compel a major reinterpretation of Royce's thought. Those early scholars—notably Ralph Barton Perry, William Ernest Hocking, and Jacob Loewenberg—created a splendid archival record of Royce's philosophy. There are, to be sure, important philosophical dimensions in the newly available incoming correspondence. Often these letters provide new data that help to clarify his congruences as well as his conflicts with the philosophies of contemporaries. For example, the four new letters of George Santayana suggest that the differences between the two men have been exaggerated. On the whole, however, my revisions of the book as an intellectual biography have been rather less affected by the new material than are my representations of Royce and his family.

Readers of this revised edition will find a somewhat modified focus. While the book is still primarily a biography of Josiah Royce, it has become, more extensively, a family history. The presentation of Katharine Head Royce is substantially modified. Her own letters, as well as those written to her by her husband, her sons, her mother, her sister, and other family members, have helped me to present her more clearly and therefore more sympathetically. Previously, believing a good deal of ill-tempered gossip and quite possibly influenced by my own warped subjectivity, I portrayed Mrs. Royce as a cold, waspish sort of person. Actually I knew very little about her and believed what others remembered, which, as suggested, was not always kind. I saw her strident personality as opposite to that of the saintly Josiah, and therefore I depicted their marriage as a failure, barely tolerated and only because of nineteenth-century codes of behavior. The new evidence leads in an entirely different direction. Readers of this new edition will find a Katharine Royce who was full of love and tenderness, a woman who was in many ways remarkably independent, yet devoted to her children and her husband, a woman who filled their home with music and each spring made her garden come alive. As they grew older, the bond between Katharine and Josiah deepened, and at the end it could truly be described as an enduring love affair.

The new material has also provided me with the means of presenting the sons—Christopher, Edward, and Stephen—in more vivid, plausible detail. From childhood to maturity, each is seen in relation to his siblings and to his parents. Most important, I can now offer a fuller account of Christopher's mental illness, the signs of which appeared in early childhood and came to a critical point at age twelve. His eventual confinement to a mental hospital and his death at age twenty-eight were tragedies for the whole family, a family that had more than its share of pain and grief. Yet through these papers, what emerges is a story of a strong, caring, supportive circle, a family that endured many dark hours, yet never lost faith or descended to self-pity.

In the interim between the first and the revised edition of my book, other developments in scholarship have influenced my rethinking of this subject. New books have been published. The two impressive volumes by Frank M. Oppenheim, *Royce's Mature Philosophy of Religion* and *Royce's Mature Ethics*, are models of probing philosophical interpretation. Robert S. Corrington's *The Community of Interpreters: On the Hermeneutics of Nature and the Bible in the American Philosophical Tradition* and Jacquelyn Ann K. Kegley's *Genuine Individuals and Genuine Communities: A Roycean Public Philosophy* in different but compatible ways bring Royce's philosophy to life, making it relevant to issues before us at the end of the twentieth century.

I have also learned much from the discussion of Royce in *Time and Reality in American Philosophy* by Bertrand P. Helm, and also from *T. S. Eliot and American Philosophy: The Harvard Years* by Manju Jain. A major contribution to the field is *Frontiers in American Philosophy*, two volumes of essays edited by Robert W. Burch and Herman J. Saatkamp Jr. Followers of American philosophy cannot give enough credit to John J. McDermott whose book, an important collection of essays, *Streams of Experience: Reflections on the History and Philosophy of American Culture*, appeared soon after mine. Professor McDermott has most recently published a moving and compelling introduction to a new edition of Royce's *The Philosophy of Loyalty.*

As a biographer, I have been most influenced by Robert V. Hine whose richly historical volume, *Josiah Royce: From Grass Valley to Harvard*, provides an abundance of wholly new information about Royce's childhood, seen against the background of California in the late nineteenth century. Through Professor Hine, we begin to grasp the presence of the philosopher's father, a man who always seems to exist in shadows. One last book that needs to be mentioned is Joseph Brent's *Charles Sanders Peirce: A Life*, a book that does not concern itself with Peirce's thought, but that provides useful new information about his oddly tortured life.

While examining the new materials in the Harvard Archives, I serendipitously came across twenty new letters by Royce to Richard Clarke Cabot and his wife, Ella Lyman Cabot. These letters, a part of a recent addendum to the Richard Clarke Cabot Papers, enabled me to clarify an important thirty-year friendship between Royce and the Cabots. Similarly, I was able to see eleven letters by Royce to William Ernest Hocking plus a number of postcards and telegrams and a single letter to Mrs. Hocking, all part of the still uncatalogued William Ernest Hocking Papers in the Houghton Library. However, my use of this material was limited due to a policy that forbids its being photocopied. I was not shown the correspondence between Royce and Daniel Gregory Mason. Some years ago Hocking acquired this material, but found it too sensitive to be used in scholarly research. His son, Richard Hocking, also forbids this use.

From what I have been able to learn about these letters, they contain nothing scandalous. The basic situation was what Henry James might have called a *donné*: a young man falls in love with a married woman and comes to Royce for advice and assistance. There must be good reasons for the Hockings' policy of secrecy, but what they are I cannot fathom. All I can say is that my book might have been more interesting if the Royce-Mason letters had been considered.

I will close these prefatory remarks with an observation about a change the reader might notice in my psychological approach to biography. Some reviewers of the first edition grumbled that the book contained too much idle speculation about the unconscious motives that might have influenced Royce's thought and actions. While I do not wholly agree with these critics, I do now recognize the merits of their objections. I continue to believe that every worthwhile biography must portray the inner being of the subject, and to do this the biographer must achieve a profound consanguinity with the person in question. Nevertheless, the first edition was no doubt heavy-handed in this regard; it was too digressive, too prone to cite psychological authorities, too clinical in its insistence on theoretical frameworks. Readers of the revised text may be relieved that the narrator does not presume to be Royce's analyst; instead he tries to relate a life story, not a case history, in ordinary language and without diagnostic jargon.

A number of people contributed time, devotion, and expertise to this project. Among these I especially and most warmly thank my technical associate, Diana Sjoberg, who several times literally saved the project. I am also grateful to the staff of the Harvard University Archives, its curator, Harley P. Holden, and four other archivists who generously and professionally assisted me in my research: Patrice Donoghue, Virginia Smyers, Danielle Green, and Brian Sullivan. To my hosts in the Westin Jesuit Community, especially the men of Faber House, I extend my warm regards and gratitude. Through them I learned the living meaning of *caritas*. I also owe a great deal to my colleagues at California State University, Northridge, who supported my work by naming me the Jerome Richfield Scholar for 1996–97. And last to my dearest Rosey, to whom this book is dedicated and without whose steady, balanced devotion it would never have been written, all love is due.

Chronology

1855   Josiah Royce is born on November 20 in Grass Valley, California, the fourth surviving child and only son of Josiah Royce (1812–1888) and Sarah Eleanor Bayliss Royce (1819–1891).

1866   In San Francisco, Royce enters Lincoln Grammar School.

1869   Royce is enrolled in San Francisco Boys' (now Lowell) High School.

1870   Royce transfers to the University of California, in Oakland, as a member of the preparatory class.

1875   Royce receives a Bachelor of Arts degree in classics with a thesis on Æschylus's *Prometheus Bound*; delivers a commencement address, "On a Passage in Sophocles."

1875–76   Royce embarks on a year's study in Germany, first in Heidelberg, then in Leipzig, and finally in Göttingen.

1876   Royce commences graduate study at Johns Hopkins University, Baltimore.

1878   Royce receives a Doctor of Philosophy degree from Johns Hopkins with a dissertation, "Of the Interdependence of the Principles of Knowledge."

1878   Royce becomes assistant under the professor of English Language and Literature at the University of California, Berkeley.

1880   Royce marries Katharine Head (October 2).

1882   Royce's first son, Christopher, is born (April 11).

1882   After publishing fifteen articles and a textbook, *Primer of Logical Analysis* (1881), Royce joins the Harvard faculty as a temporary replacement for William James.

1885   Royce publishes *The Religious Aspect of Philosophy*, based on lectures of 1883, and is appointed assistant professor at Harvard University.

1886   Royce publishes his history, *California*. His second son, Edward, is born (December 25).

1887   Royce publishes his novel, *The Feud of Oakfield Creek*.

1888   Royce suffers a nervous breakdown in February, travels to Australia, and returns to Cambridge in September. Royce's father dies (June 23).

1889   Royce's third son, Stephen, is born (May 26). The family moves to a permanent home in Cambridge at 103 Irving Street.

1889–90   Royce gives as series of lectures, "Some Noteworthy Persons and Doctrines in the History of Modern Thought," the basis of *The Spirit of Modern Philosophy* (1892).

1890–91   Royce reviews F. E. Abbot's *The Way Out of Agnosticism*, prompting the notorious "Abbot Affair"; edits and contributes articles on California history for *Century Magazine*. Royce's mother dies (November 23, 1891).

1892   Royce is appointed professor of the history of philosophy at Harvard. During the next five years, he writes and publishes essays on psychology, literature, ethics, cosmology, social consciousness, and self-consciousness.

1894   Royce becomes chair of the Department of Philosophy at Harvard for a period of four years.

1895   *The Conception of God*. Royce addresses the Philosophical Union of the University of California. Revised with a "Supplementary Essay," *The Conception of God* is reissued in 1897.

1898   Royce publishes a collection of essays, *Studies of Good and Evil*.

1899–1900   Royce presents the Gifford Lectures at the University of Aberdeen, published in two volumes as *The World and the Individual* (1899–1901).

1902   Royce is elected president of the American Psychological Association; lectures at the summer school at the University of California.

1903   Royce Publishes *Outlines of Psychology*; is elected president of the American Philosophical Association; takes a sabbatical leave during the spring semester; in the autumn gives a series of lectures at Columbia University: "Some Characteristics of the Thinking Process."

1904   Royce publishes *Herbert Spencer*.

1906   Royce gives lectures at Johns Hopkins University: "Some Aspects of Post-Kantian Idealism," posthumously published as *Lectures on Modern Idealism* (1919).

1907   Royce gives ethical lectures to the Lowell Institute, the basis of *The Philosophy of Loyalty* (1908).

1908   Royce publishes a collection of essays: *Race Questions, Provincialism, and Other American Problems*. Christopher Royce is committed to Danvers State Hospital.

1908   Royce addresses the Third International Congress of Philosophy at Heidelberg with "The Problem of Truth in the Light of Recent Discussion."

1910   The deaths of William James (August 26) and Christopher Royce (September 21).

1911   Royce delivers the Harrison Lectures at the University of Pennsylvania, "The Nature and Accessibility of Absolute Truth," preceded by John Dewey on "The Problem of Truth." Royce publishes collected essays: *William James and Other Essays on the Philosophy of Life*.

1912   Royce publishes *The Sources of Religious Insight*, the Bross Lectures presented at Lake Forest College, Illinois, in November 1911. In February, Royce suffers a stroke.

1913   Royce publishes *The Problem of Christianity*; delivers lectures at the Lowell Institute (1912) and to the Hibbert Foundation, Manchester College, Oxford University.

1914   Royce is appointed Alford Professor at Harvard University and gives an address to the Philosophical Union of the University of California: "Interpretation of the Present Crisis," published as *War and Insurance*.

1916   Royce dies (September 14).

PART ONE

The Early Years
1855–1882

Chapter One

Childhood
1855–1870

Sources of Wonder

Philosophy, says Aristotle, begins with wonder, and so begins the life of Josiah Royce. "I shall always remember," he wrote in 1900, "the surprise with which I heard my mother remark, at a moment in my childhood, when I first began to be conscious of my world, that this town and its life had the characteristics of a new community. I remember thereupon vaguely wondering, as I looked at the things about me, 'Why do they call all this new?'" The town— Grass Valley, California—had existed for only a decade when the boy began his "very frequent" wonderings about its newness. Strangely, instead of evidence of birth, he found the signs of death—rotting timber, the abandoned diggings of miners, and near his own house, the marker of a lonely grave. This world seemed very old indeed. Here were churches with their religious controversies, schools with their traditional subjects, old people with their old ways. Dimly he reflected that this town had always existed, that this sort of life had been going on for ages. "What was there then in this place that ought to be called new?" As an adult, Royce would remark that this question contained the seed of his philosophy: "I wondered and gradually came to feel that part of my life's business was to find out what all this wonder meant."

What could a boy of six or seven know of his little world in the foothills of the Sierra Nevada? He had probably been told that this town with its mountain air and evergreen was located on the lower elevations of a vast mountain wall that rose to more than 14,000 feet and extended along the eastern border of

California for 430 miles. Doubtless his parents told him of the burning desert on the eastward side of the Sierra, and of the great fertile plains beyond. Perhaps they had also told him stories of exciting city life in the East and, from their parents, accounts of rural England. Seen from his village, the sunsets he remembered were beautiful, and the wide prospects opening upon the Sacramento Valley below were impressive. He knew also that across the valley another mountain system rose, and beyond that lay the vast Pacific Ocean. As an adult, he remembered the blue summits of the Coast Range, which seemed to hide the ocean, "for whose shore . . . I, who then lived in the Sierra foothills, and had never seen the sea, used longingly to look."

Naturally he knew that the gold which had brought men to Grass Valley was principally responsible for the rapid growth of California, that a dozen years earlier, people, his own parents among them, had rushed from every corner of the earth, had crowded on boats and clambered over mountains, in search of fortune. He knew also that very few found the gold, his parents least of all.

Growing up in the 1860s, the young Royce was profoundly affected by news of the Civil War; understandably a fervent patriotism grew in him as he learned his country's history. "I heard a great deal," he remembered later, "about our war of Independence and about the deeds of Washington, . . . and the stirring events of the Civil War, that were just then occurring also filled a great deal of my childish imagination." As various pieces of the child's world coalesced, a pattern took shape, an idea of the community. The questions he asked of his world and the knowledge of it he gathered were the first efforts in a lifelong meditation on the form and meaning of the social order. Looking out from his little home pressed against the mountain wall, the boy with his sisters watched the sunsets and wondered.

A few months before his death, he took account of his life:

> I strongly feel that my deepest motives and problems have centered about the Idea of the Community, although this idea has only come gradually into my clear consciousness. This was what I was intensely feeling, in the days when my sisters and I looked across the Sacramento Valley, and wondered about the great world beyond our mountains.

If literally Josiah Royce's mountains were the physical heights that enclosed him, symbolically they were the borders of his ideal world. A native Californian, he grew up with a sense of being physically and, as a result culturally, isolated. Throughout his life, Royce was troubled, if sometimes amused, by his crudeness, the origins of which he consistently traced to his youth. Writing to a friend in 1912 about the effects of growing up in California, he remarked, "I never was, in my youth, a person 'cultivated' in any aesthetic sense; and I remain more bar-

barous as to such matters than you can easily suspect." Royce's mountains were walls of experience; the story of his life depicts him pressing against the barriers, reaching out to the world beyond. A friendless boy in a rough mining town, he grew into a shy, socially awkward, private person who seemed to find intimacy difficult, even painful; yet much of his life was spent studying the relationship between the individual and his world. Growing up in poverty with few educational advantages, he found that intellectual achievement was earned, never given, by hard and dedicated work.

But his was a time when the nation's barriers were being pushed back with remarkable success. Emerging from the Civil War, the United States found the means of corporate enterprise and learned the skills of institutional growth. The industrial revolution, which created a Gilded Age of robber barons and political corruption, also gave birth to the modern university. In science and art, indeed in every facet of intellectual activity, America achieved a thoroughly international range, and at the center of this expansion and development, Josiah Royce became a leading figure. If the western frontier of America had closed before 1890, the frontiers of the mind were just then truly opening.

It was appropriate, therefore, that Royce should be the son of pioneers. They had made the long journey from Europe to the eastern United States and across the continent to California, and he retraced their steps. But reversing their movement, Royce followed the eastward expansion of thought.

Both parents had been born in England. Josiah Royce Sr.—the family traditionally named the first son Josiah—was born in Rutlandshire, on May 14, 1812. Four years later his parents immigrated to America. They stopped first in New York, but soon afterward settled permanently near the city of Dundas on the western shore of Lake Ontario in Upper Canada—now the province of Ontario. Despite the national boundary, communities within the southern and western vicinities of Lake Ontario tended to form a cultural unity; consequently the elder Royce must always have felt closer to the Yorkers, whom he officially met at Niagara, a short distance from his home, than to the Canadians of Toronto. At some point, probably in the mid-1830s, he left Canada and settled in Rochester, New York. There he married Sarah Eleanor Bayliss on May 31, 1845. She had been born on March 2, 1819, at Stratford-upon-Avon. Her parents left Warwickshire for America when Sarah was still an infant, and settled in Rochester where she spent most of the first thirty years of her life.

Few of the specific facts concerning the childhood and youth of the elder Royce and Sarah Bayliss are known, but much can be inferred from the history of the region where they grew up. Indeed, that region had a profound, if indirect, influence on the mind of their son, for in understanding the milieu that shaped the minds of his parents, we find important clues to forces that impelled him on a lifelong philosophical quest.

During the first half of the nineteenth century, the upstate region of New York—like California during the latter half of the century—was boisterously transitional. Rich farming land and abundant sources of waterpower pinpointed the northwest corner of the state for a rapid expansion in economic activity. The key to the boom was the Erie Canal, completed in 1825, which connected the Hudson River at Albany with Lake Erie at Buffalo. Providing more than 350 miles of transportation, the canal stimulated the development of manufacturing and agriculture: rich crops of wheat and cotton were hauled into the cities where they were milled and floated east to New York City. No doubt the business interests that enticed the Royces and the Baylisses into the expanding area were related to this development. Indeed, the philosopher's grandparents were a minute part of a vast flow of population that followed the westward construction of the canal during the 1820s. This growth exceeded population gains in any other part of the country; statistics for Rochester are most dramatic: it gained, during that one decade, 512 percent.

Like their son, therefore, Royce's parents grew up in the midst of social upheavals. They, like their parents, were destined to move restlessly westward seeking the newest opportunities, the next boom. And like their son, the elder Josiah Royce and Sarah Bayliss spent their childhoods in new communities where order and chaos were frequent enemies. But as the son was fond of remarking, the stabilizing influence of tradition is always introduced with new populations; whether in New York or in California, they provide conservative motives in social development. A community, he observed, may be economically and politically new and at the same time culturally ancient. Since the upstate region was predominantly Protestant, middle-class, and Anglo-Saxon, it is not surprising that religion, education, and courts of law provided the community's standards. Indeed, in those unsettled times the church and the school generally won their battles with the saloon and the brothel. Representing these values, the Royces and the Baylisses seem to have been fairly typical of the prevailing cultural atmosphere.

But at the same time, the conservative forces affecting New York are minor when compared with the cultural uniqueness of the entire upstate region, particularly Rochester, which acquired during the second quarter of the nineteenth century an astonishing degree of spiritual turbulence. The historian for this peculiar phase of development, Whitney R. Cross, has called this region "the Burned-over District." The name describes not a natural disaster, but the religious character of the area: in the words of Lyman Beecher, the storms of flame that burned over New York were "the fire and whirlwind of human passion." Cults embraced the most extraordinary doctrines there and preached with the most unrelenting zeal. A confusing variety of sects prevailed. Utopian societies flourished: there were Shakers, Owenites, Fourierists, and a group of schismatic Quakers who called themselves the Community of the Publick Universal Friend. In Palmyra, Joseph Smith unearthed the Book of Mormon and subsequently founded the Church of Jesus Christ of Latter-day Saints.

Though the group that embraced Smith's millennial expectations was most enduring, it was but one of many adventist cults. Preaching the news of the Second Coming, adventists moved across the state with gigantic tents, addressing thousands in marathon rallies of Christian evangelicalism. William Miller— "Father" Miller—led a group of ex-Baptists into the belief that Jesus Christ would reappear to start the millennium on October 22, 1844. Anticipating the Second Coming, Millerites filled the great tent in Rochester during continuous meetings throughout October; overflow crowds took over neighboring churches and public halls, and on Sundays, it was reported, thousands lined the Genesee River to witness baptisms.

When Father Miller's vision failed, zeal found other outlets. Social and political reform was vigorous in the Burned-over District. Abolitionists locked arms with temperance fighters, while other groups pressing for reforms in education, prisons, and women's rights found willing members. Benevolent societies were created to reform prostitutes and to end adultery; dietary reformer Sylvester Graham—still famous for his cracker—taught enthusiastic Yorkers that illicit sexuality was a deliberate conspiracy against Christianity.

At the opposite extreme, religious cults advocating perfectionism were fairly common. Believing that spiritual regeneration renders one sinless and incapable of sin, perfectionists frequently took up promiscuity and polygamy as articles of faith. Stories of matrons sleeping with their ministers scandalized the Burned-over District; still, John Humphrey Noyes, notorious for his part in the "Brimfield Bundling," had some success in organizing perfectionist cults. Noyes held that the law forbidding adultery was the law of the apostasy, that the millennium had turned free sex into a sacrament. "I call a certain woman my wife," he preached, adding: "She is yours, she is Christ's, and in him she the bride of all saints." Often the leaders of these perfectionist cults were considered by their followers to be the reincarnated Christ. A certain Martin Sweet is said to have assembled a household of seven "wives," one a black woman whom he ordered into the streets with a butcher knife to murder anyone she found; three other members of Sweet's "family" were reported to have disrupted a Communion service at a neighboring church where they performed various sacrileges against the table, the cups, and the wine.

The thread that knits these bizarre zealots is their belief in the immediacy of the divine. In the Burned-over District, the faithful masses solemnly believed that the Word would become Flesh, that human beings were perfectible, that the ideal could live in the world of experience. These zealots did not, of course, always agree about the content of divine truth or the proper structure of human

8

society, but they did share—utopians, adventists, reformers, and perfectionists—a deep conviction that the ideal is not a dream to be postponed till an afterlife, but a presence that may be and is found in the midst of life.

Josiah Royce and Sarah Bayliss breathed this spirit. To be sure, their zeal did not lodge with the more radical cults, but the atmosphere that surrounded their childhood nourished a piety proclaiming that the Kingdom of God is manifest. The elder Royce, his obituary informs us, "always maintained unwavering faith in the infinite wisdom and goodness of God our Father, and in the salvation coming to us through Christ Jesus our Lord." Throughout his life, he was known for having the highest standards of Christian morality. The obituary continues:

> Amid all the unsettled conditions of those early California days, often cut off for long intervals, from Christian associations and Church privileges, Mr. Royce steadily maintained his interest in the study of the Bible, and his high standard of Christian morality. The habits of recklessness and revelry which often surrounded him in the mining camp and in the growing town, had not the slightest attraction for him. The company and conversation of the low jester, the profane talker, or the irreverent scoffer were ever so distasteful to him that he preferred a stopping place in the wilderness at any time rather than to stay among them. So strictly temperate was he in his habits that he had been known when away from home in those rough times, to suffer many hours from a sharp attack of cholera-morbus rather than go to the bar of a saloon for a small quantity of the only thing within his reach that could be called medicine.

As for his wife, Sarah, who seems to have been the author of her husband's obituary, she too was deeply pious. "Above all," her daughter Ruth said, "she was intensely *spiritual*. If the word were not so commonly misinterpreted, I would say she was a *mystic*—in the sense that Dr. Addison uses the word in his book on 'Mysticism'—'one who, believing what hundreds about him *say* they believe, simply *lives* what he *believes.*' Mother certainly lived 'as seeing Him who is invisible.'"

Here we find the spirit of the Burned-over District. For Sarah Royce, God was present in human experience: she "saw" what she believed; she "lived" her belief. Her son did not, of course, adopt his parents' evangelical Christianity or their mysticism; indeed, he explicitly, though tenderly, rejected both doctrines. On the other hand, he did not reject the idea that formed the basis of their piety, or the spirit of their mysticism. His argument with mysticism was based on its failure as an ontology to offer a consistent theory of being. His "fourth conception of being" is, in part, a correction of that failure and, at the same time, a justification of the spirit of mysticism. For Royce, as for his parents, the Kingdom of God is manifest:

And despite the vastness, the variety, the thrilling complexity of the life of the finite world, the ultimate unity is not far from any one of us. All variety of idea and object is subject, as we have seen, to the unity of the purpose wherein we alone live. Even at this moment, yes, even if we transiently forget the fact, we mean the Absolute. We win the presence of God when most we flee. We have no other dwelling place but the single unity of the divine consciousness. In the light of the eternal we are manifest, and even this very passing instant pulsates with a life that all the worlds are needed to express. In vain would we wander in the darkness; we are eternally at home in God.

Thus, though unintentionally, Royce perpetuated the tidings of the Burned-over District. Just as the zealots of the 1830s and 1840s awaited the incarnation of the ideal, Royce, a generation later, argued from a philosophical standpoint that the eternal is present in the temporal, that each experience, however trivial, is an expression of divine unity.

It is significant that the first book that Royce remembered reading was the Revelation. There were few books available in the Royces' home; his parents' travels had hindered the accumulation of household goods. Still the boy found a large-print New Testament prominently assigned to a table in the living room. Possibly with parental encouragement he read the Apocalypse "independently." If, as he added, he did not gain very clear ideas from this first literary experience, he gained something else quite as valuable: a bridge between generations. Here was the crucial text that motivated his parents' faith:

And I John saw the holy city, new Jerusalem, coming down from God out of heaven, prepared as a bride adorned for her husband.

And I heard a great voice out of heaven saying, Behold, the tabernacle of God is with men, and he will dwell with them, and they shall be his people, and God himself shall be with them, and be their God.

Here also was one of the seeds for Royce's theory of the Beloved Community. In *The Problem of Christianity*, he observed:

The well-known apocalyptic vision revealed the true Church as the New Jerusalem that was yet to come down from heaven. The expression of the idea was left, by the early Church, as a task for the ages. The spirit of that idea was felt rather than ever adequately formulated, and the vision still remains one of the principal grounds and sources of the hope of humanity.

So through the parents, we see the son. The piety and zeal that surrounded their childhood filtered through them to him who formulated their vision. Just as he was to master the arts of philosophical insight, they had experienced the vision of the Bible. It was said of Royce's father that he, at an early age, "showed much interest in religious reading." His habitual study of the Bible provided the foundation of his close familiarity with Scripture. In later life he astounded friends by reciting "from memory passage after passage on the same subject, beginning often with the earliest prophesied, and adding one quotation after another bearing upon the same point until he ended with the Book of Revelation." Such facility in biblical quotation was not acquired without institutional encouragement. Indeed a rigorous program of Bible study was central in the education of nearly every child in the Burned-over District. Sabbath schools sponsored "concerts" of prayer as annual programs that featured Bible recitations. In Rochester, during such a program in 1829, 1,700 children stood all day in the rain listening to recitations, reports of officers, and exhortations of leading religious teachers. The instruction in these Sabbath schools consisted mainly in memorization of the Bible, and since prizes were given, children were stimulated to master enormous amounts of Scripture. A seven-year-old was reported to have memorized 1,496 verses in twelve days; an eight-year-old learned 1,070 in seven days; a nine-year-old is said to have mastered 2,127 verses in ten days. Though they learned by rote, familiarity with Scripture prevailed throughout life; the lessons of childhood matured into adult piety, becoming legacies for the next generation.

Despite the father's remarkable knowledge of the Bible, he was not, so far as is known, educated beyond grammar school. The mother, on the other hand, was the intellectual pillar of the household. "A woman of fine *intellect*," Sarah Royce was by profession a schoolteacher and a graduate of Phipps Union Female Seminary. This institution, located in Albion, New York, was an ephemeral college for young ladies founded in 1833 by a Miss Caroline Phipps and recognized by the regents of the State University in 1840. Following a pattern common in such schools that flourished in the second quarter of the nineteenth century, the curriculum of Phipps offered a survey of the liberal arts and emphasized etiquette, housewifery, and religious training. When Mrs. Royce herself later established a school in Grass Valley, she introduced such subjects as spelling, reading, writing, mathematics, geography, natural philosophy, logic, criticism, moral science, political economy, and elocution. No doubt this curriculum was modeled largely on the studies she had pursued in her youth.

The religious instruction at Phipps focused on "those truths held in common by all evangelical Christians." Each student was required to own a Bible, to use it daily, and to attend public worship twice every Sunday. Great emphasis was placed on discipline and respect for authority. The young women were taught that the practices of piety and Christian morality were virtually equivalent to the proper functions of a human being. According to the published boarding regulations, "the culture of the heart, the proper control of the moral feelings, and the due observance of religious duties, are encouraged and diligently urged, as the appropriate offering of rational and immortal beings." The regulations add: "All the pupils received into the family of the Principals are regarded with parental watchfulness—the most vigilant attention being given to their health and the cultivation of their morals and manners."

Considering the distance between Rochester and Albion, it is nearly certain that Sarah was a boarding student. Such students, besides honoring these regulations, were confined to their rooms during study hours and expected to devote a portion of every Saturday to dressmaking. Although the school promised to provide a "pleasant home" as well as an "intellectual resort for the young," there appears to have been very little recreation. Daily gymnastic exercises sufficed to give some physical relief from the school's discipline. Music seems to have been the main form of entertainment. Instrumental and voice recitals were presented to the public on Wednesday evenings. The students were particularly praised for being "sweet-voiced and accurate time-keepers."

Following graduation, Sarah taught for some years at similar institutions. By 1840 Rochester, having stabilized its growth rate, offered a fair number of intellectual and cultural diversions. Newspapers and magazines were plentiful. At numerous bookstores and libraries one could find a wide variety of literature. Though most reading dealt with religious subjects, books on history, travel, philosophy, and political economy were available. The citizens of Rochester read little fiction, but the novels of Scott and Cooper were popular. There was some art, more music, and though, like their Yankee neighbors, Yorkers tended to frown on the drama, one might occasionally visit the theater for a Shakespearean or melodramatic production. There was some participation in amateur theatricals; the Rochester Dramatic Association, founded in 1832, had its following. Lecture series, sponsored by the Franklin Institute and the Rochester Atheneum, offered programs typical of the lyceum movement. Rochester, in short, had various attractions for a bright young woman like Sarah Bayliss, and more than once during her later pioneering days, she regretted the loss of eastern culture.

Her marriage to a restless husband brought this sense of loss to her life. Uprooted and often lonely, Sarah was to be remembered by her daughter as one "who thirsted for companionship and opportunities that her hard life made impossible." Her husband, on the other hand, was seized by the American Dream, enticed westward by the promise of eventual success. A daughter, Mary Eleanor, was born to the young Royces on November 23, 1846, and in the spring of 1848, the little family moved to Iowa, settling in a pleasant village near Tipton twenty miles from the Mississippi.

In the meantime, on January 24, 1848, an eccentric millwright and carpenter named James W. Marshall, while constructing a sawmill in the foothills of the Sierra Nevada, picked up a piece of rock that turned out to be gold. Marshall and his employer, John Sutter, tried to conceal their discovery, but news leaked out, and the California gold rush was on. The Royces were certainly established in Iowa when they first heard of the gold strike, for rumors of the discovery did not reach the East before August, and not until December were they officially confirmed in the president's message to Congress. Hard winters in the prairies with two vast mountain ranges to cross made an overland journey impossible before early spring. But on April 30, 1849, getting as usual a rather late start, Josiah Royce packed his belongings, his wife, and two-year-old Mary in a covered wagon and struck out, with one other party, for California.

Dragged along by three yoke of oxen and one yoke of cows, the prairie schooner began its slow, uncertain, and always hazardous journey. A copy of Frémont's *Travels* and the conflicting reports of fellow argonauts gave the Royces little knowledge of their route or of the dangers they would confront. At first they labored through mud holes that sometimes restricted their progress to three miles a day. Those "sloos" were covered with turf that broke under the weight of the wagons so that everything had to be unloaded, sometimes in rain, while the men dug out wheels sunk to the hubs. After twelve days of labor they reached Iowa City; crossing the Iowa River the next day, Sarah sadly recorded in her diary: "A pretty stream, reminding me of my own, old Genesee." After more than a month they reached Council Bluffs. It was June. That gave them three, certainly no more than four, months to complete the journey over the Sierra Nevada before the autumn snows. At Council Bluffs they lost several more valuable days waiting to be ferried over the Missouri River.

Trying to remain calm and patient, Josiah and Sarah listened with apprehension to rumors of disaster ahead, of cholera epidemics, of inadequate supplies, and of cattle starving from the lack of grass, eaten up by preceding parties. "All this we heard," wrote Sarah Royce, "and all this we talked over, but still we went on."

The Royces were among the last to cross the Missouri that summer. Bidding farewell to what Sarah called "the fag-end of civilization," they followed the Mormon Trail along the Platte River across Nebraska. They had the next sight of American life at Fort Laramie. Before that, they faced threats of hostile American Indians, an outbreak of cholera in their party, and stampeding cattle. On July 11, they passed through Laramie. For a few days they enjoyed the "sparkling waters" of mountain streams and the stunning heights of the Rockies; they were also refreshed by the social and religious diversions of prayer, reading, and occasional singing. On August 4, they crossed the Continental Divide, and by August 18, they had sighted the Great Salt Lake.

Before them were the desert and the mountains—the last but the most dangerous parts of the journey. At Salt Lake, Mormon prophets terrified them with stories of devastation. Parties divided, and the Royces, virtually alone, began the last legs of their journey on August 30 guided by two scraps of notepaper sewn together and entitled "Best Guide to the Gold Mines, 816 miles, by Ira J. Willes, GSL City." Indians threatened again, the desert wind blinded them, but the most terrible fear was thirst. On October 3, they were looking for the Sink of the Humboldt River; they had only two or three quarts of water in their cask. On October 4, they were lost and for the first time desperately thought of turning back. The landscape of the Old Testament stirred the imagination of Sarah Royce. In fantasy she became her biblical opposite, Hagar, expelled from the homeland and struggling among parched bushes with the fainting Ishmael, and when a previous camper's fire ignited a clump of sage, she bowed her head worshiping the god of Horeb. By retracing their steps, the Royces found the trail again, but even with fresh supplies of water the desert still threatened. Cattle began to die by the road. Sarah heard her husband say, "So you've given out, have you Tom?" Loosed from its harness, the ox fell dead on the ground. Only two yoke were left. To preserve the oxen, Sarah insisted on walking, and as they walked they passed the dead carcasses of cattle from previous trains strewn along the trail. Finally they reached the Carson River and stared up at the mountains before them.

The story of this desert trek must have been, at some later time, a frequently rehearsed household tale, for it figured prominently in their son's earliest dreams and fantasies, in which he saw himself repeatedly wandering in a wasteland, expelled from the hearth, terrified. Indeed, the same set of images became embedded in his rhetoric; it surfaced in his finest works where the philosopher is depicted as a searcher through a wilderness for his truthful home.

On October 12—certainly too late for a safe crossing of the Sierra—the family started to climb. Soon they sighted, a few miles off, the dust rising from an approaching party. At first they feared another attack from Indians, but luckily it turned out to be a U.S. government rescue party sent out to accompany stragglers over the Truckee Pass. The men guided the Royces through dangerous patches of snow and lent them two mules. On October 19, they crossed the highest crests of the pass, and before the end of the month, six months after their departure, the Royces were safe in Weaverville.

The self-portrait rendered by Sarah Royce in her narrative of the ordeal completely fulfills the description provided by her daughter: she was, Ruth remembered, "a *heroine* who bore all bravely for her children's sake." Distinctly maternal, Sarah had receptive, passive strength; hers was the power to endure. This is clear at the beginning of the journey when she took her place resolutely imagining the possible dangers: "If we were going, let us go, and meet what we were to meet, bravely. So I seated myself in the wagon." And so she was drawn on her "pilgrimage," as through life, by the plans and dreams of men. She followed, accepted, stood by, and occasionally supported the men, but the quest, she knew, was theirs. "Patience, energy, and courage," she recited to herself, were the virtues she must cultivate. But sometimes, prayer, humility, and a perfect renunciation gave her the strength to continue. After the first two men in the party died of cholera, Sarah was seized with fears that Mary might die or be orphaned:

> Such thoughts would rush into my mind, and for some hours these gloomy forebodings heavily oppressed me; but I poured out my heart to God in prayer, and He gave me comfort and rest. I felt a full assurance that He would not afflict us beyond our strength to bear. I committed my precious child into His hands entirely, claiming for her His promises, and His guardianship. I said from my heart "Thy will be done." Then peace took possession of my soul, and in spite of threatening ills, I felt strong for duty and endurance.

In contrast to the well-detailed character of Sarah Royce provided by her narrative, the portrait of her husband is incomplete and obscure. He seldom seems to speak, yet when he does, his conversation consists of single sentences expressing elementary ideas. Indeed, though certainly during those terrible six months Josiah was his wife's only intimate companion, he seems, at least through her narrative, to be hardly present at all. He is most often associated with physical hardship and with the cattle; like them, he is constantly laboring forward: he digs, he pulls, he pushes.

But the most peculiar, and possibly the most significant, obscurity in Mrs. Royce's story is the absence of any expressed purposes or motives for the journey. Why did they undertake such hardships? What impelled them forward? The answers are never given in terms of their ultimate goals. One should be safe in assuming that like the vast majority of forty-niners, the elder Royce intended to prospect for gold, that what drew him to California was the promise of fortune. If so, such dreams are not expressed in his wife's account of their journey or, in fact, in any surviving document.

It is entirely possible that the elder Royce had no definite plan, that California represented merely a new home with vaguely imagined new opportunities. Such a conclusion is consistent with other known details of his life. Quixotic and ill equipped to manage his affairs, he tended to bungle every chance of success. A paradigm of his lucklessness is the ironic survival of an embarrassingly apologetic letter he wrote to a certain Captain Chandler. Written from Weaverville, the letter explains what happened to the borrowed mules:

> Capt. Chandler, Sir: I send by the bearer one of the two mules that I received from your relief company with many thanks.

The other mule with one that I had of mine own, and the only one that I did own, I am sorry to say, has got away from me after I arrived at this place. Your mule, I believe, has taken the road for the S[acramento] city. I have a man who started yesterday for the city and if he finds it, will deliver it to you, in the meantime I shall continue to hunt the woods for mules in this section, hoping that I may yet find the animal, as well as my own. My family as well as myself cannot feel sufficiently grateful to the government, as well as to its officers, for the aid received; at the same time I am grieved to think that you should sustain any loss on our account. However, I have satisfaction of knowing that I had taken all the pains to watch the animal, that was possible. Please let me know if you should find and receive the mule that is lost; the mule is black, has been [ ] around the nose with the halter, and is a mare, and has fifteen feet rope on its neck.

Yours, most respectfully,

J. R[o]yce.

Of the writings of the philosopher's father, almost nothing else has survived. But the image it depicts is not a false one. He had come two thousand miles to California, he had endured every kind of hardship, yet there he was in El Dorado searching the woods for lost mules.

Mishaps continued to vex the Royces during their first month in California. For the first time, it seems, Josiah developed a definite plan. Soon after his arrival in Weaverville, he had probably tried his hand at washing out gold and had learned the uncertainties of the enterprise. The pan and the rocker were suited only for unmarried men; certainly no family could be fed on the promise of a rich strike. Josiah decided to enter the grocery business, and finding several partners, he went down to Sacramento to obtain the initial stock. In the meantime, his partners set up two tents and opened a brisk little business. But when Josiah returned, he was nearly prostrated by an attack of cholera and was unable to work for several days; just as he recovered, Sarah was laid helpless by a "powerful fever."

By the middle of December, they had decided to abandon the business and to push on to Sacramento, where Josiah planned to open another grocery store. A lot was to be purchased and a house built; this evidently was to be a permanent home. But foolishly Josiah pitched his tent on the soft green turf near the banks of the Sacramento River, and when midwinter rains came, the river began to rise. On January 9, the water spilled over its banks, and within minutes the Royces were evacuated. Sarah took Mary, while Josiah and a friend were able to carry a few armfuls of their belongings to safety before the rest was surrendered to the flood. Within a few days Josiah, discouraged with his chances in Sacramento, began discussing the prospects of moving to San Francisco. On January 15, the Royces boarded a steamer and anchored the next morning in San Francisco Bay.

For the next four years the same errant restlessness impelled the Royces to continual wandering. In this they were typical forty-niners. A historian for this period, Rodman W. Paul, has described this migratory tendency as their "one universal sin." Later, the philosopher also saw that this restlessness was a characteristic of his father's generation; indeed, his description of "the average Californian's easiest failing" offers a revealing account of his psychic heritage: "Like his father, he [the average Californian] is probably a born wanderer, who will feel as restless in his farm life, or in his own town, as his father felt in his. He will have little or no sense of social or material barriers, he will perchance hunt for himself a new home somewhere else in the world, or in the old home will long for some speculative business that promises easy wealth, or again, on the other hand, he will undertake some great material labor that attracts him by its imposing difficulty."

The Royces remained in San Francisco for about fifteen months, living at first in a hotel and then in a newly constructed tenement. Sarah evidently taught school during the year 1850–51; what Josiah did for their livelihood is not mentioned. On July 13,1850, another daughter, Harriette, was born. During the following spring the family of four moved to a farm near Martinez, which was, as Sarah remembered it, "one of the most beautifully located villages" in Contra Costa on the bay northeast of San Francisco. A son, John Samuel, was born in August 1852, but he died soon afterward. Though Sarah enjoyed the cosmopolitan atmosphere of San Francisco and the Edenic beauty of its neighboring village, financial crises spoiled the paradise. In 1852, Josiah borrowed $170 at the usurious interest of 5 percent per month. He was eventually sued twice for $210.16 and $247.52, and some of his property—two mules with harness and a wagon—was evidently forfeited. Commercial prospects again lured the Royces back to the mines.

They now opened a store in one of the little mining camps twenty miles from Sacramento. Though the adjoining river was thought to be rich in gold, a large supply of water was needed for washing it out of the banks; when, a few months later, the cost of water outran the profits from mining—a common occurrence wherever "hydraulic" mining was used—the prospectors moved on. One morning the Royces awoke to find the words Dried Up chalked on the side of the great flume, and within minutes the camp was deserted.

The Royces began to climb into the mountains. A second mining town, probably Folsom, was found the summer of 1853. Josiah's commercial plans grew more complicated. It was decided that they would open a store in the "flourishing" town but live on a homestead in the outskirts; in that way they could keep the cost of stock down by growing their own produce. However, they soon had to admit that their claim would never become an improved homestead, and since the store kept Josiah away from home many nights while his family remained unprotected from passersby, they decided to give up the homestead and move into the village. In the meantime a third daughter, Ruth, was born on   17 September 21, 1853.

In the following spring they moved again, this time higher up to a bustling town, the most permanent village in the so-called northern mines, Grass Valley. Here they remained for twelve years, and on November 20, 1855, their last child was born, a son, named for his father—Josiah.

Grass Valley

"The young Californian," Royce once observed, "is thus early used to a country that, as it were, tells its principal secrets at a glance. . . . You get," he added, "a sense of power from these wide views, a habit of personal independence from the contemplation of a world that the eye seems to own." The several descriptions that Royce later gave of his home emphasize his sympathetic response to its natural surroundings. Of these the most detailed description appears in *California*:

> In the upper foothills, where I spent my childhood, we used to live in what seemed a very open country, with not many rugged hills near us, with the frowning higher mountains far to the eastward, and with a pleasant succession of grassy meadows and of gentle wooded slopes close about us. But just beyond the western horizon that the darkly wooded hills bounded, there loomed up from a great distance two or three sharp-pointed summits that were always of a deep blue color. These we knew to belong to the Coast Range; and the far-off ocean was, we fancied, rolling just at the western base of these peaks. If now we walked a mile or two to some higher hilltop, the whole immense river valley itself seemed at the end of our walk to flash of a sudden into existence before our eyes, with all its wealth of shining and winding streams, with the "Three Buttes" near Marysville, springing up like young giants from the midst of the plain, and with the beautiful, long, and endlessly varied, blue line of the Coast Range bounding the noble scene on the west. Of course, what we could actually see of the great valley was but a very little part if compared to the whole; but the system upon which this interior region of the state was planned we as children could not fail to comprehend both very early and very easily.

The physical setting of Royce's birth and early childhood thus played an important part in forming his thought and character. In later life he placed considerable emphasis on the effect of nature upon personality. His one effort in geographical research, a paper entitled "The Pacific Coast: A Psychological Study of the Relation of Climate and Civilization," presents the argument that the native Californian, because of his region's temperate weather and its physical isolation from the rest of the country, develops a marked sensitivity to nature and distinct habits of personal independence. The argument is clearly an exercise in self-analysis, for these qualities are among Royce's own most notable traits. His enduring love of the sea and the rugged beauty of hills prompted his deepest aesthetic responses. His embodiment of pioneer independence, his constant readiness, as William James liked to say, "for everything in this world or the next" never failed to astonish his friends or perplex his foes.

These are the characteristics that developed in Grass Valley. As its name suggests, the town is situated along the grassy banks of Wolf Creek. The men of '49, on their way to Sacramento, used the valley as a kind of oasis; their stray cattle found it a place of refuge. Grass Valley's elevation of 2,690 feet ensures a brisk, but hardly fierce, climate. Though nights, even in summer, can be cool, days are seldom below freezing or above ninety degrees. The thick blanket of snow that covers the upper slopes of the Sierra Nevada is not a problem in Grass Valley, where the average seasonal snowfall is not quite two and a half feet. On occasional winter mornings one may awake to find snow on the ground, but since even in January the temperature is likely to reach fifty, substantial accumulations of snow are rare. In general, the worst weather is a drizzling rain that usually starts in November and lasts through April. Otherwise the air is dry and bright, and on a clear day one can always hear the deeply calming sound of wind in the trees.

The first settlers came to Grass Valley in 1850. Two stores were opened that year, and a handful of miners washed a little gold out of the surrounding streambeds. At first the place was called Centerville, but this boastful name had to be abandoned when the postal authorities complained that there were too many Centervilles in California. The first piece of gold-bearing quartz was found accidentally by a man who kicked a stone while carrying a bucket of water, but since miners in the early days of the gold rush usually restricted their diggings to the streambeds, the man sold his rock for five dollars—it proved to be worth a hundred. Soon afterward, during the fall of 1850, while quarrying stone for a chimney, a group of men hit an extremely rich ledge two feet thick, which yielded five hundred dollars per ton. Within a few months they mined the so-called Gold Hill Ledge for twenty thousand dollars. As news spread, claims were staked, and prospectors began to pour into Grass Valley. Mills necessary for quartz mining were constructed that winter. Before the end of the year a hotel was built, and the town, by an election collected in a cigar box, had acquired the foundations of social order—a few laws, a judge, and a constable.

By 1852 it bore the appearance of a permanent village. Sketches of Grass Valley from this period show a town of about ninety wooden buildings irregularly scattered. Most of them were concentrated on Main Street, which was one of three thoroughfares that intersected the road from Sacramento coming down a hill from the south and across Wolf Creek. At the outskirts one could make out two mills and several farms. Though there were few trees on the valley floor, the hills that rose on all sides were adorned with black oak, sugar maple, fir, cedar, and ponderosa pine.

Providing the cultural milieu for Josiah Royce's earliest consciousness, Grass Valley was a highly interesting community. To gain a clear sense of its importance, one must dispel preconceptions based on the quaint mythology popularized through the local-color sketches of Bret Harte. This Royce firmly understood; no Californian, he insisted, would confuse the romance with the social reality:

> The mining camp of Bret Harte bears much the same relation to the actual early life of California that the ideal shepherd and shepherdess so well known through a style of poetry, that once was common, may bear to the life of the actual country folks who tend their flocks. For just as the idyll is always possible, so any other romantic transformation of facts may be suggested by many different social conditions. But the real life that you find in a new country is not to be judged by any such romantic sketches. Yet what actually happened in early California is a very fair illustration to you of the way in which a new American community is formed.

In contrast to the life depicted in "The Luck of Roaring Camp," Sarah Royce, like her son, found Grass Valley to be not only a pleasant, but also a very settled and well-developed community. A number of "very good Christian people" supported three churches, a public school, and one or two social and benevolent societies. By 1855 Grass Valley claimed a population of 3,500 citizens and continued to grow during the subsequent decade despite periodic outbursts of gold and silver fever. The town had a distinctly cosmopolitan flavor; though much of the population consisted of experienced miners from Cornwall, the citizens of Grass Valley included Germans, Irishmen, Jews, Frenchmen, Chinese, and African Americans. The town's political development began with its first election in 1850 and the passage of an act of incorporation in March 1855, which approved sixteen ordinances and appointed a board of five trustees, a marshal, an assessor, and a treasurer. By the time the Royces moved back to San Francisco, Grass Valley supported more than a hundred merchants of various kinds, not counting saloon keepers, and had begun to develop a diversified program of manufacturing; in addition there were seven churches, eight schools, seven benevolent associations, two daily newspapers, three fire companies, eleven physicians, ten lawyers, four dentists, and a brass band.

Though prosperous, Grass Valley was not dull. The town was the site of sensational events typical of the Old West, providing legends that Royce undoubtedly heard recited during his boyhood. Behind *The Feud of Oakfield Creek*, Royce's only published novel, there were several tales of bloody wars with American Indians, involving superhuman heroes, hand-to-hand combat with pocket knives, the timely arrival of the U.S. Army, and bands of angry, murdering miners. Feuds over gold claims erupted in violent and sometimes fatal conflicts. Arsonists, thieves, gamblers, and murderers passed through Grass Valley; bad cards led to fists, knives, hatchets, and revolvers. As for the women, many of them, as the miners liked to say, were neither wives, widows, nor maidens. In the category, the most notorious was Lola Montez, the former mistress of Louis I of Bavaria. An actress of questionable ability—her specialty was a "spider dance"—Lola had followed the argonauts to California and had arrived in Grass Valley soon after the Royces in 1854. The miners were unimpressed with her aristocratic credentials—Louis had given her a title—and recognizing her Irish origins, despite the Hispanic flavor of her pseudonym, they dubbed her the "Limerick Countess." It is said that when a certain Henry Shipley of the Grass Valley *Telegraph* boldly ridiculed her in print, she accosted him in a saloon and lashed him with a horsewhip. It is also said that she shot her husband when he killed her pet bear.

The legend of Lola remains a tourist attraction in Grass Valley, satisfying a need for belief in the Wild West, but the development of the community deserves most emphasis. The phenomenal growth and stability of Grass Valley resulted from its peculiar geology and the resulting mining technology. The prospectors of '49 had spent most of their time washing gold in the mother lode out of sedimentary deposits—called placers. The common tools of such enterprise consisted of the pan and the rocker, or Long Tom. The pan was strictly a one-man operation, while the rocker required the efforts of two or three men working in concert. If such efforts encouraged a certain pioneer individualism, they tended to separate rather than unite communities, and since the mining camps depended on the sustained riches of the streambeds, the communities tended to dissolve as the rivers were panned out. Even the more elaborate hydraulic mining, which required the sluicing of deeper placers, failed, as the Royces discovered at the first mining camp, to produce more than very ephemeral communities.

The gold that sustained Grass Valley was in quartz deposits, very rich but extremely thin veins of igneous material often lying deep beneath the earth's surface. In mining this gold, individual effort was useless; only corporate enterprise with its vast resources of capital and technical expertise could cope with such complicated problems. Quartz mining required a variety of operations, heavy equipment, and specialized labor. As a result Grass Valley became not only a cosmopolitan but a notably sophisticated and distinctly stratified community. Mining specialists from all over the world were drawn to Grass Valley, and the pioneers of '49 were encouraged to join the labor force.

If wealth lent stability to the economy of the community, the adoption of established social order guaranteed its permanence. Exhibiting these characteristics, Grass Valley and the neighboring towns were nearly unique in the mining areas. By the time of Royce's birth the gold of Grass Valley totaled $3.5 million, but in the next quarter of a century this figure increased, throughout Nevada County, to nearly $160 million. These figures contrast sharply with the statistics for California's overall production of gold; after hitting a peak of $81 million in 1852, the annual yield dropped steadily to $17 million in 1860. If, through this process, the ideal of individual enterprise was abandoned as the town came to resemble eastern industrial cities, the compensating goal of social order was reached; and if the fortune that his father sought in making his hazardous journey to California never materialized, Grass Valley presented to a boy interested in the growth of new communities a lifetime of future thought.

Although Grass Valley gave Royce his earliest idea of community, it afforded few of the softer advantages of civilization. If its hills and trees gave him an enduring love of nature, it failed to nourish a lasting appreciation of art. Presumably he had little acquaintance with the town's only "art gallery," which maintained quarters in Gibb's Paint Store where its curator claimed to possess "the finest engravings . . . which will ornament your parlor, and improve as well as gratify your taste for the fine arts." Surely also, if the parents' religious sensibilities are indications, the theatrical attractions of Grass Valley were lost on young Josiah. He probably never saw Lotta Crabtree do her celebrated dances before adoring miners. To his friend Richard Cabot, Royce later confessed: "I never saw any beautiful object that man had made until after I was twenty years of age."

The one form of art that made a lasting impression upon Royce was music, and this he knew exclusively from his mother. Into that crude world, Sarah Royce brought a melodeon. "I sat down," she remembered, "to my melodeon and made the woods and the pretty little hills ring with some of my favorite songs." On Sundays she indulged herself "in the melodies and harmonies that brought to me the most precious memories of earth, and opened up visions of heaven. And then those bare rafters, and cloth walls became for the time a banquet-hall, a cathedral." When her son, much later, was deeply moved by Wagner and Beethoven, his mother's music could not have been wholly forgotten.

Once established in Grass Valley the elder Royce took a job as a traveling salesman, and Sarah returned to teaching. To effect her plans, she opened a "School for Young Ladies and Misses" in February 1855. Though the school was at first conducted in a single room and later moved to her home, it offered a complete curriculum in four separate classes with the goal of providing "a thorough moral and intellectual discipline." In addition to the young ladies, Mrs. Royce admitted boys, aged ten and under, and among these her son—affectionately called Josie—received his earliest education. Even later when she took a regular position in Grass Valley's public schools, Josie remained her own special student; indeed, he had no other teacher during the first eleven years of his life.

These new arrangements had the effect of bringing the mother and son into an extraordinary intimacy. Since the father was at home only for short visits, the mother was not only the boy's teacher,but also the head of the household, the figure of authority, and the symbol of family unity. His sister Ruth, ignoring any possible influence of the father, emphasized the mother's role in shaping the son:

> Of all the influences that helped in the making of Josiah Royce, the outstanding, undeniable factor was his Mother. . . . The marked religious atmosphere of the home, early familiarity with the Bible, and the constant companionship of his Mother—a companionship extending on through his college days, were influences that stand out in any study of my Brother's character, thought or writings. He was his Mother's "crown and exceeding great reward."

In most accounts of the family during this period, the father is habitually absent—"over the mountains" on business—while all activities focus on the central role of the mother. Mary, the oldest daughter, underscored the mother's place in their daily routine:

> Just before Mother was expected home from school each day, the rule was, to put it in good order, and set the table for supper; for our sitting room was also our dining room. Supper, or dinner as the city people call it, was generally a very cheerful meal for us; for as Mother had been away all day, we children had all the day's employment and pleasures to relate to her; and she, in return, often had amusing or interesting anecdotes to relate about her scholars.
>
> After supper was disposed of, the table was drawn out, the lamp placed upon it, and we all gathered around it to spend our evening.

Of the entire day, these hours were the most memorable: the anticipation of mother's return from school, supper conversation flowing between mother and children, and evening amusements of reading and more conversation. In each phase the maternal presence is central.

Mary's image of the family circle suggests not only its closeness, the mutual dependence of the mother and her children, but also its isolation from the community at large. In nearly every account of the Royces during their years in Grass Valley, they are described as having minimized or explicitly discouraged contacts outside family, church, and school. As if to confirm this impression, city directories compiled in 1856 and 1861 make no mention of the Royces. They did, in fact, live outside the town. Josiah described his home as "a farm at some distance from a flourishing mining town of the Sierras." Emphasizing the ruggedness of the terrain, he remembered that the road from town followed "a sloping plateau . . . [which] descended rapidly, winding along the edge of a ravine which gradually grew narrower and deeper as it approached my home. This ravine at one point made a sharp turn, while the road still following it was here flanked on both sides by thick groves of pine bushes." Mary's account agrees with this, but adds a sense of the idyllic:

> The house was a two story frame house painted white; it stood on the western slope of a hill, and from it we had a view of a large portion of the surrounding country; on the western, northern, and southern sides of the house was a porch, and it was a beautiful place to sit and watch the sunset. From this porch we also had a beautiful view of the orchard, and below that the broad green meadow stretched; which in its turn sloped down into a wilderness of rocks and bushes about a mile from the house.

She called the place Avon Farm, a name chosen evidently as a memorial to her mother's Shakespearean birthplace. The description of the home with its white paint, porch, orchard, and meadow makes an abrupt contrast to the flourishing mining town, the wilderness of rocks and bushes, the winding road next to the ravine. As if a bit of rural England had been preserved and transplanted, the home seems serenely agricultural in a world otherwise vexed with the turmoil of wilderness and industry.

Thanks to the careful research of Robert V. Hine, we now have a clearer understanding of the Royces' domestic economy in Grass Valley. Soon after they arrived, the elder Royce purchased a plot—approximately one acre—in town, erected a small one-story house, planted an orchard, probably apples and pears, and went into the fruit business. In 1857, two years after Josie was born in this house on Mill Street, his father, with a wealthier church friend as partner, bought a ranch consisting of 150 acres for eight thousand dollars. This farm, the Avon Farm that Mary described, included groves of fruit trees, pastures for dairy cattle, and possibly other agricultural products such as grapes and strawberries. Exactly how the farm was worked remains unclear; certainly the father's frequent absences would make it unlikely that he picked the fruit, milked the cows, or supervised those who did. In 1862 he sold his interest in Avon Farm to his partner, Thomas Barr, and evidently invested the money in a grocery store in the Nevada Comstock. He was gone for almost three years, and when he returned to Grass Valley in 1865, he had apparently lost almost everything. In the meantime Sarah and the children continued to live in the farmhouse. With another partner the elder Royce seems to have maintained a livery stable—

another abortive venture—in Grass Valley during the months before the Royces
24   moved back to San Francisco.

As the youngest member of his compact little family, Josie was "the pet, but still not a spoiled pet." His earliest portrait, a photograph taken during the early 1860s, shows a handsome boy of about five or six whose plump cheeks and double chin are remnants of baby fat. The face is solemn and slightly enigmatic. The eyes are leveled in a penetrating gaze; the lips, drawn down, seem not inclined to smile. His famous red hair—his wife, Katharine, later remembered it as "the most brilliant red I ever saw"—has been momentarily tamed, plastered down against its natural inclination. A patriotic note is suggested by his military jacket—probably a photographer's studio costume, a size too large. Fervently loyal to the North in the Civil War, Josie must have been proud of his uniform with its metallic buttons and bold stitching.

Each of his sisters took part in Josie's education, for his genius was recognized and developed at a very early age. One of the older girls taught him to read; all of them, together with the mother, were his "earliest teachers in philosophy." From Ruth, he remembered, he received "a great deal of training in dialectics": "She was three years my senior. She was very patiently persistent in showing me the truth. I was nearly as persistent in maintaining my own views." Remembering her part in these debates, Ruth said, "From his babyhood he was a *talker* and loved to talk and could *express his thoughts*." Mary emphasized his early seriousness; he was, she recalled, "almost always with a book in his hand." The Bible was most frequently read in the Royces' home; as an adult he remembered his pleasure in listening to his mother's reading of Bible stories. The family gradually accumulated a modest library as they became more settled in the early 1860s. Of Josie's taste in reading, Ruth recalled, "his first choice was history, which he read eagerly, storing up dates and statistics, battles and generals with phenomenal ease and accuracy."

Similarly his religious education was, as he remembered, "clarified and directed by the influence of my mother and sisters." Certainly his parents' evangelical idealism, which they had brought from the Burned-over District, was transmitted to the son. At first his religious interest was merely one of his childish "enthusiasms," expressing itself primarily through his fascination with his mother's readings of Bible stories. But this early intimacy with scriptural writings accompanied him through life. To George Santayana and Ralph Barton Perry, Royce seemed fundamentally a Protestant, whose discourse, as Perry remarked, always retained "a flavor of biblical allusion and of homiletic eloquence." On the other hand, Royce developed, even as a youngster, a persistent intellectual stubbornness. "I was," he admitted, "a born nonconformist." This quality appeared most decidedly in his dissatisfaction "with the requirements of observance of Sundays, which stand out somewhat prominently in my memory."

Although he later insisted that these requirements were not excessively strict, his early rejection of Christian worship endured to become a characteristic of Royce's religious sensibility. Royce never quarreled with God, but he frequently disputed with men about the ways of serving him. In these disputes, the memory of his father more than of his mother seems to have provoked his stubborn nonconformity. For Sarah Royce, Sundays were occasions of joyful song and social communion; unlike her husband, she preferred the muted faith of the Congregational church. But the religion of the elder Josiah Royce imposed a stern renunciation. Although originally a Baptist, he shifted permanently to the Disciples of Christ in 1857. "When at home," his obituary tells us, "he was in the constant habit of attending to family devotions." His son, therefore, though he did not mention the fact, might well have resisted devotion as a reaction to the regimen of his father. In this context, the son's nonconformity might be explained in terms of anger relating to the errant father's return, his disruption of household order, and his competition for the mother's affection.

But if the father was perceived primarily as a rival, the mother made the more prominent impressions on her son's consciousness. This too, however, was not altogether positive. Though her "constant companionship," reinforced by "the kindly watch" of his sisters, accelerated his education, it also tended to retard his social development. Regularly in company of women and without a vital relationship to his father, Josie became admittedly "timid and ineffective." Perhaps too watchful, Sarah discouraged her son from choosing male companions. "A mother of high ideals," Ruth said, "found few children in the small mining town whom she could invite into her home as playmates for her children." Being the family pet, Josie was too closely protected from the normal scrapes of boyhood, a fall from a tree, or a cat's scratch.

Although Ruth insisted that "he did not feel the need of boy companionship," his enduring loneliness and social awkwardness, which friends often observed in later life, certainly originated during those early years in Grass Valley. "He played much alone," Ruth remembered, "and *thought* as he played." Being unusually small, frail, rather chubby, and awkward, he was ill equipped to meet the demands of aggressive, competitive sports. At an early age he had been forced to abandon a natural left-handedness; his crude penmanship later bore the mark of that mistake, and one suspects that his dexterity in throwing a ball was similarly impaired. "He had not the ordinary boy's love for games and rough play," said Ruth; "he had no mechanical tastes and little bodily agility." Even in adulthood when he became a supporter of physical education, Royce preferred those sports, such as mountain climbing, that are practiced in solitude against impersonal obstacles, to contact sports like football as played before crowds at Harvard Stadium. Unable to compete physically, he acquired a compensating intellectual aggressiveness. With other boys his age, he adopted an air of superiority and a "considerable tendency . . . to preach down to what I supposed to be the level of these other boys." To some extent, his relentless love of polemics, which observers sometimes found to be his most remarkable trait, grew out of his youthful timidity and feelings of physical inadequacy.

In retrospect Royce tended to normalize his childhood. While admitting to minor frustrations, he insisted that he had been, "on the whole, prevailingly cheerful, and not extremely irritable." As if to prove the point Royce described himself as "stubborn" but "seldom . . . openly rebellious"; he "quarreled" with his sister, but again "seldom . . . in any violent way." Josie was undoubtedly a "good boy," good in the sense that though he might feel anger, he seldom showed it. In the Royce household emotional self-control was cultivated as one of the more notable virtues. The mother was, of course, a splendid model for the children to emulate. At Phipps she had been taught "the proper control of the moral feelings," and as her daughter noticed, she "bore all bravely"—her loneliness and unfulfilled ambitions "for her children's sake."

Consistent with this habit of self-discipline, Sarah Royce punished Josie, the only form of punishment he ever remembered, with enforced silence. When she felt his wrangles had gone too far, but when he urgently felt the need to demonstrate his truth, to prevail against the circle of dominating women, his mother—"our dear mother," as he called her—set him the task of restraining his rage and holding his tongue for an hour. It is hardly surprising that Josiah learned to express his anger in "passive resistance" and in "petty mischief," which he practiced whenever "my sisters did not succeed in keeping me under their kindly watch."

A story that he remembered as an adult adds a revealing dimension to Josiah's social development in childhood. This story was, he said, something he had read, a fragment of some larger tale, though the context, source, and author were forgotten. Vague and obscure, only this "chance bit" stuck in his memory for fifty years:

A bold bad elder boy tempted the too trustful little boy who was the hero of the story, to disobey the express commands of the hero's parents, or perhaps his teachers, and to play truant in company with the elder boy. The enticement used by the tempter was substantially as follows: "Come with me into town, and I will show you something that nobody ever saw before, and that nobody will ever see again." The trustful hero wondered, and yielded, and went. But when once the expedition had started, the somewhat insolent leader, absorbed in his own affairs, and content with keeping his follower under his control, long delayed the expected exhibition of the promised marvel. The little boy grew impatient. He had a variety of experiences, indeed; but nothing seemed to him to fulfill his expectations. At length the triumphant seducer paused at a shop, bought some nuts, and, cracking one of them, held up the kernel and said: "Did anybody ever see that before?" The hero was obliged to respond, "No." Thereupon the bad boy, instead of offering this nut or any other of the nuts to his comrade, cruelly ate the kernel and said: "Will anybody ever see that again?" and the small boy sorrowfully answered with another "No," and returned through tribulations to the path of virtue.

Such stories remembered from childhood are unavoidably symbolic. Royce repeated this one as a paradigm of the relationship between his philosophy of idealism and realism. Thus, the "trustful little boy" is associated with Royce himself, whereas his philosophical opponents are represented by the "bad elder boy." But there is much more to the story, for though childishly simple in structure, this, like all fables, is a tale of moral conflict and draws a moral conclusion. It is, in fact, a variation on the theme of original sin, the fall from innocence. The older boy is the "tempter," the "seducer"; he causes the "too trustful" smaller boy to violate the "express commands" of parents or teachers. The temptation itself consists of a promise of fuller experience, a "marvel" that can be witnessed only by stepping outside the law. Sin, evil assures innocence, is prerequisite to knowledge. This proposition is explicitly denied as the fable shows that the act of disobedience leads directly to falsehood. The moral of the tale, therefore, is that dissembling is a natural consequence of sin, or obversely, that virtue leads to truth. The little boy learns this "sorrowfully . . . through tribulations," but in the end, returning to the "path of virtue," he accepts the standards of parental authority. The results of the "fall" are fortunate: the boy has gained a knowledge of evil without suffering permanent damage; his future joy in practicing virtue will be heightened by his memory of tribulation.

As a reflection of Royce's moral training, this story is particularly revealing. It is not unlike countless other moral tales that boys of his generation found in the McGuffey readers; such stories dominated the literary fare of nineteenth-century youths and consequently made a profound impact on the American mind. Reinforcing the Bible stories that Josie heard at his mother's knee, this little fable of initiation teaches the inevitable wages of sin and the rationality of parental rule. Most important, since the boy freely and independently accepts this rule, the story emphasizes one's responsibility in fulfilling the social ideals of the family. It implies that there is no truant morality, for only by reaffirming his family ties can the boy find the path of virtue. In the ethical sense, therefore, the story illustrates the need for "loyalty" as Royce later used the term; just as he came to believe that moral individuality can develop only through dedication to socially binding goals, the little boy in the fable learns that disobedience or disloyalty leads inevitably to deception and disappointment.

If the story contains the seed of Royce's concept of loyalty, it also suggests part of the motivation that led him to philosophy. There is a danger in forcing too serious an interpretation upon a fragment remembered from childhood. Yet why, one may ask, was this fragment remembered? Royce did not himself know the answer: "I cannot tell why," he admitted, "just this incident remains alone in my mind, while the rest of the tale is forgotten." Still he did suggest that a lingering fascination with "the dialectical interest of the bad boy's unfeeling paradox" might explain the memory. A clue to the meaning of his fascination may be found in the story's ethical omission: the trickster is never defeated. Fully humiliated, the little boy is warned against the snares of paradox, but does not learn how to handle the intellectual bullies who turn sophistry into a rewarding game. Royce was to spend much of his life fighting such bullies and charlatans. Instinctively he despised them; he hated the self-serving lies of John Charles Frémont, the intellectual pretensions of the amateur philosopher Francis Ellingwood Abbot, the bullying politics of Theodore Roosevelt and imperial Germany. In different ways, each of them seems to be represented in the "bold bad elder boy." Royce hated him in fantasy and in fact; the origins of that hatred may be found in Grass Valley.

More terrifying than Josie's early fear of being overwhelmed by brute force was another fear, that of cosmic isolation, which Royce traced to his "first awakening of our personal interest in the problems of philosophy." In an undated paper, "Recent Discussions of the Concept of the Infinite," he described one of his "earliest metaphysical experiences" as a "strange dread that for a while used to haunt me, when I was nine or ten years of age,—a vague dread that seemed to be suggested to me by what I heard or read about the vast size of the physical universe." His belief in "God's power" and his reading of books on astronomy directed his fears.

> I found myself for awhile dwelling with fascination upon the tale of enormous numbers and distances with which the astronomer deals. But erelong the fascination grew painful whenever I tried to picture somehow those stellar wildernesses,—the dark interspaces between the worlds,—the clusters of stars, the systems beyond systems, the nebulae,—I came to seem so far from home; and the contemplation of the mere magnitude of Being gave me a choking in the throat, and a lonely kind of fear,—a fear which seemed all the more hopeless because nothing that I could conceivably do, or could pray God to do, or could hope for, could be expected to alter in the least the essential situation, or make this cold world of the beautiful stars and the terrible distances comfortably smaller. Nor was it the infinity of the spatial universe alone that seemed thus oppressive. I remember feeling an equal discomfort regarding the endlessness of time. I did not want to die, or to be annihilated; but the thought of living on and on, without end, came to be suggestive of the same feeling of getting far away from home. I thus felt a sort of childish tangle of mind at which it is easy to laugh. I desired to

be immortal, in the sense in which I heard about immortality from my religious teachers; but still somehow I did not want immortality to last so long, to bring one so far away from these present conditions of mother love and of home comforts that for me as for any child meant real living.

Royce noted that "all such experiences, even if mild, are, of course, in their way, pathological." He also noted that his childhood dread was "the beginning of wisdom." He went on, in the essay, to discuss the theories of Cantor, Dedekind, and Peirce, but we should not fail to recognize that Royce's metaphysics was partly, by his own interpretation, an attempt to exorcise his childhood fears.

Similarly revealing is Royce's first literary effort, written when he was eight years old, an amusing picaresque story entitled "Pussy Blackie's Travels." As the title suggests, the story relates the adventures of a black and white cat who runs away from home. At the opening of the novel, Blackie is living with the Royces in their home "on the side of a hill . . . about a mile from the nearest town." The children are given their pet names and actual ages: Mary is seventeen; Hattie, thirteen; Ruthie, twelve; and Josie, eight. Mrs. Royce is described as "a public school teacher" and "a lady of about forty five years." The father is mentioned only as "her husband—a man seven years older than herself—[who] was away at that time."

Each morning the Royces go to school, leaving Pussy Blackie alone at home. Feeling abandoned, he decides to run away. "I do wish these folks would not go away and leave me every day," says Blackie, "even if they do come back at night. . . . I'll pay them for this. . . . I'm going to run away." It is safe to suppose that the eight-year-old Josiah in identifying with the cat's feelings was projecting his own anxiety. Isolated and friendless, with a father who "was away at that time" and could be named only as "her husband," Josie could well have felt abandoned by "these folks," his mother and sisters, whose interests and values were naturally different from his. Prevented from enjoying male companionship and protected from experience with the world outside his little mountain home, Josie created Blackie's fanciful journey over the Sierra to Washoe, where he is taken in and cared for by Josie's father; then on to Salt Lake City, St. Louis, Cincinnati, Pittsburgh, and Richmond. Physically defenseless, Pussy Blackie is often the victim of natural events and predators; painfully he learns that sharp wits are necessary for survival.

The story of Pussy Blackie is, in fact, remarkably parallel to the story of the "too trustful little boy." In both stories the heroes leave home in quest of more rewarding experience; both are attacked by unforeseen superior antagonists. Most important, both stories emphasize the triumph of intelligence. Defeated, the little boy in the fable is forced to retreat to the protection of his family; the cat learns to survive by his wits. One rededicates himself to conservative social

30

values; the other sets out alone and, by cultivating intelligence, is equal to the demands of a hazardous world. If the story of the little boy suggests the origins of Royce's philosophy of loyalty, "Pussy Blackie's Travels" celebrates the survival of the pioneer spirit. Blackie's route over the mountains to the fascinating world east of California is the path of a journey that Royce himself would make a dozen years later; at the age of eight, in fantasy he was already preparing for his travels.

San Francisco

For reasons not entirely clear, the Royces decided to leave Grass Valley in the spring of 1866. Economic factors might have motivated them. Unstable conditions were described by the *Grass Valley National* in an article of August 22, 1861, "The Future of Mountain Towns." The author observed that the slump most seriously affected laborers and small tradesmen. The gradual transition to corporate control of the mines brought increased automation and, as a consequence, extensive technological unemployment. As one miner was heard to remark, "They employ fewer hands and more head work." Merchants were squeezed out by this unemployment and also by the fact that the big operators had become independent of local markets in obtaining the needed goods. Thus, though fortunes were still being dug out of the mines, the money was not being put back into the local economy, and the towns stagnated. With other forty-niners who searched relentlessly for their pots of gold, the elder Royce sought his elusive success in San Francisco. One may also suppose that the educational and cultural advantages of a larger city attracted the Royces. Josie was almost eleven years old; if he were to develop according to his abilities, he would have to be placed in schools equipped to cope with his intelligence.

For various and indefinite reasons, therefore, the Royces came down from the mountains and crossed the Sacramento Valley. Josie remembered the dry heat and the scattered oak trees that seemed to be "set out by God's hand at the creation in a sort of natural park." Mist and salt air greeted them as they approached the rugged hills near the bay, and then by ferry they reached San Francisco. For the next several years, the Royces maintained a fruit store, and behind it a home, at 1032 Folsom Street.

In contrast to the mining regions, San Francisco grew dramatically, its population increasing from 56,802 in 1860 to 149,473 in 1870. The gold rush had brought about 35,000 Americans to the city by 1850, but because of its economic isolation from the rest of the country, the prosperity and population of San Francisco remained unstable throughout that decade. Communication with the East was achieved during the sixties, first by the Overland Telegraph Company in 1861 and most dramatically by the joining of the Central Pacific and Union Pacific Railroads in 1869. Those developments created a commercial and industrial bonanza. Visitors were universally impressed with the city's tempo, its cosmopolitan atmosphere, and its cultural advantages. For a time it was a literary center, and the home of Mark Twain, Ambrose Bierce, Bret Harte, and Henry George. Compared with other coastal towns, such as Los Angeles or Seattle, San Francisco during the late 1860s was the only true metropolis in the Far West. Perhaps the clearest index of the cultural achievements of the Bay Area during this period was the foundation of the University of California, whose charter was granted by the state legislature in 1868.

The Royces lived on Folsom Street for perhaps a bit more than four years. According to Ruth, the family had to be split up "more or less by the force of circumstances," though the exact arrangement remains unclear. Their business routine does, however, seem to have taken definite shape. Each day the elder Royce loaded a fruit cart with produce and peddled his way through the streets, while the mother kept the store at home. Even Josie perhaps lent a hand to the business, for in later years Royce once referred to himself in a spirit of self-mockery as an *Obsthändler*. More important, the joke expresses depreciation of the father.

A contemporary description of the elder Royce identifies him as a notorious eccentric. One of Josie's younger acquaintances, Guy C. Earl, reported the impression that the father was "a little cracked in the head," distinctly "odd" in both appearance and behavior. Street urchins—the word *hoodlum* originated in San Francisco about this time—concluded that the elder Royce was "crazy" and consequently a suitable target for abuse. Evidently his eccentricity was related to his evangelical spirit, for instead of tending to business he spent much of his time delivering sermons from street corners. No doubt his well-known ability to quote extensively from the Bible was exercised in many of these impromptu speeches. At any rate his performances tended to drive customers away, and the fruit business, like his other ventures, was a commercial failure.

Earl emphasized the poverty and plainness of the entire family. He remembered seeing them often at a Congregational church, ill clothed, homely, with strong family resemblances. He also remembered that his friend and one of Josie's classmates, Samuel Hall, once visited the Royces to inquire about the boy's prolonged absence from school. Finding the storefront after a good walk from the city's center, Hall was directed by Josie's mother to a woodshed in the backyard. In the shed he could see daylight through the cracks; there he found Josiah recovering from typhoid fever, covered only by an old quilt and lying in a straw bed on the dirt floor.

In June 1866, Josiah was enrolled in Lincoln Grammar School, a splendid new four-story stone building, dedicated to the memory of the martyred president.

Now for the first time and thereafter Josie's education was entrusted to a battery of professional teachers; the watchful protections of his mother and sisters gave way to the rude companionship of boys. Lincoln's enrollment of 906—all boys—was supervised by sixteen teachers, two men and fourteen women. Each class was divided into two sections according to the students' proficiencies; the curriculum seems to have been quite traditional. Gymnastics and military drill were especially emphasized. Each day began with a school-yard assembly. The boys lined up by class behind a captain and a lieutenant; at the signal "about-face" they marched into the building, went to their places, and waited for the order to be seated. The same regimental tone is suggested by the daily calisthenics accompanied by singing, humming, and whistling in concert. Corporal punishment was sanctioned; one student, it was noted, was whipped twenty to thirty times for defying authority. Visitors found the "order" and "stillness" of the school "most remarkable," and gave "warm praise" to the principal and his wife for their management.

The emphasis on physical development, discipline, and submission of individuality to the group was entirely new to Josiah. It tended to deepen his hatred of bullies, particularly military bullies, and he never forgot the rough treatment he received from the other boys. "My comrades," he remembered, "very generally found me disagreeably striking in my appearance, by reason of the fact that I was redheaded, freckled, countrified, quaint, and unable to play boys' games." With irony near to bitterness he added that the boys gave him his "first introduction to the 'majesty of the community,'" which was "impressively disciplinary and persistent." His habit of "preaching down" to other boys succeeded only in intensifying his grief. Royce's memory is confirmed by Earl, who noted that because Josie was odd, poorly dressed, strange in physical appearance, and socially backward, he was a frequent butt of the other boys' teasing.

The alumni of Lincoln are decidedly proud of their school and its traditions, though it is perhaps significant that their memory of Royce has been eclipsed by their homage to more notorious graduates, David Belasco and William Randolph Hearst. Belasco is a particularly revealing counterpart to Royce. The fathers of both boys were penniless forty-niners, and oddly enough, both were fruit dealers in San Francisco during the late 1860s. Years later, Katharine Royce would describe the elder Belasco as a "gypsy Jew." Belasco attended Lincoln Grammar School from 1865 to 1871; this ended his formal education, though in later life he dramatized reality by listing himself in *Who's Who* as a graduate of "Lincoln College." In contrast to Royce, Belasco displayed an almost Grecian beauty matched with flamboyant manners. At Lincoln, he was remembered for his exceptional talent in elocution. That won him a "gold medal for tragedy" with a dramatic reading from Matthew Lewis entitled "The Maniac." By the time that Royce was entering the University of California, Belasco had already begun his famous acting career; the rest of his life is a well-known chapter in the history of the theater.

Royce and Belasco are contrasting products of the California gold rush. More overtly adapted to San Francisco in its bonanza days, Belasco capitalized on its glittering facade; Royce, on the other hand, habitually lonely and friendless, turned inward and found refuge in the Mercantile Library. Belasco accepted his world; Royce pressed against its provincial limitations. For Belasco, experience always needed to be enhanced by drama and romance; his *Girl of the Golden West* was the triumph of his vision. Royce spent his life studying the structure of experience, seeking to discover its general meaning. In *California* and *The Feud of Oakfield Creek* he renounced the legendary Golden West that Belasco promoted. These works were preliminaries to the more philosophical generalizations of *The World and the Individual* and *The Problem of Christianity*, which were for him the climaxes of his life's pursuit.

One can find the early evidences of this contrast in the two boys' responses to the Civil War and the murder of Lincoln. Both were deeply moved by the political events of the early sixties. Their school was one of the first in the country to be dedicated to Lincoln, and no doubt his memory was honored collectively by students and teachers. It inspired Belasco to write his first play, *The Roll of the Drum*, which he performed before neighborhood children in a makeshift theater he constructed in his family's basement. Royce also traced his earliest political feelings to the war and the assassination. In Grass Valley, newspapers offered flamboyant stories of Northern heroism. Royce remembered hearing a good deal about the war, but in his isolation he saw none of its direct consequences. "I remained," he said, "as vague about this matter as about most other life problems,—vague but often enthusiastic."

Since Josie's parents were transplanted Yorkers, he naturally adopted the Unionist viewpoint. His father's politics is indicated by a petition he signed in February 1858. Directed to the state legislature, the petition proposed that the testimony of Negroes in cases involving Caucasians be accepted before California courts of justice, an action that did not take effect until 1863. If therefore the elder Royce was not an outright abolitionist, he was certainly an advocate of civil rights and doubtless passed his political opinions on to his children.

At the age of ten, Josie acquired his first sense of national identity. "My earliest great patriotic experience," he remembered, "came at the end of the civil war, when the news of the assassination of Lincoln reached us. Thenceforth, as I believe, I had a country as well as a religious interest." The assassination grew in his mind and eventually was indirectly reflected in his first publication. Entitled "Is the Assassination of Tyrants ever Justifiable?" the essay was printed in the *Lincoln Observer* in June 1869. Though it was signed only with the initials "JR," there is substantial evidence, both internal and external, that it was written by Royce. The essay is an inquiry into one of the traditional subjects of political theory, and its argument is profoundly conservative. Revolution and political assassination, Josiah argued, contradict the "rules of order and decency"; regardless of a tyrant's wickedness, murdering him encourages "violence and disregard of human life." Though revolution may be justifiable when it is the act of a majority, violent acts on the part of any minority are incompatible with the ideals of democracy. An immoral and cowardly act, assassination never, as history demonstrates, serves the social good. This view is consistent with the Bible, the boy argued, which teaches respect for the ruling power and never justifies the murder of a tyrant. "The assassination of a king or ruler by a conspiracy or by a single person, except by Divine command, has never," he concluded, "done anything but harm, and from its very nature can do nothing else."

Reflecting the mind of the young Royce, this little essay reveals patterns of his thought. Even as a child of thirteen, he looked upon a single event, the murder of Lincoln, as part of a larger, more abstract and theoretical question. His idea of the community, which had expressed itself vaguely in states of wonder, now grew clearer and more complicated. The duties of citizens to the social order now became central. The confusions he saw as a child in newly developing communities, in the war fought to preserve the United States and in the murder of its president, led him eventually to conceive of the Beloved Community. He had been born to an uncertain age, when men in one place were rapidly building communities, while others elsewhere were tearing them apart. From the Civil War at the beginning of his life to World War I at the end, Royce assigned to himself the task of learning the meaning of the world and the individual.

The reports of Josiah's precocity are confirmed by the high intellectual level of this first publication. It seems to have been a sort of graduation essay, for in July 1869, at the age of thirteen, Josie was admitted to Boys' (now Lowell) High School. This institution, like Lincoln, takes pride in its distinguished alumni. One of Royce's classmates, the physicist Albert A. Michelson, became the first American scientist to receive the Nobel Prize. Under the leadership of principal Theodore Bradley, a mathematics instructor, the school offered a favorable atmosphere for scholarship. A young lady who visited the Boys' High School during September of 1869 or 1870 was impressed with its programs in rhetoric and science. She listened enthusiastically to the boys' readings of compositions and paid close attention to Mr. Bradley's demonstration of laboratory equipment. She also found a large collection of geological exhibits, including specimens of petrified rock, shells, gems, and fossils.

Although Josiah spent only one year in the high school, the experience was intellectually and socially profitable. Earl remembered that he was so quick in mathematics that he completed a whole term's work in a few days. Though excused by his teacher from further study, he worked independently in solid geometry and trigonometry, and even devised his own system of logarithms. Ruth emphasized the same spirit of independence. "He was," she said, "an omnivorous reader, and besides everything connected with his high school course, made excursions for himself into literature." She remembered his great love of the classics, his enthusiastic recitations, and the beginning of his life-long reading of German literature. Finding Goethe's *Faust*, he "seemed to revel in it with the enthusiasm of personal discovery." Among similar "epoch-marking events" Royce remembered finding George Grote's *History of Greece* in the high-school library and reading "two or three mathematical books" and "a few novels" in San Francisco's Mercantile Library. In approaching his studies with the joy of independent adventure, Josiah embodied the spirit of the intellectual pioneer. "He came to all things new to him," Ruth recalled, "apparently with the same insight—so far in advance of his age and of his companions that he saw each new world with the eyes of a discoverer—made his own observations, cut his own trails, saw more in the stupendous whole than others ever saw, and wrote his own records."

At the same time, Josie was beginning to overcome his shyness and social isolation. These traits would continue to trouble him throughout life, but for the first time he discovered the possibility of friendship with other boys his age. The unions began during the latter years at Lincoln. "I remember," he said, "lifelong friendships which I formed in that Grammar School, and which I still can enjoy whenever I meet certain of my dear California friends." Ruth insisted that he still did not seek social life, but added, "My remembrance is that it was during his adolescent period that he first made friendships with school mates that became comradeships. They were few but they lasted through the years."

A suggestion of Royce's longing for companionship, and also of his youthful imagination, is provided through a short story he wrote in high school. Entitled "A Nocturnal Expedition," it describes a dream of traveling to a seashore in Australia with a young male friend. Whether the dream was actual or imagined is not particularly important, though it does contain some elements of a recurring nightmare Royce had in the late 1870s. The story's importance lies in the feelings it expresses, the longing for friendship and the corresponding fear of its loss. The fanciful expedition to Australia—a curious destination, since Royce would actually go there in 1888 to recover from a nervous breakdown—takes the narrator far from his home and family in San Francisco; his seaside reunion with an "old schoolmate" offers him freedom to express the physical pleasures of boyhood. Even though the narrator's instinctive caution prevents him from taking to the surf with his bolder friend, he is content to watch. When the friend disappears in the waves, however, the narrator is terrified; the deep pool and the silence bring on an urgent loneliness, and as he searches for the friend, he is overwhelmed by guilt. The feeling is intensified when he is confronted by the friend's mother.

> A cold, shuddering horror seized me. I stretched forth my hand but it met nothing. I opened my eyes and darkness was all around. I groped round and at length memory came to my assistance. Not the far distant Australia, but American San Francisco, contained me. The schoolmate who had formed so great a part of my dream was now, doubtless asleep in the same city; while the voyage and its terrible results, the rolling tides, the dark pool, and the recovered garment, were all the delusions of a dismal dream, and the morning of the First of April was dawning.

This resolution is nearly identical to the ending of the remembered story of "the too trustful little boy." In both cases Josiah strays from the protections of his home in the company of an interesting, bolder friend, but through "tribulation" is happily reunited with his family. The subtitle of "Pussy Blackie's Travels" had been "There's No Place Like Home"; that again is the lesson of "A Nocturnal Expedition."

The divided emotions revealed in Josie's fictions and fantasies involve feelings of abandonment, longing for male companionship, passivity or reluctance to participate, and fear of an impending catastrophe, particularly one that separates the child from home and family. Death is, of course, the ultimate form of separation, and in "A Nocturnal Expedition," the appearance of the grieving mother shocks the dreamer from his sleep. According to Royce's memory, his earliest recognition of death was introduced by the lonely grave near his home in Grass Valley. He was preoccupied with that image throughout his childhood. It became the central detail in two essays he wrote during adolescence, and just before he died he noted it as one of his prominent early memories. The first of the two essays, entitled "The Miner's Grave," was written as a high-school composition. It is crowded with the imagery of abandonment and desolation: "Affection's hand had not been present to erect anything by which the memory of the deceased might be kept up. Only a little mound of earth, a few pine logs piled carelessly around, and a shingle, with a half-effaced inscription, distinguished the spot from the common earth around it." The burial plot is a "barren spot," a "desolate place," next to "a dusty country road." Even the young pine trees that grow thickly nearby seem to have a "horror" of the place and "studiously" avoid it. The worst horror, however, is neither the fact of death nor desolation, but the utter indifference of the world: "Few ever noticed the barren spot, near as it was to the road. And most of those who did so, simply glanced at the illegible inscription on the rude board, wondered who came to fill such an obscure grave, and with the words, 'Poor fellow' on their lips, passed on." The fear that Josiah projected into this essay is not the knowledge that one dies, but the fear that no one may care.

Much later, at different times during the 1890s, Royce explained these adolescent tensions as the inevitable shocks that accompany the growth of self-consciousness, a process, he said, that had led him to systematic thought. "The question, *Who am I?*" he observed, "contains notoriously all the issues of philosophy." In a letter to G. Stanley Hall, written in 1898, he gave a revealing account of his youthful anxieties. The new feelings that accompany adolescence, he remarked, have the immediate effect of disturbing the order of the childhood self: "Youth means a flood of new sensations, of new emotions, of novel social stimulations, and of resulting vague ideals. The old self simply gets broken up." Remembering his own youth, Royce recalled the romantic fantasies he had entertained. Life had seemed a "voyage" without a "pilot," and the safe "shore" of childhood that had been "relatively known, stable, and sure" was irrevocably lost. "I felt confident, and helpless, all at once." If having these deep feelings constituted the "grandest" part of life, they were also, as unsatisfied longings, "most dreadful." These fluctuating moods may lead a youth, Royce added, at different times to adopt an extravagant idealism or sink altogether into despair. From the social relations of childhood he had learned that "self-consciousness" means "plan, assurance, purpose, and social position." But youth "has lost hold, . . . cares no more for the old plans,—no longer is content to be a hunter or trapper (as in boyhood I had once meant to do when I should grow up)." He may wish to be a poet, a saint, a world reformer, a rebel, or an outcast; perhaps he will toy insincerely with thoughts of suicide. In the midst of his suffering he is likely to become bashful and to cherish "a lonely love for some impossible closeness of sympathy, with friends whom he sees not."

> But through all this one has the idea, the ideal, the abstract picture or ground plan, of what selfhood would be,—viz., power, courage, plan, and above all social status,—a place among the "men my brothers,—men the workers." For that ideal of selfhood one had acquired already as child. Hence you have all the materials for a fundamental problem:—Who am I? What am I good for?

In isolation, cut off from childhood and estranged from adulthood, the youth's search for selfhood, Royce insisted, eventually leads him to the problem of reality:

> Now Reality is, to any man, simply what he conceives as fulfilling the aims of his most rational Self. If a man studies science, and learns to submit, in an intellectual self-abnegation, to the hard facts, that submission comes only because he learns to see therein his most rational self-fulfillment. If a man becomes a cynic or pessimist, and pretends to abhor all reality, he learns even such abhorrence only as a sort of falsely supposed rational virtue wherein his rational aims get their best practicable fulfillment under assumed hopeless conditions. If he remains

sceptic, that is because he has not yet found himself. In brief, to seek your place in the Universe, is to be interested in the Universe; and conversely, the interest in the "whole problem of reality," involves, and means, an interest in solving the problem of who I am, of what I ideally ought to be, and of what my life means.

Royce's childhood began with wonder; it ended, or at any rate entered its final period, when mere wonder gave place to philosophical questioning. This process involved a turning inward: it began with the world and ended with the self. Youth's urgent question—Who am I?—gradually subsumed the child's vague interest in the world beyond. The world within its mountain walls, in youth became internalized, as psychic more than physical; its beyonds were sought as undiscovered components of selfhood. During the next twelve years, through the 1870s and into the 1880s, Josiah's quest would lead him halfway around the earth and back. There was, then, certainly a physical dimension to his journey. But at the same time he was engaged in a journey inward, pushing beyond the boundaries of a child's world, discovering new areas of experience, seeking and finding the answer to the question that he knew contained all philosophy.

Chapter Two

Youth and Education
1870-1878

Freshman and Sophomore

In his letter to Stanley Hall, Royce noted that the growth of self-consciousness coincides with the discovery of philosophy, that solving the problem of identity involves a commitment to an ideology. A young man's doubts, his resistance to ideology, run parallel to his search for identity. "If he remains sceptic," Royce observed, "that is because he has not yet found himself." The twin processes of finding an identity and a philosophy belong in Royce's biography, to the twelve years between 1870 and 1882. The period begins with Josiah's entrance into the University of California; it includes his graduate study in Germany and at the Johns Hopkins University, and extends into his four years as an English instructor at Berkeley. It ends when he joins the philosophy department at Harvard. He is fourteen at the start and not quite twenty-seven at the end. These years were marked by anxiety, achievement, ambition, and impatience. As he remembered his youth, it was a time of striving for "power, courage, plan, and above all social status,—a place among the 'men my brothers,—men the workers.'"

Royce was, above all, a willing and dedicated worker, perfectly suited in his time, by intellect and temperament, to push back the boundaries of knowledge. It was also his fortune to appear often at the beginnings of things when his labor was needed for new and important tasks. Lucky for him, in 1868, the University of California began operations on a tuition-free basis, and in 1870, the preparatory class carried on its rolls the name of Josiah Royce Jr.

The legal origins of the University of California were written into the state constitution of 1849, though by the mid-1860s little had been done to make that institution more than a name. By that time several private colleges had been established: the University of Santa Clara, California Wesleyan College (later the University of the Pacific), Benicia Young Ladies Seminary (later Mills College), and the College of California. The last of these institutions, with headquarters in Oakland, possessed the highest reputation. It also controlled, despite threatening debts, an attractive property four miles north of Oakland, between the forks of Strawberry Creek, in a place named for the philosopher George Berkeley. In 1866, under the authority of the Morrill Act, the state leg-islature created the Agricultural, Mining and Mechanical Arts College. But since this institution had no program, whereas the College of California was nearly bankrupt, a plan for combining resources of both colleges was devised. The key to the merger was the 160-acre tract in Berkeley. The union was suc-cessfully accomplished, and its offspring, the University of California, was legally established on March 23, 1868.

The preparatory or "fifth" class, which Josiah entered during the fall semes-ter of 1870, had fifty-five students. Admission policy stipulated that a student be at least "fourteen years of age, and . . . pass a satisfactory examination in English grammar, arithmetic, geography, and United States history." The program was, in effect, the final year of high school. Imposed by the Regents, the preparatory class failed to win the faculty's support, and partly because of this it was dis-banded in 1872. From the student's viewpoint, however, the university offered a much better education than could be found in the local high schools, and Josiah made the best of his opportunity. Under a grading system on a hundred-point scale, he earned marks of 100 in English, 93.9 in mathematics, and 79.5 in French. When one considers that his age had barely qualified him for admis-sion, that he had had only one year in a regular high school, and that he was competing with college freshmen, it is clear that Josiah's impressive marks as a preparatory student gave promise of a distinguished undergraduate record.

At about this time, no doubt partly because of Josiah's transfer to the uni-versity, the elder Royce gave up his fruit business in San Francisco, took a job as a traveling salesman, and moved his family to Brooklyn, a township now part of the city of Oakland. During the following year Josiah's college education began officially. On September 23, 1871 he was registered in the freshman class, the 115th student to be admitted to the University of California. He continued to impress his teachers by earning marks of 97.5, 78.6, and 97 in English; 93.88 and 93.43 in mathematics; and 98, 81.4, and 92 in history. He fell behind in French with scores of 85.5 and 67, while a course in drawing or drafting was a disaster with a grade of 65. In the summer of 1872 he tried to correct these defi-ciencies by taking additional work in drawing and French. His efforts, however, succeeded only modestly; his new scores were 72 and 75.

As his curriculum indicates, Josiah's freshman year was little more than a

continuation of high school, and a number of factors seem to justify his pronounced feeling that real collegiate work had not yet begun. The university was
still confined to the shabby buildings of the College of California, for construction of the Berkeley campus was in its early planning stage. The library—Royce
remembered it as "ill accessible, almost wholly uncatalogued, hastily
ordered"—was tucked away in the garret of Brayton Hall. Joseph C. Rowell—
then a student and afterward the permanent librarian—recalled that the collection of fewer than twelve hundred volumes emphasized modern poets,
essayists, and novelists. Among the modest holdings a single cause of "joy and
enthusiasm" was the latest edition of the *Encyclopaedia Britannica*.

Equally unimpressive, the university's administration was prematurely antiquated. In the absence of a permanent president the aged Henry Durant, one
of the builders of the College of California, had been given the task of holding
things together temporarily. Nor was the faculty particularly distinguished; consequently the instruction Josiah received was often slipshod. William Swinton,
a prominent English professor who was later forced into resignation because of
his habitual absence from class, eccentrically refused to correct his students'
compositions. Instead, Swinton had his youngsters read their themes aloud, and
while the students stood before the class, their instructor "simply took one of
the abominations and coolly, cruelly, dissected it with much sarcastic remark."
According to Rowell, Swinton's comments were "like Delphic responses, puzzling and unaccountable."

Josiah was largely on his own, and his main resource in those days was that
scanty collection of books in Brayton Hall. Rowell remembered him as the
"most constant reader of all, . . . who, probably because of physical limitations,
did not participate in the rather rough sports on the campus." After postlun-
cheon games of chess, Josiah habitually stayed in the library until the appointed
hour for required military drill. "It happened," Rowell added, "that the library,
considering its size, contained a very unusual number of theological and philosophical writers, and it is absolutely certain that Royce here began . . . his study
of these subjects." Many lonely hours were spent in that garret, but Royce
recalled them as "some of the most inspiring hours of my life"; the books were
"the dearest friends of my youth."

A lonely, bookish youth, Josiah learned to trust these "dearest friends" and
to minimize the importance of human friendships. Reflecting on the relative
influence of books and men, he complained that "the influence of a man over
us is commonly like the influence of a very changing weather on growing
plants." He sensed a danger in human contact, a distrust of human variability
with its unpredictable floods, droughts, and frosts; thus, Josiah relied more on
books where "ideals may be much more simply and perfectly expressed than in
any man." The discovery of Homer, the writings of John Stuart Mill, and

Mansel's *Limits of Religious Thought* became "epoch-marking events," which gave him "a new turn in life, a new insight into the world, in some important way a new being." Josiah's sister Ruth remembered him in his college days as a solitary and somewhat angry youth: "He tramped over miles of rough mountain paths and trails *alone, thinking,* and emphasizing his thoughts with flourishes and blows from his walking stick."

This image is consistent with the theme of the solitary journey that occupied a dominant place in Josiah's dreams and fantasies. Early in his college years he reported that he had awakened one morning "with a start from some long tangled mass of mournful dreams," in which he was "wandering a vast distance in search of something." As he fell back into sleep this "tangled mass" became clarified by a dream involving three successive journeys: in the first he is "idle, without a purpose, moving slowly on in a deep revery" through a crowded city street; next he is walking, alone and weary, at dusk along an abandoned country road; finally he is pushing through a wilderness of "rushing rivers," "steep mountains," and "a vast tangled forest." Each segment of the dream is dominated by the imagery of alienation. He is physically present in the world, but not a part of it; he has no role, no purpose, and no identification with the crowd. Walking on the country road, the dreamer finds himself alone with the universe, "going on, with the same oppressive loneliness." He is walking eastward into the night, searching for some "unattainable knowledge," which he pursues "in the far depths of space." The first two segments of the dream suggest strongly that Josiah was seeing himself as his father, the wanderer, the street peddler and traveling salesman, a man without power, plan, or social status.

But the dream also contains a maternal figure, a kind of Gretchen or Beatrice, a pale, dark-eyed woman, who is "gentle" and "thoughtful," whose smile seems to offer sympathy and encouragement. Josiah has a vision of this woman just before he falls asleep; she reappears for a moment on the city street and passes by silently on the country road. Finding but not possessing her, Josiah is seized by a "fierce resolution." "Life," he thinks, "shall not be an endeavor and no satisfaction. Happiness was made for man. Let me have my share." This thought leads him to the third segment of the dream. Now he is searching no longer for some ideal knowledge, but for the woman herself—"that angelic face, faultless, pitying." His journey leads him into a gothic landscape, past indifferent strangers. Finally he arrives at the tangled forest where he meets an old man who urges him to look into a stagnant pool. As he does he sees not only his own face, but also the reflection of the woman. Both faces seem to float up with a "ghastly phosphorescent light of decay." He realizes that he and the woman are dead: "We had both been indeed long numbered among the forgotten throngs of the putrefying dead." And with a shriek he awakens.

One night, still preoccupied with thoughts of death, Josiah visited an old graveyard in Oakland on Webster Street near Lake Merritt. He was drawn there by "the sorrows of parting": "Of all the many evils of our lives," he noted, "there is hardly any one that so constantly intrudes itself upon us as the ever-recurring necessity of parting from our friends." He felt as if "some evil genius" were at work to lure us into companionship only to intensify our misery by an "inevitable separation." A strange inconsistency in human nature tempts us to escape the pain of loneliness and to seek the foredoomed pleasure of love; thus, "with desperation we are forced to plunge from the one misery to the other." Feeling cheated, the victim of a cosmic trick, Josiah noted that each path of the dilemma ends in grief, but of the two the path of loneliness is much less painful: "The joys of friendship," he said, "are far exceeded by its sorrows." In the beautiful moonlight graveyard Josiah condemned emotions and life in general; life seemed "like a fever" in contrast to the "true happiness" of the moon's "cold wan, everlasting desolation."

> I leaned over the paling of one of the graves. The dark growth of bushes and grass had long since almost hidden the mound. The oak overhead cast its deep shadow upon all, and only here and there a little streak of moonlight entered and faintly lit up all. It seemed so strange to pass, from the light and merriment and bustle of Broadway so soon into this unearthly calm. Yes, what perfect stillness, not a rustle of breeze, not a ripple of water, not a single footfall disturbed the night. I felt as much alone as if in the distant extremity of some vast Scythian wilderness, alone with the thoughtful moon and the motionless dead.

Josiah's dream had left him stranded and alone with a dead past; in the graveyard, longing "to join the great company of the Dead," his despair had its fullest expression. But the other side of his ambivalence revealed a terrible fear of dying and a desire to join the living. "What refuge is there from the sorrows of parting but death, and what is death but parting from all?" Hating life and fearing death, Josiah reached a crisis of youth. Much later, while commenting on the youth's universal "problem of interpreting himself," Royce noted that the search for identity involves a "critical passing of a boundary in one's own inner world." In the graveyard Josiah approached one of these boundaries. Though his mind was filled with morbid fantasies, a "brighter side" asserted itself. Cheated by the passing love of another, Josiah began to respond to the possibility of loving and serving man in general:

> A voice seems to speak in the stillness. What if your lot is more miserable than you would wish, yet millions of beings yet unborn are to feel the sorrows that you feel. Think what a reward of your life it would be to know that you have done that which may lighten the burden of someone whom you may never see. . . . How glorious is the life that, forgetting all reward in this life or even in that to come, gives itself to the service of Humanity. Let this be the object of your life—yes, Humanity.

44

This resolution, quite unlike the "fierce resolution" of Josiah's dream, would become, under the rubric of "loyalty," a central point in Royce's idealism. It was one of several elements that he was able to preserve from the dead past. Perhaps he had been born for loneliness, but he had also been born for books, thought, and service.

In building his identity around this ideal, Josiah needed to find adult models to serve as points of comparison and subjects for emulation. Since his father was, in most respects, a defective representative of the ideal, Josiah repeatedly attached himself to surrogates. At the University of California two men allowed themselves to be adopted: Joseph Le Conte and Daniel Coit Gilman. Of the two, Le Conte was the first in time and importance. Primarily a geologist and the university's only really distinguished professor, Le Conte attracted Josiah's attention during his freshman year. Though he was not yet permitted to enroll in Le Conte's courses, Josiah hung outside the lecture room listening with fascination to the wonderful quality of the professor's southern accent and struggling to find connections between the scattered words he could hear. Eagerly Josiah anticipated his sophomore year when he could become officially one of Le Conte's students.

One evening he heard Le Conte lecture to the university on the interior of the earth. What impressed Josiah was not so much the content of the lecture as its structure. Never before had he been so impressed with "the architecture of an argument." The experience revitalized his feelings of wonder. "The union of empirical data with speculative ingenuity which the whole discussion involved appealed to my deepest instincts, as music, when first heard, awakens a sensitive young appreciation. The artistic mode of exposition charmed as an exciting story charms. And the wonder thus aroused was, for me, a beginning of philosophy."

Somewhat aloof but still fatherly, Daniel Coit Gilman was the university's first permanent president. If Le Conte offered an example of the scientist and philosopher that young Royce hoped to become, Gilman was the patrician spokesman for ideals that Josiah was just beginning to espouse. With bloodlines that reached back to the seventeenth century, Gilman was a solid member of that New England aristocracy which notoriously blends enormous dignity with vigorous independence. His biographer describes him as "a thorough Yale man," and before coming to Berkeley—he had previously turned down the presidency of the University of Wisconsin—he had been the college librarian and head of the Sheffield Scientific School. He was forty-one when he arrived in California, just at the beginning of his distinguished career as a university builder. His relationship with Royce lasted for more than thirty years, and during that time it shifted accordingly. He became in turn guardian, sponsor, confidant, and friend. But to a youth of sixteen Gilman was primarily the spokesman. "From him, in lectures," Royce later remembered, "we heard something of the ideals of the great new academic movement that was then beginning in our country." As Josiah was offering his life to the service of humanity, he must have been thrilled to hear Gilman define the work of the University of California: "It is to fit young men for high and noble careers, satisfactory to themselves, and useful to mankind; it is to bring before the society of to-day, the failures and successes of societies in the past; it is to discover and make known how the forces of nature may be subservient to mankind; it is to hand down to the generations which come after us, the torch of experience by which we have been enlightened."

With the opening of the fall term in 1872, an aura of excitement surrounded the university. Gilman had arrived during the summer, and the construction of the Berkeley campus was under way. On October 9, the entire community turned out to lay the cornerstone of South Hall. Before the ceremony, few of the students had visited the site with its magnificent, uncluttered view of San Francisco, the Bay, and the Golden Gate. It seemed a "beautiful Arcadia," and a "shrine." The gaiety of student song accompanied the procession as it left Oakland on overloaded horsecars. Midway, most of the students climbed down from their cars and walked. Gilman contributed to the sense that something altogether new was about to begin. In his inaugural address, delivered a month later, he described the future of higher education in California. The university, he insisted, was not to become "a high-school, nor a college, nor an academy of sciences, nor an industrial-school"; instead it was to be dedicated to "the promotion and diffusion of knowledge—a group of agencies organized to advance the arts and sciences of every sort, and to train young men as scholars for all the intellectual callings of life."

At this time, during Josiah's sophomore year, he was assigned to the status of "student at large." He had joined the freshman class as a member of the College of Civil Engineering, but withdrew at the end of one year. This ephemeral interest in becoming a mining engineer remains one of the curious mysteries in Royce's life; his reasons for choosing this profession and for abandoning it have never been satisfactorily clarified. His son Stephen, who did become a mining engineer, had the impression that his father had stuck to the original curriculum through his college education, that his "sole reason" for choosing philosophy originated, in 1875, through the favorable reception of his undergraduate thesis on Aeschylus.

This is not true. Except for the fact that Josiah did take a special six-week course in surveying during 1873, all documentary evidence suggests that Royce never gave serious thought to becoming an engineer after his freshman year. Indeed it is not surprising that a frail, introspective, and literary youth would quickly understand that he had made the wrong choice, nor is it surprising that his son or the father, or both, might have wished that the truth were otherwise, that only a turn of fate had diverted Royce from a career in engineering. Josiah's plan to become a builder, vigorously engaged in the world of things, and a miner, returning to a town like Grass Valley to find the gold that eluded his father, possibly offered him ways of overcoming his physical limitations and the mistakes of his parental heritage. The plan, as conceived, was the wrong one, but he did become a kind of engineer, a builder of philosophical systems, a miner of intellectual gold.

The category of "student at large" contained those who were not, in a technical sense, candidates for university degrees, though some, when they could demonstrate "considerable proficiency in knowledge," were permitted to pursue a full-time course of study. They were, in effect, special students who could enjoy all the advantages of the elective system without the obligation of following any prescribed program. Presumably Josiah's decision to move over to this special category was motivated by his uncertainty about what to study now that he had abandoned plans for an engineering career. During this year he took courses in analytical geometry, physics and mechanics, chemistry, geology and natural sciences, French, and rhetoric. Although he continued, on the whole, to do well, he remained, in some respects, dissatisfied with the quality of instruction. After receiving a miserable 53 in chemistry, Josiah struck back in the margins of his notebook by inventing a whimsical gaseous compound: "Bisulphated Carbonate of Oxide of the compound of Nitrate of the Carbonate of Potassium heated gives off gas like the Professor himself."

In his courses with Joseph Le Conte, however, Josiah never expressed any sort of irreverence. Quite the opposite. The long-awaited beginning of work with Le Conte was an illumination, an escape from Plato's cave of shadows: "The knowledge of the light grew steadily stronger, the familiarity with the true world outside the cave grew steadily more constant day by day." Le Conte's courses began with botany, moved on to zoology, and finally to geology. Josiah took them all. For three years, from the fall of 1872 through the spring of 1875, he managed to attend Le Conte's lectures in every semester. Affectionately known as "Professor Joe," Le Conte expressed a spirit that was contagious, compelling, enduring. Though Josiah was not persuaded to adopt Le Conte's naturalistic viewpoint, and though he felt that the lectures often lacked the thoroughness of modern science, he was deeply touched by Le Conte's philosophical spirit, the "artistic spirit, the love for a beautiful architecture." Le Conte taught Josiah an appreciation for the logic of science. He told his students that they would certainly forget what he said, but he hoped that they would not forget his method. Over the years an acknowledged bond of a son to his father developed between the two men. Le Conte's truth, Royce felt, had set him free. "The whole of my work," he said, "such as it is, is other than it could have been, if my teacher had never spoken. And whatever little good there is in that work is especially colored by his influence."

Something of the effect of this influence is suggested by Josiah's earliest university essays, most of which are focused on evolution. None of these essays is more than a slight and, in some respects, a puerile exercise. Yet as signals of a later development, they are noteworthy; they show that through reading and training, Josiah was becoming more analytical and scientific, relying less on a priori principles and biblical arguments. A far more interesting work, philosophically and psychologically, is the unpublished "Casual Observation of Human Nature," which Josiah composed during his sophomore year. The central concern of this essay is the age-old problem of knowing other minds, a recurrent problem in all of Royce's major works. The essay begins by inviting the reader to imagine a journey:

> When, as often happens during a journey, one is deprived of the company of friends and acquaintances, and thrown for amusement on his own resources, when his eye is fatigued with gazing on uninteresting objects, his ear benumbed by undiverting sounds, an ever attainable and constantly novel source of pleasure is before him in the quiet, unnoticed watching of those around him. Their manners, their features, their looks, their dress, and above all their conversation, may become instruments in his hands of shaping his ideas regarding their characters; and however defective these instruments may be, the mental powers cannot fail to be somewhat improved by their use, while the fancy is engaged by their variety.
>
> While it is true, as has been remarked, that this occupation is simple if viewed in the light of a recreation, yet if we desire to gain from it real additions to our knowledge, we will find considerable difficulty. An interesting inquiry rises as to the real value of this casual observation as a means of acquiring insight into the human character in particular instances, and it is to this inquiry that my essay is intended to be directed.

The inquiry leads Josiah to remark that the difficulty is inherent in the empirical method: careless, hasty, and superficial observations result in errors. On the other hand, scientists observe natural phenomena and are able to construct workable hypotheses that explain the order of the physical universe. What then are the special difficulties that arise when we observe human nature? The answer is that all such observations are "founded on a partial view of the facts"; the real facts are the other person's thoughts and feelings, and these are never directly observed. "It seems then that positive results in this research are unavailable because unattainable."

Josiah was not, however, willing to acquiesce entirely to skepticism. Though positive knowledge of human nature is limited, "negative knowledge"—knowing something of what a man *is not*—is possible. "An example of this method is the following: if we see one giving way to passion, without ourselves knowing the attendant circumstances, it might be unfair and incorrect to decide immediately that he was a person of very irascible disposition, but we might safely say that in some degree he was lacking in self-control." The essay ends with this tentative hypothesis and with the determination "to proceed in this as in all other inquiries only so far as facts will lead us, and not to sacrifice truth to pedantry."

As a technical issue in philosophy, the problem of this essay had a far-reaching influence on Royce's mature thought. Expressed in various forms, it led him to seek the mediating relationships that unite separate minds. Yet, more than this, the problem lay deep in his private emotional life, for the desire behind it is the same "lonely love for some impossible closeness" that Royce associated with his youthful crisis. The fantasy that gives rise to the problem is especially revealing. He is on some "journey," "deprived of the company of friends," "thrown for amusement on his own resources." He is surrounded by others, yet utterly alone. The loneliness tires him, numbs him, finally causes him to find pleasure by observation, "in the quiet, unnoticed watching of those around him." The fantasy does not include his meeting these people, making new friends; he remains an observer and an eavesdropper, intensely curious, wishing to know them, to share their feelings, but sensing the impenetrable walls that separate minds.

The journey is a striking parallel to Josiah's dreams and to the travels of Pussy Blackie, the abandoned pet. Seeing himself on a lonely journey, Josiah converted his anxiety into a solitary recreation and gradually into a philosophical problem. "Truth meets needs," he said much later, adding, "truth is also true." Without detracting, therefore, from the intellectual status of the problem, we may also observe that it originated in the realm of feelings. Josiah merely pushed his desire aside, and accepting the observer's perspective, he hoped "to gain from it real additions to our knowledge." He concluded that we can know only what people are not, never what they are.

Berkeley Classicist

Josiah's tendency to intellectualize his emotional energy was well established by the end of his sophomore year. The next two academic years offered him important opportunities for personal as well as educational development. During the fall term of 1873, when the university moved to its permanent home in Berkeley, Josiah enrolled in the "classical course" of the College of Letters. According to the official circulars, this program was designed for "those who desire to lay a broad foundation of literary, historical, and scientific culture as a basis for further professional study." Greek, Latin, and Hebrew now formed the core of Josiah's studies, and in them he nearly always earned marks in the 90s. In addition, he continued with French and took two courses in linguistics and one in Italian. Although he was emphasizing the humanities, he still found time for courses in mathematics, physics, astronomy, and geology.

Public recognition of Josiah's intellectual superiority began to be expressed during his junior year. In the spring term of 1874 and thereafter he was given an "Honorable Mention for Excellence in Study." In March of that year he also won the fifty-dollar first prize in an oratorical contest sponsored by President Gilman. His topic was "The Modern Novel as a Mode of Conveying Instruction and Accomplishing Reform." Competition was open to both juniors and seniors; each contestant submitted his speech at the beginning of the month, and five were selected for oral delivery on the twenty-third as part of the Charter Day celebration. Guy C. Earl remembered the event vividly:

> On the way out from Oakland to the University, I rode on the back platform of a crowded horsecar. When we arrived at a little village called Temescal, where many poor people lived, there got on to the back platform a boy. It was Josiah Royce. He was dressed, not in short pants, but his pantaloons were short, and his apparel indicated that he was very poor. The streetcar conductor evidently knew him, because he said, "I wish you success today." Royce replied in a little thin voice, "I'll do the best I can."

When they got to the assembly room of North Hall, filled with three or four hundred people, Earl was astonished to see the same odd-looking youth sitting on the speaker's platform. "He was ungainly in appearance and ungraceful in manner," Earl remembered. "He had a colossal head, with great bulging temples, crowned with a shock of red hair." Josiah was the last of the five speakers. Earl recalled that he spoke "in a plain, simple way, in a thin voice, just as if he was conversing with somebody." Josiah maintained that the modern novel is one of the more significant developments of the nineteenth century; its historical importance as "the great agent in civilizing man" lay in its tendencies toward literary realism and philosophical idealism. George Eliot was his prime example. "The first tendency is to view things as they really are, and to subject them all to law, and this demands a more careful attention to probability and naturalness; the second is toward introducing higher questions into everything. To consider the origin of the universe while analyzing the atoms, to discuss the greatest human matters, social, moral, scientific and artistic, while studying the simplest lives, this is the aim of the modern thinkers." Earl felt that the talk had gone over his head; others had been more "elegant" and "timely." But when the program was over, the odd, redheaded boy in short pantaloons had won the prize.

The public success of this contest marks a shift in the style of Josiah's life. During his junior and senior years at Berkeley, the image of the shy, frightened, and retiring boy faded into the background; it was replaced by that of an active, bold, and assertive young man. The bibliography of his publications in 1874 and 1875 lists forty items. He wrote reviews of theatrical performances and art exhibits; he described the Berkeley sunsets and advocated the formation of a chess club; he reviewed Draper's *History of the Conflict between Religion and Science* and Lewes's *Problems of Life and Mind,* eulogized Henry Durant, and wrote literary criticism of Aeschylus, Sophocles, Shakespeare, Poe, Tennyson, George Eliot, Hardy, and Turgenev. As for his academic work, the archival records show that in his senior year alone he was enrolled in nineteen different courses.

His classmates noticed the change. He was no longer "Josie" and rarely "Josiah"; now he was "Royce" and most familiarly "Josh." Now also he asserted his independence by dropping the "Jr." from his name. In February 1875, he was selected as one of five editors of the student monthly, the *Berkeleyan.* Its pages contain, besides his own numerous articles, many tributes and a lot of good-humored teasing. On one occasion his friends wrote:

> They do say that Josiah, our Josiah, has been flirting. Alas! in these days of turmoil and excitement, of rings and bribery, of Caesarism and flirting, on whom can we depend? We thought that we could lay in a supply of pool on Josiah, but the young lady acknowledges it. Vale Josiah, we will have to invest our shekels on Thad. Stevens.

The "Personals" column of another issue included the following:

> "Josh," the last of the five [editors], is hopping around in a business-like sort of a way, writing editorials, studying up for Thesis, and still considers his conscience good when he is compelled by press (of business) to "cut" only two recitations per day.—.—.—.—.

Sometimes the notes accuse Josh of "making 'mashes' on Broadway" and of warming "a whole pew in the Congregational Church," but these are clearly friendly thrusts that appreciate his oddities as well as his capacity for productive thought.

A minor incident that occurred during the spring of 1875 illustrates Royce's new assertiveness. Involving a triangular controversy between the *Berkeleyan* on one side and the *Mills Quarterly* and the Santa Clara *Owl* on the other, the incident was the first, but certainly not the last, time that Royce's outspoken prose would initiate a public quarrel. The January issue of the *Mills Quarterly* had printed two elegantly composed essays, "Will" and "Power." The next issue of the *Berkeleyan* contained Royce's "Notes on Exchanges," with an attack on the *Mills Quarterly* for its "rambling treatises, that begin in the Garden of Eden, or some equally far-off locality, take a rapid flight through the universe, and end in dream-land"; in a final lunge he accused the *Owl* of "hypercritical peevishness." The *Owl* replied by defending itself and the Mills students. In April, Royce apologized for his overly sharp criticism of the *Mills Quarterly*, but added: "The *Owl* is too poor a judge of fairness in criticism to be any authority as to the one, and is hardly in its right when it meddles with the other." The same issue of the *Berkeleyan* described a musicale and party given for the university's senior class at the Mills Seminary, noting that the hall was decorated with Chinese lanterns. With obvious glee the *Berkeleyan* also noted that "Josh's poem on Chinese lanterns is crowded out," and "it is a lie—that Royce did not want to go to Mills, that he is not 'sadder than before.'" The Mills students remained composed. The May issue of the *Mills Quarterly* compliments the *Berkeleyan*: "We appreciate the wise man's saying, 'Faithful are the wounds of a friend,' and so we accept their criticism upon our last number." The note also described the university's oratory contest of that year and praised "two finely written essays on 'Truth in Art,'" adding that "the orations . . . showed much careful thought and study. The delivery of some might be improved. The prize was awarded to Mr. Josiah Royce, of Oakland, and we tender to him our sincere congratulations."

This last reference points to a far more important event in Royce's life and one of his most impressive undergraduate efforts. The ground rules for the 1875 oratory contest resembled those of the previous year, except that this time only seniors were eligible. Contestants were required to submit their manuscripts anonymously by January 20, five of which were to be selected for oral presentation. Again the prize was fifty dollars. Royce's friends on the *Berkeleyan* seemed to view it as virtually certain that he would repeat his triumph of the previous year, and in their usual style they found another opportunity to tease: "It is a lie," they wrote in the February issue, "that Josh don't think that he will get the $50 prize—that he said he'd treat if he did—that the boys declined with thanks."

The speeches were delivered on February 26. The problem of truth in art, Royce noted at the outset, is an ancient one. The Greeks were the first to develop a coherent theory. They called it mimesis or truthful representation. Although they were never quite clear about what was to be represented, the Greeks did agree that the objects of imitation were constituted in some external reality, nature or the heavenly world of ideas. The modern age, Royce felt, had witnessed a breakup of the Hellenic conception of reality, of the harmony of God, man, and nature. Consequently the moderns are forced to start with the fragments of experience, the particulars, and work from this point toward general laws. Literature and the visual arts, he observed, do not so much imitate as distort the external world. To salvage and refine the concept of truthful representation, Royce turned to the art of music:

> From music, as such, we can demand no truthfulness in the imitation of external nature. But do we not demand a sort of truth in every musical composition? Undoubtedly we do. We expect and require a fair, a consistent, a truthful expression of some human feeling. Even the mechanical perfection that secures freedom from discord, is made necessary by this very fact. And all that we require beyond mere mechanical perfection rests on the same ground. In proportion as we understand the feeling expressed, our appreciation of music varies with the perfectness of the expression and the grandeur of the feeling itself. So the truth we demand from this branch of art, is truth in the expression of emotion.

What is true in music, he maintained, is true in all the arts: "The truth to external nature in a work of art is always subordinate to the truth in emotional expression." The distortions in the myth of Undine are necessary as means of coming to terms with human feeling. Certainly this is the case with literature; George Eliot's *Middlemarch* and Tennyson's poetry illustrate this point constantly, as do the visual arts. It has far-reaching significance, for since emotion is so central to human experience, it is inconceivable that civilization could develop without art. Art, therefore, is not a useless amusement, but a companion to science.

> The most prominent characteristic of modern life is its complexity, and its consequent want of harmony. The ideal life should be, as the ancients loved to say, like a piece of music, without a discordant tone. But this ideal . . . is beyond our power to realize, amid our confused surroundings. Our desire and our duties are ever at variance. If we strive to attain that which is higher, too often we utterly fail. If we seek harmony of life, it is but to be met with discord. . . .
>
> By the side of science, therefore, harmonious with her aim and desire, coworker in the unmeasured task of directing upwards the vast mass of Humanity, ever stands the eager, loving form of Art. The one deliberates, plans, discovers; the other encourages, incites, aids. The one seeks to alleviate and to prevent suffering; the other supports and comforts those who cannot be relieved.

Thus, anticipating his later distinction between the worlds of description and appreciation, Royce won much more than a fifty-dollar first prize; he found an enduring idealism that gave shape to the structure of his mature thought.

At the same time, as a complement to his idealistic theory of art, Royce discovered a parallel idealism in science. In 1874 George Henry Lewes published the first volume of his *Problems of Life and Mind.* Royce was particularly impressed by Lewes's chapter "Ideal Construction of Science." It gave him the path of idealism that he would later call "the world of the postulates" and still later would explore in the first five lectures of *The World and the Individual* (second series). In June 1875, reviewing Lewes's book for the *Berkeleyan,* Royce noted that science proceeds by forming simple and definite principles that help to explain phenomena, but the phenomena, because of varying conditions, never strictly illustrate the principles. According to the first law of motion, a moving body theoretically will follow a straight line. This, however, never happens; indeed, none of the so-called laws of physics and astronomy can be argued on the basis of pure empiricism. Summarizing Lewes's point, Royce noted: "Science then is ideal. Its laws are abstractions never realized in our own experience. For we can understand our own experience only by considering it piece by piece, by logically dividing it into factors which we conceive as going to make it up."

A quarter of a century later, Royce would rephrase this conclusion by pointing out that the so-called laws of nature are "interpolated series of ideal objects conceived as *between* the systems of facts that we can observe." Understanding this, Royce saw that the individual human consciousness gains renewed prominence. Lewes had shown him the error in that crude and simplistic naturalism which portrays man as the toy of the external world. Evolution, he would soon realize, is "a beautiful little dream of the intellect, coherent and doubtless in the main destined to be permanent, but still a construction of our own, useful, and acceptable only as being useful." At a time when so much was being written to deepen the conflict between science and humanism, young Royce viewed them both as congenial manifestations of the inner life.

The formation of Royce's youthful idealism had not been accomplished without a serious religious crisis. Little is definitely known about his rejection of his parents' faith, but it is clear that the experience was painful and that the theory of evolution was, for him as for most of his contemporaries, the problem that challenged orthodoxy. "I remember the failing at heart," he said later, "when I first had to throw overboard my little old creed, and felt that I must for example accept the modern theory of evolution as the real truth of nature." The acceptance of evolution introduced a period of doubt that fundamentally altered his religious perspectives. His father's eccentric zeal and his mother's mysticism were both defeated by the son's growing knowledge of scientific truth. "The individual withered," he said, "and natural selection was more and more."

The religious crisis did not, however, push Josiah into despair. Though uncertain, his mood could not be described as acutely anxious. Instead he grew stoic and, as William James would have said, tough-minded. Ironically his earliest exposure to the philosophy of religion had promoted his skepticism. At home he had learned that faith is based on mystical insight and revelation, but occasionally he had heard ministers who argued for religion on the grounds of reason. Josiah was not convinced. "I remember clearly," he said years later, "the ministrations of such men as I heard them more than once in my boyhood and in my early youth. They used to quicken my wits by the hostility which they awakened in my mind, and to arouse my boyish fury by their dogmatism." Though this form of quasi-philosophical indoctrination helped to turn Josiah in the direction of his professional calling, it certainly also drove him away from orthodoxy. "They did so by ostentatiously pretending to reason about philosophical problems, under conditions which all the while, made the spirit of leisurely and dispassionate inquiry simply impossible. They undertook to investigate; but theirs were foregone conclusions. They said, 'Come, let us reason together,' and they hurled their dogmas at me, and denounced, more or less ingeniously, all possible opponents. They in any case taught me one thing, which I have never forgotten . . . , namely they taught me that the pulpit is no place for philosophical investigation."

Remembering his religious crisis, Royce offered a generalized description of all such youthful skepticism:

> We begin, like everyone, with some traditional faith, and then, when the doubting time comes, we make some day a resolution that feeling, emotion, personal desire, impulse, subjective faith, must no longer form or influence our beliefs. . . . We carry this out consistently, and for awhile belief seems to us to be a pure matter of external evidence that is collated and revised by us, but that is in its matter received or to be received with dumb passive acquiescence. If the belief is chilling or dreadful, so are north winds and death; and we submit, or think we ought to submit, unresistingly.

On the other hand, as we have seen, he learned before his undergraduate days ended that emotion cannot be deleted from life, that even the coldest opinions are motivated by feelings. Though he knew that he would never return to his childhood creed, he also came to realize that the life of reason was partly emotional. A fuller knowledge of experience drove him back to passion, and with passion, to faith.

Royce's account of his religious crisis agrees with the records of his private reading during this period and with much of his undergraduate writing. Late in life he cited the works of John Stuart Mill and Herbert Spencer as among the principal philosophical influences of his youth. In 1874, the year after Mill's death, Royce wrote an enthusiastic memorial to the great utilitarian, praising the depth and range of his writings, and giving special emphasis to his *System*

of Logic. At the same time he praised Spencer as "the greatest thinker now living" and "the living expounder of Evolution, the far-reaching grasper of scien-   55
tific truth under every form." An exponent of natural selection during what he
later called "the storm-and-stress period of Darwinism," Royce vigorously
opposed religious bigotry. Likening antievolutionary thought to the view that the
earth is flat, he characterized the theological arguments against natural selection as

> real dangers to progress, . . . not, indeed, because the law of Evolution is in itself
> so necessary an article of faith, not because it has been indubitably proved out-
> side of a somewhat limited field, not because scientific method and the scientific
> spirit are not altogether independent of its validity; but because the prejudice and
> misconceptions which form the staple arguments against it among a certain class,
> are utterly destructive of all true views of nature, are fatal to the appreciation of
> any scientific proof, are deadly foes of both the method and the spirit of this great
> instrument of advancement.

But if young Royce opposed religious bigots, he also resisted the overzealous
attitudes of certain evolutionists. In two reviews of John William Draper's
History of the Conflict between Religion and Science, he asserted his emotional
solution to religious doubt. Draper had set out to denounce religion as an
obstruction to the growth of scientific understanding. Because of this, Royce
criticized Draper's lack of historical tolerance, his failure to consider the social
forces that had promoted conflicts between religion and science at different
times in the past. But a far more important failure in Draper's book, Royce felt,
was his tendency to treat religious feelings as equivalent to some doctrinal per-
suasion. In contrast to Draper, Royce sought to distinguish the religious life
from dogma: "Beliefs are numberless," he observed; "the spirit of Religion is
one." Any of the specific doctrines of Christianity may be renounced, but still
the motives that lead men to religion demand satisfaction. Royce identified this
theme in the earliest teachings of the church. Quoting the Epistle of James, he
approved of the view that "true religion and undefiled before God and the
Father is this, to visit the fatherless and the widows in their affliction, and to
keep himself unspotted from the world." Whatever science teaches, it cannot
conflict with religion, any more than the industrial arts can conflict with love.
Scientific discoveries may cause one to doubt specific dogmas, but the religious
life—religious longings, the need to cultivate uncontaminated spiritual values—endures. Royce learned this truth early. Gradually he came to see it as
central to the "problem" of Christianity.
    The course of Josiah's religious crisis and its idealistic resolution must have
been guided largely by the influence of Joseph Le Conte. By the 1870s the
lessons of Darwin had become the basis of the most advanced social theory, and

Royce noted, on joining the ranks of Le Conte's students, that evolution "determined the whole character of his lectures." Although the lectures were officially limited to evolution as a scientific hypothesis, Le Conte often expanded his subject to include social and philosophical issues. Royce later remembered that one of those courses contained a number of lectures on the growth of human thought. Since there was no regular instruction in philosophy at the University of California during those years, Le Conte's lectures were Royce's main introduction to speculative thought. It is hardly surprising, therefore, that Royce considered Le Conte's enlargement of geology into philosophy as "of more value than all the rest of the course put together."

LeConte was particularly pleased with his philosophical work. He was not, to be sure, a philosopher in the technical sense. Though he had "dipped into" the works of Kant, Fichte, Hegel, and Berkeley, he was repelled by their methods. Instead, his philosophical tendencies were formed under the influence of Comte's positivism and his readings in the history of scientific logic. But although Le Conte's philosophy had its roots in naturalism, he was distinctly opposed to the simplistic materialism of most early evolutionists. He gave particular emphasis to the evolution of consciousness. Whereas Spencer and his followers tended to depict all living forms as subjects to material circumstance, Le Conte was interested in the process of individuation, brought on by the growth of reason and will, through which mastery of the environment and self-determination are achieved. In the lower species mistakes are usually irreversible, but in human beings adaptation has become a conscious and willful activity. In man, Le Conte argued, natural selection has given way to rational selection.

Religious idealism was the inevitable outgrowth of Le Conte's theory of evolution. God is the "all-pervading force of Nature," working entirely within the limits of scientific understanding, lending its spirit or energy to all created forms. Evolution is the divine means by which spirit struggles upward to fulfill its individuality. With the emergence of man that process was completed. "In man," Le Conte believed, "spirit came to birth, became capable of independent life. Thus, man alone, of all the objects of Nature, is the child of God." Denying any fundamental conflict between religion and science, Le Conte felt assured that a reinterpretation of biblical cosmology would help "to reconcile the truths revealed in Scripture with those revealed in Nature." On the other hand, he hoped that his belief would not harden into dogma. The belief had been formed, he said, after years of fearful doubt, resolved finally by an act of faith. He thought of his lectures as a scattering of "seed-thoughts." "Let the seed germinate," he often told his students. "Perhaps it will bear fruit hereafter." In Royce the idea grew and branched in ways that his teacher could not have directed. It sought philosophical connections and formed new patterns, but the fruition of Royce's idealism was, to a great extent, a growth from Le Conte's seeds.

As Royce's scientific education led toward religion and philosophy, his undergraduate literary studies guided him in the same direction. We have already seen that his two prize-winning orations reached idealistic conclusions. In general, he felt, literary criticism is a philosophical activity. The critic is not one who merely "pulls to pieces," but one whose office is "quite as constructive as that of any other branch of literature." This point is most fully expressed in "The Aim of Criticism," which Josiah published in the *Berkeleyan* in May 1875. The critic may be primarily historical, philosophical, scientific, artistic, or literary, but regardless of the narrower field, the common responsibility of all criticism is to construct a conception of human experience. "He must remember that in most of what he does he is dealing with manifestations of the human mind; and that his duty is not done when he has passed judgment on the manifestations, but that he must also go behind them to find out something also about the underlying mind." In applying this principle Royce was repeatedly concerned with problems of life in the nineteenth century.

As we have seen, his interest in the philosophy of science followed similar lines. How, he repeatedly asked, have writers and thinkers addressed themselves to the problems of the age? The main feature of this age, in literature as in science, is realism: writers want to confront real life, to depict it as it is. In this respect Poe was a notable failure; his poems were like those written on "some other planet." But in the novel, modern writers came closest to fulfilling the demands of the age. Royce felt that the distinctiveness of the modern novel was its realism in technique and its idealism in content. While Hardy and Turgenev were clear examples of this tendency, George Eliot, in *Mill on the Floss* and especially in *Middlemarch*, illustrated it supremely. Answering an article published in the *Vassar Miscellany*, Royce defended George Eliot as both realist and idealist:

> It is, first of all, incorrect to say that she sets up no high ideals for others to attain to. She does. She is ever dealing with ideals. To be sure, she no sooner suggests an ideal than she makes us feel how difficult it is to be attained. She does not alter that realistic treatment of characters and facts, which is so prominent a feature in her style, to suit that ideal, or to make it seem easier of attainment. She even goes so far as to show that individuals are so unhappily under the control of circumstances, that the best efforts after the better and higher are often utterly thwarted. . . . [But] the very fact that we have such aims, that we work for them, that we are not driven from them by misfortune, is enough to make us nobler, more admirable, truly happier, than if we had remained on the lower plane of indifference.

This defense of George Eliot, with its hints of Royce's future philosophical thought, is complemented by a conception of modern tragedy that he published in the June issue of the *Berkeleyan*. Describing the difference between ancient and modern tragedy, he felt that the Greeks had regarded suffering as an exceptional and even extrahuman experience, something that happens only to gods and heroes. "But much of this," he observed, "has changed with time. We still look upon misfortunes as not necessarily the result of crime, and we still see a certain dignity in suffering of every kind, but we do not think that the dignity of tragic suffering results from the rarity of its occurrence, and we do not look upon its origin as being outside of the regular course of human events." With time, Royce believed, we have come to recognize that "to be human is to suffer," and in the nineteenth century, this recognition had become "the true spirit of modern art."

The ideology expressed in these literary studies, backed by Royce's training in classics and his growing humanistic idealism, found an expanded vehicle for expression in his baccalaureate thesis: "The Intention of the Prometheus Bound of Aeschylus, Being an Investigation in the Department of Greek Theology." Composed in April 1875, and formally presented in June, this work was undoubtedly his most impressive undergraduate effort, so impressive that, according to a family legend, it was chiefly responsible for his being given an opportunity to continue his studies in Europe.

Prometheus Bound is a problem play. Its problem, as Royce identified it, grows out of its apparent irreligion: the play glorifies the rebellious Titan and denounces Zeus, the supreme deity, as a brute. Since Aeschylus's piety is beyond question, while the implications of the play are apparently so impious, the question of the author's intention became Royce's central concern. Two solutions suggested themselves. One, which Royce found in the writings of German philologists, posits that the lost play, *Prometheus Loosed*, reconciled the contradiction by inverting the values. If this is true, Zeus is finally portrayed as the forgiving deity, while Prometheus surrenders his will to divine justice. Royce rejected this hypothesis because it lacks evidence and because it implies a serious disruption of the play's unity. The existing play so successfully and systematically arouses sympathy for Prometheus and hatred of Zeus that Royce found it inconceivable that Aeschylus intended to renounce these feelings. A second solution, the one Royce proposed, denies that Zeus is represented as God in the sense that he possesses supreme holiness. Instead he is the creator and cosmic punisher; he embodies superhuman power, which, because of its potential and unpredictable brutality, fills us with terror. Against this force, Prometheus, who represents human will and human values, heroically but tragically rebels, but his anger is directed not against the true God whom Aeschylus sincerely and deeply worshiped, but against the superior power that controls and denies humanity. The drama, then, is no an act of irreligion, but a majestic expression of Athenian humanism.

The philosophical and psychological implications in this reading of *Prometheus Bound* are vast. Though the thesis did not carry these implications very far, the meaning of Prometheus remained a problem that Royce, within the next decade, would reinterpret in "Shelley and the Revolution," in "The Decay of Earnestness," and finally in *The Religious Aspect of Philosophy*. With a different literary basis, the same issues would again attract Royce's attention in "The Problem of Job." There was much in the Titan's character that Royce could see in his own life, for one fragment of his identity was distinctly Promethean: the most desperate moments of youth, he remembered later, bring out feelings of rebelliousness, fears of becoming an outcast, and suicidal fantasies. Furthermore, the splitting of the divine father into two figures, brute force as opposed to supreme holiness, had its parallel in Royce's two images of the father—his actual father who had forced him to worship the Protestant God, against whom the son rebelled, and the surrogate father, Le Conte and Gilman, who represented humanistic values. One father punished and abandoned the son; the other helped him to rebuild the elements of selfhood. In terms of the religious issues of the nineteenth century, Zeus is the prototype of the deterministic cosmos of social Darwinism, while Prometheus represents the willful struggle of man to preserve the values that establish his identity in a hostile environment. In short, by selecting the Aeschylean drama as the text for the culminating effort of his college life, Royce was coming to terms with his own deepest anxieties and those of his age.

The same concerns and a similar conclusion were reiterated in Royce's commencement address. In April he had been chosen, as one of four student speakers, to deliver the "classical oration." At the graduation ceremony held in Berkeley on June 9, he delivered the address that he called "On a Passage in Sophocles." He began by noting the close relationship between Greek myth and philosophy:

> The fireside legend had been perhaps but a diversion, the amusement for an idle hour, but in the work of art that sprang from it was embodied life in some of its most universal forms. Indeed it was not till the Hellenic mind came to see what a treasury of instruction and pathos had been stored up in its old legends, that it began to philosophize. First came the diversion in the shape of the story, then the work of art in the shape of the drama, then the labor of philosophy in the shape of the written treatise. First Hesiod, then Sophocles, then Plato; first the tale, then the tragedy, then the illustrative myth.

The illustrative myth that attracted Royce's attention is the story of Antigone's defiance of Creon, and the passage in question is her defense. Having disobeyed the king's order by performing burial rites over the body of her brother, Antigone maintains that she was obeying a higher law: "These decrees," she says, "are not an affair of today or of yesterday, but they endure forever, and no man knows whence they spring." Those in the audience who had read Royce's thesis on Aeschylus might have been reminded of it as they listened to the young man retell the myth of Antigone. Once again he was dealing with a triangular relationship that poses a conflict between human rebellion and overbearing power, a conflict that is mediated by an appeal to a higher ideal. Eventually Royce would name this triad the community of interpretation. The passage from Sophocles, Royce believed, expresses a piety that transcends considerations of expedience, finite duty, and decorum. But can such a defiant piety, Royce asked, be still relevant today? Or have science and advanced social thought eliminated the possibility of idealism? One must agree, he admitted, that much of what we call morality has been socially conditioned by changing circumstances. But refusing to acquiesce entirely to relativism, he insisted that there remains a portion of morality "which is our property by virtue of our humanity." Like Antigone, we may not know the source of this morality, but we feel it. "This part of our nature is independent of circumstances, and because it is the result of a higher and wider experience, it is to be obeyed."

Graduate Years

The commencement exercises of 1875 made Royce a bachelor of arts, a degree restricted to those specializing in classics. The twenty-five men who received degrees on that day brought the university's total number of graduates to an even sixty. The day's festivities were, however, dampened somewhat by the earlier departure in April of President Gilman. After a brief, stormy, but productive administration, Gilman had resigned to become the founding president of Johns Hopkins. Before leaving and afterward he worked with a group of local businessmen in providing a fund to finance what Josiah called his "European expedition." Like many other American youths in the nineteenth century, Royce hoped to continue his studies for at least one year in the German universities. On June 14 he wrote to Gilman saying that he had been promised five hundred dollars and could expect about one thousand dollars altogether. "I am in good health, hopeful, and a graduate of the University. Your influence in getting me this assistance is going to be the making of my whole life."

Although Royce did not know exactly how to use this precious opportunity, he did have initial plans. They included an overland trip to New York, a voyage by steamer to Hamburg, and a period of study in Heidelberg. He was committed, at least temporarily, to Germany. If this plan was conventional, it was also a bold one, for there is no record to indicate that Royce had had any training in

the German language. Considering his poverty, it seems unlikely that he could
have afforded a private tutor; furthermore, since the university offered free
classes in German, the expense of private lessons would have been unnecessary.
Of course it is possible that he had learned German through independent study.
His undergraduate thesis does contain references to German scholarship, but
except for a title or two, he seems to have used only materials available in
English translations. It seems odd, but not uncharacteristic, that Royce
embarked for a year's study in the German universities with no more than a very
imperfect grasp of the language.

At any rate he left California early in July and was in New York by the
eleventh. Gilman himself had just sailed for Europe to gather ideas and faculty
for Johns Hopkins, but before leaving he had taken care to provide Royce with
letters of introduction to influential men in the East. One of those letters introduced him to George Dorr, a wealthy young man, only two years older than
Royce, and a member of Boston's elite social class. With Dorr's help Royce
toured the Boston and Harvard libraries. Dorr also arranged a dinner party with
leading intellectuals of Boston and Cambridge, including William James and
George Herbert Palmer. Royce arrived at Dorr's home early, wearing a threadbare suit, the only one he owned. Dorr met him in full evening dress, took one
look, and said, "Royce, I think you are right; it's too hot for formal clothes this
evening. If you will excuse me, I'll run upstairs and change." Aside from his
clothes, Royce must have presented a strange appearance. His passport, lacking a photograph, contained a highly unflattering description: age, *19*; stature,
5' 6½"; forehead, *full, broad*; eyes, *blue*; nose, *short*; mouth, *large*; chin, *round*;
hair, *red*; complexion, *florid*; face, *inclined to oval*. Many years later, after they
all had become close friends, Katharine Royce asked William James if Josiah
had not seemed awfully backward. "On the contrary," James said, "we talked
afterwards of the charm and delight of his conversation."

On July 15 Royce sailed from New York on the steamer *Klopstock* bound for
Hamburg. In Germany, following his plan, he proceeded up the Rhine and the
Neckar to the ancient city of Heidelberg. Remaining there for something less
than three months, Royce must have spent most of his time trying to master the
language. Of his first impressions and social life, little is known, but when he
returned to Heidelberg in 1908 to attend a meeting of the International
Congress of Philosophy, his mind was filled with loving memories of the university's traditions, the city's medieval ruins, and its magnificent natural setting.
As a student he seems always to have been very busy. He had hoped to increase
his income by writing articles for the *Overland Monthly*, which had already published two of his essays, "The Aim of Poetry" and "The Life-Harmony," but he
soon found that his university work left him with very little free time. A single
diversion is recorded. Gilman passed through Heidelberg in September. Royce

met him at the railway station, and together they "passed the day very pleasantly" driving over the hills into Frankfort.

With the approach of the winter term, Royce made preparations to move
from Heidelberg to Leipzig. Now, as he must have realized, the serious work
was beginning.

If Josiah's command of the German language was imperfect, his knowledge
of philosophy was not much better. Aside from Le Conte's "episodic lectures"
on the "philosophy of human thought-growth," his formal education at Berkeley
gave him no philosophical instruction. He had read Mill, Lewes, Spencer, Sir
William Hamilton, and a translation of Friedrich Ueberweg's *History of
Philosophy*. From them he had gathered some understanding of positivism, evolutionary thought, mysticism, and metaphysics, but otherwise the records show
only fragmentary notes on Kant, Hegel, and Greek philosophy. When all the evidence is counted, it is clear that as a budding philosopher, Royce was remarkably unprepared for advanced graduate work. Still, with newly born confidence,
Royce set out for Leipzig.

On October 19 he was officially registered at the university as "Josiah Royce
aus Grace Valley," an error that he remembered later as a priceless joke. In
Leipzig he settled into a boardinghouse run by a certain Frau Vogel, joined a
philosophischer Verein, and enrolled in five courses. He heard Ludwig
Strumpell's lectures on German philosophy, which included discussions of
Leibnitz, Wolff, Mendelssohn, Kant, Fichte, Schelling, Hegel, and Herbart.
The great idealistic historian Wilhelm Windelband offered a course in Greek
philosophy, which Royce attended; though his surviving notebook for these lec-
tures is very sketchy, he absorbed much of Windelband's thought from his writings during the next few years. Branching out and still interested in languages,
Royce studied Sanskrit grammar with Heinrich Hubschmann.

But his "most especial interest" was excited by Wilhelm Wundt. Royce took
two courses from Wundt: anthropology and logic. The author of the recently
published and pioneering work *Grundzüge der physiologischen Psychologie,*
Wundt was regarded as Germany's leading exponent of empirical psychology.
The course in logic was Royce's favorite. Writing to Gilman in February, he
noted: "I am hearing a course from him in Logic. In this more specially philosophic branch he has not yet written much, but he is understood to be a 'man
with system,' in Metaphysics as well as in Psychology. So in him I have a thoroughly live man, and one who will quite possibly make a powerful impression
on the thought of the next decade or so, for he is still in his younger prime."

For the foreign student, the German universities provided an atmosphere
that generated a "positively passionate enthusiasm." Nothing in the world,
Royce felt, could equal it. American society in the United States was con-
strained in its "old and narrow 'disciplinary' ideals," England was unscholarly,

and France too was backward. But Germany offered an example of scholarship that was "our master and our guide." The Germans' "admirable hospitality," the opportunities to make "immediate contact . . . with the great minds of the German world," and the "unheard of treasures of books" caused the young American to feel that Germany, not England, was his true mother country. "The air was full of suggestion," he said; it "seemed one of absolute blessing and power." If one left America with doubts about the future of the academic life, Germany made him "an idealist, devoted for the time to pure learning for learning's sake, devoted to contribute his *Scherflein* to the massive store of human knowledge, burning for a chance to help to build the American University."

There were hardships, of course. Although, by December, Royce felt that the German language had "lost most of its terrors," it still presented "plenty of difficulties." Within two months, however, finding the language "no longer a serious obstacle to understanding lectures on philosophy," he was able to drop some "special exercise work" and devote all of his time to lectures and reading. By February his grasp of German had advanced to the point that he could read Spinoza in German translation and Fichte in the original. Royce's notebooks reflect this progress. At first the notes are sparse and fragmentary; everything is written in English. Gradually as the months pass, the notes expand and grow more coherent, and the last third of each notebook is written in German. The weather was a minor irritation. For the first time in his life, Josiah had to deal with persistent frosts and heavy winter snows.

Two pieces of news from California were more disturbing. His unmarried sister Ruth was seriously ill. For a time Josiah was concerned that she might die, leaving his mother nearly alone. Soon, however, he received word of Ruth's recovery, and was able to cancel any plans of returning to the United States. Worse news informed him of an economic depression in California. In December, he told Gilman "that the succession of commercial misfortunes there keeps money at such high demand that it is just now impossible to send me any more money from there." He was nearly broke. The *Overland Monthly* still owed him something for his second article, but he had not yet heard that the magazine had just folded. Its failure was, in fact, related to the general financial crisis. A far-reaching effect of the 1873 panic, exacerbated by wild speculation in mining stocks, the depression caused a $20 million loss in agriculture and widespread unemployment in San Francisco. Though he was far from the scene of the crisis, Royce felt its effect. Gilman helped out by sending a draft on a London bank for twenty pounds, adding: "Please let me hear from you,—as to your hopes and plans, & progress."

Royce's next letter thanked Gilman for the remittance and said a good deal about his plans and progress. He had begun "to make headway in the History of German Philosophy, and also to get the first shadowy outline of that immense mass of learning and discussion, *contemporary* German Thought on philosophic subjects." Beyond this, he said, there was the summer term to think about. He was so delighted with Wundt that he thought of remaining in Leipzig. On the other hand, he wanted to hear Kuno Fischer's lectures in Heidelberg. But most of all he wanted to move on to Göttingen in order to study with Rudolf Hermann Lotze, who was, Royce understood, "the first in constructive philosophy now living in Germany." The university calendars would have, he said, considerable influence on his decision. If Lotze were to offer promising courses, he would move to Göttingen.

The decision was soon made. In March he completed his work in Leipzig, withdrew from the university on April 10, and on the nineteenth received his *Anmeldungs-Buch des Studienden* at *Georg-Augusts-Universität*. Aside from his interest in Lotze, Royce felt that he should spend at least one semester in Göttingen. The reason is obvious. Situated in Hanover, Göttingen and its university had historic connections with England. The university had been founded by George II and was widely known to be a genial host for English and American students. At Göttingen Royce continued some of the work he had begun at Berkeley and Leipzig. He heard a course on the history of ancient philosophy from Julius Baumann and continued his study of Sanskrit grammar with Adalberg Bezzenberger. He kept his mathematics fresh in a course offered by Alfred Enneper on the theory of definite integrals and heard the German side of evolutionary theory from a now-forgotten docent named Rehnisch on Spencer's Social Statics. Now also Royce began his lifelong study of Kant by attending Karl Ueberhorst's lectures on the *Kritik der reinen Vernunft*. Ueberhorst was, he remembered later, "one of the most learned and many-sided of the new philosophical doctors . . . a man who promised, as one might say, almost everything." But the greatest impact on Royce, as he had expected, was made by Lotze. Royce heard two courses from the great man—one on metaphysics, another on practical philosophy. The lectures gave Royce his first vivid example of post-Kantian idealism in the making. None of his other courses had emphasized the systematic construction of philosophy; Wundt had been interested primarily in methodology, others were concerned with the history of philosophy or the technical aspects of certain texts, but Lotze taught Lotze.

Soon after arriving in Göttingen, Royce began to make plans for the next academic year. He had hoped to spend the winter in Berlin, though his financial situation must have made the possibility very doubtful. Gilman again helped to resolve the difficulty. Johns Hopkins University was slated to open in the fall, and Gilman suggested that a fellowship for Royce might be arranged. "If you can find nothing better," Gilman wrote on March 20, "I should like to propose your coming here for a year on one of these foundations. How does that strike you?" The stipend for a fellowship would be five hundred dollars. Royce

submitted his application on April 9 and received his letter of appointment in
June. "You have the Fellowship," Gilman wrote, "and I hope it will prove a useful as well as a pleasant honor. When will you come here?" Royce replied that
he planned to be in Baltimore in late September. "I shall bring my little collection of books with me," he said, "order two or three German periodicals to be
sent to me, take care not to lose my *akademische Hefte*, and so shall be 'armed,'
I hope for what I am to do during the coming year."

Remembering his two years at Johns Hopkins, Royce was later reminded of
a passage in Wordsworth's *Prelude*: "Bliss was it in that dawn to be alive, but to
be young was very Heaven!" Under Gilman's leadership the university initiated
one of the boldest experiments in the history of U.S. higher education. Instead
of duplicating the work of undergraduate colleges and state universities, Johns
Hopkins was established as an institution devoted entirely to graduate study
and research. Before 1876 the Ph.D., except as a German degree, was almost
unknown in the United States. Academic departments, even in the sciences,
were often staffed by amateur professors, ministers, former high-school teachers, and dilettantes. But Gilman foresaw a community of scholarship that
respected specialized training, vigorous research, and head-to-head exchange of
ideas. To realize his vision he brought together a group of six professors, several
associates, occasional lecturers, and twenty-one fellows. Mutual dedication to
academic ideals created an atmosphere in which the responsibilities for study,
research, and teaching were shared by all. Although the professors constituted
the core of the teaching faculty, the fellows were also encouraged to offer
courses and give public lectures. Royce accepted the challenge at once by giving a course on Schopenhauer and constructing a series of five lectures entitled
"Return to Kant" during his first year. Describing his feelings of that time, he
later remembered his exuberance: "One longed to be a doer of the word, and
not a hearer only, a creator of his own infinitesimal fraction of a product, bound
in God's name to produce it when the time came."

This zeal for creative learning also promoted close and important friendships.
Gilman was still very much the paternal friend that Josiah had known in
California, and as a frequent guest at the president's home, Royce felt his filial
bonds to the older man grow stronger. Among the other senior men on the faculty
he was particularly attached to the classicist Charles D'Urban Morris, whom he
later described as "a fatherly friend, of the warmest, the freest, and wisest sort."
But with the younger men Royce enjoyed a companionship that was, at least in
his experience, unparalleled. He had four special friends: Hermann Brandt, an
associate in German, A. Duncan Savage, a fellow in Greek, the historian Herbert
Baxter Adams, and the orientalist Charles Lanman. Since all of them had been
students in Germany, they soon formed a *deutscher Verein*, which met at a
restaurant once a week or so for conversation in German over glasses of beer.

Lanman became Royce's primary friend, and the relationship lasted forty years. They first met at Gilman's home on October 1 and began to exchange visits immediately afterward. Like Royce, Lanman was one of the president's special protégés. Born and educated in Gilman's hometown of Norwich, Connecticut, he had graduated from Yale in 1871 and studied chemistry at the Sheffield Scientific School when Gilman was still its administrative head. But feeling a stronger attraction to philology, he earned one of Yale's early doctorates in languages and spent three years doing postgraduate research in Germany. In Baltimore, Lanman planned to offer a course in Sanskrit, and Royce, having already made a start in this field, promptly enrolled. Lanman reciprocated by taking Royce's course on Schopenhauer. Teaching each other, they formed a warm friendship during the first academic year. Though Royce lectured only on special occasions in his second year, he continued to attend Lanman's classes and as a tutorial student advanced to the Bhagavad Gita and the Vedas. For Royce this friendship was unique. His letters to Lanman reveal a degree of humorous and hearty intimacy that he offered to no one else. Lanman became his "Dearest Guru," one of the few outside his family who ever received the compliment of a letter signed simply "Josiah."

The stimulating companionship among the Johns Hopkins students is further illustrated by Royce's description of a club organized by the fellows to discuss the art of a novel. An outgrowth of one of Morris's classes, the group first met in the evenings to read Aristotle's ethics. But growing tired of the "little gnarls and knots" of Aristotle's Greek, the young men soon found themselves scattered about the room sitting on the floor. The host, a budding novelist, would usually read from his own work, and general discussion would follow. Often the topic would turn to the problem of ethics in the novel. George Eliot's *Mill on the Floss* and her newly published *Daniel Deronda* were favorite subjects. Sometimes the subjects were drawn from personal anecdotes. "But whether critics or confessors, or criticized or confessing, we were at all events amused, and as we thought, improved." The meetings invariably broke up late at night, and as the members tiptoed through darkened hallways, they were always full of joyful enthusiasm. "They were golden evenings, those, when we played with life as children with soap-bubbles, and enjoyed life as birds do a crystal mountain lake, wherein their happy forms are reflected as they fly over its surface. They care not for the unfathomed depths beneath, nor did we."

Although Royce later expressed this somewhat wistful self-criticism of his work at Johns Hopkins, his feelings at the time suggest an unbounded enthusiasm. The course on Schopenhauer is a case in point. Launched on January 16, 1877, the class met twice weekly, usually on Tuesdays and Thursdays, until the end of May. The topic was eventually expanded. When, in March, Schopenhauer was set aside in order to fit in the five lectures on Kant, Lanman began to refer to the class as "Royce's Philosophy." Aside from Morris's course on Aristotle's Ethics and another offered by John M. Cross on Plato's *Apology,* Royce's class seems to have been the only real philosophical instruction offered at Johns Hopkins during its first year, for since both Morris and Cross were classicists, their lectures were probably organized on linguistic principles. During the second year, 1877–78, George Sylvester Morris of the University of Michigan and William James were added to the staff as part-time lecturers, one giving a course on the history of philosophy and the other on psychology, "The Brain and the Mind." The fact that Royce gave the preparatory lectures to Morris's course indicates his autonomy.

Once again, as at Berkeley, Royce was almost entirely on his own, but he does not seem to have suffered much from a lack of guidance. Immediately he established a vigorous program of independent reading. Eleven well-packed notebooks tell the story. Bearing the earliest dates of October and November 1876, four notebooks are devoted to Hegel, two to Spinoza, and five to Kant. In addition there are many scattered notes on secondary sources, gatherings from periodical literature, and teaching materials on Schopenhauer. These four philosophers—Spinoza, Kant, Hegel, and Schopenhauer—made up the core of Royce's studies in his first year at Johns Hopkins.

The selection of Schopenhauer as the subject of Royce's first teaching experience is particularly illustrative of his early philosophical interests. Like Prometheus and Antigone in myth, Schopenhauer is the philosopher who represents the willful and the tragic view of life. He is, Royce told his students, "the phantom ship" of post-Kantian idealism, whose philosophy enters your "thought-horizon" when you least expect it. Royce had first read *Die Welt als Wille und Vorstellung* in Germany and recognized at once its strong and disturbing influence. In fact much of Royce's early philosophy involves an attempt to incorporate the positive aspects of the will and to accept the reality of tragedy without succumbing entirely to Schopenhauer's pessimism. Seeing this as a crucial ideological problem, with both personal and philosophical dimensions, Royce noted that "Schopenhauer is in short a thinker whom we can neither afford to lose nor be willing in all things to follow."

Royce's excitement in attacking such monumental questions and his great pleasure in the twin roles of teacher and scholar are best expressed in his five lectures on Kant. Contained in a carefully written two-hundred-page notebook with the full title "The 'Return to Kant' in Modern German Thought: Lectures with Notes and Appendices," the manuscript seems to have been composed with hopes of publication. Fifteen years later, after taking a fresh look, Royce decided that "those lectures were founded upon a serious, I might say an entire, misinterpretation of Kant's meaning." In general, as he came to believe, much of the original work attempted by university students in the 1870s was premature. This hindsight did not, however, spoil his thrill in making this first, fully developed effort in constructive thought. With a sense of being at the intellectual forefront of his age, Royce told his students that the revival of critical philosophy is not "a mere retrogressive search for the living among the dead," but "the study of a living progressive *method*." Kant had enabled philosophy to shift its concern from metaphysics to epistemology, or as the Germans had termed the new science, *Erkenntnistheorie*. The old search for a real world beyond experience should be subordinated, Royce said; instead, one should use the tools of the critical method to study the structure of experience. "The world is real for us," he observed, "because we can act in it, not because any system of metaphysics tells us that it is real." Scorning all systems of absolutism, Royce now believed that philosophy should forsake the "world of shadows" and join with psychology in an effort to develop a theory of knowledge.

The one man in the United States who could best understand and support these views was William James. Perhaps with this in mind, Royce decided to spend the summer of 1877 in Boston. His brief acquaintance with James in 1875 provided the means for renewing the friendship. They met one day at James's home on Quincy Street in Cambridge; and as Royce later remembered the event, he poured out his soul. Friends in Baltimore had been advising Royce to leave philosophy alone. There was little future in such work, they said; career opportunities were too few. But being unable to accept the practical advice, Royce was struck by the fact that James seemed to hold a different opinion. "James found me at once—made out what my essential interests were at our first interview, accepted me, with all my imperfections, as one of those many souls who ought to be able to find themselves in their own way, gave a patient and willing ear to just my variety of philosophical experience, and used his influence from that time on, not to win me as a follower, but to give me my chance." James was especially sensitive to Royce's vocational turmoil, for he too, just at that time, was working out the terms of his own professional identity. Though nearly fourteen years older than Royce, James had been fairly slow to develop. Only in the previous year had he been promoted to an assistant professorship at Harvard, and though he had begun to teach psychology, he was still known primarily as a physiologist. As a philosopher, James had done very little. Still, Royce and James—not counting that maverick, Charles Peirce—were nearly the only men in the U.S. with some grasp of contemporary European thought and its promise for the future of philosophy.

What else Royce did during the three summer months in Boston remains unclear. According to one legend he supported himself by working as a groundsman in Harvard Yard. We know that James introduced him to other Harvard personalities, including the cosmic evolutionist John Fiske. In a letter to Gilman, Royce reported that he had come to Boston "for the purpose of special studies in the libraries there." He was received most cordially at the Boston Public Library, where he was provided with liberal borrowing privileges and a private room for study. He was also given free use of the Athenaeum and the Harvard Library. No doubt he spent most of his time in those places, reading, gathering ideas, and making preliminary designs for his doctoral thesis. As his notebooks demonstrate, he read extensively in the works of Kant and the neo-Kantians. Royce had come to believe that this branch of thought, standing between materialism and critical skepticism, was the true road to the promised land. The three Boston notebooks, entitled "Notes Relating to Logic and the Theory of Knowledge," record part of this journey. Also called "Preliminaries to the Degree-Essay," the notebooks construct provisional theses on the function of thought.

Royce returned to Baltimore in late September. With his fellowship renewed, he spent his second year at Hopkins working on a series of eight lectures on the poetry of the German romantics, an essay entitled "Schiller's Ethical Studies," a long unpublished review of Francis Bowen's *Modern Philosophy*, a single lecture on "Spinoza's Theory of Religious Liberty in the State," and his doctoral thesis, "Of the Interdependence of the Principles of Knowledge." He read the piece on Schiller to the Johns Hopkins Philological Association in December and submitted it a month later for publication in the *Journal of Speculative Philosophy*. It became his first published essay since "The Aim of Poetry" and "The Life-Harmony" had appeared in the dying issues of the *Overland Monthly* three years before. The lectures were very favorably received. Gilman used his influence to recommend the introduction to the series on romantic poets for publication in *Scribner's Monthly*, while Lanman and James urged Royce to submit parts of the series to the *Atlantic*. Though nothing came of the plans, Royce saved his lectures for future use. Perhaps, in the long run, they helped Royce most by giving him ways to express and thereby to correct his own romantic tendencies. His youthful reflection in the Oakland graveyard had been, according to his definition, pure romanticism. Seeing this tendency in others, Royce was gradually able to dispose of its extravagance and incorporate its "union of feeling and reflection."

On April 2, 1878, Royce submitted his doctoral thesis in 343 holograph pages entitled "Of the Interdependence of the Principles of Knowledge: An Investigation of the Problems of Elementary Epistemology, in Two Chapters, with an Introduction on the Principal Ideas and Problems in which the Discussion Takes its Rise." The title promises an ambitious undertaking by a youth of twenty-two, and even Royce's critics must admit that his first sustained effort in philosophical inquiry is enormously impressive. At Gilman's request, Noah Porter, the president of Yale, agreed to examine the thesis: "I don't like to refuse any request which you make," Porter wrote Gilman, "& shall be ready to receive & read this Essay. I shall also be interested—as I think—in the treatment of a difficult thesis."

This work contains several positions that became the foundations of Royce's subsequent thought, but it also contains, for those accustomed to regard him as the chief absolutist of his age, one huge surprise. As for the foundations, we find Royce espousing the central doctrine of post-Kantian idealism: all that is, is in and for consciousness. Aside from experience, nothing really exists. We may posit the shadowy *Ding an sich*; indeed, all forms of rational discourse, as represented in the sciences, necessitate the construction of "ideal syntheses." So we assume that such constellations of ideas coexist permanently, but this is only an assumption. In reality, there are no independent beings. This doctrine—a dogma, in fact—guided American philosophy throughout the Golden Age. For Royce it became and remained the basis of his critique of the "first conception of being" in *The World and the Individual,* and only in the twilight of his career—in the few years following 1910—did the doctrine lose favor, break apart, and fail. Ironically the defeat was to be effected by Royce's own former students.

To grasp the significance of Royce's early achievement, one must appreciate the rampant materialism of his place and time, in which idealism seemed to be losing on all fronts, and the principles of business enterprise claimed the support of the intellectual community. The popularity of William Graham Sumner, for instance, depended largely upon his confidence in treating the "laws of science" as the determinants of things, and in treating things as the ultimate realities. Royce countered this naive conception by thrusting a spear at the epistemological heart of materialism. With things as things, he maintained, rational discourse is unacquainted; rational discourse is concerned only with ideas as they are incorporated in judgments, and judgments are acts of the will involving the identification of subjects with predicates. Human beings have sciences, not vice versa, and these sciences are developed to answer human needs and to serve human purposes.

This voluntarism is thus both idealistic and pragmatic. There is no shred of absolutism anywhere in the work, and herein the student of Royce's philosophy may be surprised. The "ideal synthesis" that underpins all rational discourse remains a postulate. We know, of course, that within a decade Royce would renounce this outlook, so it is only ironic that he should have been an originator of pragmatism.

The irony is deepened, if not obscured, by the fact that when he abandoned pragmatism he traced the origins of his absolutism to this doctoral thesis. In the preface to *The Religious Aspect of Philosophy* Royce remarked that its "questions . . . were first attempted . . . in thesis for the Doctor's degree of the Johns Hopkins University in 1878." This cryptic remark surely refers to his discussion in the thesis of the possibility of error. Suppose, Royce speculated, that two absent-minded friends have an appointment to meet on a particular day. One fellow thinks, "Today is Tuesday," while the other thinks, "Today is Wednesday." Since both judgments are independent acts of separate wills, neither is *directly* opposed to the other, and therefore neither can be an error. It would appear, then, that error, as direct opposition between judgments, is impossible. Paradoxically this conclusion not only appears to contradict common sense, but also seems incompatible with the assumptions that facilitate any rational discourse. We should be safe in believing that no opinion can be true unless its contradiction can be proven false. Royce resolved this paradox by maintaining that the judgments may be *indirectly* opposed, that there may be practical or theoretical consequences of judgments that render some true and others false. Therefore, rational discourse, with its eye on consequences, seeks not "the truth," but satisfaction of its purposes. This perspective is a very pure form of pragmatism, and as such was for the early Royce an adequate account of the grounds of scientific inquiry.

Besides the enormous intellectual growth that Royce experienced at Johns Hopkins, he found many opportunities in Baltimore for a variety of cultural entertainment. Theaters, orchestras, museums, and art galleries gave a pleasant balance and an undertone of gaiety to the university's scholarly work in libraries and lecture halls. Gilman always encouraged his people to establish personal contact with the Baltimore community, and for lighter recreation the popular boardinghouse of Mrs. DuBois Egerton became the scene of town-gown "frolics," which featured games of silhouettes and charades.

For Royce the central figure and symbol of Baltimore's social life was George Buchanan Coale, to whom Royce dedicated *The Religious Aspect of Philosophy*. A man in his late fifties, prominent in business and civic activities, Coale was founder and president of the Merchants' Mutual Marine Insurance Company. Like Gilman, Coale traced his heritage to the seventeenth century and cherished a family tradition of vigorous individualism. The first American Coale had been a Quaker preacher in Maryland, and two of his ancestors had signed the Declaration of Independence. Noted for his cultivated taste in the arts, Coale had helped to organize the Maryland Academy of Fine Arts, in which he remained active on its board of directors. He was also a member of the Baltimore Athenaeum and a prominent actor, praised for his portrayal of Shylock, in the amateur dramatic and musical productions of the Wednesday Club. To Royce, Coale was the epitome of American manhood.

Satisfying Josiah's persistent need for a surrogate father, Coale welcomed his young friend, who described himself as "an unspeakably raw little boy," into the circle of his brilliant family. One of Coale's sons, George William, was a partner in his father's insurance company; another, Robert Dorsey, was a student in chemistry preparing for a later career as professor at the University of Maryland; Coale's artistic daughter, Mary, who became one of Royce's special lifelong friends, was her father's close companion in many of his cultural pursuits. In later years, whenever Royce remembered his life in Baltimore, he invariably thought of Coale and his family. They became a model of the qualities—"power, courage, plan, and above all social status"—which were so pitifully lacking in Royce's own paternal environment, but which, in his search for identity, he was determined to possess.

It is hardly surprising, therefore, that Royce resisted the prospect of leaving Baltimore. As the summer of 1878 approached, with the end of his work at Johns Hopkins in sight, he began to drive his heels into the sand. On June 11 he reported that his Ph.D. was "about settled." President Porter had read the thesis with high approval, and G. S. Morris, who administered Royce's comprehensive examination in the history of philosophy, wrote from Michigan to say that he had read the paper "with more interest than he would feel in reading a novel, and that it only depends on the efforts of such to make great things happen in American Philosophy." On June 13 Royce received his degree, one in a group of four to obtain the first Ph.D.'s granted at Johns Hopkins. But if Royce felt the joy that is supposed to accompany great achievements, he did not show it, for he reported the event to Lanman and James in an offhand, joking, and even bitter tone. He was annoyed by the length of Morris's questions and irritated generally by the world's hostile view of philosophy. "On the whole," he told James, ". . . philosophy is a cold business. The world despises the man who engages in it, and he has to do his best to try to return the compliment."

No doubt Royce's happiness had been blunted by the uncertainty of his prospects. With no offers of employment and no means of self-support he had some reason to expect that his Hopkins fellowship might be renewed. Clinging to this hope, he planned to spend the summer reading Wilhelm Schuppe's *Erkenntnisstheoretische Logik* and Shadworth Hodgson's new two-volume treatise, *The Philosophy of Reflection*. He also hoped to write a piece on Platonic teleology in modern thought and prepare a series of lectures on Johann Gottfried Herder. In the meantime Gilman was using his influence in an effort to secure a place for Royce at Yale or the University of California.

The "call" from Berkeley arrived on July 1. It offered Royce an assistantship in English literature at an annual salary of $1,200. Though the letter also contained the vague hint that the position would provide "advantages for philosophic studies," Royce was not satisfied. The hint meant only, he felt sure, that "they will no doubt let me teach a little philosophy if I want, yea, study some even, if I give word of nothing atheistic in the presence of Freshmen." Royce hated the idea of returning to California and being diverted into the English department. The intellectual and social isolation would infect him with a kind of philosophical tuberculosis. "After all," he wrote James, "I doubt whether I can stand the (metaphysical) climate of California more than some two years. I shall grow consumptive (spiritually) and shall come East for my health. May the shade of good father Kant grant that I come not too late for recovery."

When the offer came, Royce was visiting his friend Duncan Savage in New York. He immediately wrote to Gilman for advice and three days later took his problem to Lanman in New Haven. On a dreadfully hot Fourth of July he conferred briefly with Porter, but was not encouraged. Nor did Gilman offer any means of escape. Therefore, with no other options, he returned to Baltimore, reluctantly wrote his letter of acceptance, and began to pack his books. After saying good-bye to friends, Royce left Baltimore on August 12 and made his way, full of regrets, through New York, Buffalo, Chicago, and St. Louis. The trip had its prosperous side. In St. Louis he had "a very interesting interview" with William T. Harris, the major spokesman for a vigorous circle of Hegelians and editor of the *Journal of Speculative Philosophy*. Harris promised to publish Royce's article on Schiller in the journal's October issue. The rest of the journey westward on the Union and Central Pacific Railroads was "not devoid of some little adventure." Like his mother on her overland journey thirty years earlier, Royce was particularly impressed by the fine air at the summit of the Rocky Mountains, the grand cliffs in Utah's Echo and Weber Canyons, and "the overwhelming, breath-checking sublimity" of Cape Horn in the Sierra Nevada. Even so, as the train returned him to the western side of the mountain wall, he felt like a man condemned as an exile in his native land.

The hopeful youth who had left California three years before in quest of a philosophical identity now had to face the disagreeable prospect of stepping backward into his childhood to work in a field alien to his primary interests. His was no triumphant return, but a distraction and a regression. Understandably he felt that with the completion of his education he had earned the chance to push ahead into adulthood, "to make a career to suit myself." Instead, his choice had been diverted and his moratorium had been indefinitely prolonged. In addition to these misgivings, he had left Baltimore with a pile of debts; somehow he had to satisfy his creditors and still support himself on a measly one hundred dollars a month. But on the other hand, if the future seemed unpromising, the past had been full of accomplishments. The frail, awkward "Josie" of the early 1870s, the boy afflicted with a variety of morbid dreams and fantasies, had been largely supplanted by the more confident "Josh." Now, eight years after first entering the University of California, he possessed a still newer and stronger identity: now, only twenty-two years old, he was "Dr. Royce."

Chapter Three

Exiled Apprenticeship
1878–1882

Fugitive Essayist

Royce's excursion to Europe and the eastern U.S. fixed in his mind a decided hatred of his native state. California's provinciality, its ruthless economics, its blind and selfish politics—everything, in fact, but its exquisite natural beauty—filled him with loathing. Compared with the cultural centers that Royce had just left, California had little to offer besides stock speculation, wheat ranching, political charades, racial warfare, and agitation. "Foundation for higher growth we sadly lack. Ideals we have none. Philistines we are in soul most thoroughly. And when we do talk, our topics of discussion are so insufferably finite!" As a place for philosophical thought, it was execrable. "There is no philosophy in California. From Siskiyou to Ft. Yuma, and from the Golden Gate to the summit of the Sierras there could not be found brains enough [to] accomplish the formation of a single respectable idea that was not a manifest plagiarism. Hence the atmosphere for the study of metaphysics is bad. And I wish I were out of it."

This remark prompted James to characterize Royce as "the solitary philosopher between Bering's Strait and Tierra del Fuego." Trying to encourage his young friend, James urged Royce to consider the fact of his extreme youth and appreciate his opportunity to practice the art of teaching. James sympathized with Royce's "wail" of loneliness, but pointed out that the situation could be much worse. He might have been pushed even farther afield and still be unable to support himself. "I think you are a lucky youth even as matters stand." Besides, new opportunities were always turning up. "I imagine that Gilman is keeping his eye on you and only waiting for the disgrace of youth to fade from your person."

Royce had to admit that living in California, near relatives and childhood acquaintances, offered some consolation. Arriving home on August 30 he was relieved to find that household affairs were "quite satisfactory," "peaceful and happy." His mother gave him an affectionate welcome, and though he was pleased to see that she was unchanged by his three-year absence, he was saddened to find that his father, who was now in his mid-sixties and whose strength had been declining for many years, was in "permanent ill-health." Royce said nothing about his sisters, but they no doubt were also present with warm greetings. Two of the three, Mary and Hattie, were already married and busily producing Josiah's nephews and nieces, while the family's unmarried daughter, Ruth, a recent graduate of the State Normal School in San Jose, had begun her lifetime career there as teacher and librarian.

The reunion, however, was cut short by Royce's obligation to report for work at the university on September 2. In Berkeley he found several old friends and former teachers. Besides himself, three of the university's graduates—Joseph C. Rowell, John Stillman, and William Carey Jones—were among the younger members of the faculty. Of course, Joseph Le Conte and a few other senior men were still active. But otherwise Royce had few opportunities for deeper friendships, and as he complained, he had almost no one to talk with about philosophy. The older men were absorbed in their own projects, and some even seemed to be irritated by Royce's growth into maturity. "To grow," he observed, "is something of a crime in the eyes of the stocks and stones that have attained their growth." The students were "plastic, sometimes bright, often amusing," but they could not satisfy Royce's need for companionship. A few older students resented his youth. Overwhelmed by a sense of isolation, he drifted back in thought to the happy years in Baltimore and to his closest friends—Coale, Gilman, Lanman, and James. During the next four years, so long as Royce remained stranded in California, they became the sounding boards of his hopes, fears, plans, and rage. Writing letters "to friends in the world beyond," he found a means of freeing himself from "the mental stiffness that constantly creeps over us inhabitants of Berkeley."

The one man at the university who did not exhibit symptoms of mental stiffness and who did listen to Royce was his immediate superior, the poet and professor of English literature, Edward Rowland Sill. A "fearless, devoted, and generous heart," a practical idealist who lived his beliefs, like Josiah's mother, without the need of theoretical foundations, Sill offered "friendship, counsel, and intercession," which were, Royce later recalled, "the greatest prizes that I shall ever dream of finding in life." Royce found in Sill an older man whose ideals were daily companions and taskmasters, and who refused, even for the sake of a joke, to be false to them. Once, while sportively disputing with Royce the merits of some philosophical doctrine, Sill pushed the argument aside with the remark, "If that be wisdom, may I never be enlightened!" But seeing the insincerity of the remark, he immediately retracted: "No, I will not say that even in jest. Whatever comes, may we be some day enlightened." Above even love and loyalty to his friends, Sill cherished understanding, and for that Royce made him the ultimate illustration in *The Spirit of Modern Philosophy* of the human spirit's victory over brute circumstance.

Sill had been appointed to his professorship in May 1874, to fill the vacancy left by the resignation of William Swinton; previously he had taught at the Oakland High School. This fact raises a problem surrounding his relationship with Royce. On two occasions Royce said that Sill had been "a valued teacher and adviser of my own" and "my teacher in English, during the last two years of my undergraduate life." But these statements, as they have been regularly interpreted, cannot be entirely accurate. Sill was first a member of the university's faculty only during Royce's senior year, and furthermore, the full archival records of Royce's curriculum and Sill's class reports seem to exclude the possibility that they were ever engaged in a formal student-teacher relationship. Although it is probable that they were informally acquainted during 1874–75, Sill's personal influence on Royce made its strongest impact during the years of his Berkeley instructorship.

Royce was precisely the sort of assistant that Sill had hoped to obtain. In a letter to Gilman, written on May 6, Sill had listed the qualities of the young man he wanted:

He should have a genuine love of Literature & quickness to comprehend it (I don't care so much for wide attainments in it, as for the gift of appreciation of Literature & discrimination as to it): he should know a good deal about the English Language (& to know about that he must be a good mental philosopher—more important even than the philology) & the Lat. & Greek, &, if possible, German. Finally he should be a good writer & speaker (both of these in the natural, i.e. modern style) & so the cause of it in others.

It must have occurred to Gilman that Royce was ideal for the job. Sill agreed. On September 4, two days after his assistant appeared for work, Sill wrote to Gilman in the wry tone of a man who had just purchased a product through a mail-order catalogue: "Royce has been duly rec$^{\underline{d}}$, & found to answer the description." But being also immediately sensitive to Royce's misgivings, Sill added: "He will do excellently well here, there is no doubt—only he must not stay too long in the wilderness, for his own sake. A certain period of isolation in the desert & of being tempted by the devil is probably good for any of the sons of men, but not too long. I shall look out that he is not drudged to death."

77

Royce was assigned to teach five courses in English literature, composition, and rhetoric to the freshmen and sophomores. He soon found that the classes were attentive, but their elementary needs taxed the patience more than the intellect. Restless for more challenging work, he welcomed Sill's proposal that he give a series of ten lectures on philosophy to the senior class. "These lectures," he told Gilman, "will strain all of my resources in the directions of brevity, clearness, and original work, and I look forward to the undertaking with no little interest." Presented during the latter half of the fall term as substitutes for Sill's lectures on psychology, the series extended the conclusions of Royce's doctoral thesis. "The course was," he noted privately, "dialectically a tolerable success & pedagogically a monstrous failure." This theory of logical concepts was "a kind of hybrid of Hume and Schopenhauer, with an odor of Kant about it."

Not discouraged by a single pedagogical failure, Royce continued to volunteer for extra tasks. He did that even though it irritated some of his colleagues. In January 1879, he gave the senior class a brief course on modern philosophy from Descartes to Kant, and during the spring term he reconstructed his Hopkins lectures on romanticism for the juniors. At the same time he instituted a new freshman course in logic and began to organize all of his teaching of composition around logical principles. In addition, when he and Sill managed to establish a circulating library for the convenience of the students, Royce offered to prepare a catalogue and serve as general supervisor. Somehow he still found time to write and deliver a lecture, "What Constitutes Good Fiction," at the Oakland First Congregational Church in April. Though his life was already quite full, he joined the Berkeley Club, a lively town-gown association that Gilman had founded in 1873. The group held semimonthly meetings in Oakland, and as part of its regular routine, each meeting included a paper read by one of the club's twenty-five members. Royce made his first presentation on April 24, entitled "The Practical Significance of Pessimism."

The selection of this topic suggests a good deal about Royce's emotional state at the time. Just when his loneliness was most acute, his thoughts turned to speculations about the worthlessness of life. Most of the paper is devoted to a justification of Schopenhauer's classic doctrine that life at its theoretical best is merely freedom from desire. The will, expressed through longing and strife, is the only positive element in experience, while pleasure, having a totally negative function, contributes nothing but a cancellation of pain. In theory, if all desires were canceled, the highest value of life, zero, would be attained, but in actual experience, because of a multitude of unsatisfied longings, life is predominantly painful. Accepting the truth of the doctrine that nothingness is best, Royce asked at the end of his paper: What courses of action are open? The implications of this pessimism, he answered, are twofold. First, we must learn to expect nothing from or for the self: "Labor to cast self aside, and to live in the universal life, having only this one object, that the best and highest should be attained, no matter who attains it." Second, we must abandon all hope of reforming the world: "Do not make men unhappy by telling them that were they a little more wealthy or politically a little freer, they would be happy. Tell them that they can find happiness only when they cease to seek it for themselves."

Even as Royce was publicly affirming the doctrine of self-abnegation in favor of the universal life, privately his notes on the place of the self and the components of self-consciousness were couched in language that was much more personal. These notes are contained in Royce's "Thought-Diary," which he kept for more than a year, from September 24, 1878, to December 11, 1879. Among the diary's early entries is an outline for an article on self-consciousness based on Schopenhauer's concept of the will. It seems to be a trial version of his paper on pessimism. But whereas the finished paper speaks abstractly about "the worth of love, of sacrifice, of the worship of the beautiful, of the purely intellectual delights, of the devotion to ideal aims," the notes emphasize the values of self-development and the intensity of life:

> The Pursuit of Life does not mean simply self-preservation. This is present everywhere in our volition and needs not a separate head. But to self-preservation we add the pursuit of intensity, breadth, depth of life.—This may seem at first merely a case of the pursuit of pleasure. It is not. The Will to Live takes the form of a striving after self-development, extension of experience, increase of the quantity and refinement of the quality of consciousness. Such development we consider an end in itself, and choose it without reference to the fact of its pleasure and pain. We know that it will be either pleasurable or painful, but we know not which. Yet we choose it.

Perhaps the differences between the paper and the notes are largely matters of language and emphasis. The "Thought-Diary" does agree with "The Practical Significance of Pessimism" by insisting that "the highest and most intense life is non-individual," which implies "the suicide of individualism." But though the death of the self or of selfishness is underlined in both versions, the paper couples this theme with a flaccid resignation, a desire for a total subsumption of the ego into a realm of higher and nearly lifeless ideals, while the diary reaches its conclusion with the postulate that "life is in itself a good thing . . . and since it is a good thing, the more of it, and the more intense it is, the better." One says, surrender yourself to holiness; the other says, struggle to live abundantly.

One speaks of a better life beyond the self; the other seeks its ideal fulfillment from within.

"I am a Californian . . ." Thus Royce began his "Meditations before the Gate," an essay he wrote in his diary on February 12 as a foreword to an unwritten philosophical treatise. In 1879 the view of the San Francisco Bay from the Berkeley campus was unobstructed, and as Royce looked north toward the Golden Gate, letting his eye scan the westward panorama, the scene with its contrasting images seemed to symbolize his own ambivalence: the water breaking in from the Pacific, the city obscured by haze, the dark hills, the barren ranges beyond— "these," he noted, "are the permanent background whereon many passing shapes of light and shadow, of cloud and storm, of mist and sunset-glow are projected as I watch all from my station on the hillside." It was not the nature characterized by brute force that Royce had explored in *Prometheus Bound*, but a salubrious climate that ironically had provided a setting for a vain, ignorant, and violent society. Despite that irony, however, Royce's meditations subdued his rage. He was still willing to identify himself as a Californian and to define the positive elements of selfhood in terms of the beauty of his natural environment.

The "World-Spirit," objectified in mists and sunsets, led him to rededicate his efforts to the problems of nature, truth, and right. "With these problems I shall seek to busy myself earnestly, because it is each one's duty; independently, because I am a Californian as little bound to follow mere tradition as I am likely to find an audience by preaching in this wilderness; reverently, because I am thinking and writing face to face with a mighty and lovely Nature, by the side of whose greatness, I am but as a worm."

This rededication to the values of duty, independence, and reverence gave Royce a means of clarifying his alternatives to the extremes of self-abnegation and mere selfishness. He also discovered a further clarification by making a fresh examination of Goethe's *Faust*. Adding to his "Thought-Diary" on March 10, Royce noted that "Faust's contract with Mephisto is, in Goethe's view, no extraordinary act, no great crime, but simply the necessary fundament of an active life that strives for the Ideal." Agreeing with Goethe, Royce now felt that the essence of life is activity: "*Im Anfang war die Tat.*" The act is not exclusively either force (*Kraft*) or thought (*Sinn*), but a fusion of the two. Royce revised his earlier tendency to pose total oppositions between brute power and the higher consciousness. *Kraft* is a vital component to *Tat*, while *Sinn* is realized only through *Tat*. There is, in other words, no consciousness without activity and no activity without force. To resign or to seek passivity is death. But if life implies activity, activity implies restlessness, and since life at its best is full of activity, the best life is also full of discontent. This, Royce felt, is the meaning of *Faust*: "The contract with the devil is the eternal striving of the present moment." The will to live finds its corollary in unavoidable strife.

With the coming of spring and the Easter season, Royce's depression was blended with a feeling of holiness. "This is," he noted in his diary on April 3, "in a certain sense, the holy period of the year for me." On the other hand, he was impatient with the slow progress of his thought and disturbed by "outward events" and "the atmosphere in which thought is at work." Aside from the irritations of his work at the university, Royce was annoyed by the political upheavals making the daily news in California. "The State," he noted in a letter to Gilman, "is in the heat of contest on the Constitution-question." Widespread discontent that had vexed Californians for a decade had been answered by the reframing of the state's constitution. The convention that attended to this work met from September to March and produced a final document that was, in the view of many, a hodgepodge of compromises. Royce responded with bitter irony: "That the proposed Constitution is bad, seems certain enough. But that does not secure its defeat, in fact rather recommends it to a large class of voters."

The main features of the revision—regulation of taxes, railroads, investments, and Chinese labor—were the results of factional conflicts among grangers, capitalists, and laborites. The key figure was Denis Kearney, a fierce radical and racist, the leader of San Francisco's Workingman's Party, and a man whom Royce described as an "ignorant demagogue." Kearney's favorite tactic was the "sandlot oration," in which he whipped up his listeners by urging them to take arms against the capitalists and the Chinese. He was the sort of man that Royce most passionately despised, the loudmouthed bully. Though the Kearneyites did not control a majority in the convention, they held the most powerful minority, and the finished constitution largely met their demands. "If I were to vote," Royce told Gilman, "I should certainly not hesitate as to my side, but I feel that between delay and want of interest in politics, I have lost my opportunity. It would be my first vote, and like enough my last—not that I am intending to die, but that I am unable to warm with any patriotic fire in these days of political masquerades."

The Chinese question gave Royce a practical lesson in the enormous difficulties of achieving harmony in a diverse community. "Civilization," he told Coale, "sends us out here to solve a great problem: i.e., how two races and civilizations can be accommodated side by side. And we fall to stock-speculating and wheat-raising, and leave the problem to the political hack and the strong-lunged agitator." The origins of the problem came with the gold rush and the railroads. The thousands of Chinese who came to California were generally welcomed in the 1850s and 1860s. So long as work was abundant, racial tensions were minimal. But with the widespread unemployment that followed the completion of the Central Pacific, the frustrations of the laboring class were vented on the Chinese. Easily identified by appearance, language, and custom, they became the victims of numerous pogroms, encouraged by Kearney and his followers, which leveled Chinatowns and murdered residents. Such scenes fired Royce to fury: "This I know, that this terrible Chinese question will be sooner settled by the streetcats of San Francisco, or by the sheep of the Southern Sierras, or by the coyotes of our barren Coast hills, or by the wild asses of the Oriental deserts than by this blind and stupid and homeless generation of self-ish wanderers who do the voting and talking for this part of America."

When, during the first year of his Berkeley instructorship, Royce found relief from the irritations at the university, as well as from the fury he vented on California, he was working diligently in his favorite areas of philosophy. In November he reminded Gilman that "philosophic study is still my best beloved pursuit. I regret all the hours that are not in some way devoted to it." His main task, he felt, was to fill in the gaps of his doctoral thesis and break ground for a published treatise. The "Thought-Diary" was to be the repository for new ideas, revisions, and plans, and to effect the final goal the diary records his reflections on the categories of time and space, the problem of things-in-themselves, the will, memory, the structure of thought—in short, the epistemological founda-tions of metaphysics. Progress was slow and often frustrating.

This frustration is also revealed in several unfulfilled plans for publication that Josiah projected in 1878–79. W. T. Harris had asked him to write a short review of Shadworth Hodgson's *Philosophy of Reflection* for the *Journal of Speculative Philosophy*. Royce was impressed with Hodgson's work, so much so that he was reluctant to compress his response into a brief account; even when he later tried to write a longer essay on Hodgson he felt that he was "incompe-tent to do him philosophical justice." "I think," he told James, "the public ought to 'honor' Sh. H. 'with silence' (as Kant in the *Prolegomena* thanks it for having done to him), until *The Philosophy of Reflection* has been better digested. For it is no book of a day, that work, I am sure." Hesitating to write on Hodgson, he composed instead a long article, "Of the Will as the Principle of Philosophy." He first mentioned this piece to Gilman on January 26, 1879: "I need not say that I am still restless. I am writing some, and have a long article nearly finished on the 'Principle of Philosophy'; though I begin now to have scant hope that even Harris will be long-suffering enough to print it." Two months later he told Gilman that he had sent the article, "for a trial," to the *Princeton Review*.

In this article Royce rephrased the epistemology of his doctoral thesis and continued to propound a pure form of pragmatism. His thesis runs as follows: to know is to act, to act is to will. The foundation of any successful philosophy requires a theory of knowledge concerning the external world—the world of time, space, and other minds. Knowledge entails judgments, the paradigm for which is the simple union of subject and predicate: "The earth is round." Do we find such judgments or do we make them? Clearly the latter, insisted the young pragmatist, for judgments never come ready-made. Nor is the mind a swarm of ideas that randomly become connected. No, judgments are volitional acts, and since truth results from judgments, truth itself is made, constructed, postulated. Thus, the will is the fundamental principle of philosophy.

Two other concepts—the self and experience—have been accredited as starting points for philosophy. The first is the Cartesian principle; the second was advanced by Kant. But neither is able to survive critical analysis. Absolutists and determinists may object to the volitional theory by insisting that truthful judgments are required by the nature of things: "One must believe that the earth is round." Very well, Royce answered, but this linkage of necessity to a judgment constitutes only a further judgment. Thus, the intended objection is actually a confirmation of the volitional theory.

Like so many "first works," this article suffers from the young author's attempt to say too much. Unnecessarily long and overly elaborate, the article loses its force by repetition. Royce tended to belabor every point. Since Royce's correspondence with the editors of the *Princeton Review* has not survived, their specific criticisms are unknown, but the article was rejected. So Royce set another effort aside and turned again to other work.

The summer vacation gave him the time he needed, and as his diary indicates, he filled his leisure months with reading and writing. In addition to the comprehensive book of philosophy, which he kept planning and replanning, and the article on Hodgson, which was still unwritten but not abandoned, he was working on two new projects, both in the area of logic. One was an elementary textbook for his classes at Berkeley, and the other was a treatise, "Nature of Axioms." After making some progress with the first book, he found himself "snarled on the principles between Lotze and some others." Though he made little headway with the treatise, it led him into some valuable reading of De Morgan's calculus, Boole's logic, Venn's *Logic of Chance*, Balfour's *Defence of Philosophic Doubt*, and Dühring's *Geschichte der Grundprincipien der Mechanik*. At the same time he was relieved to be able to pay off one of his debts, thirty dollars to Lanman, though he still owed something to Johns Hopkins. Altogether, in contrast to his depression and disappointments of the previous year, he entered the fall semester, 1879, and approached the new year with renewed confidence. Something had happened to him, something he never described in any detail, but which perhaps explains his happiness: he had a sweetheart.

The lady's name was Katharine Head. Three years younger than Josiah, she had been born and educated in Boston, though when she met her future husband she was a special student in modern languages at the University of California. She was the youngest child of Edward Francis Head, a Bostonian and a Harvard graduate, who had come to California in 1862 to establish a law practice in San Francisco. In 1879 he was elected to the bench as superior court

judge of San Mateo County. Known as the "blind judge," having lost his sight
during his second term, he was remembered chiefly as a keen legal scholar and
as the effective distributor of several multimillion-dollar estates.

When Royce first met the Heads, they were among Berkeley's wealthiest and
most distinguished families, special friends of Edward Sill, and like the Coales
of Baltimore, they glittered with talent. One of Kitty's half brothers, Charles, to
whom Royce dedicated *The World and the Individual*, became one of Boston's
wealthiest brokers, while an elder sister, Anna, whom Josiah had known at the
university in the early seventies, was the founder of the East Bay's best (and still
thriving) school for girls.

As for Katharine, she was quite a beautiful young lady—slim, with dark fea-
tures, and a prominent aristocratic nose. Intellectually she was a match for
Josiah. She knew Latin and Greek, and was fluent in French, German, and
Italian. In addition she wrote poetry and was an accomplished pianist. Of her
courtship with Josiah, little is known; Royce was much too reticent to discuss
anything so personal with anyone. It may be presumed that Sill, who described
Katharine as "a talented, refined, & handsome young lady," had introduced
Royce to the family. Mrs. Royce later remembered that she first saw her future
husband, shortly after his return to California in 1878, hurrying across the university library to greet his old friend, Joseph Rowell. How they fell in love
remains a secret. The first mention of anything of the sort occurs near the end
of Royce's long letter to James, January 8, 1880. All that such a momentous
experience warranted was a single sentence: "Socially I am well off, and am,
among other things, engaged to be married."

James was delighted with the news, but amazed by Royce's reticence: "First
of all," he wrote on February 3, "*Glückwünsche* as to your *Verlobung*! which, like
the true philosopher that you are, you mention parenthetically and without
names, dates, numbers of dollars, etc., etc." Royce's next letter did little to satisfy James's curiosity; again, at the end of an extended philosophical discussion,
one sentence gave scant information about his engagement: "Unless my salary
is unexpectedly increased, I cannot well hope to marry for some time." So
"Beloved Royce," as James now called him, said not one word about "the fair
Object," not even her name.

This indirect description of his personal plans and feelings characterizes all
of Royce's letters on the subject. Writing to Gilman and Coale, he mentioned
his fiancée's father—his name, profession, birthplace, and so forth—but never
Katharine. It seems almost as if Royce were marrying the family instead of its
younger daughter. Indeed, Judge Head's wealth and social position were probably involved in Josiah's attraction to Katharine: nothing so simple as greed, but
stature, honor, respectability. Certainly his future father-in-law embodied those
qualities that Royce so often found attractive in older men. In any event, Kitty

introduced new dimensions into Josiah's life, especially beauty, which he could not have created on his own. They were also united by deep intellectual sympathies, eventually by parenthood, and by a mutual passion for music, a love that they passed on to two of their three sons. Of immediate moment, in Kitty Josiah found an escape from loneliness, and perhaps because of that his literary and philosophical productivity, after the fall of 1879, increased markedly.

On November 10 he gave a talk to the Chit-Chat Club of San Francisco entitled "Shelley and the Revolution." Published during the following year in the *Californian*, this paper brought Royce to terms with the revolutionary spirit as expressed through romantic poetry. Royce had the distinct feeling, as he often said, of being somehow in the far-reaching shadows of the French Revolution. "Shelley is a poet of the age of the Revolution. To this age we still belong. Do or say or think what we will, the Revolution—political, social, moral, religious, philosophical, poetical—is all about us in the air we breathe. Escape from it we cannot."

Other intellectuals in the late 1870s might have hesitated to identify themselves with a movement that had begun on another continent a hundred years earlier, but Royce had a keen sense of being connected to its history. Reform and upheaval had always surrounded his life. The gold rush, the Civil War, the age of Darwinism, the era of U.S. academic reform, the contemporary violence of California politics—these generated in him an emotional cleavage between a desire for a better life and a demand for order. He had touched briefly on the moral aspects of reform at the end of his essay on pessimism. Shelley, whom Royce resembled both physically and temperamentally, became the representative of his ambivalence. Ignoring specific theories and movements, Royce focused his attention on the paradoxical spirit of revolution: on the one hand, it expresses "the need of the individual for fullest life, and for a better knowledge of his place in the universe," but on the other, it is fired by a "holy zeal to destroy." Shelley dramatizes the conflict in *Prometheus Unbound*, but takes refuge in the optimistic faith that fervent love must eventually overcome oppression. The ethical problem of the play resides in this groundless faith, for the hero in chains can do nothing but wait for the cosmos to fulfill its plan. "Optimism," Royce believed, "is a resort as useless as it is unfounded." But still he felt that Shelley's response to the revolutionary spirit teaches two important lessons: first, "watch and fight," expect no divine intervention, conduct your life as a hunted tiger in the jungle; and then, "endure and . . . see," give up the desire to alter the structures of life, seek instead to understand its meaning.

Royce was disappointed with his essay on Shelley. It was, he told James, "a weak essay," "an enormous diatribe." "Various things," he told Coale, "combined to make the poor thing more formless than by plan it should have been, and the whole was confused by declamation." His next effort—a talk delivered to the

Berkeley Club on January 8, 1880, entitled "Some Illustrations of the Structure and Growth of Human Thought"—did not earn a more favorable self-estimate. Writing to James immediately afterward, he described the talk as "a terribly dry and long-winded discourse." Neither judgment was entirely warranted, for in both essays Royce took useful steps toward the development of his later philosophy. The central question of his Berkeley Club address—to what extent is thought not dependent on experience?—has a direct bearing on the worlds of "power" and "postulate" in the ninth chapter of *The Religious Aspect of Philosophy*. To answer his question, Royce made use of Kant's distinction between analytic and synthetic judgments or, as Royce revised the terminology, between "descriptive" and "ampliative" knowledge. Spencer and his disciples had denied the possibility of any thought not derived from experience. According to evolutionist doctrine all thought is descriptive; it is either direct data or the result of conditioning. Whatever appears to be ampliative is really "inherited experience." But this, Royce insisted, is hopelessly inexact, for experience means direct data.

Looking for other bases of ampliative knowledge, Royce turned his attention to the sciences and found the same answer that he had first noted in Lewes's *Problems of Life and Mind*. The so-called laws of mechanics never obtain in actual experience, nor does the truth of the Pythagorean theorem depend on measurement of actual triangles. These are our constructions, our amplifications, which are never perfectly verified by experience, but which are still useful as means of organizing and comprehending our lives. The purpose of science, indeed the purpose of thought in general, is not to make descriptive notebooks of facts, but to understand experience, and this can be done, if at all, by means of ideal constructions.

As this and other earlier papers indicate, Royce's idealism was cemented in the philosophy of science. His mean and unfair judgment of the paper seems, with more justification, to have been a criticism of his audience. In California, where philosophy was "regarded as a kind of harmless lunacy," even the Berkeley Club was suspicious. With renewed irritation Royce came home, and at ten o'clock began his long letter to James, complaining of "the uselessness of trying to find a market for philosophic speculation hereabouts." He had read James's seminal essay "The Sentiment of Rationality" in the July issue of *Mind* and recognized at once its affinities with his own efforts. James's "cross-questioning of consciousness," his interest in knowing the structure and purpose of rigorous thought, suggested a future for a new school of philosophy. A similar effort had been made by Charles Peirce in six papers, "Illustrations of the Logic of Science," published two years before in the *Popular Science Monthly*. The word *pragmatism* had hardly been spoken, its lines of attack and defense had not yet been drawn, but if there were to be a new school of philosophy, Royce urgently wanted to be part of it.

Husband and Scholar

He soon got his chance. Peirce, then a resident lecturer at Johns Hopkins, had established a Metaphysical Club in Baltimore. On January 17, 1880, Allan Marquand, the club's secretary, invited Royce to send a paper. "If it is acceptable to you and to the Club," Royce replied, "I should be very glad to send on for criticism, in the course of about two months, a paper on certain problems in the Theory of Knowledge. I should call the paper an essay on 'Certainty and Reality'; as an alternative title I might name 'Of Axioms as Constitutive Principles and as Regulative Principles.' . . . You may be sure that any student so far away from fellow-students in philosophy as I now am, follows with interest, not to say envy, the work of those who can work together, and receives gratefully every account of their progress." Encouraged by Marquand's response, Royce set to work, and on May 1 he sent the Metaphysical Club a paper entitled "On Purpose in Thought." Though the subject had been slightly altered, he assured Marquand that "the discussion lies in the same field with the prospectus and covers to some extent the same ground." He also apologized for the delay, which had been caused by "requirements of other work here in Berkeley," and for the paper's length, which had resulted from a need of choosing between tediousness and a lack of clarity: "I elected tediousness and have surely succeeded in that, while I have no certainty that I have avoided obscurity."

This paper, Royce's major task during the spring of 1880 and one that has often been considered as among his most important early works, is a further elaboration of his talk to the Berkeley Club. It begins with the point made at the end of the earlier paper and reaches a more thorough statement of the same conclusion. In this it was remarkably consistent with the theories of both James and Peirce. Common sense tells us that the purpose of thought is to know the truth. But in "The Fixation of Belief," Peirce had laid the foundations of pragmatism by announcing that "the settlement of opinion is the sole end of inquiry," whereas inquiry is a struggle for freedom from the irritations of doubt. Belief, therefore, is a "habit" that meets emotional as well as theoretical needs. James, a persistent interpreter of Peirce's views for his own purposes, had maintained that "the feeling of rationality is constituted merely by the absence of any feeling of irrationality." Thought reaches for belief as a drowning man struggles for air.

Royce agreed: "Thought seeks to change uncertainty into confidence"; "Thought must be the attainment of some state of consciousness"; "The end of thought is declared to be the attainment of axiomatic certainty." But Royce wanted to go farther: Why do we make the axioms? His answer: they enable us to construct an image of possible experience; without axioms we would have no way of projecting the future. Why then do we project a future? Here Royce reached beyond mere arbitrariness. We do not *choose* to construct an image of a possible experience; that is required by the structure of thought. No skeptic can doubt the "time-axiom," for to conceive of a condition of things when time has ceased is to project some image of the future. We acquire a concept of the future simply because thought demands it; the aim and the fulfillment are one. And further, the image of the future cannot be "an independent flux of phenomena" but must be a projection of "the content of the flux" based on an ideal past and present experience, for to say that there will be a future is to say what the future will be. Thus, the axiom of uniformity is the corollary of the axiom of time. To deny this, to say that the conditions of the ideal future may fail to fulfill our expectations of uniformity, is to fall into the contradiction of saying that what we mean by future experience is not what we mean. The fallacy of naturalism, the claim that we are held fast in the grip of circumstance, is thus answered by the purpose of thought; we own the time stream; we make it in the act of thinking. Or as Royce was fond of saying, since we have made the molecules, there is no need of bowing down in mute reverence to the mystery that somehow they have made us. The task of thought, he believed, is to construct "an ideal picture of a world of experience." This is the world of the postulates.

The volitional aspect of Royce's concept of time was the paper's most arresting feature, and in advancing his claim that the time stream is not a datum but a construction of consciousness, he had a few bones to pick with Shadworth Hodgson. In letters to James and Marquand, both written in June, Royce expanded his theory and answered the criticisms of Peirce's Metaphysical Club. Hodgson had claimed that time is a "stream of consciousness"—a phrase that James later appropriated—a pure datum in which the elements of past, present, and future are presented in a seamless flow. But Royce sought to distinguish between this passive feeling of succession and the active postulating of the time stream. When I listen to the ticking of a clock or make three quick taps with my knuckle, I am conscious, all at once, of a succession, but not of discrete events, past and present. "The succession of the present moment is then indeed given, but it is not, as given, such succession as I believe to exist among the moments of the time-stream." The feeling of succession, in other words, belongs to the present moment. But when I try to remember the sound of a ticking clock a minute ago, I cease to receive data passively and begin to act. Knowledge of "the past" involves at least three elements: "immediate experience of the ceaseless change of conscious life . . . the active power which creates from moment to moment the notion of past and future experiences . . . [and] the observation of natural phenomena that are regular." The second element, the "active power" or will, is crucial. The mind receives its data, it observes and submits to uniformity, but the will creates the temporal world.

James forwarded Royce's letter to Hodgson who, in turn, wrote to Royce on June 30. Royce answered with a lengthy letter, which unfortunately has not survived, on August 7, which prompted a second letter from Hodgson on September 14. Twenty-three years older than Royce, extremely gracious in his demeanor—James called him an "incarnate angel"—Hodgson thanked Royce for his careful study of *The Philosophy of Reflection* and did his best to answer the young man's objections. Royce had wanted to know: How is knowledge or consciousness of time, as a succession, possible? Hodgson suggested that this might not be the right question and that Royce might be laboring with false assumptions:

> The *minimum sensibile* is an artificial thing. We invent it when we are trying to analyse perception, by trying to get hold of its minutest portions. It is a creature of our *attention* to the phenomena of perception. It is so just as much as the perception of larger empirical objects is, houses, trees, &c. We construct the world of these objects by *attention* to the phenomena of perception in their crude form, which is a *stream* according to me. So also we *construct* the *minima sensibilia* out of the same stream. And then, mark! because we get the *minima sensibilia* in an attempt to *analyse* the crude form, we think that *minima sensibilia* are the elements of the crude form, and *a fortiori* the elements of the world of objects made out of it. And then we imagine that consciousness comes to us in *drops, minima sensibilia;* and involve ourselves in the puzzle, How is time-perception possible? It is like pouring a glass of water away in drops, and then asking how such drops can be united into a mass of water.

Toward the end of the second letter, Hodgson proposed the following difference between the two theories:

> Where you put a *postulate* of time-succession, I put *attention,* an act of thought, the act constitutive of thought, differentiating it from perception in which it arises. Before that act, the time-succession is in perception; but only after that act is it perceived *as a time succession.* You however postulate an activity which projects the idea of time-succession, ready made, out of its own vitals; and since it does not *find* it in perception, must really *create* as well as postulate the idea. How does this differ from having "innate ideas"?

In this brief, spirited exchange, neither gave ground to the other. So far as Royce profited from the debate, it strengthened his commitment to Kantian analysis. One year later he wrote, "Mr. Hodgson is doubtless one of the greatest living masters of metaphysics, but we must suspect anything that looks like giving up the very central citadel of the critical philosophy, the doctrine of the spontaneity of intelligence. 'We can think nothing as united in the object that we have not ourselves united.' Those are Kant's golden words."

To express the moral and social counterpart of his metaphysics, Royce wrote "The Nature of Voluntary Progress." He prepared this paper for the Fortnightly Club, a faculty group of the university organized by the historian Bernard Moses and devoted to the social sciences; it was published during the summer of 1880 in the club's official organ, the *Berkeley Quarterly*. Royce liked this piece better than his other early essays on social thought: "It has," he told James, ". . . a little philosophic discussion in it." The paper is, in fact, Royce's first important effort in constructive social philosophy. According to the Spencerian doctrine, physical evolution acts by mechanical and purely involuntary means, and further, if the "laws" of natural selection are applied to the social sphere, we should expect the result to be a tendency toward greater and greater diversity. Such is the doctrine of social Darwinism.

But three years before Lester Ward's *Dynamic Sociology* took issue with Spencerism, Royce noted that social development follows the opposite course. Instead of diversity, wherever "voluntary progress" is most active, the tendency is toward simpler and more unified forms. What causes this? To answer, Royce paid a long-standing debt to his teacher Joseph Le Conte, who had maintained that in the course of human development, the growth of self-mastery through reason had supplanted natural selection. According to Royce there are two components in voluntary progress: conservatism and optimism. And just as there are varying levels in each component, the higher levels of both produce the greatest degree of progressive change in the different fields—ideological, industrial, political, and moral—of human life.

Royce believed, an apparent paradox, that the true spirit of conservatism is a prime force in reform, for the reformer, as opposed to the anarchist or the reactionary, attempts not to destroy society or preserve the status quo, but to cultivate the ideals and forms that facilitate change. Revolutions, Royce observed, often claim to be returns to former traditions. Such was the case of the early Christian church, the Protestant Reformation, the Puritan Revolution in England; such also was the case of the French Revolution, which sought to justify itself by appealing to the myth of the Social Contract. The conservative element in revolutions saves them from utter confusion; it gives them unity, rationality, and organization. Like conservatism, optimism also has its gradations. If there is the childish optimism, "the optimism of the mining camp," which says, "I shall prosper," there is also a higher faith, which requires self-sacrifice, "a faith that individual efforts, if lost for the individual himself, are not lost for his community, that the combined effect of everybody's efforts is progress and general good." This is not, however, Panglossian optimism, for the highest expressions of hope are often born of the most intense dissatisfaction.

Thus, just as conservatism is sometimes mistaken for the wildest radicalism, optimism often looks like the dreariest pessimism. These two principles are the bases, Royce believed, of all voluntary progress.

The non-Hegelian, and for that matter the non-Marxian, implications of this theory are clear. In working toward progressive development the reformer is guided by a search for unity, keeps in tune with tradition, prefers simple to complex solutions, and clings to the hope that the world can be made better than it is. This progress is not the result of a dialectical interaction between opposites, but a harmonious development through time. Royce actually had more in common with the Darwinists than with the Hegelians, for although he resisted the clichés of "competition of life" and "struggle for existence," his theory of progress is consistent with the evolutionary principles of adaptation and cooperation. Probably, he believed, we can never reach the final unity; probably we must be forever restless and dissatisfied, but this is not a justification for inactivity. The act of reaching for an ideal, of pressing against boundaries, was always for Royce the chief purpose of life.

The original insight and polemical control of these essays—"On Purpose in Thought" and "The Nature of Voluntary Progress"—surpass anything that Royce had done before 1880. This success ran parallel to the success in his personal life. Because of his meager salary and his still unpaid debts, Royce had postponed his marriage to Katharine Head. But although his income had not increased, other factors made an early marriage possible. By September, Judge Head, having decided to move permanently to Redwood City, had offered his home in Berkeley to Josiah and Katharine. This attractive offer, coupled with a plan of Royce's own parents to move to Los Gatos, prompted his decision to marry immediately. Money was still a huge problem. The possibility of earning more by instituting new programs in philosophy fell through when the university's administration refused to appropriate funds. The president informed Royce that he was welcome to teach the new courses, but would not be paid for the extra work. Among other resources Royce thought that he might add to his income by giving private lessons. All things considered, the situation favored marriage; so regardless of future bounty, Josiah and Katharine made the arrangements, and in Berkeley, on October 2, 1880, they were married.

"I am well content with the world and the future." Thus Royce wrote to James two weeks before his wedding day. Marriage settled him down emotionally, and perhaps as a result, the quantity and the quality of his work continued to increase. The second two years of Royce's Berkeley instructorship, in contrast to the first two, present the picture of a young man of twenty-five whose industry reflects peace with the world and a growing self-esteem. Writing to Lanman three months after his marriage, he exuded confidence: "As for me I

am married and happy. I wish I had my system of the universe more nearly completed. This is all that I lack." "I can hardly think of you as married," Lanman
replied; "you with boyish look and fresh heart. . . . How fortunate you are to
have fallen in love."

As planned, Josiah was earning extra money as a tutor. "Some of these
lessons," he confessed to the philologist, "are Latin lessons. (Don't be too much
frightened at that. When I *teach* Latin I try to be careful of my quantities, and
to be as good as I can.) Such is the lofty nature of my life as a breadwinner. My
contemplative existence I pursue over tea in the evenings, or on afternoon walks
on the hills that look westward out of the Golden Gate into the sea." In previous letters Lanman had echoed his friend's pessimism, but now with renewed
hope Royce brushed his concerns aside:

> As for the use of doing any work here on this doomed planet of ours, I agree with
> you that one sometimes feels despondent about the future and about the worms
> that dare to eat up the brain tissues that one is now so vigorously seeking to build
> up; but the whole solution lies here: we are alive now, and the worth our work
> now has is just the worth we choose now by our enthusiasm to give it. And pre-
> sent worth is all that concerns us. Damn the worms. We are alive now.

The same enthusiasm became the hallmark of his teaching and writing. The
academic year 1880–81 finds him at work on a number of essays, some of which
were major steps toward the completion of the "system of the universe" that he
had mentioned to Lanman. During the first week of November Royce gave a
university lecture—now lost, except for fragments—"The Ethical Aspect of
Modern Thought," which, according to the *Berkeleyan*, "was marked by the
same clearness of statement, the same depth of knowledge, and the same logical reasoning which characterize all of his productions." In December the death
of George Eliot prompted Royce to write a memorial essay on the religious
thought in her novels. Under the title "George Eliot as a Religious Teacher," he
read the paper on February 10, 1881, to the Berkeley Club and published it later
that year in the *Californian*. It was the last of Royce's several essays that he
wrote on the novelist who had influenced his youthful thought profoundly. Like
Tolstoy and Goethe, whom he also admired, George Eliot united a deep philosophical concern with a high degree of poetic vision. This quality, Royce felt,
was her main literary and religious contribution:

> If ever we have a religious philosophy, the poets on the one hand, the merciless
> skeptics on the other, will have helped the speculator at every step in his search
> for a theory. Without them speculation is a tale told by an idiot, full of sound and

fury, yet signifying nothing. George Eliot is at once speculative, skeptical, and poetic. Whatever she has done best, depends on the successful union of these three faculties.

"Speculative, skeptical, and poetic"—these faculties Royce tried to cultivate and unite in his own thought. In "Doubting and Working," published also in the *Californian* that year, he made an eloquent plea for skepticism as a vital phase in the search for truth. Anticipating the most illuminating example of "The Possibility of Error," Royce cited the famous speculation of Oliver Wendell Holmes that there are actually six persons present whenever any two are found in conversation: there are two real persons, each one's idea of himself, and each one's idea of the other. This suggested for Royce the enormous difficulties of gaining real knowledge of the world, for there would seem to be as many worlds and as many truths as there are experiences. "Every one has nooks and corners in his own mind to which he is himself more or less a stranger. Every man is an enigma to every other." The doubts that result from these difficulties cannot be easily dismissed, but must be incorporated into any philosophy:

> If you fail to doubt everything, doubt all you can. Doubt not because doubting is a good end, but because it is a good beginning. Doubt not for amusement, but as a matter of duty. Doubt not superficially, but with thoroughness. Doubt not flippantly, but with the deepest—it may be with the saddest—earnestness. Doubt as you would undergo a surgical operation, because it is necessary to thought-health. So only can you hope to attain convictions that are worth having.

What these convictions might be, Royce did not say; he saved that story for another day.

In addition to his writing and regular university work, Royce spent a good deal of time as organizer and permanent secretary of Berkeley's Psychology Club. Under his and Sill's sponsorship the club invited membership from the faculty, alumni, and advanced students. Its first meeting was held at Sill's home on November 10, and to set the group in motion Royce read a paper, "The Scope and Study of Psychology." The report in the *Berkeleyan* of Royce's part at this meeting reflected enthusiasm for the university's new undertaking: "He sketched the growth of the science from the time of the ancients, the influence of Locke and Descartes, and gave a short account of the labors of the physiological psychologists of the present day. He clearly defined Psychology and showed wherein it differed from Ethics and Logic. The paper gave rise to an interesting discussion, all members taking part." The club planned to meet twice monthly, and so long as Royce and Sill remained on the faculty, it was one of the more lively gatherings at Berkeley. On at least two other occasions Royce led the club's discussions with papers entitled "Intellect and Intelligence" (March 4, 1881) and "Association of Ideas in the Light of Theory and Experience" (March 4, 1882).

Royce's last meeting with the Psychology Club in May 1882 commemorated the work of Ralph Waldo Emerson, who had died within the past two weeks. Royce's feelings on this occasion are unrecorded, but the quality of his ambivalence can be imagined. For more than forty years Emerson had been the poet-prophet of American idealism. He had stood up against established authority, proclaimed the value of the soul against the rise of materialism, and felt the thrill of insight to be gained within the heart of nature. There was much, therefore, in Emerson that Royce admired and wanted to emulate. But on the other hand, Royce felt that Emerson's faith lacked the intellectual toughness that could make it durable. As Emersonianism declined with the rise of evolutionary theory, it remained a faith for older men such as Sill and Coale. It was no longer a young man's creed. Royce hinted these feelings to Coale in a letter of September 23, 1880:

> The men of your generation are now rare, and we young men meet you but seldom. By your generation I mean the men with the vivid sense and faith of and in the ideal value of life, as Carlyle and Emerson once taught that faith and sense, and as the whole generation of the Transcendentalists received it. We young men hear from our time no such doctrines preached. I know, as you used to say, that may be because there is no longer the need to preach and repeat what through Carlyle and Emerson has been made the common property of all; but I fear that we younger men have so much else to read and believe and puzzle over, that this heritage from the age of the Idealists comes to our minds in a very diluted, perhaps even polluted form. For my part I have needed the living man to help me in appreciating the meaning of this pure and hopeful spirit of faith, and in this way I owe you personally a good deal. Not that I am a disciple myself. The condition whose presence saves you, as you say, from Pessimism, is unfortunately lacking in my case; and though I am not properly a Pessimist, I am a dabbler in dangerous problems; and a very extensive doubter. But you emphasized, or at least greatly helped to emphasize for me one moment or element of the truth of which I sincerely hope never to lose sight. And for this I shall always thank you.

What Royce meant, he most fully expressed in "The Decay of Earnestness," published in the *Californian* early in 1881. The faith of transcendentalism as it descended from Schiller and Goethe to Carlyle and Emerson had held fast to a fundamental belief in the supreme value of the individual: "The idea that in the free growth and expression of the highest and strongest emotions of the civilized man might be found the true solution of the problem of life." Although Royce felt that this doctrine of "earnestness" was still worth preserving, and although he had placed the preservation of that faith high on his philosophical agenda, he also noted that during the twenty years after the *Origin of Species* it had decayed and in its older forms was no longer serviceable. But why had it decayed? Royce's answer was threefold. In the first place it had committed the fallacy of individualism: it had glorified the ego without taking account of its larger relationships. Represented in Shelley's Prometheus, the titanic ego stands alone in chains waiting for the day when Demogorgon will rise up to free him. The sense of powerlessness was the second failure. If, in its classical period with Schiller and Goethe, the romantic faith had proclaimed that fullness of life could be won by ceaseless toil, it had eventually surrendered to melancholy. It proved to be volitionally weak; under stress it could not find the will to persevere. And finally, it lacked theoretical strength, the intellectual capacity to resist the challenge that came from the rise of naturalism. To remedy these faults, to reconstitute the former idealism was, Royce believed, the task of thought in his generation. But he also believed that the results of evolutionary theory could not be ignored; pessimism and skepticism were parts, if only parts, of the truth. "The world is of importance only because of the subordinate place it gives to consciousness. But the cure is not in writing books against science, but solely in such a broad philosophy as shall correct the narrowness of the day, and bring back to the first rank of interest once more the problems of Goethe's *Faust* and of Kant's *Critique*."

If the faith of Emerson was the end Royce sought, the method of Kant was his way of proceeding. He spent much of his time during the summer vacation of 1880 reviewing the *Critique of Pure Reason*, and through his reading he acquired a new insight into the critical philosophy. On September 4 he made a brief but penetrating entry in his diary:

> I see Kant as I never saw him before. But we must put our problem differently. Thus says Kant: What is the relation of knowledge to its object? Thus say we: What is the relation of every conscious moment to every other? Our question may be more fundamental, and can be made so only through study of him.

On the nineteenth he reported to James that some reading in psychology had led him "back to old father Kant, whom I had neglected for a year or more." Now, Royce explained, he understood critical philosophy and could see how it might lead to constructive thought. "What I mean is this: Kant starts two great questions, one as to the objects (*Gegenstände*) and the limits of human knowledge, and one as to the structure of knowledge." Royce felt that the first question could be settled through the idealistic formula: all that is, is in and for consciousness. The *thing-in-itself* is a meaningless term, for a conception of any object outside consciousness becomes, in the act of conceiving it, a part of consciousness. Thus, critical analysis had disposed of this problem by showing that it does not exist. But to answer the second question, Royce felt, is to approach the deepest problem of philosophy. "I say deepest; for to solve the problem of the structure of knowledge would be to gain insight into everything in the range of philosophy." Outside Germany little work had been done in this field. He saw that Peirce's "Illustrations of the Logic of Science" was a step in the right direction, and James's essays in the psychology of knowledge were "a sort of propaedeutic" to the whole problem.

As for Royce's views of the subjects they were "stubborn enough . . . , only every new trial brings me against worse difficulties and into a bigger maze of puzzling questions." His paper on the purpose of thought had reached the conclusion that the active postulating of a future is a necessary condition of all thinking. Still, he felt, he had not yet reached the rock-bottom question; he had answered the *what* but not the *how*. "The deepest question is Kant's, how is experience possible? Tell us this and you have a philosophy. Leave this untold, and you stop half way. How is experience possible as a series of states known to be a series? So I put the case to myself, and here I make a beginning of all investigation."

Royce's solution begins with the point that a series known as a series is possible only if each state of consciousness knows every other state. This in turn is possible only through postulates, for experience as passive reception gives only the present moment. "Only spontaneity constructs the world in time." The ultimate datum is the present moment, which unites the passive and the active, the simple reception of immediate consciousness and the construction of a temporal world beyond. The first task of philosophy, Royce felt, is to discover "all the forms of this constructing activity, the fashion in which each of these monad-moments builds up its world." In a world of postulates the problem of absolute truth vanishes, as it does in pragmatism, for the truth is whatever consciousness, from moment to moment, can intelligibly construct. Royce also believed that these new applications of critical philosophy would encompass all areas of thought—metaphysics, mathematics, the philosophy of nature as well as ethics. "'Give me a world' is the cry of consciousness; and behold, a world is made even in the act of crying."

Royce looked upon this phase of his thought as an effort "to escape from the dogmatism of science without dropping into the fashions of the orthodox." He hoped that James would approve, but was a little uneasy about his theory's complete acceptability: "Some of this you will, I think, agree with; some of it at all events, I have learned from or through you; but I do not know whether you would approve it when you saw it stated in full. I mean to state it." James did approve. But still he was somewhat puzzled and perhaps also a little suspicious:

Your views about the structure of thought and so on are somewhat too concisely expressed for me to catch their full bearings, but you have evidently got hold of something and I hope to Heaven you will work it out. We do want some sane and educated constructive philosophizing in this country to set off against the *borborygme* and other peristaltic phenomena of the Hegelian band. Hegelianism . . . is making a very able and active propaganda here; and part of my fun this winter is trying to scotch it. I shall count on you as an ally in the common task—what you sketch in your letter as a vindication of the element of spontaneity in the construction of truth—the postulates which the moment makes. The field is fruitful, the reapers as yet but few, but everywhere else in my opinion lies *Humbug*.

No philosophy can be anything else than an attempt to *make* a certain construction work.

This was not the first time that James, in his letters to Royce, had curled his lip at the Hegelians. "Their sacerdotal airs! and their sterility! Contemplating their navels and the syllable oum!" His colleague George Herbert Palmer was James's favorite example of "the white winged band" of Hegelian prigs. Perhaps James had already identified the taint of this tendency, as yet undeveloped, in Royce and was giving advance warning that he disapproved. At any rate his charge of "*Humbug*" and his insistence on the workability of truth set the grounds for the famous "battle of the absolute" in the next decade. Royce also had his reservations about James's thought. When, a year later, James published his "Reflex Action and Theism" in the *Unitarian Review*, Royce told Coale that he had read and admired the article; "yet," he added, "in some points I differed." James had developed his fideism with an approving quotation from Goethe's *Faust*: "*Gefühl ist alles*." Alluding to this remark, Royce answered James: "Not *Gefühl* but *Gedanke* and *Gefühl* are everything." But not wishing to appear priggish, he hastened to reassure his friend: "I need not say that this *Gedanke* is not the Hegelian *Denken*. And yet I am no subjective idealist of the old-fashioned sort. Not *myself* is the ultimate truth, but Consciousness as such." Though neither Royce nor James had landed a solid blow, the first round of their match had begun.

For the moment, however, they were only sparring with hooks and jabs, content to emphasize the larger areas of their agreement. Royce was unwilling to reach beyond his postulates, and James was delighted to find one who echoed his thoughts. This delight led James to use his influence in getting Royce out of California. In the spring of 1880 James had recommended Royce for a position at the University of Minnesota, though nothing came of the effort. At the same time Sill was doing what he could to find Royce a professorship in the East. Writing to Gilman in April, Sill had high praise for his junior colleague:

About Royce: is there not some opening for him with you, or failing that, do you not know of some one of the reputable colleges where he could be Prof. of Logic, or Rhetoric, or Eng. Literature—or all of them together? As I have said to you before, I don't believe this is a good place for him. . . . If he were after an Eng. Literature position—permanently—of course he c'd have mine after a while; but he doesn't want that, unless it should be right away as a mere temporary stepping stone. . . .

I like to have him here, myself—it is only his needs that I am thinking of. The planet doesn't have a first-rate mind alight on it every year, & I w'd like to see this one properly environed. And this—as none knows better than you—is a miserable place for such a thing before it has "come to forty year."

Royce is successful with his classes. He works with them faithfully; & while he doesn't take-on another's policy and plans easily . . . , I confess I like better to see him independent. There is none of the "mush of concession" in him, but I value him the more for that. He is successful as a teacher & ought to be in a better place.

The records of Gilman's correspondence provide no evidence that Sill's appeal was answered. This silence, however, may be partly explained by the fact that Johns Hopkins already had at least four preferred candidates for the expected chair of philosophy. G. S. Morris and C. S. Peirce were on the scene, and G. Stanley Hall would soon join them. During the next few years, these three competed for the chair that Hall eventually won. Doubtless also, Gilman still hoped that William James might be persuaded to leave Harvard. Certainly any of these candidates had more visible accomplishments than Royce. Furthermore, Gilman's scientific training made him faintly suspicious of speculative inquiry; philosophy could best serve the university, he felt, by emphasizing psychology, pedagogy, and logic. If Royce remained Gilman's protégé, the president was disinclined to sponsor his return to Baltimore, nor was he sensitive to Royce's profound dissatisfaction with California. His letters to Royce—cordial, yet faintly ceremonial—eluded the issue that preyed upon the young man's mind. On February 29, 1880, for instance, Gilman wrote to congratulate Royce for "continued intellectual activity. . . . You seem to have abundant opportunities to employ your talents; & I hope we shall see in print frequently results from your versatile & comprehensive reflections." The president, it seems, was too engrossed with his own administrative prospects to worry much about his young friend in Berkeley.

The next year seemed to offer better prospects. On March 25, 1881, James sent Royce the news that Andrew Peabody, Harvard's professor of ethics, had resigned. This, along with other anticipated changes in the philosophy department, suggested the possibility of a new assistant professorship. The salary would be two thousand dollars on a five-year contract. Nothing was certain, but James urged Royce to get his dossier together and make application:

> I am sorry I can give you no more definite account of what will occur. Nothing yet is definitely known by me or anyone else. I only want you to put yourself on record in the *event* of a new man having to be called. . . . There are many other candidates with open mouths swimming around the door, and you must not be disappointed if nothing ever comes of it.

On April 3 Royce wrote back to say that he had cooked a "pretty pudding" including reprints of his articles, programs of lectures, annual reports from Johns Hopkins, an abstract of his paper "On Purpose in Thought," and had arranged to get testimonials from colleagues and former teachers. "I may therefore be regarded as swimming about with open mouth among the rest." On May 8 James announced the disappointing news that "the Harvard chances of a vacancy are for the present nil." All prospects for changes had blown over. James hoped that Royce would not be discouraged, and looking on the brighter side, he added that "one more year may upset everything again, and your application made now will keep."

If Royce wrote an answer to this letter, it has not survived. His disappointment, though he had tried to prepare for it, must have been acute. But as usual in such periods, Royce kept silent, refused to dissipate his energies in self-pity, and went to work. In April he had published an essay, "Before and Since Kant," in the *Berkeley Quarterly*. It was primarily a historical survey commemorating the centennial of the *Critique of Pure Reason* and compressing all of modern philosophy from Descartes to the present into seventeen printed pages. Although it also contained hints of Royce's views on the structure of knowledge, they were not fully developed, and he was content to limit his paper to fairly elementary issues. James admired this work; together with the essay on George Eliot, it showed that Royce had "the gift of popularizing." Still, James told him, he hoped for "something more technical and dense from your pen."

International Debut

These hopes were soon fulfilled. In April 1881 Royce sent a paper to *Mind* critically opposing the so-called mind-stuff theory as formulated by W. K. Clifford and further expounded by F. W. Frankland. This theory, one of those forgotten monisms of the nineteenth century, was an attempt to resolve the mind-body problem by claiming that nature is full of spirit. Specifically it claimed that each atom is a union of mental and physical substance called "mind-stuff," and that this stuff is the unconditioned thing-in-itself. Clifford had reached this opinion on the grounds that if evolution is traced backward from man, it is impossible to say at any point that mental activity (feelings) ceases; the continuity of the series, he argued, suggests that each speck of matter contains an elementary feeling—an "eject" as opposed to an "object"— which can exist wholly beyond human consciousness. "The universe," Clifford believed, ". . . consists entirely of mind-stuff." Royce had long puzzled over this theory; as early as October 1878, he had projected an essay on Clifford's view of the *Ding an sich*. He strongly suspected that it was merely a new version of scholastic nonsense, reminding him of Prospero's "such stuff as dreams are made on."

It was an essay by Frankland, however, that provoked Royce's attack. Frankland had hazarded the conjecture that motion is mind-stuff, that mass and velocity are correlative to volume and intensity of feeling. Such views were clearly at odds with Royce's settled view that all existence is for consciousness and consequently at odds, he felt, with all genuinely critical thought. "Almost they are persuaded that all existence is for consciousness, when lo! off they shoot on a tangent and discover that consciousness itself is made up of a mass of elements that are not for consciousness at all."

Royce's paper, "'Mind-Stuff' and Reality," was published in *Mind* in July 1881. Composed wholly with the negative intent of destroying Clifford's hypothesis, it gave the world of English philosophy its first contact with the tough-minded Californian. Royce's quarrel with "mind-stuff" was threefold. In the first place, speaking pragmatically, he observed that such monisms habitually speak in loose metaphors about the two "faces" or "sides" of reality, but fail to demonstrate that the theory has any practical consequences: even if "motion *is* Mind-Stuff," the theory that alleges this tells us nothing more than what physical science, without mind-stuff, teaches. At best, it substitutes a dead word for a living problem. Worse still, it undermines the conception of space, for if the world is composed of elementary feelings, one is put into the absurd position of speculating about the "hardness" of particular sensations, the "distance" between them, and their "paths." Finally and most important, the doctrine of atomic minds is unable to explain how these ejective facts are combined. When atoms form a molecule, the compound exhibits new qualities that cannot be explained as a mere sum of the elements. So also consciousness is more than an aggregate of feelings. But mind-stuff, according to the theory, is the unconditioned thing-in-itself; how this ultimate and unalterable material could be grouped so as to produce complex states, such as self-consciousness, must remain an ontological mystery that this hypothesis cannot explain.

James admired this essay. Years later, in his *Principles of Psychology*, he drew heavily on Royce's arguments to back up his own attack on mind-stuff. Royce, in turn, was pleased to have James's approval. "Your comments," he wrote in August, "on my article, or rather squib, concerning 'Mind-Stuff' encourage me a good deal." The encouragement reinforced Royce's confidence in several other projects. He was planning to write a sequel to his article in *Mind* showing what the purposes and requirements of an adequate ontology might be.

In the meantime he had written a second paper on Kant's first *Critique*. This piece had been read for him at the Kant Centennial in Saratoga, New York, on July 6. His major accomplishment, however, during the summer of 1881 was the publication of his first book, *Primer of Logical Analysis for the Use of Composition Students*.

A modest preface explains that the *Primer* is a "very elementary and fragmentary little work . . . intended in the first instance for some of my own students in English Composition." While acknowledging the latest work of Sigwart, Lange, Boole, Jevons, and Venn, Royce made no claims of discovering new insights or methods in logic. "Little or no genuine originality is attempted in these pages. Of logic as a philosophic science they tell nothing." It was a brief book of only seventy-seven pages, and as Royce insisted, it was a textbook in logic only so far as logic provides a useful basis for the study of rhetoric. "The immediate aim of these lessons is therefore to form and to direct the habit of reflecting upon the meaning of speech."

No doubt this was the textbook that Royce had begun during the previous summer. It was published by the San Francisco firm A. L. Bancroft and Company, and its circulation was limited. It did, however, win a favorable review in *Mind*. The reviewer approved of Royce's attempt to join logic to its "sister-disciplines," grammar and rhetoric, and recognized that he had gone beyond the traditional schemes of logical forms and into the new symbolic logic. It was, the reviewer added, "a very clear presentation of the modes of logical statement adopted by some of the modern reformers; and even philosophical students of Logic will find many instructive hints strewed through these pages. The *Primer* has the appearance of a first sketch, which, it may be hoped, the author will both extend and fill in."

While Royce's philosophy was gaining some little international recognition, his professional status in California was growing progressively more unpleasant. Several colleagues and Regents viewed the *Primer* as a transgression of departmental boundaries and voted that Royce must confine his teaching to the traditional materials of English composition. Nor did he get much support from the university administration.

Following the resignation of D. C. Gilman in 1875, the university's presidency had been assumed by Joseph Le Conte's brother, John. First a professor of physics, John Le Conte had a relationship with Royce that was the opposite of the one that his brother had established. As a student Royce had taken eight

courses from "Professor John," and his marks—ranging from 86 down to 53—
were the lowest he had received in any single discipline. These scores are puzzling, for throughout his life Royce often startled his friends with his detailed
knowledge of physical science. It seems likely that deeper personal conflicts
separated the two men; if so, they were intensified during the years of Royce's
instructorship. To make matters worse, John Le Conte was an extremely ineffective president. He had none of Gilman's charisma, and during the course of
his administration, 1875–81, the office of the presidency grew flaccid and the
university in general seemed moribund. The blame settled on Le Conte. In fact,
almost everything that can happen to a college president happened to him:
financial crises, student uprisings, faculty dissent, interference by the Regents,
opposition by rival factions among citizens—all this made Le Conte's presidency impossible.

Royce was on the edges of these conflicts. Early in his years on the faculty
he had decided to stay out of campus politics. "I attend Faculty meetings but
seldom," he once remarked, "and seldom find myself lifted nearer heaven when
I do." He shared the widespread disapproval of the president, but his angriest
feelings were directed at the Regents: "Our Regents," he told James, "a miscellaneous and comparatively ignorant body, are by fits and starts meddlesome,
always stupid, not always friendly, and never competent or anxious to discover
the nature of our work or of our ability." The best course, he felt, was to remain
detached, if at the same time contemptuous.

But he could not escape some involvement. His closest friends on the faculty, Sill and Moses, were the leaders of the anti-LeConte forces, and it was
rumored that their candidate for the presidency was the classicist and dean of
the faculty Martin Kellogg. Sill's part in the struggle against the president
remains to be clarified, but on one occasion he was the object of an erupting
scandal. Among the contentious issues was Le Conte's unsuccessful attempt to
ban secret fraternities. In the middle of the factional quarrels the fraternities
charged that Sill had bribed them to move in opposition to Le Conte. Royce
saw this petty conflict as one more illustration of the folly of political involve-
ments. "You see, Sill," he told his friend, "all this comes from your determined
fashion of casting pearls before the swine." "Ah, Royce," Sill countered, "you
never know in this world whether you were really casting pearls at all until you
feel the tusks." Royce would soon forget the politics behind this incident, but
he remembered Sill's remark as an important lesson in loyalty.

The turmoil in the university came to a head during the summer of 1881. In
May the Regents' Committee on Instruction and Visitation recommended that
the office of the presidency and the chair of physics be declared vacant. Le
Conte resigned in June but was allowed to retain his professorship. At the same
time Kellogg was nominated but did not win the Regents' approval. Instead,

after five ballots, they chose the principal of the San Francisco Boys' High School, William T. Reid. A graduate of Harvard with a strong recommendation from Charles William Eliot, Reid was obviously a compromise between those who wanted a man of academic repute and those who demanded an end to chaos. If Royce was not exactly enthusiastic over the Regents' choice, he was at least relieved by the change in the university's administration. On August 28 he wrote to Gilman: "Pres. Reid was inaugurated last Tuesday amid general good will. The task before him is no easy one, but I think that the Faculty will cordially support him in most of his acts. Personally I like Mr. Reid very well, and hope that he will make an uncommon success."

Not that Royce intended to stay. In the next breath he repeated his desire to find an academic post elsewhere: "My own anxiety to get away from California continues, and I am doing what little I can to finish work that shall be some evidence of qualification to teach philosophy." In a letter to James written four months later he reported further progress and gave a clear account of the state of his philosophical opinions:

> I have three articles on the point of appearing, one in *Mind,* one in the *Journal of Spec. Phil.,* one in our own *Californian.* All three are efforts to state aspects of what I take to be the proper *Fortbildung* of Kant. The sum of them all is that ontology, whereby I mean any positive theory of an external reality as such, is of necessity myth-making; that, however, such ontology may have enough moral worth to make it a proper object of effort so long as people know what they mean by it; that philosophy is reduced to the business of formulating the purposes, the structure and the inner significance of human thought and feeling; that an attempted ontology is good only in so far as it expresses clearly and simply the purposes of thought just as popular mythology is good in so far as it expresses the consciousness of a people; that the ideal of the truth-seeker is not the attainment of any agreement with an external reality, but the attainment of perfect agreement among all truth-seeking beings; that ethical philosophy is the highest philosophy.

These three articles—"Mind and Reality," "Kant's Relation to Modern Philosophic Progress," and "How Beliefs Are Made"—bring the earliest phase of Royce's philosophy to its climax.

The essay on Kant, the same that had been read at Saratoga, states its thesis in the last sentence: "The one conclusion that this paper has in a very hasty way tried to maintain, is that the critical philosophy, as a negative assault upon all ontological dogmatism of the theoretical reason, still stands fast, and that progress therefore lies in a reform of the Kantian *Kritik* by means of a new and yet more critical definition of experience and of the work of thought." The two parts of the thesis suggest the structure of the paper. In the first half Royce con-

sidered a handful of popular ontologies—mind-stuff, pure materialism, panlo-
gism, alogism, and the philosophy of the unconsciousness—concluding that all
of them are self-contradictory. The proof of this charge was admittedly incomplete, for Royce was content merely to name the ontologies and to suggest a few
of their difficulties. His more serious purpose came with the second half where
he turned to the theory of knowledge. Here his purpose was to show that the
critical method makes any ontology, regardless of its claims, logically untenable.
Repeating the substance of his earlier letter to James of September 19, 1880,
Royce observed that the two great questions of Kantian philosophy are, first,
"How can and does the knowing activity form or affect its matter?" and second,
"Is the matter anything apart from the forming activity?" As before, he insisted
that the answer to the second question disposes of ontology; analysis of the first
reveals the structure of knowledge. What can be said about reality? Sense data
are real; so are their forms in extension and succession; real also are the acts by
which we construct a world of possible experience. These acts have three
forms: acknowledgment of the past; acknowledgment of other conscious beings
and of their possible experience; and anticipations of the future. The objects of
these constructions, as things apart from consciousness, are not conceivable,
for to conceive is to construct; on the other hand, these objects, as things
acknowledged or anticipated, are real, for they are the products of our projec-
tions. Therefore if ontology fails, two fields of philosophy remain open: epistemology, which can continue to study the forms of intellectual activity, and
ethics, which can direct our postulates by clarifying their values.

What world is best? If it is our world—if we make it—we must choose.
Royce was not opposed to ontologies as ethical postulates; critical philosophy,
as he said, makes its "negative assault upon all ontological dogmatism of the
theoretical reason," upon what James would later call the "block universe." But
if properly understood, Royce believed, ontology is a game we play. At best it is
myth, and as such, as a means of locating ourselves in the world, it is useful and
even necessary. The question then becomes: What myths will satisfy our needs,
and will, in the largest sense, work? This is the subject of "Mind and Reality."

Ontology states that human experience agrees with external reality. To para-
phrase Spencer: "To each necessary relation *a:b* in human consciousness, there
corresponds a relation A:B in the external world." Berkeley's familiar ontology
maintains that internal impressions are caused by an "*Omnipresent Eternal
Mind*"; moreover, God fulfills his purpose by creating the world. Royce felt that
the theological aspect of Berkeley's doctrine was "question-begging" and "non-
essential." Nevertheless, Royce offered as a hypothesis, but only as a hypothesis, a doctrine that otherwise agrees with Berkeley: "*Our thought is true by
reason of its correspondence to the facts of an actual consciousness, external to our
own.*" Thus, the hypothesis conforms to Berkeleyan idealism except that the

"universal consciousness" is proposed as the counterpart, not the cause, of human experience. Can we make this hypothesis work? Yes, Royce answered: it is conceivable that the universal consciousness contains all actual and possible experience, that what it actually knows, I might know. Suppose a man looking at a candle:

> In the world-consciousness there is the group of states c, c', c'' . . That is the real candle. In the world-consciousness there is also the group of states h, h', h'' . . That is the "cerebral image" of the candle, a physiological fact. Finally, according to the laws of reality, the existence in the world-consciousness of the facts h, h', h'' . . grouped as they are, has co-existent with it the group of ideas C in the man's mind. This group C corresponds more or less completely to the group c, c', c'' . . as that group exists beyond the man's mind, in the, world-consciousness. The group C is the man's idea of the candle. Such is our hypothesis in a nut-shell.

Thus ends the first half of Royce's essay. His next purpose, as he had told James, was to tear the myth apart and show how it was made. How can one refute idealism? Not by appealing to data—by kicking rocks and avoiding precipices—for the external world is never more than a present moment of consciousness and an active construction of a larger reality. Verification by common sense fails, for it attempts the impossible task of converting data into nondata. Scientific naturalism tries a more sophisticated approach: the external world, it argues, is the cause of consciousness. The particular sensation a is said to be the result of a molecular vibration V. This V stands entirely apart from a and in no way resembles it. But, Royce observed, in addition to the sensation a, I also have the idea v, which corresponds to V. Is the resemblance of V and v also known through the postulate of causality? A naturalist might answer that without the assumption of a cause for a, it would not be possible to conceive the idea v. But, Royce replied, I cannot conceive of v without first postulating its counterpart V. First I make a world of molecules (V), then I experience a particular sensation (a), and finally conclude (v) that the molecules caused the sensation.

> The conception of reality furnished by the search for causes is thus always subordinate to the conception of reality furnished by our first postulate. This first postulate is, that our ideas have something beyond them and like them. So at each moment of my life I postulate a past and future of my own, like my present consciousness, but external thereto. So my social consciousness, my original unreflective tendency to work with and for other beings implies the postulate of the external existence of my fellow-men, like myself and like my ideas of them. So to the present intuition of the space in the retinal field or at my finger tips I join the

postulate of an infinitely extended not perceived space, like the perceived space, and like my space-ideas.

Royce likened his position to "modern phenomenism," the central doctrine of which is that the meaning of the external world is contained in "the possible and actual present, past, and future content of consciousness for all beings." However, Royce felt, this doctrine suggests a paradox: possible experience is limited to consciousness, and yet it is postulated as something more than the actual experience of any finite being. To complete this theory, Royce returned to the hypothesis that he had outlined at the beginning of his paper: "For the sake then of expressing one aspect of our fundamental postulate, we shall suggest what of course never can be proven, that all the conceived 'possible experiences' are actual in a Consciousness of which we suppose nothing but that it knows these experiences, or knows facts corresponding in number and in other relations to these experiences."

James had some doubts about the soundness of Royce's Saratoga paper. The first half, he felt, was first-rate, but though he would not say he disagreed, he found the constructive argument obscure. On the other hand, "Mind and Reality" won his unbounded enthusiasm. Four years earlier James had written "Remarks on Spencer's Definition of Mind as Correspondence." In this seminal essay he had attacked also the deterministic side of Spencer's ontology. Because Royce had offered his "universal consciousness" only as a hypothesis—calling it a "game," a "dream," a "soap-bubble," a thing that "never can be proven"—the essay aroused no hostility in James. Quite the contrary:

> *Bravissimo!* Your "Mind and Reality" has stayed by me and nourished me for three days. I, in all sincerity, don't believe anyone in America or anyone in England short of Hodgson, could have written a thing in which a subject so profound and important is so lightly handled and has air so let in through all its interstices, and behind it. I find in you the combination of play with earnestness which is so refreshing in philosophic writing, but which so few fellows have. . . . I think the point that interested me most was your treatment of Cause vs. Counterpart, which formulated the issue and solved it in a way quite new to me.

The article had appeared in the January issue of *Mind*; James had written on the fifteenth. At the same time Royce was flying high, full of fun and confidence. Even the "dry unmerciful California northers" were not dispiriting. James had offered to write a letter to President Reid telling him about the luminary he had teaching in the university. "Luminary," Royce countered, was not perhaps the best description; red-haired men were always a little tender about that word. James had also praised Royce above the better-known English philosopher T. H. Green: "Poor, feeble, dismal, serious Green, how the transcendental ego oppresses him!" Royce, on his side, was confident that his attack on "mind-stuff" had stood up to rejoinders from F. W. Frankland and T. Whittaker. He was acquiring international stature. For Royce, the sense of finally coming into his own seemed almost a fair compensation for his nearly four years of suffering in the desert.

Though James admired "Mind and Reality," he might have found as much to agree with and more to inspire him in "How Beliefs Are Made." It was here, it seems—not in James's work but in Royce's—that the phrase "will to believe" first appeared. Common sense asserts—especially in an age of evolutionary thought—that beliefs are inherited or otherwise determined by experience. Royce recalled that a friend had once insisted that his prejudices had been formed passively. "I can will to walk or eat," the friend had said; "but I cannot will to believe. I might as well will that my blood should circulate." Royce took the opposite viewpoint, that "beliefs are . . . in part the expression of our will." The mind, he argued, in the act of knowing is not a sponge. People are responsible for their creeds as well as for their conduct; in fact, their creeds are a part of their conduct.

Writing for a popular audience, Royce promised to suppress the metaphysical side of his argument. Consequently his purpose was practical and his method was psychological. What happens when we form opinions? There are, he answered, three phases of the process: attention, recognition, and construction. Making use of Wundt's experiments, Royce observed that each of these phases involves a modification of sense data. When we give attention to any subject, our consciousness actively edits and organizes its sensations in an effort to achieve the greatest simplicity and unity. With the same principle, recognition completes the work of attention. Drawing from past experience, we predicate meanings that lend a feeling of familiarity and give coherence to present data. This too is an act of the will. Finally our world reflects the interest we take in it. We construct a past and future; we create "symbols of a real universe" and the general truths that make it meaningful. In the deepest sense, Royce concluded, we are morally responsible for the world, for it is just this world that we have chosen. The mind, therefore, is not a "mere note-book," nor can men be reduced to "mere registering machines." If we are serious in our search for truth, we must be willing to trespass "on the borderland of ethics," and if we must live with prejudices, we must also assume a responsibility for them.

With the completion and publication of these essays Royce achieved a new level of maturity. Though he had not yet produced the comprehensive treatise that he had been planning for many years, he had most of the components, for later in The Religious Aspect of Philosophy he would incorporate substantial sections from "Mind and Reality," "Kant's Relation to Modern Philosophic

Progress," and "How Beliefs Are Made." The winter of 1881–82 provides, there-fore, a convenient signpost by which a chart of Royce's philosophical develop-ment can be constructed, and as if to indicate his awareness of this achievement, he chose this moment to review the path of his intellectual growth. It was not so much a path, he felt, as a circle. "We students of today run through a certain circle of thought, well-known to our elders, but affected in character for us by the peculiar environment of modern ideas in which we move." This remark was contained in a pre-Christmas greeting that Royce sent to Coale on December 5. The circle moves, he said, from faith to doubt and back to faith.

From his parents Royce had received a set of traditional beliefs; when these no longer served his needs, he turned to the theory of evolution and resolved to seek truth in "dumb passive acquiescence." But soon he found that even the axioms of geometry have an ethical meaning. So gradually Royce was led back to the heart. "In fact," he told Coale, "I am more and more inclined to connect philosophy very closely with the heart itself." If the old creed was dead, part of its spirit could be retrieved, and if skepticism had failed, it was still useful as a challenge to faith and an exercise in humility. "The individual," Royce believed, "ought to wither, but not in favor of natural selection, but in favor of life as a whole." Thus, the early phases of Royce's faith and doubt contributed vital ele-ments to his later philosophy. Ideology, he had learned, is formed by reordering a child's world; beliefs, he would eventually say, are interpretations: they draw from the past its meaning and devise a world that can serve the future.

As one of his most personal statements, Royce's letter to Coale was a kind of confession. The uniqueness of their relationship facilitated such exposures. But the letter also contains something even deeper than spiritual autobiography. Near the end Royce described a dream:

> I wish very much that I could see you and talk with you. Once in a while I have a dream of your house, especially if my neglect as a correspondent happens to weigh on my conscience. I wander in my dream about Baltimore, live there maybe for some time, and fear to go near you lest you should have forgotten me. Then I go, clamber into the house by the front window or walk in without knock-ing, feel frightened and confused, cannot explain myself, am afraid to see any-body, hear you all perhaps in another room and cannot enter, or meet you and have nothing to say; but withal am very much delighted to have found the place once more, and to have actually succeeded in making a visit. I wake up highly amused, and resolve to write forthwith.

A psychoanalyst would probably say that Royce's final amusement was his defense against fear. Certainly fear—mentioned three times in the description—

is the dream's dominant emotion. A deeper analysis might suggest a latent primal scene, not indeed reducible to coitus, but a scene of an early, always haunting, search for a missing father. As for the sources of this anxiety, two are suggested: fear of being forgotten and fear of having his uninvited entrance discovered. One word encompasses both fears: *rejection*. The dream is by no means the only indication of this fear; it crops up in nearly all of Royce's letters to Coale, and it appears also in different forms in many of his letters to James and Lanman. The fact that the fear was irrational only indicates its deeper sources. Like the story of Pussy Blackie, like the miner's abandoned grave, like also the many dreams and fantasies of the solitary voyage, this dream expresses Royce's most persistent anxiety. He goes to Baltimore to find a home, his true father's home. But when he arrives, he learns that he is unwanted. Locked out, he sneaks in by the window like an outlaw. Still unable to get to the father, he feels frightened, confused, hears voices from another room, but cannot enter; finally he meets the father, but has nothing to say. If it is true that the child lives on in the adult, Royce's dream suggests a child's fear of being excluded, locked out. Josie's father was always away on business, "over the mountains." Royce repaid him for this absence: his father was an *"Obsthändler,"* a fruit peddler, the object of little boys' ridicule. But Josie kept searching, and the search led him beyond the mountains, across the world, and finally into the mind of philosophy.

At the end of April James presented Royce with his long-sought opportunity, an instructorship at Harvard. Having been granted a sabbatical leave for the next academic year on half pay, James was required to find a suitable replacement who would be willing to teach for the other half of his salary, $1,250. James offered the job to Royce. The teaching assignment would include three courses: elementary and advanced psychology plus a course on the British empiricists. The appointment would be temporary, but if Royce proved to be a successful teacher, a renewal might be offered and eventually an assistant professorship. James asked Royce to weigh the risks and to telegraph his decision.

Royce wasted no time fretting about risks. An egg in Cambridge, he felt, was better than a brood of chickens in Berkeley. On May 1 he wired his acceptance. But when James then presented Royce's candidacy to President Eliot, there was trouble. Eliot began to vacillate. He had some second thoughts about Royce, and he felt free to disregard faculty recommendations in matters of appointment. James suspected that Eliot's favor was shifting to Jacob Schurman, the future president of Cornell, then a professor at Nova Scotia. The appointment of Schurman would be "safe," but with Royce, Harvard might capture the "highest prize." Still, so little was known about Royce, and Eliot wondered why California did not make him a better offer. The final decision was postponed for three weeks, during which James kept Royce informed. Finally near the end of the month Eliot's preference settled on Royce. The appointment was made official, and on June 2 Royce sent President Reid a brief letter of resignation.

Determined to sever all ties to California, Royce had not asked for a year's leave of absence: he was quitting and not coming back. With this act Royce not only relinquished his instructorship, but also abandoned any chance he might have had to gain the newly endowed but unfilled Mills professorship in philosophy. Katharine supported her husband's decision. She had friends and relatives in Boston, and moreover, she actually preferred the sharp eastern climate to balmy California. One more thing prompted their resolution: the young Royces had a son. "I have now a little son," Royce told James, "three weeks old, who, with his mother, is doing wonderfully well. I shall be overjoyed at the thought of bringing him up in an Eastern atmosphere."

With characteristic reticence Royce had said nothing in any of his letters about Katharine's pregnancy. Twice he mentioned that his wife was "in rather poor health," but he said nothing more about the nature of her condition. In December, following a difficult and dangerous second trimester, Judge Head let the secret out that Kitty was expecting a baby in April. "She thinks people don't know & hides the little basket of things she is making." Each of Katharine's pregnancies, in fact, was accompanied by complications that caused her husband and parents considerable alarm. But, as Royce soon learned, she was strong. On April 11, 1882, in a letter to a friend, Edward Sill announced the birth: "There is a small boy at the Head house, born this morning early, & all well." Getting a telegram from Josiah, Kitty's mother, Eliza, wrote to congratulate the young parents and particularly her daughter: "We are very glad and thankful over the good news from you this morning. I did not sleep till towards morning, thinking of you hopefully and happily for the most part with tender memories of your birth-day my daughter, and tender and loving hopes of your future with your baby." Eliza then mailed the cheerful news to Anna: "It seems too good to be true, that after so much ill health, everything should have gone so exceptionally well, such a short labor, and a large fat baby."

The parents named him Christopher—nicknaming him Coco—and like most firstborn sons, he was their special prize. In the next few years Coco's first words, his toys, his books, his bouts with the piano filled Josiah and Katharine with parental joy. When, twenty-eight years later, his life ended in horrible tragedy, their loss was almost unendurable.

But in 1882 Royce felt that no impediment could stop his progress. With the birth of his son, the publication of recognized works of philosophy, the appointment to the faculty of America's most prodigious university, everything was running his way. "What becomes of me and my family after the end of a year does not appear," he told Gilman, "but I am very willing to take risks in a good cause." By mid-June Royce had already begun to make plans for the move. Mrs. Royce wrote Mrs. James about housing. When James learned that Royce planned to bring his family to Cambridge, he was astonished and also perhaps a little fearful that he had encouraged too much confidence. It might be better, he suggested, "for this first experimental year," if Royce were to leave his wife and child with her parents. Expedience, economy, and hygiene, James felt, would make this a more sensible plan.

Royce was resolute; no bridge for retreat would be left standing. On August 14 he wrote to Lanman, who had preceded him to the Harvard faculty, that he expected to travel by rail, leaving California on September 4. His final task at the university would be to supervise entrance examinations. "I go to Harvard," he said, "with a mixture of trembling and impudence that will doubtless be charming to witness when I arrive. Doubtless I shall blunder through a year in some fashion, and I shall hope at all events to make no enemies, unless it be my ugly face and my Californian barbarity." On September 10 Lanman met the train and made a note in his diary: "Went to Boston to meet Royce, & wife & babe in arms. They arrived from San Francisco well."

They were also greeted by Kitty's affluent half brother, Charles. Hoping to save the Royces from grubbing for cheap housing, he had already made some arrangements. "How splendid of Charlie to get a house ready," wrote Eliza to her daughter. "It is most generous & good of him and I hope Josiah will find himself large minded and generous enough to be able to let you accept it comfortably & so give Charlie the real pleasure of his gift. It would hurt & grieve him to have difficulties thrown in the way." At first Josiah may have tried to assert his independence, but he soon relented. By the first week of October the Royces were ensconced at 14 Sumner Street, a comfortable and fairly new house, which they shared with a widowed landlady. For Josiah's convenience, it was a five-minute walk from the Harvard Yard. Charlie must have been generous indeed, for Kitty's letters to her mother described a spacious home with rooms on the first and second floors. There was a place for Katharine's piano in the parlor and another for Josiah's books in a separate study.

Eliza warned Kitty that she must not become a slave to domesticity. "Do a judicious am't of shirking," the wise mother advised. "If you are dragged down, the others must suffer too. Refresh yourself with your music,—go to concerts— avail yourself of all opportunities to meet pleasant people & not let yourself grow old before yr. time." Katharine clearly took this advice to heart, for throughout the rest of her life she remained a strong, independent woman as well as a devoted wife and mother.

To the extent that it is possible to establish divisions in a person's life, it is safe to say that Royce's move to Cambridge marked the end of his youth. Naturally there were many issues and tensions, both personal and philosophical, which were still unresolved and which affected his entire life. In very concrete terms he faced the immediate task of proving his worth to Harvard. On the other hand, he had achieved his educational goals, he had won a degree of professional recognition, and he had sought and found a fundamental system of belief. With a good deal of grumbling he had submitted to the unpleasant task of working outside his chosen field in a place that he associated with childhood. But as Royce sometimes remarked, troubles can be good things if one can learn the hard lessons they teach. In this case the reward for unpleasant labor was self-confidence and capacity. Not only did Royce feel that he was ready to take his place in the world, but the world was now willing to accept him.

As a measure of this growth it is illuminating to compare Royce's earlier essay "The Practical Significance of Pessimism" with the later "Pessimism and Modern Thought." Though the two works belong to Royce's Berkeley period, one was written during his first year, while the second was the product of the last. A comparison of the two essays provides a means of noting the development of the more personal aspects of his thought. Not that the second piece is a radical departure from the first; in major points of doctrine, they agree. In both, Royce insisted that the motives behind pessimism are real and that the proper response to this reality involves a surrender of the self to a larger consciousness.

The differences appear in Royce's view of how the worth of life is to be estimated. As we have already seen, the first essay takes a quantitative approach. Arguing in concert with Schopenhauer, Royce maintained that pain adds something to life—namely, restlessness—while pleasure merely subtracts: in an ideal life, if all longing were satisfied, if, in mathematical terms, each plus were canceled by its corresponding minus, this ideal existence would amount to zero. As a quantity, therefore, life is worthless. On this point the second essay disagrees. Do not tell me, Royce said, that a certain experience—say, a walk in the mountains—was a failure because the sum of the experience brought more pain than pleasure. I may still feel, despite the cuts and bruises, that the whole experience was worthwhile, and this feeling turns with indifference from the most exacting balance sheet. The value of life, according to Royce's second essay, is to be estimated in terms of goals. Can they be defined? Do they conflict with each other? How can the conflicts be resolved? Can the ultimate goals be attained? These four questions, Royce maintained, comprise the issues involved in the evaluation of life. He felt that the first two questions presented no obstacles. Goals can be defined, and with definitions it can be seen that the goals often do conflict, both within and between individuals. The doubtful areas are focused in the last two questions. Hegelians and evolutionists give answers that appeal to external efforts. In time, they maintain, all conflicts will be resolved, for the world progresses toward universal harmony. Royce found this solution unconvincing. The evidence of social and natural history argues, he felt, that there is no steady progress; at best the tendency is cyclical, in which the individual is constantly striving toward goals while the universe as a whole is governed by an endless process of growth and decay.

To solve the problem of conflicts, we must turn inward, for only through unselfish self-knowledge can the ultimate goal, freedom from conflicts, be known. The paradoxical nature of this belief is difficult to unravel; indeed, Royce spent a major portion of his life trying to make it clear. What he meant was that the deepest sense of one's own significance agrees with the whole meaning of life. To know oneself is to become aware of the universal consciousness—"the great ocean of conscious activity below, about, and above." The problem of identity and the problem of reality are the same. Royce admitted that this doctrine is not logically demonstrable; its truth is something that one might feel only in isolated moments of supreme peace. The rest is strife. So Schopenhauer was right: life is a process of unrest. But the goal, as opposed to the process, of life demands an end to warfare and a search for inner and outer peace.

Peace is hard to come by. No one knew that better than Josiah Royce. Four years before, when he was traveling from Maryland to California, the warring conflicts within him produced an anger that he wished to escape through self-abnegation. Labor to cast the self aside, he had said. But this did not alleviate his pain. Later he found the strength to sink deeper into the self, and through self-knowledge he found the conscious life he sought. The young man who was about to start his brilliant career at Harvard had grasped a sense of his identity and an ideology that could give it voice. Instead of computing life's pains and pleasures, he was concerned with the values of whole experiences. *"This life is my life."* When one can say that, Royce observed, he reaches a rich moment, perhaps the richest, for it tells him that he lives never apart, but always within the ocean of life itself.

PART TWO

Years of Achievement
1882–1900

Chapter Four

Success and Crisis
1882–1888

The Religious Aspect of Philosophy

> We in the Atlantic states, by position, have been commercial, and have
> . . . imbibed easily an European culture. Luckily for us, now that steam has nar-
> rowed the Atlantic to a strait, the nervous, rocky West is intruding a new and con-
> tinental element into the national mind, and we shall yet have an American
> genius.

Ralph Waldo Emerson spoke these words eleven years before Royce's birth. At
that time California was still a possession of Mexico, the continental railroad
was a dream, and "manifest destiny" a political slogan. Yet Royce fulfilled
Emerson's prophecy. Only a few months before Royce arrived in Cambridge to
take up his instructorship, Emerson had died quietly at his home in Concord.
For almost half a century he had been the chief spokesman for American philosophical idealism. Now that heritage fell to Royce. The great differences
between the two—differences in training and personality—produced in Royce
a much-revised idealism. In fact, he distrusted Emerson's transcendentalism.
The "universal consciousness," he had argued, is a postulate, nothing more.

Yet for reasons that cannot be easily explained, Royce soon fundamentally
revised his theory. In fewer than six months after joining the Harvard faculty he
presented a series of lectures entitled "The Religious Aspect of Philosophy." In
the third of these, speaking of the "universal consciousness," he struck the word
"postulate" and inserted "necessary assumption." With this, Royce inched closer
to absolute idealism.

By 1882, Harvard was already well into its most critical phase of development. Royce called this the "storm and stress" period, and as he recognized, the figure behind this growth was Charles William Eliot, whose tenure as president had reached its thirteenth year. Like Gilman, Eliot had a scientific background, and through his efforts Harvard was transformed from a parochial college into a great university. His plan called for enlarged professional schools, graduate programs, and a faculty of experts. College teaching was still primary, but a professor was also expected to engage in specialized research and become a producer of knowledge. The age of amateur professors had ended; under Eliot's leadership, power belonged to the academic workers. As the president would soon learn, Royce was perfectly suited to Harvard's future.

But as far as philosophy was concerned, this growth had barely begun. As Charles Bakewell once noted, in earlier years "philosophy was the handmaid of theology, and its chief concern was to explain, and try to make intelligible, the accredited beliefs." Even in 1882, philosophy was still considered a luxury. By that time only two men had earned doctorates in philosophy at Harvard: G. Stanley Hall in 1878 and Francis Ellingwood Abbot in 1881. When Royce arrived, he found one graduate student, Benjamin Rand, the department's future librarian. George Santayana was a freshman. Only ten courses were offered, all undergraduate, and they were taught by a staff of four instructors. Besides Royce, who replaced James, there were George Herbert Palmer, the aged Francis Bowen, and Francis Greenwood Peabody, who held a split appointment with the Divinity School.

Royce's assignment included an elementary course in logic and psychology, an advanced course in Locke, Berkeley, and Hume, and another advanced course in psychology. He had fifty students in the elementary course, about twenty in the British empiricists, but only two in psychology. Preparation of lectures took up all his time—but he loved it. "Harder and more delightful occupation I have never found," he reported to James. "I am on the whole very happy and very hard driven." He liked the students. Though they were not especially industrious, they were "manly and intelligent." They asked good questions and sometimes answered well, but Royce hoped to get closer to them, to have them speak their thoughts frankly, to give him "some intelligent and merciless criticism."

As for family life, they were healthy, Christopher was growing vigorously, but sometimes they were a little lonely. Lanman, still a bachelor, helped to make the Royces feel at home. Palmer was "cordial and very genuinely friendly." He and Royce took walks together and made "little visits." Soon they were "doctoring up the transcendental Ego in various ways, and giving . . . rival diagnoses of the poor fellow's case." Royce was struck by Palmer's dignity; he was "so precise and *streng*" that Royce wondered how "he can endure my slip-shod Western manners."

Palmer remembered Royce as "a picturesque figure, a prodigious scholar, a stimulating teacher, a heroic character, a playful and widely loved friend." Admittedly his appearance was strange. His clothes defied all standards of fashion. He was squat and stout, his round freckled face seeming to sink into his shoulders, and everyone was astonished by his red hair. James liked to say that Royce had an obscene exposure of the forehead and that his face resembled illustrations in medical books. But to Palmer, this "elfin figure with the unconventional dress and slouching step, that face which blended the infant and the sage" had its own peculiar beauty. No one who knew him would want one feature changed. Royce and Palmer liked each other instantly, and though as the years passed each knew the other's shortcomings, their friendship was never seriously threatened.

If Palmer was willing to tolerate this rude Californian, Mrs. James was not. Almost from the outset she disliked Josiah—and especially Katharine—intensely. She entertained them only once during the year, and complained bitterly that they were hardly adequate substitutes for her absent husband. One of these complaints, voiced presumedly in a letter to William, prompted this condolence from her illustrious brother-in-law:

Your situation seems to me most unnatural [wrote Henry James], but I hope you bear up under it. . . . I am afraid you don't from the ghastly Royce couple—as the report of your impression of them which William has transmitted to me, seems to warrant me in calling them. What terrible people and above all what a terrible infliction! I hope you will not scruple to *pull them off*—as I had to do those fatal plasters with which I had saddled my chest last spring, when William and you sprang to my rescue! They must be really a dreadful couple of plasters! Abandoned by your husband who leaves you two Royces in his stead, you seem to me, dear Alice, very greatly to be pitied, and I assure you that I think of you with tender sympathy. I shall never, in future, embrace any man's philosophy till I have seen him—and above all till I have seen his wife.

With his alarming appearance and controversial manners Royce was soon a recognized curiosity in Harvard Yard. He was also known to be a great talker. If you were in a hurry, it was not wise to ask Royce even a simple question, for it nearly always provoked a lecture. A vivid illustration of this tendency is recorded through the memory of the poet and essayist John Jay Chapman, an undergraduate in Royce's first year at Harvard. One winter evening Chapman had attended a symphony concert in Boston and afterward went to Park's, an oyster house famous for its lobsters and musty ale. Looking across the table, Chapman was startled to see "a kind of fairy." It was Royce. "He was a miniature figure, well compacted, with an enormous red head which had a gigantic aspect, as if he were Kant or Beethoven, and also an infantile look like that of an ugly baby." Suddenly Royce began talking. There were no preliminaries, no introductions— it was as if Royce had known Chapman all his life. "You were inside," Chapman remembered, "though you didn't know how you got there; and I remember wondering how I got there and where I was." They talked for half an hour, and afterward Royce insisted that they walk back to Cambridge. A fierce wind was blowing. Chapman was sure that Royce would catch pneumonia, for his over- coat was threadbare. "I forget the rest," Chapman added, "except my strong impression that he was very extraordinary and knew everything and was a bum- blebee—a benevolent monster of pure intelligence, zigzagging, ranging, and uncatchable. I always had this feeling about Royce—that he was a celestial insect."

This portrait is most remarkable in its contrast with the impression that Royce had made in California. All of his earlier timidity seems to have van- ished. Instead of holding back or retiring behind a cover of self-doubt, Royce now moved forward into direct combat, challenging all comers. He was, as James noted, "ready for everything in this world or the next." Hence Chapman's impression that Royce was "the John L. Sullivan of philosophy." Another comparison, frequently made, was that he was a "perfect little Socrates." Those who stopped him in the streets were subjected to the most exacting cross-examinations; he broke through all opposing arguments, spotted contradictions, and made every debater feel helpless and irrational. Most went away with the feeling that truth has meaning only through its place in the uni- versal consciousness.

The need to express this truth in public soon found its outlet. At first he had been determined to postpone all private study and writing in favor of teaching. But he also knew his future at Harvard depended largely on the favorable impression he might make on the academic community. To form such an impression, nothing would serve better than a series of public lectures. By the middle of the winter, busily writing and making arrangements, he constructed four lectures. He called the series "The Religious Aspect of Philosophy."

Palmer once told a story that fills in the background to these lectures. Though as Palmer remembered the incident it occurred two years later, the cir- cumstances seem to fit 1882–83 better than 1884–85. President Eliot, sympa- thizing with Royce's financial problems, hit on the idea that he might give a course of Lowell lectures for a fee of one thousand dollars. A conference was arranged between Royce and Augustus Lowell at which the offer was made. But suspecting Royce of heterodoxy, Lowell insisted that he sign a declaration of faith. It was required by the founder's will, Lowell explained. Royce refused. "He could accept no creed as a condition of receiving money," Palmer said, "nor could he be sure that his own understanding of these doctrines was in accordance with that of the founder." Those few who knew of the incident persuaded Royce to go ahead with his plans and present the lectures at the university.

The series was given in Sever Hall from March 1 to March 29, and according to reports in the *Crimson* each lecture, especially the third, commanded a large audience. Lanman attended the entire series; it was, he noted, a "splendid success." The four lectures were divided into two parts. The first two were devoted to ethics and the philosophy of nature; the third lecture caused a stir. Here Royce began by summarizing his ethical thesis:

> Act as if all the consequences of thy act, for all beings, were about to be forthwith realized to thy own consciousness. . . . Our characters as they grow must tend towards a final self-surrender to the work of humanity, so that we become to our own better insight nothing but drops in an ocean of life, existing to take our little part in the common movements of the whole. We thus must see ourselves as little members of a vast body, as little fragments of a mighty temple, as single workers whose work has importance only by reason of its relations to the whole.

This belief concurs with all of Josiah's earlier moral philosophy, but to provide a religious framework for this belief he quoted Matthew 25: "Inasmuch as ye have done *it* unto one of the least of these my brethren, ye have done *it* unto me." Jesus promises himself in the Last Judgment, not as a dealer of rewards and punishments, but as a universal moral consciousness. Can such a belief be justified epistemologically? To answer this monumental query, Royce unveiled a new theory: an argument for an absolute mind based on the logical possibility of error.

The effect of this on Boston Brahmins is illustrated in an anecdote told about Edward Everett Hale, author of *The Man without a Country*. After hearing Royce lecture, Hale stopped a friend on the street to ask about "this striking young man from California." "Well," he went on, "he seems noticeable, surely. What do you think I heard him doing in a lecture the other afternoon? Why, nothing less than showing that our human ignorance is the positive proof that there is a God—a Supreme Omniscient Being!"

As we have already seen, the germ for this theory was planted in Royce's doctoral thesis. At some later time, presumably in 1882, he returned to the theory while taking notes on Herbart's psychology:

> Herbart's method is somewhat analogous to the Cartesian. Both begin well, both fail in procedure. One good way of beginning a theory of knowledge is with the question how is error or doubt (Descartes) or illusion (Herbart) possible? But the next step should be to conduct the inquiry not into the metaphysical (or physical) conditions of error, but into the logical conditions, its *conditiones essendi* not

existendi. Thus the road might be opened to absolute truth, or if not, then to the understanding of the presuppositions upon which all thinking depends.

Royce launched his argument with a paradox: in some sense any sincere statement is true. To illustrate, he said, consider the fable of the two knights describing a shield between them. One says the shield is gold; the other says it is silver. Both statements are sincere and in that sense truthful, yet each accuses the other of lying. Perhaps we should observe that neither knight has expressed himself fully; each should have said, "To me it is gold," or "To me it is silver." But this omits situations in which we feel that certain truths ought to be accepted by all. When we say that the moon has no atmosphere, we mean to express more than a private opinion: we mean that everyone's idea of the moon ought to agree with the real moon. Here then is the central problem of "Mind and Reality." Taking away the knights' shield, we can recast their argument. One says, "I see that you are afraid of me, for my idea of you agrees with my idea of a badly frightened fellow." The other protests and the war begins. Obviously the first knight errs in failing to understand the other's state of mind. But how is error possible? The logical conditions, Royce answered, are these: a statement is false only if it fails to agree with its object, but its object is, in any case, whatever it intends to have as an object. Hence the paradox of subjective idealism. So long as truth is relative to persons, so long as my thought is limited to my ideas, any sincere statement is truthful and error is impossible. To eliminate the paradox, Royce introduced the absolute:

> So thus we come to the definition of that assumption upon which all thinking, all controversy, all the postulates that we previously studied, all science and all morality, depend, viz., the assumption that error is possible. I assert that disagreement, as well as agreement of my statements with their objects, has meaning only for a consciousness, for a thought, to which both [of] the related terms are present. If my thought has objects outside of it with which it is to agree, those objects and that agreement can have meaning, can be possible, only if there is a thought that includes both my thought and the object wherewith my thought is to agree, that includes them even as my thought includes and reduces to unity the various ideas that go to make up any one of my assertions. Thus then in the ordinary commonplace assumption that a statement of mine can agree or fail to agree with its real object, when this object is wholly outside of me: in this assumption, without which you can stir no step, is contained implicitly the assumption that all objects of all assertions, that all things, spiritual and material, are present in their true nature to an all-embracing intelligent thought of which mine is simply one subordinate part or element.

Royce urged his listeners to treat this argument only as a hypothesis, but to him it became much more. The search for merely useful postulates was nearly finished; now Royce felt that he held the key to the universe: "I know no other view that offers any chance of a philosophy."

The favorable reception of these lectures not only tended to solidify Royce's position at Harvard, but also gave him his chance for publication. In the spring of 1883 he submitted his manuscript to Houghton Mifflin. The firm's editor, Horace E. Scudder, offered some encouragement and suggested several plans that might be arranged. Royce preferred a plan by which the publisher would assume all risks, but make no payments to the author until the costs were recovered. He also knew that the lectures needed extensive revision, expansion, and clarification. "I shall therefore try to reconstruct the lectures," he wrote to Scudder on May 24, "in some such way as you suggest, and shall be glad to have the opportunity of submitting the result once more to your consideration."

In the meantime Royce took advantage of the spring vacation to arrange a trip to Baltimore. He was anxious to visit with old friends, especially Coale and Gilman. He also wanted to renew his relationship with the university and to try out his new theory on the Johns Hopkins philosophical community. There were now three philosophers on the faculty: G. S. Morris, Charles Peirce, and Stanley Hall. Royce was invited to give a talk, probably the third lecture from his recent series. Hall, whose animosity toward Royce's philosophy grew in succeeding years, took a mixed view. Writing to James in May, he praised Royce as "not only the best man of his age in this country but the best I know anywhere." On the other hand, Hall was disturbed to note the tendency toward absolutism: "Judging from a . . . talk Royce gave my men here Palmer has quite swung him over to his subtle Hegelianism. I hope next year . . . you are able to have him more to yourself. You will disenchant him. He is far too able a man to be sterilized in it."

Regardless of Hall's fears of sterilization, the general estimate of Royce's philosophy was positive. By the end of his first year at Harvard, it was decided that he should have a second. To make room for Royce, Palmer took a sabbatical leave in 1883–84. In mid-June Royce returned briefly to California, presumably to wrap up a few dangling business affairs. By August 10 he was back in Cambridge ready to begin preparation for the fall semester. He was to repeat the elementary course in logic and psychology; in addition he was assigned to Palmer's advanced courses in ethics and metaphysics. He also supplemented his income by teaching in the "Annex"—Harvard's future Radcliffe College. Aside from teaching, the proposed book on religious philosophy was his major project. As reported to Coale, it was to be "founded on old lectures and essays of mine rewritten and joined with whatever new things come into my head." He hoped that the result would be neither too dry nor too dangerous.

During this second year at Harvard, in March 1884, he found time to present a series of three lectures sponsored by the Harvard Philosophical Club, "Certain Ideals of Right Conduct and Their Value for Society." These lectures gave further weight to the growing view that Royce was indispensable. The *Harvard Advocate* described the series as "practical as well as ethical in its nature, . . . something both layman and philosophical student could take an interest in." "Dr. Royce . . . ," the article concluded, "showed his usual control over his subject, and those who listened and received benefit from his words will remember the occasion with pleasure. The lecturer is a bold and original thinker, and whatever he says is always clear and to the point."

One of Royce's more ambitious efforts in social philosophy, this series of lectures was written at a time when great changes were beginning to take place in life in the United States. The old doctrine of laissez-faire, which had given justification to a government ruled by millionaires, was being challenged; the Gilded Age had run its course. Five years before Royce spoke, Henry George had written *Progress and Poverty*; five years afterward, Edward Bellamy published *Looking Backward*. In 1883 Lester Ward's *Dynamic Sociology* made a drastic revision of the evolutionary philosophies of Herbert Spencer and William Graham Sumner; three years later a forgotten Herman Melville began *Billy Budd*, his tragic fable of innocence, evil, and established authority. In the political sphere, 1884 was the year of the Mugwump. For twenty years public tolerance of political corruption had enabled the Republican Party to retain control of the government. By the middle 1880s, however, a new generation of intellectual leaders was determined to bring about an era of reform. Forming the vocal nucleus of the independent Republicans, these so-called Mugwumps focused their objections on the party's official candidate, James G. Blaine, whose reputation, as a political opportunist supported through the spoils system, effectively illustrated much that was wrong with the U.S. As a result the independents withheld their support from Blaine, and the opposition candidate, Grover Cleveland, was elected, the first Democratic president since James Buchanan.

Though Royce took no active part in the campaign of 1884, his lectures expressed the ideals of the independent viewpoint. He began by reviewing the varieties of the "new socialism" that had spread across Europe and begun to exert an influence in America. Spencerian liberalism, supported by appeals to classical economics, had maintained that free and open competition was the key to human evolution. According to this view, state interference, particularly governmental charity, endangers human progress. It curbs personal freedom; it rewards indolence at the expense of industry. But the younger social philosophers had opposed this doctrine with the ideals of the welfare state. Royce shared some of their feelings. Widespread poverty in the cities, destruction of the environment everywhere—these, he felt, were real problems that required extensive reforms in housing, welfare, transportation, conservation, and education. To achieve the goal of providing the better life for all, personal freedom, he believed, should be sacrificed.

On the other hand, he distrusted the reformers' tendency to treat society as a sum of parts, a mere aggregate of individuals. Instead he advocated an "idealistic socialism," the central doctrine of which is that society is an organism, and that as a whole it has a moral value peculiar to itself. Too often, he felt, reform becomes an "aimless blundering," some attempt to achieve a higher and broader level of happiness by restructuring institutions. The real problems of humanity, he maintained, are not social or political, but moral and religious. The task of reform is to teach people that their redemption lies in selfless devotion to the whole. How? By myth? Perhaps, but better by the simple insight "that human life is there before you, and needs your help, whether you want to help it or not." To grasp this insight is to be drawn deeper into the problem of the worth of life, not as a meaningless unorganized mass, but as a whole. If socialism is to guide the future, Royce insisted, it must aim to be more than a new scheme to reorganize society: it must seek to know life's ideal value, just as one recognizes the unity in a work of art, and with this knowledge to reform the world.

Within a week following the conclusion of these lectures Royce received President Eliot's offer for a third year as an instructor with the promise of an assistant professorship whenever a vacancy might occur. Though pleased with the prospect of finding a permanent place at Harvard, Royce was disappointed with the proposed arrangement. Instead of a regular appointment in philosophy, he was to teach a half course, to be offered in the fall term, on philosophical theism. The compensation for this course would be five hundred dollars. For the remainder of his appointment he would take charge of the forensics program in the English department and teach another half course in oral discussion, making a total income of two thousand dollars. Royce disliked the requirement of further distracting work in English, and he wrote Gilman for advice. Might there be, he asked, some opportunity to give lectures in philosophy at Johns Hopkins or elsewhere during the spring semester? Gilman firmly advised Royce to accept the assignment to forensics "or to do any work in the literary department for which you are able."

> I know it is hard to be diverted from one's chosen work, to have a vocation *and* an avocation; but I think that the best men have most of them been developed under such difficulties. . . . Moreover I don't believe you will regret, at this very stage of your career, being forced to consider the essentials of the best English style & I am sure as a teacher you can do a great deal for young men.

The mentor concluded: "I think you are fortunate to see your way forward, at no very distant day, to so good a place, as from your letter I suppose is awaiting you." Gilman did not mention the turmoils within the Hopkins faculty—the soon-to-be-announced promotion of G. Stanley Hall as professor of psychology and pedagogics, the abrupt and unexplained firing of C. S. Peirce, or the decision to terminate G. S. Morris. Royce, in any event, understood that his future at Harvard was his best prospect, and in May 1884, he accepted Eliot's offer of a split appointment in forensics and philosophy.

At about the same time, Royce finished his revisions of *The Religious Aspect of Philosophy*. Reopening negotiations with Houghton Mifflin, he sent the manuscript to Horace Scudder. "I cannot tell whether he will recommend it for print," Royce told Gilman, "but you see that I have it pretty well finished." Though cautious, he was also confident, and he thanked Gilman for all the help he had given in the past. In November he wrote to Coale saying that the book had "passed all the dangers of much rewriting, of much weeding out and of much burning up, and having fought its little fight with a ferocious publisher, has at last peacefully entered that publisher's fold." Part of the fight involved money. Since such books rarely became commercial successes, Houghton Mifflin insisted that Royce pay for some of the production costs. Still he was pleased to have finished the book on schedule and to have his chance of gaining attention from the philosophical world.

With its dedication to Coale, *The Religious Aspect of Philosophy: A Critique of the Bases of Conduct and of Faith* was published on January 25, 1885. When Gilman received his complimentary copy, he was happily reminded of their first meeting in Oakland, interviews in Berkeley, their stroll through the hills above Heidelberg, the years at Johns Hopkins, and in short "your growth in all good things,—faith among the rest." As expected, the book was a commercial failure. Like Gilman, who had to admit that he had read only a few pages, just enough "to see the scope of your volume," few readers had the time or ability to peruse Royce's dense and tightly reasoned text. In philosophical circles it did not do much better. Royce soon grew irritated with the few reviews he had seen—one called him an "atheist," another a "learned ass"—and longed for some penetrating criticism. Oddly enough, *Mind* ignored it. In the United States Charles Peirce wrote a probing review at the request of the *Popular Science Monthly*, but for some reason the editor refused to print it. "I was a long time over the book," Peirce told James, "& wrote I thought something really very good, for me."

James became the book's chief publicist. Privately he told friends that it was "one of the very freshest, profoundest, solidest, most human bits of philosophical work I've seen in a long time. In fact, it makes one think of Royce as a man from whom nothing is too great to expect." He was particularly impressed with the "brand-new" argument for absolute idealism: "I confess [it] seems to me a very strong one, and leaves me hardly knowing what to think. I can't see my way to refuting it." Though James still had many reservations, he was forced to acknowledge, in a review published in the June issue of the *Atlantic Monthly*,

that Royce had fashioned an apparently insoluble quandary from which idealism might be the best escape. In future years James would find his own way out
of the "tight trap," but for the moment *The Religious Aspect of Philosophy* earned
his highest praise:

> Never was a philosophic work less dry; never one more suggestive of springtime,
> or, as we may say, more redolent of the smell of the earth. Never was a gentler,
> easier irony shown in discussion; and never did a more subtle analytic movement
> keep constantly at such close quarters with the cubical and concrete facts of
> human life as shown in individuals. . . . Everything in Dr. Royce is radical. There
> is nothing to remind one of that dreary fighting of each step of a slow retreat to
> which the theistic philosophers of the ordinary commonsense school have accus-
> tomed us. . . . The Thought of which our thought is part is lord of all, and, to use
> the author's own phrase, he does not see why we should clip our own wings to
> keep ourselves from flying out of our own coop over our own fence into our own
> garden. California may feel proud that a son of hers should at a stroke have
> scored so many points in a game not yet exceedingly familiar on the Pacific slope.

Quite a different assessment was advanced by Shadworth Hodgson, who,
writing to James, sharply criticized Royce's logic. In concluding his argument for
absolute idealism, Royce had written: "All reality is reality because true judgments can be made about it." To Hodgson, this means that "existence depends
on something *subsequent* to itself," and this amounts to the curious fallacy, *ante
hoc ergo propter hoc*. Royce had sent a complimentary copy of his book to
Hodgson, and the gift prompted two letters in which the elder philosopher
renewed his suspended, still unresolved, but friendly controversy with the young
American. Hodgson objected to his having been identified—on page 362—as a
"post-Kantian idealist," and he further distanced himself from Royce's conclusions: "I cannot render intelligible to myself the *absolute* in any form whatever.
. . . I cannot imagine thought except as either being itself a thinking being, or else
as belonging to a thinking being; and I cannot imagine a thinking being except as
finite." Hodgson found contradictions and faulty assumptions throughout Royce's
argument, and admonished him for ignoring logical foundations "to busy yourself
with the superstructure"—that is, with applications to religious thought.

> In fact, it is the very fact of not analysing the logical conceptions, which your
> book contains, to the uttermost, so as to see what consequences they really in-
> volve, that I most object to. . . . I mean that there is a great deal of plain & simple
> analytical work to be done, before you can profitably come to such questions as
> those of your book, the Infinite Thought in the Universe, & the "Agnosiology," or
> Limits of Thought.

As we shall see, this criticism would become increasingly a focus in discussions of Royce's philosophy throughout his life, and up to and including the present day.

The Religious Aspect of Philosophy is a homily in the form of a philosophical argument. It is also a kind of prose *Divine Comedy*. The paths to heaven, it insists, lead through hell: moral insight rises from despair; absolute truth is founded on skepticism. These two paths, the ethical and the metaphysical, give the book its organization. Book I, "The Search for a Moral Ideal," describes a dialectical journey through the ethical inferno. In the first five chapters Royce established a dilemma and reduced both sides to skepticism. Tracing the history of moral philosophy from the Greeks to the present, he outlined a struggle between ethical realism and idealism. The error of the realism lies in its determination to objectify values in facts: its "lofty *Ought*" becomes a "paltry *Is*." Expressing the ethics of evolution, the realist "resembles . . . a man who should try to show us that the truth of the law of gravitation clearly indicates that we all ought to sit down." The idealist, on the other hand, tries to preserve values without objective support. If this attempt protects the volitional element in ethics, it exposes the moral philosopher to the charge of capriciousness and in the end makes him a skeptic. Life becomes ceaseless moral warfare within and between individuals. We are little bundles of ambivalence unable to explain that even our faithlessness is unworthy. All moral principles are shattered into a spray of conflicting aims; each will is tragically opposed to every other; each feeling is estranged from all others.

With these conclusions, so familiar in the writings of modern existentialists, Royce felt that he had touched the source of moral doubt and, at the same time, that he had found "the very life-blood philosophy." For if despair is the upshot of moral conflict, despair itself is full of moral implications. "Absolute ethical skepticism, if it were actually possible without self-destruction, would still presuppose an end, namely, the effort to harmonize in one moment all the conflicting aims in the world of life." The one aim, therefore, that is not shattered is the search for peaceful harmony. To achieve this goal, the "illusion of selfishness"—the belief that my life is more real than any other—must be put aside, and with it, all forms of individualism. *"The Other Life is as My Life."* With this insight one must work to advance the spirit of harmony, to do whatever will help others share the insight, and finally to organize life into a common universal will. Royce was far from optimistic. Philosophy, he insisted, offers no panacea for the world's ills. Regardless of theoretical solutions, the warfare continues. On the other hand, philosophy can clarify issues and open useful passages. "Let us," he concluded, "get all the satisfaction from philosophy that we can. In truth we shall never get too much."

Book II, "The Search for a Religious Truth," seems initially not more hopeful. What can we know of the external world that can satisfy our need for a religious truth? The first answer is "the world of the powers." Faith in such a world worships fact and force as such, professing, as it were, that an apple's partial rottenness confirms its universal soundness. Royce reviewed the popular varieties of this creed—evolution, monism, dualistic theism, and the old empirical argument from design. In every case he found an attempt to brush the problem aside. The world as power, he maintained, is "a vast wreck of colliding molecules," "a huge mass of inexplicable facts." Each sign of evolution is matched with dissolution, every good is yoked with evil, design with chaos. Thus, the religion of power ends in doubt.

"The world of the postulates" represents a deepening of the skepticism. We believe we have no real knowledge of an external world: it is not a datum, but a postulate. If, as a postulate, the world of power has no religious significance, perhaps another hypothesis will suffice: "a deeper faith in something that is eternal, and behind or above the world of the senses." This attempt establishes the volitional character of reality and opens the way to idealism. Seen in this light, "the world is no more merely dead, or merely external. It is ours and for us." And if we choose the world, why should we not choose the best world that we can make? Answering this need, the "universal consciousness" is offered as a postulate.

Up to this point Royce's philosophical standpoint is identical with that espoused in his Berkeley period. Indeed, extracted and revised sections of his earlier essays—"Pessimism and Modern Thought," "Doubting and Working," "Kant's Relation to Modern Philosophic Progress," "Mind and Reality," and "How Beliefs Are Made"—form the backbone of the first three chapters of the second book. The revisions, however, tend toward absolutism. The postulate of idealism in "Mind and Reality" is a doctrine that "never can be proven"; in the tenth chapter of *The Religious Aspect of Philosophy*, this phrase becomes "we have not yet proven."

The skepticism of "the world of the postulates" amounts to the following objection: "You put the model all-embracing thought M in a relation to the poor human thought *h*, in which no transfer of thought really takes place, but still you give to *h* the command that it shall copy M. Then you postulate that which is by your hypothesis unknowable, namely, that this correspondence has been attained, and this empty postulate you call a philosophy." Royce admitted that this analysis is formidable. "But," he added, "like all philosophical skepticism, rightly understood it will be our best friend."

The world of the postulates is a world of relativity. Explaining the biographical background of his philosophy, Royce said that he had "passed through and long tried to hold and to rationalize this doctrine of Relativity." But finally he was caught in a fatal paradox: relativism can be reduced to the claim that the statement, "There is no absolute truth," is an absolute truth. Royce admitted that Kant's theory of knowledge can be reduced to the same absurdity. Kant, as Royce understood him, came to the result that knowledge of reality is founded on a union of thought and perception. "The necessity of any judgment amounts then only to what must be summed up in the words: *So the present union of thought and sense makes things appear.*" Beyond the present moment, all is postulate.

Royce believed that this relativism could not withstand a skeptical attack. "The thought that says, 'No judgment is true beyond itself,' is that thought true beyond itself or not?" An affirmative answer acknowledges a truth beyond itself; a negative answer denies the principle of relativity; a relative answer, one that neither affirms nor denies, fails to establish the principle as a truth. But the world of the postulates must be a true world; otherwise it is meaningless. "Twist as one will, one gets not out of the whirlpool of thought."

So whether the world is viewed as power or as postulate, all is doubtful. What then is skepticism? A thoroughgoing doubter maintains that any judgment may be an error. But what is error, and how is it possible? To answer, Royce laid down two principles of logic. First, only judgments, not merely single ideas, can be errors; second, a judgment can be an error only if it disagrees with its intended object. Statements about the unknown or the unknowable cannot be errors, but only nonsense; an infant cannot make errors in integral calculus.

This preliminary spadework enabled Royce to approach two classes of error. First, there are errors about other minds. Imagine a conversation between John and Thomas. Borrowing again from Holmes's *The Autocrat of the Breakfast-Table*, Royce observed that there are at least four persons present: the real John, the real Thomas, John's idea of Thomas, and Thomas's idea of John. If John forms a judgment about Thomas, about whom is he thinking, the real or the ideal Thomas? Plainly the latter, for John's Thomas is the only Thomas that is a possible object of John's thought. If the judgment is an error, about whom has John erred? Not about his Thomas, for his idea, being his, is always true. Nor about the real Thomas, for he is an "eject," a thing-in-itself that never enters anyone's consciousness. If, moving to the second class of errors, we ignore Thomas and discover John forming judgments about his own experience, past and future, we encounter the same difficulties. At each moment John knows only his present impression of past and future. None of John's judgments can reach beyond the present, for the real past and the real future, just like the real Thomas, can never be intended objects. Hence, all truth is subjective, and therefore error seems impossible.

But, everyone must protest, error is not only a possibility, but a daily reality. Yes, but how can this reality be explained? Perhaps John's errors can be known to a third party. Perhaps when John's checking account is overdrawn, the bankers or their computers will show him his error. But these mediators, as finite beings, are prisoners to the same subjectivity that besets John. To solve the problem by denying the possibility of error, one becomes entangled in the contradiction of relativism, asserting that the opinion that there is an error is itself an error. The only solution, Royce insisted, lies in the existence of an infinite actual judge, an absolute thought, that contains all truth and all possible error:

> Let us then drop this natural postulate, and declare time once for all present in all its moments to an universal all-inclusive thought. And to sum up, let us overcome all our difficulties by declaring that all the many Beyonds, which single significant judgments seem vaguely and separately to postulate, are present as fully realized intended objects to the unity of all-inclusive, absolutely clear, universal, and conscious thought, of which all judgments, true or false, are but fragments, the whole being at once Absolute Truth and Absolute Knowledge. Then all our puzzles will disappear at a stroke, and error will be possible, because any one finite thought, viewed in relation to its own intent, may or may not be seen by this higher thought as successful and adequate in this intent.

In abandoning the world of the postulates in favor of the absolute, Royce acknowledged his deep affinities with the older romantic idealism of Emerson. His answer to the world of the powers had been Emerson's poem "Good-bye, proud world! I'm going home." The search for a home, an image central in Royce's rhetoric, was a continually pressing motive of his life. His path often diverged from Emerson's; their methods were often poles apart. But in the end they came to a similar belief. To conclude "The Possibility of Error," he found another appropriate quotation from Emerson, in the poem "Brahma": "Truly," said Royce, "the words that some people have thought so fantastic ought hence forth to be put in the text-books as commonplaces of logical analysis:— 'They reckon ill that [sic] leave me out; / When me they fly, I am the wings, / I am the doubter and the doubt.'"

Royce had introduced the problem of the possibility of error in his doctoral thesis in order to provide an epistemology for "reasoned discourse"—such as the sciences demand. This discourse, he had insisted, requires us to construct "ideas in themselves," but the construction is "arbitrary," "unprovable," and useless as a metaphysics principle. The revision of this theory in 1885, though it retained its epistemological character, made Royce both a metaphysician and a religious philosopher. The "absolute thought" became another name for "God," infinite and omniscient. Explaining the logical motives for the revision, Royce described himself as a trapped beast, "a prey to that bondage of absolutism." Concerning the psychological motives, he said little or nothing. But in reviewing the first thirty years of his life, and in projecting the final thirty, we can identify many of the psychological components—social, historical, and parental—that made religious thought his destiny. Like Dante—*nel mezzo del cammin di nostra vita*—he had lost the straight path, but found a new one: to God.

Two Studies of California

Long before the publication of *The Religious Aspect of Philosophy*, Royce was tempted to launch another lengthy project. The Houghton Mifflin Company had begun publishing a series of state histories under the general title "American Commonwealths." The volume on California had been assigned to William Watson Crane Jr., a Bay Area lawyer and amateur historian, a member of the Berkeley Club, and one of Royce's older friends. But suddenly, in August 1883, Crane died. Horace Scudder, the series general editor, turned to Royce, who was astonished. He had never dreamed of such a thing. Still, there was much in the offer that attracted him. The money was good, and the deadline was flexible. The book would not need to be a comprehensive study, but could be a collection of essays "on the general tendency and lessons of the various historical periods." Royce was especially attracted by this last condition. As a philosopher he felt that his "airy studies" would be helped by his being forced to interpret a set of concrete facts, and as a Californian, he welcomed the chance to sort out his ambivalent feelings toward his native state.

To help him make a decision, Royce wrote to his friend and former colleague Bernard Moses, professor of history at the University of California:

> What I wish to trouble you with is the question, whether you really think that I should do right to undertake that task as a mere accompaniment of other work, as a thing for leisure hours, and whether you would expect to find as the result of it a respectable book that could be of any real use for the purpose of the proposed historical series. . . . If considering all the drawbacks you still think it reasonable for me to try, I should be glad to know the fact. If you do not think that I have any business to assume such a responsibility, your opinion would have much weight with me in making up my mind. Please tell me plainly.

Moses's reply has not survived, but it must have offered encouragement, for by the beginning of 1884 Royce had begun his research. "The book will be a sidework," he told Coale, "an amusement of idle hours, not an attempt to do expert work; but then even such amusements are pretty serious things, and I do not want to do it ill."

Through previous publications Royce had made the acquaintance of Hubert Howe Bancroft, the San Francisco publisher who had gathered the world's most

complete collection of documents on the history of California. Bancroft's plans
included a series of monumental studies of the Pacific coast, and his unique   131
library was to form the basis of his works. The Bancroft Library had grown to
such size that it filled a warehouse building in San Francisco, on Valencia near
Mission Street, just at the northern edge of Bernal Heights. The building was
also filled with a staff of assistants whose jobs included the actual writing of
"Bancroft's Works." Bancroft himself was content to be editor, promoter, and
publisher, and though his name alone appeared on the title pages, his books
were mainly the work of his assistants. Chief of these was the library's supervisor, Henry Lebbeus Oak.

Royce obtained permission to spend the entire summer of 1884 in the
Bancroft Library, and through this arrangement he and Oak became fast
friends. There was much to see, but the most interesting documents that Royce
found were included in the papers of Thomas O. Larkin, the U.S. consul at
Monterey in 1846, the year of the conquest. As the official representative of the
United States, Larkin had been privy to the government's policies, and his
papers suggested that John Charles Frémont, the principal figure in the seizure
of the Mexican province, had deliberately disobeyed his orders by making war
on the Californians.

Frémont as a soldier had been a romantic figure, and during Royce's childhood he was already a legend, universally saluted as the "pathfinder of the
West." Like many others, Royce's parents had been guided by Frémont's well-
known *Report of the Exploring Expedition* in their overland journey to the coast
in 1849. Frémont's subsequent careers, as owner of the rich goldfields of the
Mariposa Ranch and as the first presidential candidate of the Republican Party,
were equally impressive. During the Civil War he had been known as the exotic,
if somewhat incompetent, general of the Union army in Missouri.

Royce loathed the sentimental hero, the military bully, the egotistical liar,
just as he later came to despise these qualities in Theodore Roosevelt. He was
determined to explode the Frémont myth, and he obviously took rich pleasure
in doing so. The myth was a part, as Royce became gradually convinced, of a
family plot invented by Senator Thomas Hart Benton, the soldier's father-in-
law, and his daughter Jessie, the wife of "the gallant captain." A fierce prophet
of "manifest destiny," Benton was determined that California must be part of
the United States. Frémont was equally determined to realize his personal
ambitions as the conquering hero. The document that exposed Frémont's
duplicity was a memorandum from Secretary of State James Buchanan to
Consul Larkin delivered by secret agent Archibald Gillespie.

By October 1845, the United States and Mexico were on the verge of war.
Seeing, if not engineering, this inevitability, President Polk and Secretary
Buchanan devised a plan to acquire California peacefully. Operating in secret,

Consul Larkin was to deepen the antagonism between the Californians and Mexico; at the same time Larkin was to encourage their friendship with the United States and to let them understand that "should California assert and maintain her independence, we shall render her all the kind offices in our power as a Sister Republic," and further, that "if the People should desire to unite their destiny with ours, they would be received as brethren." Gillespie delivered these instructions to Larkin at Monterey in April 1846.

In the meantime, Captain Frémont of the U.S. Army Topographical Engineers had been sent to California with a party of about sixty soldiers. Officially his purpose was to find the best railway route to the Pacific coast, and on those grounds he obtained the permission of General José Castro to winter his troops in the inland valleys of California. From the outset, however, Frémont's behavior suggests that he was more interested in provoking the Californians than in surveying their land. Gillespie, as he was instructed, repeated the contents of the Larkin dispatch to Frémont; both soldiers were ordered to assist Larkin in carrying out the intrigue. Instead, Frémont moved his party to the Sacramento River near a group of American squatters, and encouraging their already well-developed hatred of the Californians, he exchanged rumors and offered strategic advice. On June 10, the settlers seized a band of horses from Lieutenant Francisco Arce; they then set off for Sonoma where, on the morning of June 14, they captured General Mariano Vallejo, his brother, Salvador, and two advisers. Here they also raised the Bear Flag, proclaimed a new government, and sent the prisoners to Frémont. War was unavoidable. Joining the settlers at Sonoma, Frémont organized them into a company of volunteers and took the war into the south. By that time the United States was officially at war with Mexico. Commodore John D. Sloat arrived and seized Monterey. Within a few days the U.S. flag was flying over Monterey, Sonoma, San Francisco, and Sutter's Fort. The inefficient Californians were unable to mount any significant resistance. The end came at the Cahuenga Pass near Los Angeles on January 14, 1847.

Seeing immediately the disparity between the Larkin dispatch and Frémont's actions, Royce initiated a series of careful investigations during the next year. Before leaving San Francisco, he disclosed part of his findings to his former classmate and colleague William Carey Jones. As Frémont's nephew, Jones was interested in clearing the reputation of his illustrious relative. On his return to Cambridge in September, Royce wrote Jones a long letter with a series of detailed questions about his uncle's part in the seizure of California. The questions were transmitted to Frémont, and through Jones's mediation, Royce arranged two interviews with the general and his wife.

Their first meeting was held in December at Frémont's home on Staten Island. Royce found the general "well-preserved, a pleasing old gentleman, quiet, cool, self-possessed, patient, willing to bear with objections of all sorts, but of course not too communicative." Mrs. Frémont, on the other hand, was "very enthusiastic, garrulous, naively boastful, grandly elevated above the level of the historical in most that she either remembers or tells of the past." Proceeding very cautiously, Royce asked if Frémont, before opening hostilities, had known of Larkin's secret mission, and if so, why he chose to undermine the plan. At the first interview, the general not only denied all knowledge of the dispatch, but agreed with his wife that it was absurd and impossible for it ever to have existed. He had been directed, Frémont insisted, by explicit, though secret and unwritten, orders to obtain California by any means available. Throughout the conversation Royce had "the precious dispatch" in his pocket. "I thank you most heartily," he told Oak, "for one of the keenest delights of my life, in that, through your kindness and Mr. Bancroft's I was enabled to sit there and hear these two distinguished historical characters demonstrate that this dispatch, which so nearly affected them both, was yet nonexistent, impossible, absurd, a fantastic bit of nonsense."

Despite, however, the indisputable existence of the dispatch, Royce was willing to entertain the possibility that Gillespie, contrary to his official testimony, had not informed Frémont of Larkin's mission, or that Buchanan had deliberately set two contradictory policies in motion with the expectation that one or the other would succeed. After reviewing the documents and considering their implications, however, Royce rejected this hypothesis in favor of the conclusion that Frémont was simply lying. Indeed, Frémont eventually admitted that he had known about Larkin's mission from the outset, but decided that "this idea was no longer practicable, as actual war was inevitable and immediate"; fearing also a plot by England to seize California, he resolved to act "discreetly but positively." Mrs. Frémont added the suggestion that Senator Benton had prompted the hostilities: "Polk and Buchanan," she told Royce, "were simply nonexistent for my Father when he had his own plan to carry out."

Royce's dealing with Frémont suggests the image of a mouse cornering a cat. He allowed the general and his wife to think of him as "a very small-minded historian." He asked questions and recorded their answers; he appeared puzzled, but kept his secret, watched patiently as Frémont hanged himself in his own noose.

After the publication of *The Religious Aspect of Philosophy*, in 1885, Royce spent most of his time on *California*. In March Mrs. Frémont sent him a few comments on their interview, though they added little new information. In April he visited Washington to examine the Department of State Archives. The trip, he told Scudder, was an "excellent success." There he found official copies of the Larkin dispatch and related documents. They left little doubt about the government's plans to win California peacefully, and consequently gave Royce "the means of applying the thumb-screw to the Frémonts." Without authentic proof of the government's secret intrigue, they would, Royce was sure, merely evade his charges. "Now," he told Oak, "I look for fun." On April 14 he drafted a long letter to Mrs. Frémont revealing his evidence, challenging her and the general to give some explanation. With a logician's skill he abandoned the role of the "small-minded historian" and pressed his argument with an antinomy between Larkin's mission and Frémont's policy of the Bear Flag:

> This one policy says: "Intrigue peacefully with the Spanish Californians." The other says, "Take possession of the province forcibly if the least chance offers." The one policy runs: "Assure the inhabitants that they are our brethren, that we shall cordially welcome them as such if they will cut loose from Mexico, that they ought so to cut loose, that they may expect in such case 'kind offices' from us, that their prosperity lies with us, and that we will fight at their sides against the English should the English come." The other policy determines deliberately upon beginning war against these very people, in order to conquer their territory from them. It offers them no "kind offices as a Sister Republic," seeks not to induce them to separate peaceably from Mexico, undertakes no intrigues with their chief men, but, on the contrary, seizes their government's horses when a band of these pass near, takes possession of Sonoma, and after seizing prominent men as prisoners, prepares for war to the end. No one could recognize the policy of the Larkin dispatch in the gallant and vigorous "disregard of red tape" with which General Frémont courageously assaulted the authorities whom Larkin was "prudently to warn." The antithesis is perfect.

The Frémonts did not react. Instead they replied with good humor, thanking Royce for his trouble and promising "a full and careful answer as soon as the General shall be free from an *immediate and pressing piece of business.*" In the meantime Royce pieced his facts together and began to write the book. By July he was tired of waiting for an answer, so while passing through New York on college business, he arranged a second visit with the Frémonts. Royce still hoped that the general, now that the truth was in the open, might have "some revelation to make." "But no; cordial he still was, dignified and charming as ever, and the good Jessie sat calm and sunny and benevolent in her easy chair, but alas, he lied, lied unmistakably, unmitigatedly, hopelessly. And that was his only defence."

To answer Royce's evidence, Frémont merely repeated his claims that he had never known of Larkin's mission and that his secret instructions were opposed to any peaceful intrigue. The government, he added, must have lied to him. Royce remained a skeptic. Of course, he had to admit the possibility that Frémont's memory, not his original plan, was at fault. But this bare possibility did not alter Royce's conviction. "Now I have utterly surrendered myself to the view that he alone is the deceiver about the matter. And this last interview confirms me."

Sending Katharine and Coco to Newburyport for the summer, Royce spent all his time on *California*. "It is a pity," Katharine wrote to her mother, "that he cannot spare time to go to N-port with me and lounge about in the woods." Royce hoped to meet a self-imposed deadline of October 1. On August 8 he mailed Oak a draft of "The American as Conqueror: The Secret Mission and the Bear Flag." It was, he joked, a "symphonic poem" that he might have titled the "Pathfinder and the Settler" or "Frémont's League with the Devil." This became the second chapter of the completed volume, and without question it was Royce's most enduring piece of historical research. With some show of modesty he admitted that he had little original evidence to offer; the whole chapter amounted to "an elaborate attack on Frémont's honor." Later in the month Royce decided to give him a chance for a final word. On the twentieth he wrote to Mrs. Frémont promising to let her examine the proofs of his second chapter before publication. "In case you choose to add any brief note or comment upon what I say, I shall thereupon be glad to print the same in your name, worded just as you desire, in the book, as note or appendix." Once again his letter was answered with silence. Meanwhile he plunged ahead with the composition of the remaining five chapters.

In the process Royce encountered a painful experience that might prove a useful lesson to any philosopher, the lesson that historical truth depends on facts. "It is fearfully hard," he told Oak, "to tell the truth in these things." Repeatedly he was forced to destroy pages of his manuscript, finding that his summaries and interpretations violated the sources. "If California history were only philosophy! For the Infinite, as philosophy deals with him, never talks back, leaves no documents on record, and always stands still to be counted. You need not interview him; he is entirely indifferent to all the lies you tell about him; and your reader is as well and as little up in the secret history of him as you are. That is the sort of thing to deal with, something submissive and plastic!!"

During the second week of September 1885, with a substantial part of his manuscript complete, Royce attended a meeting of the recently formed American Historical Association at Saratoga, New York. There he presented—"without opposition or mishap"—an abbreviated version of his second chapter entitled "The Secret History of the Acquisition of California." He was in the mood for a holiday, and the power he felt as a result of personal achievement made the whole meeting seem like a hilarious farce. "There was very little history present," he told Oak, "and much fooling." President White of Cornell read a long paper on the history of cometary theory and proved "the wholly novel and wondrous historical truth that people, and especially divines, used to be—

superstitious about comets." This, Royce noted, was a contribution to the history of civilization "just as the foam on a glass of beer is a contribution to the world's supply of nourishing food." Another paper, one by Herbert Tuttle, was a bibliographical summary of current research on Frederick the Great. Goldwin Smith spoke on "*'tendencies,'* viz. the tendency of Canada, or of the Protestant Reformation, or of anything else you please in history, to be, or to become something or other that only a clever man can understand." Royce spent his time with other members "drinking beer and punch, writing reams of letters to the press, and discussing absolutely everything that did not concern us." There were two or three other meetings in Saratoga at the same time, so the town was "a perfect madhouse," and the service was bad. On the other hand, since his paper was well attended, Royce had few serious complaints.

Back in Cambridge he continued his work on *California* and prepared to resume teaching. He missed his October 1 deadline, but hoped soon "to clear my hands of this cloying and delicious California preserve before I go to the other work. I have had my fingers in it too long already for a good child of Pres. Eliot, and shall need a scolding soon if I am caught in the mischief." Actually the work dragged on into December, when finally he delivered his manuscript. It was published in the spring of 1886.

Royce dedicated his book "To my mother, a California pioneer of 1849." The work involved, in fact, a great deal of collaboration between the son and his mother. Anticipating his research in the spring of 1884, he asked her to write down some of her memories of "old times," and she complied by sending him a few "scraps." He asked for more, hoping that they would delve into those memories when he could be close to her in the summer. In December she sent him an extraordinary memoir, which he used throughout his book. Through Sarah Royce, her son was able to document the flavor of the gold rush, told from a woman's perspective, emphasizing the role of families and religion in forging communities. Thanking his mother for her efforts, Josiah wrote: "It is so straightforwardly and sensibly, and withal so earnestly written, that it is in itself a very valuable and readable document, apart from its use to me. I shall make it a point to get it printed sometime and distributed as you desire. It will help me meanwhile much." Sixteen years after Royce died, his mother's memoir, given the title *A Frontier Lady*, was finally published, with a foreword by Katharine Royce, by the Yale University Press. Here Katharine poignantly wrote: "Wherever she was, she made civilization."

The full title of Royce's history—*California from the Conquest in 1846 to the Second Vigilance Committee in San Francisco [1856]: A Study of American Character*—suggests the work's two central aspects. First, the scope is limited to the first decade of U.S. interest in California. Thus, except for some preliminary remarks on the Spanish period, the book emphasizes the conquest, the gold rush, the San Francisco vigilantes, and the land feuds. Second, as the subtitle indicates, the entire work is controlled by a central thesis. This thesis, profoundly philosophical in its orientation, is stated in the final paragraph:

> After all, however, our lesson is an old and simple one. It is the State, the Social Order, that is divine. We are all but dust, save as this social order gives us life. When we think it our instrument, our plaything, and make our private fortunes the one object, then this social order rapidly becomes vile to us; we call it sordid, degraded, corrupt, unspiritual, and ask how we may escape from it forever. But if we turn again and serve the social order, and not merely ourselves, we soon find that what we are serving is simply our own, highest spiritual destiny in bodily form. It is never truly sordid or corrupt or unspiritual; it is only we that are so when we neglect our duty.

As can be readily observed, this thesis is consistent with the conclusions of *The Religious Aspect of Philosophy* and the earlier lectures on social idealism. Like other philosopher-historians—Voltaire, Hume, and Marx—Royce found events to illustrate his theories. Throughout *California*, he was determined to learn how, in the concrete, the individual American mind responds to the needs of society as a whole. That there is, or may be, an ideal organic unity of national experience is an assumption that lies beneath each topic considered.

Like the lectures of 1884, *California* is written from the viewpoint of a political independent, and like *The Religious Aspect of Philosophy*, it descends into an inferno of the persistent evils in American life. Greed, deception, factionalism, mob violence, legal hypocrisy, racism, and a righteous compulsion to defeat the freedom of weaker nations—these themes make a moral drama of the events described in *California*. In studying each historical phase Royce was concerned primarily with the forces and behavior that promote or disrupt the growth of new communities. Naturally he saw the conquest as a disruptive phase brought on by the private and often conflicting interests of a few individuals. He sneered at Buchanan's underhanded scheme to win California peacefully, he laughed at the settlers' childish attempt to whitewash their selfish intents, but he growled at Frémont's policy of war, his determination to win personal glory by violence, mendacity, and disobedience.

The American character, Royce observed, is a little squeamish. Other nations have never troubled their consciences before seizing foreign territory, but the U.S. must feel innocent and justified when it sheds the blood of peaceful neighbors. Such squeamishness produces hypocrisy. Our national conscience, Royce observed, prevents the left hand from knowing what the right hand is doing, when both are doing mischief. "And so, because of its very virtues, it involved itself in disastrously complex plots."

In reviewing the history of the gold rush, Royce focused on "the struggle for order," the positive theme of *California*. The main factors, he insisted, that retarded social harmony were the racial hatreds that motivated the conquerors and the individualism that placed wealth above responsibility. Placer mining, which prevailed during the early years of the gold rush, attracted large numbers of men without families and without any enduring concern for institutions. Working alone or in small parties with "pans" and "rockers," these miners moved from camp to camp, following rumors and their own dreams of fortune. Gradually as more advanced techniques were introduced—such as quartz mining in Grass Valley—corporate enterprise encouraged permanent social development. The "town" inevitably replaced the "camp." Women arrived; families grew; churches and schools were established; communities flourished.

Royce's interest in popular justice allowed him to study another aspect of the struggle for order. The early history of California afforded two famous examples: the cases settled by the ubiquitous Judge Lynch in the mining areas and the vigilance committees in San Francisco. One illustrated a capricious lawlessness; the other showed the collapse of a community's structure. Both, like Frémont's war, were disruptive forces that had been varnished with a thick layer of romanticism. As a historical realist with a strong moral concern, Royce was determined to get at the facts and study their consequences.

Among the numerous lynchings, he paid extra attention to one that occurred at Downieville in 1851. This case, as it seemed to Royce, was peculiarly horrible, for it led to the hanging of a Latina who, in a fit of rage, had murdered an Anglo-American. As was common in other lynchings, the woman and her lover were tried before a hastily elected judge and jury, which seemed to be impressed by the popular shout "Give them a fair trial and then hang them." Royce viewed this sort of "justice" as another illustration of the Anglo-American's need to satisfy conscience by superficially and insincerely respecting a mere form of social order, a form that permitted the "Great American Mind" to disguise its bigotry and disregard of human life.

The history of the vigilantes, though much more complicated, revealed, as Royce viewed the events, a similar instability characteristic of new communities. The second of these vigilance committees was organized in 1856 following the murder of James King "of William" by James Casey—editors of rival newspapers. Facing the threat of mob vengeance and having little faith in local government, a committee of prominent citizens set up their own courts and appointed a special police force. Seized by the committee's police at the sheriff's jail, Casey was promptly convicted of murder and executed. Afterward the committee persisted in efforts to reform municipal politics by ridding San Francisco of ballot-box stuffers and in general by preparing a suitable atmosphere for a return to orderly government. If in the long run, Royce observed, the

vigilantes failed to eliminate the criminal class, they did, through their own mis-
use of power, awaken men's consciences and stimulate the growth of lasting
institutions. The instances of lawlessness, mob violence, lynchings, and especially the vigilance committees taught Californians and, as Royce insisted, still
teach us "the sacredness of a true public spirit, and the great law that the people who forget the divine order of things have to learn thereof anew some day,
in anxiety and in pain."

Royce concluded *California* with a brief chapter entitled "Land-Titles and
Politics." Like the turmoil that resulted from popular justice, the land feuds
revealed the inefficiency and hypocrisy of California's legal institutions, the tendency of selfish men to settle their quarrels with violence, and the pious racism
of Anglo-America's dealings with the Spanish Californians. Repeated and generally successful attempts to defraud the *rancheros* of their land resulted in
"doubt, insecurity, retarded progress, litigation without end, hatred, destruction
of property, bloodshed." For Royce this phase of history illustrated, as did the
others he emphasized, that where greed and lies destroy communities, political
institutions alone are ineffective; finally, the social order and, through its
means, humanity can be saved only by "voluntary and loyal devotion."

The concept of loyalty is woven through most of Royce's works. Today the
word may seem quaintly Victorian, but we should not too hastily dismiss it as
nonsense. His history is a striking illustration of this principle—or rather of its
antithesis, for with few exceptions *California* is a study of disloyalty. The evil
that Royce persistently described is the form of individualism that seeks personal gain at the expense of social harmony. But the individualist is not really
an individual; disloyalty, he said later, is moral suicide. Thus, Captain Frémont
refused to follow his instructions when they conflicted with ambition. Similarly,
the gold hunters of 1849 refused to build communities and failed to subordinate
their private interests to the needs of humanity; instead, they seized the land,
lynched "foreigners" and, when convenient, used institutions for personal gain.

Only Consul Larkin and William Coleman of the vigilance committee
emerge as loyal men. While recognizing their imperfections, Royce presented
them both as selfless, responsible partisans of the social order. Neither was
wholly right, for moral purity was not a real option for either. But presented with
a variety of inevitable conflicts, they strove, in the words of *The Religious Aspect
of Philosophy*, to organize life and to extend the moral insight. Each attempted,
given the circumstances, to adopt the course of action that would enable citizens to accept their own responsibilities and to see that their best interests
could be fulfilled through "reverence for the relations of life."

When a child, Royce had viewed the early days of California as a time of
"fine and rough labors, amusements, and crimes." But when he wrote the history of this period, a lesson struck him "personally . . . with a quite unexpected

force." He learned that mere facts—even faults, however blatant—reveal "a process of divinely moral significance."

After *California* Royce did not return immediately to philosophical writing. Instead, in a letter to Milicent Shinn on August 7, 1886, he announced that he and Katharine were doing "a good deal of work this summer, of a light sort, but such as makes my pen swing a trifle." Though he was usually quite candid in discussing his work, Royce did not on this occasion choose to admit that he was writing a novel. Nor did he tell Henry Oak the whole truth: "You may ask me," he said, "why I'm so occupied in summer vacation. I wish I knew. I think it has something to do with earning my living." There was, in fact, no mention of the novel in any of Royce's letters until September 25, when he sent Scudder a finished manuscript. The title of "the promised novel" was *Just Before Nightfall*, and to justify its "portentous length," Royce explained that it was not a philosophical treatise. "There are two bloody fights, three heroes, two heroines, several villains, and almost no morals in the book."

If one is astonished to learn that the philosopher wrote a history, the effect is doubled by the discovery that he also wrote a novel. Actually Royce's three books are closely interrelated. Just as the history illustrates his moral idealism by grounding the theory in fact, the novel portrays a tragedy that occurs when ideals are separated from actions. In Berkeley, during the late 1870s, Royce had given a lecture entitled "What Constitutes Good Fiction," in which he had maintained that "the Novel deals with real life, if not with real events or with real persons." Agreeing with the doctrines of literary realism as espoused by his friend William Dean Howells, and by William James's brother, Henry, Royce had argued that the most vital constituent of the novel, aside from technique, and that which ultimately justifies it, is its successful study of character: "In properly studying character," he had said, "the Novel accomplishes the end of idealizing human life. For in the evolution and in the interaction of individuals consists the great active whole we call Life. To understand the individual lives is the stepping stone to the understanding of Humanity."

Though Royce probably expected that writing a novel would be an easy task, a thing "to finish . . . in short order," it became "a spiderweb of a job . . . ; and it stuck onto my fingers more and more as I tried to get it off them." The work was hampered by the exceptional heat and humidity of the summer, and by Kitty's illness brought on by her second pregnancy. She served as both muse and amanuensis. For recreation they took boat rides on the Charles, but otherwise they generally stayed at home. By the end of the summer Royce was "half-dead." October revived him, and looking back at his novel, he "sometimes felt very vain, although the thing is poor enough stuff now it is all done." Negotiations with Houghton Mifflin dragged on until late December; a change in the title to *The Feud of Oakfield Creek: A Novel of California Life* was decided in January, and the first edition of fifteen hundred copies was published in April.

The main plot of the novel concerns a land feud between a band of populist settlers and a San Francisco millionaire. Readers have always recognized a parallel between the fictional scene of conflict and an actual bloody shoot-out that occurred at Mussel Slough in 1880. There, Leland Stanford and the Southern Pacific Railroad, with support by the U.S. Marshal, attempted to install "jumpers" on lands occupied by settlers. Frank Norris appropriated the same scene of violence in *The Octopus* (1901). Royce was much absorbed in the history of California land suits. They were among the great public issues debated during his youth, and as we have seen, the final chapter of *California* explores some of their implications.

In 1885 he had also written a piece for the *Overland Monthly* on the Sacramento squatter riots of 1850. Returning to this article later, he noted that it was concerned "not so much [with] the special problem as to the best form of land ownership, as the still more universal question of the conflict between abstract ideas and social authority, at a moment when the order of a new society, and the eternal conflict between the private and the universal Selves, had to be settled, for the time, by men of energy, of idealistic temper, and of very fallible intelligence, just as we to-day have, as men and as citizens, to solve our own analogous problems." The problems of philosophy, he explained, take shape in actual experience; the deepest questions of metaphysics arise in the midst of life.

Like Royce's historical works, *The Feud of Oakfield Creek* is philosophical. In the tradition of George Eliot, Hardy, and Tolstoy—the novelists he most admired—Royce told his story as an illustration of social, ethical, and religious problems. The conflict between Alonzo Eldon—"Stanford in disguise," wrote one California reviewer—and Alf Escott, a populist leader, is a study of two distinct types of individualism. Both exhibit the qualities of the pioneer: they are durable, fearless, direct, and above all self-reliant. Archetypes of the legendary "rugged individualist," they have served with Frémont in the seizure of California, developed the state's resources, fought American Indians at Washoe, and weathered the political storms of the West's early history. But the individualism of Eldon expresses itself in ruthless competition motivated by jealousy, pride, and greed. His loyalties never extend beyond himself and his family circle. Unwilling to accept public defiance, Eldon severs his old friendship with Escott and brutally retaliates.

Escott, on the other hand, is an individualist with intelligence and conscience for whom independence and self-mastery provide the sources of ethical behavior. Understanding the importance of impersonal social virtues, he is willing to risk a friendship in an effort to organize the life of the community. Such loyalty has caused Escott to lose his professorship and finally to forfeit his own claim to the Oakfield Creek property in order to prevent a land war. Significantly, he tells the story of the American Indian fight at Washoe as a minor event in his life, as a fight for mere personal survival, whereas Eldon tells the same story as a fulfillment of his highest ideals. In Escott's view, the quarrel at Oakfield Creek is vastly more important, for here the entire community, not merely its individual members, is at stake.

Eldon and Escott are again set in contrast with respect to larger philosophical questions, for they represent two divergent tendencies of idealistic thought. Paradoxically it is Eldon who embodies an unworldly, impractical idealism. We learn that despite his lifelong commitment to capitalistic enterprise, he has become a convert to Henry George's theories of landownership and harbors a secret belief in socialism. "A glowing lover of the theoretic life," Eldon plans to endow a great museum and research center (*vide* Stanford University), which will "labor to investigate, to systematize, to rationalize, and to propagate the doctrines of the higher socialism." There are, then, two opposite facets of Eldon's character: one is the dreamer who sees himself as a sort of modern Kubla Khan; the other is a shrewd "leader of men, whom the very dogs on the streets knew a great way off, and revered as a man of might, but not of mercy." This total separation of the theoretical from the practical is a clear violation of Royce's belief that no theory is worthwhile unless it is critically derived from experience and leads to action.

But where Eldon has failed to make his philosophy an integral part of his life, Escott has succeeded. Ideals, as Escott knows them, are not adopted and rejected on the grounds of convenience and expedience; they are not vague goals set aside for the present to be realized somehow in future generations. They are concrete and practical guides of conduct; the absolute struggles through individual finite lives to fulfill its ultimate purposes. This belief, implicit throughout the novel, is stated directly in the final chapter, when a young idealist raises a question about the meaning of life. Escott responds:

> Live to hold on and fight, my boy! What have I lived for? You know my doctrines as well as I do. The great Spirit needs brave children. We are all of us poor specimens of what he's looking for. But alas! he can make us no better. For if it were he that made us better, we should be worth nothing. We alone can give ourselves the bravery that he wants. And so, bad as we are, our game is his game, if we only stand up to it, and fight for our side. That's the whole story of life. . . . The world is the home of brave men, and the prison of cowards.

As a realistic social-problem novel, *The Feud of Oakfield Creek* shares more with Howells's works, *The Rise of Silas Lapham* and *A Hazard of New Fortunes*, than with the California local-color sketches of Bret Harte. Like Howells's novels and Norris's *The Octopus*, Royce's fiction is based on actual events and on historical record. Oakfield Creek is nominally fictional, but its geographical description clearly identifies it as Walnut Creek. Royce moved the Mussel Slough affair north and made it parallel to actual land feuds in Contra Costa County. A similar feud broke out in that area during the 1870s when a San Francisco lawyer, H. W. Carpentier, who had acquired a large part of El Sobrante de Castro, instituted suits of ejectment against squatters who claimed that they were living on public land. Between 1878 and 1881, when the title was finally confirmed, it was the scene of the bloodiest fights in California history.

Aside from the parallels to California history, Royce might also have had the Haymarket Riot in mind. On May 4, 1886, the nation was stunned by the news that during a passionate speech in Haymarket Square, Chicago, someone threw a bomb at the police, killing several, and provoking the police to fire on the crowd, killing many more. Howells was deeply affected by the event. Royce, who visited Howells during the summer while writing his novel, could not have been indifferent to the riot's implications and might well have seen that the issues and events at Haymarket were very similar to the confrontation between the populist mob and established authority in the final chapter of *The Feud of Oakfield Creek*.

Quite probably none of Royce's other writings so clearly reveals his political views. He was certainly no activist and may even be said to have had little faith in the democratic process. In the novel we have no simple struggle between men of goodwill and their enemies. The evil is in the system that permits men like Eldon to attain vast political power through the possession of great wealth. The counterforce, represented in the settlers, the mob, is a different sort of evil. Their strength is in numbers, but they are quite as mindless as their antagonist. In such a hopeless conflict, men of insight are doomed. Royce condemned both the robber baron and the populist. Once again, as in *California*, his politics were those of the independent Republicans. But it is important to recognize that *The Feud of Oakfield Creek* is not a novel of social reform; it is a tragedy that depends on our seeing the gap between the ideal and the actual. No program is offered. A solution through the values of loyalty, love, honesty, and independence remains sound, but at achieving success for the community it is wholly ineffective.

The scant critical reception of Royce's novel was polite but unenthusiastic. Though impressive for its ambitious structure, the book was a failure in execution. A youthful Bernard Berenson reviewed it for the *Harvard Monthly*, and his criticism remains the best description of the novel's flaws:

> Great fault may be found with the telling of the story. It is prolix, unnecessarily long, and full of repetitions. . . . Mr. Royce is at his weakest when he is least dramatic, and when he attempts what ought to be an incisive analysis of the more subtle of his characters. . . . Tom [Eldon's son] is a mere shadow. We are told that

he was "clever," "charming," and affable. We do not believe it for a moment. I doubt whether Mr. Royce, were he a painter, could have painted Tom's portrait. Indeed, Mr. Royce never quite succeeds in giving us a complete picture. . . . The newest thing in the book, perhaps, is the great part that very slight misunder-standings play in it; and for that, although Mr. Royce has not made as much of it as he might have, we can not commend him too highly.

Though other reviewers praised the *Feud* highly—the *Nation* found it "ster-ling"—sales were weak. After two years, fewer than one thousand copies had been sold, and the book soon disappeared from the American literary horizon, thus ending Royce's brief career as a novelist. As George Santayana later remembered, he bore his failure in "silent disappointment."

The Devil in the Brain

The academic year 1885–86 had brought Royce a degree of permanence. On April 8, 1885, he received President Eliot's appointment to an assistant pro-fessorship for a term of five years at a salary of two thousand dollars. "My next academic year," he told Scudder, "the first that sees me in a permanent position, will be an especially exacting one, since I shall have to work out courses that will take a definite and settled place in the curriculum." During that year Royce taught two courses in the philosophy department: elementary philosophy, using *The Religious Aspect of Philosophy* as a text, and the philosophy of nature—a discussion of Spinoza, monism, and Spencer's theory of evolution. In addition, he was still assigned to forensics and oral discussion.

As if to celebrate his promotion Royce rented a more comfortable house at 20 Lowell Street, in a quiet and cheerful neighborhood off Brattle, a few steps from the Charles River. Despite financial constrictions, Josiah and Katharine grew increasingly content with their lives. The lively social world of Boston and Cambridge offered them many entertainments, particularly music, which was always their favorite recreation. Kitty took piano lessons and they bought tick-ets to concerts whenever their budget allowed. They also acquired a circle of friends in the Harvard community, and occasionally the great mansions of the Brahmins were open to them.

Josiah's reputation as a conversationalist soon made him a darling of the Bostonian grandes dames at whose soirées he regularly performed. Chief among these ladies was Mrs. Charles Dorr, the mother of George Dorr whom Royce had met in 1875. Molly, as Mrs. Dorr was known to her friends, is well described by Jack Chapman. "She lived," he said, "in the heart-secrets of others. She had been a friend of Emerson and Margaret Fuller. She gave large dinners and caused her guests to change places in the middle of the meal, called all women by their first names and all men by their last names." From her seat at the head of a long dinner table, Mrs. Dorr would call out in a low-pitched but authoritative "growl": "Edith Everett, you have talked long enough to Lowell. Let him come up and tell me about his experiences in England. Royce! tell me your story about the snake-eaters." Chapman added that someone once said "that if the Virgin Mary should come to Boston, Molly Dorr would drop in at the Bell household and say . . . 'Helen, dine with me tomorrow. *Mary'll be there!*'"

In their own home the Royces gave musicales at which their friend the composer Charles Loeffler sometimes performed. Privately their household was temporarily increased by the arrival from California of Josiah's niece, Eleanor Ingraham, Mary's teenage daughter, who had lived with the Royces in Berkeley and now joined them in Cambridge while attending high school. The eldest of seven surviving children in a poor working-class family, Ellie was welcomed as "a tall young niece," according to Katharine, "with a 'booful' great forehead and eyes."

But it was Christopher, now three years old, who became the focus of the parents' doting attention. He was a "jolly fat boy," who could "laugh very heartily and behave very wickedly." As Katharine remarked, "My little big boy grows in strength, beauty and brightness, also in stubbornness." "The latter I can stand," she added, "since he has not inherited any ugly temper." Writing to her mother-in-law, she noted, "The child inherits all of your & Josiah's persistence, & has not as yet always the wit to turn it in the right direction." Josiah agreed that Christopher had "nothing unearthly about him." "His mind is still as free as a bird's." Coco was particularly attached to his mother, whom he called "Kitty Kitty mum mum" and "you little Pussy thing." "You would be amused," she told Milicent Shinn, "to see how the little creature worships me."

This devotion brought out Christopher's talent for music, which was evident before his second birthday, though at the same age he was somewhat slow to develop speech. Before he could play he sat beside his mother at the piano, turning the pages at the right places. If she made a bad mistake in one of his favorite pieces, he would scold "with a long mournful Oh-h-h-h." Like his father, Christopher grew up with few playmates. He spent much of his time playing horsecar conductor alone, but his mother's music became "the most interesting of all games." Even as a toddler, Christopher was endowed with remarkable imagination and sensitivity. "I must tell you," Katharine wrote to her mother, "how little Coco behaved yesterday over some music that he specially liked." As she was playing "a very fascinating" mazurka by Chopin, Katharine came to a "bewitching, pathetic air way down in the bass notes," and when she was finished, there stood Christopher "with tears running down his cheeks, but smiling like an angel." "I like that part to go in there," he said, "I like it *very* much." So to see what else he might say, she played it again. "Now they're all sleeping in the dark in their cribs all night," he said, sobbing but still smiling, when she came to the soft, sad passage. "Now they're shutting the door." Evidently the music made the child think of babies asleep in the dark. Then realizing that he had been weeping, he trotted off to his bedroom to find a handkerchief.

Josiah told him stories and gave him an early, perhaps too early, introduction to philosophy. Once Christopher found a picture of a centaur in an almanac. "O mama," he said, "this man has broke his horse." "I tried," Royce said, "to introduce the suggestion that this horse had broke his man; but as Coco resisted all efforts to introduce that aspect of the subject, I gave it up." Christopher also had some quotable things to say about his father's book: "It says Religious Aspect outside, but it don't say it inside." And once after a walk he told his mother that he had seen "a boy riding on a red beelosopee." He meant "velocipede," adding, "It hadn't got any religious aspect."

As these little domestic tales suggest, Royce in 1885–86 was more relaxed than ever. After the publication of *California* he felt "unutterably lazy," and attempted little besides writing a few reviews and keeping up with his college work. The critical reception of his second book, however, even more than that of the first, was disheartening. Reviewers chastised Royce's form as lacking proportion and uniformity, and his style as "unidiomatic, awkward, and ambiguous." They attacked his historical methods, and even denied that the book was history; instead, according to one critic, it was an irritating discourse on the moral defects of the national character. Reacting to Royce's conclusions, most of the reviews, he noted, were "*a priori.*" The critics had received the book with fixed views about what it should offer, and were angry when they were not fulfilled.

The unsigned review in the August issue of the *Overland Monthly* was most stinging. A chauvinistic defense of California and of Frémont as its conqueror, the review accused Royce of "misjudgment," "sermonizing," "bad taste," and "pedantry." Without controverting the evidence, the anonymous critic maintained that Frémont had answered questions "courteously and fully," but that Royce had used "the General's own statements somewhat as a judge on the bench might deal with a crooked witness in charging a jury." "It is hardly necessary," the reviewer concluded, "to specify the verdict which must be given upon this book as a whole. It shows the results of considerable labor, and of good intentions; but as literature and as history, it is, on the whole, a failure."

Oak succinctly answered this hostile critic in the *Overland*'s September issue. In his own defense, Royce brushed off the criticism of his style with the remark that "one's style is like one's person, and however much or little it may be really chosen, it seems very natural to one's self, and very odd, sometimes to one's neighbors." As for the more ferocious attack in the *Overland Monthly*, Royce tried to maintain good humor. If—he told the magazine's editor, Milicent Shinn—he had the right to criticize Frémont, then surely Frémont's partisans should be entitled to have their say. He also felt it was safe to ignore the a priori critics. They seemed to have wanted Royce to write something more or different. "One had to select," he said. "I selected, after much labor and consideration, the conquest, one of the most significant events of our national history at the period in question; the formation of the state, one of the most remarkable undertakings of its sort; the gold period; and the vigilance-committees. What would one have me do?" If his views were sound, they would stand up; if not, the critics would find the errors. "If my book," he added, "ever comes to be read by anybody, for what it distinctly offers, on its title page and elsewhere, I don't fear the result." Even today some of the original criticism persists: Frémont's recent biographer, Andrew Rolle, characterizes Royce as "callow," "opinionated," and "moralistic."

Aside from the serious criticism, *California* had at least one comic repercussion. A certain Lieutenant J. B. Whittemore of the California militia, a grandson of Commodore Sloat who had been relieved of his command for having vacillated before seizing Monterey, wrote to say that he had "read with successive feelings of astonishment, scorn, resentment, indignation and contempt" Royce's "ignorant, mendacious, and malicious *attempt* to asperse and belittle the character . . . [of] Rear-Admiral John Drake Sloat, U.S.N." Royce had revealed the story of Sloat's vacillation and described him as a "morally timid man." Whittemore countered by calling Royce a "coward" and insinuated that he was subsidized by the English government. "The grandson, you see," Royce told Lanman, "makes up for the grandsire's defects of temperament." The little incident prompted Royce to develop in a letter to Lanman an elaborate mock-heroic fantasy:

Of course I shall have to give him satisfaction, you see. For this from a soldier, with his card accompanying the document, means a challenge soon to follow. But now you see also that the spectacle of this fellow (doubtless six-footed, straight as an arrow, a dead shot, a master with the sword) towering at one end of the Field of Honor, with sword or pistol, and poor me, with a weapon that is like "to kill me deader behind than him before," cowering and chattering my poor teeth in limitless misery at the other end—this spectacle, I insist, is not somehow just what it ought to be. Hence, after consulting with my friends, I have resolved, at the suggestion of one of them, when the challenge comes, and I have a choice of weapons, to choose Dynamite. . . .

—My will is just in the process of making. To you I bequeath . . . any MS relics, that may be found among my papers, of those happy days of youth when we studied Sanskrit together. Think of me occasionally when you wonder what has become of some book in your library, or why your bank-account is so plethoric. Forget not to drop a tear.

My poor family, all unconscious of their swift-coming fate, are absorbed in the frivolities of pianoes, clocks, nonsense-stories, and huckleberry pie. There is nobody as yet who realizes the truth but myself. Farewell! A last farewell!! If I had served my God as I have served my bank-account!!

Whittemore's anger was pacified without further incident. The story is recounted here primarily to show Royce's sense of humor at a time when he was attacked by hordes of adversaries. As all opponents eventually discovered, Royce, though physically slight, could take blows as well as dish them out.

About this time, Royce found a new rival: Francis Ellingwood Abbot, a man nearly twenty years older than Royce, a friend and Harvard classmate of Charles Peirce. Following his graduation in 1859, Abbot had entered the Unitarian clergy, but soon resigned to lead the "free religion" movement. He became minister of the Independent Church in Toledo, Ohio, where he edited the *Index*, a weekly journal devoted to his cause. Returning to Cambridge, he submitted a thesis in 1880 for a Ph.D. in philosophy, which was rejected on the grounds that much of it had been previously published. In a somewhat revised form the thesis was resubmitted the following year when it gained the department's reluctant and highly guarded approval. By that time Abbot had abandoned the pulpit in favor of teaching. In Cambridge he established the Home School for Boys and awaited the call that never came to a professorship at Harvard.

Abbot's good name and independent income gave him access to the fringes of the Harvard community. He first met Royce at James's home on January 18, 1884. His diary, which he kept faithfully and abundantly throughout his life, describes the event in some detail:

Elegant dinner. Talk all on philosophy. Royce is a good talker, though he thinks he is an idealist when all he means is theist. I never see a logical idealist—i.e. one who dares to follow out idealism to solipsism. James is brilliant, but skeptical of discovering truth by thought. I get little satisfaction in talking philosophy with the adepts: they have all got hardened to the new radical philosophy that is only just beginning to be.

It is clear that Abbot disliked and envied Royce on sight. Royce was a professional, one of the "adepts," a spokesman for the "new radical philosophy." Abbot, on the other hand, was deeply involved in the past. The thinkers of the earlier nineteenth century won his sympathy; his heroes were Emerson,

Wendell Phillips, Francis Bowen, and Theodore Parker. In Abbot's sense, Royce had no family, no history at all. Worse still, Royce held the inside track on the academic post that Abbot coveted. In 1886, "in a sort of despair," he went so far as to offer President Eliot an endowment for a "Professorship of Scientific Research" on the condition that he would be its first incumbent. The offer was refused.

This effort to buy his way into academia colors many of Abbot's projects. In 1885, the year of *The Religious Aspect of Philosophy*, Abbot finished a book, *Scientific Theism*, a revision of his Harvard thesis, which he submitted to Houghton Mifflin. Rejecting the manuscript, the officers of the firm pleaded that commercial reasons made publication unfeasible. They still balked when Abbot offered to pay all costs, so he turned to Little, Brown and Company, where all arrangements were settled within a few minutes. The book was published, at Abbot's expense, in November, and his mood at the time reflected a mixture of wild confidence and black despair:

> My book is printed. . . . In my own soul, I *know* it is the greatest book in phi-
> losophy since Kant's "Critique of Pure Reason," and in time it will be recognized
> as such. But I shall not live to see that. I expect either neglect or windy opposi-
> tion—no just appreciation whatever. This small volume, wrestled by sheer will
> out of hostile fate, is the seed of the world's future belief and faith.

The grandiosity of these remarks characterizes most of Abbot's philosophical undertakings. Knowing that he was the greatest philosopher of the century, he concluded that all disagreements were helpless and even jealous misunder-standings. Such responses suggest, to say the least, that Abbot's judgment was unbalanced, or as James once candidly put it, he was "simply *insane*."

Receiving a gift copy of *Scientific Theism*, James was sickened with the thought that a man could burden his whole life to produce a book that was utterly indigestible. James's criticisms, though mild and sympathetic, infuriated Abbot. When his son Everett, a Harvard student, received a low grade in one of James's courses, Abbot felt personally attacked. "James cannot answer my argu-ments, or even understand my book, as his letters proved; and this is his mean revenge."

Peirce's review in the *Nation* prompted a similar response. The article, Abbot felt, was guilty of "stumbling over the book very blindly." Peirce had identified its thesis as an attempt to deduce theism from the principles of science. He praised the effort and admired Abbot's "energetic dualism," but found the argu-ment evasive, fallacious, self-contradictory, and incompatible with scientific methods. "Strange," Abbot retorted in his diary, "that there is so little real philo-sophic insight or originality in America—not even keen or valuable criticism!"

Royce's criticism was the sternest. His review in *Science* depicted Abbot as a well-educated but harmless incompetent whose philosophy reveals a "not uncommon, but highly amusing state of mind." The position of *Scientific Theism*, Royce argued, is that of an objective idealist who claims that "the universe *per se* is an infinite self-consciousness," but everywhere in his book Abbot attacked idealism as tending irresistibly toward solipsism. The situation reminded Royce of a certain music critic who hated all of the best concerts he had heard, because in reality he hated music. Royce was especially irritated to find a book that reached a conclusion so nearly his own, but that defended its beliefs "by some very halting empirical arguments, and by a few scholastic word-puzzles." The importance of any philosophy, he insisted, lies not in its conclusions, but in its formal demonstration. Abbot's demonstration, Royce observed, was "vague," "comical," "antiquated," and "uncritical." This review, published in April 1886, left Abbot silently furious. Their quarrel was far from over, but for its resumption and conclusion, one must look ahead five years.

Philosophically, the academic year 1886–87 was uneventful. Royce was probably more exhausted by the work of previous years than he admitted, and as a consequence he undertook no new book-length projects. A few articles and reviews on California history were about all that he could manage. No doubt his teaching consumed most of his time. He was still director of forensics, besides which he taught an introduction to logic and psychology and repeated his course on the philosophy of nature. In addition, for the first time the philosophy department offered three courses exclusively for graduate students. Royce taught the course in metaphysics.

Beyond his university work, perhaps as a result of James's interest, he became a member of the newly founded American Society for Psychical Research. As chairman of the Committee on Apparitions and Haunted Houses, Royce worked toward ridding the society of its superstitious element. At his request the committee was reconstituted as the Committee on Phantasms and Presentiments. Thus, Royce hoped, psychical research might put less emphasis on ghost stories and begin to make genuine headway in parapsychology. He hoped to go even farther into the study of neurosis, dreams, and fantasies:

> The merely sane man . . . is very superficially known to science. The insane man proper has for years been studied by specialists. But of the fantastic man, the dreamer, of the man who lives a perfectly sane life in all but just some one or two realms of his mind, but who in these realms indulges in some sort of abnormal fancies, or is the helpless prey of some oppressive and diseased emotion or dream, of him we know in a scientific way far too little. . . . This wide and vast border-land region of human consciousness we need to study . . . to follow types and show laws whose study shall lead us into yet other parts of that romantic and

unexplored country. No one who realizes how closely the normal and the abnormal are joined in human life, how complex and delicate are their relations, how subtle and significant are their mutual influences, should hesitate to aid in any promising research in so profoundly and tragically important a province of the human spirit.

In family matters the major event of 1886 was the birth of the Royces' second son on Christmas Day. "What are you going to name the new boy?" Katharine's mother wrote. "I do not ask to name him, but you both know what I would like to have him called." Agreeing to the wish, the parents named him Edward for his maternal grandfather. "Ned," as he was known to the family, became, like Christopher, a gifted and accomplished musician, but as it eventually appeared, he too was emotionally vulnerable.

Remarking to Coale that his novel was "pretty sure to appear during the spring," Josiah was pleased to have two births to announce. "The baby is, of course, the real treasure, although it behaves so far only like a small mouse and sleeps as well as it ought." Christopher thought Neddy's arrival a miracle. His parents suggested that Santa Claus had delivered the baby. With this idea, his father noted, Christopher developed his own theory. "Santa Claus came, namely, to the house, to fetch Christopher's presents, and chancing to look upstairs, saw some baby clothes, in good number and order, in some drawers. 'Ah,' said the good Santa Claus, 'these people must be wanting a little baby.' Whereupon the old fellow trudged back whence he came, found a baby, and brought it to the house for mama."

In the letter announcing Edward's birth, Royce told Coale that he hoped to visit Baltimore sometime in the spring. By February it was Coale who planned to visit Royce in Cambridge. Those plans, however, were never fulfilled, for by March 5 Coale was dead. At almost the same time Royce learned that Edward Sill had died on February 17. The two deaths left Royce speechless. In a copy of *The Religious Aspect of Philosophy* inscribed and dedicated to Coale, Royce had added a quotation from Schiller "about the good things that flit away in this changing world." Now, feeling the whole impact of his loss, Royce must have remembered those lines. Coale and Sill had been his chief models of the idealistic temper, of lives dedicated unselfishly to enduring values, of the complete manhood that Royce struggled to attain for himself. "I shall," he assured Coale's widow, "bear my recollection of his words and of his spirit all my life, and I deeply wish that I could in any way live up to what he has suggested to me." Remembering Sill, Royce cited his friend as an example of the effort to organize life. "Science is, or ought to be, poetry, and poetry is knowledge, and the humanity of the future will not divide life, but will unite it. To bring such manly unity into his own life was his constant effort, and he perpetually invited others to join in the truly humane task that he wanted to have proposed to men of this so divided and unhappily specialized generation."

Royce's correspondence then lapsed for four months. By the middle of the summer the early signs of a nervous disorder had appeared. At first Royce was not inclined to take his symptoms very seriously. They were, he explained, the results of "some harassing temporary vexations." To get his mind off the problems, he visited the Dorrs at their summer home, Oldfarm, in Bar Harbor, Maine. The atmosphere was full of gaiety, and Mrs. Dorr became "a minister of comfort, pure and simple." Still Royce felt emotionally depleted. His enormous success in the past several years had been achieved at great cost. Though his books had brought academic security, their critical reception was disappointing, and the need to support a growing family on a tiny salary was a constant source of irritation. Probably also the deaths of Coale and Sill made a deeper psychological wound than he suspected. Something inside, he felt, was dying.

With the resumption of teaching in the fall, Royce was much altered. Eliza Head was "quite anxious about Josiah's health." This she wrote in a letter to Katharine in response to a telegram signaling a family crisis. In several of the surviving letters from Eliza to Katharine during this period, passages have been excised—cut out, torn out, or expunged with heavy black ink. Royce no longer seemed the pugnacious, teasing bumblebee that Chapman had described. Instead, he resembled a figure in Pre-Raphaelite art—subdued, pale, and limp—and he himself described his state as "an absolute negation of all active predicates of the emotional sort save a certain (not exactly 'fearful') looking-for of judgment and fiery indignation." He compared his feeling to a line from Coleridge's "Dejection": "A grief without a pang, void, dark, and drear." It seemed also like the dullness that Tolstoy had described in his *Confession*. "I felt," Tolstoy had written, "that something had broken within me on which my life had always rested, and that I had nothing left to hold on to, and that morally my life had stopped. . . . I did not know what I wanted. I was afraid of life; I was driven to leave it; and in spite of that I still hoped something from it." Quoting these lines in *The Varieties of Religious Experience*, James described this condition, borrowing a clinical term from Théodule Ribot, as *anhedonia*, an almost total loss of passion associated with fantasies of suicide.

Royce had become the "fantastic man." His depression, apparently aggravated by insomnia, increased during the fall, and by February it was clear that he could not continue. Blaming himself, he told Gilman that he had "joined the too great army of scholarly blunderers who break down when they ought to be at their best." He felt strangely well most of the time and remarked that "nobody meeting me on the street would call me ill, but the little devil in the brain is there all the same." He tried to assure his mentor that there was no reason to be seriously alarmed. The breakdown was a mere "mishap," the result of "carelessness," and needed only "a long sea voyage all alone." Royce added that he actually enjoyed the opportunity to study his own mental states and found the experience "peculiarly edifying, instructive, and even fascinating." But in truth, he was so sick that he had to dictate this letter to Katharine who served as his amanuensis. "I am very sorry to hear," Gilman replied, "that you are going into retirement for awhile,—but doubtless you are right." He advised rest, communion with nature, the Gulf Stream, deep sea currents, "but for pity's sake," wrote the hardheaded Gilman, "don't study your own mental states,—however 'fascinating' they may be." President Eliot also sympathized and arranged to grant Royce an immediate leave of absence on half pay. The illness intensified his financial anxiety, but this was helped by a gift from an unnamed friend and a loan of $350 from Lanman.

With Royce going on leave, the Harvard administration sought ways to reorganize the courses of instruction. Forensics with its staff of assistants could take care of itself, Royce's elementary and graduate classes could be rearranged, but his advanced course in the philosophy of nature presented a more difficult problem. Eliot and James suggested that Frank Abbot might be acceptable as a temporary replacement. Though Abbot's war with Royce was still smoldering, superficially they remained cordial. Since both belonged to the same committee of the American Society for Psychical Research, they continued to meet occasionally. "Royce is all gas," Abbot had remarked after one of these meetings in October. In November he had carried his anger into the public with a denunciation of Harvard philosophers as promoters of agnostic "dry-rot."

Still, if Abbot was not the man that Eliot would have chosen, the press of time made careful choice impossible. On February 8 Palmer offered the job to Abbot. Astonished, Abbot at first refused, pleading that his commitment to the Home School prevented extra teaching. Royce, with some hope that Abbot might reconsider, wrote him the next day:

> I write to say that I am heartily sorry that you could not accept the work. I am glad that you were asked to do so. You know how we differ, and how freely we both have expressed the difference. Yet I am so sure of the value of the clash of minds, and I have so true and hearty a respect for your mind, that I deeply regret that, whatever happens, my class will miss the stimulus and the moral support which your presence and your enthusiasm would have given them.

By that time, however, Abbot had already decided to accept the appointment. His reply to Royce three days later was a typical mixture of fawning and insincere humility: "The audacity of my daring to undertake such a task overwhelms me; I shall only rattle round in your shoes. . . . As to your class, they will barely tolerate me even if they come at all. Too well I understand my own unfitness to carry on your work. . . . As to our 'differences' etc., I shall have nothing to say; *my* work is constructive and controversial only in the most general way." Privately he accused Eliot of duplicity and saw the appointment as a way of joining the Harvard faculty through one of its side doors.

By this time Royce was making the final arrangements for his trip. He had decided to take a leisurely sailing voyage to Australia, and the square-rigged *Freeman*, scheduled to sail from Boston on February 25, was his choice. Lanman gave him a collection of ocean charts and a three-month supply of tobacco; James offered mineral water, figs, and a batch of French novels. Royce took along a few books of his own—some light reading in mathematics and mechanics, and James Martineau's newly published A *Study of Religion*. Lanman noted that a "horrid storm" was blowing as the bark sailed out of Boston Harbor and headed into the South Atlantic.

Now, quite literally, Royce faced a test of survival. A long period of depression accompanied the first weeks of the voyage. It was not exactly a misery, but a deep sense, like a deeper version of his earlier pessimism, of the utter worthlessness of life. Alone with his books and the sea, he read, he ate his meals of salt codfish and beef, but wondered why he bothered, why he did not simply jump overboard. His mind was clear, and his habits of analysis helped him to intellectualize his despair. "It was," he told James, "a diabolically interesting nervous state." "In the deepest of my nothingness I read mechanics, and mathematics, and Martineau, and even Casanova, with an impartial insight into the essential nothingness of definite integrals, easily conquered maidens, and divine laws—one and all." While gazing dispassionately into his soul's darkness, Royce felt that Martineau's optimism was at best a suitable model for the ironies of Swift and Voltaire. "The absence of the tragic element in M's religion," Royce noted, "is, in the case of so warm-hearted and sympathetic a man, highly characteristic. The simplicity of his world, and especially of his moral world, is as marked as its purity, serenity, and pitiful kindliness. There is no room here for the devil."

Instead of passing through the Suez Canal, the *Freeman* took the classic route around the Cape of Good Hope. Once in the latitudes of "the roaring forties," Royce's mood changed. On April 5 Royce sketched an outline for a new treatise, a large book with three parts and seventeen chapters, entitled "The World as Paradox and as Ideal." As the outline suggests, it would be an enlargement of his objective idealism, but would deal more with the concrete problems of individual freedom, will, and nature than he had previously attempted. He was delighted with the prospects for his new theory, feeling that it "does more to make the dry bones of my 'Universal Thought' live than any prophesying that I have heretofore had the fortune to do." Though the book was never written, the substance of Royce's plan became the germ for his distinction between "description" and "appreciation" in the twelfth chapter of *The Spirit of Modern Philosophy*.

On May 21 Royce computed the course of the *Freeman* as about five hundred miles out of Melbourne, the capital of Victoria. Within two or three days he would disembark. It was time to write letters to friends and to offer the cheerful news of recovery. The "head-weariness" was entirely cured, he told Scudder, and the passage as a whole had been "very jolly and prosperous." Royce enjoyed his companions, particularly the ship's captain, a Yankee and Cape Cod man, who had a certain inclination toward the contemplative life. Sitting on the deck and enjoying the tropical air, the two men discussed metaphysics and astronomy. "Well," the captain said, "sometimes it seems to me like nothing so much as a dream. Don't it ever occur to you that perhaps the whole thing above there, and our life too, is a dream of ours, and perhaps there ain't anything anyhow, that's real?" Royce admitted having had such thoughts. "Well now," the captain returned, "what do you teach your classes at Harvard about all this?"

"There was a countryman," I say, "from Cape Cod, who went to Boston to hear Mark Twain lecture, and to delight his soul with the most mirth-compelling of our humorists. But, as I have heard, when he was in Boston, he was misdirected, so that he heard not Mark Twain, but one of Joseph Cook's Monday Lectures. But he steadfastly believed that he was hearing Mark. So when he went home to Cape Cod, they asked him of Mark Twain's lecture. 'Was it very *funny?*' 'Oh, it was *funny,* yes—it was *funny,*' replies the countryman cautiously, 'but then, you see, it wasn't so damned *funny.*'—Even so Captain," say I, "I teach at Harvard that the world and the heavens, and the stars are all *real,* but not so *damned* real, you see."

As the lightheartedness of this anecdote seems to indicate, the playful Socratic side of Royce's temperament had reasserted itself. "I don't know of course how I shall feel on land," he told James, "but here in my place of safety I seem to myself to be entirely cured." In fact, he felt quite as sound ashore as at sea. The seven weeks spent in Australia and New Zealand gave him more than a recuperative holiday; they also offered "charming studies in human nature and in politics." He left feeling not only happier, but also wiser and more mature.

As a Californian, Royce was better prepared to appreciate Australia than most Americans. The sea, the coastal cities of Melbourne and Sydney, the mountains behind, and the deserts beyond—all suggested the place of Royce's childhood. The early history of California also had its Australian counterpart. Exploration in both places had been effected through foreign occupation; the discovery of gold had opened the way for development of both; the struggle for order with many political disruptions had been, Royce observed, the motive that led both California and Australia out of chaos. Even Australia's forests of gum trees were familiar sights to a native Californian. Yet to Royce, Australia, beyond the cities, had a harsh, gaunt aspect. Like many other visitors, he found it "weird, startling, dream-like—a rebellion against conventional forms of beauty in nature—impressive, admirable, but not what even the most experienced traveler would have expected." These natural and historical features, he believed, had influenced the development of Australia's national character and political institutions. He was struck by the fact that Australians put little stock in individualism. Instead, he noted, "the colonies show a degree of conservatism, of public spirit, of social discipline, of cheerful conformity to the general will of the community."

The national character was profoundly idealistic, but not in the Emersonian tradition. It could be "all fire and ferocity" or "bitter as gall," but it seldom lost "faith in the value of faithfulness"; if it "could not believe in many men," it "did believe in human life." Royce admired the Australians' public spirit and felt that it put most Californians to shame. In politics this spirit expressed itself in rudimentary socialism. State ownership of railroads, economic planning, and welfare programs were beginning to be accepted facts of Australia's political life. Finding a concrete effort to achieve the idealistic socialism that he had defended in 1884, Royce cheered the experiment. Though he feared that some of Australia's innovations were doomed, like political versions of Dr. Frankenstein's monster, he was not prepared to condemn the efforts outright. "Highly organized life," he said, "is as much the goal of all our efforts in this world as it is an unattainable ideal wherever nature does not accomplish for us the most of the work of organization. State socialism usually seems to be an effort to make live things out of dead theories." Australia, he felt, would soon demonstrate "the most remarkable experiments in State Socialism that have ever yet been seen."

Royce was especially fortunate in meeting several of Australia's leading citizens. Through letters of introduction from his friend Richard Hodgson, an Australian who had recently come to Boston as secretary of the American Society for Psychical Research, Royce met Alfred Deakin, joint leader of a coalition government in Victoria and Australia's future prime minister, and Sir Saul Samuel. Deakin was two years younger than Royce, and they became close friends immediately. "He was," Royce remembered, ". . . a young man, nervously active in temperament, cheerful, inquiring, speculative, unprejudiced, . . . an admirer of America and of good society, a lover of life, of metaphysics, and of power." Royce could hardly have found a more agreeable companion, and he was impressed that such an intelligent and versatile man had been chosen for a position of power. If Deakin had been born in California, Royce thought, "he might have written something as shadowy as *Progress and Poverty*," but he would never have been elected to high public office. Together Royce and Deakin visited the Blue Mountains of New South Wales where their "talk found all questions open and attractive—from the Moral Order to the conduct of Melbourne newspapers, and from Telepathy to the Chinese problem." Though they never met again, the friendship between the two men was kept alive by occasional correspondence.

Sir Saul, the elderly agent-general for New South Wales, was different. "His puns are bad, and his ideas lack genius," Royce told Deakin, "but his temper was perfect, and he was a charming travelling companion." Sir Saul accompanied Royce to the north island of New Zealand where they visited Auckland, Wellington, and the Hot Lakes. In the volcanic region Sir Saul's conversation was "exclusively devoted to his carriage springs and to brandy and soda (in their relations to gout), but still he never really grumbled after all. I liked him extremely." Royce's health continued to improve in New Zealand where he found the scenery "very jolly" and the climate "very tonic." "I . . . seem," he told James, "to have recovered my wits pretty completely."

On July 16 he took the steamer *Alameda* out of Auckland and reached San Francisco early in August. On his arrival Royce learned that his father had died from a stroke on June 23, though his letters do not manifest more than a trace of grief. His main concern was with the surviving members of the family, and especially with Ruth who was convalescing after a very serious and prolonged illness. His mother and sister now faced a financial crisis, and Royce blamed himself for being unable to help. "So I once more," he told James, "have cause to feel that when we play with our strength, we hurt more people than one. But I won't let myself be discouraged. The devil has had his own in my past. Perhaps he won't have so much in my future. We shall see." James replied that he was encouraged by the news of Royce's "cure" and dismissed all thoughts of any relapse. "By Jove, old man, if you ever *do* relapse, it will be the sorriest sham and suicide that ever disgraced humanity. You mustn't, you can't, with your gifts. If you do I'll strangle you with my own hands."

Looking over the Harvard announcements for the next year, Royce yearned for work. Without mentioning the fact, he doubtless also missed Katharine and the boys. Christopher was now six, and little Neddy at one year, eight months, would be toddling about. After spending three weeks with his mother at Los Gatos, Josiah took a train northward via Mount Shasta and then eastward on the Canadian Pacific. By the first week of September, more than six months after his departure, he was safely home again in Cambridge.

Royce's journey could be described as an odyssey. Certainly it had heroic aspects: the challenge of the sea, strange islands to visit, new people, an Ithaca and a Penelope waiting at the end. But in a sense the voyage was more like

Dante's descent into hell. In theoretical terms *The Religious Aspect of Philosophy* had prepared the chart for the route that Royce was bound to follow. As mentioned at the beginning of this chapter, he was heir to Emerson's idealism, but he refused, unlike the master, to answer doubt with slogans or to escape pessimism with the compensating belief that "the Devil is an ass." Royce needed to experience tragedy. At the end of his book he attempted to answer the emotional objection to his theory. Suppose, a critic might say, the absolute does exist, suppose each man's duty requires an endless devotion to the ideal, but what would be the worth of life if the absolute in its boundless freedom should reject the ideal? What if God actually sanctions evil?

Royce answered with a fable:

> At worst we are like a child who has come to the palace of the King on the day of his wedding, bearing roses as a gift to grace the feast. For the child, waiting innocently to see whether the King will not appear and praise the welcome flowers, grows at last weary with watching all day and with listening to harsh words outside the palace gate, amid the jostling crowd. And so in the evening it falls fast asleep beneath the great dark walls, unseen and forgotten; and the withering roses by and by fall from its lap, and are scattered by the wind into the dusty highway, there to be trodden under foot and destroyed.

The solution, Royce briefly maintained, lies in the fact that the King has richer treasures in his palace; he simply does not need the child's gift, is unmoved by human yearning.

This tragic fable could give no lasting comfort to Josiah. The child brings a bouquet of roses through a hostile crowd, but the father locks him out, refuses to acknowledge him or his gift, rejects his love. The painful truth that the child learns is that his father lives apart in his home with a love entirely his own. But Royce needed a God who lives and suffers with human beings. No mere problem solver, Royce's absolute gradually became a God of redemption and deliverance.

Chapter Five

Phoenix
1888–1895

Recovery and Conflict

Royce associated his breakdown with fire: he felt burned to the earth. But he soon rose from the ashes, and his career soared. In a span of seven years he attained his professorship, wrote two books, and produced dozens of speeches, reviews, and articles. By 1895 he was, without doubt, the most noteworthy philosopher in the United States.

"I feel like a bent bow, all ready to twang." Thus, Royce described his state of health on September 6, 1888. At home in Cambridge he felt "perfectly restored," and though he still made occasional use—"a trifling use, at long intervals"—of sedatives, his sleep was "very sound and cheerful," "almost as sound as it was in my boyhood." Looking forward to the last decade of the century, he projected "about ten years more of solid work." James was equally delighted: "Royce is back from his voyage round the world, as fresh as a new-born babe, and as full of promise."

He did not plunge recklessly into labor. The breakdown, caused by extreme fatigue, warned him to protect his health by establishing a routine, which he followed for the rest of his life, of brief holidays and solitary excursions. In fact, the academic year 1888–89 was relatively quiet. His major literary effort was a two-part essay, "Reflections after a Wandering Life in Australasia," which he wrote for the *Atlantic Monthly*. In addition, he kept up his association with the American Society for Psychical Research and assisted his friend Felix Adler in plans for the further development of the Ethical Culture Society. In Philadelphia on January 25, he gave a speech to Adler's group entitled "The

Practical Value of Philosophy," in which he supported a proposal for a popular "School of Philosophy and Applied Ethics." Other speaking engagements included appearances before the Harvard Club in Cleveland and the Yale Philosophical Club. Royce placed no great stock in these efforts, the last of which—"The Fundamental Problem of Recent Philosophy"—was arranged on very short notice. He condensed the substance of his course on the philosophy of nature, dictated a "pyrotechnic display" to a stenographer, and read it with minor revisions. "My chief esoteric aim and intent," he remarked offhandedly, "was by way of intercollegiate courtesy, to confound the Yale intelligence. I unquestionably succeeded herein, and then, reflecting that anything was good enough for a New England Unitarian country parson, I persuaded my friend J. H. Allen to print it." Allen, as editor of the *Unitarian Review*, published the essay in two parts under the revised title, "Is There a Philosophy of Evolution?" "The essay prepares the way for a more philosophical discussion, at some future day, of the relations between teleology and mechanism . . . ," Royce told G. H. Howison. "I think I have some light on that whole topic, although . . . doubtless you will declare that I keep my light pretty dark. Remember the circumstances, however. Someday I hope to do better."

The details of Royce's plans are contained in the notebook he began aboard the *Freeman* in April. In subsequent elaborations he revised his prospectus several times, but always projected a large treatise in several books with twenty or more chapters. It was to be a defense of absolute idealism with further applications to the philosophy of nature. On October 31 he sketched a series of twenty-one theses designed to reconcile the contradictions between the world as universal thought and the events of physical reality. This effort led, on Christmas, to a new outline and a fully elaborated plan under the title "The Philosophical Problem of the Present Day," seen as a comprehensive system such as he finally achieved in *The World and the Individual*. The four books of the treatise were planned as a historical critique of naturalism, a defense of idealism, consideration of philosophical paradoxes, and an outline for a hypothetical cosmology. On July 3 Royce revised the plan with a new title, "Outlines of a System of Philosophy," and a week later he decided to give the whole effort a more personal tone by designing the treatise as "A Philosophical Confession."

Though the specific forms of these ideas never developed beyond planning stages, the notes provided the bases for Royce's philosophical work in the 1890s. As for his teaching in 1888–89, he was still on the books as director of the forensic program in the English department, while in philosophy he taught the elementary course on logic and psychology as well as his regular class on the philosophy of nature. But his greatest satisfaction resulted from his graduate seminar on Kant. The Harvard graduate program in philosophy now supported three regular seminars: James on psychology, Palmer on ethics, and Royce on metaphysics. With seven students Royce focused his course on the *Kritik der reinen Vernunft*, read in the original, and he was "delighted to deal at last with men who were fairly free in their German, and who would read an article on Kant in German without whining and without the dictionary." With the training of a new generation of American philosophers embarked, Royce was gratified to be at the helm. A year later, speaking before the Harvard Club of Minnesota, he announced the end of the "old-fashioned American college, with its fixed course, and its neglect of higher professional studies in science and in the humanities." In the future, he believed, the university must turn its attention "to the production of ripe scholars and well equipped investigators, for they will be the leaders, the guides, and the inspirers of its younger students."

By the middle of the summer Royce, "greedy of a good rest," accepted an invitation from the Dorrs to escape alone to Maine for the whole of August. In conversations at Oldfarm, Mrs. Dorr presented Royce with an attractive proposal. She and Sarah Whitman wanted to sponsor him in a series of popular lectures on modern thought. Royce no doubt saw the possibilities of increasing his income and also making a trial of his newest ideas. Though he feared that he might be overworked by the end of winter, he anticipated the lectures as "both a delight and a rest." He accepted, and as plans developed, he agreed to give twelve lectures on a weekly basis beginning in December 1889. Under the general title "Some Noteworthy Persons and Doctrines in the History of Modern Thought," he proposed to treat Spinoza, Leibnitz, Berkeley, Kant, Fichte, Hegel, and Schopenhauer. The series would attempt, he suggested, to give "some idea, not of the technical details of their systems, but of their personal attitude towards the world, towards the ideals of life, and towards God." As a conclusion, he planned "to characterize some of the problems of modern life and philosophy" and also "to suggest something of my own attitude." The lectures, begun as scheduled in mid-December, were his most demanding extra-collegiate task of 1889–90.

Also and abruptly, after a year and a half of relative peace, Royce entered a new period of intense controversy. In 1890 he initiated two separate projects that brought him into conflict with his former nemeses, John Charles Frémont and Francis Ellingwood Abbot. Both quarrels began innocently. Robert Underwood Johnson of the *Century Magazine* engaged Royce as contributor, editor, and general consultant for a series of articles on California. Anticipating trouble, Royce warned Johnson against giving much space to the history of the conquest. "Beware, I should say to any fellow-student of those days, beware old Frémont's withered branch, beware the awful avalanche of yarns that the Sloat family, the children of the settlers and the like, have in store.—But I don't desire to seem officious. You no doubt already know far more of the troubles than I have ever had occasion to know. I only venture my word of sympathy."

The second controversy grew out of Royce's connection with Felix Adler and the Ethical Culture Society. In 1890 the society launched the *International Journal of Ethics* with Royce as founding editor in charge of theoretical ethics. The first issue contained his stinging and soon notorious review of Abbot's new book, *The Way Out of Agnosticism; or, The Philosophy of Free Religion*.

Royce's penchant for controversy had by no means been abated by his breakdown. Especially in his thirties, the Mephistophelean strain in him ran very strong, and recognizing it, he once described himself, quoting Goethe, as the *"Geist der stets verneint."* His feud with Abbot, quickened perhaps by envy on both sides, erupted with Royce's bitter denunciation. Abandoning the gentle satire of his earlier review, Royce accused Abbot of carelessly, if unconsciously, plagiarizing his "American theory of universals" from Hegel; at best his system was Hegelian without the subtlety of the original. In his conclusion Royce seemed intent on destroying Abbot's reputation:

> Results in philosophy are one thing; a careful way of thinking is another. Babes and sucklings often get very magnificent results. It is not the office of philosophy to outdo the babes and sucklings at their own business of receiving revelations. It is the office of philosophy to undertake a serious scrutiny of the presuppositions of human belief. Hence the importance of the careful way of thinking in philosophy. But Dr. Abbot's way is not careful, is not novel, and, when thus set forth to the people as new and bold and American, it is likely to do precisely as much harm to careful inquiry as it gets in influence over immature or imperfectly trained minds. I venture therefore to speak plainly, by way of a professional warning to the liberal-minded public concerning Dr. Abbot's philosophical pretensions. And my warning takes the form of saying that if people are to think in this confused way, unconsciously borrowing from a great speculator like Hegel, and then depriving the borrowed conception of the peculiar subtlety of statement that made it useful in its place,—and if we readers are for our part to accept such scholasticism as is found in Dr. Abbot's concluding sections as at all resembling philosophy,—then it were far better for the world that no reflective thinking whatever should be done. If we can't improve on what God has already put into the mouth of the babes and sucklings, let us at all events make some other use of our wisdom and prudence than in setting forth the "American theory" of what has been in large part hidden from us.
>
> I speak plainly. Moreover, I give this work a treatment whose minuteness is wholly out of proportion to the value of the book criticized. Were I writing for expert students of philosophy, this paper would have been much briefer. But I write for the general reader, as well as for the expert. And, I repeat, nothing less than the foregoing fulness and plainness of speech is due to Dr. Abbot's rank as a public teacher, and to his well-earned reputation as a man who wants to

advance the cause of sound religion. That cause, by his practical labors, as editor and counsellor, by his personal devotion to high ideals, by his heroic sacrifices in the service of duty, he has long indeed advanced; and I trust that he will very long continue to do so. But if we will philosophize in public, we must be content to be judged by formal criteria of a very impersonal sort. If not every one that saith Lord! Lord! is a good servant of the Lord, surely it is equally true that not every one who preaches a lofty creed and lives up to it can give even an American theory of why he holds it. And, in judging of the actual work of philosophical writers, we must lay friendly esteem aside in so far as it is necessary to do so for the cause of the "greater friend." In brief, in estimating these matters of the accuracy and fruitfulness of our reflective thought, we must show no mercy,—as we ask none.

The "Abbot affair"—as it is usually called—was exacerbated by the fact that *The Way Out of Agnosticism* was a revision of lectures that Abbot had given at Harvard as Royce's substitute in 1888. Though Abbot had denied all deliberate intent to provoke a controversy, it is clear that he saw Royce as his special enemy. Writing to a former student in November 1889, while the book was being serialized in the *Ideal*, he apologized for the shortcomings of the lectures, adding, "It was no fault of my class in Phil. 13, if they could not take in the tremendous meaning and strength of the argument I outlined: they had their heads stuffed beforehand with too much philosophical nonsense." A month later Abbot's exaggerated confidence and feeling of persecution reached a point of frenzy:

> If I can get a *fair hearing* from the *cultivated classes* at home and abroad, I know that there is a great future for this thought. I labor under the great disadvantage of not holding an *academic position*, and of being a mere *private American*. . . . No friend is at my back—I am only a lonely thinker tabooed in my own country; but I *know* the transcendent value of my thought, its coherency, power, and adaptation to the age.

Obviously Royce's review, as all were soon to realize, struck Abbot when he was psychologically, if not intellectually, defenseless.

Like *Scientific Theism*, *The Way Out of Agnosticism* was published by Little, Brown and Company at Abbot's expense. The book appeared in February 1890, and by October, when he first reacted to Royce's review, Abbot was furious. "Did you know," he wrote to his friend George Iles, "we have a 'liberal' Pope, qualified to excommunicate any and every one from the 'liberal' church and to give 'professional warning' against your poor friend to the 'liberal-minded'? If not, read Prof. Royce's unspeakable review of my last book in the first issue of

Adler's *International Journal of Ethics*. Really, I did not know we had so arrant an ass in America." In other letters Abbot described the review as an "impertinent article . . . a literary outrage." "Royce oversteps the limits of legitimate book criticism, when he presumes to denounce me as an impostor or advertise me as a quack—which is what he in effect does. It is a cheap way of feigning to answer arguments beyond his ability to master."

As his first move Abbot wrote a strongly worded reply entitled "Dr. Royce's 'Professional Warning,'" which he sent to the journal's managing editor, S. Burns Weston, on January 21, 1891. Abbot admitted that his article was "severe and caustic," but in light of Royce's "most malicious and slanderous" review, he felt that the journal would be duty-bound to publish it. Though the reply proved to be more abusive than the review, Adler and Weston agreed to publish it if Abbot agreed to remove the offensive language and if Royce were allowed to print a rejoinder in the same issue. Royce prepared his answer—"The 'American' and the Hegelian 'Theory of Universals'"—in which by means of parallel quotations he demonstrated that the two theories were substantially the same.

Abbot tentatively accepted the editors' first condition but was wholly opposed to the second, and his fury was rekindled when he learned that they insisted that his reply be approved by Royce before publication. Writing to Weston on February 19, he repeated his demand that the reply must be published in an issue separate from the rejoinder and rejected the idea that Royce should have any editorial authority. "I am thoroughly disgusted with this man's impudence, cunning and cowardice, and decline to have any dealings with him whatever. In this matter his is the libelous assailant, and I refuse to have him manipulate my defense. In this article, he wound up with the declaration: 'We must show no mercy,—as we ask none.' But here he is, refusing to stand up and take his whipping like a man."

A few days later he wrote again to say that upon further reflection, he had decided to permit no rejoinders at all. On February 26, Adler and Weston made a new offer: they proposed the arrangement of a special supplement in the April issue that would print the reply with Royce's rejoinder and, if Abbot wished, his final brief retort. Thus, Abbot was to have the last word but, Adler insisted, since Royce was in charge of theoretical ethics, nothing could be published in this department without his consent.

In the meantime Abbot had consulted an attorney, Robert M. Morse, about the possibility of bringing a libel action against Royce. Though Morse advised that the case was weak, Abbot was not convinced. During the spring, he began writing a pamphlet entitled *Professor Royce's Libel: A Public Appeal for Redress to the Corporation and Overseers of Harvard University*, and on June 11 he met with Louis Brandeis, then a Boston attorney, for advice on the legality of his position. Brandeis, as it turned out, was related to Adler by marriage, and there-

fore he was interested in finding a peaceful solution. A meeting was arranged
between Abbot and Adler, but neither was inclined to alter his stance. By that
time Royce had also retained a lawyer, Joseph B. Warner, a move that Abbot
took as a sign that Royce was "evidently scared out of his wits." In his letters
and visits to Abbot, Warner pleaded for restraint, suggesting that the reply be
printed in July without reference to libel. To this request for changes, Abbot
answered: "Not a comma." On June 20, Abbot informed Warner that Adler had
definitely rejected his article. Abbot also enclosed the following card, which he
demanded that Royce sign:

165

> I. I admit that I have no knowledge whatever of any "extravagant pretensions"
> made by Dr. Abbot "as to the originality and profundity of his still unpublished
> system of philosophy."
> II. I admit that Dr. Abbot did not consciously or unconsciously "borrow his
> theory of universals from Hegel" or "sin against the most obvious demands of lit-
> erary property-rights."
> III. I unconditionally retract my "professional warning to the liberal-minded
> public concerning Dr. Abbot's philosophical pretensions," acknowledge that it
> was groundless and unjustifiable, and apologize to Dr. Abbot for having published
> it in the *International Journal of Ethics*.
> IV. I authorize the publication of this retraction and apology in the next num-
> ber of the *International Journal of Ethics* without note or comment.

If Abbot seriously expected Royce to endorse this retraction, he was, of
course, mistaken. Instead, Royce replied that though he could not alter his
opinion of Abbot's book, he would apologize publicly for the tone of his review
and for the personal injury it had caused. Rejecting this offer as "self-conceited
officialism," "insolent," and "obtuse," Abbot proceeded with his demands for
total vindication. In October, with the advice of a new lawyer, he published his
pamphlet and sent copies to the university's governing boards.

At that point Charles Peirce joined the controversy. Though he had not read
either the book or Royce's review and though he felt that Abbot's views were not
particularly original, he did agree that the statement that they had been borrowed from Hegel was ridiculous. "I have long had the opinion," he told Abbot,
"that Royce is one of the large tribes of philosophical blunderers." Delighted to
gain so powerful an ally, Abbot welcomed Peirce's offer to write something in
his defense. On November 12, the *Nation* printed a letter from Peirce, charging
that Royce had libeled Abbot and that he had used unfair means to stifle
Abbot's reply. "Thus, it was a brutal, life-and-death fight from the first. Prof.
Royce clearly perceived this. . . . Dr. Abbot, on the other hand, stood like a
baited bull, bewildered at such seemingly motiveless hostilities."

Peirce's letter brought James into the fray. Taking Royce's side, as did Palmer who found Peirce's letter "absurd," James wrote to his brilliant, eccentric friend:

> If you knew Royce as I do, and had seen the whole evolution of his side of the business as I have, you would see how simply comical is the notion of there being any element of intellectual rivalry with Abbot in his attitude. The animus of his article was *objectively philosophical*; but being a man of mass he can't do a thing briefly or lightly, and "laid it on" thick enough to justify a sore feeling on Abbot's part. Abbot's view that its animus was personal persecution is however simply silly; and I am surprised that you should treat it as plausible. . . . For my own part, Abbot's soreness is excusable, but his rabid personal tone is simply pathological. . . . I have tried my best to have rational discussion with him. But when objection is made to any of his views, he stops the conversation by saying that he doesn't expect any of his contemporaries to understand him.—Posterity however will "do him justice." His philosophy surely must seem to you the scholastic rubbish which it seems to me and which it seemed to Royce. Why not speak out one's mind about such rubbish?

At the same time James printed a public answer to Peirce's letter in the *Nation*. Leaving aside the issue of Abbot's originality, James argued that Royce was not guilty of libel or unfairness: the journal had offered Abbot a reasonable opportunity to defend himself, but he had rejected it; and further, James insisted, any author should expect that his critics will handle him without gloves. When Peirce was presented with a copy of this letter two days before its publication, he wrote to James with some irritation:

> I am sorry you should see fit to sneer at my impartiality. . . . I know the two men equally well. I was a classmate of Abbot's, but saw little of him, & his manners were always forbidding. I have been told Royce's manners are also bad; but I have never felt it. Royce is about the only person who ever paid me a compliment in print. In the branch of philosophy which I have most studied, logic, I think on the whole better of Abbot, since things he sees that Royce does not are more rarely discerned. . . . But your treatment of the principal question, that of the propriety of criticism like Royce's, I will say to you in secrecy that it seems to me a little sophistical. . . . [Royce] makes much of his [Abbot's] bad taste in regard to style and capitals, etc. He repeatedly adverts to his pretentiousness. He practically accuses him of ignorance in philosophy. His *general tone*, which cannot be denied, is that of contempt. That there may be no mistake after *much* of this he at length says he "warns the public" against him! What can this mean? . . . Now *will Royce say he did not mean this?*

In the war of letters Royce also caught a piece of crossfire from John Dewey, then on the faculty of the University of Michigan. Writing to James in response to the *Nation* exchange, Dewey spotted a moral inconsistency between the high aims of idealism and the bad ethics of reviewers:

> The unfortunate personal direction which the Abbot-Royce controversy has assumed suggests one remark which fortunately is not personal. Both Mr. Royce and Mr. Abbot profess to believe in the organic character of intelligence—which means (if it means anything) that the individual *qua* individual is the organ or instrument of truth but not its author. If this is so, a book can only be one thing: a piece of news, an event in intelligence. This discussion of the book is then (*per* theory) an attempt to place the book as this piece of news, as a contribution to intelligence, just as the discussion of a political event is its placing in its outcome or relationships. And yet—and yet! Or is philosophy, at least idealistic philosophy, a Pickwick Club where things are true in some special sense—where the organic character of intelligence is true *as philosophy*, but not in specific action? . . . This inquiry has been bottled up in my mind so long that it now discharges at you as the most convenient target. Besides you at least have never joined the Pickwick Club.

The "Abbot affair" had entered its second year of controversy. Throughout this time, Royce had refrained from public discussion of the matter. But when James showed him the Peirce letter, he decided to write at length, defending the journal's policies and the justice of his review. He was satisfied on two points: first, that the journal had given Abbot a fair chance to reply, and second, that the book was carelessly and unconsciously Hegelian. As for the propriety of his manners, Royce was also convinced that plain speech in criticism is essential to philosophical progress, but on the other hand, he regretted, now more than ever, the pain that he had caused. Somehow Royce had supposed that he "was meeting an armed man," who would receive a stern judgment as "a tribute to his high mindedness." "The result has proved that I was assailing a man of the most sensitive tenderness."

Other letters in the *Nation* by Warner and Abbot added fire to the quarrel. In January the Harvard Corporation and the Board of Overseers met to give "full consideration of the case," deciding that "official action in such a matter should not be taken by the University." Before that, President Eliot wrote to Abbot to give his private impressions of the controversy:

> Dr. Royce's review has, to my thinking, an undesirable tone throughout. It is intended no doubt to be amusing; but it seems to me below the dignity of the subject and not respectful enough towards you as an older scholar in his own

Department. I believe this, however, to be the result of an error of taste and judg-ment on his part, and not the result of unkind or envious feeling. He is himself hearty, comfortable, successful and thick-skinned; & is not disquieted by adverse criticism, or even by ridicule. He has experienced a great deal of both, and is by no means disposed to take shelter from either. He, therefore, does not weigh his words with sufficient care. . . . Your appeal to the two Governing Boards of the University seems to imply a desire for some academic censure upon Professor Royce. I cannot but think that the great importance of a perfect academic free-dom for Professors, with both tongue and pen, must have momentarily been obscured in your mind. This freedom seems to me about the most precious thing in Harvard University.

Officially thwarted, Abbot shot his final round at the university in a second pamphlet, *A Public Remonstrance Addressed to the Board of Overseers of Harvard University: Is Not Harvard Responsible for the Conduct of Her Professors as well as of Her Students?* The board merely received the document and ignored it. Thus, the duel ended.

John Chapman ridiculed the whole affair with a burlesque closet drama entitled *The Two Philosophers.* It was, Chapman's subtitle says, "a quaint, sad comedy." In some respects, however, the concurrent and subsequent events were even sadder. On November 23, 1891, as the affair was reaching its climax of publicity, Royce's mother died. With characteristic reticence, he suffered his grief in silence. Palmer went to him and remarked sympathetically that it must be hard to take two blows at once. "No," Royce replied. "Each is bad, but there is a gain in having them together. They lean up against each other, and when I become sore over one, the other gives change." Except for this, Royce emerged from the conflict without visible scars, but Abbot was ruined.

As the years passed Abbot grew progressively more isolated and embittered, giving all his efforts, till the very end, to his last book, posthumously published, *The Syllogistic Philosophy; or, Prolegomena to Science.* Among his many hysteri-cal fantasies, Abbot was morbidly fixated on the third year of each decade. His brother had been killed at Gettysburg in 1863, his father had died in 1873, his mother in 1883, and his wife in 1893. On October 23, 1903, the tenth anniver-sary of his wife's death, Abbot went to her grave and committed suicide.

While the "Abbot affair" was raging, the controversy over the seizure of California continued in the pages of the *Century Magazine.* By comparison, this affair was less notorious, but still it had its vexations. As part-time editor, Royce corrected a few misunderstandings; as contributor, he published new docu-ments supporting the conclusions of *California* and answering the objections of his critics. In the first of these, "Light on the Seizure of California," Royce attempted to show that there was no "race" by the English navy to seize

California. The threat of such a plot had always been one of the main points in Frémont's defense.

Further evidence against Frémont was provided by the papers of Rear Admiral John B. Montgomery. As commander of the *Portsmouth* anchored in San Francisco Bay during the summer of 1846, Montgomery received letters from Larkin and Frémont. In "Montgomery and Frémont: New Documents on the Bear Flag Affair," Royce used the letters to demonstrate that no one in northern California outside Larkin's circle had any information about the Mexican War before the first week of July. The point was crucial, for Royce's old friend William Carey Jones had argued that Frémont's hostilities were quite possibly spurred by his knowledge that the war had actually begun. On the contrary, the documents showed that Frémont had joined the settlers at Sonoma more than a week before he could have known about the war. Worse still for Frémont's case was his candid denial of having any private instructions beyond Larkin's peaceful mission. On June 16 Frémont had written to Montgomery saying that "the nature of my instructions and the peaceful nature of our operations do not contemplate any active hostility on my part even in the event of war between the two countries." He further announced his decision to abandon explorations and move his party back to Missouri. These documents merely added new weight to Royce's already settled conviction that Frémont was a liar and that he had acted deliberately against his instructions.

Still Royce was baffled by the private motives hidden beneath Frémont's public life. A few months after the general's death in 1890, he published a summary article in the *Atlantic Monthly*. It was, Royce said, "the most cold-bloodedly cussed thing that ever I attempted." But in contrast to Royce's attack on Abbot, his "Frémont" was gracefully, if aggressively, executed. Maintaining that Frémont's reputation depended wholly on his role as "Conqueror of California," Royce summarized his evidence, arguing that the feat had been accomplished through duplicity and disobedience, and that Frémont's role in the conquest was actually insignificant. Frémont had become a romantic legend, a fictional hero, like one of Arthur's knights who had "escaped from a book, wandering about in the real world when he was made for dreamland." Recalling his meetings with Frémont, Royce wrote that he presented the surface impression of a "charming and courtly manner"; he was thoughtful, gracious, self-possessed, but behind the mask lay some "deep purpose [which] seemed always to have remained in reserve." Why, Royce wondered, had Frémont turned his life into a fairy tale? His deeds were known, but his motives, with the rest of his personality, were hidden. "And yet, after all, one whose destiny was so marvelous, so shadowy in its splendors, so obscure in its intrigues, so paradoxical in its contrasts between truth and fiction of the whole, will very long remain a puzzle and a delight to his history-reading countrymen. Of his true character, I insist, I can form only this halting and problematic estimate. . . . The real man behind that public life it is that I find so curious and baffling an enigma, as all others have found him."

Royce expected that his essay would "make some people wroth." If so, it did not provoke a public outcry. On the other hand, his quarrel with the Frémonts reached a new stage with the posthumous publication of the general's "The Conquest of California" in the April 1891 issue of the *Century Magazine*. In the essay Frémont finally admitted that he had known about Larkin's mission from the beginning, but he also defended his actions by appealing to the historian George Bancroft, who had been secretary of the navy under Polk. In a series of documents, dated September 1889, Bancroft insisted that only he among cabinet officers had authority to issue orders to armed forces on the Pacific coast at the time of the conquest, and that Gillespie had been instructed to let Frémont understand that he had a free hand to take possession of California.

Seeing that Bancroft's testimony, though given forty years after the event, added a "rather factitious weight" to Frémont's defense, Royce assembled his evidence for a final retort. He felt that Bancroft's statement was inconclusive and that new evidence could show "my old indictment to be stronger than ever." Appealing first to Johnson and then to Scudder for space to print his rebuttal, Royce promised that only "a very brief statement" would be needed "to set the thing at rest for all future students." Furthermore, he hated "to see what the less-informed public will regard, in many cases, as a conclusive refutation, go unmentioned, at the very moment when my own view is so near its final confirmation for all who are well-informed." Neither the *Century* nor the *Atlantic* was inclined to give more space to the controversy. Scudder suggested the *Nation*, which did print Royce's letter to the editor in May. Under the title "The Frémont Legend," Royce summarized the issues, showed that the general's final statement contradicted his earlier story, and proceeded to refute Bancroft's claims. A new document—Bancroft's instructions to Commodore Sloat in October 1845—indicated that the Departments of Navy and State were both pursuing a policy of peaceful intrigue, for Sloat was ordered to communicate frequently with Larkin and "do everything that is proper to conciliate towards our country the most friendly regard of the people of California." Royce concluded, therefore, that Bancroft's belated approval of Frémont was merely an unhistorical afterthought, and with obvious fatigue he ended by hoping that the legend would soon disappear. It was his last word in the controversy.

Family Interlude I

While these two controversies were raging, the Royce household prospered. A third son, Stephen, was born on May 26, 1889, and possibly to accommodate a household of five, the family moved to a larger home. A lot was selected in a newly subdivided tract known as the Norton Estate, and nowhere in Cambridge could the Royces have found a lovelier neighborhood. Bounded on the south by Kirkland Street, on the west by Francis Avenue and Harvard properties, and on the east by Somerville, the estate of thirty-four acres had been a wedding gift in 1812 to Andrews Norton, professor of divinity at Harvard, from his father-in-law, Samuel Eliot. An elegant house, Shady Hill, was enlarged and refenestrated so as to face Cambridge. In 1889 Norton's son, Charles Eliot Norton, another distinguished Harvard professor, parceled some of his land and sold it to friends. Royce chose a comfortable 90-by-117-foot lot, which became the site of his family's permanent home at 103 Irving Street. Lots to the south were purchased by Judge Jabez Fox, and two doors from the Royces, William James bought three parcels. The following year Charles Lanman built a house nearby in the same tract at 9 Farrar Street. Across the street from the Royces a house was soon built by the divinity professor and Unitarian minister, Edward Cummings, the father of the future poet, e. e. cummings. Over the years the Norton Estate has become one of the most remarkable neighborhoods in the United States. Never a demesne of the leisure class, it has always been a refuge for artists and intellectuals, people who work with their minds, and some of the most talented and accomplished men and women in the U.S. have found a home there.

On his meager salary alone, Royce could not have bought land that must have cost about $2,500 and built a house for more than $4,500. Once again he had help from Katharine's family, for the records show that on April 10, 1889, Norton sold the lot to Charles Head. Records also show that Charlie held a mortgage on the property for $5,000 and that for several years Royce made small payments toward the interest on the loan. It seems, however, that the debt was eventually canceled and the property was given to Josiah and Katharine by their generous relative.

On April 29 Royce filed a building permit. The house was constructed during the following summer and was ready for occupancy by the end of September. It was a substantial three-story cross-gabled house, designed in the colonial-revival style. The first floor contained a parlor, dining room, kitchen, and library; four bedrooms and a large nursery were on the second floor; three additional rooms, probably servants' quarters, were located above. A wood-frame exterior was softened by a broad piazza, second-floor balconies, and a sharply pitched roof. An ample yard provided room for gardens that Katharine would annually fill with flowers. In all, the home was large and functional, and unlike the Victorian styles of some neighboring houses, it had a candor suited to Royce's character.

A year and a half followed without vicissitudes in family affairs, but in 1891 the Royces were struck by ominous and tragic changes. They learned in May that Josiah's mother, seventy-two years old and living with Ruth in San Jose, had been accidentally knocked against a wall by a reckless man in the post office. She suffered a deep gash over one eye and general trauma. Within days her condition worsened. She became pale and weak; lost her appetite; had chills, palpitations, cold hands and feet, and shortness of breath. Although doctors assured the family that with proper rest and care Mrs. Royce would regain her normal vigor, she continued to decline, wracked by attacks of bronchitis. On May 27 she confessed that her eyes and nerves were too weak for much writing, though she tried to keep a stream of letters flowing to family members. Sarah had hoped to see Josie—"my precious Sonny Boy"—once more, but she was resigned that her hope might not be realized. As always, her trust in God was absolute.

Still weaker in June, having become almost totally dependent, she sent her son a final blessing: "The Lord's light and truth and love be with you, my darling boy." There was some discussion about her entering a sanitarium, but she remained till the end at home under Ruth's care. In the middle of the summer she felt better, and in September she briefly rallied. After that, silence. On November 23—three days after his thirty-sixth birthday—Josiah received a telegram from Ruth: "Mother died peacefully at nine fifteen this evening."

In July and August of 1891 Katharine decided to escape the Cambridge swelter and took the boys, with two servants, to a rented house in the Cape Cod village of South Yarmouth. Her letters to Josiah, who stayed behind in rooms at the Colonial Club, related news of Coco, Ned, and the baby, the social life of the community, birthday parties and clambakes. Four-year-old Neddy was beginning to be curious about language, the letters and words in newspapers, and his mother was sure he "shows every sign of being an apt pupil." When a violent thunderstorm frightened him, he said he would take an air ship to "Papa of the Angel to have that noise stopped." The baby Stephen threatened another child with ultimate doom: "I'll tell Mama not to love 'oo." It was, said the amused mama, "the worst threat he knows."

For Christopher, then nine years old, the vacation at South Yarmouth was a living hell. The local boys took cruel delight in tormenting and abusing him. One boy smashed the crystal of Christopher's watch by knocking him off his bicycle and pounding him. Another boy, when Coco and Katharine were out rowing, followed them, taunting and splashing them with water, laughing victoriously as they were forced to disembark. And again, one day a gang of about two dozen bullies cornered and threatened Christopher until an adult intervened and saved him from a beating. On other occasions he was the instigator of trouble. One afternoon he verbally abused the chief servant and cook, Margaret Hurley, by repeatedly yelling "Bad Margie!" and encouraging his little brothers to yell it. When he refused to stop, Katharine threatened him with boarding school and finally sent him to bed without supper. The next morning Christopher went to Margaret sobbing, kissed her, repented, and picked his mother a can full of blueberries as a peace offering.

More evidence of Christopher's behavioral problems surfaced about that time. The principal of the private school he attended, Jeanette S. Markham, gave a mixed assessment. In one undated letter she reported that Christopher was doing very well. A fast learner, notably in French, he was given special private lessons. "He seems ambitious and earnest," she wrote, "and is a satisfaction to everyone of us." However, she cautioned his parents against sending Christopher to a boys' school where students were rushed through their lessons and peer pressure was more intense. In another letter Miss Markham was troubled by Christopher's habitual tardiness. Though warned that he must appear at school on time, he continued to be late, so finally one day, after repeated tardiness, he was sent home. The principal noted that Christopher was often lost in daydreams, and she suspected that was the cause of his being late to school. Otherwise he was "most sweet and obedient." Miss Markham continued:

> The only way that he ever really troubles us is by being at times dreamy and absent-minded in the time that we give him to study his lessons. This causes us much anxiety because we earnestly wish to train him to work in the right way. On my part I am often possessed by painful doubts as to how much he ought to be interfered with when he is lost in his own thoughts, whether it is not harmful to him to be continually pulled up and made to locate a town or to work out a trick in an arithmetical problem. But to do this is the traditional duty of a teacher and the duty I try to do. If I am not right, perhaps you will tell me.

From our vantage point, we may infer that the child's dreaminess had passed beyond normal limits and that he was beginning to lose his grasp on reality.

In December 1891 Christopher was treated by a Boston physician, Dr. Hamilton Osgood, for nocturnal enuresis and a host of undefined behavioral problems. It was a most unusual case in that it involved the use of posthypnotic suggestion to counteract Christopher's bed-wetting. French researchers, followers of Jean Martin Charcot at the Salpêtrière in Paris and Hippolyte Bernheim at Nancy, had just begun in the 1880s to reclaim the scientific validity of hypnosis for psychotherapy. Bernheim was particularly a pioneer in the applications of suggestion, and it is clear from Osgood's two letters to Royce that both of them were conversant with Bernheim's theories and techniques. Royce might have learned about the new science of suggestion from William James whose *Principles of Psychology* (1890)included an important, up-to-date chapter on hypnotic phenomena. James wrote, "The most important class of post-hypnotic suggestions are, of course, those relative to the patient's health—bowels, sleep, and other bodily functions."

Also unusual as a therapeutic technique was the instruction from Osgood to Royce to act as a kind of associate practitioner:

> You must continue the treatment patiently at present. Christopher reaches a limitation a good deal this side of the depth into which I wish we could plunge him. Do not try to force that barrier but strictly suggest that he will tomorrow go deeper & that he will sleep longer. During hypnosis use argument, persuasion and command. "You love *me*, you are glad to obey Dr. Osgood's wish—*therefore*, you will abandon this habit. As your father I forbid it & Dr. Osgood wishes me to do so etc."
>
> While he is naturally asleep, go to him and gently put yourself *en rapport* with Christopher and suggesting [*sic*] that he *cannot* wake, that now he is just where you can help him greatly. Then pressing lightly over the bladder, suggest that there will be no trouble, that power has come to him during sleep, that he will have *no desire* to make water unless he is wide awake, when he will at once get up.

Evidently the treatment was not entirely successful, though Osgood believed that some progress had been made. "Moral results seem undeniable," the doctor reported, whatever that means.

Those who really knew Christopher found him clever, talented, and bold, but still in a way, odd, vulnerable, and pitiful. He was a gifted and promising student, but withdrawn into a dream world. He was the defenseless cornered victim of ruffians, but he was also a little hero who once dived from the pier to rescue his helpless brother. Over the years Josiah and Katharine continued to hope for the best, clinging to a belief that all of Christopher's troubles would eventually pass, refusing to face the brutal truth until the early tragic end.

The Spirit of Modern Philosophy

Although the Frémont and Abbot affairs tended to divert Royce's energies, his professional life prospered. The lectures on modern thought, despite Royce's initial misgivings, were enormously successful. Immediately after the first lecture Richard Hodgson wrote,

> You're a d____ fool! I hear from Mrs. Dorr that you are afraid your first lecture wasn't a success. It was splendid. I spoke with several ladies briefly before I left—they were delighted. I talked with [Barrett] Wendell as we walked away together! He was amazed. I talked with Mrs. Jack Gardner yesterday—she was ravished. What in the name of thunder & the milky way do you mean?

When Palmer received complimentary tickets, he wrote,

> I am not sure whether I sh'd thank or blame you. . . . Even a Californian must be subject to the Category of Quantity, & six courses of Philosophy seems to me a sufficiency without adding a seventh. . . . I am coming down on Tues. night to see how you do it.

Royce repeated the course twice, published excerpts on Hegel and Schopenhauer in the *Atlantic*, and in 1889 settled arrangements with Houghton Mifflin for the publication of the entire series. He stewed over the title, but finally settled on *The Spirit of Modern Philosophy*. At the same time, plans to establish the *Philosophical Review* under the sponsorship of the Sage School of Cornell University promised to give Royce an influential vehicle for his latest theories. At the request of the journal's editor, Jacob Gould Schurman, Royce suggested that he might submit one of three articles: a study of Kant's development, an essay on the logical characteristics of a philosophical hypothesis, or something on the place of teleological conceptions in modern cosmology. On this last topic, Royce promised "some rather fresh shadings." Looking also ahead to his next book, he planned to write a study of the life and intellectual development of Goethe. Though this work, if begun, was never completed, Royce went so far as to arrange a contract with the Century Company to publish a series of six articles that would form the basis of a full-length biography.

Enlarging his activities at Harvard, Royce became, by President Eliot's appointment in 1890, the chair of the Faculty Committee on the Normal Course. Through this committee Eliot fulfilled his aim to expand the university's curriculum into teacher training. Royce accepted his appointment on August 25, and added a few reflections concerning the kind of program that might be devised. "There is," he insisted, "no such thing as a science of Paedagogy, just as there is no such thing as a science of business life, or of executive skill, or of marriage, or of domestic economy, or of life in general." The training of teachers should be a practical affair, involving primarily a series of "object-lessons." But further, he felt, a teacher should be a "naturalist, fond of mental life for its own sake, and delighting in the examination of its wealth, its mechanism, its dangers, its caprices, and its growth. To such a study, we might help to 'introduce' a young teacher (in the German sense of that word,—*'einleiten'*). As for a 'philosophy of education' in any other sense—the Lord deliver us therefrom." In the first issue of the *Educational Review* Royce developed these views further, and in November he presented the committee's report to the Harvard faculty. This report established a program of "the history and art of teaching" within the division of philosophy and led eventually after several administrative reorganizations to the establishment of the Harvard Graduate School of Education in 1920.

Clearly Royce had become an indispensable member of the Harvard community. That was made especially clear when, on March 28, 1891, he was offered the chair of philosophy at the new Leland Stanford Jr. University. Writing on behalf of that institution's benefactor, the incoming president, David Starr Jordan, specified a salary of $4,000 (increased to $4,500 twelve days later) with assurances that graduate programs, research materials, and opportunities for publication would be supported. At first Royce was tempted and asked Jordan for a fortnight to evaluate the offer. There was much to recommend the position. His salary would be increased, and he was, at last, willing to consider living in California where he and Katharine would be close to family and old friends. On the other hand, he distrusted Leland Stanford and questioned Jordan in detail about matters of tenure, academic freedom, and ultimate authority.

Royce had good reason to be concerned about these matters, for it was no secret that Stanford had been portrayed as the ruthless Alonzo Eldon in *The Feud of Oakfield Creek*. At first Jordan equivocated. He promised that he would not personally interfere with academic freedom, but perhaps there was a subtext in his vision of a university comprised of men with "virility and force," men loyal "to the work and to each other . . . men who will build—rather than critical men." When pressed, on April 26 in a letter marked "Confidential," Jordan admitted that Stanford had de facto control over the university. The charter provided that only the president could remove a professor, but Stanford, while alive, would be the sole trustee and could eliminate any program simply by vetoing its budget. Furthermore the founder's religious convictions—for example, the soul of man is immortal; the laws of the Creator are wise and beneficent— were written into the charter and would be important tenets in the mission of Stanford University.

By the time Royce received those chilling revelations, he had consulted with President Eliot and members of his department, presumably James and Palmer. All agreed that Royce was important to Harvard's future, and they urged him to stay. "These representations," he told Jordan, "have been at once unexpectedly strong in their friendliness . . . and have also been accompanied with promises, not of immediate, but of comparatively early and unexpectedly prompt promotion." Various financial obligations, including the encumbrance of a heavily mortgaged house, also held Royce in Cambridge. On May 7 he declined the offer, explaining that he had tried to make his decision "a matter of duty." "I seem . . . to owe a greater debt to the office that I now fill. That is the whole case." Royce did not bother to mention his objections to the precarious terms of the appointment or to the philosophical dogmas he would be obliged to defend.

Thus, for approximately a year and a half—from the autumn of 1890 to the spring of 1892—Royce was involved in a bewildering variety of affairs. Besides teaching his classes and attending to family matters, he lectured, wrote articles, served as editor of two magazines, did committee work, prepared for a libel suit, contracted to write a biography, rejected a prestigious chair of philosophy, damaged one reputation, destroyed another, and enhanced his own. No similar period in Royce's life shows so much activity, but surely the climax of this phase was the publication of his fourth major work, *The Spirit of Modern Philosophy*. Seeing the contradiction between the destructive and creative aspects of this period, Royce turned the whole thing into a joke. William Roscoe Thayer had teased him about the "Abbot affair," offering his service as a bodyguard or a second in a duel, and adding that if Royce meant to confess his sins to the Corporation in the Appleton Chapel, Thayer wanted a seat in one of the front pews. "The world has got so many more headaches than laughs from metaphysics, that it owes you a heavy debt." Royce answered by offering Thayer "a bit of commercial speculation":

Abbot, as you know, goes for me in November.—Chas. Peirce, a friend of mine, backs him up in the *Nation*. The controversy will now rage unchecked for a month. Jokes, squibs, objurations, fury, spite, envy, malice, evil-speaking, back-biting, rage, "professional warnings," "libels," shouts of "imposter," appeals to Corporations, courts, the Public, the Moral and the Divine and the Diabolical Law, will go on far into December.—Holy Christmas will bring a lull. But in January the *Journal of Ethics* will tear open the wounds of all half-recovered combatants, will pour in venom, and will arouse more moans, sobs, shrieks,—and cries of "no mercy asked or shown!"—Thus January will pass. In February—lo! my *Book* will appear, &, *sell like hotcakes*. Children will cry for it. Grocers will give it away with every ten bars of soap.—And then (speak softly!! Don't give the secret *out*!!)—*Peirce, Abbot, & I*, will divide the proceeds of the sales amongst us. Mind you—keep mum. But that's the contract. Libel me and I'll libel you, and the public will be green enough to buy.

In a much more serious mood Royce dedicated his book tenderly to Mrs. Dorr. "The lectures," he wrote to George, "are so largely hers, that I but render dues." Touched by the dedication, she wrote back:

One word at parting, one last word of love and thanks for all your goodness and friendship shown to me and mine—

I feel as if we were going forth on a real pilgrimage, out into the unknown, in search of the unknowable, out into the far regions whence come all the deepest soul searchings of our wonderful heredity.

For say what you philosophers may, in your deepest souls you know that our birthright *is* spiritual, and that, in spite of all material obstructions, thence we come and thither we go.

Though Royce depreciated his book, finding it "a halting and fragmentary thing," it was, of all his works, the most complete stylistic success, and therefore it remains also the most accessible of his books for the general reader. Like *California*, *The Spirit of Modern Philosophy* is history with a thesis: "You philosophize when you reflect critically upon what you are actually doing in your world. What you are doing is of course, in the first place, living. And life involves passions, faiths, doubts, and courage. The critical inquiry into what all these things mean and imply is philosophy." Thus, philosophy was for Royce what literature was for Matthew Arnold: a criticism of life.

Despite the book's historical slant, its most interesting and enduring material is to be found in the last four lectures where Royce suggested features of his own theory. Concluding his task as "mere chronicler," Royce brought his readers back to Kant.

He held that all judgment is essentially only an appeal to my own deeper Self, and that all knowledge depends on my unity with my deeper Self. This seems to me the profoundest truth of philosophy. What Kant did not make clear was what this, my deeper Self, is. . . . Who, then, is this Self, and what manner of life is this he writes in this book, itself merely a waif from the lost tales of endless time, just as the endless time also is merely an illusory form wherein the Self is pleased to embody and manifest this truth? Its illusory form is not wholly an illusion. For the Self is all that is, and his world is the chosen outcome of his eternal reality.

This position is clearly identical with that outlined in *The Religious Aspect of Philosophy*. Indeed the first two lectures of the second part of *The Spirit of Modern Philosophy* are hardly more than restatements of the argument for absolute idealism against the "unknowable" of naturalism. On the other hand, Royce's emphasis on "the deeper Self" gave that argument a different metaphor, and it was something more than a new image for an old idea. Previously the absolute had been an "all-embracing Thought," which Royce usually described as something *above and around* the finite consciousness; in *The Spirit of Modern Philosophy* the infinite mind was something profound *within*. Consequently Royce's argument on the possibility of error acquired a somewhat modified form. "You are in doubt, say, about a name that you have forgotten, or about a thought that you just had, but that has now escaped you. As you hunt for the name or the lost idea, you are all the while sure that you mean just one particular name or idea and no other." When you find the name or idea and recognize it, you might say, "Oh that . . . was what I meant all along, only—I didn't know what I meant." But, Royce insisted, you did know in the deep consciousness what the momentary self had forgotten. This simple experience illustrates Royce's argument that error is possible only if it is part of a larger truth. "The deepest problem of life is, 'What is this deeper self?' And the only answer is, *It is the self that knows in unity all truth.*"

Royce admitted that this version of his argument for the absolute lacked the more thorough proof of his earlier statement. In *The Spirit of Modern Philosophy* he was content to give only the barest outline of the argument and to refer his readers back to *The Religious Aspect of Philosophy*. But with the twelfth lecture Royce went beyond mere summary of earlier doctrines and brought to partial fulfillment the line of speculation that he had begun aboard the *Freeman* in 1888. As he had told James at that time, the new theory gave life to the "dry bones" of his "Universal Thought." Understandably Royce had been dissatisfied with the sterility of the absolute, for in the earlier work it exists primarily as a problem solver, a mind that merely possesses all truth and error. How it might satisfy emotional needs, *The Religious Aspect of Philosophy* does not make clear. But with the shift in emphasis to "the deeper Self" Royce found the means of understanding a broader range of experiences.

There are two ways of regarding experience, the outer and the inner. One is permanent, the other is fleeting; one is universal, the other is private. In Royce's terminology, these are the Worlds of Description and Appreciation. Descriptions are volitional and categorized; they can be reproduced at pleasure according to accepted forms of experience. I can, for example, describe my hat in terms of size, shape, color, and texture, but how my hat feels to me when I find it among others in a darkened cloakroom is indescribable. Descriptions, therefore, are "public property," and as such they belong to "the kingdom of natural sciences"; appreciations are "essentially dumb." "I can't tell you," Royce cited as a further example, "much about the curious minor feelings of vague depression that once followed, in my own case, an attack of influenza." Thus, so far, the World of Description seems real while the World of Appreciation remains illusory or, at best, confined to the arts and poetry. And yet, Royce maintained, the primacy of description is itself an illusion, for were we able to communicate directly with other minds by means of appreciation, the World of Description would become altogether superfluous. We value science, in short, because it affords an effective bridge between minds: useful but limited, finite, and mediate.

Also partial, for every description contains a primal appreciation. When I think of another human being, in strictest terms I can describe only an unconscious entity, "a quivering mass of molecules," but when I speak of my friend, I do not mean these facts, I mean his inner life. If I appeal to him as witness of my description, I refer to his appreciative self. I assume, in other words, that his experience has the same reflective content as mine, for without this assumption there would be no point of choosing him as my witness. And further, without a witness, descriptions are meaningless:

> Without the multitude of genuinely interrelated experiences, no true similarities, no describable universality of experience; without the facts of appreciation, no laws of description; without the cloud of witnesses, no abstract and epitome of the common truth to which they can bear witness. Destroy the organic and appreciable unity of the world of appreciative beings, and the describable objects all vanish; atoms, brains, "suns and milky ways" are naught.

Here then is an acknowledged world of appreciative selves, where each dwells apart in "monad-like privacy," in "windowless isolation of momentary consciousness." And yet within this seemingly unintelligible world, descriptions are made, witnessed, and verified. How is this possible? Idealism answers: "The reality that I attribute to my friend, the genuine external existence . . . ,—all this is unintelligible except in so far as one recognizes that we seemingly isolated and momentary beings do share in the organic life of the one Self." Thus, the absolute is implied by a paradox: this is a world of encapsulated minds, yet this is also a world of shared experiences. We live behind the walls of reflective consciousness, but within the walls we are united.

So the World of Appreciation is not composed solely of impulses and vague feelings. In the deepest sense it is the world of ideals, and like the World of Description, it has its own principles and categories. Among these are self-consciousness, interrelated interests, mutual dependence, objective worth, and purpose. Who am I? What is my relation to my fellowman? What are my true aims? In terms of description these questions are meaningless, but the appreciative self, as part of the universal consciousness, finds answers to the extent that it gains a fuller sense of its identity. "The more of a self I am," Royce insisted, "the more and the deeper do I know its truth." So too the World of Appreciation is the realm of freedom. As unconscious beings we are driven by external forces and irrational impulses. But with self-knowledge, with full awareness of the deep complexity of the inner life, we are free to choose. "In so far as we are clearly conscious of our own choices, we ourselves are part of the world of appreciation. We are then, ourselves, conscious bits of the Self. Our wills are part of his freedom. And hereby we too are free." This "deeper Self," the Roycean absolute, is not a spirit remotely detached from the world, but an active will that expresses its aims in the free choices of conscious beings.

This doctrine answers naturalism. Physical law, evolution, and determinism, belonging to the World of Description, are the phenomenal "notes" but not the "melody" of life. Royce steadfastly maintained that science is essentially myth that imperfectly symbolizes the universe. But an appreciation of history in terms of evolution involves, even hypothetically, an imaginative transcendence of time. We live like those who stand on the shore of a limitless ocean of appreciation; we describe a pebble and a wave or two, but know that vast depths, solitudes, and storms remain beyond unexplored. The meaning is seen only as waves breaking on the beach, as evidences of a restless life. We call these waves evolution, but to the extent that we are in touch with our own depths, we know also that much remains undescribed.

The same doctrine provides insight into the problem of evil. In the final lecture Royce turned to "the great 'antinomy' of the spiritual world." On the one hand, evil seems to be an inevitable consequence of the finite will. This is Schopenhauer's point, that life involves endless care, longing, and strife. But on the other hand, the absolute has chosen this imperfect world as the expression of its total perfection. There are several ways of resolving the paradox. The simple optimist seeks to deny, in Panglossian style, that evil is real; at best he toys with simplistic theories of human perfectibility, or at worst he uses his faith as a justification for active immorality. There is also the mystic's resignation, which accepts the reality of finite evil but refuses to consider it a problem. The infinite perfection of the divine, the mystic believes, excludes us; we must endure and if possible ignore our misery while meditating on God's transcendent goodness. Though the two views seem to represent opposing moral philosophies, they actually agree in depriving life of any ethical significance. "What we do here," Royce observed, "our work, our purposes, our problems, our doubts, our battles, all these things have for the mystic as for the optimist no essential meaning."

Struggle, even foredoomed and tragic struggle, is the key to Royce's solution. "We win only by risking defeat; we have our courage only by conquering our fear; we can triumph in life only by transcending the pains of risk and of conflict even while they are in us and part of us." But why should life be a struggle? Would not the world be better without it? No, Royce answered, good is the product of moral conflict: only the sinners can be saints; only by defeating evil can we make claims on the realm of the good.

Finally, Royce broached the subject of the ultimate tragic vision. "The worst tragedy of the world," he observed near the end of his lecture, "is the tragedy of the brute chance to which everything spiritual seems to be subject amongst us—the tragedy of the diabolical irrationality of so many among the foes of whatever is significant." It is this "capriciousness of life" that leads men to pessimistic despair. Royce had no easy solution. Much of life is indeed irrational and capricious; we must live thus just as we must stand before the ocean of appreciation. But if idealism offers any insight, it is that God is our own true self. Our sufferings therefore are his; he is crucified in our flesh, and in us bears the sins of the world. "What in time is hopelessly lost, is attained for him in his eternity."

It is perhaps significant that the newest features of *The Spirit of Modern Philosophy* were outgrowths of Royce's mental breakdown. That experience, he had noted, was "edifying, instructive, and even fascinating." No doubt what he learned was a fuller sense of the mind in crisis, and that was a moral as well as a psychological lesson. Quoting Hegel, he wrote that true pessimism belongs to the man who "has once feared not for this moment or for that in his life, but who has feared with all his nature; so that he has trembled through and through, and all that was most fixed in him has become shaken." This is the experience of nothingness, and this is precisely how Royce had described his crisis. On his quest for health he had read James Martineau and been struck by the shallowness of an ethic that refuses to include the devil. Royce had, of course, always opposed this sort of superficial optimism, but he had never before been the devil's prisoner. Anguish, then, not merely a theorized pain, but engulfing personal anguish gave Royce his concept of "the deeper Self," showed him the emotional world of appreciation, exposed him to the tragedy of brute chance. Though he still held to his old ideals, he also now recognized the need to sink lower into the depths of despair.

Unlike his earlier books, *The Spirit of Modern Philosophy* was a commercial success. Published early in 1892, the first edition was nearly exhausted by the middle of March. Young George Santayana, soon to be one of Royce's severest critics, wrote a warm letter of appreciation:

> I have been waiting to thank you for your book, which I got long ago, until I had read enough in it to have some just sense of the value of the gift. I perceive now that it is much more than a mere record of your lectures, as we heard them; a thousand things that one overlooked or forgot in the hearing stand out in the printed page and stick in the memory. It is marvellous to me that you should have been able to write a book so full of enthusiasm and humanity in circumstances of such external pressure and distraction. I have read the appendices with special care, and feel much enlightened by them not only in regard to Hegel, but even in regard to Kant. Many things that are vaguely before one are not made really known until one comes upon the just and brief expression of them. It must be a great satisfaction to you to have brought into the world so attractive and inspiring a book, and I am grateful to you for having sent me a copy of it.

In the meantime Royce was giving a new series of nine lectures, "Some Recent Tendencies in Ethical Doctrine." "I suppose," he told Mrs. Dorr, "that another book may result." Though this expectation was not fulfilled, Royce did repeat a part of this series to the Summer School for Cultural Sciences at Glenmore, New York, in the Adirondacks.

The sponsor of this enterprise, founded in 1889, was a jovial Scotsman and minor philosopher, Thomas Davidson, a man whom James described as "a knight-errant of the intellectual life." He had come to Boston in 1875, but migrated to St. Louis where he taught Greek and became a convert to Hegelianism. Soon, however, he was attracted to the priestly philosopher Antonio Rosmini-Serbati, and by the time he returned to the eastern seaboard Davidson had dedicated his life to the perpetuation of the Rosminian doctrines of contemplation and service. Quixotic, robust, aggressive, he was also tender and open-minded; he was, in short, one of those "pluralistic idealists" that James always found irresistible. His friendship with Royce began in the spring of 1892 when Davidson first opened *The Spirit of Modern Philosophy*. The book, he said, is "lively, stirring, brightening . . . admirable . . . fresh & lucid," but he could not accept its basic metaphysical theory. "After all your most perspicacious statement, I do not see the slightest ground for believing that what I call my world is of my creation, or that, if it were, that would explain my consciousness of it." In answering this objection, Royce tried to clarify his position: "I don't mean that 'I *as unconscious being*' construct anything, but only that I *in so far as I am not now conscious of myself* am the true possessor of the outer or objective truth of things; i.e. my other or fuller and complementary consciousness is such a world-possessor."

Two months later, having finally finished Royce's book, Davidson wrote again, now stating his own metaphysics in opposition to "tragic" modern philosophy:

> If you said that all selves have a unity in something that is higher than any self, & that is apprehended by some faculty higher than self-consciousness, then I could understand you. That is the position of all true mystics, & the very meaning of mysticism, or God-consciousness. But such a position gives eternity to the individual "selves," & revokes the "tragic" element from life. That is my position. God is not the rest of me, or the whole of me: He is the source of me: He is the super-self self-maker.

Not surprisingly Royce answered by patiently explaining that "the seeming differences between your view and that of 'modern philosophy' can hardly be irreconcilable. . . . In fact I suspect that, despite endless differences in terminology, we cannot be far from agreement." In subsequent letters Davidson explained his fundamental opposition to rationalism. "Ultimate problems of human life," he insisted, "will never be solved by reason. . . . The fact is, it must be *acted* out, not *spoken* out."

184

At Glenmore, Davidson tramped through the woods, drank Scotch whisky, sang ballads, quoted Dante from memory, and talked endlessly about everything. Though Royce once sneered at "that noisy fellow," and though he had to exercise great patience in correcting some of Davidson's crude misunderstandings of *The Spirit of Modern Philosophy*, he too became a friend of the man if not of his philosophy. "I grew very fond of him," Royce told James. "I . . . sat up with him nights till we were both talked blind, and broke all the rules of his sacred community at Glenmore."

The Harvard Quintet

With his visit to the mountains, the success of his book, and the end of debilitating quarrels, Royce's life entered a new phase. A calm mood prevailed, as the energy that had sparked his feuds with Abbot and Frémont was channeled into productive labor. This phase, which lasted through the rest of the decade, culminating in *The World and the Individual*, was clearly evident by the autumn of 1892. As an outward sign of this change, at the end of August, President Eliot told Royce that he would soon be promoted to a full professorship. As a title, Eliot suggested "Professor of Metaphysics." Royce winced: this title, he admitted, "would be very painful to me, owing to the somewhat accidental and crabbed history of that word." He preferred the simple title "Professor of Philosophy." As a compromise they agreed on "Professor of the History of Philosophy," and in this form the nomination was sent to the Overseers in October.

For a moment it appeared that some members might use this issue as a means of reopening the Abbot affair, but the nomination passed without much discussion, and the appointment with an annual salary of $3,500 was approved in November. Writing a letter of thanks to Eliot, Royce summarized his first ten years at Harvard. "I am . . . like so many other bookish people, a pretty sensitive person; and accordingly I feel all the more, whether I show it or not, the large mindedness that has seen beyond my shortcomings, the patience that has borne with my incompleteness, the personal strength that makes life for me, as for so many other young men in this place, confident, cheerful, inspiring." In a letter of congratulations, Palmer wrote, "What a triumph it is! & what power it shows in him who had won it! Recall the risks you ran when you left California, the many hard years of poverty after your appointment. . . . It is superb! an ethical triumph, not merely a material one."

At the same time, beyond Royce's personal success, his department entered "the golden age of American philosophy." George Santayana was now on the staff as instructor, and Hugo Münsterberg was the newly appointed professor of psychology. With those appointments Eliot assembled his celebrated "quintet": Palmer, James, Royce, Santayana, and Münsterberg. But if they deserved that designation, they certainly did not always perform together in harmony. Indeed they were a group of odd bedfellows whose differences in background, temperament, and intelligence made each a striking contrast to the others. Palmer, the senior member and department chair, traced his family's heritage on both sides to seventeenth-century Puritans; James, the grandson of an Irish immigrant, who became a millionaire, was the son of a minor transcendentalist; Royce embodied the faith of California pioneers; Santayana was a transplanted Spaniard; Münsterberg had been imported from Germany. Each was unique and each placed a strong value on his individuality.

The students, according to Charles Bakewell, recognized them as characters in Dumas's *Three Musketeers*: "Royce, the all-knowing Athos; Münsterberg, the enthusiastic Porthos; Palmer, the subtle and diplomatic Aramis, always with some important plan in the making. James was the dashing, adventuresome D'Artagnan, while Santayana, who never quite belonged, was the remote and elegant Duke of Buckingham." You could tell the differences, Bakewell continued, by the appearance of their libraries. Royce's books spilled out of the cases on the floor; on his desk, piled with German works and periodicals, a scattering of loose manuscripts gave the impression of a book in the making. James's spacious library breathed the air of civilized ease; a small writing table in a corner proclaimed that scholarship was always subordinate to life. The desk in Palmer's room never showed more than a page knife and an inkwell; his books, like his mind, stood upright in their places and always maintained stoic order. "Oriental" was the word for Münsterberg's overfurnished library, which maintained its foreign identity as the workshop of one who had come to speak the truth to a nation of barbarians. The appearance of Santayana's library is not described, an omission that seems to confirm his distance.

Of the group Santayana was most mysterious. Like Royce, he had come to Harvard in 1882, but as a freshman rather than as an instructor. He had been born in Madrid in 1867, though by a peculiar set of circumstances he lived most of his life in and around Boston. During his undergraduate years, he absorbed Royce's philosophy, which he gradually came to distrust and finally to despise. "Royce," he remembered, "had a powerful and learned mind, and it was always profitable, if not pleasant, to listen to him: not pleasant because his voice was harsh, his style heavy, repetitious and pedantic, and monotonous preoccupation with his own system intolerable." Graduated in 1886, Santayana went abroad for two years on a Walker fellowship, and in Germany, he said many years later, he lost his faith in the sort of philosophy that Royce represented. Nevertheless, on his return he told Royce of his desire to write a dissertation on Schopenhauer. "The wise Royce shook his head. That might do, he said for a master of arts, but not for a doctor of philosophy." Royce suggested Lotze. Santayana still preferred Schopenhauer or even Hegel, but he took the professor's advice and set to work on what he soon felt was a tiresome and profitless task. In 1889 he received Harvard's fourth Ph.D. in philosophy, and in that year he also joined the faculty. Still, and throughout his tenure, he maintained a bachelor's independence, preferred student friends to colleagues, fashionable ladies to either, and in general viewed the world of Harvard Yard with Olympian irony.

Santayana and Münsterberg shared a feeling of being foreigners in the U.S., but in every other sense they were aliens to each other's interests. One was descended from Catalan aristocracy; the other was the son of a wealthy lumber merchant, a Jew converted to Christianity. One wrote sonnets; the other was dedicated to experimental science. Professionalism, which the Spaniard loathed, the German cultivated with a passion. Münsterberg's world was steeped in quarrels, hurt feelings, suspicions, and petty jealousies. Born in Danzig in 1863, he earned his Ph.D. under Wundt at Leipzig in 1885, and an M.D. at Heidelberg two years later. Established at Freiburg as a *Privatdozent*, he began to publish pamphlets showing his results in experimental psychology. Through these early papers, in 1890 he came to the enthusiastic attention of William James who was then correcting proof for *Principles of Psychology*.

Two years later James asked Münsterberg informally if he might be interested in joining the Harvard faculty in charge of the psychological laboratory and graduate instruction in that area. James explained the situation: "We are the best university in America, and we must lead in psychology. I, at the age of 50, disliking laboratory work naturally, and accustomed to teach philosophy at large, altho I *could, tant bien que mal*, make the laboratory run, yet am certainly not the kind of stuff to make a first-rate director thereof. We could get younger men here who would be *safe* enough, but we need something more than a safe man, we need a man of genius if possible." Münsterberg, James was convinced, was the man. The appointment would be a professorship for a term of three years, after which something permanent might be arranged. Within a few months all was settled, and in August Münsterberg, his wife, and children were sailing to America.

Their first months in Cambridge were hectic. The elaborate plans that Royce made for their lodgings proved "unideal, and faded like streaks of the morning cloud when once he began to warm the sky with his presence." Royce liked Münsterberg immediately, "but of course," he told Eliot, "the problem of making a foreign family comfortable is, for him and for me, a rather puzzling one." After two days of house hunting he got them settled in a "sad little house . . . where the rats do congregate, and daily do take counsel on his stairways to devour his tender infants." Münsterberg's teaching was "an immense success . . . and the lovely Frau (of whom we are all fond) spends her time in devising ways to induce the rats to bite at her traps, and in trying to make up her mind to be fond of tomatoes, and to pronounce *th* without being overcome with chagrin at having to stick out her tongue in the act. On the whole they are an ornament to Cambridge, and *very* lovable." Their lives were further saddened, however, by the death of Mrs. Münsterberg's father and by an attack of diphtheria that struck Münsterberg in February. Throughout these trials, mere preludes to a stormy career, Royce was their closest friend, unofficial guardian, and comforter.

In general Royce passed the academic year 1892–93 very quietly. He published two important articles, "The Implications of Self-Consciousness" and "The Knowledge of Good and Evil," wrote a large number of reviews, and gave a series of lectures, "Topics in Psychology of Interest to Teachers," in which he first explored the function of imitation in ego formation. He still, however, felt a little uncertain about the directions he wished to follow. The projected but unwritten biography of Goethe was set aside in favor of a new plan to translate Hegel's *Phänomenologie des Geistes.* James's publisher, Henry Holt, already had Royce under contract to edit a volume of selections from the Hegel work, but feeling that this "would be *only* a temporary text-book, soon, no doubt, to be superseded," Royce wanted to bring out the entire book.

Holt listened, hesitated, tested the market, but finally decided against the project. His antipathy to Hegel was clearly the decisive factor, for as he told Royce, the question involved a balance between the scholarly value of the enterprise and an anticipated loss of a few hundred dollars. "The answer to this is that if I were to devote that amount of money to the dissemination of philosophical ideas, they wouldn't be Hegel's. Such spasmodic reading and listening as I have done regarding him, haven't yet even made me aware that he had any; and there seems pretty strong evidence that if he had, he didn't know what they were himself." Throughout the negotiations, which were finally terminated in the summer of 1893, Royce scorned all commercial interests, an attitude that Holt understandably found irritating. "Dear old Royce!" he wrote to James in July. "He was in my office the other day professing that the one effort of his life was to 'keep free from the business virtues.' He has succeeded pretty well . . . , yet the free range of his 'philosophy' is not much hampered by such clogs as consistency, coherency and adaptation to an end. I kind of love the wambling cuss, nevertheless."

Royce was not, it seems, especially disappointed by the publisher's decision; he was chiefly concerned with teaching and departmental affairs. He missed James, who was in Europe on a sabbatical, but their companionship was kept alive with a bright and newsy correspondence. A large enrollment at Harvard kept Royce busy in the classroom, while outside he became the adviser to an assortment of "sorrowful hearts," including a young poet, and a nihilist. "Over these I brood and psychologize." The poet—Harvard had a bumper crop that year—deposited "the entire entrails of his spirit" in Royce's library. "And there they lie now, among other things of the spirit, waiting a quiet hour." The nihilist, a young Bulgarian named Stoyan K. Vatralsky, had escaped to the United States after several scrapes with the police. Later described as the "Tolstoy of Bulgaria," Vatralsky wrote poetry and propounded a mystic socialism. He appeared at Harvard with a thesis on Spinoza and was made a special student. To James, Royce wrote,

> He has read absolutely everything that is radical, and in Russian too, so that you can't refute him. He is already a terror of my life. After lectures he gathers round me, outstays all other questioners, and talks Darwin, Spencer, idealism, mathematics, socialism, everything till I flee. Then he accompanies me homewards. My brain whirls, I groan inwardly, I long for a little deep interstellar silence,—but in vain. At last, as I hurry and hobble along, hastening to be free, he says kindly "But I detain you." "No, No," I cry and to prove it take to my heels. The last I hear, as the spectre pursues me past Memorial Hall is: 'But I don't agree with Spencer, bud yed I do dink dat Indegration. . . .'"—At night, whenever the floors crack, I lie dreading the emissaries of the Russian police who, as I doubt not, are already spying on this ill-starred intimacy.

In his relations with his colleagues Royce exercised his new authority as a senior professor in the department by taking the lead in personnel and curricular matters. There was a ticklish situation with Münsterberg's laboratory assistant, Herbert Nichols, whose appointment was soon terminated. Writing at length to James, Royce tried to give a balanced evaluation of Nichols's qualities. He was a likable person—"brilliant, industrious, full of ingenuity and of ideas, learned in his way, and ambitious without limit"—but as a colleague and scientist, he was a "spontaneous variation." "He is an agonized and agonizing bundle of sensitivenesses, suspicions, wild and over-confident hopes, speculations, despairs, plans, self-assertions, apologies, and extravagant hypotheses." In short, Royce could not recommend even a satellite existence for Nichols in the brilliant constellation of Harvard philosophers. Perhaps, he added, Nichols would do better at a small college. Palmer and Münsterberg apparently agreed, and even James, who habitually sided with downtrodden waifs, concurred. "I entirely agree," he wrote Royce, "with all you say about his oughting to have an autonomous position in a smaller college. He is too cranky and crude on the side of his *allgemeine Bildung* for the fierce light that beats upon our professorial thrones in Harvard University."

Another minor but more amusing event of the year involved a skirmish between Royce and Palmer over the elementary course in philosophy.

Traditionally this course, which Palmer especially prized, was designed as an introduction to the principles of logic, psychology, and metaphysics. Coming to despise the course and feeling the power of his professorship, Royce hoped to effect a reorganization along historical lines with attention focused on the central problems of philosophy. "The Dept. met the other day," Royce told James in March, "I with heart on fire to kill Phil. 1, which I had this time grown to hate deeply, Palmer with the usual sacred desire to serve the eternal and to dish you and me." The meeting was also attended by Münsterberg, a noncombatant still weak from diphtheria, Francis Peabody, "timidly righteous . . . with the air of trembling hope," and Santayana, "who has suddenly grown to seem indispensable, to all the future work of the dept." Santayana and Royce condemned the course. Palmer listened to the arguments with "saintly calm," but threatened to take the issue to Eliot. As a compromise they agreed to keep the old course, but to let Royce set up a competing program of his own.

"My plan, you see," he told James, "is to lead to a breaking up of Phil. 1, which I intend to bleed so badly that it will be glad, another year, to be put out of its misery." He further urged James to have nothing to do with Palmer's course. "The President will write urging you to engage in Phil. 1. Be as firm as you can, and keep out of it. *Und wenn die Welt voll Palmers wär'—es soll uns doch gelingen.*" James was hugely amused by Royce's account and immediately sent a postcard in reply: "Next to living in the light of your dear eyes, living far eno' away to get such letters is the greatest boon life can bring me. I giggled so over it at my hotel bkfet. table this A.M. that they nearly put me out of the dining room.—But I am deeply sorry for this sinister intelligence it conveys, and have just written to Palmer to say that since the sacredness of Phil. 1 as the only portal has been violated by the erection of your new course he must count me out of it altogether."

The Psychosocial Ego

Though kept "in hard harness" during 1892–93, Royce was philosophically inactive. This academic year was, in fact, an interlude that ushered in a new phase of thought, giving a social dimension to his concept of the self. Anticipating this growth, he identified the needs of the present age in "The Outlook in Ethics," an omnibus review published in 1891:

> Let us suggest the unity of these varied tendencies of recent literature by means of a very obvious contrast that distinguishes our age from one former time of subjective analysis. . . . The principal ethical purpose of [subjectivism] . . . was to free the human subject from the unjust bondage of convention and authority; while

for us that aim is already, in theory, accomplished, and what we most need is to hunt out in a man's heart the passions that shall serve to tie him once more, and more clearly, to his fellows and to the social order.

The problem, as Royce came to see it, involves a distinction between the individual and individualism. In "Self-Reliance" Emerson had become the prophet of individualism, proclaiming that all truth and value reside in the primitive ego, "the aboriginal Self," that lies beneath the laminations of social experience; the poet, the philosopher, or the "representative man," Emerson had maintained, functions as mediator to liberate the self from social bondage. Royce too saw the importance of mediation, but for him social interaction performs the creative act that Emerson renounced. Self-consciousness, Royce insisted, results from social experience: whatever a person is, whatever it may aspire to become, it owes to the community. "Could he grow up alone with lifeless nature, there is nothing to indicate that he would become as self-conscious as is now a fairly educated cat." Now and for many years, indeed for the rest of his life, Royce devoted a major part of his efforts to the task of understanding the individual's social relationships.

The Columbian Exposition of 1893 gave Royce a platform. Proclaiming U.S. cultural maturity, the Chicago World's Fair sponsored a series of "congresses," in two of which—education and philosophy—Royce played central roles. He was a prominent member of the Advisory Council for the Philosophical Congress, and in that capacity he traveled twice to Chicago, in June to help with advance arrangements and in August when the meeting opened on the twenty-first. According to a report in the *Philosophical Review*, Royce was "constant in attendance, and ably seconded the chairman in making the discussions suggestive and profitable." His paper, "The Two-Fold Nature of Knowledge: Imitative and Reflective," was cited as one of two that "called forth especially lively interest."

Much impressed by the beginnings in social psychology made by J. Mark Baldwin, Royce became a convert to the view that the ego is formed, not given, as children discover their place in a historical and cultural setting. Newborns have no self-consciousness; this they acquire only by imitating the social consciousness. Ego formation, Royce maintained, is a social process; language, motor activity, customs, values—all in short that comprises the self is the result of imitation. The process goes on through life, and at each stage of development the private self is dependent on the social self. "When I feel particularly integrated with the social consciousness, when I can engage in successful imitations, my own identity seems particularly strong and I feel clearly in touch with reality; but when I utterly fail for a while to comprehend my fellows, I begin to wonder whether, after all, I am not myself mad."

In all previous works, including his most recent paper, "The Implications of Self-Consciousness," Royce had maintained that selfhood is attained by reflectively discovering itself in the world of thought. Without rejecting this conclusion, he now added a phenomenological—or as he termed it, a "teleological"—basis of knowledge. Reflection is rooted in imitation; viewed in terms of psychological development, the absolute expresses itself in the social order.

During the next two years Royce published a series of major essays in which, from different viewpoints, he examined the problem of self-consciousness and the imitative functions. The enormity and complexity of the problem led Royce into psychology, pedagogy, and aesthetics. To gather data, he asked the readers of the *Century Magazine* to send him their observations of imitation in infancy and childhood, and with Münsterberg's help he designed a laboratory experiment to test the importance of imitation in adult learning. During the summer of 1894 he spoke to the National Council of Education on the imitative functions in child development, and in March of the same year he delivered a paper to the Medico-Psychological Association of Boston, "Some Observations on the Anomalies of Self-Consciousness."

In this paper, published in the *Psychological Review*, Royce outlined a theory of self-consciousness and illustrated it with a discussion of mental illness. Personality, he maintained, implies a boundary between the ego and the non-ego: "If a man regards himself, as this individual Ego, he always sets over against his Ego something else, viz.: some particular object represented by a portion of his conscious states, and known to him as his then present and interesting non-Ego." Self-consciousness, in other words, is acquired through its contrast with social consciousness. Whenever this contrast is removed or weakened, personality tends to disappear; the typical delusive states and identity confusions of psychopathology are always associated with a loss of social consciousness. If it is true, then, that the ego depends on its contrast with the non-ego, the origin of self-consciousness must be found in the earliest social experiences of childhood.

Royce observed that the normal child leads two lives: in one he is naive, egotistic, unreflective, a bundle of appetites and passions; in the other he imitates, plays games, acquires language, learns the use of tools. Though the two lives are intertwined, only the second implies self-consciousness. Gradually the child's ego activities extend beyond the simpler forms of imitation: he acquires habits, adopts roles, absorbs values; he also learns to question, to rebel, to compete. Normal development implies, in short, a progressively more complicated structure of relationships between the ego and the other, a structure that grows steadily more internalized, so that whether the ego is at war or at peace, whether the non-ego is immediately present or represented by conscience, the self remains a social entity whose life gets meaning and sharpness of definition only by witnessing its mediating counterpart.

This theory and its application to mental disorders resulted in a striking, but unfortunately incomplete, anticipation of modern ego psychology. A decade before Freud, at a time when mental illnesses were traditionally viewed as resulting from lesions of the nervous system or from hereditary defects, Royce offered a psychosocial explanation of both normal and abnormal conditions. Royce had an impressive ally in James, whose *Principles of Psychology* had attacked reductive materialism, but still, though a scientific landmark, James's book merely analyzed the self into its constituents.

The value of Royce's theory rests in its attempt to give a unified conception of self-consciousness and its anomalies. Admitting the possibility that abnormalities of the ego can be explained from a variety of viewpoints, Royce insisted that delusive complexes involve the *"maladies of the social consciousness."* Regardless, in other words, of the presence of physiological causes, severe mental illnesses—hallucinations, paranoia, schizophrenia—all take the form of a conflict between the self and the other. The theory has obvious weaknesses, among which are a lack of clinical experience and of any suggestions for therapy. But as a philosopher's excursion into an undeveloped field, Royce's paper provided a basis for future work in psychoanalysis. His friend and physician, James J. Putnam, one of Freud's earliest defenders in America, was profoundly influenced by Royce's theory. As the most respected and enthusiastic publicist for psychoanalysis in the United States, Putnam repeatedly cited Royce's concept of the self to complement and sometimes to correct the views of orthodox Freudians.

Royce's interest in psychopathology is further indicated by his paper "The Case of John Bunyan," which he presented at the second annual meeting of the American Psychological Association in 1893. In Bunyan's autobiographical *Grace Abounding to the Chief of Sinners* Royce found illustrations of mental development. The case involved neurasthenia, irritated by a lifetime of nightmares and fantasies, the most painful of which was a dialogue between the sufferer and the devil. Bunyan was constantly tormented by an "other self" who tempted him *"to sell Christ."* The impulse became insistent, but, Royce noted, this alone cannot cause pain, for the state of health normally involves a variety of highly urgent impulses: to breathe, eat, sleep, and so forth. To result in suffering, the impulse must conflict with one's self-conceived relation to the environment. Skepticism, for example, is not inherently morbid, for the professional doubter experiences no pain; but when the religious man doubts—when, as in Bunyan's case, his thoughts are mocked by an inner voice—the suffering may become intolerable. Royce felt that too much attention had been given to the physiological and hereditary aspects of mental disorder; too much also had been made of the specific manias and phobias of psychopathology.

Focusing on the interaction between the self and its environment, Royce noted that Bunyan's tempter was an "inverted conscience" and that the dynamics between the positive and negative aspects of the self are among the most potent factors in personality development. In the normal state the child's presented with a perceptive and associative "overwealth," which, because it facilitates selection, is both useful and necessary. The child adapts to the environment, answers the call of insistent impulses, and assembles the elements of selfhood—a complex process that implies that he is reaching toward a set of aims, a relationship to the world. But despite the positive aspects of this process, the rejected fragments come together as a potential intruder into one's chosen plan of life. In a state of health, this intruder, Royce believed, is either repressed or harmlessly "segmented," while in abnormal cases it rises to challenge the positive self, and may, as in Bunyan's case, become uncontrollable.

However such crises are caused, they involve, then, a union of incoherence and resistance, or contradictory impulses to destroy the ego's adjustment or to banish the destructive element totally. Royce took hints of a possible resolution of the conflict from Bunyan's "cure." The process was threefold. First, by surrendering to the tempter, Bunyan entered a long period of melancholic despair. This means of escaping the crisis proved to be merely transitional, for gradually he came to recognize his tempter as a foreign element whose control over the positive self need not be final. Thus, understanding became Bunyan's second step toward recovery. The last step in the process was resignation, a slowly achieved ability to live at peace within the conflict. Surrender, understanding, and resignation—these, especially understanding, would eventually be Royce's means of coping with personal tragedy.

To develop the more philosophical aspects of the theory, Royce published two sequential articles in the *Philosophical Review*, "The External World and the Social Consciousness" and "Self-Consciousness, Social Consciousness and Nature." Originally proposed as a single essay in 1891, this contribution was postponed twice, and the first paper was finally delivered to the journal three years later as an outgrowth of a talk that Royce gave to the Princeton Philosophical Club in February 1894. The reason for the delay, an exceptional one for Royce, is indicated in a letter to the editor, J. G. Schurman: "My former intent was to send you . . . [an article] on Teleology. In front of that sleeping princess there has grown however so thick a forest of Causation that I must first, I find, hew my way through that, after the fashion indicated, but not developed, in my chapter on the World of Description & the World of Appreciation in my recent book. A paper on Teleology would then follow, in some later number."

The idea of externality originates in social consciousness. Such is the thesis of Royce's first essay. As an infant plays with his fists he is, in a sense, beginning to deal with external reality but, Royce insisted, this experience lacks one element essential to a mature concept: the assurance that the external world exists for other minds with whom we share a social relationship. To illustrate, Royce considered the doctrine that whatever is real must be determinate. Without criticizing the logic of this principle, Royce insisted that determinateness is based on verifiability, which in turn depends on social consciousness. The experience of something indeterminate is common enough—the loose change in one's pocket, the clicking of a ratchet. These, we say, are nevertheless real, *publicly* real, for we can count, determine, verify the items in experience. We can, in other words, convert an appreciative feeling into a description. What is meant by the external world, therefore, is whatever can be included in the social consciousness; the communal factor alone differentiates externality from inner experience: the statement "It is night" can be shared; "I am sleepy" cannot.

A child begins with a world of fascinating objects, the ideas of others which he hopes to possess, but gradually he learns that these are beyond him, that their *esse* and *percipi* are disengaged. This is the beginning of dualism. Though the child also learns that he and the other imitate common objects, he eventually recognizes the enormous gaps between experiences. What I and my friend witness must necessarily be different, yet the same. Here, Royce believed, is the source of the tertium quid—"the external object as it is for itself." Social consciousness is organized around the faith that there are objects that are not exclusively *mine* or *his*, but *ours*, and though this faith is epistemologically suspect, it receives concrete warrant from the fact that we are able to describe such objects with considerable success. Thus from the viewpoint of social psychology, dualism makes sense, but for a criticism of this conclusion, one must turn to philosophy.

The second essay outlines a "return from Dualism," collapsing the distinction between mind and matter. Here Royce advanced a chain of theses resulting in the startling claim that nature, like human experience, is "conscious, organic, full of clear contrasts, rational, definite." If self-consciousness depends on social consciousness, it follows that a belief in the reality of other minds, other experiences, cannot be denied without also sacrificing the ego. This social consciousness is manifested by "phenomenal expressive movements," which accompany and signify the inner life of other human beings: I watch a man eating and conclude that he is hungry. The expressive act of another is always witnessed in context, inseparably and contiguously connected to nature (the food he eats, for example), so that it is impossible to conclude the one set of facts (eating) is meaningful, and another set of facts (the food) is not. It follows, then, that if my fellow human beings are real, "the whole phenomenal nature-order" with which they are continuous is also real in the same sense, namely, "as inner finite experience." Traced outward to include all phenomena and backward to include even the dim evolutionary past, nature, by the principle of continuity, is seen always as a manifestation of the social consciousness. Nature, to be sure, does not speak to us, yet when we describe it, we mean no dead fact, but a facet of our ideal, socially manifold life. "A real being," Royce insisted, "can only mean to me other experience than mine; and other experience does not mean deadness, unconsciousness, disorganization, but presence, life, inner light."

As an implication of social consciousness, based only on continuity, this theory of nature lacks the force of conclusive proof. Admitting this, Royce acknowledged two objections: one insists that the proof goes too far, the other that it omits too much. To answer the first criticism, that nature as other experience exceeds the limits of human verification, he observed that such can be urged against any cosmology. Evolutionists, who might be expected to exert the greatest opposition to Royce's theory, commit the same fallacy when they assume that nature exists independently beyond human experience. What is it, then, that forces us to transcend? This, he maintained, is the sole issue, and to resolve it, he pointed to the peculiar psychological force of continuity, for if one denies the concept of nature as other experience, one forfeits also the whole chain of existence that leads to and includes self-consciousness. The second objection, Royce felt, is more cogent and interesting. A continuous system of experience implies a set of related processes, but an objector might insist, the theory fails to show the relationship between the worlds of human consciousness and the processes observed in nature. Charles Peirce, by his theory of "Tychism," had suggested that natural laws can be interpreted as gradually acquired habits. Though this analogy presents one parallel between the two worlds, Royce declined to accept it fully as a satisfactory explanation of the missing relationship. Not regularity, he insisted, but irregularity—not habit but adjustment—is the sign of conscious life. Where, then, with its habitual tendencies, does nature exhibit evidence that it adjusts to changing circumstances? The problem is difficult because man and nature exist on different temporal levels. A man will adapt to new conditions in a very brief period, but a planet may take millions of years to adjust its routine. The difficulty is compounded by the limits of our apperceptive span. This limitation, established by arbitrary and socially conditioned boundaries, makes it impossible for us to observe extremely quick or extremely slow changes. This fact, however, suggests a new hypothesis: *"Why may not just such facts be represented by experience which accompanies our own, and which is just as real as ours, but which is characterized by another apperceptive span?"* It is possible, in other words, that the physical world is a realm of life which exists within a vast apperceptive span, analogous to our own subliminal experiences, but which like them escapes our observation. By this hypothesis the doctrine of evolution can be interpreted as the beginning of a "universal sociology," which defines the social relationships among all finite beings and unites each individual, human and extrahuman, in the whole natural world.

The Conception of God

Despite the enormous accomplishments of his first dozen years at Harvard, Royce remained fairly obscure in philosophical circles. Few had paid him the compliment of opposition, and as he clearly understood, a philosopher's stature depends on attention, scrutiny, debate.

The long-delayed debate was arranged by George Holmes Howison, Mills Professor of Philosophy at the University of California. In 1889, Howison had established Berkeley's Philosophical Union, and from the first Royce had been a corresponding member. Though Howison and Royce had been distant friends since 1884, their relationship had been troubled by personal, professional, and philosophical rivalries. Like others, Howison had been thwarted in his ambitions for a Harvard professorship by Royce's youthful success. To be sure, Howison never reacted with the fury of Frank Abbot or Stanley Hall; still, to be superseded by a man who was more than twenty years his junior and whose manners were often characterized by a bluntness bordering on insult must have vexed the genteel and immensely dignified Victorian. Howison's tenderness won the sympathy of James who felt "almost guilty" about his preference for Royce, while Howison stewed privately over Royce's "needless disrespect" and "galling" criticism.

Royce, in fact, was sometimes ruthless in his exposure of Howison's blunders, and though both shared an idealistic outlook, Royce complained that Howison's thought was obscure and fragmentary, and that his "multipersonalitarianism" had failed to show that God was more than the individual or the collective selves of the finite world. Howison, on his side, felt that Royce's absolutism implied "the logical obliteration of the individual being." Still, both men appreciated the value of sharp contrasts, especially when opposing views confronted each other on the same platform, and to bring this about, Howison devised a plan that would acknowledge the importance of Royce's philosophy and also submit his views to the test of scrutiny. On September 13, 1894, he officially invited Royce to deliver the university's commencement address in May on some aspect of "philosophic evidence for the existence of God." To prepare for this address by the university's most distinguished alumnus, the Philosophical Union planned to devote a full year's study to *The Religious Aspect of Philosophy*.

On September 23, Royce thanked Howison for the invitation but explained that a commencement address in May would be highly inconvenient. Would a presentation either in February or at the beginning of the academic year in August be possible? Howison was sorely disappointed; everyone, he explained, wanted Royce for commencement, but when Royce insisted, Howison graciously relented. By October 11 all was settled. Royce would appear late in August to give not one address, but at least four of them on different and somewhat technical aspects of his philosophy. Howison warned him that the audience might be "very superficial"; there were a few "real philosophical students," but many would attend out of "primitive curiosity." "And yet you mustn't 'water' your address to the assembly *too* much."

Royce was especially interested in the possibility of speaking in his native state to an audience of trained thinkers. "After all," he remarked, "I confess that I am fairly tired of being so little *but* a grinder out of lectures in popular form. I long to meet at closer quarters students who like serious, business. The general public is good,—very good,—but alas one tires of the long distances that part lecturer and hearer on public occasions." As for the specific subjects, he planned the main address, "The Conception of God," as a restatement of his argument for the absolute. "The kernel of the book would remain unchanged as to its essence. But it is above all the method of the book that I should never repeat—a method that has led and will lead to many unnecessary misunderstandings." The most irksome of these misreadings was the view that Royce had argued for the absolute as a mere postulate. To correct the error, he planned to launch immediately into the crucial argument and to omit the preliminary and transitional stages of theory. "In brief, then," he told Howison, "I should, throughout the book, restate my case in a wholly new way; and I should say very much that my book left unsaid. In the light of what I should add, many would find my doctrine looking very different. The Thought-category would be still emphasized; but I should also lay stress on another element of reality, viz. the element that Fichte called *Leben*. The 'world of the powers' I should indeed respect no more than of old; but the interpretation of the Absolute would be more obviously teleological than, to many readers, it seemed then."

The academic year 1894–95 was full of absorbing work that brought several new experiences into Royce's life. Then he replaced Palmer as departmental chair for a period of four years; then also he initiated a soon famous and influential course on metaphysics. An ambitious undertaking, this course, according to the published catalogues, covered a full range of topics: "The fundamental problems of Theoretical Philosophy considered constructively.—The Problem of Knowledge.—Realism and Idealism.—The Problems of Causation, Freedom, Teleology, and Theism." Philosophy 9, as the course was numbered, which Royce taught throughout his remaining twenty years at Harvard, marks his gradual shift to the teaching of constructive theory in preference to courses designed along historical lines. The textbook was F. H. Bradley's *Appearance and*

Reality, published in 1893 and first noticed by Royce in the *Philosophical Review* a year later. He admired Bradley's work, seeing it at once as a similar but competing version of his own objective idealism, and for many years he struggled to absorb the book while resisting its shortcomings.

Under Bradley's influence, Royce broadened his concept of the absolute to include all "experience" as opposed to mere "thought." He approved of Bradley's way of reducing the world of appearance to self-contradiction, but felt that his constructive argument was obscure and confused by metaphorical language. The special defect of *Appearance and Reality*, Royce repeatedly insisted, was Bradley's refusal to develop the concept of self-consciousness: "The usual idealistic method of seeking in self-consciousness for the concrete and unmetaphorical instance of the true form of unity in variety has been deliberately rejected by our author. . . . The present reader can only insist that, carefully as Mr. Bradley has indeed examined the categories of thought and object, the categories which are more specifically those of self-consciousness have been treated by him with a curtness and an inadequacy wholly unworthy of his own skill and experience."

As Royce acknowledged, "The Conception of God" was composed partly with Bradley in mind; indeed the great emphasis he gave to the problem of self-consciousness during the middle 1890s grew out of his initial response to *Appearance and Reality*.

Royce worked on his California address and three additional papers—"On the Conception of Will as Applied to the Absolute," "On Some Aspects of the Empirical Psychology of Self-Consciousness," and "Considerations on the Metaphysics of the Individual Self-Consciousness"—during the year and finished them in July. All four papers, he told Howison, were restatements of how "the thing now lies in my mind" rather than mere defenses of the earlier doctrine. "I hope that these fragments,—more or less hot from the oven, would be better for your purpose than any pawing over such bits of cold victuals as your Union will have left after devouring my book, would be."

Royce planned his trip as a vacation. After thirteen years of academic success in the East, his old hatred of California had faded away. Now the prospect of seeing friends and relatives, of being celebrated by his alma mater, seemed delightful. "I anticipate a good time," he told Howison, "and shall try to earn my board." Preparations for the excursion were, however, disturbed by a family mishap. In June, just as he had finished his college work, Katharine broke her leg in a bicycle accident. Medically the fracture was not serious, but as a result Royce had to supervise a multitude of domestic chores, and since he was never a master in stewardship, the household reminded him of a dismantled ship. "Nurses, doctors, and the rest of the crew have passed in procession through the house, and as for me, in view of the natural capriciousness of domestic service at such times, I have had to 'keep a dog and do my own barking.'" The accident forced him to cancel his plans to visit Davidson in the Adirondacks, but he still held fast to his commitment in California. He set out during the middle of August and arrived in San Francisco a day or two before his scheduled appearance on the thirtieth.

Both in the life of Royce and in the history of the University of California, that event was a milestone. He alone among its alumni had achieved a national reputation in intellectual circles, and Californians to show their appreciation filled the Harmon Gymnasium to capacity, leaving hundreds outside, long before the meeting was called to order. The day before, the campus newspaper had set the ceremonial tone for the evening's discussion: "The homecoming of Professor Josiah Royce is an event which is viewed with just pride on the part of his *Alma Mater*, and he will find his younger brethren in the old halls exulting in the distinction which in winning for himself he has conferred upon her and upon them. We will all be on hand to welcome him, every one of us knows how to appreciate that distinction towards which the ambition of us all should be set."

As Royce stood on the platform, he was surrounded by three generations of philosophers: his colleague Howison, his former student Sidney Mezes, and his beloved teacher Joseph Le Conte. In the audience also a fourth generation was represented in the undergraduate A. O. Lovejoy. But it was Le Conte's presence that most deeply moved Royce, and in his opening remarks he paused to remember the lectures and counsel that had been among his earliest sources of light, guidance, and inspiration.

> This teacher it was, I may say, who set before me, in living presence, the ideal, still to me so remote, of the work of the thinker; and whenever since, in my halting way, I have tried to think about central problems, I have remembered that ideal of my undergraduate days,—that light and guidance and inspiration—and the beloved teacher too, whose living presence in those days meant the embodiment of all these things. It is a peculiar delight, ladies and gentlemen,—a wholly undeserved boon to have this opportunity to come face to face, in your presence, with Professor Le Conte, and to talk with you, and with him, of questions that are indeed called vexed questions, but that he first of all taught me to regard with the calmer piety and gentleness of the serious reason.

"We mortals question." Any question involves a gap between an idea and its object. On the other hand, to think of God is to conceive of an omniscient being in whom the two factors are fully united, an absolutely organized experience that possesses the final answer to every possible question. Does such a being exist? Agnosticism answers that ultimate reality is unknowable. Knowledge depends on experience, and experience depends on events in the nervous system. As before, Royce countered with the argument that the very limits implied by human ignorance also imply the existence of the absolute. But in restating this argument he first returned to the pragmatic analysis he had outlined fifteen years earlier in "On Purpose in Thought." To doubt is to feel some irritation which knowledge would satisfy. "What you and I lack, when we lament our human ignorance, is simply a certain desirable and logically possible state of mind, or type of experience; to wit, a state of mind in which we should wisely be able to say that we had fulfilled in experience what we now have merely in idea, namely, the knowledge, the immediate and felt presence, of what we now call the Absolute Reality."

Moving to the second stage of his argument, Royce reached back even farther to an idea he had first recognized when he read Lewes's *Problems of Life and Mind* in 1875: "What science says is simply that there is a sort of indirect and organized experience which reveals more of phenomenal truth than can ever be revealed to our direct sensory states as these pass by." Immediate experience is indeed a "heap of fragments," yet knowledge contains more than the mere fragments reveal. Atoms and geological periods may never be experienced directly; they are the "conceived realities of constructive science." So science does not pronounce a "verdict" against idealism, but provides precise models of organized experience toward which doubt irresistibly reaches. The body of knowledge we call science is, therefore, an ideal world. "It is linked to our actual experience by the fact that its conceptions are accounts, as exact as may be, of systems of possible experience, whose contents would be presented, in a certain form and order, to beings whom we conceive as including our fragmentary moments in some sort of definite unity of experience." This linkage is crucial, for unless science is connected to a world of fact, organized thought is nonsense. Furthermore, since direct experience remains fragmentary while science is characterized by form and order, the two realms are linked by contrast. "Thus all of our knowledge of natural truth depends upon contrasting our actually and stubbornly chaotic individual and momentary experience with a conceived world of organized experience, inclusive of all our fragments, but reduced in its wholeness to some sort of all-embracing unity."

To know that any opinion is false is to have some larger, contrastive, and mediating experience that identifies the error. To say further that an absolutely organized experience is merely an aim, not a reality, is also to presume some final experience in which the nonreality of the absolute is known. Since no finite thinker could claim such knowledge, the skeptic gets trapped in the paradox: "That there is nothing at all beyond this limited constitution must, as a fact, be present to this final experience." If therefore one professes to know any reality beyond immediate data, as science does insist it knows, then one must also acknowledge the existence of the absolute.

Newspapers called the discussion that followed Royce's address "the great debate," "a battle of the giants," "the most noteworthy philosophical discussion that for many a day has taken place in this country." Sidney Mezes spoke first. Fresh from the Harvard graduate program—he took the Ph.D. in 1893—Mezes remembered that Royce had always taxed his students with one basic responsibility: that they should learn to disagree with him. The requirement was "desperately difficult," for the teacher's logic seemed so overwhelming that any attempt to disagree with him left one feeling wholly unreasonable. Nevertheless, though he accepted Royce's argument, Mezes still felt that the doctrine had an important shortcoming: it offered no warrant for the conclusion that the "Absolute" is "God." From the first this had been one of the most common and widespread objections to Royce's theism. The line of reasoning from the possibility of error reached the conclusion that the absolute thinks all thoughts, answers all questions, accounts for the causal world of physical phenomena, and includes the present inner experiences of discrete individuals. But does this range of experience satisfy a need for religious truth? Mezes thought not. A chronosynoptic being, the absolute reduces the past and future to an eternal present. The moral struggle, which gives to human life its deepest religious significance, is, therefore, in the life of the absolute a fait accompli. Mezes could not understand how Royce's theory could deal seriously with the problem of evil or with the triumph of goodness, for to the absolute all problems are synoptically solved. Mezes believed that the essence of goodness is progress, and insisted that the Roycean world denies the reality of progress. A man may struggle, win or lose, but a complete being must remain aloof from all earthly struggles. Thus, if removed from the realm of moral conflict, the absolute cannot be a moral agent.

Joseph Le Conte, seventy-two years old and making one of his last public appearances, also avoided a direct collision with Royce's argument. "I can only admire, not criticise," Le Conte said as he opened his brief remarks. Le Conte's philosophy was generously supplemented by faith. For him science presents possible justifications of religious beliefs that have emotional origins. So as a naturalist, Le Conte constructed an independent argument—"a rough and ready way"—by taking hints from science as analogies of religious truth. A perfect observer, Le Conte began, examining the brain of another human being, would find a complex world of tissues, cells, molecules, and atoms. But the being observed, reflecting on his own mental life, would witness an entirely different set of facts: he would find a world of consciousness, selfhood, personality. By the same token it is not unreasonable to postulate that an unobserved subject is behind the veil of the whole objective universe. If so, this subject would have to be an "infinite personality," for only a complete, self-conscious, and self-existent being could include the cosmos.

This speculation gave Le Conte the outline of a worldview through which he attempted to solve the problems of evil and immortality. The solution to the first problem, he believed, was the same that Royce had advanced. Evil is the real and necessary means to the attainment of holiness, for without a moral struggle and without the freedom to choose right or wrong, life loses its ethical significance. Thus, though he agreed with Mezes that ethical struggle is essential to any religious view of life, Le Conte had a very different interpretation of Royce's ethical doctrine. For Le Conte, evolution is the prime example of purposeful conflict; viewed as the embodiment of divine aims, it results in a progressive growth of rationality. He was further convinced that man, the rational being, represents the achieved goal for which epochs of suffering and defeat had to be endured. The process continues, so evil remains the "spur"—a popular metaphor among evolutionists—that urges men toward moral and rational development. The problem of immortality finds its solution on the same grounds. Evolution, Le Conte suggested, can be likened to the reproductive process: nature is God's impregnated womb, so man, in an almost literal sense, is the Son of God. Mortality, then, would be a form of divine infanticide. Man needs God, but equally God needs man: *"Without immortality, this whole purpose is balked—the whole process of cosmic evolution is futile."*

Howison concluded the evening's discussion with his paper, "The City of God, and the True God as Its Head." Accepting the role of an elder brother in the philosophical family, Howison disputed, as Mezes and Le Conte had not, the fundamental tenets of Royce's philosophy. A self-styled "pluralistic idealist," Howison pitted his beliefs against "monism." Epistemologically the clash originated in Royce's assumption that the religious and the philosophical conceptions of God are the same, or that the former can be constructed from the materials of the latter. Howison disagreed, and in expressing his disagreement he revealed his deeper affinities to romantic transcendentalism. "Reason," for him, was more than *"natural-scientific experience"*; "complete reason," as he preferred to call it, included also a moral aspect that adds vision to reflection. "In this complete reason, or Conscience, the single spirit sees itself as indeed a *person*—a self-active member of a manifold *system* of persons, all alike self-active in the inclusive unit of their being; all independent *centres of origination*, so far as *efficient* causation is concerned; all moving from "within," i.e. each from its own *thought*, and harmonised in a society of accordant free-agents, not by any efficient causation, but by the operation of what has been called, since Aristotle, *final* causation—the attraction of an Ideal Vision, the vision of that CITY OF GOD which they constitute, and in which, reciprocally, they have their being. . . ."

Thus, in this rather effusive, murky, and old-fashioned language, Howison gave the outlines of his philosophical system. His "CITY OF GOD" is not, as in Royce's philosophy, simply "God," but a heavenly society of finite persons whose lives are freely independent of their creator. Since Royce's argument draws no boundaries between the finite and the infinite selves, Howison charged that such a conception is reducible to the pantheistic formula: *"I am He."* Furthermore, since the case for the absolute is derived from self-consciousness, Howison also charged that Royce could escape from pantheism only by plunging into solipsism.

Acknowledging that these charges were merely disputes over labels, Howison next moved to a more penetrating criticism of Royce's method. The assumption behind this method is the axiom, which Royce had first articulated in his *Primer of Logical Analysis*, that truth and consistency are equivalent. That is, to say that a statement is true means that it is free from self-contradiction. Since, as Royce had said, the denial of the absolute contradicts itself, the opposite view, that the absolute does exist, must be true. Thus, the existence of an objective reality is deduced from the true account that we can make of its ideal nature. It was this deduction of the objective from the subjective that Howison found unwarranted. The same criticism, we may remember, had been made ten years earlier by Shadworth Hodgson. Why, Howison asked, was Royce unwilling to remain a skeptic? Why *must* the absolute save us from endless contradiction? The answer, Howison believed, lay in the strategy of the argument: it was Royce's method to apply "a clinching dialectical thumbscrew for the torture of agnostics." Speaking to the unbeliever, but not to the believer, Royce was in effect saying: your doubts are doomed, for either you must surrender the grounds that make doubt possible or you must admit that your doubts are included in an absolute truth. This choice, which Howison characterized as a choice between solipsism and pantheism, is arbitrary, and it is a real choice only for the agnostic. To the believer, the problem is hardly relevant. At best, Howison insisted, the absolute is the *"witness* of God in my being, but it is not God himself."

The whole discussion, especially when it touched on clear differences of opinion, was for Royce the most delightful of evening entertainments. Thanking Howison, he mentioned "the hospitality and the undeserved honor of my so delightful visit," "the thoughtful care and unexampled generosity of welcome." Howison was equally gracious: the Philosophical Union, he said, "had the best of the bargain." Responding to Howison's contribution, Royce found the paper "profoundly interesting," "tantalizing," but fragmentary. "Why don't you put this multipersonalitarianism once for all into its final argumentative rights by a complete and technical statement? That would be one of the most fascinating books of the century, for us who love dialectics, as well as truth. I doubt not that that point of view ought to get its fullest hearing. Why do you forever put us off with fragments? Still, I am thankful even for the fragments."

Because of Katharine's accident, Royce had to confine his visit to California to a fortnight. His hostess was his sister-in-law, Anna Head, and his time was filled, when he was not lecturing, with social engagements of various sorts. To smaller meetings of the Union, Royce gave his three supplementary addresses on September 2, 4, and 6. After lecturing at Stanford University on September 11, he left California and was back in Cambridge before the end of the month. After a brief rest, he plunged into the complicated tasks of preparing for a new academic year.

The summer of 1895 completes another phase of Royce's life. Compared with earlier and later segments, the period from 1888 to 1895 seems, at least on the surface, markedly impersonal. Neither his quarrels nor his publications reflect direct light on his inner world. In his letters one finds little comment on personal or family matters; important events such as the birth of his third son and his mother's death pass unmentioned. And of course, the heaviest shroud of secrecy covered the early signs of Christopher's mental instability. What is most emphatically revealed during this period is professional growth, a development from youthful obscurity to national prominence. "I am quite an unknown young college professor," he told Deakin in 1889, but he could not have repeated those words in 1895. By that time the name "Professor Royce" had become, in intellectual circles, a household word, generally acknowledged to be one of the most original, formidable minds of his age.

Often his words reveal only the dimmest shades of feeling. Powerfully armed, the public Royce was a man committed to theoretical scrutiny. Perhaps his chief intellectual concerns—his persistent search for the absolute, his emphasis on the problem of self-consciousness, his attention to psychological anomalies—are outward manifestations of deeply felt needs or wishes. Perhaps also his professional quarrels with Frémont and Abbot were darkly rooted in his personality. "At heart," he had told President Eliot, "I am . . . a pretty sensitive person."

In the early 1890s Royce had served unwittingly as a catalyst in a love affair between Richard Cabot and Ella Lyman. Richard was a physician and a Harvard alumnus, destined to be one of the most influential members in its faculty of medicine. Ella had attended Radcliffe. Both had their "first taste of speculation" in *The Religious Aspect of Philosophy*, and both had gravitated as disciples to Royce. As always, he listened to their questions, encouraged their independent thinking, and freely gave his time to them as mentor. When they announced their engagement, they saluted Royce as "a sort of philosophic father": "each of us holds to a certain kind of intimacy with you and through you to each other." To this Royce replied:

The more sacred ties of life are beautiful in themselves, and worthy of all the sympathy that one naturally gives them, even when they are viewed merely as the good fortune of those who experience them. But when to this aspect another is added, and when to the beauty of the work of art, which every deeper friendship ought ideally to be, or to become, is added the charm of a devotion of the two friends to a common, difficult, and most honorable task,—well, the onlooker must not only sympathetically enjoy the joy of the friends, but take a still deeper delight in their love of service.

That under such circumstances I am remembered as forming any part of the foundation of such life and work as you carry on together, is an undeserved, but well appreciated honor. You were both born to philosophy. I was but driven to it by perplexity and by defect of insight. How little I care for the mere form of what I happen to have printed, you both know. If you can use this or that of mine as a basis, polemical or constructive, of your own work, I shall be glad.

I thank you both again for your good will in remembering me at such a time. I wish you both every joy. I greet you both with affection.

In the marriage of Richard and Ella Cabot, Royce was touched by a sacred and beautiful blending of thought and feeling.

A year earlier Royce had written a piece parallel to this: "The Problem of Paracelsus," which he presented to the Boston Browning Society on November 26, 1893. Although the essay was published twice, it has received scant attention. Thomas Davidson did write a long letter to Royce about this piece, including an insightful observation concerning its personal subtext: "How good your Paracelsus is! I read it yesterday with the deepest interest. I wonder if you know how deeply your own mental experience colors all your estimates."

The subject is Browning's *Paracelsus*, a poetic drama that depicts the perennial conflict between the head and the heart. Browning's poem belongs to the Faustian tradition. Its hero, historically a sixteenth-century Swiss physician, represents man the knower to the exclusion of man the lover. In this role Paracelsus becomes the professor and wandering scholar who aspires to infinite knowledge, but commits the tragic error of attempting to delete all tenderness from his life. If not a god, he will be the "king," despising the chaos and weakness of human feeling, seeking power by speaking to God without mediator. For Paracelsus, this goal must be totally won or totally lost: "For now 'tis all or nothing." He sees the danger in this course, but the prize is worth every risk, even that of losing his own soul. During his early travels, the scholar meets the dying poet Aprile who represents the opposite goal of love:

> *Paracelsus*. I am he that aspired to *know*: and thou?
> *Aprile*. I would *love* infinitely, and be loved!
> *Paracelsus*. Poor slave! I am thy king indeed.

God is knowledge, says Paracelsus. No, says Aprile, God is love. One would compel the world to surrender its secrets; the other would fill the earth with beauty. Paracelsus is deeply moved by Aprile's dying speech, but misinterpreting its meaning, he seeks merely to subsume passion in the larger quest for knowledge. Not love but hate becomes his ruling passion, as in the end, after a wasted life, he understands. "I gazed on power till I grew blind." The great quest for knowledge in things outside human feelings, Paracelsus finally sees, is doomed: "To know even hate is but a mask of love's."

Royce was not Paracelsus. Browning's hero is an occultist, a dreamer not a thinker, whose tragedy originates in the belief that truth resides in the world of power. With Browning, Royce agreed that God is found in one's "deeper Self," in the world of appreciation, not description. On the other hand, Royce was not Aprile. The artist touches deep feelings; his life of intense creativity is the path to knowledge. But though Royce accepted this doctrine consciously, and though he struggled to be guided by it, he found the union of thought and feeling exceedingly difficult, if not unattainable. As the discussion following "The Conception of God" had shown, the absolute is primarily a knower who combines, like Paracelsus's God, "dim fragments . . . in some wondrous whole." Royce had promised Howison that his restatement would "lay stress on . . . the element that Fichte called *Leben*," but the result, except for some verbal differences, did not convince his listeners that "absolute experience" was really more than "absolute thought."

As much as he hated the designation and fought against it, Royce was an intellectualist whose philosophy was more in tune with Paracelsus's monism than with Aprile's pluralism. By contrast Davidson saw the problem posed by Browning resolved in passion: "To me intellect is only a light which guides the footsteps of love, which alone grasps reality, by becoming one, & yet not one, with it." Feelings, Royce had said, are at best a heap of fragments. Accepting this truth, he always insisted, is the first step toward understanding. Very well, says Aprile, cherish your feelings, create with them, adorn the world with form and song. But for Royce feelings were problems. Still, despite his intellectualism, he also believed that thought without feeling is worthless, that God is neither knowledge nor love, but both. At the end of Browning's poem, Paracelsus on his deathbed suggests the path that Royce, during the next twenty years, would follow:

> Let men
> Regard me, and the poet dead long ago
> Who loved too rashly; and shape forth a third
> And better-tempered spirit, warned by both.

Royce's search for this "third spirit" ended with *The Problem of Christianity*.

The Battle for the Absolute
1895–1900

James, Peirce, and the Legacy of Hegel

On the afternoon of March 16, 1896, after a heavy snowfall, Royce left the college library. He had been writing a second paper on Robert Browning—"Browning's Theism"—scheduled for Boston later that month. A philosophical poet, Browning attracted Royce by his insight into fundamental human problems, particularly the problem of man suspended between "power" and "love." Royce found that his conception of God agreed in substance with Browning's intuitions: "That divine life, completed in God, incarnate in man, is much hidden from us by death, but is somewhere fully seen as good, when viewed in the light of the attainment and wholeness of the external world." Perhaps, on turning for home, Royce was thinking of this when he met James, and together they trudged through the damp, ankle-deep snow toward Irving Street. Soon they were arguing about the external world. What they said on this afternoon has vanished with their frosty breaths, but no doubt they explored the clash between monism and pluralism. Fragmentary experience presupposes a universal self, Royce might have insisted. An attractive hypothesis, James would have replied, but unnecessary. The wet snow spilled over their shoes, but they ignored it, and since the problems of philosophy are not solved in minutes or years, they lingered at James's gate in the twilight to continue the battle, which they never concluded, for the absolute.

Such battles belong to a realm where history blends with legend. Cambridge still echoes with stories of the debate between Royce and James—one rounding the pieces of experience into larger wholes, the other digging his heels into the sands of fact. On horsecars and street corners they presented a spectacle of modern academic heroes, each frail in appearance, yet massively equipped with intelligence and determined never to surrender. Observers, respecting the sanctity of the argument, kept off at a safe distance, but collected words and phrases for memoirs like relics left on a battlefield. Once at a peak in the debate heads turned to hear Royce shriek: "But what if the devil should swallow the whole world?" On public occasions they carried each other's books into lecture halls before delighted audiences, quoting bits of text, countering with devastating rebuttal. Still, though each labored to reduce the other's theories to fantastic nonsense, theirs was really a lovers' quarrel; they had been friends for twenty years, and in the fullest possible sense, James was chief among those, outside his family, that Royce wholeheartedly loved.

Exactly when the battle began cannot be determined. They slipped into it without plan or prearrangement. For years people had been coming to James with complaints about Royce. Henry Holt had been irritated by the fact that "somehow he can't help being a Hegelian." "I don't know what that is, and don't believe he does. And it always makes me melancholy to see a man of his splendid literary and critical make-up ignoring his real powers and trying to be something else." Jack Chapman had similar misgivings. "I am concerned about Royce," he wrote to James after a party. "I never heard a man talk so much nonsense in one evening—and a man too who is such a splendid fellow—a unique nature—and a very wonderful mind. . . . He said he was writing a paper on Originality and his conversation betrayed some of the things he is going to say in it.—One was that everything was imitative. In art you 'imitate the ideal.' This ought to be stopped."

No doubt James received such outbursts with a smile. Royce, he continued to assure everyone, was "powerful," "promising," "glorious," "a great success," "a perfect little Socrates, for wisdom and humor," "ready for everything in this world or the next." "He is a wonderful genius," James wrote F. H. Bradley in 1895, "to me as Hyperion to a Satyr!" When more serious criticisms appeared, James became Royce's champion, insisting that the critics had "failed to grasp the full force of his argument . . . the depth and importance of it." Such, at least, was James's attitude in 1888, but five years later, upon reading D. S. Miller's criticism of Royce in "The Meaning of Truth and Error," James was stung with "bewilderment and jealousy." Miller's essay helped James to see that "any definitely experienceable workings" could replace the intentions of the absolute mind. "With the help of God," James promised Miller in 1893, "I will go at it again this winter, when I settle down to my final bout with Royce's theory, which must result in my either actively becoming a propagator thereof, or actively its enemy and destroyer. It is high time that this more decisive attitude were generated in me, and it ought to take place this winter."

The story of this "final bout" is partially told in the margins of James's copies of *The Religious Aspect of Philosophy* and *The Conception of God*, where he lashed Royce's works with critical annotations. From the first he had both admired and resisted Royce's logic; years passed before he was able to sustain a vigorous resistance. In the 1890s he squared off against Royce's arguments and fought him every step of the way. Struggling with the absolute, James took a hint from the objection that Hodgson and Howison had independently advanced: that there is no warrant for the conclusion that a seemingly consistent hypothesis is necessarily true. Belief, said James the pragmatist, can never be an obligation, can be only a partial satisfaction of doubt.

James emerged feeling that Royce's thought was essentially loose. "There isn't a tight joint in his system; not one." James had also become impatient with Royce's "unit of discourse"—"the full hour lecture with some slopping over into the next"; if you tried to isolate some definite point, "his invariable reply is to restate his whole system, so it doesn't pay to object." This criticism of Royce's lavish manner—aesthetically similar to the one William notoriously leveled at his brother's late novels—was solidified after 1898–99 when he used *The Conception of God* as a textbook. He had supposed Royce to be an unassailable logician: "I thought," he told Miller, "that a mind that could talk me blind and black and numb on mathematics and logic . . . must necessarily conceal closeness and exactitude of ratiocination that I hadn't the wit to find out. But no! He is the Rubens of philosophy. Richness, abundance, boldness, color, but a sharp contour never, and never any *perfection*."

Thus, the battle for the absolute had its origin and reached its climax between 1893 and the end of the century. By the spring of 1896, when we found Royce and James arguing in the March snowstorm, each had come to a turning point in his philosophical career: Royce, fresh from his triumph in California and approaching his prime, was forty years old; James, though he seemed much younger, was fifty-four. Both men had already earned lasting places in the history of thought, but their best work was ahead of them. In 1896 James was known primarily for *The Principles of Psychology*; his philosophical views—self-described as "higgledy-piggledyism"—were scattered in periodicals, and he had done little to pull them together. As the midwife of pragmatism James was still unknown. But in June, perhaps partly because he had finally broken free from Royce's logic, James published "The Will to Believe," which became in the next year the title of his first collection of philosophical essays. In the preface to this volume James outlined the doctrine of radical empiricism, the philosophy of "ever not quite":

> After all that reason can do has been done, there still remains the opacity of the finite facts as merely given, with most of their peculiarities mutually unmediated

and unexplained. To the very last, there are the various "points of view" which the philosopher must distinguish in discussing the world; and what is inwardly clear from one point remains a bare externality and datum to the other. The negative, the alogical, is never wholly banished.

James was now publicly on record as the opponent of absolutism, and to widen the gap in 1898 he traveled to Royce's home ground of California to deliver a lecture, "Philosophical Conceptions and Practical Results." Speaking to Howison's Philosophical Union, he first used the word *pragmatism* and formulated its creed.

While Royce was fighting off James's theories, he also sometimes had to defend himself against Charles Peirce. A frequent visitor to Cambridge, Peirce came to lecture on metaphysics in the spring of 1892, and James, who was unable to attend the series, missed hearing Peirce's "godlike talk at Royce's." During the following autumn, Peirce returned to give a course of twelve lectures to the Lowell Institute entitled "The History of Science." Royce had enormous respect for Peirce's mind, and he frequently went out of his way to bring him into professional circles. In 1893, when Peirce circulated a prospectus for a twelve-volume treatise, *The Principles of Philosophy*, together with an edition of Petrus Peregrinus's *On the Loadstone*, Royce offered an enthusiastic endorsement of the project. "As you know," he told Peirce, "I have long wished to see the task of whose first results you have already given some very important though still, as I know, but fragmentary indications, put into adequate and permanent form." Acknowledging their disagreements, Royce emphasized the "cheerful conflicts of philosophical students," which he personally enjoyed and found "perfectly compatible with the admiration that I feel for you." Peirce's views were "so novel, so stimulating, so profound, . . . so ingenious . . . that I only express my natural appreciation of your genius when I say that I deeply desire to see the finished product, and I am sure that the enterprise deserves the support of every lover of philosophic progress in this country."

This plan, like all of Peirce's major undertakings, was doomed. Though far ahead of his time, among his contemporaries he was the poor cousin of the philosophical world, a man whom no university would tolerate, no publisher would trust, and no audience could comprehend. Royce and James were exceptions, but even they sometimes found Peirce's theories obtuse and his peevishness exasperating. Still, though they must have suspected that the case was hopeless, both urged President Eliot to offer Peirce a temporary appointment as instructor in 1895 for the course on the philosophy of nature. "He is the best man by far in America for such a course," James wrote on March 3, "and one of the best men living."

Writing in his official capacity as departmental chair, Royce echoed James's sentiments, describing Peirce as "a man of extraordinary mark in just that line of learning and research," adding that "no person . . . in this country . . . could compare with him (after James) in freshness of views, and breadth of information, about the questions studied in that particular course." Anticipating objections, Royce admitted that Peirce had a reputation for being a difficult person and an ineffective teacher. "I don't feel afraid as to the former point. As to the latter, I am disposed to think that in his most chosen field of work, and in one course of lectures, he might prove more successful than he could do as a general teacher. Besides, the importance of his present views would be worth some pedagogical sacrifices."

There were, Royce admitted, other unmentioned, perhaps unmentionable, objections to Peirce, and these no doubt figured prominently in Eliot's dissent. "I was sorry to dissent from C. S. Peirce," he told James. "All that you say of . . . [his] remarkable capacities and acquisitions is true, and I heartily wish that it seemed possible for the University to make use of them." Thus, despite his strong recommendation, Royce was unable to bring one of the most brilliant philosophers in the United States to the Harvard faculty.

Peirce was somewhat less enthusiastic in his judgment of Royce. Their collisions were sporadic, but their differences, though expressed with mutual esteem by both parties, appeared early and went deep. Peirce's criticism of *The Religious Aspect of Philosophy* ("a good introduction to Hegel!") revealed a sharp disagreement. Royce's commitment to formal logic had caused him, Peirce insisted, to slight the volitional aspect of knowledge as well as the simple needs of the religious life. "Dr. Royce admits in words that belief is what a man will act from; but he does not seem to have taken the truth of his proposition home." No ordinary man, Peirce observed, will take dialectics to heart; most, like Huckleberry Finn (Mark Twain's work was published a month after Royce's), are content to act as Christians without bothering much about the metaphysical bases of their faith. Royce's elaborate procedure also reminded Peirce of the humorist John Phoenix, "who after purchasing 365 solar compasses and a vast amount of other paraphernalia, in order to ascertain the distance between San Francisco and the Mission Dolores, stepped into a grocery and inquired how far it was, and, returned 'much pleased at so easily acquiring so much valuable information.'"

Royce's alleged Hegelianism has been a vexing problem in the interpretation of his philosophy. To James, *Hegelian* suggested the prig ("the white-winged band of seraphim"), while to Peirce, it meant an effort to cover the simple but real problems of life with a blanket of intellectualism. In short, as a term loaded with unpleasant connotations, *Hegelian* became another name for saintly pedantry, and being pinned with such a label was a constant source of irritation for Royce. From first to last, in each of his major books, he labored to cast it off, but his contemporaries, like many readers in the present day, ignored his denials. In the spring of 1896, Frank Thilly, a philosopher on the faculty of the University of Missouri, wrote to inquire into the matter, presumably with the intention of publishing something concerning Royce and the Hegelian system. "I think myself ill described as an Hegelian," Royce answered, "just as I think myself ill described as a Kantian, or a Spinozist, or a follower of Socrates." Admitting that he had learned a good deal from Hegel, as from the others, he objected to the tendency to classify all schools of absolute idealism as Hegelian. "Hegel," Royce felt assured, "would have despised me."

> Now I make very little of the series of the Hegelian Categories, and so very little of the system as such. Nor have I any system of categories to apply to all topics. I hold in entire contempt the "Philos. of Nature," and care nothing for the Hegelian technical Psychology (as such), nor anything for the characteristic technicalities of either the *Religionsphilosophie* or the *Rechtsphilosophie*, or the *Aesthetik*, or, but why particularize? I have fully explained what I regard as the *positive* value of Hegel in my *Spirit of Mod. Phil.* I did not there write down what I have in the way of bones to pick with Hegel. Why should I?

Royce felt that his philosophy should be described as "post-Kantian, empirically modified, Idealism, somewhat influenced by Hegelian, but also not uninfluenced by Schopenhauerian motives, with a dash of Fichte added." If readers insist on calling Royce a Hegelian, they should, he said, add some prefix like "Neo-," "Pseudo-," "Semi-," "Hemi-," or even "Pleistocene-."

Of course, on the other hand, there is merit in recognizing Royce's affinities to Hegel, and if it can be said that he had a Hegelian period, that period would be the 1890s. This is clearly indicated by his teaching. For nine years—from 1889 till 1898—Royce focused his seminar in metaphysics on the development of the Hegelian system with particular emphasis on the *Phänomenologie des Geistes.* "I am an admirer of that book," he once told Harris, "and mean to do what I can to make others feel the beauty of its analyses, whose value is by no means conditioned upon an acceptance of Hegel as a whole, or upon any theory as to his progress in his later works." The students were expected to read the *Phänomenologie* in the original German, and Royce planned to treat it as "a sort of *Wilhelm Meister*, as it is, and . . . discuss its historical background at some length." Hegel, he told Howison, "will never be to me what he is to you, . . . but a very interesting fellow, after all." One student remembered that Royce told the seminar that to read Hegel you had to acquire his vocabulary, but you could do this only by reading him: "It was like going to a concert and being told that admission tickets would be given to you as you passed out."

The seminar on Hegelian metaphysics, which Royce conducted one evening a week in his home, was open to any interested person. The Cabots, as well as other nontraditional students, regularly attended, participated, and were always welcome. Chapman recalled such evenings with nostalgia: "You could loaf down the avenue in Cambridge after supper and enter a little arena of wisdom, where a small company was sitting in eager silence; and you could join in the discussion and challenge the champion if you had the brains." William James did have the brains, and when he attended the seminar, his contest with Royce became an exciting public event. But even this zest for polemics had its limits, and after one of these meetings, James grew melancholic and was heard to mutter as he walked out: "Nothing here but intellectual sawdust."

The Principle of Individuation

If the drawn-out battle for the absolute suggests a life of academic leisure, such an impression is deceptive. "I can't see far ahead or behind just now, in this whirl of daily business," Royce wrote in December 1895. As department chair Royce attended to a plethora of administrative details, including the management of a powerful faculty. A letter from Palmer—on sabbatical leave in Europe during 1895–96—gives some flavor to the details that concerned Royce. No one cared so much about the department as Palmer; it was, he said, "the son of my soul" and "the great engine so dear to me." Writing from Venice on March 20, he admitted having "a monstrous appetite for home news," which Royce satisfied. "I shall wish to know," Palmer wrote, "each occasion when James swore, Ladd was fussy, Santayana superior, or you long winded."

Santayana's future was becoming a pressing and, to Palmer, a "puzzling" issue. A man like Santayana who seemed "principally to exist for himself" had slim chance of earning tenure at Harvard; he would have to be recognized, Palmer insisted, as "a force in the College." Royce, the great believer in community, no doubt agreed with Palmer on this point. Then there was the problem of Santayana's specialties—aesthetics and medieval philosophy—neither of which had attracted sufficient numbers of interested students. In the previous spring he "tended toward ethics," but now he announced that he would become a specialist in Greek philosophy and took a sabbatical leave the following year to study Plato at King's College, Cambridge. "But," the arch Palmer observed, "I think he makes a mistake in getting a fourth ruling passion. It will give the appointing powers a dangerous impression of instability." And finally, with a sly sexual insinuation, Palmer added, "Nothing, except marriage, is so likely to increase his serviceability."

Actually, as Palmer admitted, he preferred to see his "fosterling" Charles M. Bakewell in the position reserved for Santayana. Bakewell was "masterful, lucid, comprehensive & loveable." For years Palmer and others had encouraged him to study Greek philosophy with the expectation of teaching it at Harvard. He might have succeeded earlier had not "certain scandalous stories" ruined his chances. Palmer now had no doubts about Bakewell's moral character. "I know of no man of his years," Palmer averred, "so likely to stimulate his pupils helpfully." "And at any rate we cannot allow [Santayana's] new mistress to be snatched from one who has been faithful to her for years." Furthermore and finally, unlike Santayana, Bakewell was "clubbable." In Harvard's philosophy department, Palmer firmly believed, "no self assertor must be allowed a place." Three more years would pass before this delicate question would be resolved.

In 1895–96, aside from his regular college work—teaching and administrative duties—Royce was kept busy with the preparation of the Augustus Graham Lectures on Theism, which he delivered at fortnightly meetings of the Brooklyn Institute of Arts and Sciences from January 5 to March 1. The lectures covered three main areas: the argument for absolute idealism, the ethical significance of theism, and religious implications of evolution. In the first of his five lectures he compared the history of theism with modern tendencies; thus, three traditional conceptions of God—the "ethical monotheism" of the Old Testament, Aristotle's omniscient God, and the mystic theism of the Orient—were paired off against scientific theism, agnosticism, and constructive idealism. This last tendency was developed extensively in the second lecture, in which Royce borrowed heavily from his Berkeley address.

In these and in his two concluding lectures, where he also incorporated passages from previous publications, Royce had little to add to his already familiar philosophy, but in the third lecture, "The Moral World as the Revelation of God," he introduced and for the first time explicitly developed a new concept: loyalty. "What aspect of our life brings us," he asked, "even in its very fragmentariness, nearest to a glimpse into the divine fullness of life?" Rejecting the idea that the ethical significance of life can be imposed by any external authority, Royce sought a self-determining principle of moral individuality. "The real question is now as to your loyalty. And that is something whose absolute worth you can know just as well as God can know it. For here is a worth that is wholly dependent upon your self-conscious act of choice. You have moral worth not by virtue of what has been given to you, but by virtue of your conscious and intended stewardship in your use of the gift." The key phrase here is "conscious and intended stewardship," for, Royce maintained, one becomes a moral individual by becoming aware of aims and by choosing to serve them. Loyalty, in short, allows a human being to enter the world of value. "Loyalty," he said, "involves the self-conscious choice to give my life meaning as I alone can mean it. By choosing to be loyal I discover my moral worth, myself as a moral being."

William James had argued that the philosopher cannot guide the moral life, that no supreme good can direct the world of value. Royce's answer to the argument was that without loyalty, it is inconceivable that a person could have a moral life.

Thus in the middle 1890s, without repudiating his theory of the absolute, Royce began to emphasize the idea of the individual, which added a volitional aspect to his philosophy that many felt he had neglected. No doubt the challenge of Howison's personalism, the daily battles with James, and the annoying charge, which came from every corner, that Royce's individual was obliterated by his Hegelianism gave him a personal motive for providing the individual with a definite place in the foreground of his system. "It is a long story," he told his former student Mary Calkins, "and one that I have long rather kept in the background."

Royce first noted this direction in a letter to Gertrude Stein, then a student and organizer of the Philosophy Club at Radcliffe College, on March 27, 1896. Stein was arranging a series of talks for her club and asked Royce if he would participate. Royce agreed and suggested that his paper "Browning's Theism" might be suitable. On second thought he offered also a new paper, "The Principle of Individuation," which he was preparing for a talk at Princeton. "This latter is a more technical paper," he explained, "but is still adapted to a pretty general, if philosophically studious, company, on the problem, 'What do we mean when we call any object an Individual?' or 'What constitutes Individuality?' This problem is a pretty one, and is of practical interest to people who desire to call their souls their own."

Among the students who attended this talk in May, a few must have been astonished to find that so central a problem as individuality was prefaced by a short course in scholasticism, for Royce devoted the first two-fifths of his paper to what he admitted might seem an "ineffective and wearisome" discussion of the subtle differences between Thomas Aquinas and Duns Scotus. Royce apologized for that, but insisted that the subtleties "constitute an almost indispensable introduction to the study of our problem." His strategy was to sharpen the issues of the argument by isolating two opposing definitions of the individual. One, represented by Thomas, gives us the empirical individual, the segmented fact of immediate experience. We say that any identifiable fact is an individual because we find it separated from every other fact. But, Royce observed, segmentation will not serve as a principle of individuation, for universals—such as black and white, cause and effect, rest and motion—can also be segmented. If, in short, all individuals are segmented objects of knowledge, not all segmented objects of knowledge are individuals. The second definition, which Royce assigned to Scotus, gives us the logical individual. This definition escapes the difficulties of empiricism by showing that individuals, unlike universals, cannot be predicated to mutually exclusive classes: "philosopher" can be both "Athenian" and "Milesian," but "Socrates" cannot. Thus, uniqueness defines the logical individual. Royce preferred this approach, but found new obstacles that prevent the logical individual from being more than a mere abstraction. Thought can specify a set of characteristics—a person's fingerprints, for example—but it cannot determine that these are the characteristics of a unique individual; definitions give us types of individuals, but they do not individualize. If we take the problem back to the empirical world, we find that experience is equally helpless. "So far, then," Royce concluded, "the antinomy seems complete. Thought, as such, cannot define uniqueness, and must appeal to experience; experience, as such, cannot present uniqueness, but must leave that, as being either an intelligible type or nothing, to thought."

But Royce was not willing to surrender to the paradox. When we invoke the principle of uniqueness, we mean that the individual is the object of our exclusive interest. In the order of a child's development, the knowledge of universals precedes that of individuals; at first the child perceives a world of undifferentiated oneness and only gradually learns to recognize the many. What facilitates this perception of the individual? To answer by way of illustration, Royce asked his audience to imagine a child who is crying because of a broken toy. If offered a duplicate, the child cries harder; the very presentation of another toy like the broken one seems to intensify his grief. Why should this be? What prompts the child to renounce his first world of universals in preference for the unique? The answer is both simple and poignant: the child has loved his toy, loved it exclusively and will accept no other. Thus, a parable gave Royce a route of escape from his antinomy: "This practical, this passionate, this loving, this at first thoughtless dogma of love, *There shall be no other*, is, I insist, the basis of what later becomes the individuating principle of knowledge."

Call it love, call it will, it is in any case a passionate caring about the world that individuates it. This toy, this flower, or this face is an individual not because experience tells me it is segmented or because logic says it is unique, but because I take an interest in its being segmented and am uninterested in the possibility that it may not be unique. Once this is understood and accepted, it follows that I am individuated in the same way: I am this person for whom the individuals matter; they express my interests, my aims, my purposes, and insofar as I acknowledge my aims, I am an individual. According to Royce, therefore, individuality is an ethical concept, and its corollary is loyalty: "Be loyal, indeed, to the universe, for therein God's individuality is expressed; but be loyal, too, to the unique. Be unique, as your Father in Heaven is unique."

In addressing the female students of Radcliffe on the problems of individuality, Royce was perhaps reminded of a comment he had made ten years earlier on a similar problem that women (in this case, Victorian women) face when they take up philosophy:

> I think, to sum up my view in the briefest form, that the supposed difficulty that women are said to meet in forming abstract ideas, and so in grasping philosophical subtleties, does not exist, in case of young women who chance to be interested in philosophy. The true difficulty, however, which such young women do meet with in their study of philosophy, is rather a moral than an intellectual one: it is a certain fear of standing alone, of being eccentric, of seeming unduly obstinate in thought. This fear makes them, in the long run, too docile followers of a teacher or of an author, and so hinders their freedom of constructive thought. Now eccentricity of thought is, indeed, never the ultimate goal of philosophic study; but it is a necessary stage on the way to real success in thought. And this stage young women are less apt to reach.

Gertrude Stein, however, was never "too docile"; she, at least, was one member of Royce's audience who had no fear "of standing alone, of being eccentric, of seeming unduly obstinate in thought." Nor did Mary Calkins exhibit any of those fears. The first woman to become president of the American Philosophical Association, Calkins taught philosophy at Wellesley. As a graduate student at Harvard under the special tutelage of Royce and Münsterberg, she had shown that she was equal to any man in the program, but though she completed all requirements for the Ph.D., the Corporation declared her ineligible because of sex. When a compromise was proposed, that she should be awarded a doctorate from Radcliffe, Calkins stood up for her right to be treated without discrimination and firmly refused the degree.

A woman, therefore, with a strong individual will, Mary Calkins was one who could respond both personally and philosophically to Royce's discussion. Shortly after hearing the lecture, she showed Royce her notes and asked for more light. He answered with a long letter in which he attempted to clarify his argument. Calkins had seen the "appreciative" aspect of the theory, but had failed to recognize its "descriptive" side. It is easy to see how her view might have been formed, for to say that the world is individuated by exclusive interest suggests strongly that the category of the individual belongs always and only to one's private world. It is true, Royce insisted, that the individual is indicated by its "value" rather than by its "image," but from this it does not follow that individuation is confined to subjectivity. Individuality may also be a public value. Society, for example, may take an exclusive interest in a person's fingerprints.

> To be sure, there are numerous conscious ideas, of an appreciative, as well as of a descriptive type, which appear early in life, & to which there actually correspond,

in the physical world as viewed by other men, the objects called by developed thought, in the ordinary and conventional sense, individuals. . . . But my point is that of every such individual, and of its individual *haeccitas*, we have, and can have, only an essentially general idea, to which, to be sure, only one object in the world of common sense chances to correspond, but which nothing *in consciousness*, or in the conscious value of the idea itself, prevents from being separately exemplified by thousands of individuals.

Thus, Royce persisted in his view that the idea of the individual—whether a description or an appreciation—is "a limiting concept," known, if at all, by its mysterious and unconscious rivalry with the other. "But just for this reason none of us ever quite knows what constitutes the individual as just this unique individual, because the exclusion of the 'other' is negative, and a product of considerations of which we are not fully conscious. Hence, I say, a true and *positive* knowledge of the individual is the goal, not the beginning of knowledge; and we have positive knowledge, in any grade, only of the universal, of the type, the general structure, the definable law of our objects."

With "The Principle of Individuation" Royce achieved the most remarkable extension of his metaphysical theory since *The Spirit of Modern Philosophy*. For years he had been stressing the central importance of the individual; for years he had also been promising his critics an outline of the voluntaristic side of his absolutism. Luckily this development coincided with Howison's plans to bring out an enlarged edition of *The Conception of God*. As Howison explained his proposal on August 24, 1896, he planned to reprint the original symposium and to add a new section in which Royce would "make any reply to the criticisms that appeared in the pamphlet along with the Address."

"I am a little sorry," Royce answered on the thirty-first, "to see my poor paper get into permanent form." He was also somewhat reluctant to press toward "the always untidy 'finish' of a human argument"; the most instructive aspect of the discussion, he felt, was his disagreement with Howison, and that might prove more stimulating if left open and unresolved. Furthermore, it would be impossible to retrieve the form of the original argument. "*That* affair, so far as my poor scribble went, is, for me, over. I can no longer take the literary tone of that evening."

On the other hand, Royce was interested in writing "a new philosophical paper, standing alone," which might undertake two efforts: "(1) To restate my central argument (the 'Possibility of Error' sort of dialectics) at some length in a *technical* form, such as my paper, as it was, forbade; (2) To expound, in answer to you (if I must answer) my present definition of individuality,—a definition which might, after all, reconcile us." Giving a satirical hint of this subject and also another sharp thrust at Abbot, he promised "a startlingly 'original' (let us say 'American') theory of individuality, which I regret to be unable to publish 'in time to influence the fall elections.'" "That is the best I can do," he concluded. "So then, would such a new essay, founded on the discussion of that evening, but, free in form, serve your purpose,—in scope to be as indicated above? If so I can help you." After hearing from Howison again, Royce wrote on September 21: "I accept the conditions proposed in your letter, & will proceed to prepare my paper."

Plans and Distractions

At the same time, following a brief but delightful visit to Mrs. Dorr at Oldfarm, Royce was prepared to start a new academic year. His letter of thanks to his hostess this time was unusually affectionate. "With a feeling of great refreshment," he wrote on September 20, "as of one who has seen and shared a new experience of life, I find myself this morning returned from your home. It is always good to be with you, and it has never been better than on this occasion." He needed the vacation, for the work to be done in the next year was enormous.

Royce's administrative duties in his third year as department chair took up a good deal of time, but in addition he reported that he was lecturing "16 hrs a week, in Harvard, Radcliffe, & elsewhere." In the fall semester he took charge of the lectures on logic and philosophy in the department's elementary course; he also repeated his advanced course in metaphysics and initiated his highly influential advanced course in logic, which stepped beyond the traditional methods of induction and deduction into the new area of symbolic logic. On the graduate level his tasks were compounded by a trade he made with James. Since James wanted to teach a course in Kant, Royce surrendered his metaphysics seminar and took over the course in psychology.

In November he was pleasantly distracted from his work by a visit from Joseph Le Conte and his daughter Caroline. As Royce's houseguest, Le Conte entertained Cambridge audiences with a lecture on the higher aspects of evolution, while his daughter added finishing touches to the manuscript of her book, *The Statue in the Air*. "They are both unique people," Royce told Mrs. Dorr. "LeConte, 74, yet full of life, thought and insight, a geologist, and yet much more than a geologist; his daughter, slight, eccentric—a lonely, yet on the whole, despite moods, sensitiveness and imperfect constitution, a happy nature—a not uninstructed lover of art, a thoughtful dreamer of airy visions, without poses, and unlike, in some respects, the other dreamers whom we see."

Royce became convinced that the Le Contes should meet his friend at Oldfarm, and at her request they made a trip to Maine, where, he assured her, "whatever the weather, the leaflessness of the trees, or the nearness of winter, it would be a great pleasure to them, and, I hope, to you." As expected, the visit was a great success. Mrs. Dorr encouraged Caroline to publish her book, and enlisted the artistic advice of Sarah Whitman. Royce, acting as literary agent, opened negotiations with Horace Scudder and the Riverside Press, but when the plans failed to work out, he arranged publication with George Brett of the Macmillan Company.

Getting back to his own work in December, Royce mailed his supplementary paper to Howison with an apology:

> Why the delay? Alas, you came in upon me, with your kind demand, at what proved to be the most distracted moment of my year. How hastily I promised, how foolishly I hoped to be prompt, you now know. Fate intervened at once. My term's work opened, my house unexpectedly filled with guests (LeConte & his daughter were two of them for ten days; but there were others before them); and everything rushed at me pell-mell, saying "Do this, don't forget that." I liked the guests, but I didn't like the jobs. I struggled, squirmed, lost some sleep, got a cold and a swollen jaw, lectured, did administrative work,—in short did whatever we indolent fellows here are accustomed to do,—all *but* finish my essay. Now you have it at last. I am now quite well again,—guestless, but not exactly at leisure.— You won't like the essay; it is too long, too unequal, too hasty, too unsound. But one thing is sure; I won't improve it; and I shall thank you immensely for this chance to print it.

Entitled "The Absolute and the Individual," this paper of more than two hundred printed pages is a book in itself. But hastily written and admittedly formless, the essay was a potpourri of leftovers. Much of it, the first and the last sections, was loosely assembled from the unpublished parts of the "minor papers" that Royce had given in California, peppered here and there with replies to his critics. The real substance and lasting importance of the whole was, as he had anticipated, provided in part 3, "The Principle of Individuation." The editorial responsibility now belonged to Howison, who found the task of bringing out another man's book an exacting and irritating ordeal. Nevertheless the revised edition of *The Conception of God* was published by the Macmillan Company in the fall of 1897.

Before that, however—in fact as soon as he had mailed his paper to Howison—Royce became involved in a delicate administrative problem respecting Hugo Münsterberg. When, in 1895, Münsterberg had completed his three-year appointment, Eliot offered him a permanent professorship, and granted a two-year leave of absence so that he might return to Freiburg before making a decision. Early in January 1897, word reached Cambridge that Münsterberg was being considered for the chair in psychology at the University of Zurich. As department chair, Royce had the job of discovering the facts and, if possible, luring Münsterberg back to Harvard: "Over here," Royce wrote, "there are those (and I am one of them) who want you to return to us, not only in the interests of science, but in the interests of our own warm friendship for you, of the affectionate memory that we keep of you, and want to renew." These assurances proved unnecessary, for by the time Münsterberg received Royce's letter the negotiations with the Swiss government had probably already broken down.

Still, because of a deep commitment to the fatherland, Münsterberg was unwilling to face the prospect of a tenured life in the United States. Instead he proposed a special arrangement by which he would come without his family for the fall term only, compressing the entire year's work into a semester, and return to Germany each spring. After conferring with James and Palmer, Royce informed Eliot that they were agreed that the proposal was unacceptable. Experimental psychology was catching on in all of the universities in the U.S., competition for the best students was getting stiff, and if Harvard expected to maintain its place of academic leadership, the laboratory needed a permanent, full-time director. Everyone sympathized with Münsterberg's ambivalence and they wanted him back, but not at the cost of the department's program or its internal harmony.

> Thus we want M. to come [Royce wrote to Eliot], but we cannot sacrifice every-thing to secure even him, although our personal fondness for the man, and our hearty belief in his value as a colleague and as an investigator, are unchanged, and have been too often and too freely expressed to need further insistence here. Nobody can ask so many interests, however, to be sacrificed to his convenience as M. still finds it necessary to ask. We hope that he will not insist on his demand.

But anticipating that Münsterberg would insist, Royce had already opened negotiations with Mark Baldwin of Princeton. Royce and James had great respect for Baldwin's abilities, and Baldwin in turn was more than willing to join his friends at Harvard. This precaution, however, proved unnecessary, for soon after Münsterberg received Eliot's firmly worded letter of March 3, all was settled:

> We have come to the unanimous conclusion [Eliot wrote] that it is not in the interest of the University to accede to the precise proposal which your letter con-tains. . . . I ought also to say to you frankly that the University will not be content

to have you return hither without "burning your ships." . . . On account of the shortness of the time which now remains before the issue of the announcements for next year I must beg you to cable a Yes or a No as soon as you have made up your mind on the proposal contained in this letter.

Münsterberg cabled, "Yes," and Eliot replied, "Welcome."

Though Münsterberg was safely back in the Harvard fold, Royce found that the pressure did not let up until the end of the spring term. "Our official tasks have been very complex and severe of late," he reported. "We had, for instance, six candidates for the doctorate to examine. There was much committee business. There were countless literary tasks." The spring was further complicated by a trip in May to New Orleans where Royce delivered a series of lectures. He felt very tired and postponed all work until the beginning of July. Even then his time was parceled out to professional obligations; on the sixteenth he went to Kansas City to lecture.

As compensation for his industry, events took a pleasant turn that promised to change the whole course of his career: he had been appointed to give the Gifford lectures at the University of Aberdeen in 1899 and 1900. At first James had been invited, but feeling unequal to the task, he had refused. But in refusing James recommended Royce. This provoked an outburst from Alice James in a letter to her favorite brother-in-law, Henry: "Royce!! *He* will not refuse, but over he will go with his Infinite under his arm, and he will not even do honour to William's recommendation."

Regardless of the merits of this judgment, it seems true that Royce never thought of rejecting the invitation. W. R. Sorley, on behalf of the Gifford Foundation, first mentioned this possibility in a letter to Royce on April 6. On May 8 the nomination was introduced at a meeting of the Senatus of the University of Aberdeen. A number of names were submitted, there was a long discussion, but finally Royce was appointed unanimously by consensus; there was no vote. The agreement stipulated that Royce would deliver twenty lectures, divided evenly in two successive years, on the subject of natural theology. The pay would be £500, possibly more, for each series. Remembering the previous unpleasantness with the Lowell Institute and Stanford University, Royce probably winced when he read Lord Gifford's definition of natural theology:

> The knowledge of God, the Infinite, the All, the First and only Cause, the One and Sole Substance, the Sole Being, the Sole Reality, and the Sole Existence, the knowledge of his Nature and attributes, the knowledge of the relationship which men and the whole universe bear to Him, the knowledge of the nature and the foundation of ethics or morals, and of all obligation and duties thence arising.

Sorley assured him, however, that "complete freedom is left to the lecturer as to his method & results."

The press of work kept Royce close to his writing desk throughout summer. "There is no chance of my being able to get up into the mountains this summer," he told Davidson. "I wish I could come, and I shall think of you often; but life grows more exacting rather than less." Commitments were piling up. Aside from the Gifford appointment, Royce was scheduled to give a series of ten lectures to teachers entitled "The Social Factors in the Development of the Individual Mind" at Boston University during the next year. He had also promised to write fifteen articles for Baldwin's *Dictionary of Philosophy and Psychology*. "From now on," he told the editor in June, "I pledge some working hours of each free time to your task, until something has been done." This later earned him Baldwin's praise: "Josiah Royce, the voluminous, was always ready, always accommodating and prodigiously industrious." "The copious Royce," he said, ". . . took all the space offered him, revelling in the intricacies of Greek and Kantian terminology." These articles, however, as Royce suggested, were minor efforts that he squeezed into his daily routine. No doubt Royce's main job that summer was the revision and arrangement of his first collection of essays, *Studies of Good and Evil*.

But eight months would pass before that book was ready for publication. In the meantime, the revised edition of *The Conception of God* appeared. Writing to Howison in October, Royce thanked him for extra copies, said that he was pleased with the book's format, and praised the "extremely judicial introduction." He was disappointed, however, to note that once again Howison had failed to make his own position clear. "And now if you will only buckle down to the job and tell the whole story of that City of God of yours right out, so that one can really make out what sort of a place it is, I shall be glad indeed." Royce could not see that God could be part of Howison's world: either everyone is his own unique deity, or else God is merely the name of the collective whole. "I know of course that you can't really mean either of these things, but I indicate the helplessness of my mind by suggesting the question." As for his own contribution, Royce had momentarily lost interest in it: "I cheerfully resign it now to its fate, & care little therefore.—I now go on to my Gifford Lectures,—my next task."

Though Royce's teaching load and committee work in 1897–98 were lighter than they had been during the previous year, he found little time for leisure. "No fooling so far this winter," he said succinctly in February. He had less than a year to prepare his first series of Gifford lectures, and no doubt, as an enormous amount of surviving notes and trial outlines still testifies, he devoted almost every free moment to the task. But on the other hand, Royce's most finished work of the year was done in the somewhat distant fields of social and educational psychology. On January 15 he launched "The Social Factors in the Development of the Individual Mind," which he continued each Saturday morning till the end of March. Before that, during the Christmas vacation, he gave a talk to the American Psychological Association at Ithaca, New York, entitled "The Psychology of Invention," and on February 6 he began a series of "Cambridge Conferences," on "Some Aspects of Social Psychology." This latter series was given on successive Sundays, and as he said by way of introduction, it was substantially the same as his Saturday lectures. In April, declining an invitation from Ella Cabot, he wrote a litany of his commitments for the rest of the spring and summer:

> I have made a very great many extra engagements this year, and I seem somewhat, although I don't suppose seriously, to have overtaxed my strength. My Gifford Lectures for next winter lie ahead of me, almost untouched. I have engagements in Washington and in Springfield early in May, for extra lectures. In Washington, I am to lecture twice in July, again, before the Nat'l Educ'l Assoc. I have to make extra preparations for several such occasions. Meanwhile, my unfulfilled promises to editors are numerous; and much of that sort remains to do, very soon, in addition to all other calls. I have already begun dropping out some of my concert evenings,—although I keep my concerts as faithfully as I can.

Royce did not place a high value on any of these efforts, and it appears that he did not actively seek to publish them. "The Psychology of Invention" is a case in point. The topic had been assigned to him by the association's president, and it was not, Royce said at the outset, "one which I myself should have chosen to discuss." The paper was published in the *Psychological Review*, but apparently only because the editors, Cattell and Baldwin, requested it. "As it is," Royce told Cattell, "I think it a very unfinished piece of work, and only print it because you and Baldwin say so. For my part, I don't like my own crudeness, and yet seem fated to stay crude."

While depreciating his efforts, Royce drew renewed inspiration from the work of Charles Peirce. For nearly a year James had labored to bring Peirce to Cambridge for a series of lectures. This task was made exceedingly difficult by the fact that Peirce seemed determined to speak on the most abstruse topics in logic, which James and Royce both agreed could not be understood by more than three members of the audience. To them, Peirce replied that anything worthy of attention in philosophy depends wholly on logic, a field unfortunately that Harvard had absolutely neglected.

After a brisk exchange of correspondence the lectures were finally arranged as a series of eight "Cambridge Conferences" entitled "Reasoning and the Logic of Things." They began at the home of Mrs. Ole Bull on February 10 and continued on a semiweekly basis until March 7. When the lectures were finished, James was full of praise. "They have been a great success," he wrote Peirce, "everyone speaking of them with greatest admiration. . . . I have just been walking home with Royce, who is extraordinarily full of appreciation."

It is possible that Royce took Peirce's admonition to heart, for in the next year he redesigned his seminar in metaphysics and retitled it "The Problems of Logic and Epistemology." Three years later Royce had not forgotten his appreciation of these conferences. He told James in 1901, "Those lectures of poor C. S. Peirce that you devised will always remain quite epoch marking for me."

The newly devised seminar in logic proved to be one of the most radical and effective curricular innovations in philosophical pedagogy. In a letter to Ella Cabot, Royce explained his plan and expectations. The seminar would be a community of scholars, with each member at work on an independent project while exploring, with others and for the collective benefit of the group, the logical foundations of the inquiry.

> The Seminary in Logic, so far as you and Dr. Cabot are concerned, shall be one whose service is perfect freedom. I mean to vary the topics a good deal, and as I know very little worth knowing as yet about the subject, despite my years as a teacher of it, I shall be glad if we learn a little together,—anywhere in the vast field.
>
> Whatever previous announcements imply, the plan will be a topical one, rather than the following of any one book. The comparative study of various kinds of concepts and methods, is just now my ideal,—a sort of comparative morphology of various thinking processes, and of their results,—stress laid rather on the . . . structure of various concepts. I should suggest that you might take up the problem of the Logic of Ethical Conception, e.g. what, if anything, is the essential difference between the conception of an *Ought* and the conception of an *Is*?

Besides attending to philosophical and psychological matters, Royce still had the burden of being department chair. In 1898 his term was in its fourth and final year, and one of his last duties concerned the future of George Santayana, who had spent the previous year on a leave of absence in England. Before leaving, Santayana, an instructor for seven years, let it be known that he intended to resign if not promoted. In the meantime he had published his first philosophical work, *The Sense of Beauty*, which had been favorably reviewed in the professional journals.

It is not surprising that Royce seems to have had mixed feelings about Santayana's book. Richard Cabot wrote Royce, remarking that *The Sense of Beauty* "seems to me a wonderful thing, though I differ from it, as I suppose you do, about as radically as it is possible to differ." Roscoe Thayer had asked Royce to review Santayana's volume for the *Harvard Graduates' Magazine*, offering anonymity should Royce prefer, but five months later, when Thayer renewed his request, the review was still unwritten, and in fact was never published.

In any event, the time for a tenure decision had come, and accordingly Royce wrote to Eliot on January 21, recommending that Santayana be "not only retained, but advanced, next year, to an Assistant Professorship." Palmer had some doubts, but James, Münsterberg, and Royce were agreed on four points: "His book, the extremely marked and cordial reception that it has won, from decidedly competent judges, his slow but now unquestionable growth as a scholar, his wholly unworldly, but very steadfast devotion to his work, his really distinctive position among us, as differing from us all, in a very wholesome way, in influence and in doctrine these considerations, weighed together, now seem to me and I believe to James & Münsterberg in their present force, to outweigh any of our former doubts."

Eliot, however, had his own misgivings, and possibly with the support of Palmer, he responded by asking if Charles Bakewell, Santayana's replacement, might not be a better prospect. In his answer to Eliot, Royce acknowledged Bakewell's strengths, but insisted that between the two, Santayana would be "a better investment for the University." A statement endorsing Santayana's promotion, signed by Royce, Palmer, Münsterberg, Everett, and James, was submitted to the president on January 27. If Eliot still doubted, he finally agreed, and the May issue of the *Philosophical Review* printed the announcement of Santayana's promotion.

Discussions of Royce have never emphasized his term as department chair. A tacit assumption has been that he was too engrossed in philosophical idealism to give much attention to administrative details. The facts, however, disprove this view. During his four years as chair his department passed through a crucial period of expansion that provided the basis for its enormous prestige in later years. Royce took a special interest in the graduate program, which prospered under his leadership, facilitating a marked increase in the production of young scholars who became the teachers of future generations of philosophers. "Our seminars contain larger numbers than usual," he reported in 1896, "and the men are exceptionally strong." He also hoped to assist in the development of new fields of knowledge, fields that cut across traditional departmental lines, questioning "the decidedly accidental and artificial chasms" that tend to isolate the various fields of graduate study. Long before the university was prepared to take his proposals seriously, Royce envisioned a future in which the social sciences—or as he termed them, "the Anthropological and Sociological Sciences"—would develop and organize "all the academic studies thus relating to Man." Instead of merely waiting for this to happen, Royce promised that his department would take the initiative in devising plans for new programs leading to the doctorate in social science.

But perhaps Royce's greatest skill as chair was revealed in his handling of the department's two personnel crises, the cases of Münsterberg and Santayana. In the first case he had to deal firmly with an unpredictable and overdemanding colleague; in the second he had to protect a brilliant, but independent young man from conservative forces. Royce's actions in the two cases show that he recognized a subtle difference between them: Münsterberg's scientific skills could be duplicated, but Santayana, whose distinctiveness was so inextricably connected to his temperament, was irreplaceable. It is especially to Royce's credit that he saw and insisted that Santayana's independence, hostile to all forms of absolute idealism, was a prime reason for his promotion. Thus, the department that Royce handed back to Palmer in 1898 was still intact and stronger than before.

Studies of Good and Evil

At the end of February 1898, Royce promised Mrs. Dorr that his *Studies of Good and Evil*, published by D. Appleton and Company, would appear within "a few weeks." The book was already in type, the proofs were corrected, and the introduction, which Royce wrote last, had been sent to his editor, Ripley Hitchcock, two weeks before. Though a collection of miscellaneous essays written on a wide range of topics and for different audiences, the volume was controlled, Royce believed, by a unifying thesis. He identified this central concern in his introduction by answering the persistent charge that idealism has little to do with the actual world of human affairs, that it fails to meet the practical test of making a difference. "If idealism means anything," he insisted, "it means a theory of the universe which simply must not be divorced from empirical considerations, or from the business of life. It is not, as many have falsely supposed, a theory of the world founded merely upon *a priori* speculation, and developed solely in the closet. It is, and in its best historical representatives always has been, an effort to interpret the facts of life."

Royce's *Studies* is best approached as a response to the problems of his age, a turbulent decade bound by the works of two transplanted Vikings, Jacob Riis and Thorstein Veblen, whose immigrant voices were new to American letters: in 1890, *How the Other Half Lives* presented a grim portrait of urban poverty; in 1899, *The Theory of the Leisure Class* dissected the barbarism of the rich. With the panic of 1893 the surfaces of established power cracked, and the land was overwhelmed with a scoriaceous flow of discontent. "Coxey's Army" marched upon Washington; William Jennings Bryan seized control of the Democratic Party; Jane Addams's Hull-House became a center for social reform; in Homestead, Pennsylvania, strikers fought pitched battles with state militiamen and Pinkerton detectives hired by Carnegie Steel. Meanwhile politicians ignored the protests, set the government on an imperialist course, restricted immigration, annexed Hawaii, and kept an expansionist eye on the Philippines. The old century was dying, and so, many felt, was the old America.

What could a philosopher's "theory of the universe" say about this? For more than ten years Royce had kept his politics in the background. The Mugwump revolt of 1884, an early signal of discontent, helped to shape the social criticisms of *California* and *The Feud of Oakfield Creek*. Royce was appalled by violent protest; he had little faith in schemes to restructure institutions. A larger view was needed. The philosopher's contribution, he believed, belongs to the realm of historical and theoretical understanding. Above the many faiths by which men seek to change the world, Royce believed most in the efficacy of intelligence.

The book opens with "The Problem of Job," an address that Royce had prepared for a ministers' convention in Concord, Massachusetts, during the fall of 1896 and published in the *New World*. Always one of Royce's most popular essays, "The Problem of Job" won the enthusiastic approval of Richard Cabot who found the ideas "very beautifully set forth" by "the hand of the master." At his summer home in Dublin, New Hampshire, Cabot lent the article to fellow vacationers, and was interested, as well as amused, by their reactions:

> A graduate of Harvard '94, attempting a literary career—thoughtful—somewhat "gauche"—is entirely satisfied with it. His mother a really brilliant Bartimorean— agrees with it "as far as it goes" & admits that she can go no further & that she is using the same arguments with a neurasthenic niece. She thinks there is a higher *inclusive* point of view which she is unable to state. A St. Louis artist of 25 brought up 1/2 Catholic 1/2 Unitarian with a dash of Spencer is delighted with the boldness on the negative side, but is not yet ready to pronounce on the positive doctrine. (Later: She finds it all in Rabbi Ben Ezra—true but not new!) So the touch stone does its work & I gather the harvest with great glee.

The problem of Job is the problem of undeserved suffering, experienced by those who fully subscribe to Christian theology. Royce was quick to point out its contemporary relevance: "But what is to-day as fresh and real to us as it was to our poet is the fact that all about us, say in every child born with an unearned heredity of misery, or in every pang of the oppressed, or in every arbitrary coming of ill fortune, some form of innocence is beset with an evil that the sufferer has not deserved."

There are, Royce suggested, four possible solutions to the problem. First, pure naturalism. According to this viewpoint, evil—whatever one chooses to call evil—is a phenomenon to be studied, like all others, by science. Royce paid scant attention to this solution, except to notice that it avoids the real issue by abolishing the teleological character of Job's problem. In his fifth essay, "Natural Law, Ethics, and Evolution," Royce made his position clearer by showing that a purely descriptive ethics is impossible. The second solution takes the form of a modified naturalism. Evil, say some evolutionists, is a discipline, a means toward progress. Toothaches, war, famine, penitentiaries—these constitute "the dirt of the natural order," the present evil we owe to the distant good. Job should recognize that his suffering is necessary so that some good, somewhere, sometime, may prevail. But where, Royce asked, is the necessity? If God is both good and free, why does he introduce evil into the world? "An answer to Job," Royce insisted, "must show that evil is not a physical but a logical necessity—something whose nonexistence would simply contradict the very essence, the very perfection of God's own nature and power." The third solution attempts to satisfy this requirement. Evil, according to this view, is the necessary condition of moral freedom: unless we are free to do evil, we are not wholly free. But, Royce insisted, although this thesis can explain evil to the sinner, it offers no comfort to the innocent sufferer. Perhaps, the voice of free will may answer, the facts are not fully known, perhaps in some way beyond understanding Job actually deserves to suffer. If this is the case, Royce retorted, moral values are absurd, for if evil is a matter of individual responsibility and if justice hides behind an inscrutable veil, it follows that each man is a stranger in a world he can never hope to understand. To call this a moral world amounts to outright cynicism.

The crucial error in this solution, Royce maintained, the error even in Job's religious outlook, is the conception of God as a being external to human experience. To this error, idealism answers:

> God is not in ultimate essence another being than yourself. He is the Absolute Being. You truly are one with God, part of his life. He is the very soul of your soul. And so, here is the first truth: When you suffer, *your sufferings* are *God's sufferings*, not his external work, not his external penalty, not the fruit of his neglect, but identically his own personal woe.

Royce did not pause here to give a proof for absolutism, though the sixth paper in the volume, "The Implications of Self-Consciousness," offers a restatement of his favorite argument. But if one can assume that the absolute does exist and that evil therefore has a teleological meaning, the question becomes: "Why does God thus suffer?" Life, Royce insisted, entails a state of tension, but life, including the divine life, also entails a moral struggle. "I maintain that this organization of life by virtue of the tension of manifold impulses and interests is not a mere accident of our imperfect human nature, but must be a type of the organization of every rational life." Thus if pain endures, it may also be mastered, and it is for this that God chooses to suffer, indeed, must suffer: "Without suffering, without ill, without woe, evil, tragedy, God's life could not be perfected."

The second, third, and fourth papers in the *Studies* supplement this thesis with concrete examples. Bunyan, Tennyson, Faust, Mary Magdalene, and Raskolnikov help to illustrate it. Only the wretched, Royce believed, the psychopath, the mature pessimist, the tempted seeker, the prostitute, the murderer—only, in short, the sinner can rise to sainthood:

> It is Dostojevsky's hero in *Crime and Punishment*, just before he gives himself up to the police, whose eyes are truly open. This is the lesson of countless works of art in which the moral tragedy is portrayed. However coolly planned beforehand, the crime is still relatively blind. The still cooler and far deeper intellectual insight of later moments lifts the ransomed criminal above himself. He reads now the lesson of his case; but he reads only to condemn. His intellectual function is itself, if his eyes get opened, the beginning of a moral function.

The insight that assists the organization of life is primarily an insight into the self and its relationships. "What is it to be conscious? What does self-consciousness imply? Such are the questions with which philosophical idealism begins." To answer, Royce constructed a theoretical center for his work—essays five through nine. These papers, the crucial parts of which we have already noted, outline the argument that the self cannot be understood outside its relationship to God, nature, and society. Royce felt that ethical thought in his age was hampered by two factors, by naturalism which emphasizes the limits of human consciousness and by a corresponding failure of humanism to discover the structure and meaning of these limits. Royce was particularly irritated by the popularity of the naturalistic novel. "You all know," he had said in the Graham lectures, "how the author of some such book presented, with all his hard earned pathological skill, his own version of the problem of evil, as if he were the first person with insight since the days of Cain. . . . I cannot but deplore, and also to find grotesquely amusing, . . . the sort of pretended literary wisdom that is especially proud of its inability to think, and that patiently and lucratively prowls amidst ghastly facts, not for the sake of the search for real truth, but merely for the sake of emphasizing and of imparting its own weak-minded bewilderment." The "laws" of cosmology, Royce continued to maintain, have not made us; we have made them: "For nature we know, as a fact, only through our social consciousness, and the social consciousness is ethical before it is physical, appreciates more deeply than it describes, recognizes nature for rea-

sons which are, in the last analysis, themselves ideal, and is conscious of novelty, of progress, of significance, in general of the human, in ways which, in the
last analysis, make the whole cosmical process a mere appearance of one aspect
of the moral world. . . . The 'cosmos,' in the sense of empirical science, is a con-
ceptual product of the human mind."

The concluding three papers in this work enlarge on the central theme to
make applications through history and biography. Anticipating that the reader
might be puzzled by the inclusion of these pieces, especially by the philosopher's selection of an early article on California local history, Royce remarked,
"That the issues of the passing moment are also the issues of metaphysics, and
that the eternal problems are met with in the midst of the temporal, is the
familiar lesson for the sake of which I have ventured to introduce this paper into
the present series."

The story of the Sacramento squatter riot of 1850 appealed to Royce as a
miniature study of the populist mind. The article had been published originally
in the *Overland Monthly* in 1885 when Royce was finishing *California*, and the
fact that he saved it for his *Studies of Good and Evil* indicates his conviction that
the people of the United States had still failed to learn its lessons. In some
sense also, Royce's essay is autobiographical, for his parents had stopped briefly
in Sacramento before moving on to San Francisco in 1850. The elder Royce had
missed being a part of the riot by a few months; nevertheless, the son's interpretation of the event probably drew on childhood memories of family legends
and the popular idealism that his father represented.

Insignificant and even comic by itself, the event involved a brief rivalry
between factions contending for possession of the land. One party—the
landowners, who had bought their property from the eccentric John Sutter, who
claimed a vast but poorly surveyed Spanish tract—stood for "law and order"
backed by a hastily organized militia. The squatters, on the other side, appealed
to the "higher law," and their appeal incorporated the racist doctrine that properties of foreigners—meaning Sutter and the Spanish Californians—belonged
to U.S. citizens by divine right. Thus each party, though motivated largely by
greed, claimed to be following the dictates of the ideal. Their zeal led to public
meetings and eventually to bloodshed. The protagonist of the tale was a certain
Dr. Charles Robinson, later the governor of Kansas and a man deeply influenced by the radicalism of New England transcendentalism. Robinson became
the chief agitator on behalf of the squatters, and his popular, misguided idealism provided Royce with the key to his lesson: our national character, he
argued, is dedicated to a lofty and abstract idealism, but if this quality saves the
Anglo-American from rank materialism, it also leads to holy war and makes him
a very dangerous person when brought face-to-face with the concrete problem
of social existence:

That patient loyalty to the actual social order is the great reformer's first duty; that a service of just this erring humanity, with its imperfect and yet beautiful system of delicate and highly organized relationships, is the best service that a man can render to the Ideal; that he is the best idealist who casts away as both unreal and unideal the vain private imaginings of his own weak brain, whenever he catches a glimpse of any higher and wider truth; all this lesson we, like other peoples and generations, have to study and learn.

Contrasting approaches to the book's thesis were provided in the essays on Meister Eckhart and Jean Marie Guyau, the mystic and the agnostic, one who sought spiritual union with God, the other who grounded his philosophy in the facts of experience. The two are linked by a mutual insistence that thought, regardless of technicalities or conclusions, must always reflect personality. "You must continually reinitiate yourself," Royce said, "into the mysteries of your own philosophical doctrine. It must become and remain a personal as well as a technical matter with you." Eckhart, he noted, was "disposed to be always afresh dependent upon his own personal experience." Guyau, in the tradition of Montaigne, drew philosophy from life's intimate details. For Royce, the true idealist—today we might say, the true existentialist—can never separate thought from action, or principle from selfhood.

Though Eckhart ran the risk of heresy, he refused to abandon his independence, maintaining at the end of a sermon: "If nobody had been here then I still must have preached it—to this stick." The mystic's quest entailed not a loss of personality, but its fulfillment: "You cannot be in union with God," Royce observed, "unless in the very union, you remain you." This is idealism in the most practical, personal sense.

Guyau's views counterpoise those of Eckhart. The author of *L'irréligion de l'avenir* (1887) presaged the end of organized faith. Nevertheless, Royce maintained, ideological nonconformity can be the very essence of true religion. "The world has a right to your service, but never to your conformity. This is due to God alone, and you can only express it in your personal way." To be in harmony with truth as you see it and to follow its dictates—that, for Royce, is the lesson of idealism. "It is a marriage." To illustrate, Royce noted that Guyau had once experimented with the Buddhist regimen of strict diet and meditation. As a result, his life acquired a certain ethereal charm, but lost its earthy savor. Guyau abandoned the experiment, invoking the mountaineers' motto: "Follow the asses." "They do not understand mountain scenery," Royce concluded, "nor the heavens above; but here on earth they somehow know the road."

On May 5, 1898, the *Nation* announced the publication of *Studies of Good and Evil*; the same issue described one of the most decisive battles of the Spanish-American War in which Admiral Dewey's forces destroyed the Spanish fleet in the Philippines. The war had been coming for more than three months. The explosion of the battleship *Maine* on February 15 produced a wave of hysterical patriotism whipped up by the yellow journalism of Hearst and Pulitzer. With prophetic insight, Royce's book—particularly in its analysis of the squatter riot—explored the dangers of the sentiments that accompanied his country's entry into the war. "Such incidents," he noted in reference to the riot, ". . . may seem petty, local, transient, accidental, but their meaning is permanent, and they will recur, over and over, and perhaps on a constantly grander and grander scale, as long as our national history lasts." Royce was not convinced, however, that the U.S. would heed his warning, so his first reaction to the war was cloaked with irony. "I fear somewhat," he told Hitchcock, "that the war may spoil the sale of my book in Spain! But of course we all have to bear our share of the common burden. And at all events, I suppose that we shall all have to dispose of our 'castles in Spain' to the lowest bidder, regardless of cost. I hope that you don't own many. Alas, all my worldly goods are much of that sort."

This detachment was typical of Royce's statements about U.S. expansionist policies. Many of his colleagues—and academics generally—were more outspoken in their pacifism. One could sympathize with the Cuban affair, they often said; there, at least, it seemed clear that the tyranny of the Spaniards was intolerable. But how could the nation justify its attack on the Philippines? From the West Coast President Jordan of Stanford wrote protests against the alleged atrocities of the U.S. soldiers and claimed that the war was the fault of the U.S. all the way. "I rejoice," Royce told Jordan, "to see what stand you take as to the Philippine business, and I wish that I could see how to take part in the fight effectively myself,—the fight I mean against militarism."

Aside from his indirect comments in *Studies*, however, Royce did not find the way. In Boston, the feminist reformer Anne Whitney tried to enlist his protest against imperialism. Following an announcement that the government intended to serve its armed forces with bread in wrappers marked "Remember the Maine," Whitney, as a member of the committee on ethics of the Women's Educational and Industrial Union, circulated the following petition addressed to the secretary of the navy:

> We, the undersigned, citizens of the United States, considering that the ostensible and only justifiable motive for entering upon the war with Spain, was the deliverance of a neighboring people from oppression, and ourselves from relations to them that had become intolerable, wish to express our abhorrence of the spirit of vengeance manifested in such a war cry as "Remember the Maine"; and beg you to refuse to purchase goods of any kind bearing this motto; and in all ways to discountenance the use of this or any other motto calculated to foster the spirit of savagery against which we are contending.

Whitney sent a copy of the petition to Royce for his signature, but despite the fairly temperate language of the protest, he refused to sign. "I do not," he answered, "approve of many of the motives by which I find men actuated at every time of popular and passionate excitement." He opposed the war, or at any rate he opposed the spirit of vengeance that surrounded it, but at the same time he believed that one can best pacify violent emotions by ignoring them. One cannot move the hearing impaired toward a taste for music nor the angry man toward tolerance by preaching peace. Whitney's petition, he felt, could only further confuse the emotional atmosphere by stirring up hatred and misunderstanding. Furthermore, he told her, war is not totally evil; it also encourages the virtues of loyalty, sacrifice, patience, and self-restraint. "These," he insisted, "are the best means of serving humanity. . . . This is the time to serve our country otherwise than by arousing new hatreds, through protests that are as certain to be misunderstood by passion as they are to be justified, by and by, by the enlightenment that peace will bring."

Royce's apparent reluctance to take a partisan stand against the war, or to speak out against social injustice generally, often exasperated his friends. "Poor babe," said John Jay Chapman who was then involved in reform movements of all types. "He claims the privilege of not worrying over politics on the ground that he has more important things to attend to." When Chapman heard that Royce was going abroad, he romanticized the excursion. "Let him have no money. Let him come in grinding contact with life. Let him go to Greece and get into a revolution—somewhere where he can't think—I mean do this thing he does, which is not thinking. Let his mind get full of images and impressions, pains, hungers, contrasts—life, life, life—he's drawing on an empty well."

Chapman also remembered arguing with Royce at a party in the mid-1890s. "Toward the end of the feast," Chapman said, "I fell into a conversation with Royce as to the duty of the philosopher toward practical politics. Royce immediately constructed a cabin for the philosopher, crawled into it, and maintained that he would never come out of it." The discussion continued until Royce announced his departure, and as he was leaving, Chapman pursued him to the banister with a clenched fist. "There's no philosophy in the world, anyway," he cried.

The Four Conceptions of Being

Wars, petitions, and clenched fists notwithstanding, Royce would not be deterred from his life's work. Davidson invited him to lecture at Glenmore, but Royce begged off. "No," he wrote on June 23, 1898, "there is no chance that I can come to lecture this summer at your delightful place. The Gifford Lectures are on hand for this summer's preparation and my other tasks are numberless." Even an urgent invitation from Mrs. Dorr had to be refused. "The Gifford Lectures are rapidly approaching," he explained. "They are, or ought to be, in a purely technical or academic sense, the effort of my life." Naturally he felt the pressure of ambition, but more than that he viewed the lectures as a religious responsibility—"a very sacred task"—involving his duties as a "servant" of Harvard and the "high trust" of friends. "I must live up to it."

By the end of the first week in August, Royce could report that "the work is now in full swing" and that he had reached "a very critical place in amassing my materials." With the general plan laid out, he was working on "the purely mechanical scholarly preparation of the technical part of the lectures." It was a fairly lonely job that required "just brute time, the mere succession of hours, with continuity," and accordingly Royce spent his time in the solitude of his study, working in the college library, writing, taking long walks, poring over logic, pursuing suggestions, gathering notes and ideas. "From now on," he told Mrs. Dorr, "I must stay pretty much alone, except for my family, until I have something to show."

The work continued into the fall. "Even now," he wrote on October 23, "I have no time to do more than breathe and work, and sleep between times." Harvard made liberal accommodations to Royce's need for freedom. He was relieved from undergraduate teaching until the spring term when he was due to give the elementary lectures on the history of modern philosophy and a half course on the rationalists of the seventeenth century. He did, however, continue to direct his seminar, Philosophy 20C, which now emphasized the problems of logic and epistemology. James helped to lighten Royce's teaching load by taking over the advanced course in metaphysics. With freedom from teaching, he kept on schedule, and before Christmas he was ready to begin his momentous excursion.

The labor had been costly. Toward the end, he hinted some signs of renewed nervous exhaustion. By the time he reached Aberdeen, however, Royce was able to reassure James. "Cares have all slipped out of mind for the time," he wrote, "& I am making a very good vacation of it." The visit was a social as well as a philosophical occasion. Royce had never before visited Great Britain, so before heading north he spent some time sightseeing in London, Cambridge, and Oxford, where he also met many of the philosophers whom previously he had known only by work and reputation. Unfortunately the Oxford idealists, Edward Caird and F. H. Bradley, were "invisible . . . owing to holidays," and in London he missed a chance to visit with Henry James. "I found no time to meet your brother," Royce told William. "This I regret, but shall try to pay him my respects when next I go to London." Evidently, however, he did not.

"Safely launched" on January 11, 1899, the ten lectures were delivered at the rate of three per week through February 1. As its title, *The World and the Individual*, suggests, the scope and the volume of this work were tremendous. The two series into which it is divided command more than a thousand pages, and together they undertake the construction of a complete system. In accordance with the intent of the founder's will, Royce opted to examine the whole range of topics in the philosophy of religion. Thus, he designed his first series in the form of an ontological quest, "a philosophical inquiry into first principles." Asserting the primacy of "Idea" over "Fact," he announced his subject and his method: "I am one of those who hold that when you ask the question: What is an Idea? and: How can Ideas stand in any true relation to Reality? you attack the world-knot in the way that promises most for the untying of its meshes." Aside from Charles Peirce, no one in the U.S. and few in Great Britain had grappled with fundamental problems in this way, or done it on such a comprehensive scale. Clearly Royce approached *The World and the Individual* with a sense that it was not simply another book, but *the* book.

The "four historical conceptions of being" suggested by the subtitle of the first series are realism, mysticism, critical rationalism, and constructive idealism. Royce considered them in order, analyzed their arguments, and tested their results. When speaking of being, the realist means an independent object that does not depend on, is not changed by, and is not necessarily related to any idea of the object. It may be known, but the knowing makes no difference. The distinction between idea and object can, however, be misleading, for as Royce indicated, ideas are also objects and therefore are, according to this definition, real beings. If o is a person, o's ideas are parts of his independent existence; another person, when he thinks about o's ideas, has the same relationship to them as he might have to any other object. Apparently, the idea of o, like o itself, is an independent object. Either can change or vanish altogether without altering the other; they are mutually independent, unrelated entities. Let o therefore be the world, and let the idea of o be the doctrine of realism. It follows that realism can have nothing to do with reality. Each is an entity existing alone without the remotest possibility of finding a relationship to the other. By its own theory, Royce believed, realism is destroyed. "In brief, the realm of a consistent Realism is not the realm of One nor yet the realm of Many, it is the realm of absolutely Nothing."

Mysticism, the second conception of being, is "the logically precise and symmetrical correspondent" of realism. Whereas the latter is concerned only with "external meanings," the former defines existence in terms of its "internal meanings." The mystic's being is immediate; independent beings are illusions.

Both traditions are full of paradox, but whereas the realist is frustrated in the attempt to escape the antinomies, the mystic actually seems to glory in them. Mysticism, to the extent that it has a philosophical basis, tends toward skepticism—or more precisely, toward fideism. "Believe not those prattlers," the mystic says, "who boast that they know God. Who knows him—is silent."

Royce opposed realism with all of his polemical skill, but he treated mysticism as a most appealing doctrine. Countering the realist who claims to stand on the bedrock of empirical fact and practicality, Royce insisted that the mystic is "distinctly an empiricist," whose longing "to end this disquietude" makes him also "a decidedly practical thinker." On the other hand, mysticism cannot offer a sound ontology. Thus, mysticism reaches the same outcome as realism: "Precisely, then, as we dealt with the realist by pointing out that his ideas are at least as real as their supposed independent objects, so now we bring the mystic's case to its close, by pointing out that his Absolute, in its abstraction, is precisely as much, and in exactly the same sense of the terms a Nothing, as, by his hypothesis, his own consciousness is."

The fault of realism and mysticism is that both are totalistic: being for one is all outer; for the other it is all inner. The third and fourth conceptions of being attempt to reconstruct the world of ideas by uniting the internal and external meanings. Reality, Royce insisted, is *such as to be fitted to be known.* Critical rationalism is an alternative to realism. Admitting that the conception of an independent being is untenable, a former realist might redefine his theory in terms of the validity that objects give to their ideas. This rationalist resolves the problem by appealing to the objects of "possible experience." With this phrase Royce denoted the range of objects that are "relatively external" but "not wholly separable from internal meanings"; they are neither things-in-themselves nor facts of a merely private consciousness. Such objects are met in everyday life, just as they are the central concerns of moral philosophers, scientists, and mathematicians. If, for example, I say that the price of tomatoes is forty-nine cents per pound, I refer to a truth whose validity can be tested and verified. Prices, pounds, and tomatoes are not independent objects. They stand to be recognized, they are "stubborn," but if they are not recognized, they vanish. Reality, for the critical rationalist, is what we do or will experience when certain conditions are met.

Royce traced the history of this third conception to the Greek and scholastic philosophers, but Kant, he observed, gave the theory its most intelligible form. It should be clear also that validity is the trademark of pragmatism. Royce did not disagree. Indeed this third conception of being perfectly describes Royce's philosophy of the late 1870s and early 1880s. "What is, gives warrant to ideas, makes them true, and enables us to define determinate, or valid, possible experiences." If this is "not the final truth, it is," Royce admitted, "unquestionably, as far as it goes, true." It fails, on the other hand, because such truth is too exclusively and abstractly universal. Whatever is, Royce insisted, must ultimately be an individual.

How shall we define truth? Royce analyzed the answer of critical rationalism on two levels. First, truth is *"that about which we judge."* In formal logic the statement, *"All* A *is* B," means that the real world contains no A's that fail to be members of the class B. It does not assert that any A exists, but only that if it does exist, it is B. *"Omnis Determinatio est Negatio,"* said Spinoza. At best, reasoning on the basis of universals can define the world by stating what it is not; it voids alternative truths and posits the real in terms of what survives. The facts of experience can help to complete this conception of reality. Royce noted that Peirce and others had attempted to unite the internal and external meanings of ideas with particular judgments, such as *"Some* A *is* B." But particular facts are not individuals. An empiricist may speak of the "crushing force of experience," but the validity of facts is always relative to ideas. Empirical data can refute a hypothesis in particular cases, but cannot show that it is absolutely invalid.

Thus far, as Royce readily acknowledged, his analysis of critical rationalism closely paralleled the argument advanced in "The Principle of Individuation." Thought, confined to universals, can conceive only of types of being; experience, confined to facts, can relate only to particulars. Uniqueness, the hallmark of individuality, evades both. What the third conception of being lacks is any explicit attention to the purpose of thought. It claims that "true" means a *"Correspondence between any Idea and its Object."* Correspondence implies resemblance. We say that a map resembles its corresponding territory, but in what way does a ledger resemble a series of business transactions? Royce answered that purpose alone makes correspondence meaningful: "The idea is true if it possesses the sort of correspondence to its object that the idea itself wants to possess." "Ideas are like tools," said Royce the pragmatist. Just as one cannot say that a hammer is better than a screwdriver, an idea is never true or false aside from the purpose it intends to fulfill.

"What is, or what is real, is as such the complete embodiment, in individual form and in final fulfilment, of the internal meaning of finite ideas." This is Royce's fourth conception of being, his doctrine of constructive idealism. It appeared in the seventh lecture, but there it was hardly an astonishing revelation, for the grounds of this conception had been laid at the beginning. The ontological quest, Royce had noted in his first lecture, involves an understanding of the way in which ideas grasp their objects. Taking a clue from G. F. Stout, whose *Analytic Psychology* he had reviewed in 1897, Royce noted that ideas are plans of action. Thus, an idea may be defined as "any state of consciousness, whether simple or complex, which when present, is then and there viewed as

at least the partial expression or embodiment of a single conscious purpose." According to the older psychology, ideas can be likened to wax impressions made by perceptions. For Royce, however, when arguing for his fourth conception of being, man is the maker of the world, and the creative agent is the will. To speak of merely valid truths, Royce believed, is to miss the deeper truth that the internal meanings of ideas are answers to needs.

So turning away from a world where ideas merely correspond to objects, Royce encouraged his listeners to seek "an embodied life," a universe in which consciousness wins its purpose, in which it wins, in the end, the presence of God. Perhaps this sounds like the rankest subjectivism, a view too simple or obscure to withstand criticism. Anticipating this judgment, Royce devoted his final three lectures to the task of synthesizing all conceptions of being into the fourth, and of demonstrating that his conclusion follows logically from acknowledged premises. The outcome of this discussion, closely paralleling twenty years of philosophical growth, was Royce's characteristic assertion that finite experience is a fragment of the whole, of an absolutely organized experience, which is at once both universal and individual. To answer his critics, Royce outlined an antinomy which he believed must be the result of any nonabsolutist skepticism. One can recognize this argument as a restatement and further development of the "proof" in the seventh section of "The Conception of God." Let the skeptic deny the absolute; let him, in other words, assert that the realm of being includes only the facts of finite experience, and nothing beyond. For Royce this assertion can be reduced to the form, "A *is all* or, *There is naught but* A." This is to say that A exhausts all possible meanings of the idea of being. But is this negative fact—the nonbeing of non-A—included in A? Evidently not. For if the doubter says that A includes non-A, he abandons his skepticism in favor of the fourth conception of being. On the other hand, if non-A is excluded from A, its nonexistence remains a fact that is not present in all experience. Thus, according to the skeptic's reasoning, all experience does not include all experience. The only solution, Royce believed, is absolutism.

From the outset Royce made it clear that he intended to couch the problems of religion in dialectical terms, and to rely mainly on the force of his argument. A faith worthy of belief, he assumed, must be able to offer a convincing theory of existence. The ontological proof, with its devices for trapping the skeptic in a fundamental paradox, typifies Royce's general method. But there is another level in *The World and the Individual*, an emotional and psychological substratum, that parallels the logical surface. The Gifford lectures involved a journey. Half of this journey was a merely physical excursion to Great Britain, but it is also perhaps significant that Royce's destination was both the center of Anglo-American philosophy and the origin of his family's history. In a symbolic sense, the trip to England was both a departure and a homecoming. We have seen repeatedly that Royce's earliest fantasies involved that same theme, suggesting a tension between leaving home and returning home. Royce expressed the philosophical purposes of his lectures in terms of the same imagery. The second half of the journey was an inner quest for ontological truth. Along the way he left his first home, the mysticism of his parents. The mystical conception of being, Royce said, leads to nothingness, but the path of the fourth conception of being leads one back to the abandoned home. Our faith, Royce insisted, is confirmed even when and especially because we doubt it. "In vain would we wander in the darkness; we are eternally at home in God."

Royce thrived in the company of "the heartiest and most keen-witted" Scots. He was delighted with Aberdeen, and his hosts responded by treating him to a brisk social and professional life, including even a "very stately" funeral procession for Henry Alleyne Nicholson, Regis Professor of Natural Hisory, with the students in scarlet gowns looking "very picturesque." Halfway through his four weeks in Scotland he learned about some serious illness at home, serious enough to prompt the exchange of cablegrams. It seems that a particularly vicious strain of influenza had struck the household, infecting Kitty, the boys, and all the servants. On January 23 Royce answered a letter from Christopher, then sixteen and already a Harvard junior, about the situation:

> You wrote in most admirable spirit, after all the illness and suffering. Fearful as the story was, and much of the news pained me, I felt quite proud of your vivid narrative, as well as of your pluck, and of your admirable characterization of your Mother's pluck; and I thank you heartily for the letter. That you all got through the horror of it, even with so much, or so little, need for the neighbors, pleases me, despite the long catalogue that you give of the neighborly aid that was actually offered. One is sorry to need help, but in your places, I should have expected to call out. . . . But things seem to have ended well, except for the "light laryngitis" that your Mother's cablegram of today ascribes to yourself. I trust that that will come to nothing. . . . It seems a shame that these things come when I am not on hand. Only had I been there, the grip might have made mincemeat of me too. As it is, I am well.

He went on to describe the weather in midwinter Scotland:

> It is never so mean as with us. On the whole it is a sort of early April in New England,—gusty, rainy, bright, mild, raw, damp, dry, sleety, &c by turns. Only the dampness predominates more than with us. I know now what "Scotch mist" means. When I go out, I consider the other people first, to see whether or no they

have their umbrellas up. If no umbrellas are spread, I disbelieve my own judgment, and conclude that it cannot be raining, although by myself I might call it
rain. If the umbrellas are spread I say, "No, it must be rain, and not mere mist."
That is what I mean by "Social Consciousness."

In addition to his main task of delivering the Gifford lectures, he also spoke
to the Aberdeen Philosophical Society on the topic "The Recent University
Movement in America." Royce gave this address on January 31; two days later
he completed the Gifford program and headed for home. After one day in
Edinburgh as the guest of the James Seths, he proceeded directly to Liverpool
and sailed for America on February 4. By the middle of the month he was back
in Cambridge, ready for work and glowing in the pride of his greatest accomplishment.

Soon after Royce took up the familiar routine of university life at Harvard,
he also resumed his battle with James for the absolute. The absolutist's
undoubted success contrasted sharply with the pragmatist's frustrations.
James's health was poor, he had complained of his inability to make satisfactory
progress in his own program of Gifford lectures, and he watched his younger
colleague win the honors while substituting for Royce in the course in metaphysics. The textbooks for this course—Bowne's *Philosophy of Theism*, Bradley's
Appearance and Reality, and Royce's *Conception of God*—gave James the basis
for testing the validity of "the alleged proofs" for the absolute and further
strengthened his opposition to Royce's philosophy. Whether or not a degree of
envy provided some of the motivation, James chose this moment to bring his
dispute with Royce to a climax with a memorandum entitled "Royce's Argument
for the Absolute."

James habitually had two interlaced quarrels with Royce: he claimed, first,
that the proofs for the absolute are full of logical mischief; and second, that
experience can be explained adequately without "lugging in" the absolute. The
memorandum presses both arguments, but is structured around the second.
Since James proposed to demonstrate that an idealist is not obliged to become
an absolutist, he entered the dispute provisionally as one who espouses
"Berkeleyan idealism pure and simple, minus God." Anything is a fact if and
only if it falls within consciousness; where there is no knowing, there is no fact.
This, James observed, is the idealistic criterion of being. An idealist can conceive of three distinct universes: one where A is the sole fact, another where A
exists along with B, C, D, etc., and finally a world where A is known to be
related to B, C, D, etc. The three worlds would then correspond to three
"stages" of relationships between A and the others: impossibility, possibility,
actuality. When, at the second stage, we say that an actual egg is a possible

chicken, we mean only that a chicken is expected. "His coming," James added in a footnote, "*makes* the truth which doesn't *exist* now; it is an error to say that any proposition about the chicken is either true or false in advance of his actual presence." So possibility is merely our way of expressing our expectations, our way of connecting the mere succession.

But Royce would resolve the first two stages into the third. The thought of a possible chicken is already an actual fact; so finally, the absolute must be inserted to explain the actuality of nonexistence. This, James argued, is the result of a verbal confusion: "The habits of our speech," he said, "tend to make the answer sound paradoxical." Such habits might lead us to speak of "unknown facts," but these, by strict adherence to the idealistic criterion, must be ruled out. Nevertheless, Royce—so James insisted—first sets the criterion aside by saying that there are unknown facts, and then uses the criterion to prove the absolute. Suppose even a totally vacant universe, and Royce would bring in the absolute as the knower of nothingness. "Hegel's logic revives: to posit nothing is to posit being, and so on through the rigmarole."

Royce's answer, a twenty-three-page letter written in March, owes less to Hegel than to Hume. To show that empiricism is its own worst enemy, he pointed out that James's memorandum unconsciously assumes three of the excluded "unknown facts": first, that A is the same in each of the successive stages; second, that the subject who thinks of A is also successively identical; and finally, that each stage is objectively a real event. To whom are these facts experiences? Not to the finite observer, for according to James's theory, the universe is known not as a whole, but as parts grasped in succession. "If all reality is known," Royce noted, "then here is an assumed reality that 'we' indeed know not, but that is known & exists only as known." It seems that three courses are open to James: he could reject the idealistic criterion, in which case his whole argument fails; he could reject the threefold assumption, in which case he must explain experience without continuity; or he could follow Royce into the realm of the absolute.

On the basis of his memorandum, James seemed most willing to take the second course. His "possible chicken" was only a name for the "actual egg"; possible experience, he said, is a prediction of a future event, and as such it is neither true nor false in the present. What, Royce asked, are the practical consequences of this theory? Are astronomers' predictions of eclipses neither true nor false? What about insurance policies, promises, plans, schedules of classes? Is there nothing real about any of these? If one says, "President Eliot will write Shakespeare's plays tomorrow" and "Tomorrow two and two will make four," are both statements neither true nor false? No one, Royce insisted, could conduct his life without assuming a continuity between present and future, but once that assumption is made, the logic of the idealistic criterion leads irresistibly to the absolute: if facts unknown to any finite consciousness are real, and if to be real the facts must somehow be known, it follows that they must be known to an infinite consciousness.

The letter suggests, despite its length, that it was written in great haste. In addition to his spring teaching, Royce spent much of his time revising the first series of his Gifford lectures and planned to devote the entire summer to the writing of the second course. "My nose will be in the neighborhood of the grindstone," he told Davidson on May 13, "if not flat against it, until the task of grinding is done."

During the previous November, Royce had concluded a "very liberal" agreement with the Macmillan Company for the publication of *The World and the Individual*, and on August 22 he sent the manuscript of the first volume to George P. Brett, the firm's president. "The lectures themselves have received much revision," Royce noted in his covering letter. "Hence the delay." Hoping to use the volume as a textbook during the spring term of 1900, he urged Brett to proceed directly with the plans for publication. Despite promises of a second volume, Royce felt that "this first course can perfectly well stand upon its own legs, as a treatise on general Metaphysics."

In the same covering letter, Royce raised another point. He was writing and had nearly completed a lengthy essay on "my relations to Bradley's *Appearance and Reality*." Would the publisher be willing to include this piece as a supplementary essay in the first volume of *The World and the Individual*? Although the contract had not provided for the printing of extra materials, Royce hoped to convince Brett that the supplement would "increase the value of my book enough to make the addition objectively worthwhile." He emphasized his debt to Bradley's book, its widely acknowledged importance, and he suggested that since Macmillan had published *Appearance and Reality*, the company might be especially interested in his essay. Admittedly the supplement would appeal mainly to technical readers, but Royce was willing to have it printed in small type so that it would add only about a hundred pages at the end of the book.

Understandably the publisher did not enthusiastically welcome this proposal. Brett proceeded immediately with plans for the production of the lectures, but hesitated for two and a half weeks before agreeing to print the supplementary essay. In the meantime, on the first of September, Royce sent a finished copy of his essay together with a more urgent appeal for its inclusion:

> In favor of printing this paper is its close relation to the most fundamental theses of my lectures, and its importance as defending my general doctrine against Bradley, and as introducing very central ideas that I cannot pause to explain at length in my Second Series, but that I must use therein. The main problem, that of the Infinite, has recently assumed new phases, which I have here discussed in

light of the most recent literature. In brief, the paper is one of the most serious and important things that I shall be able to write, or that ever I have written.

This evidently convinced Brett, for on September 10 Royce acknowledged an agreement that the supplementary essay would be included.

"The One, the Many, and the Infinite"—as the essay was finally entitled—does much more than pick bones with Bradley. It provides, as Royce had suggested, a transition between the two series of his Gifford lectures, and most important, it defends the fourth conception of being in the language of mathematical logic. Logicians in the 1890s gave a good deal of attention to the concept of the infinite, and Royce was quick to see the possible applications of this research to metaphysics. His abundant references to such vanguard philosophers as Cantor, Peirce, Poincaré, Couturat, and especially Dedekind show again that Royce, unlike many absolutists, was an astute follower of modern logic—a quality that eventually won him a degree of forgiveness from Bertrand Russell. And yet, together with a highly condensed exposition of Bradley's theory, this attention to modern logic makes the supplementary essay one of Royce's most difficult, if not impenetrable, works. If it was, as he believed, his "most serious and important" effort, it has remained the least read and understood. Even Charles Peirce, the most adept of logicians, hesitated before reading it, citing his ignorance of Bradley as his excuse.

The philosophies of Bradley and Royce, being among the last important formulations of absolute idealism, share large areas of agreement. According to both doctrines, all experience is synthesized in the universal consciousness. But whereas Royce proposed to show how this unification is accomplished, Bradley insisted that it must remain unintelligible. His central argument involves the claim that all attempts of "relational thought" end in contradiction. To make sense of experience we group qualities into relationships: we say that the qualities A and B are related by C. But since C is also an independent quality, it needs to be related by D; by the same token, D leads to E, E to F, and so on. Thus, by the process of "endless fission," thought reaches the uneasy realm of the "actual infinite"—a concept that Bradley regarded as contradictory. Royce agreed with Bradley's analysis of the process, but he denied the contradiction.

The problem with infinite systems, Royce observed, is that they are ordinarily defined negatively—as series with no last term. But to show that they are intelligible, capable of positive definition, he outlined what he called an "internally self-representative system." Such a system is one in which the whole can be represented by one of its constituent parts. Such a system is also infinite. To illustrate, Royce asked his readers to imagine that a perfect cartographer is constructing a detailed map of his own country: when his work reaches the point where he is to be represented, he will have to draw a new map, repeating with exact fidelity all the details of the first attempt. It is easy to see that this process will lead to an endless series. But the infinity of the series is not of principal importance. More and most important, Royce insisted, is the fact that the process of self-representation expresses "a single internal purpose," which is subsequently discovered to involve an endless series. What one means, then, by the concept of the infinite is not a foredoomed search for the last term, but a "positive power to image each of my thoughts s, by a new and reflective thought s'."

After detailed elaboration and mathematical illustration, Royce applied the principle of self-representation to his fourth conception of being:

> To be, or to be real, means to express, in final and determinate form, the whole meaning and purpose of a system of ideals. . . . The Absolute must be a self-representative ordered system, or *Kette*, of purposes fulfilled; and the ordered system in question must be infinite. I accept this consequence. . . . But I also insist upon several important aspects of the *Kette* in terms of which the Absolute is for me defined. And these aspects enable me to conceive the Absolute not only as infinite, but also as determinate, and not only as a form, but as a life.

The Second Series

"Getting one book through the press while writing another, isn't, in my case," Royce admitted in December 1899, "conducive to much extra writing; and my letters pile up unanswered in a vast array." He was still working on the second series of his Gifford lectures, but hoped to finish before sailing aboard the *Teutonic* on the twenty-seventh. His teaching duties were heavier than they had been during the previous year; he had his course in metaphysics and the seminar in logic, and he was also giving a course in ethics at Radcliffe. In addition, he had agreed to give the Ingersoll lecture at Harvard, his topic "The Conception of Immortality." Royce was always a worker, but his accomplishments between February and December of 1899 were, even for him, exceptional. He revised the first volume of *The World and the Individual*, wrote the important supplementary essay, corrected proofs for both of them, wrote the entire second volume, composed *The Conception of Immortality*, which was a short book in its own right, and all the while he taught a full load, and even more than a full load, of courses. Somehow he managed to do it all. James enjoyed the wisecrack that the absolute was sitting to have its portrait painted by Royce, but to many observers, it seemed that Royce had simply become the absolute.

Though the first volume of *The World and the Individual* was scheduled for publication in January, Royce had advance copies before Christmas. He intended to carry them abroad for friends in Great Britain, but one of the copies was intended as a special gift for his dearest friend James, who, on a year's leave of absence from Harvard, lay immobilized by a heart attack at his brother's house in Rye. In November of the previous year James had noticed the first symptoms. His heart had been further damaged during a hiking trip through the Adirondacks in June, and by the time of his departure for Europe in July he was a very sick man. James had hoped to spend the year writing his own series of Giffords—*The Varieties of Religious Experience*—but now, with only a few pages written, those plans had to be postponed.

"I grieved more than I can tell over the troubles that beset your health," Royce wrote to his friend on December 3, "and especially over their stubbornness in continuing to vex." He filled out his letter with small talk about Harvard, Irving Street, the Cambridge mayoralty election, and the weather. They were enjoying a fine Indian summer.

> The squirrels are numerous and very merry, and visit our windows for their daily meal of nuts in great numbers. The Warrens have imported a very clever cat, who excites the fury of the squirrels, and who hopelessly climbs the trees after them, while I, who love both cats and squirrels, in vain endeavor to persuade them all to take a monistic view of the situation. Like you, they persist in pluralism, and will listen to no reconciliation of the One & the Many.

As for "events on the higher plane," Royce spoke of his work, his second trip to Scotland, and plans for seeing James in England. "I am not very tired," he said, "but shall be glad of a little vacation."

Approaching Queenstown on January 2, Royce wrote letters to Kitty and the boys, including the youngest, ten-year-old Stephen. To amuse the youngster he included excerpts from the ship's log and inspired him with a description of the young captain of the *Teutonic*, who at thirty-four was the youngest to hold so high a command. When he reached London, Royce found a letter for him at American Express from Mrs. James, inviting him to visit for a day or so. "I want to see you badly," James had told Royce earlier, "because there are many future problems that concern us both connected with my cardiac condition."

Royce was equally anxious to see James: "An hour with you would be a delight," he said, "if I can get it." Royce took the train to Rye, and there they no doubt discussed the "problems" that James had cloaked in mystery. In the same visit Royce gave James the copy of *The World and the Individual* he had brought over. It was inscribed with a marvelous mock-heroic obituary of the author, in German, complete with appropriate quotations from Heine, De Vere, and the medieval drinking song *"Meum est propositum"*:

Here lies buried
Josiah Royce
of Grace Valley

Fruit Vendor and Ladies' Philosopher

He died from an excess of loud garrulity
Not, indeed, greatly missed by science
Nor ever, forsooth, understood by his faithful disciples
But sincerely lamented by his creditors.

Within a few days Royce and James were headed in opposite directions—one was off to Aberdeen to begin his second course of lectures, the other headed south to Costebelle-Hyères on the Côte d'Azur. There in the Mediterranean warmth James's health was gradually restored. He plunged immediately into Royce's book, emerging toward the end of the month full of praise and mischief:

> My predominating impression is of its *charming* character in being a presentation so light and flowing, of a complex and weighty *Weltanschauung*. Its ease, its unfailing clearness, its sincerity and affability so over-spread its subtlety and intricacy as to disguise them. All this is said without the slightest prejudice to my hard-heartedness in the matter of belief, for I find the arguments you use as incoercive as ever, and the Absolute still remains for me a hypothesis to be tested by its uses, rather than a doctrine to be submitted to for its credentials. But I must say that it gives me the profoundest pleasure to see how delightfully you have got yourself together in this book. It is far more of an organic whole than any of your previous statements. I don't see how you can fail, from now onward, to be recognized as the champion of Absolute Idealism for Anglo-Saxondom, and the one thoroughly original leader of that whole school of thought. The Absolute himself must get great fun out of being you.

James came to see Royce's book as a personal challenge: "It would be too careless on the part of the Absolute to leave your lectures undestroyed by mine, but it looks as if the old sinner might be going to do it."

This last remark concluded a postcard that James addressed to Royce on February 8. It also gave news of James's health, of his life in southern France, and expressed hope that "the lectures are reeling off to your heart's desire and that you feel like a regular Aberdonian townsman." By that time, however, Royce had already completed his second series and was steaming home aboard the *Oceanic*. His visit had been full, fuller even than the visit of the previous year. Aside from the Giffords, he had lectured to the philosophical societies of Edinburgh and St. Andrews, and at Glasgow, where he lectured on the "Evolution of Conscience," he was named honorary president of the University Philosophical Society.

In addition he had given two extra lectures at Aberdeen and one at Oxford. There, at Manchester College, where Royce repeated his Ingersoll lecture, he renewed an acquaintance with J. Estlin Carpenter, Cummings's friend and namesake of the future poet, and was introduced to Lawrence Pearsall Jacks, Royce's important friend and soul mate in the next fifteen years. There had been teas, dinners, receptions honoring various occasions, and the Aberdonians had finished it off by making Royce an honorary doctor of laws. "All went well enough," he told James. "Everywhere they ask about you, & regard me only as the advance agent of the true American Theory. *That* they await from you. I received endless kindness; but they have still far more, I am sure, in store for you if only fate would permit them to get at you."

Royce read the ten lectures of his second series on Mondays, Wednesdays, and Fridays, beginning on January 10 and concluding on the thirty-first. It was clearly a sequel to the first series, and as the subtitle suggested, it applied the principles of absolute idealism to the problems of "Nature, Man, and the Moral Order." The first five lectures addressed themselves to the philosophy of nature, lectures six and seven outlined the concept of the self, eight and nine turned to ethics, and the final lecture drew conclusions.

After a brief introduction to the entire series, Royce ended his opening lecture by raising a dispute with determinism—the doctrine, stated in its simplest terms, that facts are compulsory. This view has common sense on its side, but like many of the truths that claim the same alliance, it is at best half true. The missing half relates to purpose. Take the case of the jilted lover. What vexes him? The fact of his mistress's rejection, common sense answers. But this account ignores the deeper truth that the lover has actually conspired with the fact to produce his misery. He has cared, loved, willed; he has made her the object of his loving attention, the companion of his idealized future. Royce insisted that every recognition of fact has its corresponding voluntary act. The two aspects of experience can be expressed as the worlds of description and appreciation. The first series of Giffords, climaxing with the fourth conception of being, had dealt extensively with the world of appreciation. In the second series Royce first turned to the world of description, the world of external meanings where we all must live because of finite limitations.

In his supplementary essay to the first series Royce had noted that the world of appreciation, there called a "self-representative system," has the logical characteristic of "*nextness*." A different type of serial order governs the world of description: its linkage of facts depends on the relation of *"betweenness."* Royce was influenced by a "very remarkable paper" of Alfred Bray Kempe, "The Relation between the Logical Theory of Classes and the Geometrical Theory of Points," published in the *Proceedings of the London Mathematical Society* in 1890. Kempe had demonstrated to Royce's satisfaction that "the exactly definable properties of any complete system of logical classes, or 'Universe of Discourse,' are, up to a certain point, *identical with the properties of a geometrical system of points."* In the series of points $a, \ldots m, \ldots b$, it is clear that m lies between a and b. The same is true when two classes, a and b, are related to a third class, m, so that m contains all the objects that are common to both a and b, and also is contained by the class of objects that are either a or b. Graphic representation of this principle shows the sense in which m is "between" a and b (see figure). "Betweenness," in this special sense, facilitates *discrimination*— the most fundamental, Royce insisted, of the descriptive categories. *Similar* and *different* are correlative terms: things are different only within the context of their similarities, only, in other words, when there is some common ground *between* them.

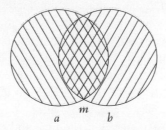

Kempe's formulation gave Royce the means for redefining the logical structure of the world of description and for solving in a fresh way the ancient puzzle of the one and the many. To most people the linkage of facts is a "dyadic" relationship, a simple juxtaposition of pairs. But Kempe had shown that the relationship is "triadic." When we want to know how any two objects are related, we must seek a third object that lies between them, as orange lies between red and yellow. Using the same examples, we might note that both red and yellow are colors. In this case, disregarding the differences, we allow a and b to blend together so that they are entirely subsumed by m. This analysis establishes the logical model for describing the linkage of finite individuals and their subsumption in the absolute. The mediating tertium quid is not only *between* the two objects, but in them—one nature with two expressions.

This leads to the working postulate upon which all scientific description depends: *"Between any two objects of the world there is always another to be found*." On the basis of this postulate it is easy to see that the theoretically possible chain of discriminations is endless. The first comparison $(a, \ldots m, \ldots b)$ may lead to a second $(a, \ldots m_1, \ldots m)$, then to a third $(m, \ldots m_2, \ldots b)$, and so on. On the theoretical plane the process will result in Bradley's problem of "endless fission," but practically speaking, the process has value, for by means of extending the chain of discriminations between a and b, our knowledge of their relationship grows more precise. Say we want to know how the English language has changed in the past hundred years. To get the answers we find the intermediaries—$m, \ldots m_1, \ldots m_2$, etc.—between a and b. In the world of description the philologist will never have to face Bradley's problem because the process will always end far short of infinity:

> And so one *could* continue indefinitely. *What* laws our discriminating intelligence and our discovery of the serial linkages shall lead us to define, this view of our world leaves us unable to predict. But that *some* laws will come to be acknowledged, this is as certain as that the serial method of interpreting the structure of our world has, within its own limits, validity.

With this last word, *validity*, Royce made the important observation that the world of description corresponds to the third, not the fourth, conception of being. In acknowledging the realm of facts, he insisted, we must also admit that they do not exhaust the problem of reality. Sooner or later, perhaps arbitrarily, the describer must cease his investigations, knowing that his method will always result in "missing links." Thus, Bradley's problem returns to vex the describer. "But," Royce countered, "the deepest principle of our procedure, even in this case, is the assurance that the One and the Many *can* be reconciled, and that the real world is the expression of our Purpose." Mere description, he said, is a "self-surrendering plan." But to appreciate the world is to see that its facts fulfill or express or represent *our* purposes.

Despite the logical technicalities of *The World and the Individual*, and all of its hard-driving polemics, we must not miss the vastly more important point that for Royce this book was a religious act, concerned in every way with the most practical moral questions of life, and of his life. No mere academic exercise, it was a bridge between centuries. Doubtless Royce—and almost everyone else—was unaware of Theodore Dreiser's *Sister Carrie*, published a few months after he concluded his second trip to Aberdeen. If Royce had read that novel, however, he would certainly have been irritated by its pseudoscientific determinism, but he might also have been deeply moved by the final pages that witness the death of George Hurstwood in a fifteen-cent flophouse, "in the blackness, hidden from view." The central issue of Dreiser's book and of Royce's book, the central issue of the twentieth century—the dream-tormented pain which Royce's philosophy addressed but could not fully exorcise—was and is the feeling of alienation.

To the child's mind, Royce observed, all is integrated; the minds of others the child meets seem related, akin to his own. But in the adult world one loses social identity, feels sundered from nature, becomes a stranger to the past and future, a stranger to God. Without in the least dismissing the importance of these feelings, Royce endeavored to show that they belong to the appearances, not the reality, of things. The naturalist makes each man an alien, oppressed *dyadically* by the unyielding forces of nature.

In his fourth lecture, "Physical and Social Reality," Royce maintained that the very concept of nature, as a complex of facts that exist apart from one's private feelings, demands the logically prior assumption that there is an organized world of social relationships. The attempt to deny this results in an extreme form of solipsism. Suppose I say that I am acquainted with some fact that no one else can know. What would you say? Probably that my privileged fact is a hallucination. What we know of nature—that is, what makes any descriptive science possible—is not its independence or its immediacy, but its presence as a mediator in social relationships, its capacity to serve as an instrument of social cohesion. "Here then," Royce observed, "is a special instance of the application of the category of the *between*. It leads to the triad: My fellow and Myself, with Nature between us." When the naturalist speaks of "the unvarying laws of nature," he should also recognize that these laws are invariant precisely because they help man to fulfill his purposes in the social realm.

The real world, therefore, contains no isolated, lifeless facts. These indeed seem, but only seem. The real world—the world of will, of values, of appreciations—is a world of social relationships, and to study it thoroughly, we need a universal sociology. This point echoes the cosmology that Royce had outlined in "Self-Consciousness, Social Consciousness, and Nature," and that, though admittedly "provisional and tentative," he still felt offered a promising philosophy of nature.

The definition of nature in terms of its place in the social order helped Royce prepare the way for an exposition of his social philosophy, where the concept of the self and its ethical relationships are central. When dealing with these subjects in the concluding half of his second series, he relied increasingly on the philosophical work that he had previously done in *The Conception of God* and *Studies of Good and Evil*.

The human self may be viewed in two ways—either empirically or teleologically. The empirical or descriptive method results in the doctrine that Royce had outlined in his essay "Some Observations on the Anomalies of Self-Consciousness": the ego is born through and bound by social interaction. Another instance of *betweenness*, imitation, is the key to the formation of the empirical ego: in imitating, Royce insisted, one performs an act of discrimination *"between the doings of some other individual and the present deeds of one's own organism."* The imitator does not merely copy the act of his model; he observes the difference as well as the sameness and, by finding the intermediaries, is able to separate the "me" from the "not-me." Thus, the ego wins its individuality through the imitative functions; while imitating, it becomes more, not less, of an individual. Seen from the viewpoint of the fourth conception of being, successive imitations become the recurrent processes of self-expression. Here, then, the empirical ego is superseded by the teleological or appreciative self. The idea of an individual self, Royce maintained, is basically an ethical idea; it is not, as Descartes's "Soul-Substance" would have it, a "Thing," but a consciously embodied "Meaning." But just as this individual meaning defines itself by its contrasting relationship to others, it also stands in contrast to the absolute. It sees itself, in the world of appreciation, as a fragment of a divine purpose:

> At this instant I am indeed one with God, in the sense that in him my own absolute Selfhood is expressed. . . . If this is my task, if this is what my past life has meant, if this is what my future is to fulfil, if it is in this way that I do God's work, if my true relation to the Absolute is only to be won through the realization of this life-plan, and through the accomplishment of this unique task, then indeed I am a Self, and a Self who is nobody else, just precisely in so far as my life has this purpose and no other.

The ethical implications of this doctrine are obvious: the individual fulfills his moral ideal by finding his true relation to God and by doing God's work on earth.

Royce clarified these implications by comparing his moral principle with the ethics of realism, mysticism, and critical rationalism. Ethical realism easily resolves itself into what is commonly called individualism. The realist's individual is an independent being; he stands alone without obligations or responsibilities, and consequently, in its extreme forms, realism has always tended to side with moral solipsism and anarchy. At the other extreme, mysticism is also unable to find the sources of moral obligation. The mystic simply "condemns all finite individuality as an evil dream," turns the moral life into an empty illusion. Correcting both of these tendencies, the critical rationalist seeks moral "validity"—through a system of laws and relationships. Royce preferred this view, but found it defective, abstract, and impersonal. Only in the fourth conception of being, he argued, do we find a moral life that is at once fully unified in the absolute and fully individuated in the finite world.

The moral "ought" that emerges from this doctrine is the principle of harmony:

Harmonise thy will with the world's Will. Express thyself through obedience. Win
thy victory by accepting thy task. The world is already thy Will absolutely
expressed. Learn this truth by conforming thy deed to an absolute law.

The homiletic style of this passage as well as its ethical insight is reminiscent
of *The Religious Aspect of Philosophy*. Indeed there is much in the final lectures
of *The World and the Individual* that suggests an earlier, and even the earliest,
Royce, the Royce of 1875 who wrote "The Life-Harmony" for the *Overland
Monthly*.

The stale odor of Royce's prose should not obscure our awareness that he
was, far ahead of his time, advancing an existential ethics. Individual freedom
is guaranteed by the fourth conception of being. Except for plants, beasts, and
robots, activity entails conscious and purposeful acts—insight and choice.
These events require "attention." Royce was uninterested in the merely inat-
tentive, the reflex action that expressed neither freedom nor responsibility in its
"invincible ignorance." But the choice of inattention—the deliberate *"narrowing
of consciousness,"* the "sin against the light"—constitutes a forfeiture of ethical
individuality. This *"viciously acquired naïveté"* corresponds exactly to what Sartre
calls "bad faith," or self-deception. Royce could not have forgotten, nor will his
readers forget, the gallant Captain Frémont whose inattention to his instructions, whose persistent refusal to acknowledge his duty, led to the violent
seizure of California. "As a man attends, so is he." To live freely and responsi-
bly with the fullest possible attention to the widest realm of values, without
deception and in harmony with the absolute, constitutes the distant aim and
only possible fulfillment of the moral life.

The final lectures treated the problems of evil and immortality. The former
had been expressed eloquently in "The Problem of Job"; the latter was a subject
Royce had held largely in the background. In 1889 Royce had read a paper at
Bryn Mawr, "The Conception of Immortality," and repeated it later in the same
year for the Free Religious Association. In a letter to Howison in 1886, Royce
expressed his already settled opinion that the question of immortality ought to
be couched in teleological terms, and in the last five pages of his supplement to
The Conception of God, he gave a brief outline of his theory. The Ingersoll lecture brought the subject into full view.

The reasons for his reluctance to publish much concerning immortality may
have involved a degree of embarrassment over the aura of superstition that surrounds the subject. Though he had flirted with parapsychology in the 1880s and
though, with James, he sometimes attended séances, Royce's theory of immortality differs sharply from the popular spiritualistic and sentimental views of his
day. It gives no credence to metempsychosis, it acknowledges no message from
the realm of the dead, nor does it send souls to heaven or find lovers reunited

in an afterlife. For Royce the problem of immortality relates logically to the inherent incompleteness of finite purposes. If any man could ever say, "My deed is done, my aims are all fulfilled," there would be no need for a continuance of life. But since no thoughtful person can say this and since every finite aim is the expression of an absolute aim, there is always an eternal need for each temporal life. The absolute needs each self immortally, for without us his internal meaning can never be satisfied. "My human form of consciousness," he concluded, "is indeed doubtless a transient incident of my immortal life. Not thus haltingly, not thus darkly and ignorantly, shall I always labor. But the service of the eternal is an essentially endless service. There can be no last moral deed."

When he wrote these words, being within a few paragraphs of finishing his thousand-page treatise, Royce might have wondered what his own next deed, mortal or immortal, would be. With the achievement of *The World and the Individual* he had reached one of life's peaks, and if at that moment he paused to see his life in perspective, he was probably gratified to find a remarkable continuity. Royce's philosophy proclaims that this collection of fragments we call life expresses a plan; so his own life, the forty-five years of it that belong to the nineteenth century, had progressed like a steadily developing plan. The boy who wondered about the world beyond his mountains had made his excursion; the young man who felt locked out and abandoned had found his way back to his home. Just as the first series of Royce's Gifford lectures ended with these emotionally important images, the second series concludes with similar words:

> This life is real through us all; and we are real through our union with that life. Close is our touch with the eternal. Boundless is the meaning of our nature. Its mysteries baffle our present science, and escape our present experience; but they need not blind our eyes to the central unity of Being, nor make us feel lost in a realm where all the wanderings of time mean the process whereby is discovered the homeland of Eternity.

Life, he had said, is a series of self-representative acts, of maps within maps. In precisely this way, Royce's book—as well as the several books that preceded this one—was a map that expressed his personal quest. One may close *The World and the Individual* with the feeling that here the quest was completed, that the plan was fulfilled, its vital questions answered, its issues finally set to rest. But no act, Royce would say, is final; all self-representative series are endless. "There can be no last moral deed."

1. *Josiah Royce in 1914*

Eisenhower Library, Johns Hopkins University

2. *Josiah Royce, circa* 1860

Harvard University Archives

3. *1875*

University of California Archives,
Bancroft Library

4. *circa 1885*

Harvard University Archives

5. *circa 1890*

Harvard University Archives

6. *Royce's mother, Sarah Eleanor Bayliss Royce*

Harvard University Archives

7. *Royce's sister, Mary Royce Ingraham*

9. *Royce's sister, Ruth Royce*

8. *Royce's sister, Harriette Royce Barney*

10. *Royce's sister-in-law, Anna Head*

Harvard University Archives

11. *Royce's niece, Eleanor Ingraham*

Harvard University Archives

12. *Josiah and Katharine, circa 1914*

13. *Royce's wife and sons (from left) Stephen, Christopher, Katharine, Edward*

15. *Royce's second son, Edward*
Harvard University Archives

14. *Royce's first son, Christopher*
Harvard University Archives

17. *Royce's daughter-in-law,*
Marion Woodworth Royce

Harvard University Archives

16. *Royce's third son, Stephen*

Harvard University Archives

18. *Royce's grandson, Randolph*

Harvard University Archives

19. Meadville, Pennsylvania, 1902.

20. With Margaret Gilman, 1902

21. *William James and Josiah Royce, Chocorua, New Hampshire, 1903*

Harvard University Archives

PART THREE

The Final Years
1900–1916

Chapter Seven

The Fading Light
of the Absolute
1900–1908

The Idealist in a New Century

As his friends sometimes remarked, Royce was best met in simple surroundings—in plain restaurants, at seminars, or breathing free in the open air—and on such occasions, seeming most himself when dressed informally, he paid slight homage to the genteel tradition. The Californian in him, emblemized in his crushed and cherished "western" hat, shunned the stylized role of the Harvard professor or the rites of academic ceremonies. His friends were understandably astonished when, on Commencement Day in 1900, Royce appeared in the full regalia of an Aberdonian doctor of laws, a degree conferred in absentia that summer. Palmer said he "came out like a butterfly in his many colored hood." The revised style fitted Royce's mood, for as Palmer also remarked, he seemed "well suffused with a sense of kindness, adventure, & triumph."

The image of Royce at the height of triumph was captured in two photographs taken at Meadville, Pennsylvania, in 1902, where he repeated the lecture series "Social Factors in the Development of the Individual Mind," previously given at Boston University in 1898. His host, Nicholas Paine Gilman, was a jovial professor at the Meadville Theological Seminary and an editor of the *New World*, which had published a number of Royce's essays. In the first snapshot Royce is standing on a garden path. His arms are relaxed, and the sense of the whole body is that of repose. The right leg, however, is thrust forward, and the head too is pointed as if he is in the act of taking a step. His once

257

flaming hair has turned to a sandy gray, but there is no other hint of age in the photograph. Instead we see here a man in his fullest maturity, composed and ready to act. His mouth is curled into a Giaconda smile, and his eyes are leveled in the direction of the pointed foot. Here is a man who settles his weight confidently, but who is already moving toward his next task. In the second photograph the philosopher is showing the inner workings of his pocket watch to a little girl—his host's daughter, Margaret Gilman, who was later a professor at Bryn Mawr. Here Royce seems older. As the child stands stiffly in her white pinafore, he appears to shrink, his face benevolent, but drawn. The expressions of both man and child as they lean toward each other are fixed intently on the clock, and for a moment they share an intimacy, united, as a Roycean might observe, by the time between them. The two photographs together present contrasting metaphors of Royce in the first decade of the twentieth century. In one we see him in his mid-forties—alert, vigorous, poised in readiness for the next phase of his life—but in the other he seems already to have passed prematurely into his role as the father figure of American philosophy.

These years brought new advances to Royce's thought, particularly in the areas of logic and ethics, but steadily, when he estimated his place in the decade, he saw it as a period of declining power. As a portent of the times, Royce found himself, during the first two years of the new century, writing obituaries. Charles Carroll Everett and John Fiske were colleagues whom Royce had known since his earliest years at Harvard. Each had been appointed to the faculty during the first year of Eliot's presidency, and though neither was an enduringly original thinker, each had been instrumental in the academic awakening of the 1870s. Both also were deeply committed to the task, which Royce continued, of reconciling science to faith. Everett—he died on October 16, 1900—was a theologian and dean of the Harvard Divinity School whose major work, *The Science of Thought*, defended religion against Darwinism. Representing the opposite viewpoint, Fiske, who died nine months later, was an evolutionist whose *Cosmic Philosophy*, which Royce would later edit, attempted to apply Darwin's theory to the development of man's spiritual consciousness. Royce probably knew that the ideas of Everett and Fiske would not survive, but as he saw in them parts of himself, he probably also felt that their deaths prefigured his own. In them he saw the beginning of an end of an era.

A greater and more personal loss came with the death of Joseph Le Conte, who died at Yosemite on July 6, 1901. Royce promptly wrote a memorial essay for the *International Monthly*. He felt, as he said at the opening of the essay, that he could finally voice the affection and gratitude which might have seemed too indelicate to express while his teacher was still living. Death had unlocked that inhibition. As Royce remembered Le Conte, he regretted his earlier reticence, and he also remembered a phrase that he had previously used in a letter to Mrs. Dorr: "In a busy world . . . our meetings with so many of our best friends are but like the encounters of ships at sea, which signal, and pass on, and are then lost to view in the wilderness of waters." Life is a lonely voyage—repeatedly that feeling haunted Royce's inner world, and no doubt he loved his teacher more than even now he could say. In the essay Royce emphasized his student years when "Professor Joe" had been primarily for him a source of inspiration. Leaving the judgment of Le Conte's work to future critics, Royce said little about the details of his thought. The personal inheritance, however, was the kind that a father can leave to his son: "He has left," Royce said, "in his ideals and in his life-work a model for an age of specialism and of divided sympathies to reverence and to follow."

While thinking and writing so much about death, Royce doubtlessly was also concerned about James. By the summer of 1901 James had, however, recovered sufficiently to complete the first series of his Gifford lectures, *The Varieties of Religious Experience*, and by the following September, when he returned to Cambridge, the two were reunited. The separation had been very painful for both men. In the previous year Royce wrote frankly to James about that feeling:

> The year to come will be very lonesome without you, and my own interest in Harvard is more bound up with my associations with you than it is with any one other interest. Philosophy I love for itself, and life for its general meaning. But Harvard originally meant to me *you*, and the old association remains still the deepest. I shall go on, and lecture; but the Department can have its real meaning to me personally only when you are here. And I ought the more plainly to say that, because I am so poor a letter writer, and so silent, that you must think me less bound up in you than I always am. My defect as a letter writer is simply a result of my writing so much otherwise. The writing centres rebel at anything but lectures and books. But the heart has its own life too, and I miss you deeply.

He filled out the rest of the letter with lighthearted news about Harvard and Cambridge. A group of teachers from Cuba had attended the summer school and "gave a very weird seeming to Harvard Square." The Cuban women were "picturesque" as they sat in rows during the evenings next to Memorial Hall, but the men with their wide trousers, swart faces, cigarettes, gestures, and shrill voices reminded Royce of "a bird store when the parrots are lively."

Irving Street also had its lively sounds. The Foxes—Jabez Fox was a judge of the Superior Court and the next-door neighbor to the Royces—had rented their house, and the eldest daughter of the new family aspired to an operatic career. "Her purposes are professional," Royce lamented, "her conscientious devotion to them is absolute, and her voice is that of Brynhilde on a charger." The professor viewed her "with profound, but somewhat timid respect" and was "not altogether comforted for the loss of our admirable Foxes." Across the street Edward Cummings had been appointed pastor of a Unitarian church in Boston. "Cummings," Royce quipped, ". . . has joined the company of the saints . . . and the neighborhood gains in sanctity daily."

There was also a rumor that Charles Lanman had "so impressed some of his Ceylonese friends with his work as editor of Buddhist Scriptures, that a shrine has been erected in his honor somewhere out there, and he is in the way to be worshiped with special rites!"

Royce asked, "And now when you consider once more your neighbors, as these familiar names recall them to you, doesn't it make you feel ready to get back to Irving St.? Where else are to be found such judges, clergymen, apotheosized Orientalists? But I forbear. At all events, I assure you, Irving St. needs you, and will miss you until you come."

James answered his "Beloved Royce" on September 26, 1900, with the same fine mixture of genuine sentiment and good humor:

> I need not say, my dear old boy, how touched I am at your expressions of affection or how it pleases me to hear that you have missed me. I too miss you profoundly. I do not find in the hotel waiters, chambermaids, and bath-attendants with whom my lot is chiefly cast, that unique mixture of erudition, originality, profundity and vastness, and human wit and leisureliness, by accustoming me to which during all these years you have spoilt me for inferior kinds of intercourse. You are still the centre of my gaze, the pole of my mental magnet. When I write, 'tis with one eye on the page, and one on you. When I compose my Gifford lectures mentally, 'tis with the design exclusively of overthrowing your system, and ruining your peace. I lead a parasitic life upon you, for my highest flight of ambitious ideality is to become your conqueror, and go down into history as such, you and I rolled in one another's arms and silent (or rather loquacious still) in one last death-grapple of an embrace. How then, O my dear Royce, can I forget you, or be contented out of your close neighborhood? Different as our minds are, yours has nourished mine, as no other social influence ever has, and in converse with you I have always felt that my life was being lived importantly. Our minds, too, are not different in the *Object* which they envisage. It is the whole paradoxical physico-moral-spiritual Fatness, of which most people single out some skinny fragment, which we both cover with our eye. We "aim at him generally"—and most others don't. I don't believe that we shall dwell apart forever, though our formulas may.

One can exaggerate the philosophical differences between Royce and James. After all has been said about their endless battle, one must acknowledge the larger areas where they agreed. If Royce's world was "silly . . . idiotic . . . dropsical," "bloated and puffy with superfluous consciousness," James still acknowledged the aim they shared. And if they were to be linked historically in a "death-grapple," they were also united in an "embrace."

The first several years of the twentieth century were frustrating for Royce. *The World and the Individual*, though a climax in his career, had taken its toll. He was exhausted, more so than he knew or chose to admit. He had "a sense of being driven, a discomfort with the sight and presence of classes and responsibilities" that left him feeling "morally tired,—mildly aboulic, so to speak." Vacations at sea during the summers partly dispelled the fatigue. In 1900 he took a short cruise to Charleston, South Carolina, and in 1901 he ventured on to New Orleans. The destinations were fairly unimportant; it was the sea itself that Royce needed, the soothing hours alone on deck with pen and paper. The long voyage to Australia had once healed his shattered nerves; now and for the rest of his life he sought restoration in briefer versions of the same therapy. While on his way south in June 1901 he told James that he needed a period of rest before he would feel ready to face a heavy schedule of work in the latter parts of the summer. On the sea he found a way to relax, free of distractions. "And if one wants a quiet journey," he added, "I don't know any better rule than to go in whatever direction the crowd is not going."

The task to which Royce referred in his letter involved the revisions of his second course of Gifford lectures. Although he had completed the oral delivery of the series in January 1900, he continued to work on the lectures for a year and a half. The finished version, he told his publisher, was not only "revised," but "in very large part rewritten." Suggestions gleaned from the three surviving drafts of the series, together with the carefully dated notebook entries between January and August of 1901, indicate that the major revisions were made in the first two lectures where the Kempean structure of the descriptive world appears and in later sections where he applied that structure to ethical questions. It seems safe, therefore, to suppose that Royce had decided to hold back the publication of his second volume until he had managed to color the whole with the logical theory that he was just beginning to absorb. "I seem to myself," he told James, "to be on the track of a great number of interesting topics in Logic," and then alluded to the series of lectures that Peirce had given in Cambridge, during February and March in 1898, "Reasoning and the Logic of Things," calling them "epoch marking for me." After a brief visit in New Orleans Royce sped home by rail, "ready for the summer's campaign," and after two months of hard work he sent a complete and final text to the Macmillan Company on August 22. The book then moved rapidly through the press and was published before the end of November.

The "last agony" had been a struggle. "I had been confident of finishing sooner," he told Münsterberg, "but the job dragged." Altogether, from the first invitation to the final publication, it occupied almost five years of Royce's life; in sheer expenditure of time *The World and the Individual* was undoubtedly his costliest undertaking. But now that was behind him, and if he felt drained by the effort, he must also have known that, regardless of the future, he had earned for himself a secure place in the history of philosophy.

"The year was a pretty tangled one," he told James. But since, as Royce always insisted, the philosopher needs to see his theories confronted by concrete experience, the lessons of death—like the deaths of Everett, Fiske, and Le Conte—were not lost on Royce.

In the spring of 1901, he became entangled in a different and distant issue. Midway through the academic year of 1900–1901 Stanford University found itself in turmoil over a case of academic freedom involving the distinguished economist and pioneer sociologist Edward Alsworth Ross, who had been summarily dismissed by President David Starr Jordan. The case smelled strongly of political interference by Mrs. Leland Stanford, the benefactor's widow and sole trustee of the university. Ross had first angered her in 1896 by publishing *Honest Dollars*, a pamphlet in which he made an outspoken defense of Bryan's populism.

From its inception, when Royce had been offered the chair of philosophy, he had taken a special interest in the Palo Alto campus, and though he had refused the offer, he had lectured at Stanford in 1895 and had been instrumental in the appointment of his student A. O. Lovejoy to its faculty. The Ross case prompted two letters that Royce addressed to John Stillman, his college friend and former colleague at the University of California. Stillman, professor of chemistry, supported Jordan's policies. Royce cared little about the political issues in the case, but he did believe that a professor should have the right to speak his mind and that a university administrator should feel bound by duty to defend that right vigorously. "As to the principle of academic liberty," he reminded Stillman, "you know my views of old." He was referring doubtless to his 1883 article in the *Overland Monthly*, "The Freedom of Teaching." In his several discussions of this principle Royce never questioned the right of academic authority to judge the fitness of a professor, but Jordan's actions caused him to suspect duplicity and a tendency to cave in under external pressure. In his first letter to Stillman he asked for a frank explanation of the apparent contradiction between the president's first warm approval of Ross and his subsequent dismissal. Had Jordan merely compromised his own opinion in deference to the benefactor's power? Stillman's nine-page answer, though it added new information and raised doubts about Ross's competence, did not satisfy Royce with regard to the honesty of Jordan's position.

The case remained, Royce insisted in his second letter, a threat to the integrity of university life on the national level. He was sensitive to the charge

that the huge endowments presented to private institutions had political strings
attached and that these conditions tended to force professors to maintain a discreet silence on controversial matters. Ross had spoken, he had lost his job
because of his candor, and the case seemed to prove the charge that the universities were either unable or unwilling to defend their freedom against the
power of the donors.

Here was another practical illustration—not unlike those that Royce had
developed in *California* and *The Feud of Oakfield Creek*—of the conflicts that
arise when loyalty to the community is threatened. If Ross strongly resembled
the crusty Alf Escott of the novel, President Jordan took the role that Eldon's
son Tom had played; at best he was a Quixote when he should have been a
Prometheus. The incident soon disappeared from public view: Ross eventually
finished his career at the University of Wisconsin; Lovejoy also departed, in
protest, and later became a champion of academic freedom at Johns Hopkins.
For Royce too the incident was transient, but its deeper meaning was not forgotten; it remained a part of the background in *The Philosophy of Loyalty* and
The Problem of Christianity.

Several years would pass before those books were to emerge. In the meantime Royce had a great deal of other work, and he felt the pressure especially
in August 1901, when he looked forward to the next academic year. Münsterberg
had suggested that they might spend some days together at his summer home
in Clifton, but in refusing the invitation Royce noted that he would be busy
with his lectures for Philosophy 15—The Theory of Knowledge, now for the first
time to be offered as a full-year course—and that he owed "several different
things" to various editors. He meant that he still had proofs to correct for the
second volume of *The World and the Individual*, and he might also have been
involved in the completion of his fifteen articles in Baldwin's *Dictionary of
Philosophy and Psychology*. His major contributions to this work—"Greek
Terminology," "Hegel's Terminology," "Kant's Terminology," and "Latin and
Scholastic Terminology"—no doubt required of Royce more research than their
brief pages could indicate. In addition he had, as president of the American
Psychological Association, to prepare his official address, "Recent Logical
Inquiries and Their Psychological Bearings," scheduled for the midyear meet-
ing in Chicago; and looking beyond that, he was committed to a trip in February
to Baltimore where he was to receive an honorary doctorate and chair the inauguration banquet for Ira Remsen, the incoming president of Johns Hopkins.

One more commitment developed in October. In 1894–95 Royce had written a chapter on the practical and educational aspects of psychology for a popular book about hygiene entitled *In Sickness and in Health*, published by D.
Appleton in 1896. He had used this material in a series of lectures on psychology that he gave in St. Louis during January and February of 1895, but it

264   remained unpublished. The composition of this minor piece had been engrossing—in some ways, vexing—and in his last letter to the firm's editor, Celeste
Winans Herrick, he had bristled a little in annoyance with her persistent
requests for revision.

As early as September 1897 there was correspondence promising that Royce
would write a book on psychology. Ripley Hitchcock had written: "We had
hoped to have your Psychology this autumn. . . . I am very anxious to have your
most important new books on our list and hope that nothing will prevent."
However, after *Studies of Good and Evil* Royce ceased to have a working relationship with Appleton. On October 18, 1901, George P. Brett of Macmillan proposed that Royce expand this chapter into a book, one of several in the *Teachers'
Professional Library* edited by Nicholas Murray Butler. The publisher's terms
were satisfactory, and Royce probably also welcomed the opportunity to
"sketch" his psychological theory. He felt that he might be able to complete this
job during the spring of 1902, but stipulated an August deadline. The revision,
he explained, would be difficult, and a list of his mounting engagements, as he
complained a few months later, would fill "2 vols. quarto."

Overburdened, Royce looked with favor on an opportunity to spend the next
summer in California. The Berkeley president, Benjamin Ide Wheeler, suggested this possibility in a letter of September 23, 1901. He proposed a six-week
lectureship in Berkeley's summer school. In his reply accepting this appointment on the twenty-eighth Royce explained that his Gifford lectures had
absorbed all his free time for the last several years, and as a consequence he had
been deprived of vacations. "While I am in reasonably robust condition," he
added, "I have still felt that *next* year, I ought to have a decidedly longer and
clearer summer rest than I have allowed myself for a long time."

With this feeling Royce was moved to protest when he received, during the
following spring, the university's official announcement of summer courses.
George Holmes Howison had outlined the philosophical offerings in language
that strongly suggested some "scrimmage" between him and Royce as a sequel
to their famous debate of 1895. Against this suggestion Royce had a "decided
complaint":

> The untrammeled freedom to choose one's topic, and to treat it in one's own way,
> belongs of course without the least doubt to anyone in your position. I do not for
> an instant call in question that freedom, or object to it. But the right to announce
> as part of a scheme of instruction, what you yourself call in your letter to me a
> "scrimmage" with a colleague who comes as an official guest, is a right which can
> only rest upon previously consulting the person with whom you propose to have
> the "scrimmage." For a polemic announcement of this sort necessarily predeter-
> mines the plan, not only of your work, but, in some measure of mine, since it

brings students to the class with a sort of interest which I may, or again may not choose to use for the purposes of this course.

Royce went on to insist that his agreement to teach in Berkeley's summer school required no more than a repetition of one of his Harvard courses. President Wheeler had promised him a quiet summer, free of "entanglements" and "public responsibilities." Royce saw his duty as "solely to get my students to worm out of me whatever they can, in the time, in the way of help about thinking for themselves." He now had no desire for controversy, and let Howison know that he would decline to participate in polemics: "I hope that you will not expect more than a passive, and perfectly cheerful acquiescence, on my part, in your right and duty to set forth to your students exactly what you think proper. I shall try to confine myself to telling my own story, without joining any public issue, of any sort with you."

As Royce was soon to admit, he had entirely misunderstood his friend's intentions. Howison was too ill to engage in heavy polemics; he had never actually expected that, and his letter to Royce explaining his position was enough to bring forth an extended apology. "I now see," Royce wrote just before setting out for California in June, "that my interpretation of the intended situation was wholly wrong, and I have no wish, at this time, to defend the grounds of that interpretation, as I then made it. Enough, if the interpretation was my blunder, the complaint founded thereon by me entirely falls to the ground. I am sorry indeed that my blunder caused you pain." Giving a clue to the motivation behind his outburst, Royce explained that the Gifford lectures had exhausted his once abundant supply of zeal in public debates. "The long and somewhat straining job of the past five or six years has left me perhaps too anxious to avoid for the time any unnecessary public discussion. I like to be criticized. But I don't like any longer the responsibilities of controversy, where I can escape them."

There was perhaps another kind of strain that Royce did not mention, but that certainly was and increasingly became a source of private annoyance. The effort of writing *The World and the Individual* had been great, but the experience of unrewarded effort must have been greater. To Palmer, it was "a masterpiece, the greatest treatise on its subject in our language." Close friends like the loyal Cabots also praised it. The first volume prompted Ella Cabot to write:

> We value very greatly this book from you. It is a peculiarly rich possession, for much of our life with you is bound up in it. . . .
>
> Your formulation of the four modes of Being has very vividly lighted up that realm for me, and the discussion of the Infinite grows more & more significant as I meet it in different realms.

The official criticism, however, though polite, amounted to a categorical rejection. He had struggled to the top of his profession only to find himself the acknowledged master of a dying philosophy. Instead of bringing the world around to his belief, Royce merely created a wave of reaction.

Wendell Holmes, the newly appointed associate justice of the Supreme Court, gave Royce's first volume a rapid perusal. It was, he told William James, "very able," but perhaps, he also said, it might better be called "thimblerigging with the Divine." Holmes's feeling that Royce's argument was little more than a logical trick led, probably at about this time, to what Chapman characterized as "a curious Bostonian cockfight"—an afternoon's entertainment at the home of Sarah Whitman:

> Professor Royce and Judge Oliver Wendell Holmes were pitted against each other to talk about the Infinite. Royce won, of course, somewhat after the manner of Gladstone—by involving the subject in such adamantine cobwebs of voluminous rolling speculation that no one could regain his senses thereafter. He not only cut the ground from under everyone's feet; but he pulled down the sun and moon, and raised up the ocean, and everyone was shipwrecked and took to small planks and cups of tea.

Here, as always, Chapman was more in touch with the comic side of Royce's character than with his deeper feelings. Chapman's Royce was a persistent controversialist, impervious and indestructible.

Other critics more readily perceived Royce's weaknesses. "The ideas are very beautiful," Charles Peirce told William James. "The logic is most execrable." Peirce objected to Royce's equating of the absolute with God. "The Absolute," he said, "is, strictly speaking, only God in a Pickwickian sense, that is, in a sense that has no effect." And yet Peirce did not write off the book as a failure. In two reviews published in the *Nation* he made it clear that he saw *The World and the Individual* as the beginning of a long-awaited development: the union of religious philosophy with modern mathematical science. As such, he predicted, Royce's book "will stand a prominent milestone upon the highway of philosophy."

> Prof. Royce has inaugurated a vast reform, affecting not only the philosophy of religion but every department of metaphysics, and consisting in sweeping away all the vaguenesses and vagaries that now prevail in that science and replacing them by such exact ideas as Weierstrass and Cantor have begun to introduce into mathematics. No other man in the world, prominently before the public, is half so capable of working this matter out as he.

Peirce repeated this judgment in a private letter to Royce, mixing his praise with a now famous and often quoted piece of advice:

> Now as to your work generally, the introduction of exact ideas into metaphysics makes it one of the very most remarkable performances in the whole history of philosophy. I cannot admit that you have solved the problem; but you have taken a seven-league stride toward it; and at your age, with the best years of philosophic study before you, the philosophic world may hope that you will yet accomplish the great achievement of bringing metaphysics up into the company of the peacefully progressive sciences. It appears to me that the time is ripe for it and that you are the man to do it.
>
> Your present solution of the problem is I believe on the right track. The relation between the individual & God must be something like what you say. It is a sublime conception, fit to satisfy the heart of man in life and in the hour of death. But aside from the impression which is left to me that it is only one side of the matter, there are various philosophical ideas to which it does not do justice, and to meet which it has to be deeply amended. I should think you would inevitably find out what these are. But the great danger which everybody interested in the progress of metaphysics must be interested in your avoiding is that of your logic remaining in its present violent conflict with the logic of all the successful sciences. I entreat you to study logic.

Peirce felt that Royce's exposition was full of "innumerable vague and unsatisfactory points"; among them was his blindness to the fact that the philosophical realist maintains that there is a difference between *being* and a *representation of being*. Royce, Peirce insisted, had blurred this elementary distinction and so had constructed his argument around a false definition of realism. He had failed, the critic continued, to refute the realists with the logic that they themselves recognize as valid.

Peirce noted that Royce's work was most cogently addressed to those who were already converted to absolute idealism. Realists, on the other hand, would remain unconvinced: "If you drive them into a corner," Peirce observed, "they will simply modify their admissions so far as may be necessary to avoid self-contradiction."

This prediction soon proved true, for during the next decade a school of thought, calling itself the "new realism," drew its forces together to attack Royce's central beliefs. As a vanguard of this reactionary movement, its titular leader Ralph Barton Perry published one of his earliest essays, "Prof. Royce's Refutation of Realism and Pluralism," in the April 1902 issue of the *Monist*. Echoing Peirce's warning that realism would simply decline to accept Royce's definition, Perry insisted that the realist "would never recognize as descriptive of himself, Professor Royce's statement of the *absolute mutual separateness* of idea and object." Independence, Perry maintained, is not reciprocal: the object *o* is independent of the *idea of o*, but the *idea of o* is not independent of *o*. "The realist," said Perry, noting Royce's alleged fallacy, "would contend that the *idea of o*, as a psychological entity, was independent, not of o, but of another idea, the idea of *idea of o*."

Since Royce's whole argument against realism demanded a reciprocal independence between ideas and their objective referents, realists had an opportunity to attack him that they doggedly pursued. Sweeping aside Royce's detailed critique of the possibility of error and rejecting his central dictum that all reality is some form of consciousness, Perry sought to restore the commonplace of realism that ideas are derived from actual experience and that to know them to be either true or false we must refer our ideas to the world of empirical fact.

Just as *The World and the Individual* became a target for the "new realists," it also gave the pragmatists some useful practice in philosophical marksmanship. It was, however, neither Peirce nor James who first took advantage of this opportunity. Peirce, noting the volitional aspect of Royce's theory, had emphasized his affinities with the "pragmatistic spirit." James refrained from public criticism; even in *The Varieties of Religious Experience*, which was consciously motivated by the hope of overthrowing Royce's monism, he admitted "momentary evasion" of his philosophical duty ". . . by not even attempting to meet Professor Royce's arguments articulately."

On the other hand, John Dewey, who was in the process of shedding his neo-Hegelian skin and giving coherence to the "Chicago School" of instrumentalism, did not hold back. Dewey wrote two remarkably judicious critiques of Royce's volumes for the *Philosophical Review*. In the first of these, he passed rapidly over the dispute between Royce and realism; he summarized the chapters on mysticism and ignored totally the long supplementary essay. What most interested Dewey was the argument by which Royce passed from critical rationalism to constructive idealism, and it was in this transition that, the critic felt, Royce had failed. This failure was due in part to "an elaborate misinterpretation" of the rationalist's position: Royce had jumbled the Kantian terms "real," "valid," and "possible experience" so that they were no longer distinguishable. This had led to an "oscillation" between "validity as immediate but fragmentary" and "validity as universal, ideal but infinite." Royce, so Dewey maintained, "blows hot and cold upon our 'finite' experience": on the one hand, he says that our experiences are meanings fulfilled in absolute reality, but on the other, he says that finite experience is inadequate, merely universal, or indeterminate. Dewey insisted that these two views were incompatible, or as he put the matter more positively: "What we need is a reconsideration of the facts of struggle, disappointment, change, consciousness of limitation, which will show *them*, as they actually are experienced by *us* (not by something called Absolute) to be significant, worthy, and helpful."

Santayana was another dissenter. Although he had privately ridiculed *The World and the Individual*, particularly the Supplementary Essay—calling it "a nightmare" and comparing the absolute as a self-representative system to "Jonah eating a whale"—he wrote to Royce with studied restraint and much politeness. The book, he said, "seems to me to make your doctrine more approachable for those of us to whom it is not a native conviction, and the supplementary essay gives it more definition, I should say, than any of your previous works had done." Nevertheless, he had at least one crucial objection:

> I don't see, for instance, how the third and fourth conceptions escape a kind of realism in that they still seem to make one part of the system of things *representative* of other parts and of the whole, not included in the given part, and seem to be related to it only by a third person—the philosopher himself. For the *existence* of the completion of my life is no datum of my life itself, although the *demand* for that completion may be such a datum.

So far as is known Royce did not respond to these criticisms. The once pugnacious enfant terrible now often avoided disputes and allowed his critics' objections to stand unanswered. Dewey's criticism must have been particularly distressing.

Both Peirce and James had, on various occasions, made the same objection to the idealist's solution: the pragmatic onslaught against Royce persistently made much of the charge that the absolute was a deus ex machina that had little relevance to everyday life. James once described the absolute as "a useless excrescence on a universe that is already large enough."

Royce might have hoped that his second volume would satisfy Dewey's concern, but the opposite was the case. "I am still bound to say," Dewey remarked in his second review, "that my most careful study of the new volume has only strongly reinforced my conviction of the contradiction inherent in the old." He still charged that Royce's concept of finite experience was "question-begging" and that his whole metaphysical outlook was "permeated with this illusion of double vision, of reduplication." Worse still, Dewey saw in Royce's cosmology—as outlined in the conclusion to his fifth lecture, "The Interpretation of Nature"—nothing but "vague analogies" and a "highly precarious proposition" which could only "bring philosophy into disrepute." Dewey felt that Royce was too willing to speculate about what might lie beyond consciousness and too little disposed to deal with "the actual warp and woof of our experience." He could sympathize with Royce's predilection to treat ideas as plans or purposes, but he insisted that these are constructed in response to human restlessness and must be relevant to it. In his *Studies in Logical Theory* (1903) Dewey's colleague A. W. Moore repeated and clarified this criticism of Royce's absolutism: "It is when the idea as a purpose, a plan, born out of this matrix of restlessness, begins to aspire to the absolute system, and attempts to ignore or repudiate its lowly antecedents, that the difficulties concerning fulfilment begin."

Through the years Royce had grown accustomed to bearing his critics' judgments in silence; this time as usual, he said nothing.

Family Interlude II

Rumors still echoing through Cambridge suggest that people in general—especially students and neighbors—found it impossible to describe Royce without reference to his family and its turmoils. He remained that shy, strange, lonely man, sometimes mistaken for a university janitor. Katharine, on the other hand, stood out. She performed magnificently at social events where she was habitually surrounded by circles of worshipful students. At one small reception she was holding a conversation with the gifted African American student, W. E. B. Du Bois:

> We ceased conversation for a moment [Du Bois later recalled] and both glanced across the room. Professor Royce was opposite talking excitedly. He was an extraordinary sight: a little body; indifferently clothed; a big red-thatched head and blazing blue eyes. Mrs. Royce put my thoughts into words: "Funny-looking man, isn't he?" I nearly fainted.

This anecdote accords with Rollo Brown's memory that Katharine was "a vivid personality . . . with picturesque speech which she did not hesitate to employ." She called the little boys in the neighborhood "rats" and "muckers"; "war paint" was her name for cosmetics; and a future ex-daughter-in-law was a "vampire." She was devoted to music and language. When William James came to borrow a translated Aristotle, Kitty, with a wicked smile, handed him a volume in Greek. Tender souls recoiled when she stripped away their pretensions, but tougher students encouraged her incisive tongue:

> Metaphysics—what did she think of metaphysics? Well, had they heard of the old game of hunting the doll? You take a doll upstairs, and then you take it on up to the attic, and then you go back into a dark corner and find a trunk and put the doll deep down in the trunk. Then you go back downstairs and say, "I wonder where the doll could be." And you begin turning up rugs and moving furniture all over the first floor; and then you go to the second floor, and throw everything off

the beds and out of the linen chests and the closets; and then you go on up to the attic and empty out everything up there; and finally you say, "Do you suppose it could be in that old trunk?" and look there, where you knew it had been all the time. That was metaphysics.

The students who heard this parody felt elevated by the discovery that the professor's rhetoric was matched by his wife's sense of the absurd. "Philosophers!" she once protested. "I think philosophy is *drivel*, absolute *drivel*." To prove her point she opened a volume at random and read a few sentences. "Can you imagine anybody writing anything like that?" When asked about her marriage to a great philosopher, she answered: "Just like being married to any other fellow when you didn't know what he was talking about."

Estlin Cummings sketched a vivid tableau of Josiah and Katharine. Though Cummings's memory belongs to a later period, it seems a timeless portrait of their married life:

> I myself experienced astonishment when first witnessing a spectacle which frequently thereafter repeated itself at professor Royce's gate. He came rolling peacefully forth, attained the sidewalk, and was about to turn right and wander up Irving, when Mrs. Royce shot out of the house with a piercing cry "Josie! Josie!" waving something string like in her dexter fist. Mr. Royce politely paused, allowing his spouse to catch up with him; he then shut both eyes, while she snapped around his collar a narrow necktie possessing a permanent bow; his eyes thereupon opened, he bowed, she smiled, he advanced, she retired, and the scene was over.

Cummings turned the same scene into a poem that first describes a stripper named "dolores" who is built like a Rolls-Royce. The poem concludes:

> while softly along Kirkland Street
> the infantile ghost of Professor
> Royce rolls
>
> remembering that it
>
> has for
> -gotten some-
> thing ah
>
> (my
>
> necktie

Despite his enormous dialectical power, there was something curiously infantile, soft, and peaceful that endured in the adult Royce. Katharine, by contrast, seems best described in terms of strength, protection, and motherhood.

As one of the neighborhood children, Estlin Cummings had many opportunities to observe the Royces, and his impressions were shared by his playmates. The professor was their favorite. Betty Thaxter found him "very gentle" and "off in a world of his own"; she "wasn't at all sure whether he was God or Santa Claus." Concerning Mrs. Royce, however, the children had no illusions. They saw her as a woman of "very high temper" who was constantly chasing "rats" out of her yard and who seemed "to take a certain pleasure in getting children into trouble by tattling to their parents about anything they had done." The older boys, Billy and Aleck James, were her special enemies. Once Katharine, who never forgot their distant Irish heritage, was seen chasing them down Irving Street, shaking her fist and shouting: "Paddies!" In retaliation they organized a "Riot Club" devoted to keeping "her life well-stirred up." They devised an ingenious means of vexing her by stringing a line across the street so that a passing carriage would trip her doorbell. But their most famous prank—one that according to some versions of the story was invented by her own son Christopher—thwarted Mrs. Royce's plans for a social tea. A few moments before the scheduled event they hung a funeral wreath on her front door: the guests, perceiving a death in the family, turned away.

Trusting rumors, one can get a distorted impression of the waspish Katharine Royce and the stress she imposed on her marriage. Recent evidence, on the contrary, suggests that Josiah and Katharine were deeply united as husband and wife, as parents, and in other family relationships, and their love for each other deepened as they grew older. The death of Kitty's mother is a case in point. In October 1900 Eliza Head came to Cambridge to spend the winter with Katharine and with other family members and friends in Boston. At seventy-two and a widow for ten years, Eliza had already suffered "a long period of invalidism." By Christmas she relapsed. Medical examination revealed a host of problems including acute kidney failure. From March to May she was confined to her bed, and the last two weeks were the worst. "Then indeed," Josiah confided, "death showed his teeth, and the end was pathetic enough." Katharine bore most of the care, and in letters to her sister, then vacationing in Greece, she insisted that there was no need for Anna to return only to stand by the death bed. Eliza died on May 6. With Kitty's well-tested resilience she needed only a quiet summer for recovery. As for himself, Josiah "was not especially out of sorts, once our season of winter cares had passed away into the quiet grey mood that death leaves behind it when the aged die."

Josiah's sisters and their families were intermittent problems. Mary, his eldest sister, had married Ossian Ingraham, a jovial mechanic and a hard-drinking man.

They lived in terrible poverty. She died in 1889 from pneumonia, having given birth to eleven children, seven of whom survived, including Eleanor, who lived with Josiah and Katharine in Berkeley and Cambridge, and who worked later at the Stanford University Press. Harriette, or Hattie, was married to Charles S. Barney, then divorced, was always unstable, worked as a secretary, and was a constant drain on Josiah's emotional and financial resources so long as he lived. Ruth, by far the most reliable of the three sisters, was the librarian at the State Normal School in San Jose.

By 1900 the younger boys, Ned at thirteen and Stephen at eleven, were sent to summer camp. Christopher, newly a graduate at eighteen from Harvard and an avid bicyclist, was off on his own, riding forty-five and even sixty-five miles a day. At about this time Royce assured James that the "boys have had reasonably good health." None of them, however, was really robust. Family correspondence relates with some alarm various bouts with childhood illnesses. Stephen suffered from asthma, and Ned seems to have been physically weak throughout his life. Obviously the parents were concerned about the boys developing physical stamina, and summer camp with its healthy outdoor life seemed the answer. The effort proved worthwhile. Returning from a day's visit to Stephen, "Popps" wrote, "I have reached home safely, and have told your Mother all about you. She is glad to hear how well you have done." Concerning a proposed hike into the mountains, however, Josiah and Katharine were adverse to giving permission: "She and I both think that, in view of the doubts and difficulties of the mountain trip, you had better not go upon that."

Ned and Stephen returned to camp each summer for the next few years. In 1901 Christopher, still cycling during the summers, visited Ned; "Fuffy," Stephen's nickname for Katharine, described the splendid success of the camping experiment: "Coco has been down to Gloucester one day and found Ned very brown & fat & healthy & a grand swimmer."

Sometimes she wrote about her seemingly idyllic summer life with Josiah:

> Papa and I had a perfectly ideal visit with the Palmers at Boxford. We had two lovely walks in the woods, all pines and ferns and moss and the dearest brook. And in the midst of it all was a circular spot clear of everything but moss called the Fairies' Ring.—Then we went with quite a party through the woods to a dear little lake & all went swimming, & had a picnic supper afterwards, & then drove home through the deep woods with a good natured shaggy horse called Hobson, who poked his way where there seemed to be almost no path just like a sheep.

Such attentive, lyrical appreciation of the world's beauty permeates many of Katharine's letters. "Mamma," Josiah once wrote to Ned, "seems very content with her garden, which is indeed lovely; and the robins, bees, hummingbirds,

274 &c. agree with us in thinking it a very good place." To Katharine, the world resonated with music; it was scented with flowers, animated with people and with pets—cats, white mice, rats, canaries, pigeons, and goldfish.

Of the two Josiah was more distant and lonely. Time and again he searched through the house, as in his earlier dream, for the love that always eluded him. Browning's poem "Love in a Life" provided the words for Royce's feeling:

> Room after room,
> I hunt the house through
> We inhabit together.
> . . . .
> Yet the day wears,
> And door succeeds door;
> I try the fresh fortune—
> Range the wide house from the wing to centre.
> Still the same chance! She goes out as I enter.

Royce once quoted lines from this poem to illustrate the tragic mystery of the individual. An individual, he had observed, is never an object of abstract thought or of finite experience. We individuate by loving, but love expresses aims that can never be wholly fulfilled. The lover of Browning's poem cannot find his beloved because she is what he wants her to be; exclusively she belongs to his ideal world and cannot be touched. "Individuality is something that we demand of our world," Royce said, "but that, in this present realm of experience, we never find." "The unique eludes us; yet we remain faithful to the ideal of it; and in spite of sense and of our merely abstract thinking, it becomes for us the most real thing in the actual world, although for us it is the elusive goal of an infinite quest." Royce's need to generalize, to give a universal meaning to his personal feelings, nearly conceals this confession of the enormous and crushing tragedy of his life. A neighbor and former student remembered that his "loneliness was a solitude of cosmic proportions."

Locked doors and empty rooms are images that haunted Royce's dreams. And yet he continued to search. "This finite situation has its own perplexing and beautiful irony," he wrote. "We rise above our helplessness even as we confess it; for this helplessness hints to us that our real world is behind the veil." These thoughts are found in *The Conception of Immortality*, the one book he dedicated to "K. R."

California Sojourns

On June 19, 1902, Royce left for his six-week stint at the University of California. He was distressed when he heard that his departure coincided with

William James's return to America from his second series of Gifford lectures in Edinburgh. "It was heartrending," Royce wrote from Chicago the next day, "to have all my arrangements made for leaving Cambridge, just in time for the California engagement, and then to learn that you were to arrive at about precisely that moment."

James's arrival had been preceded by *The Varieties of Religious Experience*, an advance copy of which Royce got from James's son Harry. He soon lost the book, however, by lending it to President Eliot, who evidently forgot that he had borrowed Royce's sole copy of his friend's work. "So much for Eliot's variety of religious experience," Royce quipped. "But to lose the book thus," he added, "gave me still another 'variety,' from which I haven't recovered yet. The few hours spent over your book gave me great delight. It is a wonderful thing."

On the same day, still in Chicago, Royce wrote to Charles Peirce, apologizing for his seeming neglect and giving an overdue answer to two letters, those of January 19 and May 28. In the first of these letters Peirce had made an appeal for help; in the second he had offered assistance. The appeal was a request for Royce's support in an application that Peirce was submitting to the newly formed Carnegie Institution in Washington. Peirce had outlined and partially written a treatise entitled *Minute Logic*, but to complete the work he needed a grant to cover living expenses, books, typing, and a subvention. Royce welcomed this plan and hoped that he might be able to influence Daniel Coit Gilman who, following his retirement from Johns Hopkins, had become the first president of the new foundation. As Gilman had envisioned the Carnegie Institution, it was designed to encourage "unusual talent" and "secure the publication of very extended memoirs, for which there is at present no adequate provision." These purposes probably encouraged Royce to feel that a means for promoting his friend's work had finally arrived.

Royce assured Peirce that he would help him in every possible way. In fact, in February he had had a lengthy conversation with Gilman in Baltimore; the subject of Peirce's application had been the main point of the interview, and Royce had urged the president to act favorably. Then in March, after reading two chapters of the proposed work and a prospectus for the whole, Royce had sent Gilman a detailed letter, emphasizing Peirce's preeminence among American logicians and his need for institutional support. Royce felt that he could state the argument for the first point objectively, but he put the case for the second in terms of personal sympathy:

> As to Mr. Peirce's need of assistance in order to complete the proposed work, there seems to be no doubt. Here of course plainness of speech is necessary. Mr. Peirce is a worker whose personal eccentricities are not unknown to you. He has never been able to fit into the official plans of other men for any great length of time. He has not been either the most frugal or the most provident of scholars.

He is now obliged to earn a living by various literary and other tasks that do not contribute to science. He lives more or less from hand to mouth, and probably has no savings. He is past sixty years of age. While he seems still capable of rapid and skillful production, his powers cannot indefinitely continue to respond to the calls made upon him. Unless he is aided to complete what I regard as his great task, his later results will be lost to the world. What I have lately seen of these results convinces me more than ever that they ought not to be lost.

Not only in this letter, but also in a conversation with the secretary of the American Academy of Arts and Sciences, Royce continued to support Peirce's case. Despite his good intentions, however, Royce was forced to admit that his "power to be of aid is indeed small." Peirce had already anticipated a failure, believing that his enemies, the "microscopical microbes," would prevail. In the next several months his apprehension was confirmed. For a time it appeared that a grant might be forthcoming. A plan was devised whereby the Carnegie Institution would establish a trusteeship administered by Royce, Dewey, and G. S. Fullerton, who were to supervise the work and make payments to Peirce as he completed segments of his manuscript. Even this cautious arrangement ran into trouble. In May of the following year Peirce learned that his application had been formally and finally rejected.

Royce probably did not know the depth of Gilman's animosity toward Peirce. From Joseph Brent we learn that on the occasion of his visiting Christine Ladd-Franklin, Gilman was told that Peirce was a guest in the house; whereupon the distinguished gentleman marched out, saying "he would not remain under the same roof with so immoral a man." Clearly, to Gilman, Peirce's deficiencies went far beyond "personal eccentricities."

Peirce's offer to assist Royce was made as a suggestion that the two men might spend the summer of 1902 together. The idea was that Royce should move his family to Peirce's home in Milford, Pennsylvania, where they could undertake a program of cooperative study in logic and Hegelianism, each teaching the other in his specialty:

We have [Peirce wrote] a large house up here in this beautiful country. There are four large bedrooms vacant, an extra study, and lots of other room inside and out. Now if you would bring your family up here for the summer, servants and all, dividing expenses as easily as could be arranged, you and I could pitch in to the logical problems and I am sure I could make it well spent time for you, while with all you should teach me of Hegel etc. I am equally sure it would tremendously benefit my own work.

Royce thanked Peirce briefly for the invitation. It was a "kind proposal" and "very attractive . . . rendered extremely so by my wish to make some real progress before long as to some logical questions about which you, of all men, could best enlighten me."

It is certain that Royce found a more restful summer in Berkeley than he could have expected at Milford. He appeared on the coast during the last week of June. Before settling in at Berkeley he delivered a Phi Beta Kappa address entitled "Provincialism" at the University of Iowa on June 10 and made a short detour to San Jose where he delivered a commencement address at the State Normal School (now San Jose State University) and where he also undoubtedly visited with his sister Ruth, whom he had not seen for seven years. For this occasion Royce selected an address that he had originally prepared for Founder's Day at Vassar College on April 28, 1899. Its title was "On Certain Limitations of the Thoughtful Public in America."

The selection of this particular speech is indicative of Royce's mood in the summer of 1902, a mood that became gradually more dominant in his life and writings during the next decade. He had reached the age when people tend to look backward, when instead of anticipating the future, they seek wisdom by examining the past and reiterating the insights they learned in youth. Returning to California's Bay Area, Royce brought memories and reflections, warnings and beliefs, which his mind had been incorporating since his student days more than twenty-five years earlier. His address at San Jose was full of autobiographical details and retrospective attitudes; perhaps the most important of these was his repeated use of the same passage from Sophocles that had formed the basis for his commencement address at Berkeley in 1875: "These things," says Antigone, "are not of to-day or of yesterday, and no man knows whence they came." His faith that events in our lives are subject to higher laws had been and remained the central doctrine of Royce's philosophy.

The United States is "a nation of idealists." That was Royce's thesis, though he doubted the soundness of some forms of idealism. The Puritans, he asserted, were idealists; so were the signers of the Declaration of Independence, and even the Civil War had been inspired by idealism. But Royce, who has often been compared to Socrates, wholeheartedly accepted the Socratic creed that the unexamined life is not worth living. In quoting Spinoza, Royce also accepted his advice: "Human affairs are neither to be wept over nor to be laughed at, but to be understood."

The danger he foresaw in American civilization was not due to materialism; rather, the danger was the pursuit of vague ideals, and accordingly he warned his audience about the hazards of the amorphous idealism that feeds on empty dreams. That was not a new insight for Royce, but a thoroughly settled conviction, one that can be traced to *California*, *The Feud of Oakfield Creek*, and other works. Unlike Henry Adams who felt that older ideals had been overrun by the new technology, Royce believed that the fundamental idealism of the people of the United States had increased during the years following the Civil War:

"Numerous forces," he insisted, "have been at work to render us as a nation more thoughtful, more aspiring, and more in love with the immaterial things of the spirit." The utopian economics of Henry George and Edward Bellamy, as well as the extravagant populism of Bryan, provided Royce with his clearest examples. Populism, he believed, "had its origin quite as much in practical idealism as in material distress. Its fundamental motives were in considerable measure philanthropic, humane, and, in an abstract way, vaguely large-minded." This vagueness, Royce insisted, is the chief limitation of the intellectual class in the United States. Thought must be critically steadfast; mere earnestness is not enough. And yet too often the thoughtful public in the U.S. is attracted to novel schemes and fads; it floats from doctrine to doctrine, feeling for each the same temporary enthusiasm that a new play, an exhibition of new pictures, or a political party might inspire.

Royce saw that there are two contending types of idealism in the U.S., one which works consciously and relentlessly to know the truth, another which is content to live in fantasy. In American literature the two idealisms have been repeatedly portrayed and pitted against each other; they are embodied in the contrast between Ishmael and Ahab, Huckleberry Finn and Tom Sawyer, Nick Carraway and Jay Gatsby. It is the same contrast that Royce drew in the characters of Alf Escott and Alonzo Eldon, and that, he had maintained, was the core of his dispute with Abbot. Perhaps Royce also had in mind some memory of David Belasco, his former schoolmate who had risen to the heights of theatrical fame in New York. Within a few years Belasco would produce *The Girl of the Golden West*, an extravagant melodrama which presents life in the California gold rush as a triangular conflict involving a virgin barmaid, a mustachioed villain, and a gentleman thief. Royce knew the true story of the mining towns, and he abhorred the popular tendency to envelop that history in a false romance. The virtues he urged his audience to cultivate were those of the Protestant ethic that his parents had taught him, the virtues of study, faithfulness, resignation, and work. "Learn to wait," he said at the end of his address, "to believe in more than you see, and to love not what is old or new, but what is eternal."

Having come to cherish what he had learned from experience, Royce spent much of the summer in nostalgic repose. Established at 2401 Le Conte Avenue, a street named in memory of his beloved professor, he doubtless found that his rooms satisfied his simple needs for "a sound sleep and a good bath." He spent a good deal of his time with Ruth, Hattie, and his five Ingraham nieces, including Eleanor who was now a young woman of thirty-three. He also wrote to Katharine "constantly." Writing to Stephen in summer camp, she said he should "write a fair share of your letters to Papa, as he seems lonely out there." Indeed Josiah did complain about the "lectures, dinners, conferences, receptions, and all the other drearinesses of such a job." In one of his letters to Stephen, he praised his son for becoming a "good woodsman" and admired his descriptions of mountain hikes and wildcats. He went on to describe an excursion by railway up Mount Tamalpais with his sisters and another outing on an army tug to Alcatraz where he was given a grim tour of the military prison and then a happier visit to the naval installation on Goat Island.

On June 30 he helped to launch the summer session by giving an address to the first university meeting. As Royce's title, "The Old and the New—A Lesson," suggests, he was mainly interested in drawing a contrast between the university as he remembered it in the early 1870s and the same institution thirty years later. The speech was rich in autobiographical detail. Royce emphasized his relationship to Le Conte and Gilman; he recalled also his youthful love for the books he found in the university's tiny library. An important part of his argument was that a few great men and a handful of books can make a foundation for a great university. Royce wanted to impress his audience with his belief that progress cannot be measured wholly in terms of material accomplishments. Buildings and other resources are not the university; the university consists in the loyal work of its members.

Two weeks later, in a letter to Münsterberg, Royce described his routine, acquaintances, and general impressions:

> I lecture on Metaphysics here, at the Summer Session; see friends; hob-nob a little with Baldwin; keep out of the way of the summer school women students whose name is Legion; watch the sunsets; and revel in youthful memories. Howison is at Shasta Springs—invalided. He has given up doing anything at the school. Baldwin's family occupy Bakewell's house. Montague is faithful, and has matured a good deal, showing signs of improvement. California, as a State, seems to me not to have progressed as it ought; but the University, at all events, is in a wholesome state of progress. Wheeler works like Hercules.

Baldwin—that is, James Mark Baldwin, the psychologist—rendered a somewhat different portrait of Royce at that time. Just after describing Royce's enormous capacity for argumentation, Baldwin gave this thumbnail sketch:

> Royce and I lectured side by side one summer in the University of California. Driving to a San Francisco hotel on arriving we were besieged by reporters asking for our opinions of California. Royce was ready—no catching Royce! Had he not, a Californian, written a book on his native State? I shrank in fear behind him.

It seems that the paradoxical sides to Royce's character were still yoked, one side that sought peace and tried to stay out of trouble, the other side that welcomed controversy and was ready for all comers. If, as he grew older, the peaceful side became more persistent, on occasion he could still make the sparks fly.

In his letter to Münsterberg, Royce did not mention any writing that he might have been doing. It is nearly certain, however, that he used his free time in Berkeley to press forward in the writing of *Outlines of Psychology*. He had hoped to complete the book by the end of the summer and had set for himself the goal of finishing in August. In June he saw that he would be unable to deliver the manuscript before September 1. A letter to Brett explains the reasons for his delay:

> When you first urged upon me the task, and I consented, I said that I should act as promptly as possible, but that it would be hard to be as prompt as you wished. I have since worked on the matter when I could. But the great mass of novelties in Psychology makes the task harder than I expected.

Evidently the summer in Berkeley was not entirely restful. "I think," wrote Katharine, "they have lionized him a little too much out there & he has not had as much quiet as he wanted." He returned home on August 12, and a few days later Katharine wrote a very tender letter to Ned and Stephen:

> Papa & I have had two good outings together. On Friday we went boating on the Charles at five o'clock & took our supper with us & ate it way up above Riverside & came home at nine o'clock. The light was soft & pretty & we came down river by moonlight. . . . Papa seems very pleased to be at home again & very much satisfied with me & with the house.

At home Royce continued working on his *Psychology*, and the task proved to be even more demanding than his letter to Brett admitted. Eventually he needed another extension of five months. In the fall he took on the additional job of editing and writing a long introduction to a new four-volume edition of John Fiske's *Cosmic Philosophy*. Finally, on February 4, 1903, he mailed a revised and final manuscript of approximately a hundred thousand words to the Macmillan Company. He was not especially proud of the result. It was, as he said to James, "my poor little *Psychology*."

Indeed the book has been almost wholly ignored by modern historians. Nor did Royce seem to expect that the book would have more than a momentary popularity. It was, he explained in the preface, an elementary treatise designed to give teachers some guidance in understanding the processes of learning. That use was soon exhausted. What remains, the most recent scholarship seems to agree, is the insight the book gives into the psychological bases of Royce's meta-

physics, for the really distinctive feature of *Outlines* is its discussion of the volitional aspect of consciousness. According to the fourth conception of being, the   281
real world is the fulfillment of an absolute purpose. In *Outlines* Royce persistently argued—and meticulously illustrated the point—that there is no mental
life that is wholly receptive. Sensory perception and habit, as well as mental initiation, involve and express the will. "Thought," he said, meaning consciousness
in general, "is either action or nothing."

The reader of *Outlines of Psychology* will surely recognize Royce's debt to
James, and this perhaps gave the two friends a topic for discussion when they
met again in September. The Jameses were installed at their summer home in
Chocorua, New Hampshire, where they were enjoying their first full reunion in
four years. Royce paid them a visit in August, and afterward he wrote to Mrs.
James a warm letter of thanks:

> Two things stand out with special prominence in my mind as I look back upon
> my brief but very delightful visit at your beautiful home;—first, the satisfaction
> that I felt in finding my beloved colleague so strong and well again, so free of
> movement about the woods, and so heartily his old self; and secondly, my sym-
> pathy with you yourself as I saw you with all the family once more together about
> the same table. Such good things seemed so far off when I saw you at Rye. And
> now I have seen the fulfilment of what you then so patiently were working to
> accomplish. I thought of you for so long after my visit at Rye with such sorrow for
> your divided household and your long waiting, that it was especially joyous this
> time to witness the fruition of your labors. As for my visit with James, I hope that
> my cantankerousness didn't weary him too much. I dearly love to argue about
> some things, but I hope that he didn't find me unbearably disputatious. I thank
> him much for his good care of me.

This letter was written from Irving Street on September 9. For the rest of
that month Royce worked on the Fiske project and also probably spent a good
deal of his time looking over his class notes in preparation for the fall semester.
His teaching load would be one course lighter than it had been in the previous
year. His advanced logic was to be omitted; that left him with a half course in
elementary logic, the advanced course in metaphysics, which he reduced to a
single term, and the graduate seminar in logic. The cutback was doubtless the
result of Royce's having been granted a sabbatical for the spring term in 1903. It
was to be his first leave of the sort in twenty years of teaching at Harvard. To
provide for a smooth transition into the spring term, it was decided that Royce
would share his teaching in the seminar with Richard Cabot. The two men
worked closely together in the fall term; in the spring Cabot directed the seminar on his own.

Royce planned his sabbatical leave so that he would be as free as possible from toil and minor irritations. To achieve this end, he decided to take a month-long steamer cruise to California by way of the Isthmus of Panama. Ordinarily Royce would have preferred to travel alone, but on this occasion he took fourteen-year-old Stephen with him. They set out on the first leg of the trip, on board the *Seguranca*, from New York on February 6. Since the Canal had not yet been constructed, they had to disembark in Panama and transfer to a mail boat, which was scheduled to bring them to San Francisco on March 11. The connecting steamer did not appear as promised, so they did not reach California until the eighteenth. Royce had a strong and generally distasteful impression of this first part of his voyage. He loved the natural beauty of the coast, especially the huge volcanoes, but the food was bad and the prolonged delays at each port were tedious. The poverty and vice of Central America appalled him. He was disgusted by some of his fellow passengers, by the "ragged and pompous officialism" he found in the ports, and by the "squalid degradation of the common folk." "It is a land," he told James, "where nothing decent appears to the passing stranger to be going on." And yet, he added afterward, he was glad to have had the experience.

Waiting for Stephen when they arrived in California was a letter from "Mamma." She had taken a bicycle ride one morning and her mind was full of images of springtime:

My dear little Stephen

This morning I rode round the pond, and the water was that wonderful deep blue that only comes with pure air & a brisk wind. I heard three sorts of bird songs, but am too green to specify the kinds. Anyway they were lovely and they mean spring. Also muckers are playing marbles & girls are skipping their ropes, & the brown & cream colored flutterbys are out so spring is coming. The pigeons have fresh gravel—pounded oyster shell, which Ned pounded for them. . . . The other day Yellow Puss carried a chop bone all the way down stairs & gave it to Christopher, remarking prrmeow, as if he were her kitten. . . . Mysie was over today & sang two or three dear little songs for me. She was very sweet & dear. Yesterday I saw a very tall pretty girl coming along Irving Street & she waved her hand and smiled and who should she be but Sue Taber, prettier and sweeter than ever—coming to see me. She sent her love to you, & so did Mysie. Coco says he would like to see you in a room with them both to see which you would run to first. Well, deary boy I hope you are well and happy, and don't forget about de Fuffy—Be good to Papa always—

With very best love
Mamma

From San Francisco he went to San Jose to see Ruth, and then to Glenwood in the Santa Cruz Mountains where he spent much of his time out of doors enjoying the beautiful woods and mountain torrents. "As you may well imagine," he wrote to Münsterberg from Los Gatos in April, "I am neither seeking nor finding any great intellectual experiences in these parts." Moving lazily southward, Royce spent a month in Avalon, Santa Catalina. Stephen's chronic asthma was the principal reason for the move, and the island provided an excellent climate for the relief of his nightly wheezing. The whole atmosphere was one of restful indolence. "Here," Royce told James, "we now abide in a cheap little cottage by the shore, row occasionally in our rented boat, read our Latin or our Logic, according to our age and our business, loaf a good deal, wash dishes a little, eat also part of our meals at restaurants, and look out upon a very peaceful sea, in excellent weather."

From time to time he read the proofs for *Outlines of Psychology*, but he was in no hurry to finish his work on "that not very promising book." He spent the main part of his time on logic, which he felt was considerably more promising. "Logic," he wrote to James, "treated in the main as an empirical science of the morphology of the concepts in actual use in human thinking, and of the reasoning process also in actual use, looms up before me more and more as the thing to be worked upon." He assured his friend that logic is thoroughly "pragmatic": "For all thinking is doing; and logic might be defined as the science of the forms of conduct, so far as they are not so confused by passion as to be unconscious forms of conduct."

Pragmatism and Personal Crisis

Leaving Catalina toward the end of May, Josiah and Stephen continued their restful tour of California. They stopped at Yosemite in June and probably spent a few more weeks with relatives in the north. By mid-July they had returned to Cambridge. Royce had expected to be "quite hungry for work," and soon after his arrival he made arrangements which guaranteed that his time would be well occupied. George Brett asked Royce if he would be Macmillan's consultant in the areas of philosophy and psychology. In 1901 Royce had turned down a similar request, but now he consented. Immediately Brett started sending manuscripts that Royce read and criticized. The work consumed a great deal of time, and the compensation was precious little, usually fifteen dollars for each assignment. The extra money to be earned from this enterprise was perhaps less important to Royce than the satisfaction he felt in being an effective leader in American thought. Without question Macmillan was the most distinguished publisher of philosophical works in the U.S., and during the ten-year period of Royce's consultantship, he had a large hand—as both invisible patron and severe critic—in determining which books would reach the public.

The arrangement was initiated in July. During that month Royce also agreed to give a series of lectures at Columbia University in February. F. J. E. Woodbridge, who made the proposal, had suggested that Royce might deliver as many as ten lectures in the field of metaphysics. By mutual consent the plan was scaled down to a series of five, and reflecting Royce's current interests, it was also agreed that the program would focus on the relationship between metaphysics and logic. The construction of these lectures became his major undertaking in the fall of 1903. Under the general title "Some Characteristics of the Thinking Process," Royce attempted to introduce the new logic into philosophical discussions. The bulk of his lectures bore such technical titles as "Classes and Classification," "Relations and their Types," "Ordinal Concepts and Ordered Series," "Concepts of Transformations," and "Concepts of Levels." In conclusion Royce suggested the revolutionary importance of modern logical research and challenged philosophy to modify its procedures in accordance with these findings.

Thus, in his Columbia lectures Royce anticipated directions for philosophy in the twentieth century. Acquiring a more logical outlook, philosophy would tend to ally its interests with mathematics; it would become more specialized, more technical, and consequently less popular. Gradually it subordinated its interest in what Royce and others called "the philosophy of life," and became generally suspicious of speculative or constructive philosophy. In the process it lost most of the wide audience enjoyed by the so-called Golden Age of American Philosophy.

Although Royce wanted to lead philosophy in this direction, he did not welcome these consequences. His own work, from the turn of the century till the end of his life, tended to follow two separate paths: one was concerned with the abstrusities of logic; the other was more involved in questions of social and metaphysical thought. Often he protested that the two paths were really one, and he persistently tried to unite them, but the reconciliation seems to have remained clearer in his own mind than he could make it to an observer. "The lesson of mathematics," he once observed, "that by rational creative activities we come to participate in the very being of an uncreated world is the great common lesson of art, of morality, of religion, and of philosophy."

A concrete effort to unite the two paths can be seen in Royce's creation of the Philosophical Conference in 1903–4. Taking its name from a semiofficial group that had been organized in Cambridge in the 1880s and 1890s, the conference was an informal gathering of friends that met fortnightly at Royce's home. Membership included Richard and Ella Cabot, Mrs. Glendower Evans,

Frances Hall Rousmaniere, W. E. Hocking, Reginald Robbins, George Dorr, Mary Calkins, and others. Royce planned and coordinated the meetings with the hope that the conference would be free of the structure imposed by a regular university course. The central purpose of the gatherings was to make practical applications of speculative problems. At the first meeting on October 19, Royce presented an "Introductory Statement," in which he gave the background to his idea of the Philosophical Conference, offered some suggestions for its procedures and, most important, expressed his philosophical credo:

> I believe that the modern developments of purely logical technique offer great prospects for the future of philosophical theory. Newman used as the motto of his "Grammar of Assent" the well known statement that God has not been pleased to save his people by the dialectic art. Now I do not myself accept this thesis. I think it probable that at least some of God's people will in the near future be saved, in part, by Symbolic Logic. The means of grace are numerous; and amongst the "varieties of religious experience" I believe that there are some in which the use of mathematics finds, and in future will find, a considerable place. I think then very highly of technical research; and it is far from my purpose, in this presence, to make light of such research. Yet I do also insist that the final justification of all technique lies in its power to save somebody, or to save some vital interest of humanity, from the practical calamities which confusion and unreasonableness may entail. Technical researches may indeed bake no bread. They are not required to bake bread. But in the house of spiritual endeavor they must so work as, in the end, to pay for their board and lodging. It is in fact with logic somewhat as it is with automobiles. I am fond of logic; and personally I hate automobiles. But the justification of both, as artful devices, depends upon the same fundamental principles. If there be anybody,—say a messenger, a physician, a businessman, a traveller,—who propels his automobile for the glory of God or for the service and salvation of man,—then such an one is justified. My dislike for automobiles is due to the fact that those who drive them commonly seem to my prejudiced eyes to be unconcerned for the salvation of anybody. But I am ready to consent to let formal logic be tried by the same standard, although here I look for a different verdict. At best logic can only be a part of life. It must be judged by its power to serve the whole. And what I say of formal logic holds true also, as is obvious, for any other branch of technical inquiry, whether philosophical or non-philosophical.

In adopting this pluralistic view of human salvation, Royce hoped that the conference would vigorously defend the right of each member to differ with the others. Everyone, he said, should "ride his or her own hobby, but with the intent to edify the rest."

William James gave a paper on John Dewey and the Chicago School at the group's second meeting, but otherwise he seems not to have been a regular participant. Indeed, James turned a critical eye on the whole enterprise:

> The "Conference" is a queer illustration of the Cabots' inability to live without Royce. They give up his "seminary" which they have frequented for years past— and then find themselves so disconsolate, that they must creep in again by the back door, and ask him to found an epi-seminary under the name of "conferences" in which the old work can go on.

This satirical description of the conference suggests not only James's hostility toward it, but also its basic opposition to his theories. Throughout the year the group focused most of its attention on the "religious consciousness," and although the "varieties" of belief were emphasized, the drift of these discussions edged toward monism. That was made clear in Royce's concluding remarks presented at the last meeting in the spring of 1904. The central problem in religion, he insisted, is to have a faith that is both personal and universal: "The problem is everywhere the same, how to keep our personal and practical relation to things and to other beings, whether these are in the visible or the invisible world,—how to keep these relations, I say, definite while still defining a relation that will have the genuinely religious dignity and absoluteness." Tying this problem directly to a criticism of *The Varieties of Religious Experience*, Royce observed that James's God was like a "subliminal telephone service." If the analogy is a fair one, it would seem that the "central office" works so badly that no sensible person would subscribe to it. On the other hand, if we wish to interpret the phenomena of religious experience in a "deeper sense," if we want to know "how God really works," we are asking more of James than he is able to offer.

It is clear that Royce was ready to pick up the gauntlet which James and the other pragmatists had thrown down. To make an important defense of his philosophy against his critics, Royce delivered a presidential address at the third annual meeting of the American Philosophical Association held at Princeton University on December 30, 1903. His title was "The Eternal and the Practical." Reviewing the current literature, Royce cited, as among the "several very notable volumes . . . of pragmatism," James's *Will to Believe*, Dewey's *Studies in Logical Theory*, and F. C. S. Schiller's *Humanism*, but disputing their claim to newness, Royce observed that the issues of pragmatism are ancient. He also reminded his colleagues that he had begun his philosophical career as "a very pure pragmatist," and he insisted that he still subscribed to a number of viewpoints most often associated with that school of thought. Specifically Royce noted that his absolutism and their pragmatism share a disagreement with realism: both are post-Kantian in that they take the real world to be a construction of consciousness rather than a set of facts barely given in and independent of experience. The failure of pragmatism, however, lies in its inability to justify its theory of knowledge on purely pragmatic grounds:

287

> There are those who often speak as if they were pure pragmatists. Yet their doc-
> trine has always another side; and the existence of such additions as are often
> made to doctrines that at first seem to be pure pragmatism shows, I judge, that
> there is some difficulty involved in leaving the problem of knowledge just where
> our previous exposition has so far left it. Something is still lacking to complete
> our picture of what we call truth.

Royce maintained that his position was a modified pragmatism; his thesis was this: "Everything is practical; and everything seeks nothing whatever but its own true self, which is the Eternal." In his defense he outlined a seven-point critique, which bears a striking resemblance to his earliest argument for absolutism in *The Religious Aspect of Philosophy*: (1) "every judgment . . . is a constructive response to a situation"; (2) "we need the judgment to be . . . not only ours but true"; (3) "this need for truth is the need that there should be other points of view . . . to confirm one another, and unite in one system of truth"; (4) "these various points of view . . . must be conceived as belonging to, and as being included within, a single self"; (5) "in so far as we conceive this self as like ourselves transient, passing, variable,—its inclusive constructive judgments become . . . like our own, not genuinely true, but only special points of view"; (6) "in order to conceive our judgments as true, we need to conceive them as partial functions of a self which is so inclusive of all possible points of view regarding our object as to remain invariant in the presence of all conceivable additional points of view, and so conscious of its own finished and invariable purpose as to define an ought that determines the truth or falsity of every possible judgment about this object"; (7) "the need for the Eternal is consequently one of the deepest of all our practical needs."

Royce's argument did not, however, impede the opposition, nor did the pragmatists heed his warning that absolutism would be the logical outcome of their premises. Josiah Royce notwithstanding, pragmatism took its own course and enjoyed during the four years between 1903 and 1907 one of its most vigorous periods of expansion. The climax of this movement was the publication of James's *Pragmatism*, a book that many readers have felt best expresses the philosophical mood of the Progressive Era. The result, in the words of Morton White, was "The Decline and Fall of the Absolute."

Corresponding to this philosophical decline, there appears, between the summers of 1904 and 1907, a conflict in Royce's personal life, an impending family crisis and tragedy.

On February 25, 1904, Christopher wrote an odd letter to Stephen. From its content it is clear that Christopher was then teaching mathematics at some university in New York City where he was addressed as "Professor Royce." The letter is coherently composed and gives amusing accounts of students who come to Christopher's room for private lessons or to listen to him playing classical piano. What is baffling about this letter is its uniqueness: not only is it the only letter of Christopher that has survived, but it is also the only mention, anywhere, of the fact that he was at any time a "professor" of mathematics. Later, on June 19, Royce wrote to a Professor E. R. Hedrick of the University of Missouri saying that his sister-in-law, Anna Head, had mentioned a vacancy in the mathematics department. The position would be that of an assistant. Royce proceeded to recommend Christopher without mentioning that he had had any relevant previous teaching experience:

> I write only to say that I believe that he has a fair chance to make a reasonably good assistant in mathematics; and that I am prepared to answer whatever questions you wish to ask about him. He is 22 years old, Harvard A.B. 1900, A.M. 1903,—a student of Mathematics and Music. His record can at pleasure be put at your disposal in whatever way you wish, in case you desire to consider his application.

The letter was placed in an envelope, addressed but unstamped; obviously it was not mailed.

In early July, the family—except for Ned, who opted for summer camp— went to Nantucket for a brief vacation. Writing to Ned, Katharine said it was "really lovely . . . so cool . . . very restful." Christopher and Stephen set out to explore the island on bicycles, but abruptly returned after only two days. "Christopher's interior works didn't prosper," Katharine cryptically explained.

There is also evidence of a strained relationship between Josiah and Ned. When in California in the spring of 1903, Royce wrote a stern letter to his second son, scolding him for bad marks, especially in physics and algebra. Ned was then finishing high school and would soon enter Harvard. His father was distressed because "the whole evidence seemed to indicate neglect on your part,— not incapacity, but that old tendency to do all sorts of things instead of the job that is at hand." The letter amounted to a lecture on the importance of developing sound work habits:

> For as your habits are now trained, so you are to live all your days. That you please or displease *me*, is but a symptom of how things stand. The great matter is whether you in the end really please God and yourself,—two persons who, as you already know, ought to be in very intimate union in your life if you are to be successful.

Josiah was also annoyed to learn that Ned so wanted to return to camp in the summer that he managed to get a promise, that if his parents were unwilling to pay, he could go on a "scholarship." That is not a scholarship, Royce retorted, it is charity, and he refused to accept it. "I must beg you to be more careful about how you tell strangers about what you wish that papa would do for you. What you must have said, puts me almost in the position of having my son ask outsiders for good things."

In the summer of 1904 another letter suggests that the father-son relationship had not improved. Josiah noted the "official return of your marks in the Freshman year." It was a lackluster performance at best: B's in English and German, a D in history, an A in music, and a C and a B in mathematics. "It is good to see them in black and white," Josiah stated, then added somewhat ambiguously, "and to know you so well on in your Sophomore year." Ned had written letters to Katharine and Stephen, but none to Papa, who noted this lapse: "I fear that you don't want to write me." Josiah, however, closed the letter with reassurance of fatherly love: "I hope that you are a good brown poet by this time, in your camp outfit and in your woodland life, and that the world is as full of beauty to you as your dear good heart can find it."

Royce did not repeat the Philosophical Conference in 1904–5. Apologizing to Richard Cabot for the omission, Royce wrote, "This has been so far a year of Logic and the flying moments. . . . I have missed my old philosophical friends much; but I have been nowise able to control the disposition of my time." He continued, nevertheless, to offer his philosophy freely to the Cabots whenever they asked. To Ella, in April 1905, he wrote a long, tightly reasoned philosophical letter on the morality of truthfulness. In being truthful, he explained, "one really means to be true to one's real world in whatever expression one makes."

> But in no one act, and by no one word of mine can I ever express the whole truth of any situation as I see it, or as I mean it to be; because all finite acts, especially all human acts, are inadequate to express my whole meaning. . . .
>
> Since then it is impossible to secure, by any one act of mine, that my true meaning gets to be conveyed to another man, I can only undertake, constantly, and with all sincerity, to serve the *whole* truth, as best I can, by each act of mine, so far as that act expresses me, and expresses my view of the truth.

Again, in May, he answered Richard's and Ernest Hocking's several questions concerning our knowledge of the goodness of God:

> God is good, but unless you take the trouble to find out that fact for yourself, and in your own way, you will not find it out at all. And, owing to the magnitude of the goodness, the trouble of finding it out is considerable. The task lasts a long

time, in fact, forever. It is my task. I "drop stitches," throw away work half-done, forget, ignore, repent, learn, rise, grow, &c. because I am to become infinite in my own way, and because I am to come to view that as God's way only through first learning it to be mine. Hence my trust in God involves an endless discontent with all my own fragmentary views of myself and of him. Why am I a fragment?—Answer: because it is well that God should learn (as he eternally does learn), just *my* way of becoming infinite through overcoming imperfection. Have I prophetic insight into God's will? No; I have only whatever good sense to guide me upwards I can get in the school of life as I go along. Shall I disagree, fight, struggle? Yes.—Why if all is good?—Answer: because I thus win my right to see the good in my own way. Shall I help, harmonize, agree, resign myself, submit, trust, and so on?—Yes, whenever that helps my brothers and myself to see better our relation to God.—In a word, the being of God is one,—the seeing of God is manifold. Therein lies the pluralism and the conflict.

To further promote his philosophical development, Royce initiated three important innovations in his teaching schedule. In 1904–5 and again in 1905–6 he continued his battle with pragmatism by sharing the teaching of Philosophy 9, Metaphysics, with William James. Using *The World and the Individual* as their textbook, James taught pluralism during the first term while Royce defended monism in the spring. The experiment, James said, was like a love affair between Siamese twins, but it was also like a war between hostile armies fighting in parallel trenches. During the same two years Royce took over the teaching of Philosophy 8, Kantian Philosophy. This assignment provided a background for his Baltimore lectures in 1906, "Some Aspects of Post-Kantian Idealism," or as they were called when posthumously published, *Lectures on Modern Idealism*. Finally, beginning in 1904 and in successive years until 1909, Royce taught two courses in the Harvard Summer School of Arts and Sciences. Both courses were designed for teachers, and one of them developed eventually into an introductory course in ethics, which, as Royce noted in 1908, gave him an opportunity to break ground for *The Philosophy of Loyalty*.

By working in these areas Royce was dealing in different ways with the ethical and metaphysical issues raised by pragmatism. However, it was logic, particularly its relationship to science and mathematics, that gave him his greatest satisfaction. During the summer of 1903 Royce composed but never published a fifty-five-page essay on "Mr. Bertrand Russell's Problem of 'The Contradiction,'" an ambitious undertaking, for *The Principles of Mathematics* had just appeared. He also welcomed an opportunity to read a paper, "The Sciences of the Ideal," at the St. Louis World's Fair in September 1904. On April 29, 1905, he presented a paper, "The Relation of the Principles of Logic to the Foundations of Geometry," at a meeting of the American Mathematical Society.

This paper, published in the July issue of the society's *Transactions*, contains what is probably the most technical discussion to be found in any of Royce's published works; so technical is it, in fact, that only those specially trained in mathematical logic can hope to follow the argument or estimate its significance. Nevertheless Royce felt that he had made an important discovery that extended and corrected the logical theory of Alfred Bray Kempe. Royce had continued to work on the Kempean logic since he had first made use of the material in the second volume of *The World and the Individual*, and in September he sent reprints of this article to Kempe and Peirce.

Peirce had flattered Royce two years earlier, saying that he was best equipped to "accomplish the great achievement of bringing metaphysics up into the company of the peacefully progressive sciences." To do this, Peirce had insisted, Royce needed to resolve several problems in logic. Clearly Royce believed that he had taken steps to that end, so probably he expected that his paper would win from Peirce an expression of approval. Instead, while admitting that he had read only a few pages of the article, Peirce issued several bluntly stated objections. Parts of Royce's discussion, he insisted, were "*absurd*"; they were founded on "a weaker variation of Kempe's argument."

Royce kept his patience through two letters, explaining where he felt Peirce had misinterpreted his theory. But when Peirce replied that he was too busy to read the letters, Royce concluded his correspondence with a final clarification and a rare exposure of anger: "I shall of course never trouble you further with letters so long as these cannot be read. I send this merely as a last deposit so to speak, against the day when you may have time to find out what it is that I *have* said." Obviously insulted, Royce could not understand why his old friend had so flatly rejected him. In a letter to James, however, Peirce revealed that he was in a state of great psychological stress. His wife was suffering from some sort of mental disorder, and he too felt that his grasp on reality was failing. "It is very true," Peirce confessed, "that my own mind is out of gear."

Royce was also under stress, but unlike Peirce, who was sinking to total devastation, Royce continued to function on the surface with a calmness that gave no hint of inner tension. Certainly those who gathered at Johns Hopkins to hear his "Post-Kantian Idealism" lectures in January 1906, and those in Emerson Hall who heard him repeat the lectures at Harvard a month later, witnessed a trained analyst who deftly and dispassionately clarified the most obtuse points of metaphysics from Kant to Hegel.

Lectures on Modern Idealism, as the series is known in its published form, invites a comparison with *The Spirit of Modern Philosophy*. As popular histories of philosophy both works cover the same ground; both were designed to acquaint the public with the theoretical antecedents to Royce's system of absolute idealism. Hence in both works Kant and Hegel became the major figures. To the general reader, the earlier work has remained the more accessible. It has the advantage of being comprehensive without requiring technical background, and it is written in a style distinguished by vivid descriptions and penetrating irony. Professional philosophers, however, have found the *Lectures* to be the more interesting and enduring work.

Royce delivered ten lectures. In two of them, the third and the tenth, he developed his own ideology. For the purely historical parts of the series, Royce apportioned two lectures each to the philosophies of Kant and Schelling, but he devoted four lectures, nearly two-fifths of the book, to Hegel. Thus Royce, who had been frustrated during the early 1890s in his attempt to edit an English translation of *Phänomenologie des Geistes*, now found in his *Lectures* an outlet for the material that he had stored up for more than a decade.

As a historian Royce noted that to interpret the theories of modern idealism properly, one must appreciate the social factors that influenced thought in the late eighteenth and early nineteenth centuries. Only in the context of the Enlightenment, the French Revolution, and the Napoleonic period can the philosophies of Kant and the post-Kantians be understood. Royce then focused on a more contemporary issue, for a thread that runs throughout the *Lectures* brings the past into the present by relating the older forms of absolute idealism to pragmatism:

> Our idealists were, one and all, in a very genuine sense what people now call pragmatists. They were also, to be sure, absolutists; and nowadays absolutism is supposed to be peculiarly abhorrent to pragmatists. But of the historical, and perhaps also of the logical relations of pragmatism to absolutism we shall see more hereafter. What I now emphasize is that all these thinkers make much of the relation of truth to action, to practice, to the will. Nothing is true, for them, unless therein the sense, the purpose, the meaning of some active process is carried out, expressed, accomplished. Truth is not for these post-Kantian idealists something dead and settled apart from action. It is a construction, a process, an activity, a creation, an attainment. *Im Anfang war die Tat.*

To demonstrate this point, Royce examined the pragmatist's conception of truth. According to this view a thought *becomes* true when it satisfies some finite need. Royce agreed that true ideas must refer to needs, but he denied that truth could stand alone on these grounds. Total relativism, he argued, is in fact self-contradictory. It implies "that every finite life actually finds its fulfilment in an Absolute Life, in which we live and move and have our being." Idealism, Royce said in conclusion, "is not merely a collection of eccentric opinions . . . , but is at least unconsciously what I hope it will more and more consciously become, the expression of the very soul of our civilization."

This hope remained unfulfilled. Instead, his old friend and rival William James enjoyed the greater part of public recognition. In the autumn of 1906 James gave his now famous Lowell lectures on pragmatism, and in the early months of the following year he repeated the series at Columbia to enthusiastic audiences of more than a thousand. Published in May 1907, *Pragmatism: A New Name for Some Old Ways of Thinking* made further erosions into the popularity of Royce's philosophy. Royce declined to review the new book for the *Boston Transcript*, pleading that he intended "to discuss that work in other connections and places, and am very busy now." In a letter to James he related "one criticism" of *Pragmatism*: he objected mainly to the book's flippant tone, which he felt had given the nonprofessional public the false impression that pragmatism is "a splendid joke, a brilliant *reductio ad absurdum* of all attempts at serious grappling with any philosophical issue." Never throughout his adult life had Royce doubted the worth of vigorous analytical thinking; to instill in others a sense of that worth was his life's mission. The rise of pragmatism, he feared, would bring not only the decline of the absolute, but also the extinction of philosophy itself. Royce concluded this letter with an expression of sadness that the letter alone does not wholly explain. "Meanwhile," he said, "no criticism of mine is hostile.—Life is a sad long road, sometimes. Every friendly touch and word must be preciously guarded. I prize everything that you say or do, whether I criticize or not."

A single sheet marked "(2)" is all that remains of this letter to William James. Whether by carelessness or deliberate intent, the first half has not been preserved. In any event, the missing half of the letter signifies the dark side of the moon in the Royce family history.

In April 1906 there was another, distant and totally unexpected family concern. On the eighteenth San Francisco was struck by a devastating earthquake; unabated fires broke out, and in three days one-third of the city was leveled, five hundred were dead and thousands injured. Josiah's main concern was for his sisters and nieces. Anna Head came remarkably to the rescue. She located the Ingrahams and invited all five unmarried young women to live at her school, noting that they would need clothing and "ready money." "I shall keep a hotel here this summer," she told Josiah. "My school is open and a good many girls [are] coming back." Some of Royce's friends, including Charles Eliot Norton, made generous contributions. In thanking him, Royce praised Anna, whose school—a "Noah's ark"—had become a center of the relief work.

But by that point the major concern was Christopher. A Harvard A.B. with Honors in 1900, by far the youngest member of his class, he immediately entered graduate school, specializing in mathematics, physics, astronomy, and music. In 1903, he was awarded an A.M. degree. Strikingly handsome—blessed with his mother's dark features—Christopher was posed at that time for a photograph, holding a tennis racket. Except for his penetrating, uncanny gaze, he appeared to be a normal, exceedingly attractive young man.

Stories concerning Christopher's mental instability were whispered in Cambridge. When a boy, he notoriously doused James Russell Lowell as the old gentleman passed through Irving Street in a victoria on a visit to Shady Hill. In a parallel legend Christopher is reported to have embarrassed his mother at a social tea given by a certain "Mrs. A." Finding the hostess and her daughter unbearable, Christopher had finally blurted out: "Mother, take me home. Mrs. A is a fool, and her daughter is a damn fool." "Well," his father is supposed to have said when Christopher repeated his remark, "I think you caught the distinction." Katharine's concern was revealed in family correspondence where she cautiously mentioned Christopher's moderate success in social activities, sleep, and diet.

After his abortive attempt at teaching mathematics in 1904, Christopher worked at real estate and finance, probably with the help of his uncle Charles Head, but teaching continued to be his intended profession. In 1905–6 he enrolled briefly in Harvard's Educational Division, but did not complete a single course. His parents became especially concerned about Christopher's mental condition during the spring and early summer of 1906. At that time they believed that he simply needed rest and might profit, as his father had, by journeys taken alone and under his own care. In the winter of 1906–7 he was well enough to live in New York City where he was engaged in business, but at the end of April he broke down and was brought home. The disorder was so serious that he had to be put under restraint and was treated by a battery of specialists. He was not violent, his intellect was still sharp, but he suffered from acute depression and psychotic delusions.

In July 1907, Stephen wrote to his mother from the Harvard Engineering Camp in Ashland, New Hampshire: "Please tell dear old Coco that if he ever feels blue I hope it will do him some good to remember that Deucy loves his Coco." In August, Papa wrote Stephen that he was leaving for "a brief and long promised visit to see my sisters. Poor Ruth needs badly, I fancy, a little comfort and company." He added, "Christopher's affairs are much the same. No real news to report."

At the end of the month, Katharine wrote the youngest son: "You will be surprised that Christopher is at home, having a very happy pleasant visit all alone with me. I love to have him and am most glad of this chance to give him the companionship without other distractions." Ned came home briefly, but she dispatched him quickly. "I sent him off again, to be alone with Coco, which seems to be just right & happy for now." For a week or two, mother and son played the piano, lounged on the piazza, took walks, rode the bicycle, and engaged in other peaceful amusements. In the meantime Josiah was enjoying the outdoors on Mount Hamilton, near San Jose, with Ruth and Hattie. Obviously a crisis was imminent.

Royce still hoped that his son might have an early recovery. After returning from California, on October 6 he sent Christopher down to New York with a letter of introduction to George P. Brett. Omitting all comment regarding his son's medical history, Royce asked Brett if Christopher might be employed in any way by a publishing firm. "He has a *little* capital, and is a young man of steady habits. He is, as a man of long training as a student, no man of the world. In the business world he is so far unpractical. Yet he has in him the making of a useful servant of a serious enterprise, if he finds and pursues a steady practical employment." Christopher appeared at Brett's office on the next day, presented his letter, and made an appointment for further discussions that evening. He did not, however, keep the appointment, and with his failure his father seems finally to have accepted the desperate seriousness of the case.

Three months later Josiah and Katharine admitted that their struggle for Christopher's sanity had been lost. On January 9, 1908, they had him committed indefinitely to Danvers State Hospital. Josiah also on the same day reported most of these facts in a long letter to James. The confinement had been made necessary, he explained, because Christopher's delusions had led him into a romantic attachment to a neighbor's family, and his actions in this relationship could no longer be controlled at home. The "patient" or "C. R."—as Royce now called his son—was judged to be suffering from either dementia praecox or a developmental defect. Royce knew enough psychiatry, as the science was then understood and practiced, to recognize that the case was nearly hopeless.

We have fought our fight, and lost. We shall keep on fighting, and try not to make any outcry. . . . I try to keep objective, to work up to my limit in order to meet the extra expenses (as, so far, I have done), to be of service in my job even if I can't be successful, to hold on to my two other boys (who are so far very dear and promising), and,—incidentally to find or to teach a little that may be worthwhile in the way of truth. I don't ask comfort. The only comfort to look for is not of this visible world. But at least I am not a "shallow optimist," nor do I take more than the necessary "moral holidays," nor do I change my mind as to our problem of evil because I am hard put.—But the poor boy will probably never see any of the light that I had been longing and fighting to have him see. And the way is a long and dark one for us all.

On January 21, 1908, the Boston *Post* reported that Josiah and Katharine Royce petitioned the probate court of East Cambridge to appoint a guardian for Christopher, and in compliance with legal requirements they alleged that he was insane and incapable of taking care of himself. Prescott F. Hall of Brookline was named as guardian. Royce was fully resigned to the fact that Christopher's disease was incurable. It was probably, he now acknowledged, an inevitable hereditary dysfunction, predetermined at birth.

The following day Royce wrote to his young friend Ernest Hocking whose infant son had just died. Always a philosopher, especially with young people who followed his thought, Royce again addressed the problem of Job. Why do we suffer? Why do the heavens rain such misery upon innocent heads? Royce offered two answers: one, metaphysical; another, existential. In the first, the metaphysical thesis, Royce insisted that we never see the whole of reality. Over each instance of suffering, a "larger dome" overarches and supplements our finite grief. "I believe in the supplement," Royce affirmed, "but I have no sort of right to conjecture about its details,—its time, its place, its manner, its contents." In the second, the existentialist formulation, Royce insisted that suffering is the source of our creative insight:

> Grief is our greatest opportunity for creation. Grief has created all the world's highest religious thought, all that is noblest in poetry, all that is deepest in human relationships. Love without grief is a dream of fancied,—often hopelessly misconceived—bliss and perfection. Love that grief has illuminated and glorified, knows for the first time the way to a genuine spiritual world,—knows that what it has sought and now afresh seeks is eternal just *because* nothing in this poor sense world is able to give us the embodiment that love demands.

In 1882 when Christopher was an infant and Royce came to Harvard the world was full of boundless expectation. In 1908 Christopher was in Danvers at the age of twenty-five, and Royce was just over fifty. His boy's life was wrecked, and it seemed that his own life's work had been passed over. Royce began to feel very old. "As for me," he said a few months later, "I am an oldish professor, who stoops a little, and carries too many books about, and plans many books that I do not write. I am already supposed by younger colleagues to be an old fogey. The 'Pragmatists' wag their heads and mock when I pass by. My colleague James, who although so much my senior, is eternally young, has all the interest on his side,—even although he is now an emeritus professor. I am rapidly passing into an early but a well-earned obscurity of professorial old age."

Chapter Eight

Loyalty, Logic, and Love
1908–1910

The Philosophy of Loyalty

In the first eight years of the twentieth century, the years that followed Royce's masterful achievement in *The World and the Individual*, his life and work descended from zenith to nadir. During this period he published only two books, his least ambitious and most disappointing ones: *Outlines of Psychology* and *Herbert Spencer*, both of which he wrote halfheartedly in compliance with specific requests from his publishers. His work in logic was promising, but most of it went unnoticed, and his two fine series of lectures— "Some Characteristics of the Thinking Process" and "Some Aspects of Post-Kantian Idealism"—were eclipsed by the rise of pragmatism. Thus, he passed through a phase of his life in which he received many honors and much recognition, more for work already accomplished than for a future that anyone expected. It was as if he and his books had been retired to history. The tragic story of Christopher seems a metaphor of Royce's decline: from hopeful beginnings to premature collapse.

Royce, however, was unwilling to accept retirement. As we have previously seen, he had an astonishing resilience, an ability to force pain to serve as a source of insight. The next phase of Royce's life, though it was to be scarred by still greater personal tragedies, became his most mature period. In the five years between 1908 and 1913 he published five major books, and at least two of them—*The Philosophy of Loyalty* and *The Problem of Christianity*—are often cited as his most enduring contributions to modern thought. Among the principal characteristics of Royce's philosophy in these works are his subordination of absolutism to community relationships and a growing indifference to cosmology in favor of the more immediate issues of daily life. Now he advanced the theories for which he has been accurately recognized as a precursor of existentialism. From a biographical viewpoint it is significant that Royce's emphasis on this more humanistic side of his philosophy was concurrent with a series of terrible shocks to his private life, shocks that brought him down from the Olympian heights of abstraction and put him in closer contact with his feelings. In his own words, the result of this shift in emphasis was "a new attainment . . . a new growth."

Near the end of 1907, during the four weeks between November 18 and December 12, Royce read a series of eight lectures at the Lowell Institute in Boston, simultaneously presented at Yale, "The Philosophy of Loyalty." In the same period he went through the agony of Christopher's breakdown. On the lecture platform the professor outlined an orderly system of ethics, telling his audience that real life involves a steadfast devotion to conscious purposes; at home the father dealt with his son's madness and witnessed the defeat of their dreams. Still, no one who heard these lectures and no one who read them in the book published four months later could have guessed that they had been presented under tremendous emotional strain. Royce habitually kept his personal affairs beneath the surface in his books, and *The Philosophy of Loyalty* was no exception.

Nevertheless it was one of Royce's most personal works. Indeed a lifetime of thought and passion went into the lectures; perhaps because of that, he had his formulation so clearly in mind and gave the lectures in such polished form that he was prepared to offer them immediately to his publisher. In 1906 and 1907 he had outlined an ethical theory focused on purposeful activity in his summer-school courses at Harvard, and repeated substantially the same theory in the series "Loyalty as an Ethical Principle" at the University of Illinois. Royce had first explicitly advanced the concept of loyalty to his Graham lectures (1896), and ten years before that he had made it the guiding moral principle in *California* and *The Feud of Oakfield Creek*.

Looking back into his childhood, we can recognize the origins of this philosophy in his earliest writings: his grammar-school essay on the assassination of tyrants, his undergraduate thesis on Aeschylus, and his commencement address on Sophocles. In the realm of dreams and fantasies the obverse of this ideal—disloyalty—can be seen where Josiah's fear of abandonment was represented by the images of locked doors, empty rooms, unmarked graves, lonely voyages, and desert places. When he later remembered these feelings of alienation, Royce gave the impression that he had recovered from his childhood terror, and yet there is an abundance of material to suggest that the feelings persisted. Undoubtedly Christopher's mental illness revived those feelings. If it is true that parents often search in their children for ways of repairing the

injuries of their own childhoods, it is also true that Royce saw his son's disintegration as a painful reminder of his own unrepaired grief. But when parenthood
failed, philosophy served, and in *The Philosophy of Loyalty* Royce presented his
version of a world unified and redeemed.

For many twentieth-century readers, a barrier to acceptance of Royce's theory has been a merely semantic difficulty. *Loyalty* has acquired a bad reputation:
it conveys the stale odor of the Victorian era; we associate it with imperial gov-
ernments, political oppression, militarism; we suspect that it is only a mask for
the slave's devotion to his master. This kind of loyalty dehumanizes; it requires
blind obedience, violation of conscience, denial of individuality. But these
implications are incompatible with Royce's meaning. As he used the term, loyalty is intensely personal; it is, indeed, the only way that personality can be ethically expressed; it is nearest to what people mean today when they speak of
commitment.

In his opening lecture Royce articulated his fundamental thesis: loyalty
entails a *"willing and practical and thoroughgoing devotion of a person to a cause."*
Here, as in Royce's other major works, he insisted that the true self, the real
being, is a life struggling to fulfill its chosen plan. The loyal life is neither wholly
personal nor wholly impersonal; it is lived, rather, through the dynamic interre-
lationships between the private and the social selves. On the one hand, as
Royce believed his principle of individuation had demonstrated, having a plan
and struggling to fulfill it make one an individual. But on the other hand, commitment requires self-sacrifice, for no act is loyal which seeks to gain a purely
personal advantage. If you would attain selfhood, Royce insisted, you must,
through your freely chosen devotion, renounce selfishness. Thus, the principle
that defines the ego also shows the emptiness of egoism: "If you wholly decline
to devote yourself to any cause whatever, your assertion of moral independence
will remain but an empty proclaiming of a moral sovereignty over your life, without any definite life over which to be sovereign."

It is clear that the philosophy of loyalty is opposed to popular individualism.
Emerson had maintained that "imitation is suicide," a dictum based on his
belief that primitive intuitions are the sole guides to moral behavior. Royce
countered this principle with the observation that the self, particularly the ethical self, results from social relationships, imitative functions. Should one hypothetically strip off his social self, nothing human would survive. And since,
therefore, identity or self-consciousness always depends on institutional relationships, one discovers and expresses individuality in acts that fulfill social purposes. Hence, replacing the Emersonian dictum is the Roycean counterpart:
"Disloyalty is moral suicide."

So just as there is no purely individualistic morality, there is no individuality
at all without the commitment to purpose that is the hallmark of loyalty. Royce's

book belongs to the casuistic tradition that announces the discovery of the sum-
mum bonum, and his claim that "loyalty" attains the goal of the search for an
ethical universal is founded on the metaphysics of the fourth conception of
being. What is real, he had insisted, is the expression of a purpose; in exactly
this sense, loyalty—Royce's comprehensive term for purposeful commitment—
is the beginning, the only possible beginning, of a real moral agency.

> Reverberating all through you, stirring you to your depths, loyalty first unifies your
> plan of life, and thereby gives you what nothing else can give,—your self as a life
> lived in accordance with a plan, your conscience as your plan interpreted for you
> through your ideal, your cause expressed as your personal purpose in living.

Conversely, the person who renounces his loyalty abdicates his role as a moral
agent. Herein Royce answered James, whose pragmatism leads to the denial of
all ethical universals. Act, James had advised in "The Moral Philosopher and the
Moral Life," so as to preserve the greatest fraction of ideality at the least cost.
Royce insisted that the pragmatist, whose fundamental expediency provides no
guide for making qualitative value judgments of one ideal over another, must
choose his acts on the basis of the mere quantities of value available; thus, he is
one who cries *"cash, cash"* in a world that is morally bankrupt. *The Philosophy of
Loyalty* warns that there are no ideals, fractional or otherwise, that can exist outside the human will whose commitment gives them life.

But commitment to what? Surely, a critic may remark, aims are ethically
unequal. Did Royce mean to argue that every loyal act is good or that evil is
nothing but mere aimlessness? Such an argument is belied by experience, for
history and contemporary events abound with examples of individuals deeply
committed to evil purposes. In his opening lectures Royce was disinclined to
judge the relative merits of various causes, but in the third lecture he met the
problem head-on. Admitting that some causes are good while others are evil,
Royce proposed a test by which one may determine the moral value of any act.
If any loyalty is good in that it promotes moral being, one should act, Royce
maintained, so as to advance the cause of loyalty itself. In short, be loyal to loyalty. At any moment a person may confront an ethical dilemma, having to
choose to be loyal to one cause at the cost of some other. At an ethical cross-
road the true loyalist will disregard all private interest as well as the personal
fortunes of all other individuals—friends, relatives, or loved ones. Knowing that
he owes his loyalty to their loyalty, not to their fortunes, the loyalist will do
whatever may assist others in their continuing struggle to be loyal. Such is
Royce's moral formula: "Find your own cause, your interesting, fascinating, personally engrossing cause; serve it with all your might and soul and strength; but

so choose your cause and so serve it, that thereby you show forth your loyalty
to loyalty, so that because of your choice and service to your cause, there is a   301
maximum of increase of loyalty amongst your fellow-men."

At the beginning of the penultimate lecture "Loyalty, Truth, and Reality,"
Royce quoted excerpts from a letter he had received from a "dear friend" raising questions and stating objections to the ethical theory that had so far been
advanced. We now know the friend to be Richard Cabot, and his letter, dated
December 3, the day after the sixth of the eight lectures had been presented,
needs to be considered in its entirety. Cabot felt that Royce had separated loyalty, an abstract relationship, from the real world of individual objects worthy of
loyalty; he had, in other words, placed the emphasis on the means instead of
the end:

> As I have listened to your lectures on loyalty and checked off point after point
> of agreement I find myself going off in [an] attempt to state somewhat differently
> the doctrine of the object of *ultimate* loyalty. Perhaps all that I am thinking will
> be discussed in your final lecture but even so we ought to be hearing its voice in
> *all* the lectures as we hear the sea in the distance.
>
> *"Loyalty to loyalty" doesn't seem ultimate.* It sounds like the 3rd rather than the
> 4th concept of being. Is it not loyalty to all *objects* of true loyalty that is our ulti-
> mate duty? The object not the relation, the universe & the devotion to it not the
> devotion alone is the object of our ultimate devotion. We seek the Whole always
> & we are loyal to our search, & to all who are seeking it in their own way &
> degree. Is it not the glory of the Goal that lends dignity to all loyal search,—our
> own or others'[?] It is because of this goal that we cheer on all we [*sic*] pursue it,
> not simply for the faithful pursuit (=loyalty) taken in itself. It is because of what
> we believe of their end that we are so glad of all the loyalties which make it pos-
> sible to attain that end. The port gives value to the courses steering for it.
> Loyalties are such courses & there are many courses to many ports. Except for
> our knowledge of the value of their destination & of all life lived in quest of that
> destination, should we be anxious to urge all seekers along their courses?
>
> It is true that we know little enough about the port,—the end, the goal of our
> own or anyone else's search but is it not *that little* which gives value to the whole
> shooting match?
>
> Loyalty is a relation. We seek an individual. Can we be loyal to anything,—
> ultimately,—except that individuated universe which is the object of all love & all
> knowledge?
>
> I have never succeeded in differing from you save where I misunderstood you.
> Doubtless it is so now. But if so—others of your audience need also (in good
> time) to be shown how rightly instead of wrongly to understand you on this point.

Royce appreciated the importance of Cabot's objection. The problem reminded him of the parable of the talents in Matthew 25 where the faithful servants continue to do their absent master's work. Any "mere moralism"—that is, an ethical system without metaphysical roots—will have "a certain mystery about it." It requires blind faith in the goodness of the cause. But Cabot demanded knowledge of "the glory of the Goal," without which loyalty is a worthless moral principle. The remainder of this lecture consists of Royce's attempt to connect ethics to metaphysics. The good that one pursues resides, he argued, not in the loyalist, but in the cause, and since causes always have social applications, they cannot be limited to individual human beings, but must be part of the "unities of spiritual life in the universe." Thus: "Loyalty has its metaphysical aspect. It is an effort to conceive human life in an essentially superhuman way, to view our social organizations as actual personal unities of consciousness, unities wherein there exists an actual experience of that good which, in our loyalty, we only partially apprehend."

Thus, with a shift from ethics to metaphysics, *The Philosophy of Loyalty* offers, by way of conclusion, two additional definitions of its basic terminology: "*Loyalty is the will to manifest, so far as is possible, the Eternal, that is, the conscious and superhuman unity of life, in the form of the acts of an individual Self.*" And again, borrowing a phrase from James: "*Loyalty is the Will to Believe in something eternal, and to express that belief in the practical life of a human being.*"

It is noteworthy that Royce relegated this feature of his theory to his final lectures. Perhaps he wished his audience to understand that loyalty is primarily a practical guide to action, a guide that, in its merely pragmatic usefulness, can stand apart from the philosopher's speculative system. This is noteworthy because it was the first time in any of Royce's major works that he invited his readers to accept one part of his thought without also subscribing to absolutism. Viewed as a rhetorical strategy, this arrangement of material suggests that Royce had become sensitive to critics who had prophesied the doom of his philosophy precisely because it insisted on cosmic inclusiveness. Royce continued to regard the metaphysical aspects as indispensable, but with *The Philosophy of Loyalty*, he was beginning to be willing to let the absolute take care of itself, and to enter the twentieth century.

Royce ended his work with a discussion of tragedy and the meaning of situations where loyalties are defeated. The experience of a "lost cause" teaches that temporal life is too imperfect to realize the fulfillment of the ideal. But tragedy does not turn the loyalist into a cynic, nor does he deny his pain by accepting some "shallow optimism." The tragic hero—Hamlet, for example—experiences his pain and loss as spurs to action; his loyalty intensified, he strives to repair the world. For Royce, whose "lost cause" was a daily experience throughout the autumn of 1907, tragedy was a source not only of grief, but also of knowledge. "The *loyal*, and they alone, know the one great good of suffering, of ignorance, of infinitude, of loss, of defeat—*and that is just the good of loyalty*, so long as the cause itself can only be viewed as indeed a living whole. Spiritual peace is surely no easy thing. We win that peace only through stress and suffering and loss and labor." They also know that just as loyalty entails strife, strife is an entailment of all consciousness. As we suffer, God also suffers. This, Royce believed, is the meaning of the great Christian fables of the Crucifixion and the Resurrection.

Concluding his Lowell lectures during the second week of December, Royce promptly sent the manuscript to the Macmillan Company with whom he had already reached an agreement for publication. The contract guaranteed Royce a royalty of 15 percent on the first three thousand copies, 20 percent thereafter, and a $250 advance. On December 23, George Brett wrote to acknowledge the receipt of the package and promised that typesetters would be put on the job immediately. The first batch of proofs, he advised, would be sent to Royce before the close of the winter vacation.

Christmas was traditionally a special event in the Royce household. A huge tree was lighted with candles in the nursery, and the professor played Santa Claus for all the neighborhood children. On Christmas the Royces also celebrated Ned's birthday. This year, however, the joyful spirits were no doubt ruined by the final agony of Christopher's breakdown. Royce knew, even in early November, that he would have to stay close to home during the next several weeks. Writing to James McKeen Cattell, he said that he would be unable to attend the annual meeting of the National Academy of Sciences in New York. In this letter Josiah made no mention of his son's illness, but excused himself on the basis of his commitments to work. Like his Protestant forebears, Royce placed a high value on his role as worker. In times of great personal turmoil—and especially with the mounting family crisis—he sought distraction from anxiety in labor.

But he knew also that he could not turn away from the problem. Financially the whole dreadful affair had been a disaster. Royce estimated that he had spent $1,850 on the case in one year, from August 1906 to August 1907. Undoubtedly most of the money earned from his Lowell lectures and from his ethics course at Yale ($1,500) was dissipated by the payment of these bills. "I earned that, & was glad to do so," Royce told James. "But the money might have been thrown into the sea for all the good it did to the poor boy." James responded, when he learned of Christopher's illness, by making a sizable gift that enabled Royce to establish a fund held in trust "for the patient's future benefit." The father seems to have accepted, as well as he could, the hopelessness of the case, but still he regarded "with peculiar horror" the possibility that his son might have to bear the additional burden of a future life as an indigent cripple. James's gift sustained Royce by providing a safeguard against the boy's becoming a helpless pauper.

It is not surprising that Royce's memories then drifted back to the point, precisely twenty years earlier, when he had experienced his own mental collapse. Central to this memory was his delightful and restorative visit to Australia in the spring of 1888. So when *The Philosophy of Loyalty* was published in April 1908, Royce seized this opportunity to renew his friendship with Alfred Deakin, the statesman and companion on his unforgotten journey through the mountain wonderland of the antipodes. Royce had the Macmillan Company send Deakin a presentation copy of the book, and soon afterward he wrote a letter to his old friend celebrating those memories that stood out "clearly . . . encouragingly . . . pleasingly" of their travels together, their talks, and the host's kindness and hospitality. Royce felt old and forgotten. Perhaps, it crossed his mind, Deakin would not remember him. But still Royce needed, though the expression was admittedly difficult, to tell the statesman how much he cherished their friendship and his youthful reminiscences:

> What a place the meeting, and your presence and personality, have since occupied in my life, I can hardly tell you. It is partly the inability to make my feeling clear that has kept me from much writing. For, being a lonely and abstract student, I have no sort of return to offer you, who are an empire-builder, and a man of affairs. I hear of your long career of service with delight and admiration;—not indeed with envy, for I am a student, and love the life apart from affairs;—but I can fully appreciate the world's work, if I cannot do such work; and I reverence the power that has made you so long a leader in your country's affairs.

Deakin's long service in public affairs might have served as a living model of loyalty, and Royce was led into a comparison between Australia's parliamentary system and the U.S. presidency. Royce was offended by the storms and gimmicks of Theodore Roosevelt's second administration. In the U.S., he observed, popularity and power are quickly depleted, whereas the Australian government had somehow, as in the case of Deakin, the capacity to foster the longevity of its political leaders. Struck by the hypocrisy of Roosevelt's scheme for the "Great White Fleet"—soon scheduled for a visit to Australia—Royce felt that his own "very tiny and silent book" might serve better than the "vast and noisy" gunboats as a U.S. citizen's "word of greeting about our common ideals." "If you have time to look at it some day," he said at the end of his letter, "—for an hour or two,—remember that its author still loves you."

In the same letter Royce spoke of *The Philosophy of Loyalty* as "a sort of last expression of ideals." The rhetoric of this premature obituary was, however, effectively canceled by news of the book's reception. The reviews in the popu-

lar journals were overwhelmingly positive, the initial sales were brisk, and as
Macmillan planned for an early reprinting in August—there were to be a total
of seven reprintings before his death in 1916—Royce laid plans for a supplementary volume of essays. This he first proposed in a letter to George Brett on
March 20. When the publisher returned from Europe in May, he asked Royce
for a more detailed plan. Brett was hesitant. His business managers warned that
collected essays do not sell. Brett relayed these doubts, but Royce persisted.
Clearly the professor had finally mastered the commercial arts. Negotiations
over the contract continued into late July when Brett, hoping to retain Royce as
his principal philosophical author, capitulated on every issue.

Race Questions, Provincialism, and Other American Problems was conceived
as an auxiliary to *The Philosophy of Loyalty*: "In the light of that philosophy,"
Royce stated in his preface, "I therefore hope that the various special opinions
here expressed may be judged." The five essays in this volume, two of which
deserve special notice, represent Royce's social philosophy between 1898 and
1908. At first glance the topical range of this material makes the book seem diffuse. Royce attacked racism, defended provincialism, criticized sentimental
idealism, examined relationships between climate and culture, and finally
applied the philosophy of loyalty to physical education. Originally each essay
had been a lecture prepared for a specific occasion: "Race Questions and
Prejudices" (Chicago, Philadelphia, and New York Ethical Societies, 1905–6);
"Provincialism" (University of Iowa, 1902); "On Certain Limitations of the
Thoughtful Public in America" (Vassar College, 1899); "The Pacific Coast"
(National Geographic Society, 1898); "Physical Training in America" (Boston
Physical Education Association, 1908).

But despite the disparities the book has a thesis. As an effort in the "philosophy of life," it attempts to cut through the sterile sands of mere abstraction and
to place Royce's theory on the bedrock of practical relationships. Countering
the charge that idealism has no useful applications, he hoped to show the wide
range of his interests and the efficacy of his thought in dealing with concrete
social issues. To promote this thesis, Royce separated himself from popular idealisms, specifically the ideologies of Henry George and Edward Bellamy, and
expressed "profound contempt for deliberate excesses in the work of reasoning."
Theory, as always, he respected, but when theories are reduced to formulas as
guides to social action, nothing can result but mischief.

A case in point is the theory of race, espoused by certain otherwise eminent
thinkers in the so-called Progressive Era. Industrial societies, racists maintained, had reached the pinnacle of cultural evolution, and this growth had
been made possible by the extraordinary capacities of the Teutonic race. Royce
was quick to perceive this notion as a debasement of the theory of evolution, an
exercise in self-aggrandizement, a childish illusion, analogous to a fear of snakes

and mice. Answering the hysteria of the "yellow peril" or the "black peril," Royce suggested that the "white peril" is a far greater threat to humanity. Surely if the Romans had had the "gentle arts" by which we seek to Americanize the world— "unlimited supplies of rum, of rifles, and of machine guns"—the "superior" Germanic peoples to whom the modern age pays homage would be extinct. History is written by the victors; hence the silent victims provide unanswered examples of their inferiority to those who oppress and kill them. "For my part . . . ," Royce concluded, "I am a member of the human race, and this is a race which is, as a whole, considerably lower than the angels, so that the whole of it very badly needs race-elevation. In this need of my race I personally and very deeply share. And it is in this spirit only that I am able to approach our problem."

Warning that racism leads to cultural strife, Royce hoped that provincialism might contribute to communal reunification. Royce identified three evils of the modern age: alienation, which excludes minorities from communal relationships; leveling, which reduces everyone to "a dead level of harassed mediocrity"; and the mob spirit, which requires individuals to forfeit personal judgment in favor of a collective identity. "I should say to-day that our national unities have grown so vast, our forces of social consolidation have become so paramount, the resulting problems, conflicts, evils, have been so intensified, that we, too, must flee in the pursuit of the ideal to a new realm." The province—the domain, the home—was for Royce the realm of strength, inspiration, salvation. An "elastic" term, a *province* may be a town, a neighborhood, or even an entire region. Whatever its geographical boundaries, a province is characterized by unified customs, languages, and culture. Most of all, it possesses "unique wisdom," generated and guided by shared belief which strengthens selfhood and directs a people to the fulfillment of its mission. For Latinos today, "*la raza*" accurately expresses the Roycean concept of provincialism. As an antidote to the faceless crowd of the future—"incomprehensible monster, in whose presence the individual loses his right, his self-consciousness, and his dignity"—the individual may, Royce affirmed, be saved by the province.

Logic, Religious Philosophy, and the New Realism

In the summer of 1908, Stephen, a nineteen-year-old junior at Harvard and a future mining engineer, had his first job working in a mine in McGill, Nevada. There he was given charge over a crew of miners, and the work was brutal. As one raised in the privileged world of Cambridge, Stephen was shocked by the coarseness of the West. At the end of July he wrote an anguished letter to his parents complaining about "the filthy Greeks and the bad smells, and the disappointing wait for a change of job."

His affectionate father responded in a letter dated August 5: "I need not say what loving sympathy it arouses, nor yet need I tell how heartily our dear Kitty joins with you in your sense of how intolerable, for the time, the situation that you describe is." Yet for Royce, fresh from his *Philosophy of Loyalty*, the "situation" was a rough-and-ready test of early manhood. He was gratified that Stephen was determined to complete the job. "I want you to know, at once," wrote the philosopher in the spirit of loyalty, "how despite the gloominess of the momentary situation, I am moved with a genuine delight in the fact that you are not a quitter . . . and are going to win the essential thing, viz. the power to meet conditions as they arise, and to fight it out on this line if it takes all summer."

This letter, while it applies the principle of loyalty to an instance within the family, ends wistfully, noting Ned's departure for his two-year absence in Europe, reiterating the theme that haunted Josiah's thoughts of empty rooms and, of course, the always unmentioned absence of the beloved Christopher:

> Well, it rains, and Ned leaves us this evening, and the nights are often lonesome now, and the shadows are sometimes pretty deep. But we love Stephen, and his voice when it comes back to us, as it will, is one of the sweetest things that we ever hear. So keep our precious one for us, and it isn't long, after all, before home and you will be together again.—Lovingly
> Josiah.

In September, Royce traveled abroad and presented the keynote address as representative of Anglo-American philosophy to the Third International Congress of Philosophy at Heidelberg. The congress was to be divided into a series of general sessions, each featuring a leading speaker from one of the four official languages: English, Italian, French, and German. Others assigned to these honorific posts were Benedetto Croce, Henri Bergson, and Theodor Lipps, though illnesses prevented Bergson and Lipps from attending. Aside from the honor which this invitation entailed, Royce doubtless welcomed the opportunity to revisit the city where he had begun his study of German philosophy in 1875 and to renew his acquaintance with his old professor, Wilhelm Windelband, who officiated as president of the congress.

Reports of the Heidelberg congress indicate that pragmatism was the dominant theme, and that the discussions, particularly those touched off by a paper from F. C. S. Schiller, were marked by "bitterness" and "fury." In Schiller's acrimonious letters, before and after, he accused Royce of Spinozist optimism. Such comments brought pragmatism into the forefront of the discussions.

In his paper, "The Problem of Truth in the Light of Recent Discussion," Royce engaged the issues of the debate. It was one of his more incisive criticisms of the pragmatic theory of truth. There are, said Royce, speaking in the context of 1908, three historical and current "motives": pragmatism or instrumentalism, individualism, and the theories resulting from modern logic that, as he foresaw its long-range implications, would lend support to the doctrine of absolute truth. The first set of theories—those advanced by James and Dewey—places the search for truth in the more general framework of biological evolution. To the instrumentalist a true idea is a successful adaptation to the requirements of surrounding circumstances; truth therefore changes and grows according to one's needs. This claim amounts to relativism, and Royce gave this theory the same scrutiny for which his earliest philosophical work is remembered. Does pragmatism claim that its theory is subject to the same flux that unsettles all rigid theories? If so, it follows that pragmatism will fail to satisfy future needs—pragmatically. A theory of truth, Royce insisted, must be true, not merely as a moment in thought, but true for all, always. Needing help, pragmatists may supplement their theory by appealing to the inner structure of thought. This is individualism, and for Royce, James was its most impressive exponent. Locked into subjectivity, the individualist must admit that vast realms of knowledge—past time, other minds, the physical world—cannot be verified by immediate experience. To escape this predicament James argues that lacking "cash," we are free to accept certain truths on "credit." Spotting this as a false analogy, Royce attacked James's metaphor. In the commercial world, notes of credit have value only in that they can be converted to cash; a banker can, whenever he chooses, liquidate his assets. But in the bank of truth James would have us accept on credit certain beliefs that are inherently unredeemable. Obviously any bank that adopted James's prescription as policy would find itself soon in desperate circumstances. Thus, from individualistic caprice we turn to the methodology of logic and the exact sciences.

Royce's first move on these lines involved a reassertion of his long-standing conviction that "there is no pure intellect." With pragmatism he agreed that ideas are plans of action; with individualism he also agreed that the grounds of truth are found within the structure of consciousness. But that there are "absolutely true propositions," he argued, is the plain result of science and logic. The classic model of an absolute truth is a proposition any denial of which results in the reassertion of that proposition under a new form. Royce illustrated his absolutism by rehearsing the Euclidian theorem which states that there is no last number in an ordinal series of whole numbers: the argument that there is a last number in the series merely provides the means of constructing another number which can follow the "last" one. Here is the same logic underlying *The Religious Aspect of Philosophy*, where Royce had maintained that the denial of absolute truth must itself be an absolute truth. Royce still held to this argument, and he still shared with Peirce the hope that metaphysics would eventually take its place with science. Citing Dedekind, Frege, Russell, and others, he predicted that modern logicians would make an increasing impact on modern thought, correcting the limitations of both instrumentalism and individualism. Nevertheless the polemical thrust of Royce's paper was considerably softened by his concluding belief that all three motives must be unified in a single theory of truth, a synthesis designated as "Absolute Pragmatism."

Royce welcomed the opportunity, afforded by the congress, to get back into the swing of technical philosophy. Needless to say, he also enjoyed the freedom that his absence from the cares at home gave him, and he made the most of his brief holiday. From Germany he traveled to Italy, spending a few days in Rome before turning homeward to America. On the voyage home, on the Cunard liner *Caronia*, as on the way over on the Cunard *Pannonia*, Royce kept a notebook, the contents of which confirm his rededication to logical research. Preserved here are sixty-one pages of a connected discussion entitled "Properties of Circuits in the Logical System" and described as notes preparatory to a new treatment of the theory advanced in his earlier paper on the principles of logic and the foundations of geometry. "This time," he noted, "I look towards Projective Geometry proper." Thus, Royce returned to work on the planned, but never completed, study of logic, the fragments of which, covering the last ten years of his life, still lie massed and unorganized in his surviving papers.

Restless to move on, Royce signed and dated his preface to *Race Questions* on October 16, 1908, but left the remaining details, as well as much of the editing and rewriting, to Katharine. Before the book was published, Royce's attention had shifted first to logic, then to religious philosophy, and finally with *The Problem of Christianity* to a synthesis of the two.

It was "a logic year," he told Paul Carus. In addition to Philosophy 9, Metaphysics, Royce taught three courses in logic ranging from elementary (Philosophy C) to advanced (Philosophy 15) to graduate (Philosophy 20C). The seminar had been, by 1908, converted permanently to the study of the logical foundations of scientific methodology. With this work he hoped to contribute to a philosophical future that would concentrate on "logical analysis" and tend toward confirmation of absolutism. The first half, at least, of his prophecy proved true.

These notebooks and his letters of this period give the strong impression that Royce had survived the worst of the anguish caused by Christopher's breakdown. He was productively occupied, and that was enough to make him, momentarily at least, content. "I have been trotting along," he told Professor Frank Thilly of Cornell, "trying to catch up with my correspondence, and other business, which are running some distance ahead of me, like a trolley car that will not stop." Thilly had invited him to participate in a symposium entitled "Realism and Idealism" at the December meeting of the American

Philosophical Association in Baltimore. Royce answered this challenge with the air of a man who was willing to give that trolley car a chase: "I will take part in a discussion of Realism, Idealism, Pragmatism, Anarchism, or (if you prefer) Eddyism and Psychotherapy, or whatever else you will." Sensing that the "New Realists" were about to make their move, he was not certain that his defense of idealism would be successful. "I don't think that anything I can say will be of much use," he told Thilly, "but I am willing to try."

If this did not reflect a mood of self-confidence, it was a closer approximation than Royce had been able to manage for some time. In March 1909 he wrote to Richard Cabot with renewed vitality. The letter contained a contribution to the program in social welfare that Cabot had initiated at Massachusetts General Hospital:

> Having just looked over your interesting Report of the Social Service Dept. (a sort of Purgatorio and occasionally Inferno, wherein the visits of you and of your workers seem to appear more useful than was Dante's, since, if I am right, he got nobody out of either place except himself)—I am moved to enclose a cheque. It is little. I should have sent one before, and a larger one now, were it not that I have had, and still have, other investments to make in the problem of evil,— investments some of which are sad enough.

It is clear that Royce was still grieving, and still paying, for the loss of his son's mental health, but that loss only increased his compassion for the suffering of others. The letter also shows that Royce was sensitive to the beauty of his surroundings. He noted that he was giving an evening course, sponsored by the Lowell Institute, twice a week at the new Harvard Medical School—"a marvelous marble wilderness, which serves as a fine frame to set off the winter stars when one approaches it from Longwood Avenue. . . . You must have a hard time to live up to your buildings, you medical men!"

Though preoccupied with specialized topics in mathematical logic, Royce still found time for religious philosophy. In the spring of 1909—March 18 and 25, and April 1—he participated in a series of conferences, sponsored by the Harvard Y.M.C.A., on the question "What Is Vital in Christianity?" At about the same time he revised the presentation and delivered it as a Phi Beta Kappa address at Vassar College. Published later during the same year in the *Harvard Theological Review*, this paper was a major breakthrough in Royce's thought, seen by him almost from the first as a preliminary effort in a much larger and long overdue study of the relationship between his philosophy and Christianity.

He had, of course, written abundantly on the philosophy of religion. He tended always to perceive philosophy as an enterprise that serves religious purposes; his style strongly resembled homiletic and scriptural writings, and he was a profoundly religious person. But was he and was his philosophy in any sense Christian? Royce had kept this issue in the background. Certainly he did not subscribe to the views of any particular orthodoxy, nor was he affiliated with any established church. The Ethical Culture movement was the only form of institutionalized religious activity with which he was associated, and in that he was at best an irregular member, a critic more than a faithful participant. In his youth Royce had rejected the traditional doctrines of belief; still there was much in the Christian faith of his parents that he had incorporated, and in the autumn of his life he began to reexamine that heritage. According to his parents' belief, the Kingdom of God is manifest; God is here and now, about and within us. Royce reinterpreted this doctrine and built his philosophy upon it. In "What ss Vital in Christianity?" it became the bedrock of his faith.

What gives a living relevance to Christianity and without which it cannot survive? Is it a program of religious behavior—prayer, sacramental observances, good works? Or is it a state of consciousness—an attitude of worship, reverence, and piety? To answer adequately, Royce maintained, one must construct an "interpretation of life" so as to comprehend "action" as well as "thought," for the vital element in any religion cannot be exclusively either a moral or a metaphysical doctrine. In Royce's age the moral, social, and political aspects of Christianity were popularly emphasized by the advocates of the so-called Social Gospel. Taking its material primarily from the Synoptic Gospels, this view was based on the thesis that the teachings of Jesus contain the essential features of his religion. Radically interpreted, these teachings call for a social revolution in which the meek and the poor shall inherit the earth, the mighty shall be cast down, and all worldly kingdoms shall dissolve before the sovereignty of divine presence. By learning these truths and practicing them, and thus by working to accomplish the revolution, we may become, according to this view, true Christians.

Royce found this argument "profoundly unsatisfactory" and "essentially incomplete." He had little faith in the efficacy of social movements. Answering the appeal of his friend Cabot, he had, as we have seen, responded by making a small contribution, but he remained unwilling to become deeply involved in politics or social reform. He tended to regard such efforts as "trivial," and most of the petitions mailed to him were returned to their senders, unsigned. When Brander Matthews urged him into a scheme to revise English orthography, Royce declined: "I have too many serious issues to attend to as it is, without burdening my soul with a promise regarding one further complication of life." This episode, though unimportant in itself, illustrates Royce's suspicion of those who would change the world piecemeal. A critic of the Progressive Era, he closed his door to reformers, reasserting that the real problems of life demand religious solutions.

312

Maintaining that Christianity cannot be reduced to its practical uses, Royce emphasized "the two cardinal doctrines" of the Fourth Gospel: incarnation and atonement. Interpreted symbolically, the first doctrine teaches that "God is the conscious meaning that expresses itself in and through the totality of all phenomena. . . . Like the Logos of the Fourth Gospel, this entire world is not only with God, but is God." This, however, ushers in the deepest and most tragic of religious paradoxes: "Why, . . . if the world is the divine life embodied, is there so much evil in it,—so much darkness, ignorance, misery, disappointment, warfare, hatred, disease, death?—in brief, why is the world as we know it full of the unreasonable?" The doctrine of atonement provides the answer. "The value of suffering," he insisted, "the good that is at the heart of evil, lies in the spiritual triumphs that the endurance and the overcoming of evil can bring to those who learn the hard, the deep but glorious, lesson of life." Each of us must relive the sufferings of Christ, for the Crucifixion, like the Nativity, is a metaphor of our union with the Divine. So with us God suffers because otherwise there can be no redemption. He descends into our lives, and scalded with our pain he suffers through the redemptive process in three forms: endurance, love, and loyalty. Nailed to these forms, we are the crucified; we also are the redeemers.

In citing this belief as the vital element in Christianity, Royce was making a profoundly personal statement. More than expressing a need to reconstruct his religious heritage, it helped him to explain the "bad dreams which fill our finite life." With this opaque reference to his dreams, Royce clarified the underlying motive that made his faith in God so urgently necessary. The dominant self-image haunting his childhood was that of the homeless wanderer. Wherever he appeared, the wanderer was ruthlessly punished with humiliation and death. Royce's philosophy responded to the terror that his dreams and fantasies knew best, making a telling statement about the human condition: to live is to suffer, but to suffer alone is unbearable. Only a God who would share his pain could satisfy this child's cry of anguish.

An ideology is not only a means by which one can repair the damage of childhood; it also arms the believer against the pain of future grief. It is no mere coincidence, therefore, that the composition of "What Is Vital in Christianity?" preceded by a year and a half the almost simultaneous deaths of William James and Christopher Royce. Anticipating the double shock of these losses, the philosopher had renewed his religious commitments, uniting his griefs with those of the suffering God. Before facing this new crisis, however, Royce had one good year relatively free of personal trouble.

He returned to Europe for a vacation in the summer of 1909 from July 10 to September 4. No doubt one of his purposes was a two-week visit with Ned, now twenty-two and a 1907 Harvard graduate, who was beginning his second year studying music in Berlin at the Stern Conservatory. If Josiah corresponded with

Ned during these years of study abroad, none of their letters has survived; there are, however, several letters from Katharine. In them she kept Ned informed of family happenings and dealt out motherly advice. "Keep proper shoes on your little Neddy feeties and if you love me don't use your eyes in bad light." Interlaced between what she called her "solicitous mummums," Kitty reported on her projects in philosophical translation. With Josiah's encouragement and technical assistance she had already completed a first-draft translation of *Problemi della Scienza* by Federigo Enriques, published by the Open Court Publishing Company in 1914. In the autumn of 1909 she was "hammering away" at Eugen Kuhnemann's massive study *Schiller*, which Ginn and Company brought out in two volumes in 1912. Translating this work, she told Ned, was "about as encouraging as picking Memorial Hall to pieces with my fingernails," and she relished the thought of making Kuhnemann "sit down on a pin." Nevertheless it is clear that Katharine enjoyed her work and the opportunities it afforded, even though much of it was done under the patronage and supervision of her husband.

One of the highlights of Josiah's vacation was an excursion with Ned to Bayreuth where the two music lovers attended productions of the *Ring*, *Lohengrin*, and *Parsifal*. The philosopher and his son had an additional incentive to attend this particular festival because of their personal friendship with Karl Muck, one of its most distinguished conductors, whom they had known during his two years as visiting director of the Boston Symphony. Ned and his father traveled on to Munich together and then back to Berlin before Josiah caught his steamer home from Rotterdam. The strain in their relationship seems to have abated considerably. Writing to Stephen, Josiah reported that "Ned is doing well, and has improved in a good many ways. I think that his second year will be much more effective and practical than his first year; and his first year has been one of really good and sound work so far as I can make out." He then added, "Ned and I are in substantial harmony of spirit."

"Papa," Katharine reported to Ned on September 30, "is in fine health and spirits, for which I am most grateful." He and Stephen had just returned from a three-week sailboat cruise to Cape Cod, Martha's Vineyard, Buzzard's Bay, and Newport. "They had a good time and came home fonder of each other than ever." Stephen was more of an outdoorsman than Ned. He told his mother that he was doing a good deal of the physical work on the boat while "Papa does logic and such." Earlier that summer he had taken a job at the Monarch Mine in Murray, Idaho, and seems to have enjoyed the work more than in the previous year. "You would laugh to see me standing almost on my head," he wrote to "Fuffy," "drilling a hole by pounding on a drill with a four pound hammer." "I am getting so 'tuff' you wouldn't recognize me. I scratch matches on my face."

Resettled in Cambridge, Royce began to prepare for the academic year 1909–10 in late September. In addition to teaching part-time at Yale he was scheduled for his standard set of classes with one exception: instead of teaching metaphysics, he picked up two half courses, one on Kantian philosophy in the fall and another on contemporary philosophical issues in the spring. In this sequence Royce reviewed his earliest philosophical commitments and criticized his current adversaries—the pragmatists, the realists, and the individualists. These teaching assignments, especially the latter, proved to have larger implications, for during this year Royce was made to face squarely one of the most pressing challenges of his career.

The story of this conflict was later told succinctly by one of its participants: "At the meeting of the American Philosophical Association held in New Haven in 1909 five [later there would be six] of the younger members who either read papers or took part in the discussion, found, quite without premeditation, that they were fighting on the same side against a common foe." Idealism, specifically Royce, was this unnamed foe, and the six realists were W. P. Montague, W. B. Pitkin, W. T. Marvin, E. G. Spaulding, E. B. Holt, and R. B. Perry. Four of them read papers that directly or indirectly took issue with Royce's idealism; afterward they corresponded and decided to band together. In 1910 they published in the *Journal of Philosophy* a series of brief position papers entitled "The Program and First Platform of Six Realists," and two years later they fleshed out their apologia and attack on idealism in *The New Realism: Cooperative Studies in Philosophy*.

Of the several discussions at the APA meeting in 1909, the paper read by Ralph Barton Perry, "The Ego-centric Predicament," was the most important, for it cut right to the heart of Royce's idealism. In 1880 Royce had announced in a letter to James that all existence is conditioned by consciousness, that it is absurd and self-contradictory to entertain thoughts about objects outside thought, and further that if the world is composed exclusively of actual and possible experiences, the chief remaining task of philosophy is to discover the structure of experience. Such was Royce's earliest conviction, and for nearly thirty years this principle had guided most constructive thought at Harvard and throughout the nation. The importance of Perry's analysis was that it challenged the first stage of Royce's argument, giving the impression that if this challenge could be sustained, the rest would collapse like a house of cards. With Royce, Perry agreed that one cannot separate the known from the knower. Egocentricity is ubiquitous and indispensable. But from this it does not follow that existence is a form of experience. Though it is a fact that anything known is something known, the fact is trivial and proves nothing. It is not a proposition, but a methodological predicament. Armed with this apparent refutation of Royce's system, the new realists pursued their investigations with the reassurance that only two options remained for Royce: solipsism or realism.

At different stages of the attack Royce responded by depreciating his opponents. "Spaulding's papers," he said, for instance, "are conscientious. Like Herbart (as Schopenhauer described him), Spaulding *'ist einer der seinen Verstand verkehrt angezogen hat.'* Otherwise he is all well enough." Royce also ridiculed the entire group with a parody of the "Ten Little Indians":

> *Six Little Realists*
> Six little Realists a creed demurely did contrive;
> But one of them asked what it meant;
> —And then there were five.
> Five little Realists in joy called new their ancient lore;
> Till one of them found out its source;
> —And then there were four.
> Four little Realists at play—each with an Entity;
> But one said: "Mine's the prettiest";
> —And then there were three.
> Three little Realists that talked the very best they knew;
> But one of them began to *think*;
> —And then there were two.
> Two little Realists that preached in quite a learned tone;
> Until the audience, waking up;
> —Diminished them to one.
> One little Realist, in a world from which all sense had flown;
> Observed his own "predicament";
> —And then there were none.

Royce vented his frustrations somewhat more effectively in "The Reality of the Temporal"—a paper he presented to the same meeting of the American Philosophical Association. Assisted by a childhood memory, he depicted the realists in the role of the "bold bad elder boy" who misleads the "too trustful little boy." In the story as Royce remembered it, the elder boy cracked a nut, opened it, and ate it, thus claiming to have shown "something that nobody ever saw before, and that nobody will ever see again." Royce applied the story to his present situation:

> The lessons of my story seem indeed manifold. I am a little reminded of this
> tale, for instance, when I hear that there is nowadays a form of the New Realism
> which has obtained a very novel insight into the nature of Time, and when I later
> discover that the new theory is that the time world is one wherein novel events
> are always occurring,—events that nobody ever saw before, and that nobody will
> ever see again. I watch such theories crack their nuts and produce the kernel, and
> then I sometimes wish that I were not so far from the home of sound reason as

some of them want me to wander. To be sure, they have told me the truth, but in how disappointingly familiar and commonplace a fashion.

Despite this casual depreciation, the "little" realists did, in fact, pose a threat that was all but fatal, for as the popularity of realism spread, Royce was steadily pushed farther into the role of an antiquated patriarch. In his defense he could only remind his colleagues that he had silenced this bullying realism long ago, and to this end he rehearsed the outlines of his metaphysics. Time, he insisted, is real, but it is not an immediate datum; rather, the events that comprise the temporal world are constructions of the will or of the appreciative self. "*How* then can we appreciate uniqueness, individuality, novelty, whether in the sequence of temporal facts, or otherwise? I answer, as I have elsewhere repeatedly argued: Uniqueness, individuality, novelty, can be *willed* in case of our own deeds, and can be *acknowledged* in case of our interpretations of objects and of persons not ourselves. When I act, I *will* this one act. I will that it shall be this act and no other." Any follower of Royce's thought will recognize this as an old story; by 1909 few were interested in hearing it retold, and fewer were persuaded.

In a somewhat broader sphere, 1909–10 brought about a change in power and leadership at Harvard. The long tenure of Charles W. Eliot gave way to the presidency of Abbott Lawrence Lowell. A Harvard alumnus, class of 1877, a lawyer, and professor of government since 1900, Lowell had set his cap on the Harvard presidency. Royce took the change in stride, but his younger disciple, W. E. Hocking, was disappointed. He had hoped that their friend Richard Cabot might have been chosen. Languishing at Yale, Hocking feared that an appointment to Harvard would be jeopardized by the new leadership. In the past, he confided to Royce, his friendship with Cabot had worked against him. Eventually, with Palmer's retirement in 1914, Hocking made his way back to Harvard, dedicated to defending its traditions of philosophical idealism, but only after Lowell had vetoed the appointment of A. O. Lovejoy, because of his leading role in the American Association of University Professors and after Cabot promised to pay half of Hocking's salary.

Royce did not share his disciple's preference for Cabot. Their "friend," he wrote without naming him, might be both too humane and too outspoken for the job. Lowell, he felt, possessed the necessary qualities of a university president: sophistication, diplomacy, and ruthlessness. With Lowell, Royce had a respectful, distant relationship, but with the departure of Eliot the door of an era had closed. It was another sign of the end of the nineteenth century.

James, Christopher, and the Shadow of Sorrow

The arrival of Eusapia Palladino lent a note of comedy to Harvard circles in 1909. A celebrated medium, Mme Palladino accepted a challenge from Hugo Münsterberg for a scientific examination of spiritualism. Münsterberg was convinced that she was a humbug and regarded her popularity as a threat to the foundations of experimental psychology. William James shared his colleague's suspicions, but he privately felt that Münsterberg was a "buffoon" and publicly accused him of a "shallow dogmatism, which . . . is in no way more scientific than that of mystical superstition." Münsterberg was determined to expose the medium's pretentions, trick for trick. A séance was arranged at which he was allowed to press his body against Palladino while she produced spirits that filled the room with table taps, gusts of wind, flashes of light, and strains from a dormant guitar. In a cabinet, however, the experimentalist had hidden one of his students, who as he reached for wires and switches, accidentally grabbed Palladino's bare foot. She screamed, and the hoax was revealed. Royce, from Olympian heights, made the most of the situation by teasing James with the following jingle:

> *The Search for Truth*
>
> (Lines written upon hearing
> of Professor Münsterberg's
> success in the investigation
> of the case of Eusapia Palladino)
>
> Eeny, meeny, miny, mo
> Catch Eusapia by the toe;
> If she hollers, then we know—
> James's doctrines are not so!

Royce circulated this among friends. Katharine sent Ned a copy, announcing it as "Papa's greatest effort."

At about the same time, Royce, James, and Münsterberg became involved in another seriocomic episode. Their friend James Mark Baldwin had been arrested in a raid at a brothel and was forced to resign from the faculty at Johns Hopkins. Baldwin may have admitted his guilt when apprehended, but he later denied the charge categorically. From Paris where he had gone to escape publicity, he pleaded his innocence in a letter to Münsterberg, claiming that he had gone to a "social club" unaware "that women were harboured there." Little was done to clear up the affair, but it deserves mention in that it shows Royce's effort to apply the principle of loyalty to a concrete situation and reveals his difficulty in maintaining a strict logic when dealing with illicit sex. Hoping not to appear prudish by condemning "an unfortunate victim of some temptation that we have no concern to judge," he was nevertheless disturbed by the rumor that Baldwin had been sneaking off with prostitutes for years. If the rumor were true and if his friend was trying to win his innocence by lying, then, Royce told James, Baldwin would be guilty of "turpitude," and having "violated his trust," he would be no longer "worthy of the moral support of the general body of his fellow workers in this country." Royce was obviously attempting to form a distinction between cases where one momentarily fails to fulfill some ethical purpose and those where one's acts betray a prolonged and deliberate plan of disloyalty. The fine line of the distinction, however, was blurred by the circumlocution of Royce's casuistry, suggesting that he was exceedingly uncomfortable in open discussions of sexual transgression.

During the last years of their friendship, Royce and James continued to rehearse their arguments with each other's theories. But as their polemics abated, they reached a rapprochement allowing each to express his affection for the other freely and to acknowledge the positive influence of their friendship. In the preface to *The Philosophy of Loyalty* Royce had written,

> Had I not very early in my work as a student known Professor James, I doubt whether any poor book of mine would ever have been written,—least of all the present one. What I personally owe him, then, I most heartily and affectionately acknowledge. But if he and I do not see truth in the same light at present, we still do well, I think, as friends, each to speak his mind as we walk by the way, and then to wait until some other light shines for our eyes. I suppose that so to do is loyalty.

When James read this "oriental hyperbole," he was prompted to answer:

> That the world owes your books to *me* is too awfully gracious a saying! But I thank you for the beauty of spirit shown and for the honour. I am sorry you say we don't see the truth in the same light, for the only thing we see differently is the absolute, and surely such a trifle as that is not a thing for two gentlemen to be parted by. I believe that at the bottom of *your* heart *we* see things more alike than any pair of philosophers extant!
>
> I thank you anyhow from the bottom of mine.

On January 18, 1910, twenty-two of James's closest friends gathered in his library for a dinner to celebrate the unveiling of his portrait by Ellen Emmet

Rand. Perhaps they guessed that it would be their last chance to pay tribute to James's irresistible warmth and power. The portrait, which now hangs in the Faculty Room of Harvard's University Hall, depicts the pragmatist at his writing desk in front of a wall of books. With his left hand on his hip he stands erect in a professorial posture holding a manuscript in his right hand with the index finger poised for a gesture. His eyes are firmly set on a point beyond the artist. Royce admired this portrait, "especially [the] eyes, brow, pose, and pleasing impression," but felt that James's "more Titanic features" were missing.

The reference to James as a Titan suggests the power and authority that Royce saw in his friend. Certainly James made no claim to the possession of such features, for with habitual self-effacement he more often attributed them to Royce. Perhaps Royce was thinking of Prometheus, the defiant fire-bearer who had haunted his youth, the demigod, the redeemer. Royce delivered a moving tribute to James at his testimonial dinner. Published as "A Word of Greeting to William James," this address tells the story, already quoted, of their first meeting at James's home in 1877 when Royce desperately needed support for his ambition to become a philosopher. Royce characterized himself as "one of James's cranks . . . for many years very much his disciple . . . [and] still in large part under his spell." He did not deny their theoretical differences, but emphasized the positive value of James's criticisms, "those wonderful, lightning-like epigrams . . . [which have] long since blasted, I hope, some at least of what is most combustible about my poor teachings." James had also, Royce acknowledged, the capacity "of fertilizing the human soil where our truth has to grow." If, to Royce, James was a Titan, he was also like his father, Royce Sr.—"frontiersman . . . gold seeker . . . home builder"—the one who had been "my creator and my support."

When Royce completed the academic year in 1910, he headed for the sea. "You know about my little voyages," he said in a letter to Münsterberg. "I find them a great refreshment, and feel as if only one who sees the wonderful tropical ocean, and the lofty cumulous clouds of the trade winds, from time to time, really comes in touch with the larger aspects of natural beauty. The sea is to me what Switzerland is to many;—only, not the North Atlantic of high latitudes,— the tropical sea is my joy." Royce needed the vacation badly, for he was in the depths of a terrible depression. His work seemed fruitless, and his family situation had worsened. "I move about, and am henceforth always to move about under a shadow of sorrow that can never be lifted."

Royce took two sea voyages during this summer, one to Costa Rica and another to Dutch Guiana. It was while he was on the second of these, on August 26, that William James died. Because the boat had no radio, Royce did not hear of his friend's death until he disembarked at Boston on September 13. It was, he said with great constraint, "an entire surprise to me." To deepen his grief, in a manner he described as "baffling," his desk was piled with letters from editors, each asking for an obituary. "After hesitating over the conflicting calls," he wrote to R. U. Johnson of the *Century*, "I simply find that, at the moment, my friend is too dear, the shock of his death is too sudden, the event is too near, for me to choose the right word." After consulting with his friend's widow, he decided to postpone all public comment on James's life and thought until he was better composed.

Though he failed to mention it in this letter of September 16, Royce had to bear up under another grief. Somehow, near the end of the first week of September, Christopher had come down with a fatal case of typhoid fever. Presumably the mental illness had so depleted his body that he was unable to fight off the infection. For two weeks the family stood by helplessly. He died on September 21. Two weeks later Katharine received a letter from Ned, who was beginning his teaching career at the Baptist College in Bryan, Texas:

> Coco is out of his troubles, but [I] can't help feeling terribly grieved, of course, as everybody does. Do you remember what Ophelia says about Hamlet— "sweet bells jangled out of time and harsh"? Coco was composed of such sweet qualities that it was a deep tragedy to see them all wasted, and to be powerless to help him by any human means. He was Mamma's best boy, and I know that, even were I able to be everything he *would* have been (I shall always attempt this, though I know it is impossible), it would not make up at all for her loss.
>
> I am very glad that everything was so sweet and consoling at the last. I wish I could have been with poor dear Coco and tried to comfort him at the last. . . . I know how wonderful the Bach and Beethoven must have been as memorials of Coco, who loved and understood and felt Bach and Beethoven so much more and better than the rest of us do.

Christopher's death, together with the death of William James, provoked in Royce a return of his predominant fears: isolation and abandonment. "The worst thing about many sorrows," he said on the evening following Christopher's funeral, "is their lonesomeness." It is not surprising, therefore, that at this moment he reached out to his oldest surviving neighbor and colleague, Charles Lanman. In a letter of thanks for the help that Lanman and his son Tom had given, Royce remembered an observation that James had made shortly after the California earthquake in 1906: "He was impressed with the fact that, because they all suffered together, and because nobody was lonesome in his grief, they all could be relatively cheerful." Actually James had said that it was by working, not suffering, together that the victims had escaped "the sense of loneliness that (I imagine) gives the sharpest edge to the more usual kind of misfortune that may befall a man." With this slight emendation, Royce made the remark speak more directly to his own grief and touched a deeper level of tragedy. His first child and his loving companion were dead; now he entered what he would later call the *"hell of the irrevocable."* Worse still, as he sat alone in the darkened house he contemplated with singular horror a world of sufferers "left alone with their dead and their lost hopes," each sealed off from the others. He decided to write a note to Lanman, his "dearest guru," but as his hand touched a stack of stationery, he did not select one of the traditional black-bordered papers, for as he explained, "the 'trappings and suits of woe' are not needed when I speak to one who understands me."

Chapter Nine

The Beloved Community
1910–1913

Because My Help Is Needed

A human community united in love. This is the theme of the last phase of Royce's life and thought. Love had always been central to his philosophy: the principle of harmony, the world of appreciation, the theory of individuation, the philosophy of loyalty are all variations on the same theme—that love gives meaning to life. As he grew older, especially after he had felt the sharp edge of tragedy and knew that death at every angle was approaching, love gained a new importance. His friends recognized that the emphasis was the result of his enormous capacity to love. "He was loved by his fellows," said Charles A. Bennett, "and the cause of it was that he loved them."

Nothing illustrates this truth more vividly than a story told by the boy who grew up on the east side of Irving Street, the future poet, Edward Estlin Cummings—named to honor the Oxford philosopher-theologian, J. Estlin Carpenter, a close friend of both Royce and the poet's father. Just before embarking on his voyage to Oxford for the Hibbert lectures, Royce wrote a note to his eighteen-year-old neighbor:

Dear Estlin:—

This is for thanks to you for the flashlight; and farewell. I shall tell Carpenter

and his house how lovely you are. When I get back we shall talk poetry, or whatever you will.

> Yours
>
> J. Royce

A scrap such as this might easily have been discarded, but the poet kept it for
the next fifty years, and in his *six nonlectures* he remembered the ensuing
promised conversation. "One ever memorable day," he said, in 1912 or 1913,
Estlin met the professor "rolling peacefully home from a lecture":

> "Estlin" his courteous and gentle voice hazarded "I understand that you write
> poetry." I blushed. "Are you perhaps" he inquired, regarding a particular leaf of a
> particular tree "acquainted with the sonnets of Dante Gabriel Rossetti?" I
> blushed a different blush and shook an ignorant head. "Have you a moment?" he
> shyly suggested, less than half looking at me; and just perceptibly appended "I
> rather imagine you might enjoy them."

In a few moments Royce and Cummings were closeted together in the philosopher's study, rich with the scent of tobacco and cluttered with blue books. The
professor found his copy of Rossetti's poems, turned to *The House of Life*, and
began to read "lovingly and beautifully, his favorite poems." "And very possibly,"
the poet concluded, "(although I don't as usual, know) that is the reason—or
more likely the unreason—I've been writing sonnets ever since."

What were Royce's thoughts when he selected these particular poems? *The
House of Life* contains the most sensuous poetry of the late Victorian era.
Rossetti had written the sonnets for his wife and buried them with her when
she died. Retrieved and published in 1870, they had prompted a savage attack
directed against "the fleshly school of poetry." Undoubtedly Royce first read
these sonnets during his youth and never forgot the passions that they first
then evoked. One of the poems in the sequence has particular significance, for
Royce had quoted the first line of it in a lecture he composed in 1907.
"Stillborn Love" commemorates Rossetti's daughter who died at birth. Royce,
we may safely presume, responded very personally to the portrayal of the "little outcast hour" who stands "mute before the house of Love." In the most personal way he understood the loneliness of a fatherless child and the grief of a
childless father.

> The hour which might have been yet might not be,
> > Which man's and woman's heart conceived and bore
> > Yet whereof life was barren,—on what shore
> Bides it the breaking of Time's weary sea?

Bondchild of all consummate joys set free,
　　It somewhere sighs and serves, and mute before
　　The house of Love, hears through the echoing door
His hours elect in choral consonancy.

But lo! what wedded souls now hand in hand
Together tread at last the immortal strand
　　With eyes where burning memory lights love home?
Lo! how the little outcast hour has turned
And leaped to them and in their faces yearned.—
　　"I am your child: O parents, ye have come!"

Cummings was certainly too young to know any of this background. He did not remember the specific poems read to him on this day, nor did he grasp the fact that this shy, courteous gentleman was satisfying his need to share his buried feelings with a boy who would not forget the lesson. This was Royce's quiet and almost unnoticed way of loving.

Almost immediately after Christopher's funeral, Royce plunged into the academic year. That was probably good for his mental health, for work—always his fortress against pain—gave him no chance to wallow in idle grief. At Harvard he was scheduled to teach his regular set of courses: logic, metaphysics, advanced logic, and the seminar in logic. Once a week he traveled to Yale where he taught an additional course on the philosophy of religion. He also made arrangements to deliver a series of three Harrison lectures at the University of Pennsylvania on February 6, 7, and 8, and to repeat these together with other material at Smith College on February 10, 17, 24, March 3, 10, 17, and 18. During the spring semester he took on a new course: a seminar in the history of philosophy entitled "Hegel's Dialectical Method." Finally, toward the end of June 1911, he gave a commencement address at Simmons College entitled "Loyalty and Insight," and presented his well-known Phi Beta Kappa address at Harvard, "James as a Philosopher." Financially as well as psychologically he needed the extra work. The bills from Christopher's final illness and funeral had left him so strapped that he was forced to ask his publisher for an advance on earned royalties. The thousand dollars or so that he earned from lecturing passed joylessly through his hands en route to the same creditors. Still, granted his need for a supplementary income, it must be allowed that for a man who was nearly broken by personal tragedy, Royce was remarkably active.

In family affairs Royce's life was also full. Ned returned from Germany engaged to be married in December. His fiancée, a distant cousin on the Head side, was a beautiful, gifted, eccentric sculptor, Elizabeth Lean Randolph. An attractive addition to the family, Elizabeth was particularly close to "Papa." Years later, with "a happy warm chill" she remembered "one most beautiful of all looks, the time he whispered that my eyes were like stars." Like Estlin Cummings, Elizabeth was a youthful seeker, and Josiah welcomed her invitation to tell a few of his deepest convictions. Given a copy of *The Philosophy of Loyalty*, she asked for a few points of clarification. Why must we live? Is there a definite purpose in life? Can we expect proof, or must we live by faith? Another philosopher might have dismissed these naive questions, but Royce was not one to reject any honest inquiry. He answered at length, offering a concise summary of his ethical theory:

> *I must live because my help is needed.* There is something that I can do which nobody else can do. That is: I can be friend of my friends, faithful to my own cause, servant of my own chosen task, worker among my needy brethren. I can thus join with the world's work of trying to make the whole situation better and not worse. And because I can live thus, I am more than a chance creature of nature. My life has sense and meaning. . . . *The* help which my friends really most want of me, is help in living "in the unity of the spirit," as lovers and faithful friends, and patriots, and all those who together are devoted to art, to humanity, to their religion, or to whatever *binds the souls of men in the common ties of the spirit,*—as all such, I say, are, in their various ways, trying to live. Whenever and however I can steadily and faithfully live in this way, I am really helping, helping not only my own nearer friends, but, by my example and my indirect influence, I am helping everybody who is even remotely related to me or influenced by me to give sense to his life. Now thus to live,—to live for the sake of the "unity of the spirit," to live for some "cause that binds many lives in one,"—to live thus is to possess what I call Loyalty.

This alone explains why, despite his terrible sorrow, Royce could not pull out. "*My help is needed.*" With this he sought to defeat the terror of estrangement. The tragedy had not destroyed, but actually strengthened his faith, and he obviously took pleasure in being able to express his rededication in a letter to his future daughter-in-law. "And whatever you tell us is most prized," he said with rare unguarded affection, "and whatever we can do to help you our dearest desire. / Yours lovingly / Josiah."

The Harrison lectures offer another illustration of Royce's continuing loyalty. Evidently written during the summer before James's death, they make no mention of this fact, but instead continue the "battle of the absolute." James surely would have welcomed this treatment, to be regarded as a still living philosopher. The officers of the University of Pennsylvania had hoped to sponsor a head-on debate between leading exponents of pragmatism and idealism. Originally they hoped to have Royce and James appear side by side, but when James declined, they turned to John Dewey. Then when neither Royce nor Dewey was "willing to lock horns openly," a compromise was struck: to have the instrumentalist present three lectures, "The Problem of Truth," in December, followed by the absolutist in February. Royce's title was "The Nature and Accessibility of Absolute Truth."

Dewey laid out, with few surprises, a popular outline of his early pragmatism and its case against idealism. Despite the title given to his series, he attempted to show that there is no problem of truth as Royce had defined it. Ideas are instruments or representatives of the meanings of things, and these meanings are determined by social procedures and consequences; truth is prescribed and sanctioned by custom. Whenever truths no longer fulfill a community's needs, other truths are found to replace them. Dewey's favorite illustration of this position was the spectacular emergence of philosophy among the Greeks: "Philosophy was born out of the inability of custom to maintain itself as a final standard of life, and out of the attempt to do by reflection the work previously done by tradition." From this viewpoint the search for truth is a special case of human evolution, and philosophy, instead of yearning for absolutes, should unite its interests with the experimental sciences. "If the pragmatic idea of truth has itself any pragmatic worth," he said at the close of his first lecture, "it is because it stands for carrying the experimental notion of truth that reigns among the sciences, technically viewed, over into political and moral practices, humanly viewed."

To the instrumentalist, an idea is a tool whose function fits its structure and whose value is found in its results. The idealist, whom Dewey found guilty of the crime of "pompous futility," finds himself "in a state of 'splendid isolation,' where the isolation is most evident and the splendor depends on the point of view." Dewey attacked the isolation of the professional philosopher in favor of a wider, more primitive humanism. He wanted to bring the problem of truth back to the simpler, commonsensical notion of "truthfulness." "Truth, in final analysis, is the statement of things 'as they are,' not as they are in the inane and desolate void of isolation from human concern, but as they are in a shared and progressive experience."

It is unlikely that Royce had read Dewey's lectures before presenting his own. Only once and without naming him, Royce referred to his opponent as a "distinguished colleague," adding: "I am here to state my own case and do not wish to waste your time by any unnecessary controversy." But since for a decade Dewey had been one of Royce's severest critics, he knew what to expect, and he answered him point for point. He denied as vigorously as possible that he was in any sense an isolated intellectualist. He insisted that thought cannot function without will, that theory cannot be separated from practice, that a man is what he does, that philosophy must learn from the methods of science, and that service to the human community is the aim of the trained thinker. Taking a more critical tack, Royce raised three important objections to the pragmatists: first, that they could not defend their theories without implicit acknowledgment of certain absolute truths; second, that their allegiance to science had been pledged without an acceptance of its logical methodology; and third, that if "workings" are the criterion of truth, the observance of the workings implies an absolute observer.

For a thesis Royce argued that pragmatism unintentionally supports absolutism. In "The Will to Believe," James exemplified his theory with the case of the stranded mountaineer whose safety can be won only by leaping across a chasm. Does he have the right to believe a truth untested by prior experience? Not only does he have that right, James answered; he has a logical obligation, for if he decides not to decide, that too is a decision. Here, Royce observed, the pragmatist has advanced a proposition that is absolutely true. Royce admitted that this observation might seem trivial, but taken in context it serves as a model for many absolute truths—the assumption of the irreversibility of time is another—which had crept into pragmatic theory. Such truths are neither remote nor barren; they are familiar aspects of daily life and have the greatest practical import.

Royce also attacked the "repeated boast" of pragmatists that their theory is an extension or application of the procedures used by empirical science—the doctrine that a hypothesis is true if it works. But this, Royce observed, is not science: "The scientific [testing] of hypotheses depends upon deducing from them the consequences which must be true in case the hypotheses are true." Peirce had repudiated this claim of pragmatism, and with his aid Royce summarized the logical characteristics of deduction and induction as they are actually used in the sciences. This exposition led him to the following conclusion:

> Our interest in all this lies in the fact that however limited to mere probabilities our knowledge of nature may be, deduction is concerned with getting to absolute truth. For the assertion that a proposition A involves a proposition B is . . . an assertion about a matter of absolute truth. One assertion implies another or it does not. A bit of deductive reasoning is either right or wrong. And the existence of the exact and deductive mathematical sciences is a proof that we have in a considerable measure a genuine access to absolute truth of the deductive type.

Royce identified the third objection as "the very core of my difference with current pragmatism." "Things as they are," to use Dewey's phrase, are events in time. But, Royce added, each event takes "its place in the whole life of the world, a life which for good reasons you conceive as infinitely complex." Citing his favorite metaphor, he asked his audience if the meaning of a sonata is in the individual notes or in the whole composition. Obviously the latter. So too the meaning of any event cannot be known apart from its bearings on other events, and to be fully known it must be grasped by a mind capable of infinite understanding. The "workings" of the world, therefore, are neither time-bound nor timeless: they are "supratemporal." And further, so long as the pragmatist refuses to acknowledge the absolute, his truth is incomplete. Of course, anyone is at liberty to refuse this conclusion, but look at the consequences:

> You may refuse to accept it. Life may seem to you to be no fit object for such a supratemporal conspectus of intent and deeds.—Yes, but the alternative is to view life simply as that trivial flow of temporal "workings" in which all flows, but nothing ever gets done. If there are deeds, if life is real, if the world in which you express your will is real at all, then there is an infinity of absolute truth such as only a supratemporal conspectus of all life and of all time can adequately observe.

Royce never published this interesting set of lectures, but in answering a letter from Ella Cabot on March 22, he explained his position and his plans for the lectures:

> You ask a fair question. The answer is brief; but the reason would be long indeed. We *can* know, *secundum quid*, what the unique purpose, meaning, truth, absolute sense of *this* deed is, exactly in so far as the deed is the object of the present individual choice. But the *secundum quid* may be limited enough. The present view may be extremely narrow. This glimpse of the absolute may be, for us, shrouded in enormous mists of ignorance.—But we have the glimpse.
>
> As to how all this can be,—as to the reasons for saying so,—I have some new papers, read this year at Philadelphia and at Smith, on "The Nature & Accessibility of Absolute Truth." A little later in the spring, when the present rush of engagements slackens a trifle, I may be in to show you some of these papers. They need revision in their present MS form. Otherwise I would send them to you to read.

This is one of the few times—perhaps the only time, in fact—when Royce admitted the imperfection of a philosophical argument that he had constructed for public presentation. Was he beginning to doubt the absolute? In any event he incorporated parts of the Harrison lectures in the fourth chapter of *The Sources of Religious Insight* and continued to insist that his faith in this doctrine never wavered. His later arguments, however, were couched in less polemical speech. At the age of fifty-five he seemed ready to grow in different directions.

The lectures at Smith College were a repeat of the Philadelphia program—rearranged, expanded, and divided into smaller pieces. Royce was no stranger to the Northampton campus, having first lectured there in 1895 and often afterward. "Acute, learned, brilliant, generous, friendly," said Professor H. N. Gardiner, "he was always a welcome and admired guest." In the spring of 1910 Royce had given a series, "Modern Philosophy of Life," which seems to have been a collection of four lectures he had on hand. His appointment in 1911 was prompted by the absence of the chair of the philosophy department. At the end of this course he agreed to add one unscheduled lecture, "Immortality," which was probably the same that he had written in 1906 and published in the *Hibbert Journal*, whose editor, L. P. Jacks, had asked for something "not too technical." In selecting this piece as the finale to his series Royce was reinforcing his conviction that life must continue because the individual's help is needed. The crux of his argument for immortality is that since life is a struggle to fulfill an eternal plan and since no finite life can achieve a final fulfillment, God needs each life to continue its spiritual existence after its physical death. "This need of mine is God's need in me and of me. Seen, then, from the eternal point of view, my personal life must be an endless series of deeds."

At the same time, an illustration of Royce's strong need to be needed was expressed in his dealings on the professional level. With the retirement of G. H. Howison at the University of California, President Benjamin Wheeler offered Royce the Mills Professorship. Balancing his commitment to Harvard against his desire to live and work among his relatives and oldest friends, Royce sought the advice of his colleagues. He was especially interested in President Lowell's opinion. When Lowell urged Royce to remain at Cambridge, the case was decided. In the letter that announced this decision, Royce emphasized the weight he gave to the president's recommendation:

> In a certain sense, as I suppose, I may henceforth regard myself as here by your appointment. At all events I wished you to have every chance to choose as to my decision; and if you had thought best, I should have done what I could for Harvard by going, as I shall now try to do by staying. Whatever other fortunes life brings, there is no doubt that to teach here is the best of all the academic opportunities for one in my calling and with my interests.—I thank you for your kind interest in the matter.

Lowell's answer to this letter gave Royce the reassurance that "the welfare of this University demands your presence." "The University," he added, "is built not of bricks, but of men; and you have long been one of the cornerstones. A dozen such men would alone make a great University."

As evidence of his sincerity, Lowell arranged to have Royce awarded the Walter Channing Cabot Fellowship. The founders of this grant provided a stipend of two thousand dollars a year to be given to a member of the Harvard faculty, but did not specify other conditions except that the money should be used "to attract and hold some eminent man to Cambridge." In April Lowell forwarded to the Corporation his recommendation that Royce be appointed for a period of three years. The terms of the award were liberal: Royce was given the money as additional income, a source for acquiring materials, or a means of relief from teaching. In a conference with Lowell, Royce indicated that the fellowship would give him more time for writing. He planned to give up extra teaching and to refuse invitations for public lectures; he also intended to take a sabbatical in 1912–13 and to hire a substitute, the following year, to do part of his teaching at Harvard. At the end of three years he hoped to have published two volumes of popular philosophy and a technical work on the connection between logic and metaphysics.

Royce's health necessitated some revision of this three-year plan. The technical work remained unpublished, but the financial and psychological boost of the Cabot Fellowship did see him through two minor works and a monumental third. During this period he published *William James and Other Essays on the Philosophy of Life, The Sources of Religious Insight,* and in two volumes, *The Problem of Christianity.* "I need not say," Royce wrote to Lowell in the summer of 1911, "how very greatly my vacation has been brightened by the kindness of the Corporation. I wish to express my deep thanks for their honor and confidence, and to add my personal thanks to you also for your very large part in giving me so much to be grateful for, and to inspire the serious work that I hope to be able to do when I return." Writing also to Arthur T. Hadley, the president of Yale, on the occasion of his being awarded an honorary doctorate at the June commencement, Royce expressed his gratitude for "the beautiful kindness with which you, and the Yale Corporation, overwhelmed me." The honor bestowed was in part Yale's recognition of the service that Royce had performed for three years as an auxiliary professor. Funds from the Cabot Fellowship enabled Royce to free himself of this extra chore.

Insight

A list of Royce's students reads like a *Who's Who* in American philosophy for the first half of the twentieth century: George Santayana, Charles M. Bakewell, A. O. Lovejoy, Mary Whiton Calkins, William Pepperell Montague, John Elof Boodin, Ralph Barton Perry, W. E. Hocking, Harold Chapman Brown, Morris R. Cohen, Horace M. Kallen, C. I. Lewis, Harry T. Costello, Jacob Loewenberg, C. J. Ducasse, and Henry M. Sheffer. From start to finish they joined a chorus that sang, with occasional dissonances, their teacher's praises. Royce, they agreed, was the supreme dialectician. He reminded Perry of a "battleship, heavily armoured . . . [seemingly] impregnable and irresistible," in contrast to James who was more like a cruiser, a submarine, or light aircraft. Students were drawn to Royce; they wanted to emulate him and minimize their objections to his system. To Lewis he was "my paradigm of a philosopher." "He had," said Montague, "an unexampled power of making abstract ideas concrete and almost sensuously vivid." Montague added that Royce had given him "the kindest and most painstaking assistance in working out my own philosophic problems."

Power and kindness were qualities that the students repeatedly attributed to their teacher, to whom they were linked by a bond of filial love. If they were dismayed by his shyness, they were delighted whenever his humor broke through. "With a solemnity belied only by the twinkle lurking in his eyes, he liked to build up some portentous narrative or fable until the whole edifice came toppling down in laughter." Once, in the middle of a lecture, a young man failed to catch an allusion to Lewis Carroll. "Your education is incomplete," admonished Royce, and taking the youth aside, he recited from memory the whole of "The Hunting of the Snark."

Students countered by constructing fictitious rumors about Royce—that he was the first man born in California, or better still, that he wrote all of his books in German and his wife translated them into English. These comic thrusts, which Royce would certainly have appreciated, were the signs of deep affection. "He was my dear teacher," said Montague, "and I longed to call him master."

Speaking for many others, Brown feared that he might injure the master by being too much opposed to his absolutism. But Royce was convinced, as the philosophy of loyalty teaches, that people must learn to think and act for themselves. Hence, tolerance became the quality that the students most admired in their teacher. "Royce proclaimed the truth volubly enough," said Loewenberg, "but he always retained a genial indulgence of opinions opposed to his own." In his capacity as Royce's assistant, Loewenberg once consulted the master about a paper in which a student had irreverently compared the absolute to a "purple cow." "He has wit, imagination, and understanding. How James would have liked his style! Give him an 'A', and compliment him on his originality." Another story, told by Hocking, illustrates the same point. In a seminar paper he sharply disagreed with an idea advanced by Royce and expected to be criticized. "Instead, when Royce handed my essay back, he pointed out the dissenting passage with the comment, 'This is your insight: you must adhere to that!'"

So one by one Royce's disciples joined the camp of opposition. As the students suspected, it probably did trouble him to find so many of his academic offspring lined up against him. He may have consoled himself with Aristotle's remark about Plato, that truth is the better friend. At any rate he certainly knew that nothing is more vital in the life of a mind than insight. It is not, therefore,

surprising that as Royce grew older, more fatherly, and more tolerant, the importance of insight grew ever clearer to him.

With insight, Royce said, we gain "a more considerate view of our life and
its meaning." More than what? In Royce's earlier philosophy the terms of the
inner life are "knowledge," "consciousness," "experience," "thought," and "will."
But in 1911 he began to give "insight" a special emphasis. Insight, he said with
less than total clarity, is a tertium quid standing between and making a synthesis of reason and intuition, or to use other elements in Royce's vocabulary,
insight joins the worlds of description and appreciation. Resisting James's "sub-
conscious," Royce continued to insist that all truthful insight must be rational,
but it encircles a wider sphere than "mere analytic reasoning." "For whoever is
to comprehend the unities of life must first live. Whoever is to be best able to
survey the landscape from the mountain top must first have wandered in its
paths and its byways, and must have grown familiar with its valleys and its
recesses. Whoever is to get the mature insight must first have become a little
child." Insight grows out of individual experience. One may have "sight" of
many things foreign to the self, but "insight" cannot be learned by rote: it is personal, intimate, authentic knowledge. The specific content of insight varies, but
its universal hallmark is its perception of "the unities of life."

Some studies of Royce's thought maintain that his final years were marked by
a gradual drift into mysticism. Although the point has been ably disputed, it is
plain that he was feeling his way toward an enlargement of his earlier theory of
knowledge. "Loyalty and Insight" is a clear sign of this tendency. Less obviously,
the same concern is the guiding principle behind Royce's tribute to the "beautifully manifold, appreciative, and humane mind" of William James. In his Phi
Beta Kappa address Royce sought a rapprochement in the battle of the absolute.
The James he now described was not the witty antagonist, but a "moral idealist"
and a "prophet of the nation that is to be." Admittedly James never described
himself in those terms, and Royce acknowledged that he still found pluralism
unacceptably chaotic. But Royce was seeking a statement in his own terms of
their deeper affinities. James "saw the facts of human life as they are, and he resolutely lived beyond them into the realm of the spirit. He loved the concrete, but
he looked above towards the larger realm of universal life."

Henry James complimented Royce on this "generous & luminous treatment
of my dear Brother's work & influence." The address was generally acclaimed.
It was published in the Boston Evening Transcript, and reprinted in Science and
the Harvard Graduates' Magazine. Soon afterward Royce decided to make it the
title piece of a collection of five essays: "William James and the Philosophy of
Life," "Loyalty and Insight," "What Is Vital in Christianity?" "The Problem of
Truth in the Light of Recent Discussion," and "Immortality."

In his letter proposing this volume to Brett, Royce announced his appointment to the Cabot Fellowship and outlined an ambitious plan for publication.
Within two or three years he hoped to offer Macmillan three additional volumes: "a proposed book on 'The Vital features (or elements) of Christianity'
[*The Problem of Christianity*], and a further book on 'The Art of Loyalty,' as well
as a more technical treatise on 'Logical Theory.'" *William James* would be "a
brief volume of rather closely related essays that, if you publish them—may well
serve as an introduction to the expected future volumes." What Royce perceived as this close relationship is unclear, for *William James* has less unity than
his two earlier collections. Nevertheless, since Royce was the brightest star in
Brett's constellation of philosophers, the publisher acceded immediately to the
proposal. The book was produced rapidly and published before the year's end.

Royce had opened negotiations with Brett for the publication of *William
James* in August 1911 as he was preparing to cross over to Scotland to attend, as
Harvard's representative, the fifth centennial of St. Andrews University. In New
York, a day or two before he sailed, Josiah wrote Katharine a letter, reassuring
her of his health and his love, and giving her an update on the schedule for the
new book:

> After a quiet night and an early breakfast, I made my way to the steamer dock,
> found my room on the *Cedric*, got my bags all safely into the room, and have now
> come to the publishers;—that is to the Macmillan Company,—for a brief call. I
> have seen Mr. Brett. All seems to be right about the book. I learn that you may
> expect galley proofs to begin in about ten days from now.—I am now going to
> return to the steamer at once. It is not far off. The outlook for comfort and cheer
> on the voyage seems to be very good,—weather fine, steamer cheerful, passenger
> list moderately small for so large a boat. I hope that you got home all safely last
> night.—Very very much love to all, & Stephen also included.

Meanwhile Royce was working on still another book, *The Sources of Religious
Insight*, a series of lectures sponsored by the William Bross Foundation and
delivered at Lake Forest College, a small coeducational Christian college
located north of Chicago on Lake Michigan. The college president, John S.
Nollen, in a letter detailing the arrangements, explained that Royce should
arrive on Sunday, November 12, 1911, and deliver his lectures daily, concluding
the following Sunday, November 19, with "The Unity of the Spirit and the
Invisible Church." In addition, Royce would be expected to give informal talks
"at our morning assembly" and meet a few times with philosophy classes. While
in Illinois, Royce also renewed his old friendship with George Herbert Mead
and lectured at the University of Chicago on "Psychological Problems Suggested
by Pragmatism," later published, in 1913, in *Popular Science Monthly*.

The idea for *The Sources of Religious Insight* originated during the spring of 1910 when Royce was asked to speak to the Yale Theological Club. He presented his lecture on May 14, and before that at Smith College on April 18. Five sources of religious knowledge were examined: revelation, mysticism, pragmatism, reason, and loyalty. In his description of "insight" Royce stressed the internal bases of religion. "The witness of the spirit must be, at least in its deepest essence, an internal witness. . . . Our knowledge of . . . [religious] truths must . . . be a sort of reminiscence, an inner memory of our lost home which arises within the spirit, and which tells us what signs and words and deeds are really worthy to be viewed as expressions of the divine truth regarding that home." The importance of Royce's spiritual homecoming, a theme so prominent in his life and thought, cannot be overestimated. To miss that theme is to miss the destined goal of his wanderings. "Insight" was the unworn path he took on his search for the lost home.

An expansion of the original paper, *The Sources of Religious Insight* unfolds in seven lectures. As Royce noted, "It is one of the easiest of my books to read,—so I fancy. And it contains the whole sense of me in a brief compass." The universal human need for redemption, or deliverance from conflict, was Royce's central theme. Such is the office of religious insight. He pinpointed this theme in his second lecture where the conflict appears in two forms: within the self, and between the self and social experience. This analysis is a striking departure from Royce's earlier and less insightful treatments, where he often described conflict in terms of some external agent. *The Sources of Religious Insight* places the conflict within, where it belongs:

> We forget one part of ourselves in our temporary absorption in some other part. And if, as our naturally complex and often conflicting motives determine, these our various lives are out of harmony with one another, we constantly do irrevocable deeds that emphasize and perpetuate the results of this disharmony. As we grow older our motives alter; yet because of our natural narrowness of interest, we often do not recognize the change. Our youth consequently lays a poor foundation for our age; or perhaps our mature life makes naught of the aspirations of our youth. We thus come to spend a great part of our days thwarting ourselves through the results of our fickleness, yet without knowing who it is that thwarts us.

Insight is redemptive in that it allows one to see, as a whole, the various disjointed parts of the self. True redemption comes with the insights that allow the self to become integrated with society. Speaking perhaps out of his personal traumas, Royce noted that "the sense of guilt may take the form of a feeling of overwhelming loneliness." Sin punishes the sinner by making him an outcast. Symbolically, Coleridge's Ancient Mariner seeks reunion by confessing his sin to the wedding guest; his "escape from the horrors of this despair, the beginnings of his salvation, date from the first movings of love in his heart toward all living beings." In *Crime and Punishment* Raskolnikov "finds the way to salvation through love—the love which the martyred Sonia teaches him—herself, as our Russian most persuasively pictures her, at once outcast and saint." Redemption, Royce insisted, is "essentially a social process," a deliverance from "a chaos of needs" to a "fulfillment, where love finds its own, and where the power of the spirit triumphs."

In the middle portions of this series, lectures three through five, Royce offered an analysis of absolutism, pragmatism, and loyalty which varies only slightly from his previous statements. But with the sixth lecture, "The Religious Mission of Sorrow," he touched a subject notable for what it biographically reveals. The sorrows and their corresponding insights are those that result from loving, from willfully involving one's life in the destinies of others. "For when you love your kind, you aim to be a factor in their lives; and to deprive you of this privilege would be to insure your total failure. But if you possess this privilege, you share in a life that, in proportion to its importance and depth and range and richness of spiritual relations, is full of the possibilities of tragedy." Hence the paradox: love, the richest experience in life, is fraught with the greatest dangers.

Royce could not have been insensitive to the personal meaning of this discussion; the tragic insanity and death of his son and his love for him that had horribly contributed to that tragic outcome were the unmentioned examples of this paradox. He did illustrate it, however, with a discussion of "The Preliminaries," a story by Cornelia A. P. Comer published in the *Atlantic Monthly* in November 1910—less than two months after Christopher's death. The plot involves a young man who encounters parental interference when he proposes to marry the daughter of a convicted embezzler. Peter Lannithorne, the convict who more than coincidentally resembles Alf Escott in *The Feud of Oakfield Creek*, is the moral spokesman of the tale. When the young man announces his desire to do the safe thing, Lannithorne tells him he wants the impossible:

"What every man in the world is looking for is the sense of having mastery over life. But I tell you, boy, there is only one thing that really gives it! . . . It comes," he said with an effort, "with the knowledge of our power to endure. That's it. *You are safe only when you can stand everything that can happen to you*. Then, and then only! Endurance is the measure of a man!"

Royce drew from the story's insight his own threefold conclusion: first, that suffering is the price we pay for leading a fully engaged life; second, that there is no safety from grief except through endurance; and third, that insight, which is the gift of love, is born in sorrow. Reading this with a knowledge of the anguish beneath it, we can understand why insight had become a central concept in Royce's philosophy.

The final lecture anticipates the greater speculation that Royce was yet to formulate: "The Unity of the Spirit and the Invisible Church." The "Invisible Church" was Royce's name for human brotherhood, *the community of all who have sought for salvation through loyalty.*" In brief outline, he maintained that this community is no mere hypothesis, but a reality like the larger experience that escapes our limited span of consciousness. Ignorance, then, makes this church invisible; loyalty is the hallmark of its membership; and Saint Paul is its apostle. Royce reserved for himself, as he stated repeatedly in *The Sources of Religious Insight*, the future task of bringing this concept of Pauline Christianity to the fore. In the meantime he preached love and tolerance for all seekers: "I have no authority to determine your own insight. Seek insight where it is to be found."

Written for a general audience, *The Sources of Religious Insight* is one of Royce's most accessible works. The original talk had been hosted by "the New Haven ladies," an informal class of philosophically minded women headed by Julia Bristol, a niece of Daniel Coit Gilman, and Agnes Hocking. In November, before leaving for Illinois, Royce sent them a typewritten copy of the entire series, and the ladies—"your little flock" as Mrs. Bristol called them—began immediately to discuss the work with "much happiness" at regular sessions.

Royce repeated the lectures at the Andover Seminary in February 1912. When Scribner's published the book in April, the Cabots, Royce's always loyal friends, greeted it with passionate enthusiasm, and in separate letters, they listed the points they most admired. Ella, deeply religious and romantic, responded most to Royce's emotional arguments. Where Royce had written concerning redemption—"If he is to be saved, something that is divine must come to be born in the humble manger of his poor natural life"—Mrs. Cabot said his words glowed "with the light from the shepherd's torches." She wondered, however, why Royce had not included love of nature as a source of religious insight. "In your book I've missed the insight that comes from our brothers the trees & thrushes, & anemones, but I think they happen to be more friends of mine (or I friend of them) than most people would feel. And great joy of fulfilment has its insight surely as well as starry-eyed sorrow?"

Richard Cabot read the book with more attention to its logical structure. Admitting that he was always unable to oppose Royce's philosophy, he listed fourteen points of approval. But like Ella, Richard also found something lacking:

> I feel . . . that something more ought to be said—(if only in the way of disapprobation)—about the place of *beauty* as a source of religious insight. I cannot doubt

that it is such & a very common one,—though doubtless it gets amalgamated with loyalty and reason in many people. Many readers of your other books have asked me why there was not more recognition of the place occupied by beauty in spiritual life.

In response to this criticism, Royce confessed to a defect that he traced to his California childhood. "Personally," he wrote, "I have *some* access to beauty especially in *two* realms, viz.; music, and nature-beauty; together with a fairly warm, but, as you know, limited access to poetry. As to music and nature— beauty, I am, and must remain, naïve, ignorant,—at best childlike." Yes, when he was alone with the hills or at sea or listening to music (though Christopher's death had clouded this appreciation with tragic associations), beauty was a source of spirituality for Royce. But feeling inept in all but a child's love, Royce chose to remain silent. Indeed, aesthetics is the one branch of philosophy to which Royce made practically no contribution. We remember that he never wrote the promised review of Santayana's *The Sense of Beauty*, and in 1913 Royce would tell his portraitist, L. Leslie Brooke, that he was ignorant of art. The comment amused Brooke who, as the sittings progressed, learned the range and depth of Royce's knowledge: "you know more about art," wrote the artist, "than I am ever likely to understand about any system of philosophy."

My Health, My Plans

During a meeting of the American Philosophical Association held at Harvard, December 17–29, 1911, Royce was embroiled in another controversy with his younger colleagues. The argument arose in a planned discussion, "The Relation of Consciousness and Object in Sense Perception," for which a committee of participants had defined the key terms—*"object," "real object,"* and *"perceived object"*—in ways that were unacceptable to all but the disciples of realism. The effect of these definitions was to create a "riot of philosophic anarchy" in which Royce became the leader of the rival faction.

Immediately after the meeting he spelled out his objections in a fifteen-page essay—"On Definitions and Debates"—which he submitted for publication to the *Journal of Philosophy* on January 5. Two weeks later he was still negotiating the publication of this article with the editor, Frederick J. E. Woodbridge, who had asked for a more abbreviated treatment. Royce answered that he saw no way to shorten the essay, but suggested that it might be printed piecemeal. "Verbal discussions . . . ," he added, "are always unwelcome to me"; and later in the letter he complained of "the irksomeness of all such discussions." One might suppose that more was troubling Royce than this. He seems to have reached the limit of patience.

Then on February 1, "years of severe strain, care, and contest with fortune" resulted in an attack of apoplexy. The stroke occurred immediately after a long walk in the snow. "What happened," he said later, "was a very minute cerebral haemorrhage, somewhere in the optic region, on the right side,—with the result of a left side hemianopsia." Although the injury to vision soon repaired itself, Royce was confined to his bed for several weeks. The Harvard Corporation helped to lighten his anxieties by voting him a leave of absence on full pay until September 1912. The symptoms of the disorder were the expected ones: "somnolence," "confusion," "depression," "moodiness," "head-aches," and "a general emotional flabbiness." To his relief there was no "motor paralysis, or serious interference with mental processes at any level," and checks of his vital organs were encouraging. Royce's doctors gave a positive prognosis, urged him to continue with his philosophical plans, and made him feel that he had "won a very fine vacation." "My general nervous condition," he felt assured, "is better than it was before I thus took to loafing."

The household situation was, however, complicated by factors that Royce chose not to mention. Ned had gone off to the University of Illinois where he served one year as instructor of music, leaving behind his wife and their son, born on December 11. Randolph, named for Elizabeth's family, was ill during his first weeks of life and proved eventually to be profoundly retarded. Sweeping aside the worst of interpretations, Elizabeth gave her husband an optimistic view of the situation in a letter postmarked February 12, 1912:

Darlingest dear—Randolph is better, Papa is better, I am better, everything does seem today to be going so nicely. Papa has been walking around the house a lot, has even been downstairs, and the doctors have said that he may read a little beginning with fifteen minutes twice a day. And then Randolph is too lovely! His smile is absolutely irresistible and he looks more and more like Nenny every day. I almost believe that his eyes are going to be blue after all. I do hope so! But even with the indeterminable color that they have now they look just like Nenny-eyes, their expression changes so suddenly an' boofully. He has gained three and a half ounces since Thursday, now weighing ten pounds exactly. This afternoon we have had a very handsome and welcome visitor. At first we thought it was Pussy Pope but it was too large. I have never seen such a superb cat, and he was very condescending and lay on Papa's bed and allowed himself to be admired and petted as though he hadn't been big enough for a menagerie.

During the next month Royce continued to improve steadily. By the middle of March he was well enough to write long letters to friends—Woodbridge, Brett, Bertrand Russell, and Alfred Deakin—relating with clinical exactitude the state of his health and his prospects for recovery. He was not in any sense an invalid, and he wanted to be regarded as momentarily sidelined but fit for serious work. "I bid fair to live a bit longer, and to do a bit." The stroke also made Royce somewhat sentimental in his longing for sympathetic companionship. "I find myself fonder of my friends than ever," he told Woodbridge, "and I hope that you will call to see me whenever you are hereabouts; and that others also will come when they can." His spirits were high, and with an unflagging sense of humor he closed this letter with a free adaptation of Lewis Carroll's "Advice from a Caterpillar":

> "In the days of my youth," his father replied,
> "I thought it might injure the brain;
> But now I am perfectly sure I have none,
> I do it again and again."

Royce assured Brett that he was "certainly not neglecting the Christianity plan." The contract for this work had been signed in January, and Royce's letter to his publisher was a full report of his progress. He had arranged to deliver *The Problem of Christianity* as a series of Lowell lectures in the spring of 1913, and he had tentative plans to use the same material in a series of Hibbert lectures at Oxford during the following summer or autumn. Far from ending his career, Royce's "vacation" provided ample time for research. "My leisure for reading on the topic of the book is giving me daily new materials. And I am sure that the delay thus forced upon me will make the book better, and will result in making it more notable than it could otherwise be."

A list of the most important of these "new materials" can be inferred from the bibliographical references in *The Problem of Christianity*. Included were contemporary works by religious philosophers and historians: Percy Gardner, *The Religious Experience of the Apostle Paul*; Ernst Troeltsch, *Die Soziallehren der christlichen Kirchen und Gruppen*; William Sanday, *Christologies, Ancient and Modern*; H. R. Mackintosh, *The Doctrine of the Person of Jesus Christ*; and Auguste Sabatier, *The Doctrine of Atonement*.

From two scientific colleagues at Harvard, Royce also gained important insights. The anatomist Charles S. Minot, who occasionally participated in Royce's seminar on methodology, lent support to the claim that the growth of science depends on its communal relationships. A younger colleague and another member of the seminar, Lawrence J. Henderson, attracted Royce's attention with a new form of the teleological argument. Henderson's theory, as advanced in *The Fitness of the Environment*, was published by Macmillan after Royce had enthusiastically recommended it to Brett. However, with due acknowledgment of the influence of these works, Royce was most indebted in *The Problem of Christianity* to the epistemology of Charles Peirce.

Partly because he had not expected this influence, Royce responded to it with special intensity. In a tribute to Peirce, Royce described his experience as that of one who had searched afar for a key idea only to find the solution nearby:

Although I long knew Peirce personally, and have been for many years interested in his theories, there were some aspects of Peirce's theory of knowledge which I never understood until, in connection with my own efforts to work out the relations of my philosophy of loyalty to other branches of philosophy, and, in particular, in connection with my review of the problem of the essence of Christianity, I was lead [sic] to reread some of Peirce's early logical contributions, and to reconsider the way in which these his earlier theories had worked themselves out in the form which some of his later studies indicate. Then I came to see, with increasing clearness, that Peirce's whole career as a student of logic and of scientific method was devoted to a few fairly simple and obvious ideas, which have nevertheless been very imperfectly understood, just as great and obvious ideas usually are neglected and misunderstood. When I hereupon tried to restate these central ideas of Peirce, I found that, if once grasped and held before one's mind, they supply one with a theory of knowledge which I ought to have understood and used long ago. I often had heard Peirce state, in his own attractive but baffling way, this theory of knowledge. I had supposed it to be fairly well known to me. Yet I had never understood its real force, until I thus saw it in the light of this new review. Then indeed, I observed its close connection with what I had been seeking to formulate in my philosophy of loyalty. I saw also how many aspects of philosophical idealism, when this Peircean theory of knowledge was brought to bear upon them, got a new concreteness, a new significance, and a new relation to the methods and to the presuppositions of inductive science. Thus, by the aid of Peirce, I was led to those considerations about the theory of knowledge which I have tried to set forth in the second volume of my *Problem of Christianity*.

The slip of the pen that caused Royce to write "I was lead" rather than "I was led" is perhaps an unconscious admission or self-accusation of stupidity. Indeed, his earlier failure to grasp Peirce's theory is difficult to explain except in terms of the dynamics of their relationship. One element of the relationship, which each occasionally disguised by bestowing elaborate compliments upon the other, was a rivalry that made them blind to each other's intentions. It was probably in 1905, when Royce ventured into Peirce's field of mathematical logic, that the feelings of rivalry had severely damaged their friendship. In a draft of a letter to James, Peirce attacked Royce's "unscientific" training and defended his own theory on the basis of "On a New List of Categories"—"my very first paper on the subject, in 1867, which is almost perfect." This claim went unnoticed by Royce until the spring of 1912 when he most certainly reread Peirce's seminal essay. Then—"fonder of my friends than ever"—Royce repaired his damaged friendship with Peirce, understood him fully for the first time, and incorporated the results. When Royce footnoted his debt, "On a New List of Categories" headed the entry.

Royce's condition improved much more rapidly than he had first expected. On June 5 he reported to Brett that he was "in very good health" and busy with the writing of *The Problem of Christianity*. The work now had its permanent title, and the structure of sixteen lectures was firmly set. Although he was not yet ready to make a public announcement, he was six months ahead of schedule and reasonably certain that his efforts would result in a short course of Lowell lectures in the fall of 1912 and a longer series of Hibbert lectures at Oxford in the spring of 1913. "The MS ought to be in the main ready for you by April, 1913." On September 6 he wrote again to Brett to say that the program of lectures was "definitely arranged."

In the meantime—between May 17 and September 1—Royce wrote the first seven lectures. Acting as his own archivist, he preserved for a future historian the precise record of his dates of composition. On four separate sea voyages aboard the steamer *Esparta*, shuttling between Boston and Limón, Costa Rica, he wrote most of this material. He worked slowly at first, spending about a month on each of the first two lectures. Then with the plan more clearly in mind, he pressed ahead, writing the third lecture in late July and completing the fourth before the middle of August. Now momentum carried him forward with relative ease; inside of two weeks on his final voyage he was able to compose the fifth, sixth, and seventh lectures. Only eight months after a nearly disabling stroke Royce had written approximately half of his most important and enduring work. Still, he could not afford to relax under the pressure of deadlines; only six months remained before he was due to present the entire series at Oxford. A sabbatical leave for 1912–13 gave him the free time he needed for the task, and as always he was ready at the appointed time.

He achieved all this not only against the odds of waning health, but also while dealing with personal and professional vexations. In June he noted the early signs of stress in Ned's marriage. The young couple had planned to spend the summer in Cambridge. Randolph was left in the temporary care of the grandparents, while Edward and Elizabeth traveled from Illinois to Pennsylvania for a brief visit with her family at Germantown. During this visit Elizabeth came down with a sudden attack of bronchitis, the reports of which hinted also of a possible tuberculosis. Josiah disbelieved this diagnosis. He was familiar enough with Elizabeth's family to know that they "held as a pious article of faith the view that she is a great and beautiful treasure who *must* be regarded as in some mysterious way an invalid." Convinced that her disorder was rooted in the psychodynamics of her relationship to her parents, Royce enlisted the help of Richard Cabot, who wrote Ned a Special Delivery letter and promised, if necessary, to pay a visit to the couple in Germantown. Royce, though he exhibited affection for Elizabeth, was most concerned about Ned who seemed unable to cope with the complicated network that surrounded his wife and her family. "He is a heartily good boy," Royce told Cabot, "and deserves a better fate."

Between the lines of the letters to his physician-friend one senses Royce's fears of a repetition of the agony he experienced in Christopher's mental illness. Josiah's anxiety was increased by the feeling that there was little he could do, except by discreet inquiries and sympathetic watchfulness, to help the situation. "Both of them are, as you see, in many ways, babes.—As I feel myself also a babe—the more so the older I grow—I cannot complain of the young people." The sense of being helplessly cut off from his loved ones found its way into *The Problem of Christianity* when he spoke of "the tragedy of love." "What constitutes, in this present world, the pathos, the tragedy of love, is that, because our neighbor is so mysterious a being to our imperfect vision, we do not now know how to make him happy, to relieve his deepest distresses, to do him the highest good."

While fighting for his son's right to a happy life, Royce became snarled in another controversy, this time with A. O. Lovejoy. With backgrounds in three universities—California, Harvard, and Johns Hopkins—the two men had overlapping careers. Royce had recommended Lovejoy for his first post at Stanford, describing him as "an admirable man,—growing, learned, resolute, ingenious, and sensible." But in his remarkable rise to philosophical prominence Lovejoy had lost sympathy with his teacher's absolutism, the arguments for which he dismissed as "dialectical hocus-pocus." This hostility surfaced in a 1912 review of Perry's *Present Philosophical Tendencies*. Praising the book, Lovejoy attacked Royce. Perry had exposed, he said, "with merciless lucidity the confusions and equivocations through which alone many neo-Kantians or eternalistic idealisms of the last half-century have acquired a speciously edifying sound." Although Lovejoy did not cite Royce by name, the target was made abundantly clear by innuendo. Royce was irritated by the indirectness of the attack and insulted by a singular reference to "the imposture in the pseudo-voluntarism of the neo-Fichteans." For many years Royce had refrained from writing book reviews or otherwise answering his critics. As recently as January 1912, he had set aside an appeal from J. E. Creighton that he answer Dewey's criticism of his Heidelberg paper. Now, however, he wrote to Lovejoy:

> On p. 634 of the current number of Woodbridge's *Journal* I find words of yours which seem to me to need a little explanation. They stand in a context in which the same thoughts as the ones which I have to ask you to explain are two or three

times repeated. As I understand the matter, you accuse some friend of yours of deliberate and willful "imposture." You repeat and vary the charge with use of the form of innuendo, in such wise as to make reply impossible. You thereby shield your attack. You in substance also appear to make Perry responsible for the same attack. I believe that Perry himself has avoided such responsibility, and is very scrupulous about fair play in polemic.

Thus, twenty years after issuing his famous warning about F. E. Abbot's pretensions, Royce found himself the object of a similar attack. The accuser had become the accused. He did not call attention to the earlier affair but, through a lapse in memory, denied it. "I have long tried,—vainly it seems, to promote mutual and kindly understanding in philosophy. Do we gain by this talk about 'imposture'?" Lovejoy saw the merit in Royce's complaint and promptly retracted the charge in a letter published in the *Journal of Philosophy*.

In a letter accepting Lovejoy's apology, Royce closed the discussion with a friendly observation about their philosophical differences. In his retraction, Lovejoy, one of the first of the modern analysts to dispose of philosophical issues by examining the behavior of ordinary language, replaced the charge of "imposture" with a criticism of "irenically-disposed philosophers" who seek to accommodate popular belief by endowing its vocabulary with unintended technical meanings. This criticism went to the heart of Royce's methodology. Philosophy, he had always insisted, is a critical inquiry into the meaning of life. His most recent studies of religious thought had led him to a theory of interpretation that gave to the philosopher the special role of discovering those meanings. Royce associated this procedure with that of Plato. "I have always acted under the influence of what Socrates says, in the *Phaedrus*, as he prepares to begin his 'palinode' about Love. . . . The popular mind is deep, and means a thousand times more than it explicitly knows. The philosopher's endless task is to find out what this deep mind means, and to tell what it means." Royce was convinced that human feelings contain truths which sober reflection must understand. In *The Problem of Christianity* he chose for himself the task of guiding the popular mind from its depths to the surface, so that it might see itself, not as through a glass darkly, but face-to-face.

The Problem of Christianity

During the first week of 1913, aboard the Cunard liner *Campania*, Royce began his eighth and final transoceanic voyage. He had presented the first part of *The Problem of Christianity* at the Lowell Institute in Boston, from November 19 to December 13, and now, with the lectures "safely stowed in my bag," he was prepared to deliver an entire series at Manchester College, Oxford, beginning on January 13—"if all goes well," he noted, aware of the risk to his health. After bidding him farewell, J. J. Putnam wrote to Katharine: "It was delightful, you may be sure, to see what seemed at first so threatening an illness, pass gradually away. I also gained a sense of admiration of your devotion & patience, which contributed greatly to the good result." Midwinter passage in the North Atlantic is notoriously stormy, but Royce passed this leg of the journey without mishap. "I am in apparently good health," he announced as his ship approached the coast of Ireland, "after finding the sea as good to me as it usually is; and I expect to be in good shape for my lecture job."

Installed at Oxford in chambers at Manchester College, next door to Jacks, he managed to get through the next three months without so much as a bad cold. His daily routine included a morning stroll for exercise in the university park. He avoided overnight trips. Getting enough sleep required special vigilance, but he participated fully in the local social life even when invitations involved late evening affairs. A friendly visit from Sir William Osler, the eminent cardiologist, was the occasion for a physical examination. Sir William pronounced Royce healthy, approved his regimen, and advised him to continue his work. "All this advice was, no doubt, unnecessary," he told Putnam, "but it was of course a pleasing added comment."

Royce's trip to England included an added academic task—that of recruitment. Harvard's once great philosophical faculty had been ravished by time. The huge vacancy in the department left by James's death was still unfilled, though Perry—chair since 1906—was his destined successor. Palmer, now in his seventies, was due to surrender the Alford Professorship at the end of the year. Likewise, Francis Peabody, an auxiliary member and patron of Social Ethics, had signaled his imminent retirement. Münsterberg was still active; he, however, and the other psychologists were pursuing directions that would eventually secure their autonomy. After 1913 the *Harvard University Catalogue* listed the curricula of philosophy and psychology separately. Almost alone Royce remained, but surely his continued health was a factor too doubtful for long-range plans.

In 1912 Santayana had been dispatched to Europe with hopes that he would attract a few gifted philosophers to America. Instead he promptly resigned. Always an alien in his adoptive nation and his profession, Santayana had come finally to deplore the "unintelligible sanctimonious and often disingenuous Protestantism" which Royce conspicuously represented. "And it is my adoration of this real and familiar good, this love often embraced but always elusive, that makes me detest the Absolutes and the dragooned myths by which people try to cancel the passing ideal, or to denaturalize it. This is an inhumanity, an impiety, that I can't bear." When Palmer forwarded Santayana's letter of resignation, in which he explained his need to work out an extensive philosophical project in total solitude, Royce sensed that his former protégé was "passing away to his own region in his own heavens, where he discourses with the seraphs of his own order and choir." Royce was "sad to be left behind." Palmer echoed this sentiment: "In such an isolated existence as he proposes I should rot."

Ambassador without portfolio, Royce carried to England a list of candidates and promised to be a more loyal emissary than Santayana. Near the top of his list were the names of R. F. Alfred Hoernlé, Leonard Trelawney Hobhouse "whom I am only to 'observe,' as I understand," and Lawrence Pearsall Jacks. Hoernlé was acquired for a temporary lectureship beginning in 1913, but Jacks immediately declined the offer of Peabody's chair. Hobhouse was reported to be "a very good teacher, as well as writer," available it was hoped, but unobservably in Italy. Royce was impressed with what he learned about younger Oxford fellows W. H. Moberly and A. D. Lindsay; others, including H. H. Joachim, were "*very* strong men, but too technical in their bearing and interest for our sort of job." J. A. Smith, presumably a name on the list, was too old, inaccessible, and "as critically dialectical as Mephistopheles." The list was crowned, since Harvard wanted only the best, with the name of Bertrand Russell.

Russell had previously agreed to a visiting post at Harvard, scheduled for the spring term of 1914. Royce had hopes of acquiring Russell permanently, but Jacks warned that this would be impossible: "Russell is the only man of scientific genius whom his ancient family has produced. The family will hold him fast." The warning, as it turned out, was well founded. "I feel," Royce reported after a long talk with Russell at Trinity College, Cambridge, on February 4, "like an unwilling but doomed bachelor who is always proposing to somebody."

Russell had told him that he was "utterly immovable for any permanent foreign appointment." They had, however, explored Russell's plans for teaching the theory of knowledge and advanced logic. "There is no doubt that Russell is a great men," Royce concluded; "and we must make the best of our half year with him." Russell, Royce later told one of his students, had received more attention than any logician since Aristotle. But more than this, again like Aristotle, Russell was a complete philosopher, particularly awake to ethical and religious thought. Recommending him to the Lowell Institute, Royce promised that Russell's course would be "of great originality, and power, on some of the general life-problems . . . 'radical' but inspiring." Royce had been especially impressed by Russell's article "The Essence of Religion." "There is a wonderful frosty atmosphere about Russell's mind just now,—an infinitely pathetic and manly and calm resoluteness: His last *Hibbert Journal* essay on 'religion' was to me like a landscape of moonlight on the snow, when a cold wave has just died out and become still. This sounds sentimental, but is not in his case, such. He has seen deeply into the dark."

Russell liked Royce ("tho'. . . . a garrulous old bore") because he listened to "whispers from another world." Both men shared, despite vast differences, a disposition to value mysticism as well as logic. "The greatest men who have been philosophers," Russell observed in 1914, "have felt the need both of science and of mysticism: the attempt to harmonize the two was what made their life, and what always must, for all its arduous uncertainty, make philosophy, to some minds, a greater thing than either science or religion."

Such is the platform of *The Problem of Christianity*. Royce delivered his lectures twice a week for eight weeks, on Mondays and Thursdays, from January 13 through March 6. His audiences were small, but he was assured that they were "as good,—on the whole—as the Oxford conditions make possible for lectures of this kind." At the close of the sixth lecture he expressed his general satisfaction. "Some very good people are present each time."

Scholars generally agree that *The Problem of Christianity* excels all of Royce's previous works. It is more personal and inviting than *The World and the Individual*, perhaps lacking its technical precision, but less magisterial and obtuse. No longer committed to a persistent hammering away on behalf of the absolute, he presented his case in clear, uncluttered prose, sharing his insights and interpretations with an expectant audience. Anyone can read *The Problem of Christianity*; it requires no special technical preparation. Like *The Education of Henry Adams*, which belongs to the same period, it forewarns the public of the lost generation. It is the nineteenth century urging the twentieth that the problems it will have to face—loss of faith, global warfare, personal alienation, political hypocrisy, and ethnic strife—can be solved only by reaffirming, historically and practically, the unity of purpose which relates the individual to the common interests of humanity.

Thus finally Royce had become a humanist, a designation that in his last years he freely embraced. He was not primarily an apologist for Christianity or its critic, though in some senses he was both. In the opening lecture he announced his intention to treat his subject "as a central, as an intensely interesting, life-problem of humanity, to be appreciated, to be interpreted, to be thoughtfully reviewed, with the seriousness and with the striving for reasonableness and for thoroughness which we owe to every life-problem wherewith human destiny is inseparably interwoven." The problems of religion, he insisted, are special cases of the issues that affect the lives of all human beings. The search for community, the burden of personal tragedy, and the hope for redemption—these, for Royce, are "the three central ideas of Christianity."

The concept of the universal community is the focal point of the entire book. Failing to grasp this concept, the reader will miss the freshness of Royce's approach to religious thought and the enduring significance of his mature philosophy. The New Testament, read in the light of his interpretation, gives different names to the community: Kingdom of God, Body of Christ, New Jerusalem. Neither Jesus, nor Paul, nor John, the author of the Apocalypse, expressed fully the meaning of this concept, yet they all agreed that the goal of the religious life, human salvation, is reached in and through communal relationships. Royce departed from the traditional exegesis of these terms by arguing that the community is to be realized not in a celestial afterlife, but here and now by laboring to satisfy one's deepest needs and to aspire to the highest ideals. This thesis, we know, is a feature of Royce's thought, which he maintained throughout his long professional life.

Another aspect of Royce's argument which invites analysis is his claim that the community is a person. "A community," he suggested, following Wundt's *Völkerpsychologie*, "behaves like an entity with a mind of its own." Although Royce introduced this only as a "fair 'working hypothesis,'" it is a postulate upon which the entire book depends. A few years later he repeated the claim, but with more emphasis: "For me, at present, a genuinely and loyally united community, which lives a coherent life, is, in a perfectly [literal] sense, a person." Such a community is "not merely an aggregate, and not merely by metaphor a person." Despite the air of mystery that hangs about this idea, Royce found it practical, concrete, not mystical, but imbued with clarity and common sense.

What conditions must a community fulfill in order to be classified as a person? A typical idealist, Royce denied that a person can be described in terms of physical properties. Personality, if anything, is a psychological phenomenon, and a person—like the individual of "The Principle of Individuation"—is the expression of a will. Hence a community can be considered a person when its members are united by shared purposes. That many can be one is not merely a paradox indulged by poets; love, as in marriage and parenthood, makes it concrete. Just as communities can hate and be hated, they also can love and be loved. Undoubtedly Royce held this belief because of his deepest psychological needs, but he did not base his discussion on these private sources. The personality of any community—and by expansion, the personality of the universal community—is clearly implied, he felt, by the modern sciences of sociology and logic.

As in "Provincialism," Royce held that a community, considered as a person, is characterized by a common language, customs, and ethical aims. Religion, as the embodiment of these aims, expresses a community's highest spiritual identity. Thus, the church, the universal community—poignantly Royce also called it the Beloved Community—is the goal of religion, and the individual's moral burden is its problem. Drawing on material published in the 1890s, Royce observed that self-consciousness linked to an injected social consciousness results in a conflict within which the self is divided. What one part of the self desires, the other condemns: hence the moral burden. Royce would have readily agreed with

Freud's thesis that social organization progresses at the cost of individual happiness, but he would have denied the claim that the superego disarms the self, rules it "like a garrison in a conquered city." For Royce, civilization has a creative function: its laws, customs, and norms offer a means, the only means, of redemption. The primitive self must perish, crucified and expelled from paradise, to be reunified and harmonized in the Beloved Community: "It is the body of Christ. The risen Lord dwells in it, and is its life. It is as much a person as he was when he walked the earth. And he is as much a spirit of that community as he is a person. Love that community; let its spirit, through this love, become your own. Let its Lord be your Lord."

This sounds like pulpit oratory, and yet Royce did not wish his lectures to be taken as a case for the "visible" church. By studying Christian thought, and even by adopting in large measure its language, he wanted to understand how this particular institution had developed as an answer to basic human needs. Repeatedly he assured his audience that he was not defending religious dogmas, but looking behind the dogmas, seeking their psychological motives. Saint Paul, Royce felt, provided the key. The apostle of Christian love had framed his epistles in the correlative contexts of guilt and atonement, and thus had touched the deepest needs of humanity, its divided self and painful search for deliverance.

The needs and their fulfillment were, of course, none other than Royce's own needs and his own unsatisfied resolution of these needs. This becomes clear in a passage where, having translated "love" into "loyalty," he announced that "the value of loyalty can readily be defined in simply human terms." He went on to describe this simple, human value: "Man, the social being, naturally, and in one sense helplessly, depends on his communities. Sundered from them, he has neither worth nor wit, but wanders in waste places, and, when he returns, finds the lonely house of his individual life empty, swept, and garnished." One thinks of the isolated, fatherless home of Josiah's childhood, the deserted grave nearby, and the boy's earliest thoughts of escaping over the mountains, his terrified dreams of wandering in a wasteland, returning to an empty, locked house.

The tension is sharpened in the next paragraph where Royce observed that the injected social consciousness not only tempers and directs self-consciousness, but also, by internalizing the outward enemy, fosters rebellion, hatred, and "spiritual death." This Royce called "the spiritual disease of cultivation." A possible escape might be found by loving some other individual. This, however, is no solution. "For such loves . . . are capricious fondnesses for other individuals, who, by nature and by social training, are as lonely and as distracted as their lover himself." The only healthy solution remaining is loyalty. By coming to terms with the divided self, by rededication to the aims of the human community, we reach, Royce urged, "the realm of grace" and the path to "atonement."

The first part of *The Problem of Christianity*, the eight lectures presented to the Lowell Institute in the fall of 1912, develops these ideas. This constitutes the psychological and ethical half of the series. In the concluding eight lectures, Royce turned the discussion to "a philosophical theory of the real world." Here he was interested in the epistemological bases of his problem and its solution. The Beloved Community, he argued, is not merely an emotional need; its reality is implied in the structure of thought.

These lectures emphasize the triadic structure of knowledge. Cognition is often assumed to entail a dyadic relationship between subject and object, the knower and the known. In the second volume of *The World and the Individual*, Royce had challenged this theory through his discussion of Kempean logic. An act of comparison always involves more than two terms: it involves also the quality *between* them.

Royce neglected the larger implication of this thought until, in 1912, he reread a few of Charles Peirce's early essays: especially "On a New List of Categories" (1867), where Peirce maintained that comparison requires a "mediating representation"; "Questions concerning Certain Faculties Claimed for Man" (1868), where he attacked intuition and introspection as sources of knowledge; and "Some Consequences of Four Incapacities" (1868), where he claimed that knowledge is acquired through communal relationships. In the first essay Peirce pointed out that the relationship between two terms (or signs) can be known only through the introduction of a third, which functions as an interpreter. For example, suppose I am searching for the meaning of *"homme"* in a dictionary and find *"man"* next to it; this familiar sign interprets *"homme"* as meaning the two-legged mammal that *"man"* also means. According to Peirce the role of the interpreter is to resolve conflict or clash between two signs by drawing them into unity.

Peirce developed the social dimensions of knowledge in the second and third essays. "No cognition not determined by a previous cognition . . . can be known"; "no facts require the supposition of [intuition]." Self-consciousness, he maintained, meaning "the recognition of my *private* self," is developed through social interaction. This is, of course, the position that Royce had held for twenty years. The contribution that Peirce brought to the theory was his explanation of self-consciousness in terms of the interpretive process. Suppose a parent warns, "Don't touch the stove, it's hot," and a child says, "No, it's not hot." The clash between these two signs is resolved when the child, touching the stove, interprets himself to himself: "No, I was wrong, it is hot." Thus, the child discovers his ignorance and error—aspects of self-consciousness—through the interpretation of testimony.

The third essay explores a concept of reality that involves a community of knowledge. Peirce launched this discussion with a criticism of the Cartesian concept of an absolutely incognizable reality. This, he maintained, is an absurdity, for what is unknowable cannot be a concept, and being meaningless cannot be real. What is real "is cognizable in some degree." Once again, Royce and Peirce had long maintained the same position. Suppose, Peirce said, that I discover that one of my ideas was an illusion; to reach that conclusion I must first have had a conception of reality, "such as would stand in the long run," as opposed to the merely idiosyncratic. "Thus, the very origin of the conception of reality shows that this conception essentially involves the notion of a COMMUNITY, without definite limits, and capable of an indefinite increase of knowledge."

Adopting Peirce's theory and adapting it to his own purposes, Royce made the concept of interpretation the foundation of his epistemology. "Man is an animal that interprets; and therefore man lives in communities." "Interpretation is, once for all, the main business of philosophy." According to the Roycean model, the process involves an antithesis, or at least a tension, between two ideas (or selves), mediated by interpretation, and thereby expressing "reality." The process also entails an infinite sequence of interpretive events and an endless variety of selves mutually interpreted. For example, suppose I render an interpretation of *Hamlet*, claiming in effect that what I say is identical to what Shakespeare says. My audience, reading both the play and the interpretation, agrees with my insight and makes its understanding of *Hamlet* identical to mine. Thus rises a triadic unity, or a mediated reality, in which the text, the interpretation, and the audience are mutually equivalent. This, in ideal form, constitutes a community of interpretation. But if as is generally the case, one interpretation conflicts with another, a further interpretation is needed, and so on endlessly.

This vast network of signs and interpretations results in a universe in which all cognition is social activity. It is not surprising, therefore, that Royce remained a severe critic of individualism. The individualist is one who wishes to eject the social consciousness and who insists that relationships be dyadic and knowledge intuitive. One thinks of Emerson speaking before the Harvard Divinity School, urging the students to "refuse the good models, . . . dare to love God without mediator or veil," or in "Self-Reliance," turning away from society and loved ones: "I must be myself." Royce insisted that the community, when its members are loyal and loving, is not the external oppressor, but the actual embodiment of our own larger being, and by joining together in interpretive acts we grow toward a fuller realization of the possibilities of our humanity. Mere conception is "sterile"; mere perception is "intolerably lonesome . . . a desolate wilderness." "When viewed as if I were alone, I, the individual, am not only doomed to failure, but I am lost in folly." On the other hand, interpretation is "essentially spiritual"; it seeks "the homeland where, perchance, we learn to understand one another."

Is this more than a sociology of human knowledge? Royce refused to develop parallels between his older absolutism and the newer "doctrine of signs." He asked his audience to listen "as if all my former words were unspoken." He did not, however, renounce the absolute: "As a fact, I still hold by all the essential features of these former attempts to state the case for idealism." And yet the rhetoric of *The Problem of Christianity* expressed a sharp departure from his previous works. By faith and faith alone Royce acknowledged the community of interpretation as the Beloved Community, the spirit and redeemer as its "core" and "central member," God as the divine interpreter. Royce gave no reasons, but abundant motives, for these beliefs. Previously he had proposed to prove his theory of a transcendent being; now the whole argument was couched in existential terms. Loneliness, misery, guilt cause human beings to cry out for redemption and deliverance. "Alone I am lost, and am worse than nothing. I need a counseller, I need my community. Interpret me. Let me join in this interpretation. Let there be the community. This alone is life. This alone is salvation. This alone is real."

For Ruth Royce this new orientation connected the philosopher to his pious and devoted mother. In a letter to Josiah on April 17, 1913, his sister wrote,

> I often think of Mother's unflinching courage, sturdy faith and self-control, and of their outcomes in triumphs. . . . Were she still here, I can well imagine how happy she would be in the results of your undertaking. And she would understand & appreciate it even better than in the old days, for she was growing & broadening all the time. . . . Most of all I rejoice that in your writings you are expressing your philosophy "in terms of life" that others can lay hold of and work out in turn in their own lives. To be helpful seems sometimes to be the *only* thing *worthwhile*.

Royce planned to publish his lectures immediately. Brett complied, and the enterprise was accomplished with astonishing dispatch. On September 6, 1912, Royce had written to him with a detailed outline of his plans. The first volume would be ready for the publisher in October, the second in December. This schedule would permit Macmillan to begin the typesetting process before the lecture series opened in England. In fact, Royce corrected the galleys of the first volume in January at Oxford. Katharine was to handle page proofs, and Jacob Loewenberg was hired to construct the index. With adequate help Royce lost no time. He had hoped to get the first volume in print by April. Actually both volumes were published simultaneously early in May.

While staying at Manchester College, between lectures, Royce had his portrait painted by L. Leslie Brooke. The original is now missing from all known collections, but in England photographs were taken and distributed to Royce's friends. Jacks hung his copy prominently in his dining room, and when he received his copies of the two volumes, he mentioned this graphic remembrance. "You sank deep into the lives of these men," he wrote, "and it is a common saying among us that of all our Hibbert Lecturers it is you to whom we owe the most."

Royce's achievement during the eighteen months following his stroke seems incredible. He was a man known for his enormous productivity, but even for him the facts provoke disbelief. There was nothing like it in his whole life. Within this period, while recovering from a disease that would have forced most people into retirement, he accomplished the major part of his research, he wrote the entire work—more than 150,000 words—he delivered the first part at the Lowell Institute, the full series to the Hibbert Foundation, and he supervised all of the necessary corrections leading to publication. The achievement is explicable, first, because of his tremendous resilience, his will to live being an important asset, and second, because of his clear conception of the work he wished to produce. The words flowed from his pen, not needing extensive revision. Such a work could have been written only by one whose whole life was bound up in it. For almost sixty years its components were inwardly constructed. Now, perhaps partly because of the crisis in his health, he was able to unite these components into a final, coherent expression of himself and his philosophy.

This chapter opened with a story told by a poet who grew up in Royce's neighborhood. The story involved a meeting between Royce and Cummings in which the older man had interpreted to the younger man the poems of Rossetti. Here is the paradigm of what Royce meant when he explained the triadic structure of the community: the youth, the professor, and the poet who had filled the professor's young years with romance. The fact that Estlin Cummings went on to become a major lyric poet suggests a confirmation that we do indeed live in a world of interpretation.

Chapter   Ten

Watchman,
What of the Night?
1913–1916

Family Interlude III

In the last years of Royce's life we become witnesses to a gradual decline of his physical stamina. A private person, he did not lay open the ravages of time and care, or the causes of grief that enclosed him. Unknown to all except intimate friends and relatives, a series of crises rocked the family. Resigned but not without hope, Royce went about his business in an aura of serenity. Some have said that his intellect suffered a similar decline, that his works lost their originality, and that he became quarrelsome, vague, eccentric. By 1915 his closest friends seemed to understand that he was dying. Because he could no longer write with a steady hand he was sometimes forced to seek assistance from typists and amanuenses, and the fact that many careless errors began to creep into his manuscripts suggests that his attention was beginning to wander. Still for the most part his mind remained lucid, he continued to take a lively interest in each new task, and there was never, even at the end, a clear sign of senility. As one devoted to intellect, Royce was spared the indignity of living on into a period of silent confusion.

Christopher's tragic death and the stroke that nearly ended Royce's career were by no means the only incursions that afflicted and engulfed the family. As an omen of what would follow, Edward Royce had decided to marry Elizabeth Randolph on December 29, 1910—only three months and a week after

353

Christopher died. In family correspondence this ill-timed wedding was scarcely mentioned, but the silence may amply describe the grief-stricken demeanor of Ned's parents at what should have been a joyous occasion. A year later a sequence of misfortunes—the birth of the retarded grandson in December, Royce's stroke in February, Elizabeth's bronchial attack in June—put stress on the entire family. Throughout these months and increasingly thereafter, Ned and Elizabeth lived apart and went separate ways, while Randolph remained, except for brief visits with his parents, in Cambridge mothered by Katharine. Futile attempts were made to teach Randolph basic skills, and for some time the entire family tried to deny the hopelessness of the case. In commenting on a visit to Cambridge in 1915, Ned spoke of "how very much Randolph has gained in intelligence and grasp, and in what splendid health he continues to flourish." After Royce's death, the rift in Ned's marriage widened, and in 1922 a Reno divorce finished it. The terms of the settlement provided that Elizabeth would take Katharine, their daughter born in 1914, and Ned would have custody of Randolph. Actually Ned never fully accepted parental responsibility for the poor boy. Randolph remained with his grandmother until 1940, when she, in her eighties, could no longer control his "rather wild attacks"—his "dashing about & roaring aloud" several times a day and often in the night. Reluctantly in February Katharine had Randolph committed permanently to the Westborough State Hospital.

Stephen's marriage was quite a different affair. Indeed in most respects Royce's two younger sons were opposites. Ned's letters to Mamma were full of comment about his musical compositions and performances; indeed he rarely mentioned anything except his professional ambitions and achievements. Physically and emotionally fragile, Edward complained sometimes of weakness in his hands and fingers that prevented him from giving recitals. Katharine stated the matter bluntly when she wrote: "Edward is never strong, looks to me always like a ghost." Stephen, on the other hand, was robust. Unlike his older brothers, he had little interest in music; his letters to "Fuffy" and hers to "'Tephen" most often dwelt on her garden or the birds, squirrels, and cats in the neighborhood. Stephen's preference for physical reality led him toward a successful career as a mining engineer.

In the summer of 1913, just as Royce was being praised by friends and family for *The Problem of Christianity*, Stephen's engagement to Marion Woodworth was announced in the local papers. The young lovers had known each other since childhood; they had attended the same elementary school in Cambridge, and when Stephen was at Harvard, Marion was at Radcliffe. Before they could marry, however, their happiness was blunted by another—fortunately a minor—family crisis. A former sweetheart, a Miss Grady, came forward with the claim that Stephen had previously proposed to her, and she definitely did not consider him released from his promise. Straight off she went to the Woodworths, made a scene, and even threatened a lawsuit. Marion was devastated. Stephen had not told her about this former attachment, and what seemed his lack of confidence in her was particularly galling. Bitterly she wrote to Stephen, who was unfortunately still on the job in Wisconsin:

> I went to your house almost dying of anxiety and grief. And there, Stephen, I upbraided your dear father for never having told me. . . . I have only to say that it was enough to break one's heart to see your father, alone. Stephen, if things come out right, as they *must*—if I am ever yours,—there is just one person in the world you can thank: your own dear father.

Things did "come out right." Within a month the lovers were reconciled, the jealous Miss Grady had vanished, and the incident was forgotten. Stephen and Marion were married on September 10, and set out immediately for their new home in Hurley, Wisconsin.

"We shall always keep in our hearts the bright & lovely picture you both made at the reception & again at the train window," wrote Katharine soon after the wedding. "We take such solid comfort in that last glimpse of you bright and happy together—with the new life lying before you." When the first notes from Hurley arrived, she burst into joyful tears. To celebrate, Josiah and Katharine spent "a morning festival together" at Fresh Pond. Secreted on a bench by rock ramparts they recalled their own youthful dreams, "dear hopes fulfilled," and for a brief hour they were young again. "Hold to your dear memories, my dear ones," Josiah wrote. "The time will come when every one of them that you have kept fresh and sweet will grow more and more precious to you as the shadows lengthen." Closing, as father and professor, he did not restrain the impulse to philosophize:

> "*Nicht Glückseligkeit, sondern Glückwürdigkeit,*" is the goal of life. And towards that goal you are now on the way,—Marion the more unerringly and swiftly, as it is her nature to do and to be;—and beside her, or nearer and nearer to her, my dear Stephen. Let them always go together on that way.—"Happiness" is a matter largely of fortune. It comes and it goes. But love, and courage, and fidelity, and unity of spirit, and *Würdigkeit,*—these are yours now, if you will, and so long as you will,—whatever your fortunes.—And these are the best of all.
>
> And so now Kitty sends me to express something for you. Your letters gave us a sweet and beautiful morning together,—a vision of peace such as we had hardly hoped again to see in this world.

Stephen and Marion would have the occasion to heed this advice much sooner than they expected to need it. Exactly a year after their wedding, Marion gave birth to a daughter. Seriously ill from the beginning, "Petsy" held on to her life for less than five months. Family members were alarmed when their letters of congratulations remained unanswered. In November the anxious parents were relieved to report that the baby seemed out of danger, but a relapse eventually followed. On January 30, 1915, Stephen wired Josiah and Katharine: "Baby dead. Acute indigestion. Ill only fourteen hours." "How lonely they will be," wrote Anna to Kitty, "with that growing & developing little soul taken away . . . and the poor body laid away under the snow." Anna was touched when she learned that Stephen and Marion had buried Petsy at Mount Auburn Cemetery close to Christopher, in a family plot that would eventually contain six graves. "I think of him oftenest as a tiny thing and even younger than she was." On Easter morning Katharine obeyed her sister's wishes, brought a wreath of baby roses for Petsy and branches of flowering azaleas for Coco. And in April Josiah visited the grieving young parents in Hurley.

Logic, Criticism, and "The Spirit of the Community"

In March of 1913, Royce had described his health as "perfectly good." In July it was "fair, if a little fussy sometimes." In September, after a restful ocean voyage that completed his year-and-a-half absence from the classroom, he resumed a full schedule of teaching. He initiated an experimental half-year course, "Contemporary Discussions of the Problems of Conduct and Religion." "Outlines of Logic" (for undergraduates), the course in metaphysics, and the seminar in logic rounded out his program. With the anticipated arrival of Bertrand Russell in the spring, the Harvard community experienced an awakening of interest in logic.

For Royce, whom Russell admired for his role in promoting this interest, it was to be another "logic year." The work for *The Problem of Christianity* had reconfirmed his long-standing belief that logic should be wedded to ethics, and he hoped now to get this always postponed aspect of his thought into print. He envisioned a "book on the relations between logic and geometry"—an outgrowth of his 1905 paper in the *Transactions of the American Mathematical Society*—"and on some general philosophical issues connected therewith." In August he offered the *Journal of Philosophy*, through Woodbridge, the first piece of the projected work: "An Extension of the Algebra of Logic." This, he assured the editor, was "neither controversial nor directly representative of any general philosophical position." It was "pure algebra" and might interest mathematicians almost as much as philosophers. Royce hoped that the *Journal* would print his series of seven articles, which he promised to produce at regular intervals during the next three or four months. The project was "nearly ready to be penned, since the researches concerned have busied me for a long time."

Woodbridge accepted the first article—published in November 1913—but raised questions about future installments. The editor's response may have caused Royce to reassess his plans for publication. Fearing that the series might be too diffuse, narrow, or abstruse, he encouraged Woodbridge to feel free in rejecting the enterprise. In any event the articles were never written.

Thanks to the excellent set of seminar notes recorded by Harry T. Costello, we can follow Royce's teaching and research in 1913–14 with exceptional clarity. Costello, whom Royce described as "modestly sententious, humorously obstinate, very original, and very telling," was the seminar's official secretary for the year. The portrait of Royce that emerges from these notes is that of a benevolent patriarch, honored and respected by both students and colleagues. Ill health prevented him from exhibiting "the pugnacity which . . . made him a terror in the 90s, a flaming red-haired apparition." The color of his hair, with his temperament, had faded, and now, as in his 1914 photograph, he could be described in terms of "the thin lips [that] quivered in a whimsical smile."

"The Seminary stands for no theories of my own. It is meant to help philosophical students to think about methods. It is no formal school of Logic. Anybody who has a rational method of doing anything,—especially a scientific method,—is invited to tell us about it." Thus, Royce had described his seminar in 1911. In 1913–14 that straightforward description still pertained. Royce gathered a diverse company of scholars, including L. T. Troland, the coinventor of Technicolor, and the future poet T. S. Eliot. Discussions touched on history, psychiatry, Einstein's theory of relativity, comparative religions, as well as on the more technical issues of modern logic. The theories of Russell and Peirce were frequently entertained, and in April, on the occasion of Peirce's death, Royce led a poignant discussion of his old friend's character and contributions to thought. In his more formal presentations, he read three papers: first, his technical piece on the algebra of logic; second, a paper on the concept of "fitness"; and finally, a discussion of three modes of scientific investigation, "The Mechanical, the Historical, and the Statistical."

The second and third of these papers belong to the philosophy of science interpreted from an idealistic viewpoint. The issues which Royce explored and to which his seminar gave its most emphatic attention throughout the year depend in part upon the controversy over vitalism prompted by the evolutionary theories of Bergson and Driesch. The older doctrines of Darwin and Spencer had tended to portray life as passive phenomena forced mechanically into certain forms by unyielding natural law. The vitalists argued that life possesses as one of its inherent characteristics a substance—an "élan vital" or entelechy—which asserts itself against the brute facts of the environment.

Royce's younger colleague Lawrence J. Henderson resisted both theories: in *The Fitness of the Environment* he had advanced the thesis, which still in general prevails among biologists, that evolution proceeds by means of an interaction between life and its physical environment. In other words, if natural selection had forced living things to adapt to the environment, there were also conditions preestablished in the earth's environment that rendered it a host fit for life. This thesis, though strictly scientific, raised certain teleological questions that fascinated Royce and caused him to speculate about the possibility of discovering finally the validation of his metaphysical doctrines. He encouraged his seminar, at which Henderson was a prominent visitor, to examine these implications, and in his own work he emphasized the conviction he had reached as an undergraduate that science requires an idealistic outlook. Scientific theory, he argued, deals neither with individual historical events nor with general mechanical laws, but with statistically defined assemblages. The work of science, Royce had previously observed, is an accurate model of a community of interpretation. Now he took that theory a step further by noting that all assemblages, mechanical and nonmechanical, exhibit certain tendencies toward wholeness, assimilation, and development. This principle of "the fecundity of aggregation" suggested a universal or cosmic evolution: "the tendency of nature towards what seems to be a sort of unconscious teleology—towards a purposiveness whose precise outcome no finite being seems precisely to intend."

In this bit of cosmological speculation Royce acknowledged his debt to Charles Peirce—particularly to his series of articles in the *Monist* (1891–93). On March 4, 1914, he sent Peirce a mimeographed copy of "The Mechanical, the Historical, and the Statistical." In his covering letter—his last, for Peirce died on April 19—Royce acknowledged his debt to Peirce and their mutual interests. In speaking to others about Peirce, he was able to make his feelings clear, and in his actions designed to preserve Peirce's thought he adequately paid his debt.

It was Royce, in fact, who played the leading role in saving the Peirce papers from oblivion. He dispatched a student, Victor Lenzen, to Milford, to obtain the collection from Mrs. Peirce, he arranged with William Coolidge Lane to have the manuscripts deposited in the Harvard Library, and he housed them temporarily in his own office in Emerson Hall. Although Royce did not attempt to edit the papers himself, he supervised the project in its earliest phase. He spoke with publishers and prospective editors, considered the suitability of various plans, wrote a memorial essay on Peirce for the *Journal of Philosophy*, and frequently during the last two years of his life made references to Peirce that helped to keep his reputation alive.

Claiming an alliance and final reconciliation with Peirce, Royce stated that his old friend had read and approved *The Problem of Christianity*. "He wrote to me," Royce noted later, "a very kind letter of acknowledgement which I deeply prize, and which shows that my so belated effort to understand and to expound the side of his opinion which was in question in this book, had received, despite his feebleness and his age, a reasonable and an unexpectedly careful, although necessarily a very summary attention, and my interpretation of him gained on the whole, his approval."

Royce certainly exaggerated the depth and quality of this response, for Peirce had almost nothing to say about *The Problem of Christianity*. In the letter he wrote with a trembling, almost undecipherable, hand on June 30, 1913, Peirce admitted that he had not been able to read more than a few pages. "I began your book with great interest but was obliged to lay it aside until I can do more in a day than I can yet." In truth, Charles Peirce was dying; his "powers," as he said, had "broken" and only with enormous effort was he able to participate in intellectual discourse. Instead of addressing Royce's theory of triads, he expounded his own—rambling distractedly, yet with flashes of peculiar insight, and enlisting his loyal friend's service as an archive for his "present opinions about Reasoning." In this presumably final metaphysical letter, Peirce gave special emphasis to *Uberty*, a term he coined from Latin, *ubertas*: fruitfulness, plenty, abundance, full-breastedness. In terms of its usefulness, "Uberty," Peirce stated, is to "Security" as "*gold*" is to "*iron*." Possibly, as Frank M. Oppenheim has suggested, Royce's "fecundity of aggregation" may add a subtle parallel to Peirce's epistemology. With regard to the fundamental triadic structure of knowledge, Peirce wrote,

> The first is pure *sensation* on which I have made an enormous amount of experiments. . . . The second element is Volition on which I made an elaborate series of observations about 1871. . . . The third kind of consciousness is *thought*, where there is always a *triad* (or a larger collection of relates.) I don't think this can take place without the help of a *sign* which stands for an *object* vaguely called up, and significant in a certain *respect*. So thought has those 3 parts at least that have to be held apart in consciousness of that third kind. . . . I find the whole doctrine of inference to be full of triads. . . . And also that the art of making explanatory hypotheses is the supreme branch of logic.

Peirce concluded his letter with an empty promise: "You may be very sure that I shall study . . . [your book] unless my end overtakes me," as it did ten months later, "on which missing that reading would be one of my principal regrets."

Although Royce received many letters of congratulation and approval, *The Problem of Christianity* did not make a considerable impact upon intellectual circles. *The World and the Individual* had prompted a chorus of opposition, but *The Problem of Christianity* was politely reviewed, warmly praised, mildly criticized, and otherwise ignored. Philosophy was already moving toward analytical climates too severe for metaphysics, and on the eve of World War I, the audiences for lectures on the Beloved Community were rapidly diminishing. Royce, who had once said that philosophies are kept alive by the critical attention they get, sensed that his was now dying, or already dead.

And then also, in some quarters of the religious community, readers were unable or unwilling to appreciate the beauty of Royce's tragic vision or his radical contribution to Christian hermeneutics. Representing the viewpoint of the popular Social Gospel, Francis Greenwood Peabody, the colleague whom Royce least respected among Harvard philosophers, made it clear that he did not agree with "your estimate of the place of pain and sorrow in the work of Christian religion. It seems to me . . . marked by serenity, victory, and peace." For Peabody the personal life of Jesus and his homilies, not the Logos of the Fourth Gospel or the Beloved Community as interpreted through the Pauline epistles, comprised the core of religious belief and social ethics. "I am an old fashioned liberal," wrote Peabody to Royce in 1913, "and quite incapable of finding the essence of my religion anywhere else than in the Synoptic Gospels. The conclusion that the essence of Christianity was hidden from the mind of Jesus and disclosed only to the later Church, seems to me, to speak frankly, to turn history upside down." Probably then most people in Protestant America agreed with Peabody.

Thus, 1913–14 was a sad interlude in Royce's life. With enormous effort he had written and published his greatest work, though its importance was unrecognized. He had tried but failed to make progress with his logical theory. Efforts to revise and reissue his book *Herbert Spencer* were also frustrated. He did accomplish important work in the philosophy of nature, and in this regard he must have been pleased to act as patron to Henderson, just as he was pleased to serve the memory of Peirce. But when he spoke compassionately about Peirce's lonely life, he must have been thinking about his own loneliness. So in the summer of 1914 he returned to Berkeley, the home of his youth.

Royce set out for California in July. Mixing business with pleasure, he spent some time with Ruth and Hattie, and then went on to the university where he was the guest of his former student Charles H. Rieber. It was then that Mrs. Rieber painted his portrait, which now hangs in the Faculty Room of Emerson Hall. The official part of this trip to California involved his appointment to the University Summer School, for which he delivered six lectures between July 20 and August 1, and a special lecture at the twenty-fifth anniversary of the Philosophical Union on August 27.

These "Berkeley Conferences" were designed to clarify Royce's published philosophy, rather than to initiate new doctrines. The six lectures were organized around the concepts of loyalty, the triadic structure of knowledge, and the metaphysics of the community. The theme of the whole series, articulated in the first lecture, was that the moral individual cannot be sundered from the social context. The characteristics of an assemblage inevitably refer to its members. Thus, if one denies the value of loyalty and concludes that mankind is contemptible, then each individual man, including the one rendering the judgment, is also in some degree contemptible. A radical individualist may seek personal salvation by divorcing all communal relationships, but this act sanctions a world of broken ties. Original sin, Royce suggested, can be interpreted as the individual's rejection of the social order. True salvation, he argued as always, is achieved through loyalty, through each person's lifelong struggle to fulfill the common purposes of humanity.

In a similar vein, but with a more concrete and practical emphasis, Royce planned his address to the Philosophical Union, "The Spirit of the Community." Although Royce did not deliver this particular piece, a substantial fragment of it, thirty-five handwritten pages, is preserved among his papers. The "spirit" named in the title of the address is a special sort of mediator. In the secular world we are familiar with "forensic mediation," as when a judge resolves a legal dispute, an arbitrator settles a conflict between labor and management, or an international issue is referred to the Hague tribunal. Royce had little faith in this device for solving human conflicts, for it is designed to heed and it actually legitimizes the contentions between two parties. It does this without fundamentally changing the disposition of either toward the other. "The greatest evil of human social life," Royce believed, "lies not in the elemental greed, the selfishness of men, but in their failure to understand one another." He also believed that this evil is an inherent danger to harmony whenever dual relationships are allowed to prevail. "Men, when they are merely related in pairs,—as buyer and seller, as lover and beloved, as a master and servant, misunderstand each his fellow, and fail, each one of the pair, to find how to make his own mind clear to his mate."

There is, however, another type of mediation in which an agent represents the interests of both parties, and forms by this representation a community of three members, "a threefold personality." Royce suggested that the insurance industry is a concrete example of this triadic activity and might conceivably be used as a model in new institutions developed for world understanding, harmony, and mutual assistance.

The Great War

But while he was speaking on behalf of the universal human community, the armies of Europe, provoked by fierce nationalism, were marching against one another. On June 28, in Sarajevo, the Austrian Archduke Francis Ferdinand was murdered by a Serbian radical. This event set in motion the forces that resulted, precisely one month later, in the declaration of war between Austria-Hungary and Serbia. On August 3, the Germans, already at war with the Russians, smashed into Belgium and turned their guns toward Paris. When Great Britain promptly intervened in alliance with France, the war was active on all fronts.

The First World War provides the context for the last phase of Royce's life. As previously noted, his earliest thought had been aroused by the great national crisis of the 1860s. At different points during adulthood he had been profoundly disturbed by wars between nations and by conflicts between rival factions within nations. Such, he had often said, are the tragic consequences of dishar-mony and disloyalty, which finally injure humanity more than the individual nations and persons involved. Loath to side with any cause, Royce appointed himself to the task of understanding the meaning of conflict, and of rendering a philosophical synthesis that might organize the peaceful energies of the human community. Considered in the context of his lifework, *The Problem of Christianity* most satisfactorily fulfilled this aim. It struck him, therefore, as a bitter irony that this accomplishment was followed almost immediately by the first global war in human history.

Like most Americans, Royce must have been astounded by the news that reached him in early August. British propaganda was particularly effective in gaining support in the United States for the Allied Powers, but Royce, who had a deep and enduring love for both England and Germany, resisted the pressure to take sides. Interpreting the war as a threat to the interests of the universal community, to which he was both professionally and personally committed, he set aside his prepared manuscript, and on August 14 he constructed an outline for a new address based in part on the earlier piece, which he entitled "Interpretation of the Present Crisis." It was published as *War and Insurance*. On August 20 he wrote to President Wheeler with this account of his plans and motives:

> Thursday evening, the 27th, I am, as you know, to deliver an Address before the Philosophical Union. I have been forced, because of the importance of that task, and because of the very grave problems which the war brings before every philosophical student's mind, to change that address very largely. I had spent a good many weeks preparing for this one occasion. At the last moment I have felt required to lay aside all my MSS and notes intended for the address to the Union. I am now rewriting the address. It will still be a philosophical (and certainly not a political or a contentious) discussion. But it will deal with problems about which I have had to think in new ways since August the first.

War and Insurance proposes, first, to analyze the cause of the war in terms of Royce's latest metaphysical formulation, and second, to apply this philosophy so as to find a concrete solution. Royce believed, and many modern historians would not disagree with him, that the central motive which provoked the war was a type of nationalism peculiar to modern democracies. Such nationalism obtains, he observed, whenever an intense love for one's own people is expressed in a murderous hatred of neighbors. Hence the warlike passions become morally indispensable, holy, and even rational. In *California* Royce had previously recorded how the proud love of the United States had led to a policy of conquest, and in *The Feud of Oakfield Creek* he had treated a similar antagonism between rival families. He believed, in short, quoting Kant, that "by nature man both loves and hates his neighbor." On the other hand, he also believed, and here his philosophy came into play, that the love-hate dynamic is a special consequence of dyadic relationships:

> Taken by itself, the mutual love of a mere pair of people tends, like physical energy, to run downhill; to be baffled by personal contrasts, to be thwarted by mutual interruptions, to give place to a consciousness of painful differences, to be worn out by time. . . . Love, when it is a merely dyadic relation between a pair of lovers, is essentially unstable and inconstant. For the two tend in the long run to interrupt, to bore, or collide each with the other.

Every dyadic relationship, Royce argued—whether between lovers, partners, neighbors, provinces, or nations—is "essentially unstable and inconstant." As a solution Royce proposed a restructuring of institutions so that triadic forms will regulate international relations. Royce envisioned the emergence of a worldwide community of interpretation, which would be characterized by its relationships of interdependence, cooperation, and loyalty. In *The Problem of Christianity* he had hoped that such a community would evolve "invisibly" as the ranks of its loyal members expanded, but in *War and Insurance* Royce became a social reformer proposing means for insuring world peace.

His plan called for the formation of an "International Mutual Insurance Corporation," based in one of the neutral countries, such as Sweden or Switzerland, and directed by an independent, financially expert board of trustees. The corporation would have no political functions, but would operate strictly according to business principles. Each member nation—ideally the membership ought to include all the nations of the world—would purchase a policy insuring it against most types of natural disasters and also against acts of war committed by other nations. In the event of hostilities, the board of trustees would conduct an investigation and assign liabilities. The nation committing the first act of violence would receive nothing, whereas its victims would receive full compensation. By this condition the system of insurance would provide a powerful incentive for nations to seek peaceful solutions to their conflicts, for the first aggressor, even if it should militarily prove the victor, would face the consequence of being held liable for war damages and, by its act of aggression, economically ruined.

Although the corporation, as Royce envisioned it, would have tremendous power to exert economic pressure upon nations and to curb their warlike motives, this was not to be its primary sphere of influence. It would function mainly, he insisted, as a moral force to promote loyalty. Being the spirit of the community, it would achieve this end by its example. One must presume, because Royce did not clarify the point, that the corporation would exemplify loyalty to loyalty, for being loyal to the interests of all members of the community, it would act so as to cause the spreading of loyalty. Thus, the insurance industry had for Royce some special, almost mystical significance. Why not banking, real estate, public relations? Royce never answered this obvious question, but perhaps the paternal aspect of insurance appealed to him.

The concept of a nation protected by an insurance corporation suggests uniquely the kind of protection that an almost helpless child demands of his father, the protection that Royce, in his earliest years, was denied. As we have previously seen, Royce sought and found this relation in his friendship with George Buchanan Coale, and it is not entirely irrelevant that Coale was by profession an insurance executive. Although this important friendship lasted for little more than a decade, Royce kept in close touch with the family, particularly when Coale's daughter, Mary Redwood, was widowed in 1906. Then, with generous sympathy, he offered his friendship to her son George, a student at Harvard and a classmate of Stephen Royce. *War and Insurance* was Royce's last, perhaps unconscious act of homage paid to the memory of his old friend. A final and ironic postscript to this tale is that Captain George Buchanan Redwood was the first Baltimore officer to be killed in action during World War I. He died in 1918 and was awarded the Distinguished Service Cross with an Oak Leaf Cluster.

In 1914–15 Victor Lenzen attended Royce's seminar and eventually became its official secretary. In his fragmentary notes Lenzen recorded his teacher's opening comments:

Agamemnon. Wonderful interpretation of life. Speaks speech of today. Dealing with fortunes of dangerous pair. Father killed daughter. Mother hate. Instinctively discovered by an artist. Interpretation of life. Of some of its most tragic aspects. Horror of war. Dangerous pair. Aeschylus more than Greek. Communities of Interpretations—Scientific—Artistic. Powerful agents to make man understand man. Difficulty. Problem of war. Lack political influence. Not expressed in man's

prosaic business. Insurance—ideal as others. Yet prosaic business. Might become
what Church could but has not. If peace comes—artists & scientists will help it
to come.

Lenzen probably did not know that Royce had taken his undergraduate
degree in classics, that he had written his bachelor's thesis on Aeschylus and
delivered his commencement address on Sophocles. And yet these notes show
that after forty years Royce had not forgotten the lessons of Greek drama. The
tragedy surrounding the House of Atreus provided him with ancient examples
of "the dangerous pair," and although his seminar was officially concerned with
comparative methods of scientific inquiry, he did not hesitate to begin the year's
academic work with an analysis of the logical structure of human relationships
upon which are based the dynamics of war and peace.

In 1914 Royce completed his Cabot Fellowship and was elevated, upon
Palmer's retirement, to the Alford Professorship. In a letter to A. Lawrence
Lowell, he reminded the president that *War and Insurance* was written in the
closing weeks of my Cabot Fellowship. . . . I, like the Barrister in the Hunting
of the Snark, 'went bellowing on to the last.'" The Macmillan Company published *War and Insurance* on September 15, and though it was sharply criticized
in some quarters, the reviews were generally favorable. The book was instantly
popular; its second edition was prepared two days after the first was released.

Royce received a number of letters warmly praising the book, but none of
these correspondents endorsed the insurance scheme. The always gracious
Palmer noted the elevated style of Royce's prose and suggested that he had been
seized by "the solemnity of the war." Barrett Wendell, while doubting the possibility of international insurance, admired Royce's ability to look beyond the present crisis: "In the midst of this world-bewilderment you . . . look ahead, . . .
think constructively, and with a big imaginative precision for which *great* does
not seem to me too serious a word." However, Royce's English correspondents—
Jacks, Leslie Brooke, and F. C. S. Schiller—were so caught up in the war that
they could hardly think beyond the present. Their world had lost its continuity;
it was "terrible" and "dark." "We need all your sympathy," wrote Jacks.

The widespread public attention to his views encouraged Royce to make several defenses, clarifications, and revisions of his plan. Early in 1915 the World's
Insurance Congress sponsored a Peace Day exercise in San Francisco. David
Starr Jordan, chair of the event, invited Royce to be a member of the sponsor-
ing committee. With his letter of acceptance on February 10, Royce enclosed an
eleven-page "Memorandum on International Insurance," in which he advanced
the thesis that "the essence of insurance is that it is a principle at once peace-
making in its general tendency, and businesslike in its practicable special application." Unlike political activities, such as diplomacy, international insurance

would not forge treaties, alliances, or federations. Those activities might continue to function, but the insurance corporation would be strictly a business, free of political entanglements.

The uniqueness of insurance enterprise in promoting the goal of world peace, Royce explained, consists in its tendency to create "a social network of complicated but beneficent relations, . . . by means of which modern society has been profoundly transformed." In essence, the triadic relationship of the insured, the insurer, and the beneficiary has the potential to promote social harmony. One who buys an insurance policy engages in "forms of social enterprise, [whereby] types of social linking, unities of human endeavor,—far-reaching social loyalties,—are made possible through insurance, in a way that no other social institution renders possible."

Royce proceeded to examine different types of actual policies as models for international insurance policies. Closing, he urged Jordan to distribute his thoughts to members of the World's Insurance Congress. The opportunity, he wrote, "is too momentous for us simply to neglect it." In a separate letter to Theodore H. Price, editor of *Commerce and Finance*, Royce sought unsuccessfully to have the memorandum published.

Another essay on the same subject was, however, published in the Sunday edition of the *New York Times* on July 25. By this time many specific objections had been voiced. What corporate mechanisms could guarantee that the trustees would remain exempt from political pressures? How, with any precision, could any nation be found responsible for committing the first act of war? How could the peace be maintained if one or several of the great powers declined to participate? One of Royce's correspondents, an insurance man by profession, expressed a more probing criticism: "By its very nature war tends to impair, and in the long run to destroy, all sorts of interests which, apart from war, have constituted or have determined insurable risks." Small, defenseless nations, as well as the great military powers, would be found to be inherently uninsurable.

To answer these criticisms Royce hit upon the idea of "reinsurance." He envisioned a vast and growing network of state insurance systems throughout the world. Any of these "companies," each with a great variety of subscribers and types of policies, could be "reinsured" against potential losses, and thus the international corporation, functioning in a manner similar to the World Bank, would deal not with the unstable political structures of nations, but with the separate insurance companies. In other words, it would insure the insurers.

Royce submitted his revised plan to two colleagues in the Harvard Graduate School of Business Administration, H. B. Dow and W. B. Medlicott, both of whom were active in the insurance business. Dow at first had doubts about the feasibility of war insurance. The weaker nations might be induced to insure themselves against invasions by the great powers, but not vice versa.

Furthermore, he pointed out that a policy whereby aggressors would indemnify their victims is inconsistent with insurance practices. Eventually he seems to have changed his position, assuring Royce that the system of reinsurance was "probably the most practical fashion of beginning the undertaking as an international enterprise." Medlicott, though also cautious, approved the plan and urged Royce to publish the article: "While to the practical busy underwriter it will doubtless appear visionary, it will set men thinking and after all where would progress be if it were not that some men can see visions that to the man constantly stirring up the dust of business ventures are completely hidden."

At the same time in a rather different type of social conflict Royce expended a great deal of time and energy. In 1913 Ned joined the music faculty of Middlebury College in Vermont, and while visiting the campus where he gave the lectures "Illustrations of the Philosophy of Loyalty" and "The Philosophy of Religion," Royce met Middlebury's president, John M. Thomas, who solicited his help in coping with interconnected financial and governance issues. The State Educational Commission had authorized the Carnegie Foundation to study these issues and to report its recommendation. This report adopted the rigid position that if the state appropriates funds to colleges, it should both own and control these institutions.

Royce was so moved by this "vicious connection between education and politics" that he wrote a sixteen-page position paper, "A Plea for Provincial Independence in Education," published in the *Middlebury College Bulletin* in October 1914. By that time the commission had already taken steps to implement the Carnegie report by eliminating all state scholarships and making deep cuts in academic programs. Royce tried to involve Harvard's Dean Byron S. Hurlbut and President Lowell in the cause, and eventually brought it to the attention of A. O. Lovejoy who in turn aroused the concern of the American Association of University Professors. In 1915 Royce wrote a second paper, an address read for him at a meeting of the AAUP, which James McKeen Cattell published in *School and Society*. For Royce the plight of Middlebury College, an institution literally fighting to stay alive, rekindled his faith in the value of provincialism:

Higher education is good because it helps the state to be a Province with an independent life of its own, with a consciousness of its worth, of its uniqueness as a member of the family of states. Even a small group of college graduates help Vermont, as a larger group of the University of California have helped California, to be conscious of itself. And every New England state has a very precious heritage of traditions, a very precious variety of civilization to preserve, to bring to its own consciousness, and to contribute to the common life of the Union. . . . The wisest way for the state to live up to its own ideal life is to make a wise use of the academic resources that it already has, with the prudently advised aid adjusted to what is worthiest in the traditions and in the ideals of the state's existing institutions.

By that point, as the war was entering its sixth month, Royce was beginning to feel a strain that made his neutrality difficult. Pro-British sentiment was running strong throughout the U.S., and his English friends with whom he corresponded regularly bent him to their cause. At Harvard his established friendships with the German members of the faculty became increasingly delicate. He was able to maintain cordial relations with Kuno Francke, the curator of the Germanic Museum, but his older and deeper friendship with Münsterberg soon disintegrated totally. Francke, German born but a U.S. citizen, was wrenched horribly by the war. Professionally committed to the spreading of German culture and convinced of the rightness of Germany's cause, he published several popular essays in which, with great restraint, he explicated his people's national character and defended its policies. Francke was obviously torn between conflicting loyalties, but endeavored to practice, as Royce was prompt to recognize, a loyalty to the larger community. For this he was condemned by radicals on both sides of the conflict. On November 22, 1914, Royce wrote to Francke:

My Dear Colleague:—

I have received and read with great interest your article in the copy of the *Atlantic Monthly* for November which you have so kindly sent me. This, as all of your interpretations of the German mind and genius which I have read, I prize, and shall always prize, very deeply. Your view seems to go to the heart of things, and to deal with genuine and deeply interesting differences between Germany and America which we must always henceforth ponder, now that you have called them to our attention. I wish indeed that all international comparisons,— whether criticisms, or self-criticisms, or efforts at reconciliation, or essays upon antitheses, were conceived in so universal a spirit, and were also so delicately appreciative of important particular traits and contrasts.

I very deeply regret whatever makes you feel, from day to day, "engulfed," as you say, in "elemental feelings and passions." I assure you that what a patriot like you, who can both feel and see, finds so engrossing, has my heartiest respect and reverence, whatever my own problems, or visions, or defects of vision, or opinions about special issues may be. These are times when the personal sympathy which a friend heartily feels, as I do, for the griefs which beset you as a patriot, may serve to help towards sustaining you in trials in which, just at the present moment, we can offer to one another only such hearty personal sympathy, such deep respect for a man's best offering towards the cause of his life, and such hope that the clear vision, the fuller comprehension of what we all are seeking, may soon be given to us all, in the light which the world's peace may bring, and which, as we all hope, will bring the world peace. . . .

> Yours Very Warmly
> Josiah Royce.

A much colder aura surrounds Royce's final letters to Münsterberg, whose political stance was delineated in *War and America*, a book published only a few days after *War and Insurance*. Münsterberg, who had never opted for U.S. citizenship, described himself as neither an American nor a German-American, but simply a German, and he called urgently for the total defeat of the Allied Powers and "the spiritual triumph of Germany." The public outrage demanding his resignation or dismissal was tremendous. Some believed that his mind had cracked under the strain. C. W. Eliot, to whom Münsterberg sent secret packets by registered mail, shared this opinion. "I must frankly tell you," Eliot wrote on November 21, 1914, "what impression your letter of yesterday produced on my mind. It seems to me to be the composition of a man who has been overwrought, and who is laboring under grave hallucinations. I beg you to consult at once the physician in whose judgment you have the greatest confidence." Others charged that Münsterberg was literally one of "the Kaiser's agents" assigned to propagandize on behalf of Germany. According to the report of Stephen Royce, Royce too eventually accepted this verdict. "Shortly before his death," wrote Stephen, "my father told me that this was all part of the plan, and that Münsterberg had been called in to the Wilhemstrasse [presumably in 1910–11] and instructed to get in the limelight so that his name should be well-known when his propaganda should become necessary to the fatherland."

Whether responding to a secret mission or acting out of his own patriotic zeal, Münsterberg was a vigorous plotter and propagandist. One of his more elaborate plans involved an effort to win ex-President Theodore Roosevelt to the pro-German cause. Roosevelt was an old friend and admirer of Münsterberg, and he was prominent among U.S. politicians as a persistent lover of the German people, but he was thought to be leaning toward the side of Great Britain. Münsterberg planned to bring Roosevelt to Harvard for a meeting with a select group of colleagues and thus to influence the ex-president's opinion. A luncheon meeting was scheduled for January 10.

Royce was invited, but declined to attend. In his first letter of refusal, dated December 17, he was evasive, if entirely cordial: "Deeply as I desire to be one of the company whom you are so kindly and thoughtfully bringing together, I feel that, at present my own personal duty as a lover and teacher of philosophy requires me to be absorbed in ideas and in the service of interests which unfit me to take part in such a discussion of European politics as you propose." When

Münsterberg pressed further with a second invitation, Royce made it clear that he would refuse to participate in any discussion at which Roosevelt was present. Royce had always despised Roosevelt, regarding him as the moral and military equivalent of John Charles Frémont. He thanked Münsterberg. "But," he added, "I knew when I replied that Roosevelt has been a sovereign, that he still feels 'every inch a king,' and that, in his presence, no one directs the course of conversation but himself." It seems clear that Royce, who once seemed ready for anything and everything, could not bear the thought of being intimidated in speech by the notorious hero of San Juan Hill. "But Roosevelt,—although I doubt whether he even remembers my existence,—would be, if I were present, the arbiter of how far and how much I should have to commit myself to and in a possible discussion of European politics."

The meeting did, in fact, take place without Royce, but Roosevelt soon thwarted its purpose by publishing *America and the World War*, in which he condemned Germany and argued that the U.S. should be prepared to enter the war on the Allied side. Within months Royce severed his friendship with Münsterberg. They had known each other and worked together for more than twenty years; in the past they had been able to work through their disagreements and misunderstandings. But the war made them enemies. According to Stephen, the emotional toll of this broken friendship was huge. "When it proved that his friend . . . was a German agent, this just about completed his heartbreak."

Royce finally severed all personal and professional relationship with Münsterberg. When the Suffolk West Association of Ministers invited him to discuss "Neutrality" at a meeting with Münsterberg, Royce wrote across the top of their letter: "Answered, . . . declining." Fergus Kernan remembered occasions when they came face-to-face on the icy duckboards in the Harvard Yard, and the furious Royce forced his German adversary off the planks and into deep snowdrifts.

If before the spring of 1915 Royce was leaning in either direction, he was siding with the Allies. The surprising attack on Belgium prompted Royce to doubt the morality of Germany's intentions. Publicly he remained neutral. However, on May 7, the day a German submarine attacked and sank the *Lusitania*, his fury was total. He abruptly dropped his nonpartisanship and sided with the Allies against the Central Powers. Now and afterward Germany was his and humanity's enemy. Not, of course, the Germany of Kant and Beethoven, but the Germany of the Kaiser and his circle, the bullies again whom he instinctively hated. John Jay Chapman applauded Royce's belated entrance into the mire of partisan politics, but he knew also that emotionally a high price was paid for this step. "He had been," said Chapman, "an interpreter of Germany, and the German villainy of 1914 [or was it 1915?] appeared to him almost in the light of

a personal insult. He rose up against it. He threw off Germany. He took the
stump." For once in his life Royce became actively and fully engaged in politics,
and he carried this commitment to his grave. Now, more than a philosopher, he
was a partisan, an orator, a reformer, striving to press his vision forward into our
own age, the final years of the twentieth century.

"It is now a relief . . . ," Royce said in June 1915, "to speak out plainly." Before
the sinking of the *Lusitania,* he had felt morally bound to silence. But since his
own friends and former students had died in that atrocity, he was freed, indeed
obliged, to proclaim his position. "Among these dead of the *Lusitania* are my
own dead." He spoke to his classes openly against Münsterberg and against
Germany. "It makes very little difference," he told them, "to anybody else what
I happen to think, but to you, as my pupils, it is my duty to say that henceforth,
whatever the fortunes of war may be, 'the spiritual triumph of Germany' is quite
impossible, so far as this conflict is concerned. I freely admit that Germany may
triumph in the visible conflict, although my judgment about such matters is
quite worthless. But to my German friends and colleagues, if they chance to
want to know what I think, I can and do henceforth only say this: 'You may triumph in the visible world, but at the banquet where you celebrate your triumph
there will be present the ghosts of my dead slain on the *Lusitania.*'"

To publicize his commitment, and especially to make his views clear to his
friends in England, Royce wrote a letter to L. P. Jacks who printed it in the
Hibbert Journal. He was no longer dispassionate in his analysis of dyadic and triadic relationships, nor was he resigned to wait for some distant, postwar solution to international conflicts. Now, unequivocally, he pointed the finger of guilt
at "the infamies of Prussian warfare." "The German Prince is now the declared
and proclaimed enemy of mankind, declared to be such not by any 'lies' of his
enemies, or by any 'envious' comments of other people, but by his own quite
deliberate choice to carry on war by the merciless destruction of innocent, noncombatant passengers." Although historians have found ample evidence to
explain, if not justify, the sinking of the *Lusitania,* Royce was unwilling to entertain any such tolerant interpretation. To him the act was simply a treachery that
expressed "utter ignorance of human nature . . . utter contempt of everything
which makes the common life of humanity tolerable or possible." It did have,
however, the one advantage of arousing public sentiment against Germany.
Royce predicted that the United States would be irresistibly allied with England
and that even "our German-American population will be wholly united with us,
as never before, in the interests of humanity and of freedom."

Royce denied that his motive was hatred. "It is not hate, but longing and sorrow for stricken humanity, which is with me, as I am sure it is with you, the ruling sentiment." Nevertheless there is an unmistakable tone of fury in this letter.
Chapman thought that Royce felt betrayed and insulted by the Germany he had

loved from youth. In addition, Royce's strong paternal feelings, expressed in his identification with "my own dead," suggests that he associated the slaughtered innocents of the *Lusitania* with his own dead or disabled children— Christopher, Randolph, and Petsy. In his philosophy the world is a loyal and loving home prepared for the family of mankind. To be forced, at the end of his life, to witness, in his own home and on a global scale, the disintegration of all his hopes—that was outrageous and unacceptable.

The Last Year

In the summer of 1915 Josiah took three Caribbean cruises aboard his favorite steamer, the *Esparta*, each time stopping at Havana and Limón. The sea gave him a restful escape from the unbearable heat and thunderstorms in Cambridge. He needed serenity in order to write the lectures for an extension course in ethics that would earn him an extra one thousand dollars. Presented in the fall at Boston University, this series, "Introduction to Ethics," has been carefully studied by Frank M. Oppenheim, who finds it exemplary of Royce's "mature ethics." In the Programme to these lectures, Royce promised to explore the problems of loyalty in light of "the Social Problems of our day," including the war and the ethical responsibilities of nations. As Oppenheim observes, this series of lectures demonstrates Royce's "mature" tendency to explore ethical issues through concrete instances.

Katharine, meanwhile, was visiting Stephen and Marion in Hurley, Wisconsin. Josiah wrote her five tender letters during their six-week separation, from July 19 to August 30, keeping her informed of his health, his work, his life aboard ship, and continually sending her his love as well as love to Stephen and Marion, and indirectly through Katharine's correspondence, to Ned and Elizabeth. "Of course it is lonesome at sea," he admitted; "but the dear birds are there; and I also made friends with a new Esparta cat to whom I daily offered objurations against the Germans." His last letter written to Katharine is most charming, subtly intimate and most revealing of Josiah's deep, abiding love for her. It conveys these feelings through a story about a black kitten, another Kitty, and one of Pussy Blackie's distant relatives:

> This time a little black half grown kitten (with one little white spot only on its throat) had joined the ship at Boston, without paying fare, but with an independent intent to view the world in its own way. I stroked it a little when we first met as we went out of port. . . . [I]t seems to have sized me up, and at once considered my room. So on the afternoon of our leaving Boston . . . I went to my room, darkened it a little, and fell into a doze. Suddenly what seemed to me in my

dreamy state a very vast monster, clawless but with cuttlefish tentacles, leaped
from the darkness and began grappling with my shirt front. I waked, pounced in
my turn across the still darkened room, and with much delight found and began
to hold the little black puss. It at once purred most rapturously, and we were very
good friends. I call it a good luck pussy, was reminded of what you have told me
about your Meph'stopples, and connected puss forthwith with the hope that
somebody is comforting you nicely at Hurley. . . . I like to be pounced upon in my
sleep, and to dream so of a soft monster with no claws,—dark and yet good
humored,—and soon to find it so friendly and purring.

The moon wanes and is good and kind. There were some excellent birds in
the north. Fewer here.

My dearest love for both the children. Give them the same. I hope that all will
go well, and that you will take your visit out to the full,—that is, till you have only
just time to get home about as I do.

Lovingly,
Josiah.

Money matters infiltrate these letters as never before in Royce's correspondence. Now indeed a steady flow of cash was distributed to Stephen and
Marion and to Ned and Elizabeth, as well as to Hattie, who had become
increasingly indigent, unemployed except when she could earn a few dollars by
sewing. The young people received most of the money—money for coal, for
rent, for furnishings, for moving expenses, for household repairs. Hundreds of
dollars flowed every month. When Stephen and Marion moved to Ironwood,
Michigan, in February 1916, Josiah sent them a check for one thousand dollars
as a down payment for a house. A few months later Ned was appointed to the
Ithaca Conservatory as professor, pianist, and conductor of the symphony
orchestra. In a letter to Katharine, Elizabeth hinted that they too would need a
house. It becomes increasingly evident that Josiah, sensing his imminent death,
was stripping his estate of resources, hoping that whatever he earned would buy
shares for future generations.

The public image of Royce in the final year of his life is ambiguous. To many
of his friends he appeared wrecked and worn out. Still he did manage to complete a full load of teaching. The preserved shorthand notes of his 1915–16 lectures in Philosophy 9 reveal a mind still focused and incisive. Although the war
remained his daily obsession, he did not abandon his research in logic. With the
help of Fergus Kernan he wrote an article on Peirce, and in the same year he
contributed three new pieces to James Hastings's *Encyclopedia of Religion and
Ethics*: "Mind," "Negation," and "Order."

To Jack Chapman, Royce "seemed to stand in a tabernacle." Age had made
him more sacred, more perfected, smaller, and wiser—"more and more like a

very ancient Chinese saint." Sometime during this last year, when Chapman "was passing through Cambridge, a New York woman who was a worshiper of sages, expressed a wish to see some one who was remarkable." Chapman's son was sent to fetch Royce. "Track him down," Chapman ordered. "If he is engaged, wait till he is free, no matter how long it takes. Explain to him the exigencies of the occasion; but don't come back without him." After nearly an hour the young man returned: "Get ready, get ready; he's coming up the stairs behind me!" Someone promptly asked Royce a question about Germany:

> Royce would not remove his coat or sit down; and he talked for an hour. He began with the Norse legends, to illustrate the German spirit. He recited with wonderful skill a poem of Edgar Allan Poe's, and he must, first and last, have mentioned about everything that could be thought of between Odin and Poe. The rest of us sat rapt and happy. There was a weight of atmospheric pressure in the room. In our minds floated memories of the great talkers of history. Perhaps Coleridge may have talked like this, or Bacon.

Chapman's story gives one the sense of Royce's twilight warmth, a vitality that enabled him to compose a final series of apologies for idealism. In the first of these, "The Hope of the Great Community," written for the *Yale Review*, he restated his understanding of the meaning of the war and his vision of a world struggling toward an ideal peace. Although all idealists claim as a rational belief that good will inevitably defeat evil, they do not—and cannot—venture to state when or where this victory will be realized. Not pausing to state the basis for this belief, Royce emphasized the uncertainties of actual life. The biological history of the earth shows that there is no sound reason for believing that human life must endure. Royce was willing to entertain the thought that as a result of the war human beings might become, if not physically destroyed, morally obsolete. In his view, therefore, the war was not a conflict between nations or national ideals, but a moral test of the worth of humanity. The outcome of the war, he insisted, would prove if there were any longer a basis for "the hope of the great community."

Although he still firmly believed that Germany had become the modern equivalent of Satan, he did not construct his essay as an appeal for its defeat. Instead he reinterpreted the Pauline doctrine of love in terms of his own doctrine of loyalty. Citing the seventh and eighth chapters of Romans, Royce criticized "the essentially disastrous life of the detached individual." As Paul insisted, we can be saved, not separately, but "in Christ Jesus"—that is, as Royce interpreted these words, through "the spirit of the universal community." He envisioned the founding of an international organization, like the United Nations, in which each member would retain its national character. It would be a religious—certainly not a political—community, but unlike any known church, it would be modeled after the U.S. corporate system. As one might expect, it would also be triadic in structure and would have insurance as its primary business.

Thus, while progressive social critics feared that the growth of corporate structures would endanger the freedom of individuals and endeavored to check this growth by political means, Royce was working in the opposite direction. He believed, in fact, that through the corporate experience "the idea of the community of mankind has become more concrete, more closely related to the affairs of daily life, has become more practicable than ever before." He was still unconvinced that the universal community was more than a faint hope, but he was convinced that "the way towards peace" through a "business-like devotion" and a "true Pauline charity"—"that way already lies open."

Royce mailed "The Hope of the Great Community" to Wilbur Cross, the editor of the *Yale Review*, in November. In that month he celebrated his sixtieth birthday. The American Philosophical Association made this the occasion of honoring him by devoting most of its fifteenth annual meeting to his philosophy. The meeting was held in Philadelphia, at the University of Pennsylvania, on December 28–30. Attendance was disappointingly light and no member of Royce's family was present, but those few who did attend heard papers from George Howison (read by W. E. Hocking), John Dewey, Charles Bakewell, Mary Calkins, W. H. Sheldon, E. G. Spaulding (read by W. P. Montague), E. E. Southard, Richard Cabot, and H. H. Horne. Royce was present for the delivery of each of these papers and made brief critical responses after most of them. Through the efforts of Cabot and Hocking, the papers were assembled with others to form a festschrift, *Papers in Honor of Josiah Royce on His Sixtieth Birthday*, which was published in the May 1916 issue of the *Philosophical Review*. This was the first time that the APA so honored one of its members.

The high point of the meeting came with a banquet at the Walton Hotel on the evening of December 29. After a round of toasts and the reading of flattering telegrams, Royce made a brief speech on his life and the main issues of his thought. These "Words," reprinted in *The Hope of the Great Community*, provide us with the best source for an understanding of Royce's early childhood and development. He spoke of his years in Grass Valley, San Francisco, and Berkeley. He emphasized his education at the University of California, Johns Hopkins, and Göttingen, the influence of Mill, Spencer, Lotze, Kant, and the romantics. Warmly he remembered Edward Sill, Joseph Le Conte, his mother, and his sisters. Surprisingly he depicted himself as a nonconformist and rebel: "So much of the spirit that opposes the community I have and have always had in me, simply, elementally, deeply. Over against this natural ineffectiveness in serving the community, and over against this rebellion, there has always stood the interest which has taught me what I nowadays try to express by teaching that we are saved through the community." It was the idea of community, not the absolute, that formed the center of his thought. He closed by reading "A Watch in the Night" from *Songs before Sunrise* by Swinburne, a poem built upon a line from Isaiah 21:

> Watchman, what of the night?—
> > Storm and thunder and rain,
> > Lights that waver and wane,
> Leaving the watch fires unlit.
> Only the balefires are bright,
> > And the flash of the lamps now and then
> From a palace where spoilers sit,
> > Trampling the children of men
>
> . . . .
>
> Europe, what of the night?—
> > Ask of heaven, and the sea,
> > And my babes on the bosom of me,
> Nations of mine, but ungrown.
> There is one who shall surely requite
> > All that endure or that err:
> She can answer alone:
> > Ask not of me, but of her.
>
> Liberty, what of the night?—
> > I feel not the red rains fall,
> > Hear not the tempest at all,
> Nor thunder in heaven any more.
> All the distance is white
> > With the soundless feet of the sun.
> Night, with the woes that it wore,
> > Night is over and done.

Royce felt that Swinburne had expressed "the spirit of that for which, in my poor way, I have always in my weakness been working." "May the light soon dawn. May the word of the poet and prophet soon come true. This is my closing greeting to you."

Before Christmas Royce had received his last letter from Richard Cabot in which the disciple summarized the influence that had extended over a span of thirty years:

What you have taught & written you have lived—no discrepancy in the aim. I found it hard to branch off into medicine, away from the path in which I followed you. Perhaps I was wrong but I think not. I still preach your doctrine, in strange places & companies, under strange guises—yet to those whom you would want me to reach—those who cannot hear you or read you.

377

I value the critical and probing side of your teaching as much as the constructive. Where you have pulled down my rickety constructions I have found the result most salutary, never discouraging.

I shall never be tempted to stop championing the truths that you teach. They are in me too deep for that. My chief difficulty is to see that there is any other philosophy in the world—any worth the name.

I am bound to you & to all belonging to you by ties of deep & mature affection. Christmas gives me the impulse, the opportunity to say so.

A few months later Royce had his last opportunity to acknowledge his debt to Cabot, the "long period of most intimate and inspiring companionship, which you have permitted me to enjoy with you. May many, as the years go on, bless you, as I do, for such inspiration and support in life and in work as I have owed to you ever since our first meeting as fellow students."

Royce's last two public appearances stood out in the memories of his contemporaries. Both were speeches delivered in Boston's Tremont Temple and sponsored by the Citizens' League for America and the Allies. "The Duties of Americans in the Present War" (January 30, 1916) and "The First Anniversary of the Sinking of the Lusitania" (May 7, 1916) are important not so much for their arguments as for the compassion, the religious zeal, and the fury they expressed. Huge audiences attended. The twenty-five hundred reportedly present at the first speech gave him a standing ovation. Both speeches were published immediately in the *Boston Evening Transcript*. Thus, the tired old professor was transformed into a "prophet," a "leader," an "inspired vehicle of a righteous imagination." Chapman remembered the appearance of "this frail and aged philosopher . . . in the role of the young patriot." "He was all righteous rage, and his lifelong voluminous metaphysical ideas were expressed in the flames and burning periods of denunciation."

Royce's words were crowded with biblical allusions and analogies. At last he was the true son of his father. The suffering of Belgium, the victims of the *Lusitania*, the cruel inhumanity of Germany—these images suggested parallels in the stories of Cain and Abel, and of Judas and Jesus. "We Americans know what the *Lusitania* outrage meant, and to what spirit it gave expression. That spirit has the 'primal eldest curse upon it—a brother's murder.' . . . And the mark of Cain lasts while Cain lives."

The treason of Judas was, for early Christianity, a fact, and a fact without which the salvation of mankind could not have been accomplished. . . . The death of Christ according to the teaching of the religious imagination of Christianity saves because, through the memory of his death all those whom, in the great words of the Fourth Gospel, the Father has given him are, or will become "One even as we" (namely the Father and the Son) "are One." So the best memorial of our dead consists in the fact that through what they have suffered those who inherit their work are brought together, are loyally united, are inspired to brotherhood and unity.

Josiah Royce died on September 14, 1916. Friends and members of the family were convinced that the war had hastened his death, and while that is certainly plausible, there is also a sense in which it kept him alive, emotionally at least, fulfilling his need for a final obsession, a deep social commitment. Without that he might have lived longer. Given more time he might have been able finally to complete his treatise on logic, but longevity, regardless of technical accomplishments, could hardly have satisfied his emotional needs. So Royce was granted a fortune which few philosophers enjoy. He was allowed at last to join thought with passion, and to know with his final breath that his life's work was swept up in an issue of global importance.

Horace Kallen was a witness to what for him was a last and lasting image of Josiah Royce. It was probably during May or June of 1916 when Kallen, who had been Royce's assistant in 1906, was revisiting Harvard Yard. Between the new Widener Library and Emerson Hall was interposed a large black limousine, and the man he met, apparently heading toward it, was Professor Royce. "His steps seemed hesitant and unnaturally short, all his movements suggested an uncertainty, a reluctance to make them. When I greeted him, his round blue eyes looked staring, and without recognition. It was a moment or two after I had spoken my name that he remembered who I was. And then he said in a voice somehow thinner, and more dissonant than I remembered: 'You are on the side of humanity, aren't you?'"

At first Kallen was shocked and hurt that his old teacher could even ask such a question. Later he thought it ironic that Royce, whose thought was so drenched in German culture, should have turned against Germany with the vindictiveness of a Hebrew prophet. But finally, after pondering the question for forty years, Kallen viewed it as a signpost to one of the "commonplaces of the philosophic enterprise": the philosopher's need to adapt his published commitments to the exigencies of his ongoing life:

We rarely take into consideration that a man's philosophy is first of all an event in his personal struggle, come to birth from his need for encouragement, for consolation, for power to endure, for compensation for failure. Its usual role is to be a vision and a weapon of his personal life, an armament against fate and fortune, insuring that among whatever other strugglers who may be seeking his hurt perhaps unto death, he shall live and not die, even also after he has died. Philosophers by occupation serve as armorers whose art is ever so to refine and perfect the visions and the weapons of their schools as to give them preponderant power. I take this to be the case with the philosophic systems of the littler as well as the great tradition, and I count Royce's not the least among the latter.

What Kallen had seen was the clash between a completed system of thought and the inevitable incompleteness of life. A philosopher can interpret events so as to force them to conform to his system, or he can revise his system as revisions are dictated by events. Royce, the architect of systems, opted to live with the events. He refused to take the moral holiday that William James had said is the coveted luxury of all absolutists.

And yet, if Hocking was right, Royce's last years were "clouded by a tragic sense of incompleteness." He had few disciples, the realists and pragmatists seemed to have won their battle with the absolute, and within a few years the positivists and logical analysts would stand at the center of philosophical circles. The young men who returned from the war in the twenties scorned the rhetoric that permeates Royce's work. Ernest Hemingway spoke for his "lost generation" when he has Frederic Henry in *A Farewell to Arms* denounce the abstract language of his leaders:

> I was always embarrassed by the words sacred, glorious, and sacrifice and the expression in vain. We had heard them, sometimes standing in the rain almost out of earshot, so only the shouted words came through, and had read them, on proclamations that were slapped up by billposters over other proclamations, now for a long time, and I had seen nothing sacred, and the things that were glorious had no glory and the sacrifices were like the stockyards at Chicago if nothing was done with the meat except to bury it.

A young Rupert Brooke spoke also for his generation in England: "The Community hasn't got a soul; you can't voice the soul of the Community any more than you can blow its nose."

Alfred Hoernlé remembered that Royce, near the end, sometimes expressed doubts about his effectiveness; his doctrines, it seemed to him, had been "stillborn": "received at best with barren respect, instead of being accepted, expounded, developed." Nevertheless, Hoernlé added, if Royce had become "a still backwater" while others were carving new channels, one earns the right to reject absolute idealism only by studying and understanding its master.

Although Hoernlé's and Kallen's reports give the impression of one near death, Katharine told her sister-in-law that Josiah was in good health, lively, and engaged in course preparation for the next year. He took two ocean voyages during the summer but required the *"most* kindly" care and attention. In spring 1916 he refused for the second time President Wheeler's offer of the Mills Professorship at Berkeley. "I greatly regret that I must decline your very kind offer," Royce wired on March 4. "My arrangements here for the coming academic year are already fully arranged. No free time remains." When Wheeler persisted, Royce sent another telegram on March 7: "With very hearty thanks for the kindness of your proposal I must repeat that my engagements for next year at Harvard are definitely made. I decline with regret your invitation." Royce apparently foresaw no interruption of his regular routine. Before the end of August, however, he was gravely ill, and for the next three weeks he was confined to his bed. On September 14 a blood vessel cracked in his brain and he died. The cause of death was listed as arteriosclerosis.

The funeral, held in the Appleton Chapel, was brief, quiet, and simple. At the request of the widow, an organ without chorus played subdued strains from Beethoven. The dignity of the ceremony suited, at least one mourner remarked, the character of Royce and the overall tone of his life. His own words might have been used in lieu of a funeral oration, for according to Stephen he slipped down to his study two or three nights before he died, and after burning many papers, he placed on his desk two sheets, the beginning of an essay called "The Cult of the Dead." The doctrine of immortality, as Royce had previously expounded it, grows out of the "fourth conception of being." It states that since no mortal life entirely fulfills its purpose, the absolute demands, for its ultimate purposes, that each individual must live immortally. In this new and final essay, however, Royce altered his claim: despite the childish superstitions that motivate a belief in immortality, the cult of the dead remains "genuine and vital . . . a part of the religious experience of men." Surviving many changes of opinion, it continues to grow, for in at least one important sense the dead are always living. They live in our memories. "So long as love and memory and record and monument keep the thought of our own dead near to our lives and hearts, so long as patriotism and the spirit of human brotherhood enable us to prize what we owe to those who have lived and died for us, the cult of the dead will be an unfailing source to us of new and of genuinely religious life."

Charles A. Bennett, who wrote the obituary for the *Philosophical Review*, remembered Royce in a way that he would have wanted to be remembered. When Bennett learned of his friend's death, he was struck with "dismay and grief." But then almost instantly a second feeling obliterated the first. "It was simply a supreme confidence that all was well with him." "He had lived too close to the heart of things for death to be anything but an episode in his life."

L. P. Jacks wrote a moving obituary for the London *Inquirer*. At his home at Manchester College, the photograph of Brooke's portrait of Royce hung over the mantelpiece, and weeks later Jacks found himself talking to it. Obviously he was unable to fully accept this finality. In November he wrote to Katharine:

> His death leaves me impoverished of a relationship with one of the most gifted and beautiful souls it has ever been my joy to know & love. *Sit mia anima cum illo* I often say to myself, but alas I am now worthy! When I enter the next world—as I hope to do—he is one of the first for whom I shall look out & if I fail to find him I shall know that I am not in heaven, or that he is in some vastly higher sphere of it, and surely he belongs to the highest. I wish I could grasp you by the hand—but I would have nothing to say & could not say it if I had, for the well of feeling in regard to him is very deep. My wife joins me in sending you our love. *Quid plura?*

Knowing something about the troubled history of Katharine's three sons, Jacks concluded by sharing his own parental concerns: "I have three boys in the thick of the war. Do you remember Owen? He has been in the front line of three great attacks & three times has been one of a handful of survivors. Is it not wonderful? They have decorated him with the Cross for valour."

The day after Josiah died, Anna wrote to Katharine offering and promising every kind of aid and support:

> I would gladly do anything I could for you. I know you have your dear sons, if only they were nearer—but perhaps you will go to one of them.
>
> If you care to come out here, I have a room all ready for you & perhaps the change & out-door life would do you good. We have a furnace with register in your room. The garden is lovely & the hills & cañons near, & many easy trips to take.
>
> Many old friends of yours and Josiah's would welcome you. I phoned this morning to Mr. Howison, Mr. Rieber & Miss Calkins. Also last night Ruth called me up to see if I had any more details. She was with Hattie. I have written to Mary [Ingraham] Compton & Ruth is in touch with the others. He was a good son and brother & I know they appreciate it even if they don't know how to express themselves. He will be widely mourned, not only for his great mind but for his personal qualities of friendliness & sympathy.
>
> I was reading the magazine he sent me—the birthday one & meant to write & thank him when I had taken in the contents more—now it is too late.
>
> My love & sympathy to the boys. Be sure & tell me if I can do anything to help you and if you need cash for instance for temporary expenses.
>
> Lovingly
> Anna

In Royce's will, Katharine was named sole heir and executrix. There was, however, precious little to inherit. Two-thirds of the home was mortgaged, he had two thousand dollars in cash, and after adding the estimated value of his copyrights, books, and manuscripts, the total value of his estate amounted to less than ten thousand dollars. Katharine continued to live in the house with her retarded grandson for many years. After Randolph was taken to Westborough State Hospital, she lived alone but continued to keep the house in good repair and was frequently entertained by neighbors and the Harvard community. The house stood empty after she left it in 1944 to spend the rest of her days at the Kirkland Rest Home. Bill James continued to look after the place, but because of a coal shortage during the war, the house was left unheated and the plastered walls, cold and damp, caved in, leaving only an external shell.

Some may see in this image of a ruined house a symbol of Royce's philosophy. His books for many years were unread, and one by one they dropped out of print. In our own age few seem convinced by his massive arguments for the absolute which once commanded attention; *loyalty* is now a word that offends. The hope of the great community and the international organization to insure peace is still unfulfilled. But having lived through two global wars, political murders, international intrigues and interventions, social uprisings, racism, environmental destruction, and the plain lies of our leaders—many may now feel that the search for a spiritual community must still direct the best hopes of mankind. The biblical Josiah was a king who tried to lead his people back to traditional beliefs, but who died in battle with a foreign invader. The other Josiah, our Royce, taught us that we are nothing if not united with the common interests of humanity. In his last year he reminded us of the words of the soon-to-be-crucified Christ. It was a prayer for a Beloved Community: "That they all may be one; as thou, Father, *art* in me, and I in thee, that they also be one in us."

One final anecdote may serve as a conclusion to the life of Josiah Royce. In the fifth lecture in the 1915 series, "Introduction to Ethics," he related a story involving Schopenhauer. Wandering in a public garden, the philosopher became suddenly excited by an idea, and when spotted by an official as an eccentric was asked, "Sir, who are you?" "I wish you would tell me," Schopenhauer answered. "That's exactly what I'm trying to find out." The meaning of the tale, Royce explained, is that self-knowledge—so central to ethics—is never fully known; its meaning and purpose are never complete. "Your self, like your happiness or unhappiness, like your failure or your success, is a history, a drama, a life quest." And so it was for Josiah Royce. In his life there was no closure, no final victory, no peaceful repose, but always the quest, often in darkness and sorrow, his quest for "the great world beyond our mountains."

Notes

ABBREVIATIONS

ALC   Autograph Letter Copy.

ALS   Autograph Letter Signed.

BWJR   *The Basic Writings of Josiah Royce*. Ed. John J. McDermott. 2 vols. Chicago: Univ. of Chicago Press, 1969.

California   *California from the Conquest in 1846 to the Second Vigilance Committee in San Francisco [1856]: A Study of American Character*. Boston: Houghton, Mifflin, 1886.

CG (1897)   *The Conception of God*. New York: Macmillan, 1897.

CPCSP   *Collected Papers of Charles Sanders Peirce*. Ed. Charles Hartshorne, Paul Weiss, and Arthur W. Burks. 8 vols. Cambridge: Harvard Univ. Press, 1931–58.

FE   *Fugitive Essays*. Ed. J. Loewenberg. Cambridge: Harvard Univ. Press, 1920.

Feud   *The Feud of Oakfield Creek: A Novel of California Life*. Boston: Houghton, Mifflin, 1887.

HGC   *The Hope of the Great Community*. New York: Macmillan, 1916.

HHL   Henry E. Huntington Library, San Marino, California.

HL   Houghton Library, Harvard University.

HUA   Harvard University Archives.

JHU   Milton S. Eisenhower Library, Johns Hopkins University.

JP   James Papers, Houghton Library, Harvard University.

JR   Josiah Royce.

JRL   *The Letters of Josiah Royce*. Ed. John Clendenning. Chicago: Univ. of Chicago Press, 1970.

JRP   The Papers of Josiah Royce, Harvard University Archives.

PC   *The Problem of Christianity*. 1913. Reprint, Chicago: Univ. of Chicago Press, 1968.

PL   *The Philosophy of Loyalty*. 1908. Reprint, Nashville, Tenn.: Vanderbilt Univ. Press, 1995.

PP   The Papers of Charles Sanders Peirce, Houghton Library, Harvard University.

PUL   Princeton University Library.

RAP   *The Religious Aspect of Philosophy*. Boston: Houghton, Mifflin, 1885.

RQP   *Race Questions, Provincialism, and Other American Problems*. New York: Macmillan, 1908.

SGE   *Studies of Good and Evil*. New York: Appleton, 1898.

SMP   *The Spirit of Modern Philosophy: An Essay in the Form of Lectures*. Boston: Houghton, Mifflin, 1892.

SRI   *The Sources of Religious Insight*. New York: Scribner's, 1912.

TCWJ   Ralph Barton Perry. *The Thought and Character of William James*. 2 vols. Boston: Little, Brown, 1935.

TLC   Typed Letter Copy.

TLS   Typed Letter Signed.

UCA   University of California Archives, Berkeley.

UCB   Bancroft Library, University of California, Berkeley.

UCLA   Josiah Royce Memorial Collection, Special Collections, Research Library, University of California, Los Angeles.

W&I   *War and Insurance.* New York: Macmillan, 1914.

WI   *The World and the Individual.* 2 vols. New York: Macmillan, 1899–1901.

WJ   William James.

WJL   *The Letters of William James.* Ed. Henry James. 2 vols. Boston: Atlantic Monthly Press, 1920.

WJO   *William James and Other Essays on the Philosophy of Life.* New York: Macmillan, 1911.

The principal collection of manuscripts is the papers of Josiah Royce in the Harvard University Archives, which is rich in unpublished material spanning JR's entire career. *The Letters of Josiah Royce*, ed. John Clendenning (Chicago: Univ. of Chicago Press, 1970), contains all of the most important letters that were known twenty-eight years ago; more than a hundred letters by JR have come to light since that time. In addition HUA has other important collections pertaining to JR; these include the papers of Francis Ellingwood Abbot, Richard C. Cabot, Charles W. Eliot, Paul Henry Hanus, Lawrence J. Henderson, Charles R. Lanman, Ralph Barton Perry, and Abbott Lawrence Lowell. The Houghton Library of Harvard University has two important collections: the James papers and the papers of C. S. Peirce. The papers of William Ernest Hocking have been deposited in the Houghton, but are still uncatalogued. The Robbins Library of Harvard University maintains a special collection of books owned by JR, William James, C. S. Peirce, George Santayana, and others; these often contain valuable marginalia. The Bancroft Library of the University of California, Berkeley, has several items pertaining to JR, as does the University of California Archives, Berkeley. The Special Collections Department of the Research Library in the University of California, Los Angeles, has the most complete collection of JR's published work, including many obscure periodical materials; UCLA has also collected important memorabilia.

There is no satisfactory edition of JR's works. *The Basic Writings of Josiah Royce*, ed. John J. McDermott (Chicago: Univ. of Chicago Press, 1969), provides, in two volumes, the best edition now available. *BWJR* 2 includes Ignas K. Skrupskelis, "Annotated Bibliography of the Published Works of Josiah Royce," which is definitive. For a useful checklist of translations and secondary works on JR, see *Revue Internationale de Philosophie* (1967), 159–82.

Users of this work will find *JRL* helpful in tracking down the sources of correspondence cited. References to JR's published works are keyed to the Skrupskelis bibliography, with date of publication and entry number in brackets.

CHAPTER 1. CHILDHOOD, 1855–1870

Sources of Wonder

Pp. 3–5:   "Autobiographical Sketch," *HGC* [1916, 5]; "Some Characteristic Tendencies of American Civilization," JRP, vol. 92; "The Pacific Coast," *RQP*, 172 [1908, 3]; *JRL*, 578.

P. 5:   For biographical data on JR's parents, I am indebted to the genealogical research of Mrs. Robert L. Hacker, JR's grandniece.

Pp. 6–8:   Whitney R. Cross, *The Burned-over District: The Social and Intellectual History of Enthusiastic Religion in Western New York, 1800–1850* (Ithaca: Cornell Univ. Press, 1950); see also Cross, "Creating a City: The History of Rochester from 1824 to 1834," M.A. thesis, Univ. of Rochester, 1936.

P. 8:   For obits. of JR's parents, see UCLA, box 1; "Tribute to Josiah Royce," *Los Gatos News*, 24 Aug. 1888; "Funeral of Mrs. Sarah Royce . . ." (unidentified newspaper clipping, n.d.; UCLA, box 1); ALS. Ruth Royce to Ralph Barton Perry, 26 Feb. 1928 (HUA).

P. 9:   *WI*, 1:427 [1899, 1].

P. 9:   Revelation 21.2–3; *PC*, 79 [1913, 6].

Pp. 10–11:   "Tribute to Josiah Royce"; Cross, "Creating a City," 113–14; for circulars pertaining to Phipps Union Female Seminary, consult County of Orleans, Dept. of History, Albion, New York; see also Frank M. Oppenheim, "Some New Documents on Royce's Early Experiences of Communities," *Journal of the History of Philosophy* 6 (1968): 381–85.

Pp. 11–17:   Sarah Royce, *A Frontier Lady: Recollections of the Gold Rush and Early California*, ed. R. H. Gabriel (New Haven: Yale Univ. Press, 1932).

Pp. 14–15:   "Gen. Riley's Civil Correspondence," 31st Congress, 1st sess. (Senate), Ex. Doc. no. 52, 106.

P. 16:   Rodman W. Paul, *California Gold: The Beginning of Mining in the Far West* (Lincoln: Univ. of Nebraska Press, 1947), 84–85.

Grass Valley

P. 17:   "The Pacific Coast," *RQP*, 186, 202 [1908, 3]; *California*, 6–7 [1886, 3].

P. 18:   *RQP* [1908, 3]; *TCWJ*, 2:146.

Pp. 18–19:   Paul, *California Gold*; *Bean's History and Directory of Nevada County, California* (1867) (HL: US38304–5); *Brown and Dallison's Nevada, Grass Valley and Rough and Ready Directory* (1856) (HHL: 2594); Harry L. Wells,

History of Nevada County, California (Oakland: Thompson and West, 1880)(HHL: 44498); Robert V. Hine, *Josiah Royce: From Grass Valley to Harvard* (Norman: Univ. of Oklahoma Press, 1992), 17–32.

P. 19: "Some Characteristic Tendencies of American Civilization," JRP, vol. 92; Sarah Royce, *Frontier Lady*, 139.

P. 21: *Grass Valley National*, 17 Aug. 1861; JRL, 577–78; Sarah Royce, *Frontier Lady*, 130, 132.

Pp. 21–22: Oppenheim, "Some New Documents," 381–82; ALS. Ruth Royce to Ralph Barton Perry, 26 Feb. 1928 (HUA).

Pp. 22–23: Avon Farm: Oppenheim, "Some New Documents," 383–84.

Pp. 23–26: Hine, *Josiah Royce*, 33–50; ALS. Katharine Royce to Ralph Barton Perry, 16 Oct. [1929?]; "Autobiographical Sketch," HGC [1916, 5]; ALS. Ruth Royce to Ralph Barton Perry, 26 Feb. 1928 (HUA); Oppenheim, "Some New Documents," 383; "Tribute to Josiah Royce."

Pp. 26–27: "The Reality of the Temporal," *International Journal of Ethics* 20 (1910): 257–59 [1910, 5].

Pp. 28–29: "Recent Discussions of the Concept of the Infinite," JRP, vol. 72.

Pp. 29–30: "Pussy Blackie's Travels," JRP, box A.

San Francisco

P. 30: HHL: 256410; "The Pacific Coast," RQP, 173 [1908, 3]; *The San Francisco Directory . . .* , comp. Henry G. Langley (San Francisco, 1867) (Schubert Hall, California Historical Society). This annual directory continues to list "Royce, Josiah, fruit, 1032 Folsom" until April 1871.

P. 31: ALS. Ruth Royce to Ralph Barton Perry, 26 Feb. 1928 (HUA); "*Obsthändler*": in a presentation copy of WI to William James: TCWJ, 1:819.

P. 31: Guy C. Earl, "Memorabilia" (UCB: C-B 822).

P. 32: "A Day at Lincoln School in 1866," Bulletin no. 31, Lincoln Grammar School Association (Schubert Hall, California Historical Scciety); "Autobiographical Sketch," HGC, 126–27 [1916, 5].

Pp. 32–33: Craig Timberlake, *The Bishop of Broadway: The Life and Work of David Belasco* (New York: Library Publishers, 1954); Lise-Lone Marker, *David Belasco: Naturalism in the American Theatre* (Princeton: Princeton Univ. Press, 1975), 13–15.

Pp. 33–34: "Autobiographical Sketch," HGC, 125 [1916, 5]; petition of J. Royce, 19 Feb. 1858, California State Archives, Sacramento; "Is the Assassination of Tyrants Ever Justifiable?" [Student Publications, 1].

Pp. 34–35:   Fannie A. Cheney, "Our Visit to the Boys' High School" (Schubert Hall, California Historical Society); *Centennial Edition of Red and White* (Schubert Hall, California Historical Society); Earl, "Memorabilia"; ALS. Ruth Royce to Ralph Barton Perry, 26 Feb. 1928, Perry Papers (HUA); JRP, vol. 96.

Pp. 35–36:   "A Nocturnal Expedition," JRP, vol. 53; "The Miner's Grave," JRP, vol. 53.

Pp. 37–38:   *JRL*, 366–73.

CHAPTER 2. YOUTH AND EDUCATION, 1870–1878

Freshman and Sophomore

P. 39:   *JRL*, 366–73.

Pp. 39–40:   Verne A. Stadtman, *The University of California, 1868–1968* (New York: McGraw-Hill, 1970).

P. 40:   For curricular information and JR's academic record, I am indebted to J. R. K. Kantor, University Archivist, and Robert E. Brownell, Associate Registrar (University of California, Berkeley).

P. 41:   Joseph C. Rowell, "The Beginnings of a Great Library: Reminiscences" (1938), (UCA); J. C. R[owell], "Recollections of an Undergraduate, 1870–71," *Occident* 7 (31 Oct. 1884): 105–6 (UCB); "The Old and the New—A Lesson," *University of California Chronicle* [1902, 2].

Pp. 41–42:   Miscellaneous notes on the influence of books and men: JRP, vol. 96; ALS. Ruth Royce to Ralph Barton Perry, 26 Feb. 1928 (HUA).

P. 42:   "An Incursion into the Regions of the Sentimental; In Imitation of Certain Novelists," JRP, vol. 53.

Pp. 42–43:   Untitled essay, JRP, vol. 53.

P. 44:   "Joseph Le Conte," *International Monthly* 4 (1901): 324–34 [1901, 3]; "The Old and the New—A Lesson" [1902, 2].

Pp. 44–45:   Fabian Franklin et al., *The Life of Daniel Coit Gilman* (New York: Dodd, 1910); "The Old and the New—A Lesson" [1902, 2]; Stadtman, *University of California*, 64.

P. 45:   William Carey Jones, "Some Recollections and Reflections of a '75er," *Occident* 7 (14 Nov. 1884): 123–25 (UCB); Stadtman, *University of California*, 63–64.

P. 45:   Stephen Royce quoted in Daniel S. Robinson, *Royce and Hocking: American Idealists* (Boston: Christopher Publishing House, 1968), 148.

P. 46:   Chemistry professor: JRP, box A.

Pp. 46–47:   "Joseph Le Conte" [1901, 3]; "The Old and the New—A Lesson" [1902, 2].

Pp. 47–48:   "Sound and Silence," *Neolean Review* 1 (Apr. 1873) [Student Publications, 2]; "Personification in Early Tongues," *Neolean Review* 1 (Oct. 1873): 1, 3 [Student Publications, 3]; "Casual Observation of Human Nature," JRP, vol. 53; "Truth": *Lectures on Modern Idealism* (New Haven: Yale Univ. Press, 1919), 257.

Berkeley Classicist

Pp. 49–50:   *Berkeleyan* 1 (Apr. 1874) [Student Publications, 6]; Guy C. Earl, "Memorabilia" (UCB: C-B 822).

P. 50:   College essays: *BWJR*, 2:1170–73.

P. 50:   *Berkeleyan* 1 (Nov. 1874): 11; *Berkeleyan* 2 (Feb. 1875): 13; (Mar. 1875): 13–14; (Apr. 1875): 14.

Pp. 50–51:   *Berkeleyan* 2 (Feb. 1875): 12 [Student Publications, 17]; (Apr. 1875): 12–13 [Student Publications, 27]; *Mills Quarterly* 3 (Jan. 1875): 12–14; (May 1875): 76–77.

Pp. 51–52:   "Truth in Art," *Berkeleyan* 2 (Apr. 1875); 3–4 [Student Publications, 22].

P. 53:   "A Word about the 'Ideal' in Science and in Art," *Berkeleyan* 2 (June 1875): 7 [Student Publications, 35]; so-called laws of nature: *WI*, 2:215; evolution a dream: *JRL*, 104–5.

Pp. 53–54:   Religious Crisis: *JRL*, 104; "The Clergyman's Relation to Philosophical Inquiry" (1904), JRP, vol. 75; cf. "Smith Lectures on Present Problems of Philosophy" (1910), JRP, vol. 78: "I remember well a conversation that I had, in 1875, with [Edward L.] Youmans, the editor of the old Popular Science Monthly of those stirring days. I recall the splendid vehemence with which he repeated: If evolution is anything, it is everything."

Pp. 54–55:   "Mill and Spencer," JRP, vol. 53; "Darwin Answered, or Evolution a Myth," *Berkeleyan* 2 (Apr. 1875): 8 [Student Publications, 24].

P. 55:   "Draper's Religion and Science," *Berkeleyan* 2 (Feb. 1875): 9 [Student Publications, 14]; "Draper and 'Religion,'" *Berkeleyan* 2 (June 1875): 8–9 [Student Publications, 36].

Pp. 55–56:   "Joseph Le Conte," *International Monthly* 4 (1901): 324–34 [1901, 3]; Le Conte, *Evolution: Its Nature, Its Evidences, and Its Relation to Religious Thought*, 2d ed. (New York: Appleton, 1897).

Pp. 57–58:   "The Aim of Criticism," *Berkeleyan* 2 (May 1875): 9 [Student Publications, 31]; "The Vassar Miscellany and 'Middlemarch,'" *Berkeleyan* 2 (Mar. 1875): 8–9 [Student Publications, 19]; "The Tragic as Conceived by the Ancients and the Moderns," *Berkeleyan* 2 (June 1875): 10 [Student Publications, 37].

Pp. 58–59:   *Bulletin of the University of California*, no. 16 (June 1875), 113–37 [1875, 2].

Pp. 59–60:   Sophocles: JRP, box H; commencement: *Oakland Daily Transcript*, 10 June 1875, 3.

Graduate Years

P. 60:   *JRL*, 45–46.

P. 61:   Undocumented story cited in J. H. Cotton, *Royce on the Human Self* (Cambridge: Harvard Univ. Press, 1954), 4; Passport, JRP, vol. 53.

Pp. 61–62:   *Overland Monthly* 14 (1875): 542–49 [1875, 1]; *Overland Monthly* 15 (1875): 157–64 [1875, 3]; ALS. D. C. Gilman to Charles Lanman, 3 Sept. 1875, Lanman Papers (HUA).

Pp. 62–63:   *Collegien-Buch*, JRP, vol. 53; *JRL*, 47–50; "Present Ideals of American University Life," *Scribner's Magazine* 10 (1891): 382–83 [1891, 14]; notebooks, JRP, box B; ALS. D. C. Gilman to JR, 27 Dec. 1875 (JHU).

P. 64:   *Anmeldungs-Buch*, JRP, vol. 53; Ueberhorst: *SMP*, 104.

Pp. 64–65:   ALS. D. C. Gilman to JR, 20 Mar. 1876; 24 Apr. 1876; 29 June 1876 (JHU); J. M. Cross to JR, 21 June 1876 (JHU); *JRL*, 50; JR to J. M. Cross, 9 July 1876 (JHU).

Pp. 65–66:   "Present Ideals of American University Life," 383 [1891, 14]; Hugh Hawkins, *Pioneer: A History of the Johns Hopkins University* (Ithaca, New York: Cornell Univ. Press, 1960), 79–93; *JRL*, 188; diary, Lanman Papers (HUA); *JRL*, 52–55, 70–71; Franklin, *The Life of Daniel Coit Gilman*, 412–13.

Pp. 66–67:   "What Constitutes Good Fiction," JRP, vol. 80; Lanman diary (HUA); Hawkins, *Pioneer*, 333–34, 187–210; notebooks: JRP, box C.

P. 67:   "The World and the Will," JRP, box C.

P. 67:   "The 'Return to Kant' in Modern German Thought," JRP, box C; misinterpreting Kant: *SMP*, 105.

P. 68:   *TCWJ*, 1:779–80.

Pp. 68–69:   "John Fiske," JRP, vol. 72; ALS. JR to D. C. Gilman, 11 Jan. 1877 (JHU); "Notes Relating to Logic and the Theory of Knowledge," JRP, box C.

P. 69:   JRP, vols. 55–57; *FE*, 41–65, 290–99; *JRL*, 51, 54.

Pp. 69–71:   "Of the Interdependence of the Principles of Knowledge," JHU [1878, 3]; typescripts of this doctoral thesis are deposited in JRP and UCLA, box 2; ALS. Noah Porter to D. C. Gilman, 15 Apr. 1878 (JHU); *RAP*, xvii.

Pp. 71–72:   Lanman diary (HUA); Hawkins, *Pioneer*, 273; G. B. Coale (c. 1819–87): see obit. *Baltimore Sun*, 7 Mar. 1887; "The Wednesday Club," *Maryland Historical Magazine* 38 (1943): 60–68; *JRL*, 106, 367.

Pp. 72–73:   *JRL*, 52–63; ALS. Horatio Stebbens to JR, 19 June 1878 (JRP); confers with Porter: Lanman diary (HUA).

CHAPTER 3. EXILED APPRENTICESHIP, 1878–1882

Fugitive Essayist

Pp. 74–75:   *JRL*, 63, 66; *WJL*, 1:202.

P. 75:   *JRL*, 61.

P. 75:   *JRL*, 62, 72.

Pp. 75–76:   Sill: *JRL*, 208; *SMP*, 465–67; *HGC*, 128.

Pp. 76–77:   Alfred R. Ferguson, *Edward Rowland Sill* (The Hague: Nijhoff, 1955), 158–59; TLC. E. R. Sill to D. C. Gilman, 4 Sept. 1878, Autograph Letters of Edward Rowland Sill, vol. 3 (UCA).

P. 77:   *JRL*, 61, 64, 67, 68–69; "The Circulating Library," *Berkeleyan* 6 (Nov. 1878): 222–24; 8 Oct. 1870 (UCA); "What Constitutes Good Fiction," JRP, vol. 80; Berkeley Club Minute Books (UCB, C-H 9).

Pp. 77–78:   *FE*, 133–54.

Pp. 78–79:   "Thought-Diary," JRP, box D.

Pp. 80–81:   California Constitution: *JRL*, 73; Kearney: *RQP*, 217; Chinese question: *JRL*, 62, 93.

P. 81:   *JRL*, 65.

Pp. 81–82:   *JRL*, 67, 69, 72, 76; "Of the Will as the Principle in Philosophy," JRP, vol. 79.

P. 82:   *JRL*, 76–77.

Pp. 82–83:   Roy W. Cloud, *History of San Mateo County, California*; P. Munroe Frazier and William L. Halloway, *History of San Mateo County, California*; E. F. Head obit., *San Mateo County Times-Gazette*, 10 May 1890 (San Mateo County Historical Association); TLC. E. R. Sill to D. C. Gilman, 26 Apr. 1880 (UCA); ALS. Katharine Royce to J. C. Rowell, 28 Nov. 1934 (UCA); *JRL*, 77.

Pp. 83–84:   *WJL*, 1:204; *JRL*, 83, 84, 92–93.

P. 84:   Shelley: *FE*, 66–95 [1880, 3].

Pp. 84–85:   *JRL*, 83, 92; JRP, vol. 80; *JRL*, 74–75.

Husband and Scholar

P. 86:   ALS. JR to Allan Marquand, 29 Jan. 1880; 1 May 1880, Marquand Papers, (PUL).

Pp. 86–87:   "On Purpose in Thought": *FE*, 219–60.

P. 87:   *JRL*, 78-83; ALS. JR to Allan Marquand, 13 June 1880, Marquand Papers (PUL).

Pp. 88–89:   ALS. Shadworth Hodgson to JR, 30 June 1880; 14 Sept. 1880 (JRP); "Kant's Relation to Modern Philosophic Progress," 375 [1881, 5].

Pp. 89–90:   *JRL*, 83–84; *FE*, 96–132 [1880, 2].

Pp. 90–91:   Marriage: *JRL*, 90–91, 92–93; ALS. Lanman to JR, 17 Apr. 1881 (JRP); JR to Lanman: *JRL*, 94–95.

Pp. 91–92:   *Berkeleyan* 10 (8 Nov. 1880): 5; *FE*, 261–89 [1881, 4]; 322–44 [1881, 3].

Pp. 92–93:   *Berkeleyan* 10 (22 Nov. 1880): 5. For other references to the Psychology Club, see *Berkeleyan* 10 (8 Nov. 1880): 4; 11 (14 Mar. 1881): 5; 13 (29 May 1882): 12; *Occident* 1 (8 Sept. 1881): 2; 1 (15 Sept. 1881): 6; 1 (6 Oct. 1881): 3; 2 (2 Mar. 1882): 3; 2 (9 Mar. 1882): 3; 2 (11 May 1882): 3.

P. 93:   *JRL*, 91–92.

Pp. 93–94:   *FE*, 300–21 [1881, 2].

Pp. 94–95:   *JRL*, 86–89; "Thought-Diary," JRP, box D.

Pp. 95–96:   *JRL*, 89–90, 105, 108; ALS. WJ to JR, 25 Dec. 1880 (JP), published with minor errors in *TCWJ*, 1:789; *WJL*, 1:205.

Pp. 96–97:   *JRL*, 83; ALS. E. R. Sill to D. C. Gilman, 26 Apr. 1880 (JHU); Hawkins, *Pioneer*, 187–210; ALS. D. C. Gilman to JR, 29 Feb. 1880 (JRP).

Pp. 97–98:   ALS. WJ to JR, 25 Mar. 1881 (JP); *JRL*, 95–96; *TCWJ*, 1:790.

P. 98:   "Before and Since Kant": [1881, 1]; *TCWJ*, 1:790–91.

International Debut

Pp. 98–99:   W. K. Clifford, "On the Nature of Things-in-Themselves," *Mind* 3 (Jan. 1878): 57–67; F. W. Frankland, "The Doctrine of Mind-Stuff," *Mind* 6 (Jan. 1881): 116–20; *JRL*, 96–97; "'Mind-Stuff' and Reality," *Mind* 6 (July 1881): 365–77 [1881, 6].

P. 100:   *JRL*, 100; "Mind and Reality," *Mind* 7 (Jan. 1882): 30–54 [1882, 2]; "Kant's Relation to Modern Philosophic Progress," *Journal of Speculative Philosophy* 15 (Oct. 1881): 360–81 [1881, 5]; *Primer of Logical Analysis for the Use of Composition Students* (San Francisco: A. L. Bancroft, 1881) [1881, 8]; review: *Mind* 7 (Apr. 1882): 311–12; G. H. Howison, "Josiah Royce: The Significance of His Work in Philosophy," *Philosophical Review* 25 (May 1916): 234.

Pp. 100–1:   Stadtman, *The University of California*, 88–92; *JRL*, faculty meetings: 73; Regents: 113; Sill: 209.

P. 102:   *JRL*, 102; 106–7.

Pp. 102–3:   "Kant's Relation to Modern Philosophic Progress."

Pp. 103–5:   "Mind and Reality."

Pp. 105–6:   *TCWJ*, 1:793–94; *JRL*, 108–9; T. Whittaker, "'Mind-Stuff' from the Historical Point of View," *Mind* 6 (Oct. 1881): 498–513; F. W. Frankland, "Dr. Royce on 'Mind-Stuff' and Reality," *Mind* 7 (Jan. 1882): 110–14.

P. 106:   *FE*, 345–63.

P. 107:   *JRL*, 10–6.

P. 108:   *TCWJ*, 1:794–96; *JRL*, 112–14; ALS. WJ to JR, 25 Apr. 1882; 18 May 1882; 21 May 1882 (JP).

P. 109:   *JRL*, 113.

P. 109:   *JRL*, 101, 103; ALS. E. F. Head to Anna Head, 27 Dec. 1881 (JRP); ALS. E. R. Sill to Alice E. Pratt, 11 Apr. 1882 (UCA); ALS. Eliza Head to Mr. and Mrs. Josiah Royce, 11 Apr. 1882 (JRP); ALS. Eliza Head to Anna Head, 12 Apr. 1882 (JRP).

Pp. 109–10:   *JRL*, 114; ALS. WJ to JR, 13 June 1882 (JP); *JRL*, 115–16; Lanman diary (HUA).

P. 110:   ALS. Eliza Head to Katharine Royce, 18 Sept. 1882 (JRP); ALS. Eliza Head to Katharine Royce, 9 Oct. 1882 (JRP).

Pp. 111–12:   *FE*, 133–54, 155–86.

Chapter 4. Success and Crisis, 1882–1888

The Religious Aspect of Philosophy

P. 115:   "The Young American," in *The Collected Works of Ralph Waldo Emerson* (Cambridge: Harvard Univ. Press, 1971), 1:229; lecture 3, "The Religious Aspect of Philosophy," JRP, box E.

P. 116:   Hugh Hawkins, *Between Harvard and America: The Educational Leadership of Charles W. Eliot* (New York: Oxford Univ. Press, 1972); "Present Ideals of American University Life," *Scribner's Magazine* 10 (1891): 385 [1891, 14]; Bakewell: *George Herbert Palmer, 1842–1933: Memorial Addresses* (Cambridge: Harvard Univ. Press, 1935), 3–43; *Doctors of Philosophy and Doctors of Science Who Have Received Their Degree in Course from Harvard University, 1873–1926* (Cambridge: Harvard Univ. Press, 1926); *The Harvard University Catalogue, 1882–83; JRL*, 121–22.

P. 116:   Lanman diary (HUA); *JRL*, 122.

P. 117:   Samuel Eliot Morison, ed., *The Development of Harvard University* (Cambridge: Harvard Univ. Press, 1930), 9–15; *Henry James Letters*, ed. Leon Edel (Cambridge: Harvard Univ. Press, 1975), 2:385.

Pp. 117–18:   John Jay Chapman, "Portrait of Josiah Royce, the Philosopher," *Outlook* 120 (2 July 1919): 372–77; *TCWJ*, 2:146; *WJL*, 1:249.

Pp. 118–19:   Morison, *Development of Harvard University*, 12–13.

P. 119:   "The Religious Aspect of Philosophy": lectures 1 and 2 are in JRP, vol. 95; lectures 3 and 4 are in JRP, box E; Lanman diary (HUA).

Pp. 119–20:   For E. E. Hale story, see G. H. Howison, "Josiah Royce; The Significance of His Work in Philosophy," *Philosophical Review* 25 (1916): 234; notes on Herbart: 3-by-9 note cards, JRP, box E.

Pp. 120–21:   "The Religious Aspect of Philosophy," lecture 3, JRP, box E.

P. 121:   *JRL*, 126.

P. 121:   ALS. G. Stanley Hall to WJ, May 1883 (JP).

Pp. 121–23:   *The Harvard University Catalogue, 1883–84*; *JRL*, 129; "Certain Ideals of Right Conduct and Their Value for Society," JRP, box E; *Harvard Advocate* 37 (29 Feb. 1884): 23; (14 Mar. 1884): 26.

P. 123:   *JRL*, 131–33; ALS. D. C. Gilman to JR, 19 Mar. 1884 (JRP).

P. 124:   *JRL*, 133, 141, 153–54.

Pp. 124–25:   ALS. D. C. Gilman to JR, 26 Jan. 1885 (JRP); *JRL*, 151; C. S. Peirce to WJ, 28 Oct. 1885 (JP); WJ to G. H. Howison, 15 Feb. 1885 (JP); WJ to Shadworth Hodgson, 20 Feb. 1885; 16 Aug. 1885 (JP); *TCWJ*, 1:772, 629; WJ, "The Religious Aspect of Philosophy," *Atlantic Monthly* 55 (June 1885): 840–43; ALS. Shadworth Hodgson to JR, 27 Sept. 1885; 20 Nov. 1885 (JRP).

P. 126:   Book 1, "The Search for a Moral Ideal," *RAP*, 33, 80, 142, 133, 138, 161, 221–22 [1885, 1].

Pp. 126–27:   Book 2, "The Search for a Religious Truth," *RAP*, 265, 288 [1885, 1].

Pp. 127–28:   "The World of the Postulates," *RAP*, 292, 332, 369, 371, 375, 387–88, 421 [1885, 1].

Pp. 128–29:   "The Possibility of Error," *RAP*, 408–20, 423, 290, 434 [1885, 1].

P. 129:   "The Eternal and the Practical," *Philosophical Review* 13 (Mar. 1904): 116 [1904, 1].

Two Studies of California

P. 130:   *JRL*, 128–29.

Pp. 131–32:   Oct. 1845: Larkin Papers (UCB).

Pp. 132–33:   *JRL*, 134–39, 141–45; J. C. Frémont, "The Conquest of California," *Century* 41 (Apr. 1891): 922–23; *JRL*, 171.

Pp. 133–35: *JRL*, 153, 155, 157–65, 165–66, 171, 172.

P. 135: ALS. Katharine Royce to Eliza Head, 31 May 1885 (JRP); *JRL*, 170, 172, 174, 178.

Pp. 135–36: Saratoga: *JRL*, 178–80, 170.

P. 136: ALS. JR to Sarah E. Royce, 24 Mar. 1884; 28 Dec. 1884 (JRP).

Pp. 136–40: *California*, 394, 119, 290–95, 344–66, 366, 368, 394 [1886, 3].

P. 140: *JRL*, 199, 202.

P. 140: "What Constitutes Good Fiction," JRP, vol. 80; *JRL*, 203, 204–6.

P. 141: "The Squatter Riot of '50 in Sacramento: Its Causes and Its Significance," *Overland Monthly*, n.s., 6 (1885): 225–46 [1885, 4]; *SGE*, 301 [1898, 8].

Pp. 141–42: *Feud*, 358–59, 437–38.

P. 143: Mae Fisher Purcell, *History of Contra Costa County* (Berkeley: Gillick Press, 1940), 127–201.

Pp. 143–44: Berenson review: *Harvard Monthly* 4 (Apr. 1887): 78–79; *Nation* 44 (26 May 1887): 453; "Josiah Royce,"in George Santayana, *Character and Opinion in the United States* (New York: Braziller, 1955), 79.

The Devil in the Brain

P. 144: *JRL*, 170; *The Harvard University Catalogue, 1885–86*.

Pp. 144–45: Mrs. Dorr: M. A. De Wolfe Howe, *John Jay Chapman and His Letters* (Boston: Houghton, Mifflin, 1937), 195–96.

Pp. 145–46: Loeffler: Lanman diary, 4 Nov. 1885 (HUA); Eleanor Ingraham: ALS. Katharine Royce to Sarah E. Royce, 11 Aug. 1884 (JRP); Coco: ALS. Katharine Royce to Milicent Shinn, Jan.–July [1885?] (Schubert Hall, California Historical Society); ALS. Katharine Royce to Eliza Head, 31 May 1885 (JRP); *JRL*, 130, 131, 147, 199.

Pp. 146–47: *JRL*, 189, 198; "Royce's California," *Overland Monthly* 8 (Aug. 1886): 222–23; H. L. Oak, "Dr. Royce's 'California,'" *Overland Monthly* 8 (Sept. 1886): 329–30; *JRL*, 189, 197–98; Andrew Rolle, *John Charles Frémont: Character as Destiny* (Norman: Univ. of Oklahoma, Press, 1991), 259–61.

Pp. 147–48: *JRL*, 194–95.

Pp. 148–49: Abbot diary (HUA); ALS. WJ to C. S. Peirce, 12 Nov. 1891 (JP).

Pp. 149–50: *WJL*, 1:247; Peirce, "Dr. F. E. Abbot's Philosophy," *Nation* 42 (11 Feb. 1886): 135–36; Abbot diary, 20 June 1886; 11 Feb. 1886 (HUA); "Abbot's Scientific Theism," *Science* 7 (9 Apr. 1886): 335–38 [1886, 1].

Pp. 150–51: *The Harvard University Catalogue, 1886–87*; "Report of the Committee on

Apparitions and Haunted Houses," *Proceedings of the American Society for Psychical Research* 1 (Dec. 1887): 229 [1887, 6].

P. 151:   Birth of Edward: ALS. Eliza Head to Mr. and Mrs. Josiah Royce, 10 Jan. 1887 (JRP); *JRL*, 203.

Pp. 151–52: Deaths of Coale and Sill: *JRL*, 148, 207, 209.

Pp. 152–53: JR's mental health: *JRL*, 210; ALS. Eliza Head to Katharine Royce, n.d. (JRP); *JRL*, 215; *The Varieties of Religious Experience* (New Hyde Park, N.Y.: University Books, 1963), 145–46, 153; *JRL*, 211; ALS. D. C. Gilman to JR, 11 Feb. [1888]; Lanman diary, 11 Jan. 1888 (HUA).

Pp. 153–54: Abbot diary, 26 Oct. 1887 (HUA); "The Future of Philosophy at Harvard," *Harvard Monthly* 5 (Nov. 1887): 47; Abbot diary, 8 Feb. 1888 (HUA); *JRL*, 212; ALC. F. E. Abbot to JR, 12 Feb. 1888, Letter Book, Abbot Papers (HUA); Abbot diary, 9 Feb. 1888 (HUA).

P. 154:   JR's annotated copy of James Martineau, *A Study of Religion*, is preserved in the Robbins Library, Harvard; Frank M. Oppenheim, *Royce's Voyage Down Under* (Lexington: Univ. Press of Kentucky, 1980); Lanman diary (7–25 Feb. 1888)(HUA); *JRL*, 211, 215.

P. 154:   Notebook: "Barque Freeman," JRP, box E.

Pp. 155:   *JRL*, 214–17.

Pp. 156–57: Australia: "Reflections after a Wandering Life in Australasia," *Atlantic Monthly* 63 (1889): 675–86, 813–28 [1889, 9–10]; *JRL*, 218–19.

Pp. 157:   *JRL*, 219; *TCWJ*, 1:802.

P. 158:   "Compensation," in *The Collected Works of Ralph Waldo Emerson* (Cambridge: Harvard Univ. Press, 1979), 2:64; *RAP*, 483–84 [1885, 1].

CHAPTER 5. PHOENIX, 1888–1895

Recovery and Conflict

Pp. 159–60: *JRL*, 225; *TCWJ*, 2:43; "Reflections after a Wandering Life in Australasia"; "The Practical Value of Philosophy," *Ethical Record* 2 (1889): 9–22 [1889, 8]; "Is There a Philosophy of Evolution?" *Unitarian Review* 32 (1889): 1–29, 97–113; *JRL*, 234.

P. 160:   "Barque Freeman," JRP, box E. See Oppenheim, *Royce's Voyage Down Under*.

Pp. 160–61: *The Harvard University Catalogue, 1888–89*; *JRL*, 233; "Professor Josiah Royce before the Harvard Club of Minnesota" (St. Paul: Press of Wm. E. Banning Jr., 1890) [1890, 6].

P. 161:   *SMP*: *JRL*, 233, 241.

Pp. 161–62: Frémont and Abbot: *JRL*, 243–45; "Dr. Abbot's 'Way Out of Agnosticism,'" *International Journal of Ethics* 1 (1890–91): 98–113 [1890, 1].

Pp. 162–63: *JRL*, 231; "Dr. Abbot's 'Way Out of Agnosticism,'" 112–13.

Pp. 163–64: ALC. Abbot to [Sempers?] 16 Nov. 1889, Letter Book, Abbot Papers (HUA); ALC. Abbot to George Iles, 29 Dec. 1889, Letter Book, Abbot Papers (HUA); ALC. Abbot to George Iles, 26 Oct. 1890, Letter Book, Abbot Papers (HUA); ALC. Abbot to Irving B. Richman, 17 Nov. 1890, Letter Book, Abbot Papers (HUA); ALC. Abbot to Everett Abbot, 3 Nov. 1890, Letter Book, Abbot Papers (HUA).

P. 164: ALC. Abbot to S. Burns Weston, 21 Jan. 1891; 19 Feb. 1891; 23 Feb. 1891, Letter Book, Abbot Papers (HUA); TLS. Felix Adler to Abbot, 26 Feb. 1891; 5 Mar. 1891, Abbot Papers (HUA).

Pp. 164–65: Abbot diary, 7 Feb. 1891; 1 June 1891; 6 June 1891; 7 June 1891; 10 June 1891 (HUA); ALC. Abbot to Joseph B. Warner, 20 June 1891, Letter Book, Abbot Papers (HUA); *JRL*, 272–73; ALC. Abbot to Joseph B. Warner, 4 Aug. 1891, Letter Book, Abbot Papers (HUA); Abbot diary, 11–23 Oct. 1891 (HUA).

Pp. 165–66: ALS. Peirce to Abbot [1 Nov. 1891?], Abbot Papers (HUA); Peirce, "Abbot against Royce," *Nation* 53 (12 Nov. 1891): 372; ALS. WJ to Peirce, 12 Nov. 1891 (JP); WJ, "Abbot against Royce," *Nation* 53 (19 Nov. 1891): 389–90; ALS. Peirce to WJ, 17 Nov. 1891 (JP).

P. 167: ALS. Dewey to WJ, 22 Nov. 1891 (JP).

Pp. 167–68: *JRL*, 285; Joseph B. Warner, "The Suppression of Dr. Abbot's Reply," *Nation* 53 (26 Nov. 1891): 408; Abbot, "Mr. Warner's 'Evidence in Full' Completed," *Nation* 53 (3 Dec. 1891): 426; memo: E. W. Hooper [Sec'y of the Harvard Corporation] to Abbot, 22 Jan. 1892 (HUA); TLS. Eliot to Abbot, 28 Nov. 1891, Abbot Papers (HUA); *The Two Philosophers: A Quaint, Sad Comedy* (Boston: J. G. Cupples, 1892); for Palmer's remarks, see Samuel Eliot Morison, ed., *The Development of Harvard University* (Cambridge: Harvard Univ. Press, 1930), 15.

Pp. 168–70: Frémont: "Light on the Seizure of California," *Century*, n.s., 18 (1890): 792–94 [1890, 4]; "Montgomery and Frémont," *Century*, n.s., 19 (1891): 790–83 [1891, 10]; "Frémont," *Atlantic Monthly* 66 (1890): 548–57 [1890, 3]; *JRL*, 257; "The Frémont Legend," *Nation* 52 (21 May 1891): 423–25 [1891, 6].

Family Interlude I

P. 171: *Cambridge Tribune*, 27 July 1889, 1–2; Arthur Gilman, *The Cambridge of Eighteen Hundred Ninety-Six* (Cambridge, 1896), 107.

P. 172: ALS. Sarah E. Royce to JR, 12 May 1891; 27 May 1891; 9 June 1891 (JRP); telegram: Ruth Royce to JR, 24 Nov. 1891 (JRP).

Pp. 172–73:   South Yarmouth: ALS. Katharine Royce to JR, 15 July 1891; 26 July 1891; 8 Aug. 1891; 30 Aug. 1891 (JRP).

Pp. 173–74:   Christopher, teacher: ALS. Jeanette S. Markham to JR, two undated letters [1891–92?] (JRP); Christopher, doctor: ALS. Hamilton Osgood to JR, undated letter; 22 Dec. 1891 (JRP).

The Spirit of Modern Philosophy

Pp. 174–75:   ALS. Richard Hodgson to JR, 20 Dec. 1889 (JRP); ALS. George H. Palmer to JR, 3 Jan. 1890 (JRP); *JRL*, 264, 265, 266–67, 272.

P. 175:   Normal Course: *JRL*, 250–52; "Is There a Science of Education?" *Educational Review* 1 (1891): 15–25, 121–32 [1891, 8]; Hawkins, *Between Harvard and America*, 253.

P. 176:   Stanford: ALS. David Starr Jordan to JR, 28 Mar. 1891; 9 Apr. 1891; 15 Apr. 1891; 26 Apr. 1891 (JRP); *JRL*, 269–70, 681.

P. 177:   ALS. William Roscoe Thayer to JR, 31 Oct. 1891 (JRP); *JRL*, 279.

Pp. 177–79:   *SMP*: *JRL*, 271; ALS. Mary W. Dorr to JR, 11 July 1891 (JRP); *SMP*, 1, 304–7, 371, 374.

P. 179:   *SMP*, 388–94.

Pp. 179–80:   *SMP*, 405–7, 410.

P. 180:   *SMP*, 412, 414, 429–30.

Pp. 180–182:   *SMP*, 437, 451, 455, 465, 471.

P. 182:   *JRL*, 211.

Pp. 182–83:   ALS. George Santayana to JR, 6 Mar. 1892 (JRP); "Ethical Doctrine": *JRL*, 287,

Pp. 183–84:   Davidson: *TCWJ*, 1:731–33, 757; ALS. Thomas Davidson to JR, 20 Mar. 1892; 9 May 1892; 15 May 1892; 26 Sept. 1892 (JRP); *JRL*, 299.

The Harvard Quintet

P. 184:   *JRL*, 295–96, 301; ALS. G. H. Palmer to JR, 17 Nov. 1892 (JRP).

P. 185:   C. M. Bakewell, "The Philosophy of George Herbert Palmer," in *George Herbert Palmer, 1842–1933: Memorial Addresses* (Cambridge: Harvard Univ. Press, 1935), 3–43.

Pp. 185–86:   *Persons and Places* (New York: Scribner's, 1944), 244; *The Middle Span* (New York: Scribner's, 1945), 152–53; Daniel Cory, ed., *The Letters of George Santayana* (New York: Scribner's, 1955), 31.

P. 186:   Matthew Hale Jr., *Human Science and Social Order: Hugo Münsterberg and the Origins of Applied Psychology* (Philadelphia: Temple Univ. Press, 1980), 46ff.; *TCWJ*, 2:138–39.

Pp. 186–87: *JRL*, 297, 300, 307

P. 187: "The Implications of Self-Consciousness," *New World* 1 (1892): 289–310 [1892, 1]; "The Knowledge of Good and Evil," *International Journal of Ethics* 4 (1893–94): 48–80 [1893, 1]; "Topics in Psychology of Interest to Teachers," JRP, vols. 63–66; ALS. JR to Henry Holt, 28 Feb. 1893 (PUL); ALC. Henry Holt to JR, 8 Mar. 1893 (PUL); Henry Holt to WJ, 24 July 1893 (JP).

Pp. 187–88: *JRL*, 300–301.

Pp. 188–89: *JRL*, 304–5; ALS. WJ to JR, 7 Jan. 1893 (JP); *JRL*, 309–12; postcard. WJ to JR, 21 Apr. 1893 (JP).

The Psychosocial Ego

Pp. 189–90: *JRL*, 313; "The Outlook in Ethics," *International Journal of Ethics* 2 (1891): 106–11 [1891, 13].

P. 190: *The Collected Works of Ralph Waldo Emerson* (Cambridge: Harvard Univ. Press, 1979), 2:27–51; "Self-Consciousness, Social Consciousness, and Nature," *Philosophical Review* 4 (1895): 465–85, 577–602 [1895, 13]; *BWJR*, 1:431.

Pp. 190–91: *Philosophical Review* 2 (1893): 752; "The Two-Fold Nature of Knowledge: Imitative and Reflective," JRP, vol. 62, printed in *Journal of the History of Philosophy* 4 (1966): 326–37; "The External World and the Social Consciousness," *Philosophical Review* 3 (1894): 540–41 [1894, 3], a partial rewrite of JR's Chicago address; "The Implications of Self-Consciousness."

P. 191: "The Imitative Functions and Their Place in Human Nature," *Century*, n.s., 26 (1894): 137–45 [1894, 4]; see also "Preliminary Report on Imitation," *Psychological Review* 2 (1895): 217–35 [1895, 5].

Pp. 191–92: "Some Observations on the Anomalies of Self-Consciousness," *Psychological Review* 2 (1895): 433–57, 574–82 [1895, 4]; *SGE*, 169–97.

Pp. 192–93: "The Case of John Bunyan," *Psychological Review* 1 (1894): 22–33, 134–51, 230–40 [1894, 4]; *SGE*, 169–97.

Pp. 193–95: *JRL*, 264, 292–93; "The External World and the Social Consciousness," *Philosophical Review* 3 (1894): 513–45 [1894, 3]. "Self-Consciousness, Social Consciousness, and Nature," *Philosophical Review* 4 (1895): 465–85, 577–602; *SGE*, 198–248; reprinted in *BWJR*, 1:421–61.

P. 195: *SGE*, 230; 243.

The Conception of God

P. 196: J. W. Buckham and G. M. Stratton, *George Holmes Howison: Philosopher and Teacher* (Berkeley: Univ. of California Press, 1934), 70, 82; Hall privately sided with Abbot against Royce (see ALS; Hall to Abbot, 6 Dec. 1887, Abbot Papers [HUA]), and twice suggested a parallel between Royce's philosophy and masturbation. See Dorothy Ross, *G. Stanley Hall: The Psychologist as Prophet* (Chicago: Univ. of Chicago Press, 1972), 2–54; *JRL*, 339, 361.

Pp. 196–97: *JRL*, 324–26, 327–29; ALS. G. H. Howison to JR, 21 Oct. 1894 (JRP).

Pp. 197–98: *The Harvard University Catalogue, 1894–95*; review of F. H. Bradley, *Appearance and Reality*, *Philosophical Review* 3 (1894): 212–18 [1894, 6]; *CG* (1897), 44ff.

Pp. 198–99: *JRL*, 333–34, 336.

P. 199: *Occident* 29 (29 Aug. 1895; 5 Sept. 1895); *CG* (1897), 4.

Pp. 199–200: *CG* (1897), 8–41.

P. 201: Buckham and Stratton, *George Holmes Howison*, 80.

P. 201: Mezes: *CG* (1897), 53–62.

Pp. 201–2: Le Conte: *CG* (1897), 67–78.

Pp. 202–3: Howison: *CG* (1897), 81–132.

P. 203: *JRL*, 338–39; ALS. G. H. Howison to JR, 17 Oct. 1895 (JRP).

Pp. 204–5: *JRL*, 230, 301; ALS. R. C. Cabot to JR, 6 Mar. [1894] (JRP); ALS. JR to Ella Lyman and R. C. Cabot, 7 Mar. 1894, Cabot Papers (HUA).

Pp. 205–6: Paracelsus: *FE*, 378–407; ALS. Thomas Davidson to JR, 14 Mar. 1894 (JRP).

CHAPTER 6. THE BATTLE FOR THE ABSOLUTE, 1896–1900

James, Peirce, and the Legacy of Hegel

P. 207: *TCWJ*, 1:807–8. Perry had access to JR's diary, now lost. See his annotated copy of *TCWJ* in HL. "Browning's Theism," *New World* 5 (1896); 401–22, reprinted in *Boston Browning Society Papers, 1886–1897* (New York: Macmillan, 1897), 34.

P. 208: ALS. Henry Holt to WJ, 18 May 1893 (JP); ALS. John Jay Chapman to WJ, 17 Mar. 1897 (JP); *WJL*, 1:249; *TCWJ*, 1:703, 755, 799; *TCWJ*, 2:146.

P. 209: See WJ's annotated copies of *RAP* and *CG* (1897) (JP); *TCWJ*, 1:810; *TCWJ*, 2:498.

Pp. 209–10: *The Will to Believe and Other Essays in Popular Philosophy* (Cambridge: Harvard Univ. Press, 1979), 6.

Pp. 210–11: *JRL*, 317–18, 332; ALS. WJ to C. W. Eliot, 3 Mar. 1895 (JP), quoted in Joseph Brent, *Charles Sanders Peirce: A Life* (Bloomington: Iindiana Univ.

Press, 1993), 243; ALS. C. W. Eliot to WJ, 26 Mar. 1895 (JP); *CPCSP*, 8:39–53.

Pp. 211–12:   *TCWJ*, 2:20; *JRL*, 346, 302–3, 234; see Raymond Calkins's annotated copy of Hegel's *Phänomenologie*, Robbins Library, Harvard University.

P. 213:   J. J. Chapman, "Portrait of Josiah Royce, the Philosopher," 372. C. M. Bakewell, "The Philosophy of George Herbert Palmer," 3–43.

The Principle of Individuation

Pp. 213–14:   *JRL*, 339; ALS. G. H. Palmer to JR, 20 Mar. 1896 (JRP).

Pp. 214–15:   Graham lectures, JRP, vols. 67–68.

Pp. 215–16:   *JRL*, 345, 339–40; "The Principle of Individuation" was incorporated into JR's supplementary essay in *CG* (1897), 217–71; *CG* (1897), 235, 248, 261, 262, 268.

Pp. 217–18:   Women in Philosophy: *JRL*, 183; for a brief but accurate account of Calkins's philosophical career, see Bruce Kuklick, *The Rise of American Philosophy* (New Haven: Yale Univ. Press, 1977), 590–93; *JRL*, 340–45.

Pp. 218–19:   ALS. G. H. Howison to JR, 24 Aug. 1896 (JRP); *JRL*, 347–48.

Plans and Distractions

P. 219:   *JRL*, 352, 675.

Pp. 219–20:   *JRL*, 348–50.

P. 220:   *JRL*, 351; Buckham and Stratton, *George Holmes Howison*, 81.

Pp. 220–22:   *JRL*, 352, 353–55; Hale, *Human Science and Social Order*, 52–55; Margaret Münsterberg, *Hugo Münsterberg: His Life and Work* (New York: Appleton, 1922), 58–60.

Pp. 222–23:   *JRL*, 360; Gifford lectures: Gay Wilson Allen, *William James: A Biography* (New York: Viking, 1967), 387; ALS. W. R. Sorley to JR, 6 Apr. 1897; 4 May 1897; 8 May 1897 (JRP); "Lord Gifford's Bequests to the Scottish Universities" (JRP).

P. 223:   JR to Davidson: *JRL*, 357; "The Social Factors in the Development of the Individual Mind," JRP, vols. 69–70; JR to Baldwin: *JRL*, 360; James Mark Baldwin, *Between Two Wars, 1861–1921: Being Memoirs, Opinions, and Letters Received*, 2 vols. (Boston: Stratford, 1926), 1:74, 82.

P. 223:   *CG* (1897): *JRL*, 360–61.

Pp. 223–24:   *JRL*, 373; *Psychological Review* 5 (1898): 113–44 [1898, 4]; *National Educational Association, Journal of Proceedings and Addresses of the Thirty-seventh Annual Meeting* (1898), 196–99, 554–70 [1898, 2 and 7]; ALS. JR to Ella L. Cabot, 11 Apr. 1898, Cabot Papers (HUA); *JRL*, 365.

Pp. 224–25:   *TCWJ*, 2:418–21; ALS. WJ to Peirce, 7 Mar. 1898 (JP); *JRL*, 422.

P. 225:   ALS. JR to Ella L. Cabot, 17 Sept. 1898, Cabot Papers (HUA).

Pp. 225–26:   Santayana: ALS. R. C. Cabot to JR, 20 Jan. 1897 (JRP); ALS. W. R. Thayer, 9 Oct. 1896; 19 March 1897 (JRP); *JRL*, 363–65.

Pp. 226–27:   "Philosophy," *Harvard Graduates' Magazine* 5 (1896–97): 228–32 [1896, 4].

Studies of Good and Evil

Pp. 227–28:   ALS. JR to Mary W. Dorr, 19 Feb. 1898 (JRP); *SGE*, iii–iv [1898, 8].

Pp. 228–30:   Job: ALS. R. C. Cabot to JR, 8 July 1897 (JRP); *SGE*, 4–5, 7, 8–9, 14, 22.

P. 230:   *Crime and Punishment*: *SGE*, 120.

Pp. 230–31:   *SGE*, 141; Graham lectures, JRP, vol. 68; *SGE*, 137.

Pp. 231–32:   *SGE*, 301–2, 325–26, 267, 281, 378, 369.

Pp. 232–33:   Spanish-American War: *SGE*, 299; *JRL*, 374, 389.

Pp. 233–34:   *JRL*, 375-76; Howe, *John Jay Chapman and His Letters*, 163, 177–78; J. J. Chapman, "Portrait of Josiah Royce, the Philosopher," 377.

The Four Conceptions of Being

Pp. 234–35:   *JRL*, 378–79, 380, 683; *The Harvard University Catalogue, 1898–99*.

Pp. 235–36:   *JRL*, 381.

P. 236:   "Introduction: The Religious Problems": *WI*, 1:16–17 [1899, 1].

P. 236:   Realism: *WI*, 1:137 [1899, 1]. For an alleged fallacy in JR's refutation of realism, see criticisms by C. S. Peirce and R. B. Perry, pp. 267–68.

Pp. 236–37:   Mysticism: *WI*, 1:179, 186, 148, 190, 195 [1899, 1].

Pp. 237–38:   Critical rationalism: *WI*, 1:201, 210, 266, 270ff. [1899, 1].

Pp. 238–40:   Fourth Conception of Being: *WI*, 1:339, 22–23 [1899, 1]; review of G. F. Stout's *Analytic Psychology*, *Mind*, n.s., 6 (1897): 379–99; *WI*, 1:387, 371–74, 427 [1899, 1].

Pp. 240–41:   ALS. JR to Christopher Royce, 23 Jan. 1899 (JRP); obit. for Nicholson: (London) *Times* 20 Jan. 1899, p. 9.

Pp. 241–43:   "Royce's Argument for the Absolute," *TCWJ*, 2:726–29; *JRL*, 382–88.

Pp. 243–44:   *JRL*, 389, 390–91, 392, 679.

Pp. 244–45:   Supplementary essay: *WI*, 1:473–588 [1899, 1].

P. 245:   *WI*, 1:545.

The Second Series

Pp. 245–48: *JRL*, 394–96; *TCWJ*, 1:459; ALS. Alice James to JR, 3 Dec. 1899 (JP); *JRL*, 398; *TCWJ*, 1:820, 812–13; postcard, WJ to JR, 8 Feb. 1900 (JP); *JRL*, 401.

P. 248: Determinism: *WI*, 2:29–30. Although *WI*, 2 was published in 1901, Skrupskelis lists it with *WI*, 1; hence both are identified in [1899, 1].

Pp. 248–50: Betweenness: *WI*, 2:77–78, 79, 88, 94–95.

P. 250: The one and the many reconciled: *WI*, 2:98–99.

Pp. 251–52: Social relationships: *WI*, 2:104–6, 167, 177, 310, 276.

Pp. 252–53: Moral implications, *WI*, 2:355–59.

Pp. 253–54: Immortality: *WI*, 1:445–52; "The Conception of Immortality," Bryn Mawr lecture, JRP, vol. 61; *The Conception of Immortality*, Ingersoll lecture [1900, 2]; *JRL*, 185–86; *CG* (1897), 322–26.

Chapter 7. The Fading Light of the Absolute, 1900–1908

The Idealist in a New Century

P. 257: ALS. G. H. Palmer to WJ, 18 Mar. 1900; 5 July 1900 (JP).

P. 258: "Professor Everett as a Metaphysician," *New World* 9 (1900): 726–41 [1900, 4]; "John Fiske: His Work as a Philosophical Writer and Teacher," *Harvard Graduates' Magazine* 10 (1901–1902): 23–33. *Outlines of Cosmic Philosophy*, 4 vols. (Boston: Houghton, Mifflin, 1903), 1:xxi–cxlix. For more on Fiske, see JRP, vol. 72.

Pp. 258–59: "Joseph Le Conte," *International Monthly* 4 (1901): 324–34 [1901, 3].

Pp. 259–60: *JRL*, 408–9.

Pp. 260–61: *WJL*, 2:136; *TCWJ*, 2:443.

P. 261: *JRL*, 407, 420.

Pp. 261–62: *JRL*, 420, 422–23; for material relating to the revision of *WI*, 2, see JRP, Logic Box 2.

Pp. 262–63: *JRL*, 420; Ross: *JRL*, 412–18; "The Freedom of Teaching," *Overland Monthly*, n.s., 2 (1883): 235–40 [1883, 1]; TLC. J. M. Stillman to JR, 7 Mar. 1901 (Stanford University Archives).

P. 263: *JRL*, 423; "Recent Logical Inquiries and Their Psychological Bearings," *Psychological Review* 9 (1902): 105–33 [1902, 4].

Pp. 263–64: "Outlines of Psychology" [1896, 3]; ALS. Hitchcock to JR, 8 Sept. 1897; *JRL*, 425, 430, 678.

Pp. 264–65: JRL, 424, 431–33, 434–35.

Pp. 265–66: ALS. G. H. Palmer to WJ, 8 Feb. 1900 (JP); ALS. Ella L. Cabot to JR, 19 Dec. 1899 (JRP); ALS. Oliver Wendell Holmes Jr., to WJ, 8 July 1902 (JP); J. J. Chapman, *Memories and Milestones* (New York: Moffat, 1915).

Pp. 266–67: *TCWJ*, 2:425; *CSPCP*, 8:75–102; *CPCSP*, 8:101; ALS. Peirce to JR, 28 May 1902 (PP); *CPCSP*, 8:101–2.

Pp. 267–68: R. B. Perry, "Prof. Royce's Refutation of Realism and Pluralism," *Monist* 12 (1902): 451.

Pp. 268–69: *The Varieties of Religious Experience* (New Hyde Park, N.Y.: University Books, 1963), 454 n. 1; J. Dewey, *Philosophical Review* 9 (1900): 311–24; 11 (1902): 392–407.

P. 269: ALS. Santayana to JR, 30 Dec. 1899 (JRP).

Pp. 269–70: Dewey, *Philosophical Review* 11 (1902): 398 n. 1; 404–5; A. W. Moore, quoted in H. W. Schneider, *A History of American Philosophy* (New York: Columbia Univ. Press, 1946), 536.

Family Interlude II

P. 270: W. E. B. Du Bois, *Autobiography* (New York: International Publishers, 1968), 143; Rollo Brown, *Harvard Yard in the Golden Age* (New York: Current Books, 1948), 46–47; K. Royce, JR's granddaughter, unpublished memoir; e. e. cummings, *six nonlectures* (Cambridge: Harvard Univ. Press, 1953), 25, 29–30; *Poems, 1925–54* (New York: Harcourt, Brace, 1954), 169; Elizabeth Thaxter Hubbard, "Mini Memories," unpublished MS; interview Esther Lanman Cushman, 1969.

P. 272: Eliza Head: *JRL*, 419–20.

Pp. 273–74: Summer camp: *JRL*, 420; ALS. JR to Stephen Royce, 27 July 1900 (JRP); ALS. Katharine Royce to Stephen Royce, 4 Aug. 1901 (JRP).

P. 274: Josiah and Katharine: ALS. Katharine Royce to Stephen Royce, 27 July 1901 (JRP); ALS. JR to Edward Royce, 5 Aug. 1904 (JRP); *The Conception of Immortality*, 27–28, 38–39 [1900, 2].

California Sojourns

P. 275: *JRL*, 435.

Pp. 275–77: Peirce: *JRL*, 436–37; TLC. JR to Daniel Coit Gilman, 26 Mar. 1902 (PP); ALS. Peirce to JR, 19 Jan. 1902 (PP); Gilman re Peirce: Joseph Brent, *Charles Sanders Peirce: A Life* (Bloomington: Indiana Univ. Press, 1993), 21; ALS. Peirce to JR, 28 May 1902 (PP); *JRL*, 436.

Pp. 277–78: *RQP* ("Provincialism") 55–108, ("Limitations") 109–65 [1908, 3].

Pp. 278–79: Family letters: ALS. Katharine Royce to Stephen Royce, 15 July 1902

(JRP); ALS. Katharine Royce to Stephen and Edward Royce, 21 July [1902] (JRP); ALS. JR to Stephen Royce, 28 July 1902 (JRP).

P. 279: "The Old and the New—A Lesson," *University of California Chronicle* 2 (1902): 92–103 [1902, 2].

P. 279: *JRL*, 438–39; Baldwin, *Between Two Wars*, 1:83.

P. 280: *Psychology: JRL*, 433.

P. 280: JR at home: ALS. Katharine Royce to Stephen Royce, 3 Aug. 1902 (JRP); ALS. Katharine Royce to Stephen and Edward Royce, 16 Aug. 1902 (JRP).

Pp. 280–81: Fiske: *JRL*, 440; *Psychology: JRL*, 444–45, 447; Bruce Kuklick, *Josiah Royce: An Intellectual Biography* (Indianapolis: Bobbs-Merrill, 1972), 102–4; *The Rise of American Philosophy*, 276–77; *Outlines of Psychology* (New York: Macmillan, 1903), 351 [1903, 3].

P. 281: James: *JRL*, 439-40.

P. 281: *The Harvard University Catalogue, 1902–3.*

P. 282: ALS. Katharine Royce to Stephen Royce, 15 Mar. 1903 (JRP).

P. 283: *JRL*, 446, 448–49.

Pragmatism and Personal Crisis

P. 283: *JRL*, 448; Macmillan: *JRL* 453.

P. 284: Columbia lectures: *JRL*, 456–57; JRP, vol. 74. JR presented these lectures at Columbia, Feb. 1–15. Following his lectures on Feb. 2, he traveled to Indiana where he gave a miscellaneous series in Indianapolis, Bloomington, and at Earlham College before returning to New York for his third Columbia lecture on Feb. 8. See JRP, box F. In November 1904, he also presented a series of three lectures at the University of Richmond: "Some Fundamental Conceptions of Science," JRP, vol. 88. The titles of these lectures suggest parallels to the Columbia lectures.

P. 284: Lesson of mathematics: "What Sort of Existence Have the Entities of Mathematics," JRP, vol. 75.

Pp. 284–86: "Philosophical Conference," JRP, vol. 73; *WJL*, 2:201; ALS. WJ to Sarah Whitman, 29 Oct. 1903 (JP).

Pp. 286–87: "The Eternal and the Practical," *Philosophical Review* 13 (1904): 113–42 [1904, 1]; Morton White, *The Age of Analysis* (New York: New American Library, 1955), 13–21.

P. 288: Christopher: ALS. Christopher Royce to Stephen Royce, 25 Feb. 1904 (JRP); ALS. JR to E. R. Hedrick, 19 June 1904 (JRP).

Pp. 288–89: Edward: ALS. Katharine Royce to Edward Royce, 6 July 1904 (JRP); ALS.

JR to Edward Royce, 30 Mar. 1903 (JRP); ALS. JR to Edward Royce. 5 Aug. 1904 (JRP).

Pp. 289–90: Cabots: ALS. JR to R. C. Cabot, 27 Jan. 1905, Cabot Papers (HUA); ALS. JR to Ella L. Cabot, 29 Apr. 1905, Cabot Papers (HUA); ALS. JR to R. C. Cabot, 13 May 1905, Cabot Papers (HUA).

P. 290: *TCWJ*, 2:443; WJ to F. H. Bradley, 22 Jan. 1905 (*Mind* 75 [1966]: 332); ALS. WJ to D. S. Miller, 10 Nov. 1905 (JP); Harvard Summer School: *PL*, v [1908, 2].

Pp. 290–91: "Mr. Bertrand Russell's Problem of 'The Contradiction,'" JRP, vol. 73; "The Sciences of the Ideal," *Science*, n.s., 20 (1904): 449–62 [1904, 6]; "The Relation of the Principles of Logic to the Foundations of Geometry," *Transactions of the American Mathematical Society* 24 (1905): 353–415 [1905, 3]. For JR's letter to Kempe, see Bruce Kuklick, rev. of *The Letters of Josiah Royce,* ed. John Clendenning, *Journal of Value Inquiry* 5 (1971): 230–31. ALS. Peirce to JR, 28 May 1902 (PP); JRL, 488–92; ALS. Peirce to WJ, 23 Sept. 1905 (JP).

Pp. 291–92: *Lectures on Modern Idealism* (New Haven: Yale Univ. Press, 1919) [Posthumous Publications, 2]; *Lectures*, 85–86, 258–59.

P. 293: *Pragmatism: JRL*, 511–12.

P. 293: Earthquake: ALS. Anna Head to JR, 25 Apr. 1906 (JRP); *JRL*, 501.

Pp. 293–96: Martin Duberman, *James Russell Lowell* (Boston: Houghton, Mifflin, 1966), 367; Leonora Cohen Rosenfield, *Portrait of a Philosopher: Morris R. Cohen in Life and Letters* (New York: Harcourt, Brace, 1962), 79; ALS. Stephen Royce to Katharine Royce, July 1907 (JRP); ALS. JR to Stephen Royce, 11 Aug. 1907 (JRP); ALS. Katharine Royce to Stephen Royce, 29 Aug. 1907 (JRP); *JRL*, 512–13; ALS. JR to WJ, 9 Jan. 1908 (JP).

P. 296: ALS. JR to W. E. Hocking, 22 Jan. 1908 (Hocking Papers, HL).

P. 296: *JRL*, 522.

Chapter 8. Loyalty, Logic, and Love, 1908–1910

The Philosophy of Loyalty

P. 298: For JR's contribution to existentialism, see Richard Hocking, "Process and Analysis in the Philosophy of Royce," in *Josiah Royce's Seminar, 1913–1914* (New Brunswick, N.J.: Rutgers Univ. Press, 1963), xxiii; John E. Smith, "The Contemporary Significance of Royce's Theory of the Self," *Revue Internationale de Philosophie* 79–80 (1967): 86–89; *JRL*, 645.

P. 298: In subsequent citations, page numbers in PL are those of the Vanderbilt Univ. Press edition, 1992. *PL*, xxiii; "Outline of Course on Ethics for

Teachers," Diary (1906), JRP, box F; Urbana lectures, JRP, vol. 76; Graham lectures, JRP, vols. 67–68.

P. 299:   *PL*, 9, 44–45.

P. 299:   Emerson, "Self-Reliance," in *The Collected Works of Ralph Waldo Emerson* (Cambridge: Harvard Univ. Press, 1979), 2:27; *PL*, 105.

P. 300:   *PL*, 178, 161.

Pp. 300–1:   *PL*, 65.

Pp. 301–2:   *PL*, 141; ALS. R. C. Cabot to JR, 3 Dec. 1907 (JRP); *PL*, 144, 166.

Pp. 302–3:   *PL*, 182.

P. 303:   TLC. Brett to JR, 23 Dec. 1907 (Macmillan Archives, New York Public Library).

P. 303:   Cattell: *JRL*, 516; ALS. JR to WJ, 9 Jan. 1908 (JP); *JRL*, 518–19.

P. 304:   *JRL*, 521–23.

P. 305:   *JRL*, 523–25, 680, 525–26.

P. 305:   *RQP*, v [1908, 3]; contempt: *RQP*, 145–46.

P. 306:   *RQP*, 53, 74, 97, 98.

Logic, Religious Philosophy, and the New Realism

Pp. 306–7:   ALS. JR to Stephen Royce, 5 Aug. 1908 (JRP).

Pp. 307–9:   Heidelberg: "The Problem of Truth in the Light of Recent Discussion," *WJO*, 187–254 [1909, 2]; *BWJR*, 2:681–709.

P. 309:   "Absolute Pragmatism": *WJO*, 254; "Properties of Circuits in the Logical System," JRP, Logic Box 6.

Pp. 309–10:   *JRL*, 681; Notebook, "Phil 15/1908–9," JRP, box F; Notebook, "Phil 9/1908–9," JRP, box F; *JRL*, 532–33; APA meeting, 1908: *Philosophical Review* 18 (1909): 182–86.

P. 310:   Social welfare: *JRL*, 533–34.

Pp. 310–11:   "What Is Vital in Christianity?" *WJO*, 99–183; Social Gospel: Ralph Henry Gabriel, *The Course of American Democratic Thought*, 2d ed. (New York: Ronald Press, 1956), 156–80; *WJO*, 130–31, 140–41; letter to Brander Matthews: *JRL*, 483.

P. 312:   Cardinal doctrines: *WJO*, 135; Logos: 168–69; suffering: 171–72.

Pp. 312–13:   Europe, 1909: ALS. Katharine Royce to Edward Royce, 30 Sept. 1909; 24 Oct. 1909; 9 Dec. 1909; 21 Jan. 1910 (private collection, James Royce); ALS. JR to Stephen Royce, 19 Aug. 1909 (JRP); Geoffrey Skelton, *Wagner at Bayreuth: Experiment and Tradition* (London: Barrie and Rockliff, 1965).

P. 313: ALS. Katharine Royce to Edward Royce, 30 Sept. 1909 (private collection, James Royce); ALS. Stephen Royce to Katharine Royce, 9 July 1909; 17 July 1909; 17 Sept. 1909 (JRP).

P. 314: *The Harvard University Catalogue, 1909–10.*

P. 314: "The Program and First Platform of Six Realists," *Journal of Philosophy* 7 (1910): 373–401; reprinted in *The New Realism: Cooperative Studies in Philosophy* (New York: Macmillan, 1911), 471–86; R. B. Perry, "William Pepperell Montague and the New Realists," *Journal of Philosophy* 51 (1954): 605–6; "The Ego-centric Predicament," *Journal of Philosophy* 7 (1910): 5–14; solipsim or realism: *The New Realism,* 9. See also Herbert W. Schneider, *Sources of Contemporary Philosophical Realism in America* (Indianapolis: Bobbs-Merrill, 1962).

Pp. 315: Spaulding: *JRL,* 552; "Six Little Realists" (JHU), quoted in Ronald Albert Wells, "A Portrait of Josiah Royce," Ph.D. diss., Boston University, 1967, 146.

Pp. 315–16: "The Reality of the Temporal," *International Journal of Ethics* 20 (1910): 258–59, 267 [1910, 5].

P. 316: Lowell: ALS. JR to W. E. Hocking, 29 Jan. 1909 (Hocking Papers, HL).

James, Christopher, and the Shadow of Sorrow

P. 317: Palladino: WJ diary quoted in Allen, *William James,* 471; "The Search for Truth" (JP); ALS. Katharine Royce to Edward Royce, 21 Jan. 1910 (private collection, James Royce).

Pp. 317–18: Baldwin: ALS. Baldwin to Münsterberg, 16 Feb. 1910 (Boston Public Library); *JRL,* 539–40.

P. 318: *PL,* xxv; *TCWJ,* 2:822.

P. 319: "A Word of Greeting to William James," *Harvard Graduates' Magazine* 18 (1909–10): 630–33 [1910, 6]; *JRL,* 539; *WJO,* 22.

Pp. 319–320: JR voyages: *JRL,* 541–42; James, death: *JRL,* 543.

Pp. 320–321: Death of Christopher: ALS. Edward Royce to Katharine Royce, 4 Oct. 1910 (JRP); *JRL,* 544; James on earthquake victims: *WJL,* 2:251.

CHAPTER 9. THE BELOVED COMMUNITY, 1910–1913

Because My Help Is Needed

P. 322: C. A. Bennett, "Josiah Royce," *Philosophical Review* 25 (1916): 843.

Pp. 322–24: ALS. JR to E. E. Cummings, 30 Dec. 1912 (HL, bMS Am 1892 [770], by permission of Houghton Library, Harvard University; Cummings Papers, (HL); e. e. cummings, *six nonlectures* (Cambridge: Harvard Univ. Press, 1953), 29–30; Rossetti quoted: "What Sort of Existence Have the Entities of Mathematics" (1907), JRP, vol. 75.

P. 324:   Harrison lectures: JRP, vol. 85; "Loyalty and Insight," *Simmons Quarterly* 1 (1910): 4–21 [1910, 3]; reprinted *WJO*, 49–95 [1911, 4]; "James as a Philosopher," retitled "William James and the Philosophy of Life," *WJO*, 3–45 [1911, 4].

Pp. 324–25:   Ned and Elizabeth: ALS. Elizabeth Royce to Edward Royce, n.d. (private collection, James Royce). *JRL*, 547–51.

Pp. 325–28:   Harrison lectures: ALS. Romaine Newbold to Herman V. Ames, 18 May 1910 (Univ. of Pennsylvania Archives); John Dewey, *The Middle Works of John Dewey, 1899–1924*, ed. Jo Ann Boydston (Carbondale: Southern Illinois Univ. Press, 1985), 6:12–68. JR's Harrison lectures: JRP, vol. 85: lecture 3, pp. 1–8, 17–18, 26; lecture 2, pp. 21, 32, 37–38.

P. 328:   ALS. JR to Ella L. Cabot, 22 Mar. 1911, Cabot Papers (HUA).

P. 329:   H. N. Gardiner, note in Scrapbook of Correspondence (Smith College Archives).

P. 329:   "Immortality," *WJO*, 297; *BWJR*, 1:401.

Pp. 329–30:   Mills Professorship: *JRL*, 553; TLC, A. L. Lowell, 6 Feb. 1911 (HUA); Cabot Fellowship: TLS. Henry B. Cabot to A. L. Lowell, 23 Mar. 1911, (Lowell Papers) (HUA); memorandum: A. L. Lowell, 4 Apr. 1911 (HUA); ALS. JR to A. L. Lowell, 16 Aug. 1911 (HUA); Yale honorary doctorate: ALS. JR to Arthur T. Hadley, 4 Dec. 1911 (Yale Univ. Archives).

Insight

Pp. 330–31:   George P. Adams and William Pepperell Montague, *Contemporary American Philosophy: Personal Statements*, 2 vols. (New York: Russell & Russell, 1962); Perry: 2:188; Lewis: 2:32; Montague: 2:139–40. Bennett, "Josiah Royce," 844–45. J. Loewenberg, "Emerson Hall Revisited," in *The Harvard Book* (Cambridge: Harvard Univ. Press, 1953), 98–100. W. E. Hocking, preface to *Royce's Metaphysics*, by Gabriel Marcel (Chicago: Henry Regnery, 1956), vii–viii.

P. 332:   *SRI*, 90–92 [1912, 5].

P. 332:   *WJO*, 49–95, 43–45; ALS. Henry James to JR, 30 June 1911 (JP).

P. 333:   Plan for publication: *JRL*, 558–60.

P. 333:   ALS. JR to Katharine Royce, 17 Aug. 1911 (JRP).

P. 333:   Lake Forest College: ALS. John S. Nollen to JR, 3 Oct. 1911 (JRP); ALS. G. H. Mead to JR, 4 Nov. 1911 (JRP).

P. 334:   "<1910> Notes for Address before Yale Theological Club, May 14, 1910," JRP, vol. 78.

Pp. 334–35:   Easiest book: *JRL*, 570; divided self: *SRI*, 49 [1912, 5]; guilt, Coleridge, Dostoyevsky: *SRI*, 66–69, 70–71, 75.

Pp. 335–36:   "The Religious Mission of Sorrow": *SRI*, 252, 249.

P. 336:   "The Unity of the Spirit and the Invisible Church," *SRI*, 280, 297.

P. 336:   ALS. Julia S. Bristol to JR, 15 Nov. 1911 (JRP).

Pp. 336–37:   ALS. Ella L. Cabot to JR, 6 July 1912 (JRP); ALS. R. C. Cabot to JR, 22 June 1912 (JRP); reply to Cabot: *JRL*, 577-78; ALS. L. Leslie Brooke to JR, 24 May 1913 (JRP).

My Health, My Plans

Pp. 337–38:   "On Definitions and Debates," *Journal of Philosophy* 9 (1911): 85–100 [1912, 3], *JRL*, 560, 562–63; stroke: *JRL*, 563–64.

P. 338:   ALS. Elizabeth R. Royce to Edward Royce, 12 Feb. 1912 (private collection, James Royce).

Pp. 338–39:   *JRL*, 563-70.

Pp. 340–41:   Influence of Peirce: "Illustrations of the Philosophy of Loyalty," JRP, vol. 84, 10–14; 1905 exchange: *JRL*, 488–92; AL. unsigned draft C. S. Peirce to WJ, n.d. [Sept. or Oct. 1905?] (PP).

P. 341:   *JRL*, 571, 581; "Voyages in 1912," JRP, Logic Box 4.

Pp. 341–42:   Elizabeth's illness: *JRL*, 574–77; tragedy of love: *PC*, 91.

Pp. 342–43:   Lovejoy: *JRL*, 389. Adams and Montague, *Contemporary American Philosophy*; Lovejoy: 2:89; *JRL*, 583–85, 586–87.

The Problem of Christianity

Pp. 343–44:   *JRL*, 587; ALS. J. J. Putnam to Katharine Royce, 14 Jan. 1913 (JRP); to Putnam: *JRL*, 596–97.

Pp. 344–45:   Santayana: *TCWJ*, 2:321, 403; *JRL*, 579; ALS. G. H. Palmer to JR, 14 Aug. [1912] (JRP).

Pp. 345–46:   *JRL*, 588–89, 590–92; Ronald W. Clark, *The Life of Bertrand Russell* (New York: Knopf, 1976), 197, 230; Barry Feinberg and Ronald Kasrils, *Bertrand Russell's America, 1896–1945* (New York: Viking, 1973), 41; *JRL*, 591; "Mysticism and Logic," *Hibbert Journal* 12 (July 1914): 780–803.

Pp. 346–47:   *JRL*, 589. In subsequent citations, page numbers in *PC* are those of the Univ. of Chicago Press edition, 1968. *PC*, 61, 71–74.

Pp. 347–48:   *PC*, 81–82; community as person: *JRL*, 646–47; Sigmund Freud,

Civilization and Its Discontents (New York: Norton, 1961), 70–71; Body of Christ: *PC*, 118.

Pp. 348–49: *PC*, 131–32.

Pp. 349–50: *Writings of Charles S. Peirce: A Chronological Edition.* Vol. 2: *1867–1871*, ed. Edward C. Moore (Bloomington: Indiana Univ. Press, 1984), 49–59, 193–211, 211–42.

P. 350: Interpretation: *PC*, 297–98, 340.

Pp. 350–51: *The Collected Works of Ralph Waldo Emerson* (Cambridge: Harvard Univ. Press, 1971–79) 1:90; 2:42; *PC*, 290–91, 357, 340, 362, 377, 404, 362.

P. 351: ALS. Ruth Royce to JR, 17 Apr. 1913 (JRP).

P. 351: Publication of *PC*: *JRL*, 581–83, 589.

P. 352: ALS. L. P. Jacks to JR, n.d. [1913] (JRP).

CHAPTER 10. WATCHMAN, WHAT OF THE NIGHT? 1913–1916

Family Interlude III

P. 354: ALS. Edward Royce to Katharine Royce, 7 Mar. 1915 (JRP); ALS. Anna Head to Stephen and Marion Royce, 6 Sept. 1922 (JRP); ALS. Katharine Royce to Edward Royce, 13 Feb. 1940; 20 Feb. 1940 (private collection, James Royce).

P. 354 Edward, never strong: ALS. Katharine Royce to Harriette Royce Barney, 1 Oct. 1919 (JRP).

Pp. 354–55: Miss Grady: ALS. Katharine Royce to Stephen Royce, 3 July 1913; ALS. Marion Woodworth to Stephen Royce, 4 July 1913 (JRP).

P. 355: ALS. Katharine Royce to Stephen and Marion Royce, 25 Sept. 1913 (JRP); ALS. JR to Marion and Stephen Royce, 16 Sept. 1913 (JRP).

P. 356: ALS. Anna Head to Katharine Royce, 12 Mar. 1915 (JRP).

Logic, Criticism, and "The Spirit of the Community"

Pp. 356–57: Health: *JRL*, 596, 604; *The Harvard University Catalogue, 1913–14*; *The Autobiography of Bertrand Russell, 1872–1914* (Boston: Little, Brown, 1967), 326; logic papers: *JRL*, 609–11.

P. 357: *Josiah Royce's Seminar, 1913–1914* (New Brunswick, N.J.: Rutgers Univ. Press, 1963), 189–90; *JRL*, 613.

Pp. 357–58: *JRL*, 554–55. *Josiah Royce's Seminar*, 165–70; "The Mechanical, the Historical, and the Statistical," *Science*, n.s., 39 (1914): 551–66 [1914, 2]; *BWJR*, 2:711–33.

Pp. 358–59: Peirce: *JRL*, 614–15; Peirce on *PC*: "Illustrations of the Philos. of Loyalty,"

JRP, vol. 84; C. S. Peirce to JR, 30 June 1913 (JRP); Oppenheim on "Uberty": Frank M. Oppenheim, *Royce's Mature Ethics* (Notre Dame, Ind.: Univ. of Notre Dame Press, 1993), 242; "Charles Sanders Peirce" (with Fergus Kernan), *Journal of Philosophy* 13 (1916): 701–9 [1916, 1].

Pp. 359–60:   Reviews of *PC*: W. A. Brown, *Journal of Philosophy* 11 (1914): 608–14; A. C. Armstrong, *Philosophical Review* 23 (1914): 71–74; H. Rashdall, *Mind*, n.s., 23 (1914): 405–17.

P. 360:   ALS. F. G. Peabody to JR, 11 Nov. 1911; 21 Oct. 1913 (JRP).

Pp. 360–61:   Berkeley Conferences: JRP, vol. 84.

P. 361:   "The Spirit of the Community," JRP, vol. 91.

The Great War

P. 362:   "Interpretation of the Present Crisis," JRP, Logic Box 4; *JRL*, 615–16.

Pp. 363–65:   *W&I*, 29, 34–35; Victor Lenzen, "Notes on Royce's Seminary in Scientific Methodology, 1914–15" (Lenzen Papers, UCB).

P. 365:   Lowell: *JRL*, 617-18.

P. 365:   Reactions to *W&I*: ALS. G. H. Palmer to JR, 28 Oct. 1914 (JRP); ALS. B. Wendell to JR, 18 Oct. 1914 (JRP); ALS. L. P. Jacks to JR, 25 Sept. 1914 (JRP); L. L. Brooke to JR, 20 Dec. 1914 (JRP); ALS. F. C. S. Schiller to JR, 3 Oct. 1914 (JRP).

Pp. 365–66:   TLC. JR to D. S. Jordan, 10 Feb. 1915 (JRP); TLC. JR to T. H. Price, 10 Feb. 1915 (JRP).

Pp. 366–67:   "Professor Josiah Royce of Harvard Advocates Insurance by the Nations of the World," *New York Times*, 25 July 1915 [1915, 5]; reprinted: *HGC*, 71–92; *JRL*, 624–26; ALS. H. B. Dow, 9 Sept. 1914 (JRP); ALS. Willam B. Medlicott to JR, 1 April 1915 (JRP).

Pp. 367–68:   "A Plea for Provincial Independence in Education; A Letter with Reference to the Report of the Carnegie Foundation for Advancement of Teaching on Education in Vermont," *Middlebury College Bulletin* 9 (Oct. 1914): 3–19 [1914, 3]; "The Carnegie Foundation for the Advancement of Teaching and the Case of Middlebury College," *School and Society* 1 (1915): 145–50 [1915, 3].

Pp. 368–69:   ALS. JR to Kuno Francke, 22 Nov. 1914, Francke Papers (HUA).

P. 369:   Hale, *Human Science and Social Order*, 175, 228; ALS. C. W. Eliot to H. Münsterberg, 21 Nov. 1914 (Münsterberg Papers, Boston Public Library); Stephen Royce: Robinson, *Royce and Hocking*, 152.

Pp. 369–370:   Roosevelt: *JRL*, 619–21; Robinson, *Royce and Hocking*, 149; Suffolk West: TLS. H. Grant Presons to JR, 7 Jan. 1916 (JRP); duckboards: TLC. W. F. Kernan to Frank M. Oppenheim, 26 Sept. 1967 (Oppenheim files).

Pp. 370–71:   Chapman, "Portrait of Josiah Royce, the Philosopher," 377.

P. 371:   *Lusitania: JRL*, 627–31.

The Last Year

P. 372:   Frank M. Oppenheim, *Royce's Mature Ethics* (Notre Dame: Univ. of Notre Dame Press, 1993), 117, 123.

P. 372:   ALS. JR to Katharine Royce, 25 Aug. [1915] (JRP).

Pp. 372–73:   ALS. JR to Katharine Royce, 30 Aug. 1915 (JRP).

Pp. 373–74:   Hastings: *JRL*, 643–44; Chapman, "Portrait of Josiah Royce, the Philosopher," 377.

Pp. 374–75:   "The Hope of the Great Community," *Yale Review* 5 (1916): 269-91 [1916, 4]; *HGC*, 25-70 [1916, 5].

P. 375:   Cross: *JRL*, 639; APA meeting, 1915: *Journal of Philosophy* 13 (1916): 97–102; *Papers in Honor of Josiah Royce* . . . , *Philosophical Review* 25 (1916): 229–522.

Pp. 375–76:   Telegrams from Lovejoy, Russell, Bergson, Loewenberg, etc.: (UCLA), box 1; "Words of Professor Royce . . . ," *HGC*, 122–36.

P. 377:   ALS. R. C. Cabot to JR, 23 Dec. 1915 (JRP); ALS. JR to R. C. Cabot, 24 June 1916 (JRP).

Pp. 377–78:   "The Duties of Americans in the Present War," *Boston Evening Transcript*, 2 Feb. 1916, 18; *HGC*, 1–13; "Professor Royce's 'Lusitania' Speech," *Boston Evening Transcript*, 8 May 1916, 13; *HGC*, 93–121. See R. A. Wells, "A Portrait of Josiah Royce," Ph.D. diss., Boston University, 1967, 188; J. J. Chapman, "Portrait of Josiah Royce, the Philosopher," 377.

Pp. 378–79:   Horace M. Kallen, "Remarks on Royce's Philosophy," *Journal of Philosophy* 53 (1956): 132–34.

P. 379:   W. E. Hocking, "On Royce's Empiricism," *Journal of Philosophy* 53 (1956): 57. Ernest Hemingway, *A Farewell to Arms* (New York: Scribner's, 1919), 184–85; R. Brooke quoted: Arthur Lane, *An Adequate Response* (Detroit: Wayne State Univ. Press, 1972), 66. R. F. A. Hoernlé, "The Revival of Idealism in the United States," in *Contemporary Idealism in America*, ed. Clifford Barrett (New York: Macmillan, 1932), 300–301.

P. 380:   ALS. Katharine Royce to Ruth Royce, n. d. [spring or summer 1916] (UCLA), box 1; ALS. Katharine Royce to R. B. Perry, 25 Nov. [1929?], Perry Papers (HUA); JR telegrams to B. I. Wheeler, 4 Mar. 1916; 7 Mar. 1916 (UCA); JR funeral: ALS. M. W. Calkins to Anna Head [Oct. 1916?] (UCLA), box 1; TLC. A. L. Lowell to [Davidson?], 4 Sept. 1916, Lowell Papers (HUA).

P. 380:   "The Cult of the Dead," quoted: J. H. Cotton, *Royce on the Human Self* (Cambridge: Harvard Univ. Press, 1954), 6–7.

Pp. 380–81: Bennett, "Josiah Royce," 845; ALS. L. P. Jacks to Katharine Royce, 5 Nov. 1916 (JRP); ALS. Anna Head to Katharine Royce, 15 Sept. 1916 (JRP).

P. 382:   JR's will (Jan. 1903) and Executor's Inventory, Commonwealth of Massachusetts, Middlesex, Registry of Probate (6 Nov. 1916).

P. 382:   John 17:21; JRP, vol. 94.

Bibliography

BIBLIOGRAPHIES

Devaux, André-A. "Bibliographie des traductions d'ouvrage de Royce et des études sur l'oeuvre de Royce." *Revue Internationale de Philosophie* 79–80 (1967): 159–82.

Oppenheim, Frank M. "A Critical Annotated Bibliography of the Published Works of Josiah Royce." *Modern Schoolman* 41 (1964): 339–65. Rev. ed. *Revue Internationale de Philosophie* 79–80 (1967): 138–58.

Skrupskelis, Ignas K. "Annotated Bibliography of the Published Works of Josiah Royce." In *The Basic Writings of Josiah Royce*, ed. John J. McDermott, 1166–1226. Vol. 2. Chicago: Univ. of Chicago Press, 1969.

SELECTED BIBLIOGRAPHY OF THE WRITINGS OF JOSIAH ROYCE

The following is a chronological list of the writings of Josiah Royce, including edited collections of his writings. This is not meant to supersede the work of Ignas Skrupskelis, whose bibliography remains standard and exhaustive, but rather to guide the reader to Royce's major works and suggest the historical development of his thought.

1869	"Is the Assassination of Tyrants ever Justifiable?" *Lincoln Observer* 2.
1874	"The Modern Novel as a Mode of Conveying Instruction and Accomplishing Reform." *Berkeleyan* 1 (Apr.): 10–11.
1875	"Draper's Religion and Science." *Berkeleyan* 2 (Feb.): 9.
	"Truth in Art." *Berkeleyan* 2 (Apr.): 3–4.
	"A Word about the 'Ideal' in Science and in Art." *Berkeleyan* 2 (June): 7.
	"Draper and 'Religion.'" *Berkeleyan* 2 (June): 8–9.
	"The Aim of Poetry." *Overland Monthly* 14: 542–49.
	"The Intention of the Prometheus Bound of Aeschylus, Being an Investigation in the Department of Greek Theology." *Bulletin of the University of California*, no. 16: 113–37.
	"The Life-Harmony." *Overland Monthly* 15: 157–64.
	"On a Passage in Sophocles." *Oakland Daily Transcript*, 10 June, 3.
1878	"Of the Interdependence of the Principles of Knowledge: An Investigation of the Problems of Elementary Epistemology." Ph.D. diss., Johns Hopkins University.
	"Schiller's Ethical Studies." *Journal of Speculative Philosophy* 12: 373–92. Reprint, *Fugitive Essays*.
1880	"Natural Rights and Spinoza's Essay on Liberty." *Berkeley Quarterly* 1: 312–16. Reprint, *Fugitive Essays*.

"The Nature of Voluntary Progress." *Berkeley Quarterly* 1: 161–89. Reprint, *Fugitive Essays*.

"Shelley and the Revolution." *Californian* 1: 543–53. Reprint, *Fugitive Essays*.

1881   "Before and Since Kant." *Berkeley Quarterly* 2: 134–50.

"The Decay of Earnestness." *Californian* 3: 18–25. Reprint, *Fugitive Essays*.

"Doubting and Working." *Californian* 3: 229–37. Reprint, *Fugitive Essays*.

"George Eliot as a Religious Teacher." *Californian* 3: 300–310. Reprint, *Fugitive Essays*.

"Kant's Relation to Modern Philosophic Progress." *Journal of Speculative Philosophy* 15: 360–81.

"'Mind-Stuff' and Reality." *Mind* 6: 365–77.

"Pessimism and Modern Thought." *Berkeley Quarterly* 2: 292–316. Reprint, *Fugitive Essays*.

Primer of Logical Analysis for the Use of Composition Students. San Francisco: Bancroft.

1882   "How Beliefs Are Made." *Californian* 5: 122–29. Reprint, *Fugitive Essays*.

"Mind and Reality." *Mind* 7: 30–54.

1885   *The Religious Aspect of Philosophy: A Critique of the Bases of Conduct and of Faith*. Boston: Houghton.

"The Squatter Riot of '50 in Sacramento: Its Causes and Its Significance." *Overland Monthly*, n.s., 6: 225–46. Reprint, *Studies of Good and Evil*.

1886   "Abbot's Scientific Theism." *Science* 7: 335–38.

California from the Conquest in 1846 to the Second Vigilance Committee in San Francisco [1856]: A Study of American Character. Boston: Houghton. Reprint, with an introduction by Robert Glass Cleland, New York: Knopf, 1948.

1887   "Bancroft's Conquest of California." *Nation* 44: 39–40.

The Feud of Oakfield Creek: A Novel of California Life. Boston: Houghton. Reprint, with an introduction by John Clendenning, New York: Johnson, 1970.

"Tennyson and Pessimism." *Harvard Monthly* 3: 127–37. Reprint, *Studies of Good and Evil*.

1889   "Bancroft's California." *Nation* 48: 140–42, 164–65.

"Is There a Philosophy of Evolution?" *Unitarian Review* 32: 1–29, 97–113.

"The Practical Value of Philosophy." *Ethical Record* 2: 9–22.

"Reflections after a Wandering Life in Australasia." *Atlantic Monthly* 63: 675–86, 813–28.

1890   "Dr. Abbot's 'Way Out of Agnosticism.'" *International Journal of Ethics* 1: 98–113.

"A Neglected Study." *Harvard Monthly* 10: 169–79. Reprint, *Fugitive Essays*.

"Light on the Seizure of California." *Century*, n.s., 18: 792–94.

"Frémont." *Atlantic Monthly* 66: 548–57.

1891   "Impressions of Australia." *Scribner's Magazine* 9: 75–87.

"The Frémont Legend." *Nation* 52: 423–25.

"Present Ideals of American University Life." *Scribner's Magazine* 10: 376–88.

"Montgomery and Frémont: New Documents on the Bear Flag Affair." *Century*, n.s., 19: 780–83.

1892   "The Implications of Self-Consciousness." *New World* 1: 289–310. Reprint, *Studies of Good and Evil.*

The Spirit of Modern Philosophy: An Essay in the Form of Lectures.* Boston: Houghton.

1893   "The Knowledge of Good and Evil." *International Journal of Ethics* 4: 48–80. Reprint, *Studies of Good and Evil.*

1894   "The Case of John Bunyan." *Psychological Review* 1: 22–33, 134–51, 230–40. Reprint, *Studies of Good and Evil.*

"The External World and the Social Consciousness." *Philosophical Review* 3: 513–45.

"The Problem of Paracelsus." *New World* 3: 89–110. Reprint, *Fugitive Essays.*

1895   *The Conception of God.* With Joseph Le Conte, George Holmes Howison, and Sidney Edward Mezes. Bulletin no. 15. Berkeley: Philosophical Union of the University of California.

"Natural Law, Ethics, and Evolution." *International Journal of Ethics* 5: 489–500. Reprint, *Studies of Good and Evil.*

"Self-Consciousness, Social Consciousness and Nature." *Philosophical Review* 4: 465–85, 577–602. Reprint, *Studies of Good and Evil.*

"Some Observations on the Anomalies of Self-Consciousness." *Psychological Review* 2: 433–57, 574–84. Reprint, *Studies of Good and Evil.*

1896   "Browning's Theism." *New World* 5: 401–22.

"Outlines of Psychology; Or, a Study of the Human Mind." In *In Sickness and in Health,* ed. James W. Roosevelt, 171–233. New York: Appleton.

1897   *The Conception of God: A Philosophical Discussion Concerning the Nature of the Divine Idea as a Demonstrable Reality.* New York: Macmillan. [Reprints the discussion in the 1895 volume, but adds a long supplementary essay by Royce: "The Absolute and the Individual."]

"Originality and Consciousness." *Harvard Monthly* 24: 133–42. Reprint, *Studies of Good and Evil.*

"The Problem of Job." *New World* 6: 261–81. Reprint, *Studies of Good and Evil.*

1898   "The Psychology of Invention." *Psychological Review* 5: 113–44.

Studies of Good and Evil: A Series of Essays upon the Problems of Philosophy and of Life. New York: Appleton.

1899   *The World and the Individual: First Series: The Four Historical Conceptions of Being.* New York: Macmillan. Reprint, with an introduction by John E. Smith, New York: Dover, 1959.

1900   *The Conception of Immortality.* Boston: Houghton.

"The Pacific Coast: A Psychological Study of Influence." *International Monthly* 2: 555–83. Reprint, *Race Questions.*

"Professor Everett as a Metaphysician." *New World* 9: 726–41.

1901   *The World and the Individual: Second Series: Nature, Man, and the Moral Order.* New York: Macmillan. Reprint, New York: Dover, 1959.

"John Fiske: His Work as a Philosophical Writer and Teacher." *Harvard Graduates' Magazine* 10: 23–33.

"Joseph Le Conte." *International Monthly* 4: 324–34.

1902 "The Concept of the Infinite." *Hibbert Journal* 1: 21–45.

"The Old and the New—A Lesson." *University of California Chronicle* 2: 92–103.

Provincialism: An Address to the Phi Beta Kappa Society of the State University of Iowa. Iowa City: State Univ. of Iowa. Reprint, *Race Questions.*

"Recent Logical Inquiries and Their Psychological Bearings." *Psychological Review* 9: 105–33.

1903 Introduction. In *Outlines of Cosmic Philosophy*, by John Fiske, xxi–cxlix. 4 vols. Boston: Houghton.

Outlines of Psychology: An Elementary Treatise with Some Practical Applications. New York: Macmillan.

1904 "The Eternal and the Practical." *Philosophical Review* 13: 113–42.

Herbert Spencer: An Estimate and Review. New York: Fox.

"The Sciences of the Ideal." *Science*, n.s., 20: 449–62.

1905 "Kant's Doctrine of the Bases of Mathematics." *Journal of Philosophy* 2: 197–207.

"The Relation of the Principles of Logic to the Foundations of Geometry." *Transactions of the American Mathematical Society* 24: 353–415.

1906 "Race Questions and Prejudices." *International Journal of Ethics* 16: 265–88. Reprint, *Race Questions.*

1907 "Immortality." *Hibbert Journal* 5: 724–44. Reprint, *William James.*

1908 *The Philosophy of Loyalty.* New York: Macmillan. Reprint, with an introduction by John J. McDermott, Nashville, Tenn.: Vanderbilt Univ. Press, 1995.

Race Questions, Provincialism, and Other American Problems. New York: Macmillan.

1909 "The Problem of Truth in the Light of Recent Discussion." *Bericht über den III internationalen Kongress für Philosophie.* Heidelberg: Winter. Reprint, *William James.*

"What Is Vital in Christianity?" *Harvard Theological Review* 2: 408–45. Reprint, *William James.*

1910 "Loyalty and Insight." *Simmons Quarterly* 1: 4–21. Reprint, *William James.*

"The Reality of the Temporal." *International Journal of Ethics* 20: 257–71.

"A Word of Greeting to William James." *Harvard Graduates' Magazine* 18: 630–33.

1911 "In Honor of Professor Palmer." *Harvard Graduates' Magazine* 19:575–78.

"James as a Philosopher." *Boston Evening Transcript*, 29 June, 13. Reprint, "William James and the Philosophy of Life," in *William James.*

William James and Other Essays on the Philosophy of Life. New York: Macmillan.

"On Definitions and Debates." *Journal of Philosophy* 9: 85–100.

The Sources of Religious Insight. New York: Scribner's.

1913   "An Extension of the Algebra of Logic." *Journal of Philosophy* 10: 617–33.

"The Principles of Logic." In *Logic: Encyclopedia of the Philosophical Sciences*, 67–135. Vol. 1. London: Macmillan.

Introduction. In *Science and Hypothesis*, by Henri Poincaré, 9–24. Trans. George Bruce Halsted. Lancaster, Pa.: Science Press.

The Problem of Christianity. 2 vols. New York: Macmillan. Reprint, with an introduction by John E. Smith, Chicago: Univ. of Chicago Press, 1968.

1914   "The Mechanical, the Historical, and the Statistical." *Science*, n.s., 39: 551–66.

War and Insurance. New York: Macmillan.

"Professor Royce on His Reviewer." *New Republic* 1: 23.

1915   "The Carnegie Foundation for the Advancement of Teaching and the Case of Middlebury College." *School and Society* 1: 145–50.

"An American Thinker on the War." *Hibbert Journal* 14: 37–42. Reprint, "The Destruction of the Lusitania," in *The Hope of the Great Community*.

"Professor Josiah Royce of Harvard Advocates Insurance by the Nations of the World." *New York Times*, 25 July, pt. 4, 2–3. Reprint, "The Possibility of International Insurance," in *The Hope of the Great Community*.

1916   "Charles Sanders Peirce." With Fergus Kernan. *Journal of Philosophy* 13: 701–9.

"Duties of Americans in the Present War." *Boston Evening Transcript*, 2 Feb., 18. Reprint, *The Hope of the Great Community*.

"Professor Royce's 'Lusitania' Speech." *Boston Evening Transcript*, 8 May, 13. Reprint, "The First Anniversary of the Sinking of the Lusitania, May 7th, 1916," in *The Hope of the Great Community*.

"Words of Professor Royce at the Walton Hotel at Philadelphia, December 29, 1915." *Philosophical Review* 25: 507–14. Reprint, *The Hope of the Great Community*.

The Hope of the Great Community. New York: Macmillan.

1919   *Lectures on Modern Idealism*. Ed. Jacob Loewenberg. New Haven: Yale Univ. Press.

1920   *Fugitive Essays*. Ed. Jacob Loewenberg. Cambridge: Harvard Univ. Press.

1950   *The Social Philosophy of Josiah Royce*. Ed. Stuart Gerry Brown. Syracuse: Syracuse Univ. Press.

1951   *Royce's Logical Essays*. Ed. Daniel S. Robinson. Dubuque: Brown.

1952   *The Religious Philosophy of Josiah Royce*. Ed. Stuart Gerry Brown. Syracuse: Syracuse Univ. Press.

1966   "The Two-Fold Nature of Knowledge: Imitative and Reflective." Ed. Peter Fuss. *Journal of the History of Philosophy* 4: 326–37.

1967   "Royce's Urbana Lectures." Ed. Peter Fuss. *Journal of the History of Philosophy* 5: 60–78, 269–86.

1969   *The Basic Writings of Josiah Royce*. Ed. John J. McDermott. 2 vols. Chicago: Univ. of Chicago Press.

1970   *The Letters of Josiah Royce*. Ed. John Clendenning. Chicago: Univ. of Chicago Press.

Secondary Sources

Collections of Essays about Royce and Other American Philosophers

Adams, George P., and William Pepperell Montague, eds. *Contemporary American Philosophy: Personal Statements*. 2 vols. New York: Russell & Russell, 1962.

Barrett, Clifford, ed. *Contemporary Idealism in America*. New York: Macmillan, 1932.

Burch, Robert W., and Herman J. Saatkàmp Jr., eds. *Frontiers in American Philosophy*. 2 vols. College Station: Texas A&M Univ. Press, 1992–96.

Creighton, James Edwin, ed. *Papers in Honor of Josiah Royce on His Sixtieth Birthday*. Special issue of *Philosophical Review* 25 (1916): 229–522.

Kegley, Jacquelyn Ann K., ed. *The Doctrine of Interpretation: Building Community Out of Conflict*. Hayward: California State Univ., Hayward Press, 1978.

In Memoriam: Josiah Royce, Born November 20, 1855. Special issue of *Journal of Philosophy* 53 (1956): 57–139.

Selected Works Relating to Royce's Life and Thought

Allen, Gay Wilson. *William James: A Biography*. New York: Viking, 1967.

Bakewell, Charles M., ed. *George Herbert Palmer, 1842–1933: Memorial Addresses*. Cambridge: Harvard Univ. Press, 1935.

Baldwin, James Mark. *Between Two Wars, 1861–1912: Being Memoirs, Opinions, and Letters Received*. 2 vols. Boston: Stratford, 1926.

Bennett, Charles A. "Josiah Royce." *Philosophical Review* 25 (1916): 843–45.

Blau, Joseph Leon. *Men and Movements in American Philosophy*. New York: Prentice, 1952.

Bradley, Francis Herbert. *Appearance and Reality*. London: Macmillan, 1893.

Brent, Joseph. *Charles Sanders Peirce: A Life*. Bloomington: Indiana Univ. Press, 1993.

Brown, Rollo Walter. *Harvard Yard in the Golden Age*. New York: Current Books, 1948.

Buckham, John Wright, and George Malcolm Stratton. *George Holmes Howison, Philosopher and Teacher: A Selection from His Writings with a Biographical Sketch*. Berkeley: Univ. of California Press, 1934.

Buranelli, Vincent. *Josiah Royce*. New York: Twayne, 1964.

Burch, Robert W. "A Transformation in Royce's View of Kant." *Transactions of the Charles S. Peirce Society* 33 (1997): 557–78.

———. "An Unpublished Logic Paper by Josiah Royce." *Transactions of the Charles S. Peirce Society* 33 (1997): 173–204.

Cabot, Richard Clarke. "Josiah Royce as a Teacher." *Philosophical Review* 25 (1916): 466–72.

Calkins, Mary Whiton. "The Foundation in Royce's Philosophy for Christian Theism." *Philosophical Review* 25 (1916): 282–93.

Chapman, John Jay. *Memories and Milestones*. New York: Moffat, 1915.

———. "Portrait of Josiah Royce, the Philosopher." *Outlook* 120 (1919): 372, 377.

———. *Two Philosophers: A Quaint, Sad Comedy*. Boston: Cupples, 1892.

Clark, Ronald W. *The Life of Bertrand Russell.* New York: Knopf, 1976.

Clendenning, John. "Josiah Royce: Literature and Humanism." In *Frontiers in American Philosophy*, ed. Robert W. Burch and Herman J. Saatkamp Jr., 215–22. Vol. 2. College Station: Texas A&M Univ. Press, 1996.

Clendenning, John, and Frank M. Oppenheim. "New Documents on Josiah Royce." *Transactions of the Charles S. Peirce Society* 26 (1990): 131–39.

Clifford, William Kingdon. "On the Nature of Things-in-Themselves." *Mind* 3 (1878): 57–67.

Cohen, Morris R. "Neo-Realism and the Philosophy of Royce." *Philosophical Review* 25 (1916): 378–82.

———. *Studies in Philosophy and Science.* New York: Ungar, 1945.

Cook, Gary A. "George Herbert Mead: An Unpublished Essay on Royce and James." *Transactions of the Charles S. Peirce Society* 28 (1992): 583–92.

Corrington, Robert S. *The Community of Interpreters.* Macon: Mercer Univ. Press, 1987.

———. "A Comparison of Royce's Key Notion of Community of Interpretation with the Hermeneutics of Gadamer and Heidegger." *Transactions of the Charles S. Peirce Society* 20 (1984): 279–301.

———. "Hermeneutics and Loyalty." In *Frontiers in American Philosophy*, ed. Robert W. Burch and Herman J. Saatkamp Jr. Vol. 1. College Station: Texas A&M Univ. Press, 1992.

Costello, Harry T. *Josiah Royce's Seminar, 1913–1914.* New Brunswick: Rutgers Univ. Press, 1963.

Cotton, James Harry. *Royce on the Human Self.* Cambridge: Harvard Univ. Press, 1954.

Cross, Whitney R. *The Burned-over District: The Social and Intellectual History of Enthusiastic Religion in Western New York, 1800–1850.* Ithaca: Cornell Univ. Press, 1950.

Cummings, Edward Estlin. *Poems, 1923–1954.* New York: Harcourt, 1954.

———. *six nonlectures.* Cambridge: Harvard Univ. Press, 1953.

Dewey, John. *The Middle Works of John Dewey, 1899–1924.* Ed. Jo Ann Boydston. Vol. 6. Carbondale: Southern Illinois Univ. Press, 1985.

———. Review of *The World and the Individual: First Series*, by Josiah Royce. *Philosophical Review* 9 (1900): 311–24.

———. Review of *The World and the Individual: Second Series*, by Josiah Royce. *Philosophical Review* 11 (1902): 392–407.

———. "Voluntarism in the Roycean Philosophy." *Philosophical Review* 25 (1916): 245–54.

Du Bois, William Edward Burghardt. *Autobiography.* New York: International Publishers, 1968.

Dykhuizen, George. *The Life and Mind of John Dewey.* Carbondale: Southern Illinois Univ. Press, 1973.

Feinberg, Barry, and Ronald Kasrils. *Bertrand Russell's America, 1896–1945.* New York: Viking, 1973.

Ferguson, Alfred R. *Edward Rowland Sill.* The Hague: Nijhoff, 1955.

Fisch, Max, ed. *Classic American Philosophers.* New York: Appleton, 1951.

Frankel, Charles, ed. *The Golden Age of American Philosophy*. New York: Braziller, 1960.

Frankland, F. W. "The Doctrine of Mind-Stuff." *Mind* 6 (1881): 116–20.

———. "Dr. Royce on 'Mind-Stuff' and Reality." *Mind* 7 (1882): 110–14.

Franklin, Fabian, et al. *The Life of Daniel Coit Gilman*. New York: Dodd, 1910.

Frémont, John Charles. "The Conquest of California." *Century* 41 (1891): 917–28.

Fuss, Peter. *The Moral Philosophy of Josiah Royce*. Cambridge: Harvard Univ. Press, 1965.

Gabriel, Ralph Henry. *The Course of American Democratic Thought*. 2d ed. New York: Ronald, 1956.

Hale, Matthew, Jr. *Human Science and Social Order: Hugo Münsterberg and the Origins of Applied Psychology*. Philadelphia: Temple Univ. Press, 1980.

Hawkins, Hugh. *Between Harvard and America: The Educational Leadership of Charles W. Eliot*. New York: Oxford Univ. Press, 1972.

———. *Pioneer: A History of the Johns Hopkins University 1874–1889*. Ithaca: Cornell Univ. Press, 1960.

Helm, Bertrand P. *Time and Reality in American Philosophy*. Amherst: Univ. of Massachusetts Press, 1985.

Herbst, Jurgen. "Francis Greenwood Peabody: Harvard's Theologian of the Social Gospel." *Harvard Theological Review* 54 (1961): 45–69.

Hine, Robert V. *Josiah Royce: From Grass Valley to Harvard*. Norman: Univ. of Oklahoma Press, 1992.

Hocking, William Ernest. "The Holt-Freudian Ethics and the Ethics of Royce." *Philosophical Review* 25 (1916): 479–506.

———. "On Royce's Empiricism." *Journal of Philosophy* 53 (1956): 57–63.

Holt, Edwin B., et al. *The New Realism: Coöperative Studies in Philosophy*. New York: Macmillan, 1912.

Howe, M. A. De Wolfe. *John Jay Chapman and His Letters*. Boston: Houghton, 1937.

Howison, George Holmes. "Josiah Royce: The Significance of His Work in Philosophy." *Philosophical Review* 25 (1916): 231–44.

Jain, Manju. *T. S. Eliot and American Philosophy: The Harvard Years*. Cambridge: Cambridge Univ. Press, 1992.

James, Henry. *Henry James Letters*. Ed. Leon Edel. 4 vols. Cambridge: Harvard Univ. Press, 1974–84.

James, William. "Abbot against Royce." *Nation* 53 (1891): 389–90. Reprint, *Essays, Comments, and Reviews*. In *The Works of William James*, ed. Frederick H. Burkhardt, 135–38. Cambridge: Harvard Univ. Press, 1987.

———. *The Letters of William James*. Ed. Henry James. 2 vols. Boston: Atlantic Monthly Press, 1920.

———. "The Religious Aspect of Philosophy." *Atlantic Monthly* 55 (1885): 840–43. Reprint, *Essays, Comments, and Reviews*. In *The Works of William James*, ed. Frederick H. Burkhardt, 383–88. Cambridge: Harvard Univ. Press, 1987.

Jarvis, Edward A. *The Conception of God in the Later Royce*. The Hague: Nijhoff, 1975.

Jones, William Carey. "Some Recollections and Reflections of a '75er." *Occident* 7 (1884): 123–25.

Kallen, Horace M. "Remarks on Royce's Philosophy." *Journal of Philosophy* 53 (1956): 131–39.

Kegley, Jacquelyn Ann. *Genuine Individuals and Genuine Communities: A Roycean Public Philosophy*. Nashville, Tenn.: Vanderbilt Univ. Press, 1997.

———. "Loyalty to Loyalty: A Plan for America Today." In *Frontiers in American Philosophy*, ed. Robert W. Burch and Herman Saatkamp Jr., 337–45. Vol. 1. College Station: Texas A&M Univ. Press, 1992.

Kuklick, Bruce. "The Development of Royce's Later Philosophy." *Journal of the History of Philosophy* 9 (1971): 349–67.

———. *Josiah Royce: An Intellectual Biography*. Indianapolis: Bobbs, 1972.

———. *The Rise of American Philosophy*. New Haven: Yale Univ. Press, 1977.

Le Conte, Joseph. *Evolution: Its Nature, Its Evidences, and Its Relation to Religious Thought*. 2d rev. ed. New York: Appleton, 1897.

Loewenberg, Jacob. "Emerson Hall Revisited." In *The Harvard Book*. Cambridge: Harvard Univ. Press, 1953.

———. "Interpretation as a Self-Representative Process." *Philosophical Review* 25 (1916): 420–23.

———. *Royce's Synoptic Vision*. Baltimore: Johns Hopkins Univ. Press, 1955.

———. "Royce's Synthetic Method." *Journal of Philosophy* 53 (1956): 63–72.

Mann, Ralph. *After the Gold Rush: Society in Grass Valley and Nevada City, California, 1849–1870*. Stanford: Stanford Univ. Press, 1982.

Mahowald, Mary Briody. *An Idealistic Pragmatism: The Development of the Pragmatic Element in the Philosophy of Josiah Royce*. The Hague: Nijhoff, 1972.

———. "A Roycean Pragmatic: Insights for Applied Ethics." In *Frontiers in American Philosophy*, ed. Robert W. Burch and Herman J. Saatkamp Jr., 267–76. Vol. 2. College Station: Texas A&M Univ. Press, 1996.

Marcel, Gabriel. *Royce's Metaphysics*. Trans. Virginia and Gordon Ringer. Chicago: Regnery, 1956.

Marker, Lise-Lone. *David Belasco: Naturalism in the American Theatre*. Princeton: Princeton Univ. Press, 1975.

McDermott, John J. "The Confrontation between Royce and Howison." *Transactions of the Charles S. Peirce Society* 30 (1994): 779–90.

———. "Josiah Royce's Philosophy of the Community." *Philosophy* 19 (1986): 153–76.

———. *Streams of Experience: Reflections on the History and Philosophy of American Culture*. Amherst: Univ. of Massachusetts Press, 1986.

Mead, George Herbert. "Josiah Royce—A Personal Impression." *International Journal of Ethics* 27 (1917): 168–70.

———. "The Philosophies of Royce, James, and Dewey in Their American Setting." *International Journal of Ethics* 40 (1930): 211–31.

Münsterberg, Margaret. *Hugo Münsterberg: His Life and Work*. New York: Appleton, 1922.

Myers, Gerald E. *William James: His Life and Thought*. New Haven: Yale Univ. Press, 1986.

Oak, Henry Lebbeus. "Dr. Royce's 'California.'" *Overland Monthly* 8 (1886): 329–30.

Oppenheim, Frank M. "Graced Communities: A Problem in Loving." *Theological Studies* 44 (1983): 604–24.

———. "Josiah Royce's Intellectual Development: An Hypothesis." *Idealistic Studies* 6 (1976): 85–102.

———. "Major Developments in Royce's Ethics after the *Problem*." In *Frontiers in American Philosophy*, ed. Robert W. Burch and Herman J. Saatkamp Jr., 346–56. Vol. 1. College Station: Texas A&M Univ. Press, 1992.

———. "A Roycean Response to the Challenge of Individualism." In *Beyond Individualism*, ed. Donald L. Gelpi, S.J., 87–119. Notre Dame: Notre Dame Univ. Press, 1989.

———. *Royce's Mature Ethics*. Notre Dame: Notre Dame Univ. Press, 1993.

———. *Royce's Mature Philosophy of Religion*. Notre Dame: Notre Dame Univ. Press, 1987.

———. *Royce's Voyage Down Under: A Journey of the Mind*. Lexington: Univ. Press of Kentucky, 1980.

———. "Some New Documents on Royce's Early Experiences of Communities." *Journal of the History of Philosophy* 6 (1968): 381–85.

Palmer, George Herbert, and Ralph Barton Perry. "Philosophy." In *The Development of Harvard University: Since the Inauguration of President Eliot, 1869–1929*, ed. Samuel Eliot Morison. Cambridge: Harvard Univ. Press, 1930.

Paul, Rodman W. *California Gold: The Beginning of Mining in the Far West*. Lincoln: Univ. of Nebraska Press, 1947.

Peirce, Charles Sanders. "Abbot against Royce." *Nation* 53 (1891): 372.

———. *The Collected Papers of Charles Sanders Peirce*. Ed. Charles Hartshorne, Paul Weiss, and Arthur W. Burks. 8 vols. Cambridge: Harvard Univ. Press, 1931–58.

———. "Dr. F. E. Abbot's Philosophy." *Nation* 42 (1886): 135–36.

———. *Writings of Charles S. Peirce: A Chronological Edition*. Ed. Peirce Edition Project. Bloomington: Indiana Univ. Press, 1982–.

Perry, Ralph Barton. "The Ego-centric Predicament." *Journal of Philosophy* 7 (1910): 5–14.

———. "Prof. Royce's Refutation of Realism and Pluralism." *Monist* 12 (1902): 446–58.

———. *The Thought and Character of William James*. 2 vols. Boston: Little, Brown, 1935. See also the reprint of the one-volume abridgment, with an introduction by Charlene Haddock Seigfried, Nashville, Tenn.: Vanderbilt Univ. Press, 1996.

———. "Two American Philosophers: William James and Josiah Royce." In *In the Spirit of William James*. New Haven: Yale Univ. Press, 1958.

Pomeroy, Earl. "Josiah Royce, Historian in Quest of Community." *Pacific Historical Review* 40 (1971): 1–20.

Powell, Thomas F. *Josiah Royce*. New York: Washington Square, 1967.

Rand, Benjamin. "Philosophical Instruction in Harvard University from 1636 to 1906. *Harvard Graduates' Magazine* 37 (1929): 296–311.

Robinson, Daniel S. *Royce and Hocking: American Idealists*. Boston: Christopher, 1968.

Rolle, Andrew. *John Charles Frémont: Character as Destiny*. Norman: Univ. of Oklahoma Press, 1991.

Rosenfield, Leonora Cohen. *Portrait of a Philosopher: Morris R. Cohen in Life and Letters.* New York: Harcourt, 1962.

Royce, Sarah. *A Frontier Lady: Recollections of the Gold Rush and Early California.* With a foreword by Katharine Royce. Ed. Ralph Henry Gabriel. New Haven: Yale Univ. Press, 1932.

Ross, Dorothy. *G. Stanley Hall: The Psychologist as Prophet.* Chicago: Univ. of Chicago Press, 1972.

Rowell, Joseph C. "Recollections of an Undergraduate, 1870–71." *Occident* 7 (1884): 105–6.

Russell, Bertrand. *The Autobiography of Bertrand Russell.* 3 vols. Boston: Little, Brown, 1967–69.

Samuels, Ernest. *Bernard Berenson: The Making of a Connoisseur.* Cambridge: Harvard Univ. Press, 1979.

Santayana, George. "Josiah Royce." In *Character and Opinion in the United States.*In vol. 8 of the Triton Edition of *The Works of George Santayana.* New York: Scribner's, 1937. Reprint, New York: Braziller, 1955.

———. *The Letters of George Santayana.* Ed. Daniel Cory. New York: Scribner's, 1955.

———. *Persons and Places: Fragments of Autobiography.* In *The Works of George Santayana.* Vol. 1. Ed. Herman J. Saatkamp Jr. Cambridge: MIT Press, 1886.

Schneider, Herbert W. *A History of American Philosophy.* New York: Columbia Univ. Press, 1946.

———. *Sources of Contemporary Philosophical Realism in America.* Indianapolis: Bobbs, 1964.

Singh, Bhagwan B. *The Self and the World in the Philosophy of Josiah Royce.* Springfield, Ill.: Thomas, 1973.

Slattery, Charles Lewis. "Josiah Royce." *Outlook* 121 (1919): 114–15.

Smith, John E. *America's Philosophical Vision.* Chicago: Univ. of Chicago Press, 1992.

———. "The Contemporary Significance of Royce's Theory of the Self." *Revue Internationale de Philosophie* 79–80 (1967): 77–89.

———. *Royce's Social Infinite: The Community of Interpretation.* New York: Liberal Arts, 1950.

Stadtman, Verne A. *The University of California, 1868–1968.* New York: McGraw, 1970.

Straton, George Douglas. *Theistic Faith for Our Time: An Introduction to the Process Philosophy of Royce and Whitehead.* Washington: Univ. Press of America, 1979.

Timberlake, Craig. *The Bishop of Broadway: The Life and Work of David Belasco.* New York: Library Publishers, 1954.

Townsend, Harvey Gates. *Philosophical Ideas in the United States.* New York: Octagon, 1968.

Trotter, Griffin. "Royce, Community and Ethnicity." *Transactions of the Charles S. Peirce Society* 30 (1994): 231–69.

Wells, Ronald Albert. "A Portrait of Josiah Royce." Ph.D. diss., Boston Univ., 1967.

Werkmeister, William Henry. *A History of Philosophical Ideas in America.* New York: Ronald, 1949.

Whittaker, T. "'Mind-Stuff' from the Historical Point of View." *Mind* 6 (1881): 498–513.

Williams, Robert R. "The Absolute, Community, and Time." *Idealistic Studies* 19 (1989): 141–53.

Woodworth, Robert J. "Josiah Royce." National Academy of Sciences of the United States of America. *Biographical Memoirs*, 381–91. Vol. 33. New York: Columbia Univ. Press, 1959.

Zedler, Beatrice H. "Royce and James on Psychical Research." *Transactions of the Charles S. Peirce Society* 10 (1974): 235–52.

Index

Abbreviation: R = Josiah Royce (1855–1916)
In the cases of duplicate names, life-span dates distinguish between individuals.

429

Lectures and Unpublished Writings. (Published texts similar to those titles listed below are identified in parentheses immediately after the title of the lectures or other writings.) "Aspects of Post-Kantian Idealism" (*Lectures on Modern Idealism*), 291–92; "Association of Ideas in the Light of Theory and Experience," 93; "Berkeley Conferences," 360–61; "Casual Observation of Human Nature," 47–48; "Certain Ideals of Right Conduct and Their Value for Society," 122–23; "On the Conception of Will as Applied to the Absolute," 198; "Considerations on the Metaphysics of the Individual Self-Consciousness," 198; "The Cult of the Dead," 380; "The Ethical Aspect of Modern Thought," 91; "Evolution of Conscience," 248; "The Fundamental Problem of Recent Philosophy," 160; "Illustrations of the Philosophy of Loyalty," 367; "Intellect and Intelligence," 93; "Of the Interdependence of the Principles of Knowledge" (Ph.D. thesis), 69–71; "Interpretation of the Present Crisis" (*War and Insurance*), 362; "Introduction to Ethics," 372, 382; "Meditations before the Gate," 79; "Memorandum on International Insurance," 365–66; "The Miner's Grave," 36; "Mr. Bertrand Russell's Problem of 'The Contradiction,'" 290; "A Nocturnal Expedition," 35–36; "The Philosophy of Religion," 367; "The Principle of Individuation" (in *The Conception of God* [1897], Supplementary Essay, Part III), 215–16, 217–18, 299, 347; "Psychological Problems Suggested by Pragmatism," 333; "Pussy Blackie's Travels," 29–30, 48; "The Recent University Movement in America," 241; "The Religious Aspect of Philosophy" (*The Religious Aspect of Philosophy*), 115, 118, 118–21; "Return to Kant," 65, 67; "The Scope and Study

of Psychology," 92; "The Social Factors in the Development of the Individual Mind," 223, 224, 257; "On Some Aspects of the Empirical Psychology of Self-Consciousness," 198; "Some Aspects of Social Psychology," 224; "Some Characteristics of the Thinking Process," 284; "Some Illustrations of the Structure and Growth of Human Thought," 85; "Some Noteworthy Persons and Doctrines in the History of Modern Thought" (*The Spirit of Modern Philosophy*), 161; "Some Recent Tendencies in Ethical Doctrine," 182–83; "Spinoza's Theory of Religious Liberty in the State" ("Natural Rights and Spinoza's Essay on Liberty"), 69; "The Spirit of the Community," 361; "Thought-Diary," 78–80; "Topics in Psychology of Interest to Teachers," 187; "What Constitutes Good Fiction," 77, 140; "Of the Will as the Principle of Philosophy," 81–82

Royce, Katharine (Kitty, Fuffy) Head (wife): assists R in writing and publication, 140, 309, 333, 351; and Belasco, 30; bicycle accident of, 198–99, 203; courtship of, 82–84; and brother (Charles Head), 83, 110, 171; compared to R, 270–72; and Enriques, 313; and granddaughter (Petsy), 356; and grandson (Randolph), 354; influenza of, 240; and Mrs. James, 117; and Kuhnemann, 313; and life with R, 280, 355, 372–73; and marriage, 90; and mother (Eliza Clement Head), 110, 152, 272; and mother-in-law (Sarah Eleanor Bayliss Royce), 136; personal qualities of, 83–84, 270–72, and philosophy, 270–71; and R's death, 381–82; and R's health, 344, 380; and R's jingle re Palladino; and R's manners, 61; and R's works: *The Conception of God*, 274, *The Problem of Christianity*, 351, *Race Questions*,

442

John Clendenning,
Professor of English at California State University, Northridge,
is a well-known authority on Josiah Royce.
He is the editor of the standard collection of
The Letters of Josiah Royce (1970).